HARCOURT

Math

Harcourt

Orlando   Austin   Chicago   New York   Toronto   London   San Diego

Visit *The Learning Site!*
www.harcourtschool.com

Senior Author

Evan M. Maletsky
Professor of Mathematics
Montclair State University
Upper Montclair, New Jersey

Mathematics Advisor

Richard Askey
Professor of Mathematics
University of Wisconsin
Madison, Wisconsin

Authors

Angela Giglio Andrews
Math Teacher, Scott School
Naperville District #203
Naperville, Illinois

Jennie M. Bennett
Houston Independent School District
Houston, Texas

Grace M. Burton
Professor, Watson School of Education
University of North Carolina
 at Wilmington
Wilmington, North Carolina

Lynda A. Luckie
K–12 Mathematics Coordinator
Gwinnett County Public Schools
Lawrenceville, Georgia

Joyce C. McLeod
Visiting Professor
Rollins College
Winter Park, Florida

Vicki Newman
Classroom Teacher
McGaugh Elementary School
Los Alamitos Unified School District
Seal Beach, California

Tom Roby
Associate Professor of Mathematics
California State University
Hayward, California

Janet K. Scheer
Executive Director
Create A Vision
Foster City, California

Program Consultants and Specialists

Janet S. Abbott
Mathematics Consultant
California

Lois Harrison-Jones
*Education and Management
 Consultant*
Dallas, Texas

Elsie Babcock
*Director, Mathematics and Science
 Center; Mathematics Consultant*
Wayne Regional Educational
 Service Agency
Wayne, Michigan

William J. Driscoll
Professor of Mathematics
Department of Mathematical Sciences
Central Connecticut State University
New Britain, Connecticut

Rebecca Valbuena
Language Development Specialist
Stanton Elementary School
Glendora, California

UNIT 1
CHAPTERS 1–4

Number Sense and Operations

TECHNOLOGY LINK

Harcourt Mega Math:
Chapter 1, pp. 17, 23
Chapter 2, pp. 47, 50
Chapter 3, p. 62
Chapter 4, pp. 78, 83, 87

**The Harcourt
Learning Site:**
www.harcourtschool.com

**Multimedia Math
Glossary:**
www.harcourtschool.com/
mathglossary

UNIT 2
CHAPTERS 5–6

Statistics and Graphing

TECHNOLOGY LINK

Harcourt Mega Math:
Chapter 6, p. 139

The Harcourt
Learning Site:
www.harcourtschool.com

**Multimedia Math
Glossary:**
www.harcourtschool.com/
mathglossary

Chapter 6

Fraction Concepts and Operations

UNIT 4
CHAPTERS 11–14

Algebra: Expressions, Equations, and Patterns

Geometry and Plane Figures

TECHNOLOGY LINK

Harcourt Mega Math:
Chapter 16, pp. 358, 364
Chapter 17, p. 386
Chapter 18, pp. 399, 404

**The Harcourt
Learning Site:**
www.harcourtschool.com

**Multimedia Math
Glossary:**
www.harcourtschool.com/
mathglossary

Chapter 17

Chapter 18

Measurement: One and Two Dimensions

TECHNOLOGY LINK

Harcourt Mega Math:
Chapter 19, pp. 422, 425
Chapter 21, p. 461

The Harcourt Learning Site:
www.harcourtschool.com

Multimedia Math Glossary:
www.harcourtschool.com/mathglossary

Chapter 21

Solid Figures and Measurement

Chapter 22

Chapter 23

UNIT 8
CHAPTERS 24–27

Ratio, Proportion, Percent, and Probability

Chapter 24

Chapter 25

Chapter 26

Chapter 27

Algebra: Integers and Graphing

TECHNOLOGY LINK

Harcourt Mega Math:
Chapter 28, p. 632
Chapter 29, pp. 653, 657
Chapter 30, pp. 670, 683

The Harcourt
Learning Site:
www.harcourtschool.com

**Multimedia Math
Glossary:**
www.harcourtschool.com/
mathglossary

Chapter 30
ALGEBRA GRAPH RELATIONSHIPS

UNIT 9 WRAP UP

STUDENT HANDBOOK

Why Learn Math?

▶ Building Success Now

Math is used in youth sporting events when marking the playing field, recording the playing time, and keeping the score of the game. ▶

▲ Math is used when you spend money for entertainment.

You measure weight and capacity when you cook. ▼

You will use the mathematics that you learn in **Harcourt Math** every day. The skills you learn will help you **build success** both now and in the future.

▶ Building Success for the Future

▲ A carpenter uses math to measure lengths, widths, heights, and angles.

You will need math to determine the amount of paint and other supplies needed to decorate your home. ▼

▲ A paramedic uses math to read and understand life saving machinery and administer medication.

Have a great year and enjoy learning Math!

PRACTICE WHAT YOU LEARN

It's in the Bag

PROJECT In each unit of this book, you'll do a project that will help you practice the math skills you've learned. Make the Bi-Folder below to hold some of these projects.

Materials

- **2 large brown grocery bags**
- **Markers**
- **Scissors**
- **Wide clear packaging tape**
- **Construction paper**
- **Glue**

Directions

1. Lay the bag in front of you with the flap facing you. Cut across the flap, close to the fold, about $\frac{1}{8}$-in. from the edge. Cut down the two sides to open the bag flap.

2. Lift up the flap and push the bottom of the bag flat. Replace the flap and tape on both sides to make the first pocket. (*Picture A*)

3. At the top opening of the bag, draw two diagonal lines, each about 3-in. long, from each corner and cut down them. Cut straight across to connect these lines and cut the piece off. This forms the second bag pocket. (*Picture B*)

4. Follow these same steps on bag 2. Glue construction paper inside each pocket for color.

5. Tape the two bags together down the middle of the inside and outside. Tape the end pockets closed. Decorate the front and inside of the bags. (*Picture C*)

6. Label the inside "PROJECTS."

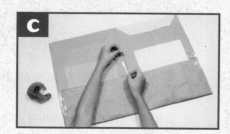

SHOW WHAT YOU LEARN

Taking a test is one way to show what you've learned. Being a good test taker is like being a good problem solver. When you answer test questions, you are solving problems.

Each time you take a test, remember to:

- Listen carefully to your teacher's instructions.
- Read all the directions.
- Pay attention to where and how to mark the test.
- Read the problems carefully.
- If you don't understand a problem, read it again.
- Mark or write your answers clearly.
- Answer questions you are sure about first.
- Work quickly but carefully.
- If you finish early, go back and check your work.
- Relax and do the best that you can.

Draw a Diagram

Eight basketball teams will play in a tournament. A team is out after it loses once. How many games does a team have to win in order to win the tournament?

Analyze   There are 8 teams. If a team loses, it is out of the tournament. If a team wins, it keeps playing.

Choose   You can *draw a diagram* to show which teams play in each game of the tournament. Use the diagram to show each pair of teams playing against each other.

Solve   Use the diagram to pair up the 8 teams. Make up a winner for each game. Then show the next games until the tournament has a winner.

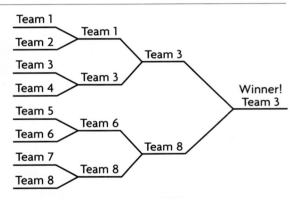

So, a team must win 3 games to win the tournament.

Check   Follow Team 3 through the tournament listing. Count the number of times it wins.

Problem Solving Practice

1. **What if** half as many teams play in the tournament? How many games will have to be played to determine the winner?

2. After the game, the teams have sandwiches at their coaches' houses. You can build your own sandwich with lettuce, tomato, and ham. How many different ways can you stack the 3 fillings to make a sandwich?

Make a Model

Alice has three pieces of ribbon. Their lengths are 7 in., 10 in., and 12 in. How can Alice use these ribbons to measure a length of 15 in.?

Analyze

Each of the three ribbons is a different length. No ribbon is 15 in. long, but you can combine the ribbon lengths to measure 15 in.

Choose

You can *make a model* of each piece of ribbon. Then you can organize the ribbons to show new lengths.

Solve

When you put two pieces together, you can form lengths of 17, 19, or 22 in. All of these are too long.

One Way
Alice can place the 7-in. piece above the 10-in. piece to show that the 10-in. piece extends 3 in. beyond it. Then that 3 in. piece and the 12-in. piece together will make 15 in.

Another Way
Alice can place the 7-in. piece above the 12-in. piece to show that the 12-in. piece extends 5 in. beyond it. Then that 5 in. and the 10-in. piece together will make 15 in.

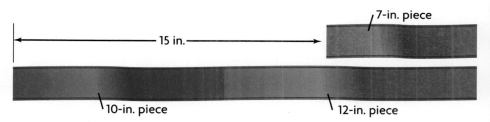

Check

Check that you used the correct lengths for the ribbon pieces. Then add the lengths of the two longer pieces and subtract the length of the short one. The result is 15 in.

Problem Solving Practice

1. Draw pictures of models you could make to measure other lengths with the three pieces of ribbon.

2. **What if** Andy is building a stand by using four cubes? He stacks the cubes, one on top of the other, and paints the outside of each cube (not the bottom). How many faces of the cubes are painted?

Predict and Test

Margaret sells tickets to a pizza dinner at her school. An adult ticket costs $3.50. A student ticket costs $2.50. Margaret sells 10 more adult tickets than student tickets. She collects $155 in ticket sales. A total of 450 people attend the pizza dinner. How many student tickets has Margaret sold?

Analyze

Student tickets cost $2.50 and adult tickets cost $3.50. Margaret sells 10 more adult tickets than student tickets. Her sales are $155. The number of people at the dinner is given, but this information is not needed.

Choose

You can use *predict and test* to solve. Use number sense and the needed information to predict how many student tickets Margaret has sold. Then test your prediction and revise it if needed.

Solve

Make a table to show each prediction and its result. Be sure you have 10 more adult tickets than student tickets each time.

PREDICTION		TEST	
Adult	Student	Sales	
20	10	(20 × $3.50) + (10 × $2.50) = $95	too low, revise
40	30	(40 × $3.50) + (30 × $2.50) = $215	too high, revise
30	20	(30 × $3.50) + (20 × $2.50) = $155	✓ correct

So, Margaret has sold 20 student tickets.

Check

Check that each multiplication is correct: 30 × $3.50 = $105, and 20 × $2.50 = $50; $105 + $50 = $155. The answer checks.

Problem Solving Practice

1. The sum of Margaret's age and her younger brother's age is 18. The difference between their ages is 4. How old is Margaret's brother?

2. Tables for the pizza dinner are set up in 3 rooms. One room has 11 tables to seat 98 people. Some tables are for 8 people, and others are for 10 people. How many tables for 8 people are set up in this room?

Work Backward

Joe and his brother Tim go shopping. At the toy store, they use half of their money to buy a video game. Then they go to the pizza parlor and spend half of the money they have left on a pizza. Then they spend half of the remaining money to rent a video. After these stops, they have $4.50 left. How much money did they have at the start?

Analyze

You need to find how much money they had at the start. You know that they had $4.50 left and that they spent half of their money at each of three stops.

Choose

Start with the amount you know they have left—$4.50—and *work backward*. Knowing how much they have left will help you calculate first how much they spent to rent the video, then how much the pizza cost, then the price of the video game, and finally how much money they had at the start.

Solve

amount they had left → $4.50

$4.50 → twice that amount before a video → 2 × $4.50 = $9

$9 → twice that amount before a pizza → 2 × $9 = $18

$18 → twice that amount before a video game → 2 × $18 = $36

So, the amount they had at the start was $36.

Check

Put $36 in the original problem to check the amount they spent at each stop.

$36 ÷ 2 = $18, $18 ÷ 2 = $9, $9 ÷ 2 = $4.50

The amount they had left matches the amount given in the problem.

Problem Solving Practice

1. The Lauber family has 4 children. Joe is 5 yr younger than his brother Mark. Tim is half as old as his brother Joe. Mary, who is 10, is 3 yr older than Tim. How old is Mark?

2. If you divide this mystery number by 4, add 8, and multiply by 3, you get 42. What is the mystery number?

Make an Organized List

At Fun City Amusement Park you can throw 3 darts at a target to score points and win prizes. If each dart lands within the target area, how many different total scores are possible?

Analyze

If all 3 darts hit the center circle, you get 30 points. This is the highest score. If all 3 darts hit the outside circle, you get 6 points. This is the lowest score. If the 3 darts hit a different combination, other scores are possible.

Choose

Make an organized list to determine all possible hits and score totals. List the value of each dart and the total for all three darts.

Solve

First consider all 3 darts hitting the center circle. List the value of each dart and the total score. Then consider 2 darts hitting the center circle and the third dart hitting a different circle. List the value of each dart and the total scores. Do the same for 1 dart hitting the center circle and no darts hitting the center circle.

3 Darts Hit Center	2 Darts Hit Center	1 Dart Hits Center	0 Darts Hit Center
10 + 10 + 10 = 30	10 + 10 + 5 = 25	10 + 5 + 5 = 20	5 + 5 + 5 = 15
	10 + 10 + 2 = 22	10 + 5 + 2 = 17	5 + 5 + 2 = 12
		10 + 2 + 2 = 14	5 + 2 + 2 = 9
			2 + 2 + 2 = 6

So, there are 10 possible scores.

Check

Make sure that all possible combinations of scores are listed and that each set of scores in the list is different.

Problem Solving Practice

1. The Yogurt Store at Fun City sells 3 flavors of yogurt: chocolate, vanilla, and strawberry. You want to get a scoop of each flavor in a waffle cone. In how many different orders can the scoops be arranged?

2. How many ways can you make change for a quarter by using dimes, nickels, and pennies?

Find a Pattern

A contractor can build stairways to a deck or patio with any number of steps. She uses the pattern at the right to build them. How many blocks are needed to build a stairway with 7 steps?

Analyze

As the number of steps increases, so does the number of blocks. You must find the number of blocks needed for a stairway with 7 steps.

Choose

You can *find a pattern* for the number of blocks needed. For each stairway, count the number of blocks to make each step and then find the total number of blocks. Use the pattern to find the number of blocks for 7 steps.

Solve

The pattern shows that the number of the step in the stairway is the same as the number of blocks needed to make it. The 2nd step is made with 2 blocks, the 3rd step is made with 3 blocks, and so on.

Number of Step	Side View	Number of Blocks	Cumulative Total
2		2	2 + 1 = 3
3		3	3 + 2 + 1 = 6
4		4	4 + 3 + 2 + 1 = 10

So, a stairway with 7 steps has 7 blocks in the 7th step, 6 blocks in the 6th step, and so on. The total number of blocks is 7 + 6 + 5 + 4 + 3 + 2 + 1 = 28 blocks.

Check

Sketch a stairway with 7 steps. Check the number of blocks needed. The number in the sketch matches the answer.

7 + 6 + 5 + 4 + 3 + 2 + 1 = 28

Problem Solving Practice

1. A cereal company adds baseball cards to certain boxes of cereal. Cards are added to the 3rd box, the 6th box, the 11th box, and the 18th box of cereal. If this pattern continues, how many boxes will have baseball cards in them when a case of 40 is ready to be shipped? Explain.

Describe the pattern and find the missing numbers.

2. 1, 4, 16, 64, 256, ■ , ■ , 16,384

Problem Solving Strategy Review 7

Make a Table

In math, Mrs. Laurence gave her class a 100-point test. Students who score 80 or above are eligible to join the Math Club. The test scores are in the box below. How many students scored 80 or above? How many students scored below 80?

90	83	80	77	78	91	92	73
62	83	79	88	72	85	93	84
75	68	82	75	94	70	98	82

Analyze

You have the test scores for the class. You need to find how many students scored below 80 and how many students scored 80 or above.

Choose

You can *make a table* and tally the test scores. This organizes the data and makes it easier to answer questions about the scores.

Solve

Make a two-column table for the range of scores. As you read each test score, place a tally mark across from the appropriate range. Be sure you end up with 24 tallies, one for each student.

SCORES	TALLIES
60–69	||
70–79	卌 |||
80–89	卌 |||
90–99	卌 |

Now use the table to answer the questions.

SCORES OF 80 OR ABOVE	SCORES BELOW 80
8 students scored 80–89.	8 students scored 70–79.
6 students scored 90–99.	2 students scored 60–69.

So, 14 students scored 80 or above, and 10 students scored below 80.

Check

Recount the tallies in each row and check your addition.

Problem Solving Practice

1. Starting at 3:00, the director will give each student 5 min to try out for the talent show. The students, in order, are Ben, Tarek, Jan, Ed, and Frank. At what time does Frank start?

2. Kelly reads stories to children at the library. There are three sessions, each lasting 45 min, with 30 min between sessions. If Kelly starts reading at 10:00 A.M., at what time does she finish?

Solve a Simpler Problem

Make a table of the first 2 odd numbers and their sum, the first 3 odd numbers and their sum, and so on. How does the table show a pattern? What is the sum of the first 20 odd numbers?

Analyze

You know how to begin finding sums for the first 2 odd numbers and the first 3 odd numbers. You need to find a pattern in the table to help you find the sum of the first 20 odd numbers.

Choose

You can begin by *solving a simpler problem*. Start with sums for the first 2 odd numbers, followed by sums for 3 odd numbers, 4 odd numbers, and 5 odd numbers.

Solve

Organize the data in a table and look for a pattern in the sums.

ODD NUMBERS	SUM	PATTERN
1 + 3	4	2^2
1 + 3 + 5	9	3^2
1 + 3 + 5 + 7	16	4^2
1 + 3 + 5 + 7 + 9	25	5^2

The table shows a pattern in the sums that relates to square numbers. Extend the pattern in the table to 20 odd numbers.

6 odd numbers → $36 = 6^2$

7 odd numbers → $49 = 7^2$

8 odd numbers → $64 = 8^2$

20 odd numbers → $400 = 20^2$

So, the sum of the first 20 odd numbers is 20^2, or 400.

Check

Extend the table a few more rows to check that there really is a pattern of square numbers. For example, find sums for the first 9, 10, 11, and 12 odd numbers. The answers check.

Problem Solving Practice

1. Martha has 5 pairs of slacks and 4 blouses for school. How many different outfits can she make with these items?

2. What is the least 5-digit number that can be divided by 50 with a remainder of 17?

Write an Equation

A school district can afford to build a gym with three basketball courts with an area of 18,700 square feet. The gym needs to be 110 ft wide to leave walking room around the courts. How long will the gym be?

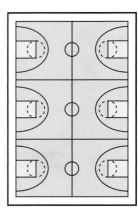

Analyze

The gym is rectangular. To find the area a rectangle covers, you multiply the length by the width. You know the area and the width of the gym and need to find its length.

Choose

You can *write an equation* for the area of the rectangle. Begin with the formula for the area of a rectangle. Use the numbers you know to find the missing number.

Solve

You find the area of a rectangle by multiplying its length by its width.

$$A = l \times w$$ *Write the formula.*
$$18{,}700 = l \times 110$$ *Replace A with 18,700 and w with 110.*
$$l = 18{,}700 \div 110$$ *Write a related division equation.*
$$l = 170$$

So, the length of the gym should be 170 ft.

Check

Place your answer in the original equation.

$$A = l \times w$$
$$A = 170 \times 110$$
$$A = 18{,}700$$

The product matches the information in the problem.

Problem Solving Practice

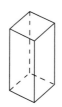

1. A rectangular box of crackers has a volume of 128 in.^{3} The area of its base is 16 in.^{2} What is the height of the box?

2. The perimeter of an isosceles triangle is 70 cm. The sides of equal length each measure 28 cm. What is the length of the unknown side?

Use Logical Reasoning

Christine, Elizabeth, and Sharon like different sports. One girl likes to snow ski, one likes to run track, and the other likes to swim. Elizabeth is a good friend of the girl who likes track. Sharon is shorter than the girl who likes to ski. Elizabeth does not like to ski. Which girl likes which sport?

Analyze

You know that there are three girls and that each one likes a different sport. Clues will help you determine which girl likes which sport.

Choose

You can *use logical reasoning* to solve this problem.

Solve

Make a table. List the sports and the names of the friends. Work with the clues one at a time. Write "yes" in a box if the clue applies to that girl. Write "no" in a box if the clue does not apply. Only one box in each row and column can have a "yes" in it.

a. Elizabeth is a good friend of the girl who likes track, so Elizabeth does not run track. Write "no" in the appropriate box.

	ski	track	swim
Christine	yes	no	no
Elizabeth	no	no	yes
Sharon	no	yes	no

b. Sharon is shorter than the girl who likes to ski, so Sharon does not ski. Write "no" in the appropriate box.

c. Elizabeth does not like to ski. Write "no" in the appropriate box. With the other sports eliminated, Elizabeth must be the person who likes to swim. Write "yes" in the appropriate box. For Christine and Sharon, write "no" in each box under *swim*.

So, Christine likes to snow ski, Sharon likes to run track, and Elizabeth likes to swim.

Check

Compare your answers to the clues in the problem. Make sure none of your conclusions conflict with the clues.

Problem Solving Practice

1. Brent, Michael, and Tim always order their favorite pizzas: pepperoni, three-cheese, and sausage. Brent is allergic to pepperoni. Tim is going to see a movie with the boy who likes sausage on his pizza. Mike does not like meat on his pizza. Which kind of pizza does each boy order?

Compare Strategies

Mrs. Hagen is eager to plant her spring garden. She wants to plant 24 tomato plants in a rectangular array. For each plant, there will be a 1-foot square of space. How many different arrays can she make?

Analyze

There are 24 plants to be put into a rectangular array. You need to find how many arrays are possible.

Choose

Lexi and Jake use different strategies to solve this problem. Lexi chooses to *draw a diagram*, and Jake chooses to *write an equation*.

Solve

Lexi's Way: Draw a Diagram

Lexi uses graph paper to draw diagrams of rectangles to show all possible arrays. Each rectangle represents a garden that covers 24 square feet. The rectangles are 1×24, 2×12, 3×8, and 4×6.

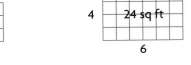

Jake's Way: Write an Equation

Jake uses the equation $A = l \times w$ for finding the area of a rectangle to identify the different rectangles that could be formed. Each length and width needs to be a whole number.

$A = l \times w$ *Think: What are the factors of 24?*

$24 = 1 \times 24$
$24 = 2 \times 12$
$24 = 3 \times 8$
$24 = 4 \times 6$

So, Lexi and Jake both find that Mrs. Hagen can choose from four rectangular arrays.

Check

Lexi can do the problem Jake's way, and Jake can try it Lexi's way.

Problem Solving Practice

1. Mr. Sargent is buying math games for his class. One game costs $2.95, one costs $3.75, and one costs $6.00. He wants 6 of each game for his class. What is the total cost of these games?

2. How many triangles are in the figure at the right?

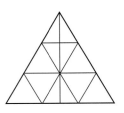

Multistep Problems

The Enrichment Program Committee at the Franklin School orders 500 T-shirts to sell at the school Field Day. Each T-shirt costs the school $4.20 and sells for $13.50. All 500 T-shirts are sold. After paying for the T-shirts, the school has passed its goal of raising $4,000. How much money has the school made?

Look at the facts in the problem. T-shirts cost $4.20 each and sell for $13.50. The committee orders and sells 500 T-shirts. You need to find how much money has been made after the costs are deducted. You know your answer should be at least $4,000.

One Way

First subtract to find how much the school has made on each T-shirt.

money earned on 1 T-shirt: $13.50 − $4.20 = $9.30

Then multiply to find the total earned.

money earned on 500 T-shirts: $9.30 × 500 = $4,650

Another Way

Find the total sales and subtract the total cost.

Total sales: 500 × $13.50 = $6,750

Total cost: 500 × $4.20 = $2,100

Total earned = $6,750 − $2,100 = $4,650

So, the school has made $4,650 on the sale of the T-shirts.

Problem Solving Practice

1. At the school Field Day, frozen yogurt cones sell for $2.25. Lin buys one for herself and one for each of her 4 friends. How much change does she get back from $20?

2. Fran is making a cabinet for her shell collection. She buys 3 boards at $2.75 each and 4 hinges at $0.99 each. What is the total cost of the supplies?

3. Mrs. Smith bought bread for $0.98, eggs for $1.17, ground turkey for $3.18, and 3 bunches of carrots for $0.65 each. She gave the clerk $10.03. How much change should Mrs. Smith receive?

CHAPTER 1

Whole Number Applications

≡FAST FACT • SCIENCE

NASA has launched more than 100 shuttle missions from the Kennedy Space Center. One of the space shuttle missions launched in 2000 was STS-89.

PROBLEM SOLVING To the nearest hour, the STS-89 mission lasted 211 hours. About how many hours longer than the STS-89 mission did the STS-98 mission last? Use the bar graph to find out.

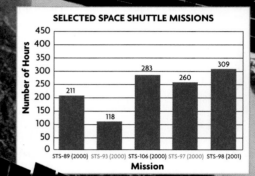

SELECTED SPACE SHUTTLE MISSIONS

Check What You Know

Use this page to help you review and remember important skills needed for Chapter 1.

☑ Multiply and Divide

Find the product.

1. 2×736 **2.** 7×503 **3.** 4×862 **4.** 6×831

5. 8×422 **6.** 2×836 **7.** 5×438 **8.** 5×409

9. 3×543 **10.** 4×684 **11.** 2×986 **12.** 9×376

Divide.

13. $459 \div 7$ **14.** $815 \div 5$ **15.** $235 \div 6$ **16.** $444 \div 3$

17. $525 \div 5$ **18.** $906 \div 4$ **19.** $639 \div 9$ **20.** $277 \div 8$

☑ Round Whole Numbers

Round to the nearest thousand.

21. 2,467   **22.** 5,609   **23.** 28,500   **24.** 299

25. 34,831   **26.** 19,089   **27.** 6,136   **28.** 43,712

29. 134,612   **30.** 217,501   **31.** 59,832   **32.** 539,513

Round to the nearest ten thousand.

33. 51,677   **34.** 228,260   **35.** 12,435   **36.** 78,562

37. 639,108   **38.** 40,500   **39.** 90,499   **40.** 381,810

VOCABULARY POWER

REVIEW

round [round] *verb*

A word may have more than one meaning in the same subject. In mathematics, *round* can mean "to increase or decrease to the nearest unit." Write another meaning *round* can have in mathematics.

PREVIEW

clustering
underestimate
overestimate

 www.harcourtschool.com/mathglossary

Place Value

Learn how to use place value to express, compare, and order whole numbers.

The length of Pluto's orbit is 22,955,012,169 miles. Each digit in a number has a place value. The value of a digit is determined by its position in the number. The value of the first digit 2 in 22,955,012,169 is 2 × 10,000,000,000 = 20,000,000,000 since it is in the ten-billions place.

PLACE VALUE CHART											
Billions			**Millions**			**Thousands**			**Ones**		
Hundreds	Tens	Ones	Hundreds	Tens	Ones	Hundreds	Tens	Ones	Hundreds	Tens	Ones
	2	2,	9	5	5,	0	1	2,	1	6	9

When you read and write numbers, you are using place value.

Standard form: 22,955,012,169

Expanded form: 20,000,000,000 + 2,000,000,000 + 900,000,000 + 50,000,000 + 5,000,000 + 10,000 + 2,000 + 100 + 60 + 9

Word form: twenty-two billion, nine hundred fifty-five million, twelve thousand, one hundred sixty-nine

You can use place value to compare and order whole numbers.

EXAMPLE 1

Compare 537,437,641 and 537,438,006. Use < or >.

537,437,641   537,438,006
537,437,641   537,438,006
So, 537,437,641 < 537,438,006

Start at the left. Compare the digits in the same position. The thousands digits are the first that are different. 7 is less than 8.

EXAMPLE 2

Order 467,703,522; 476,703,520; and 436,703,521 from least to greatest.

Compare every possible pair.
467,703,522 < 476,703,520   467,703,522 > 436,703,521
476,703,520 > 436,703,521

So, the list of numbers in order from least to greatest is 436,703,521; 467,703,522; 476,703,520.

Think and ▶
Discuss
Look back at the lesson to answer the question.

1. **Explain** how to compare 3,214,220,201 and 3,214,230,201.

Guided ▶
Practice
Write the value of the blue digit.

2. 37,951,252   3. 861,740,213,903   4. 4,350,217

Write the number in expanded form and in word form.

5. 351,040   6. 814,300,579   7. 135,040,234

Compare. Use < or > for each ●.

8. 8 million ● 80 thousand   9. 762,317 ● 762,399

PRACTICE AND PROBLEM SOLVING

Independent ▶
Practice
Write the value of the blue digit.

10. 987,450,317   11. 38,777,810,413   12. 43,952

TECHNOLOGY LINK

More Practice:
Harcourt Mega Math
The Number Games,
Tiny's Think Tank,
Level A

Write the number in expanded form and in word form.

13. 23,005,000   14. 740,050,000   15. 4,649,340,070

Compare. Use < or > for each ●.

16. 75 million ● 65 billion   17. 1,359,214 ● 1,359,124

18. 39 thousand ● 23 thousand   19. 31,012,367 ● 31,021,367

Write the numbers in order from least to greatest.

20. 24,127,256; 24,172,265; 24,127,265

21. 324,480,125; 324,480,127; 324,480,521

Problem Solving ▶
Applications
22. **≡FAST FACT** • SCIENCE The maximum additional weight a space shuttle can carry into space is 65,000 lb. Use < or > to explain whether a shuttle can carry a 59,978-lb weather satellite.

23. The cost of the space shuttle *Endeavour* was approximately one billion, two hundred million dollars. Write the amount in standard form.

MIXED REVIEW AND TEST PREP

24. Write $\frac{12}{18}$ in simplest form.

25. Divide. 414 ÷ 8

26. Write six-tenths as a decimal.

27. Compare. Use < or >. 0.091 ● 0.13

⭐28. **TEST PREP** If 3 pencils cost $0.72, how much would a dozen pencils cost?

A $1.44   **B** $2.16   **C** $2.88   **D** $8.64

EXTRA PRACTICE page 30, Set A

Estimate with Whole Numbers

Learn how to estimate sums, differences, products, and quotients of whole numbers.

The longest throw of a flying disc was about 712 ft, made by Christian Voigt in 2001. Carmen, David, and Leona each threw a disc. Is the total distance of the three throws close to the record distance?

You don't need an exact sum to answer the question, so estimate.

NAME	DISTANCE
David	134 ft
Leona	148 ft
Carmen	183 ft

$$
\begin{array}{rcr}
134 & \to & 130 \\
148 & \to & 150 \\
+183 & \to & +180 \\
\hline
 & & 460
\end{array}
$$
Round each number to the nearest ten.

The estimate, 460, is not close to the record distance of 712 ft, so the total distance is not close either.

Vocabulary

clustering
underestimate
overestimate

Remember that when rounding, you look at the digit to the right of the place to which you are rounding.
• If that digit is 5 or greater, round up.
• If that digit is less than 5, round down.

Use **clustering** to estimate a sum when the addends are about the same.

EXAMPLE 1

Estimate $1,802 + 2,182 + 1,999$.

$3 \times 2,000 = 6,000$ *The three addends all cluster around 2,000, so use 2,000 for each number. Multiply 2,000 by 3.*

So, the sum is about 6,000.

You can use rounding to estimate a difference.

EXAMPLE 2

Estimate $31,928 - 20,915$.

Round to the nearest ten thousand.	*Round to the nearest thousand.*
$\begin{array}{r} 30,000 \\ -20,000 \\ \hline 10,000 \end{array}$	$\begin{array}{r} 32,000 \\ -21,000 \\ \hline 11,000 \end{array}$

So, both 10,000 and 11,000 are reasonable estimates.

You can show an estimate by using the "approximately equal to" symbol, ≈.

5,125 − 1,920 ≈ 3,000   *Read: 5,125 − 1,920 is approximately equal to 3,000.*

An estimate that is less than the exact answer is an **underestimate**. An estimate that is greater than the exact answer is an **overestimate**.

366		370	*Round up.*
+198		+200	
564	*Exact answer*	570	*Overestimate*

144		100	*Round down.*
×123		×100	
17,712	*Exact answer*	10,000	*Underestimate*

EXAMPLE 3

Students set up 28 rows of 36 seats each for a talent show in the school cafeteria. About how many programs should the school print for the show?

Estimate 28 × 36. To make sure there are enough programs, find an overestimate.

$$
\begin{array}{cc}
28 & 30 \\
\times 36 & \times 40
\end{array}
$$
→ *Round each factor up to the nearest ten.*

$$
\begin{array}{r}
30 \\
\times 40 \\
\hline
1,200
\end{array}
$$
Multiply. Because each factor is rounded up, the product is an overestimate.
28 × 36 ≈ 1,200

So, the school should print about 1,200 programs.

Remember that compatible numbers are numbers that divide without a remainder, are close to the actual numbers, and are easy to compute with mentally.

To get a closer estimate in Example 3, round only 28 to the nearest ten. Since 30 × 36 = 1,080, it is a closer estimate.

To estimate a quotient, use rounding or compatible numbers.

EXAMPLE 4

The employees of the Briar Creek office building have collected 1,545 lb of paper to be recycled. The building has 36 offices. About how many pounds of paper, on average, did the employees in each office collect?

Estimate 1,545 ÷ 36.

1,600 ÷ 40   *4 is compatible with 16, so use 1,600 ÷ 40.*
1,600 ÷ 40 = 40   *Divide. 1,545 ÷ 36 ≈ 40*

So, the employees in each office collected an average of about 40 lb.

Math Idea ▸ Some of the strategies you can use to estimate are rounding, clustering, and compatible numbers.

19

Think and ▶ Discuss

Look back at the lesson to answer each question.

1. **Explain** why 6,000 + 1,500 is either an overestimate or an underestimate of 6,108 + 1,524.

2. **Explain** how to estimate a quotient by using compatible numbers. Give an example to illustrate your answer.

Guided ▶ Practice

Estimate the sum or difference.

3.	723	4.	2,940	5.	4,480	6.	5,449
	+819		3,140		4,100		4,869
			+2,834		+3,967		+4,834

7.	667	8.	8,855	9.	34,855	10.	67,184
	−133		−2,268		−11,268		−49,650

Estimate the product or quotient.

11.	36	12.	59	13.	48	14.	490
	× 9		×33		×29		× 66

15. $321 \div 4$ 16. $1,544 \div 28$ 17. $4,156 \div 64$ 18. $8,429 \div 39$

Independent ▶ Practice

Estimate the sum or difference.

19.	1,700	20.	293	21.	5,765	22.	43,643
	2,008		348		5,948		+84,211
	+2,324		+343		+6,324		

23.	389	24.	3,556	25.	44,123	26.	667,184
	− 43		−3,339		−29,512		−249,650

27. $17,809 - 2,145$ 28. $321,059 + 42,950$

Estimate the product or quotient.

29.	364	30.	53	31.	482	32.	1,874
	× 12		×41		×299		× 582

33. $1,844 \div 22$ 34. $3,575 \div 56$ 35. $6,435 \div 529$ 36. $21,416 \div 521$

37. $4,135 \times 784$ 38. $62,217 \div 4,889$

Tell whether the estimate is an *overestimate* or an *underestimate*. Then show how the estimate was determined.

39. $352 + 675 \approx 1,100$ 40. $4,134 + 47 \approx 4,100$ 41. $96 \times 19 \approx 2,000$

42. $709 + 151 \approx 850$ 43. $291 \times 28 \approx 9,000$ 44. $25 \times 29 \approx 900$

Use estimation to compare. Write < or > for ●.

45. 614×41 ● $21{,}119 + 1{,}899$ **46.** $18{,}391 \div 19$ ● 59×21

47. $4{,}012 - 3{,}508$ ● $3{,}624 \div 6$ **48.** $12{,}283 + 19{,}971$ ● $209{,}910 \div 7$

49. 711×63 ● $28{,}520 + 16{,}990$ **50.** 513×52 ● $29{,}190 - 1{,}986$

Problem Solving ▶ Applications

Use Data   For 51–52, use the table.

51. About how many more library books does Harvard have than the University of Illinois at Urbana?

52. Estimate the total number of library books at Yale and the University of California at Berkeley.

53. The theater of the Natural Science and History Museum was filled to capacity for 276 shows. The theater holds 36 people. How many people attended the shows?

54. ✎ **Write About It**   Is it easier to use rounding or compatible numbers to estimate $756 \div 74$? Explain.

55. Two numbers, each rounded to the nearest hundred, have a product of 60,000. What are two possible numbers?

LARGEST UNIVERSITY LIBRARIES IN THE UNITED STATES (2000)	
Library	**Books**
Harvard University	14,190,704
Yale University	10,294,792
University of Illinois–Urbana	9,302,203
University of California–Berkeley	8,946,754
University of Texas	7,783,847

MIXED REVIEW AND TEST PREP

For 56–58, find the perimeter and area.

56.

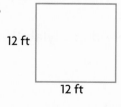

12 ft

12 ft

57.

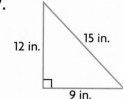

12 in.   15 in.   9 in.

58.

10 cm

3 cm

⭐ **59. TEST PREP**   Ms. Cannon baked a total of 60 apple and blueberry pies. She baked a dozen more apple pies than blueberry pies. How many apple pies did she bake?

A 18 **B** 24 **C** 36 **D** 48

⭐ **60. TEST PREP**   Allen and Mei began working at the same time. It took Allen 50 min to mow the lawn, while Mei took $1\frac{1}{4}$ hr to paint the fence. How much longer did Mei work than Allen?

F 85 min **G** 65 min **H** 35 min **J** 25 min

EXTRA PRACTICE page 30, Set B

21

Addition and Subtraction

Learn how to add and subtract whole numbers.

Round to the nearest thousand.

1. 3,841   2. 2,490
3. 7,450   4. 8,500
5. Add. 4,256 + 1,725

PROGRAM	YEARS	TOTAL HOURS IN SPACE
Mercury	1961–1963	54
Gemini	1965–1966	1,940
Apollo	1968–1972	7,506
Skylab	1973–1974	12,352

Remember that you add when joining groups of different sizes and subtract when taking away or comparing groups.

During the early years of space flight, the total time United States astronauts spent in space increased with each program.

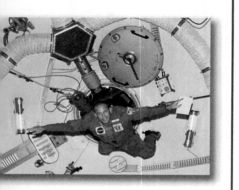

EXAMPLE 1

How many hours did U.S. astronauts spend in space from 1961 to 1974?

Find 54 + 1,940 + 7,506 + 12,352.

Estimate to check for reasonableness.

Round to the nearest thousand. | Find the sum.

```
    54          0           54
 1,940      2,000        1,940    Compare your estimate.
 7,506  →   8,000        7,506    21,852 is close to 22,000, so
+12,352   +12,000      +12,352    the sum is reasonable.
           22,000       21,852
```

So, U.S. astronauts spent 21,852 hours in space.

EXAMPLE 2

How many more hours did U.S. astronauts spend in Skylab than on the Gemini missions?

Find 12,352 − 1,940.

Estimate to check for reasonableness. | Find the difference.

```
 12,352      12,000       12,352    Compare your estimate.
− 1,940  →  − 2,000      − 1,940    10,412 is close to 10,000, so
            10,000       10,412     the difference is reasonable.
```

So, U.S. astronauts spent 10,412 more hours in Skylab than on the Gemini missions.

• Find 39,472 − 20,124. Estimate to check.

Think and ▶ Discuss

Look back at the lesson to answer each question.

1. **Explain** how you know whether to add or subtract when solving a word problem.

2. **Explain** why it is a good idea to find an estimate before or after you find the exact answer.

Guided ▶ Practice

Find the sum or difference. Estimate to check.

3. $835 + 604$ 4. $6,901 + 342 + 67$ 5. $40,190 - 13,982$

PRACTICE AND PROBLEM SOLVING

Independent ▶ Practice

Find the sum or difference. Estimate to check.

6. $9,500 - 289$ 7. $21,670 + 14,704$ 8. $31,227 + 56,995$

9. $\begin{array}{r} 999,999 \\ +111,385 \end{array}$ 10. $\begin{array}{r} 987,654 \\ -456,789 \end{array}$ 11. $\begin{array}{r} 50,000,000 \\ -\ 3,604,381 \end{array}$

TECHNOLOGY LINK

More Practice:
**Harcourt Mega Math
The Number Games,**
Tiny's Think Tank,
Levels B, C

Solve.

12. $1,485 + 2,019 + 1,310 + 3,665 + 798$

13. $43,875 + 81,420 - 38,288 + 12,108 - 23,990$

Problem Solving ▶ Applications

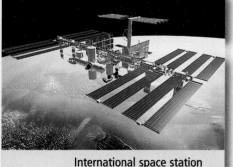

International space station

Use Data   For 14–15, use the graph.

14. How many more calories are in 1 cup of almonds than in 1 cup of carrots mixed with 1 cup of raisins? Estimate to check.

15. 📖 **Write a problem** that uses data from the graph and that can be solved by adding or subtracting.

16. When the international space station is completed, it will be 290 ft long, which is 206 ft longer than Skylab. Skylab was 41 ft longer than Mir, the Russian space station. How long was Mir?

CALORIES

Calories in 1 Cup

Almonds 849, Apples 73, Carrots 46, Raisins 419

Food

MIXED REVIEW AND TEST PREP

17. $6,785 + 4,521$

18. Complete. 36 in. = ■ ft

19. List the factors of 24.

20. List the first six multiples of 9.

⭐ 21. **TEST PREP** Which is a prime number?

   A 15   **B** 27   **C** 31   **D** 50

Multiplication and Division

Learn how to multiply and divide whole numbers.

Sometimes you can multiply to solve a word problem.

EXAMPLE 1

Sixth-grade students sold 132 books of carnival ride coupons. How many ride coupons did they sell if there were 18 in each book?

Multiply. 132×18 Estimate. $130 \times 20 = 2,600$

Remember that you multiply when joining equal-sized groups, and you divide when separating into equal-sized groups or when finding how many in each group.

$$
\begin{array}{r}
132 \\
\times\ 18 \\
\hline
1\ 056 \\
+\ 1\ 320 \\
\hline
2,376
\end{array}
$$

Compare the exact product to your estimate. Since 2,376 is close to the estimate of 2,600, the exact product is reasonable.

So, the students sold 2,376 coupons.

You can omit the zero placeholders when you multiply. Just be careful to put the products in the right place values.

Correct
$$
\begin{array}{r}
132 \\
\times\ 18 \\
\hline
1056 \\
+\ 132
\end{array}
$$

Incorrect
$$
\begin{array}{r}
132 \\
\times\ 18 \\
\hline
1056 \\
+\ 132
\end{array}
$$

EXAMPLE 2

Season tickets to an amusement park are on sale for $125 each. On the first day of the sale, the amusement park sold 12,383 tickets. How much money did the amusement park receive for season tickets that day?

Multiply. $12,383 \times 125$

Estimate. $12,000 \times 130 = 1,560,000$

$$
\begin{array}{r}
12,383 \\
\times\ \ \ \ 125 \\
\hline
61\ 915 \\
247\ 66 \\
+1\ 238\ 3 \\
\hline
1,547,875
\end{array}
$$

Compare the exact product to your estimate. Since 1,547,875 is close to the estimate of 1,560,000, the exact product is reasonable.

So, the amusement park received $1,547,875.

• What if each season ticket cost $215? How much money would the amusement park have received for season tickets that day?

Sometimes you have to use division to solve word problems.

EXAMPLE 3

Remember that the procedure for dividing is divide, multiply, subtract, compare, and bring down.

Mrs. Lopez is redesigning the company cafeteria to seat 540 employees. Each table in her design seats 12 employees. How many tables will she need?

Divide. 540 ÷ 12

Estimate. 480 ÷ 12 = 40

```
      45
12)540
   −48↓
     60
   −60
      0
```

Compare the exact quotient to your estimate. Since 45 is close to the estimate of 40, the exact quotient is reasonable.

So, Mrs. Lopez will need 45 tables in her design.

• What if each table seats 10 employees? How many tables will Mrs. Lopez need?

Sometimes a division problem has a zero in the quotient.

EXAMPLE 4

A school collected 2,568 newspapers. The newspapers were bundled in packages of 25. How many packages of newspapers did the school bundle?

Divide. 2,568 ÷ 25

Estimate. 2,500 ÷ 25 = 100

```
      102 r18
25)2,568
   −25
     06
    −0
     68
    −50
     18
```

Compare the exact answer to your estimate. Since 102 r18 is close to the estimate of 100, the exact quotient is reasonable.

So, the school bundled 102 packages of newspapers.

In Example 4 there is a remainder. Some calculators allow you to show a whole-number remainder.

2,568 [÷R] 25 [=] [102 R18]

You can express a remainder with an *r*, or you can express it as a fractional part of the divisor or as a decimal. The quotient and remainder in Example 4 can also be expressed as $102\frac{18}{25}$ or as 102.72.

Think and ▶
Discuss

Look back at the lesson to answer each question.

1. **Explain** why the school bundled 102 packages of newspapers instead of 103 packages of newspapers in Example 4.

2. **Tell** the different ways to express the remainder for the division problem $153 \div 6$.

Guided ▶
Practice

Multiply or divide. Estimate to check.

3. $1,113 \times 712$ 4. $2,115 \div 72$ 5. $16,225 \times 219$

Multiply or divide.

6. $\begin{array}{r} 13 \\ \times 14 \end{array}$ 7. $8\overline{)432}$ 8. $12\overline{)144}$ 9. $\begin{array}{r} 962 \\ \times\ 40 \end{array}$

10. 159×340 11. $7,658 \times 111$ 12. $7,044 \div 14$ 13. $1,068 \div 19$

Independent ▶
Practice

Multiply or divide. Estimate to check.

14. $2,250 \div 18$ 15. $4,904 \times 196$ 16. $193,200 \div 46$

17. $7,021 \times 498$ 18. $249,900 \div 49$ 19. $24,587 \times 71$

Multiply or divide.

20. $16\overline{)1,664}$ 21. $\begin{array}{r} 298 \\ \times\ 89 \end{array}$ 22. $\begin{array}{r} 5,233 \\ \times\ 238 \end{array}$ 23. $52\overline{)728}$

24. $4\overline{)412}$ 25. $\begin{array}{r} 380 \\ \times\ 55 \end{array}$ 26. $\begin{array}{r} 2,382 \\ \times\ 12 \end{array}$ 27. $24\overline{)626}$

28. $\begin{array}{r} 327 \\ \times 123 \end{array}$ 29. $26\overline{)2,314}$ 30. $68\overline{)24,820}$ 31. $\begin{array}{r} 5,470 \\ \times\ 240 \end{array}$

32. $29\overline{)13,253}$ 33. $\begin{array}{r} 6,378 \\ \times\ 291 \end{array}$ 34. $\begin{array}{r} 2,009 \\ \times\ 562 \end{array}$ 35. $120\overline{)10,080}$

Divide. Write the remainder as a fraction.

36. $5\overline{)49}$ 37. $7,349 \div 20$ 38. $386 \div 15$ 39. $4\overline{)3,385}$

40. **ALGEBRA** What is the least whole number, n, for which it is true that $n \div 8 > 542 + 258$?

41. **ALGEBRA** What is the least whole number, n, for which it is true that $70 \times n > 29,000$?

42. Yuji's parents bought an entertainment center for $1,176. They plan to pay for it with 14 equal monthly payments. How much will each payment be if a $3.50 service charge is added every month?

43. Lincoln Middle School had a car wash to raise money. The students charged $3.00 for every car and $5.00 for every van. If they washed 23 cars and 18 vans, how much did they earn?

44. **?** **What's the Error?** Describe the error. Then solve the problem correctly.

$$\begin{array}{r} 62 \text{ r}15 \\ 49\overline{)30{,}395} \end{array}$$

45. **Vocabulary Power** How you pronounce *estimate* depends on whether it is used as a noun or a verb. Write one sentence using *estimate* as a verb, and one sentence using it as a noun.

MIXED REVIEW AND TEST PREP

46. How much more than 96,784 is 142,981? (p. 22)

47. Complete. 4 lb = ■ oz

48. Order 804, 824, 818, and 803 from least to greatest.

⭐ **49. TEST PREP** How many meters are in 1,800 millimeters?

A 0.18 m **B** 1.8 m **C** 18 m **D** 180 m

⭐ **50. TEST PREP** Teresa is buying perfume for her mother. The prices are $16.19, $15.89, $15.99, and $17.00. How much will she save by buying the least expensive instead of the most expensive?

F $0.01 **G** $0.11 **H** $0.81 **J** $1.11

PROBLEM SOLVING

LiNKUP to Reading

Strategy • Use Context Many word problems contain words such as *more than, fewer than, twice as many,* and *total.* Be sure to interpret these words within the context of the problem before you choose an operation.

Use Data For each problem, write the words that help you choose the operation. Then solve the problem.

1. How many more calories will you burn in 1 hr by skiing than by hiking?

2. On Saturday, Connie spent an hour in gymnastics class and then walked for 1 hr. How many total calories did she burn during these two activities?

3. Clara burned half as many calories while raking the lawn for 1 hr as she did while jogging for 1 hr. How many calories did she burn while raking the lawn?

CALORIES BURNED PER HOUR	
Activity	Calories
Walking (at 2 mi per hr)	112
Gymnastics	128
Hiking	191
Jogging	224
Cross-country skiing	326

EXTRA PRACTICE page 30, Set D

PROBLEM SOLVING STRATEGY
Predict and Test

Learn how to use the strategy *predict and test* to solve problems with whole numbers.

You can solve some problems by using your number sense to predict a possible answer. You should then test your answer and revise your prediction if necessary.

There were 25 problems on a test. For each correct answer, 4 points were given. For each incorrect answer, 1 point was subtracted. Tania answered all 25 problems. Her score was 85. How many correct answers did she have?

Analyze

What are you asked to find?

What facts are given?

Is there any numerical information you will not use? If so, what?

Choose

What strategy will you use?

You can use the strategy *predict and test.* Use the given information and your number sense to predict about how many correct answers Tania had. Then test your prediction, and revise it if necessary.

Solve

How will you solve the problem?

Make a table to show your prediction, your test of it, and any revisions you need. Be sure that the total of correct and incorrect problems is 25.

PREDICTION		TEST	
Correct	**Incorrect**	**SCORE**	
23	2	$(23 \times 4) - 2 = 90$	*too high, so revise*
21	4	$(21 \times 4) - 4 = 80$	*too low, so revise*
22	3	$(22 \times 4) - 3 = 85$	← *correct*

So, Tania had 22 correct answers.

Check

What other method could you use to solve this problem?

What if Tania's score were 65? How many incorrect answers would she have?

PROBLEM SOLVING STRATEGIES

| Draw a Diagram or Picture |
| Make a Model |
| ▶ **Predict and Test** |
| Work Backward |
| Make an Organized List |
| Find a Pattern |
| Make a Table or Graph |
| Solve a Simpler Problem |
| Write an Equation |
| Use Logical Reasoning |

Solve by predicting and testing.

1. Rodney bought a total of 40 oranges and apples. He bought 14 fewer apples than oranges. Use a table to show how to find the number of each fruit he bought.

2. The Mighty Tigers soccer team played a total of 25 games. They won 9 more games than they lost, and 2 games ended in ties. Use a table to show how to find the number of games they won.

3. The perimeter of a rectangular garden is 40 ft. If the length is 6 ft more than the width, what are the length and width of the garden?

   A $l = 12$ ft, $w = 6$ ft

   B $l = 13$ ft, $w = 7$ ft

   C $l = 6$ ft, $w = 12$ ft

   D $l = 7$ ft, $w = 13$ ft

4. The perimeter of a rectangular lawn is 32 yd. If the length is 3 times the width, what are the length and width of the lawn?

   F $l = 18$ yd, $w = 6$ yd

   G $l = 12$ yd, $w = 4$ yd

   H $l = 6$ yd, $w = 18$ yd

   J $l = 4$ yd, $w = 12$ yd

MIXED STRATEGY PRACTICE

5. Rosalia waters her tomato plants every other day. She waters her pepper plants every 3 days. If she waters both on April 20, what are the next three dates on which she will water both?

6. Stacy spent a total of $28.45. She bought a ticket for a basketball game for $8.50, food for $7.95, and some T-shirts for $6.00 each. How many T-shirts did she buy?

7. Sam has 98 baseball cards. This is 2 more than twice as many as Paul has. How many cards does Paul have?

8. Use the table below. If the pattern continues, how many miles in all will four runners run on the fifth day?

Each Runner's Training Schedule

| Day | 1 | 2 | 3 | 4 | 5 |
| Miles | 2 | 6 | 10 | 14 | — |

9. Melina and her two sisters collect stamps. Melina has twice as many as her older sister, who has 33 stamps. Melina has three times as many as her younger sister. How many stamps do they have in all?

10. ❓ **What's the Question?** The sum of the ages of Jeff, Elijah, and Stefan is 41. Jeff is 14 years old. Stefan is 3 years older than Elijah. The answer is 12 years old.

11. The train that leaves at 11:45 A.M. usually arrives in New York City 34 minutes after that. Today it arrived at 12:24 P.M. How late was the train?

Set A (pp. 16–17)

Write the value of the blue digit.

1. 539,046,172 **2.** 303,931,035 **3.** 502,634,253 **4.** 400,137,492

5. 5,786,902 **6.** 4,683,579 **7.** 361,017,382 **8.** 34,045,162,000

Compare. Use < or > for each ●.

9. 529,387 ● 529,391 **10.** 1,078,411 ● 107,841 **11.** 304,654 ● 304,586

Order from least to greatest.

12. 223,056; 223,704; 223,001 **13.** 21,346,672; 21,346,627; 21,364,672

Order from greatest to least.

14. 547,153,414; 574,165,220; 575,443,090 **15.** 2,636,313; 2,363,313; 2,533,313

16. Write a 10-digit number greater than 4,245,912,368 that has a 7 in the hundred millions place.

Set B (pp. 18–21)

Estimate.

1. 589 +342 **2.** 865 −383 **3.** 8,926 +1,674 **4.** 8,960 9,043 +8,756 **5.** 3,406 − 792

6. 4,496 ÷ 51 **7.** 47 × 98 **8.** 321 × 43 **9.** 3,552 ÷ 58 **10.** 6,251 ÷ 12

Tell whether the estimate is an overestimate or underestimate.

11. 848 + 692 ≈ 1,550 **12.** 398 × 66 ≈ 28,000 **13.** 317 − 67 ≈ 230

Set C (pp. 22–23)

Find the sum or difference.

1. 6,343 − 1,145 **2.** 19,826 − 3,517 **3.** 22,912 + 84,718 **4.** 532,047 + 36,603

5. 26,001 − 4,282 **6.** 242,338 + 67,116 **7.** 876,543 − 345,678 **8.** 400,000 − 15,492

Set D (pp. 24–27)

Multiply or divide, writing any remainder as a fraction.

1. 83 × 62 **2.** 16)869 **3.** 45)1,675 **4.** 458 × 194

5. 24,852 ÷ 57 **6.** 216 × 34 **7.** 52,206 ÷ 21 **8.** 3,186 × 15

1. **VOCABULARY**   An estimate that is less than the exact answer is a(n) __?__ . (p. 19)

2. **VOCABULARY**   A way to estimate a sum when all of the addends are about the same is __?__ . (p. 18)

3. **VOCABULARY**   An estimate that is greater than the exact answer is a(n) __?__ . (p. 19)

Write the value of the blue digit. (pp. 16–17)

4. 4,347,380   5. 54,300,245   6. 265,538,236   7. 31,402,674,346

Compare. Use < or > for each ●. (pp. 16–17)

8. 13 million ● 31 million   9. 60,325 ● 60,235

10. 41,123,478 ● 41,132,478   11. 263,015,102 ● 263,105,102

Estimate. (pp. 18–21)

12. $\begin{array}{r} 593 \\ +724 \\ \hline \end{array}$ 13. $\begin{array}{r} 1,420 \\ +5,791 \\ \hline \end{array}$ 14. $\begin{array}{r} 935 \\ -549 \\ \hline \end{array}$ 15. $\begin{array}{r} 2,371 \\ -1,456 \\ \hline \end{array}$ 16. $\begin{array}{r} 43,816 \\ -39,972 \\ \hline \end{array}$

17. 48×6 18. 308×67 19. $374 \div 7$ 20. $276 \div 42$ 21. $3,764 \div 591$

Find the sum or difference. (pp. 22–23)

22. $\begin{array}{r} 4,762 \\ +39,038 \\ \hline \end{array}$ 23. $9,724 - 286$ 24. $\begin{array}{r} 50,031 \\ -\ 9,352 \\ \hline \end{array}$ 25. $\begin{array}{r} 737 \\ 4,650 \\ +11,821 \\ \hline \end{array}$ 26. $\begin{array}{r} 678,040 \\ -329,193 \\ \hline \end{array}$

Multiply or divide. (pp. 24–27)

27. $\begin{array}{r} 526 \\ \times\ 42 \\ \hline \end{array}$ 28. 123×12 29. $2,250 \div 18$ 30. $\begin{array}{r} 189 \\ \times 108 \\ \hline \end{array}$ 31. $40\overline{)3,206}$

Solve. (pp. 28–29)

32. At school during spirit week, Ming sold a total of 36 red and blue ribbons. She sold 6 more red ribbons than blue ribbons. How many of each color did she sell?

33. Colton worked two days on a project for school. He worked a total of 195 minutes. If he worked 45 minutes longer on the first day, how long did Colton work each day?

NUMBER SENSE, CONCEPTS, AND OPERATIONS

1. Mount McKinley is located in Alaska's Denali National Park. The park's area is 4,740,907 acres. Which of the following is 4,740,907 written in words?

   A four million, seven hundred forty thousand, nine hundred seven

   B four million, seven hundred forty, nine hundred seven

   C four million, seventy-four thousand, nine hundred seventy

   D four billion, seven hundred forty thousand, nine hundred seven

2. Coach Martinez bought 18 basketballs for $288. If you bought 5 basketballs at the same price per basketball, what would the total cost be?

   F $16   H $80

   G $30   J $90

3. There are 126 milligrams of calcium in 1 cup of cottage cheese. In 1 cup of whole milk, there are 165 more milligrams of calcium than there are in 1 cup of cottage cheese. How much calcium is there in 1 cup of cottage cheese and 1 cup of whole milk combined?

   A 204 milligrams   C 417 milligrams

   B 291 milligrams   D 456 milligrams

4. **Explain It** Jorge bought 3 CDs for $18 each and a bottle of juice for $3. About how much did he spend? Explain your estimate.

   > **TIP** **Get the information you need.** See item 4. Use information you know about the prices of these items to make your estimate.

★ **MEASUREMENT**

5. The table shows the time it took four students to run $\frac{1}{2}$ mile. How many minutes did it take Kay to complete the run?

Student	Lee	Kay	Matt	Keith
Time (sec)	325	300	294	360

   F 3 minutes   H 5 minutes

   G 4 minutes   J 6 minutes

6. The more a package weighs, the more it costs to mail it. Which of the following weights would cost the **most** to mail?

   A 30 kilograms   C 3,000 grams

   B 300 grams   D 300 decigrams

7. Which is the **best** estimate of the length of a real school bus?

   F 10 inches   H 10 yards

   G 10 feet   J 10 miles

8. **Explain It** Each square below represents 1 square foot. ESTIMATE the area of the triangle. Explain how you made your estimate.

   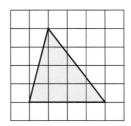

   SCALE

   ☐ = 1 square foot

DATA ANALYSIS AND
PROBABILITY

9. Sarah surveyed 200 people who said they plan to vote in the election for mayor. Which of the following is the **best** estimate of the percent of undecided voters?

VOTERS' CHOICE

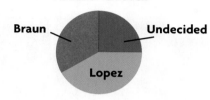

A 10%   **C** 25%

B 15%   **D** 50%

10. In presidential elections in the United States, each state has a certain number of electoral votes. The table shows the number of votes for five southern states in 2000. What is the mean number of electoral votes for these five states?

PRESIDENTIAL ELECTION 2000					
State	LA	MS	AL	GA	FL
Electoral Votes	9	7	9	13	25

F 9   **H** 16

G 12.6   **J** 25

11. Explain It The picture shows a basket of apples. If you closed your eyes and took an apple at random, what is the probability that it would be red? Explain how you found your answer.

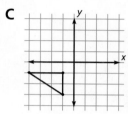 GEOMETRY AND SPATIAL SENSE

12. Which figure shows a rotation of triangle *ABC* around the origin?

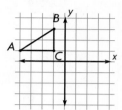

A 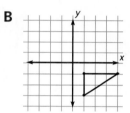   **C**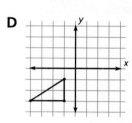

B   **D**

13. The perimeter of the poster shown below is 72 inches. What is the area of the poster?

12 inches

F   18 square inches

G   288 square inches

H   432 square inches

J   720 square inches

14. Explain It Egypt's Great Pyramid of Giza is a square pyramid. Describe its shape. In your description, include how many faces a square pyramid has and what their shapes are.

CHAPTER 2

Operation Sense

≡FAST FACT • SCIENCE A bird can reach almost any part of its body with its beak because it has an extremely flexible neck. The bones in the neck are called cervical vertebrae. Most birds have more cervical vertebrae than humans or other mammals. The number of cervical vertebrae that flamingos have can be written as $4^2 + 8 \times 2 - 13$.

PROBLEM SOLVING About how many times as many cervical vertebrae does a flamingo have as a human?

CERVICAL VERTEBRAE

Animal: Human, Owl, Pigeon, Swan, Calif. Condor

0 2 4 6 8 10 12 14 16 18 20 22 24 26

Number of Cervical Vertebrae

Check What You Know

Use this page to help you review and remember important skills needed for Chapter 2.

✅ Repeated Multiplication

Find the product.

1. $3 \times 3 \times 3$

2. $2 \times 2 \times 2 \times 2$

3. $4 \times 4 \times 4$

4. $5 \times 5 \times 5 \times 5$

5. $10 \times 10 \times 10 \times 10$

6. $9 \times 9 \times 9$

7. $8 \times 8 \times 8$

8. $6 \times 6 \times 6$

9. $7 \times 7 \times 7$

10. $10 \times 10 \times 10$

11. $4 \times 4 \times 4 \times 4$

12. $5 \times 5 \times 5$

13. $3 \times 3 \times 3 \times 3 \times 3$

14. $2 \times 2 \times 2 \times 2 \times 2 \times 2$

15. $6 \times 6 \times 6 \times 6 \times 6$

✅ Use Parentheses

Evaluate the expression.

16. $(4 + 7) + 9$

17. $5 \times (6 + 2)$

18. $(1 + 7) \times 4$

19. $(7 + 8) + 3$

20. $4 + (7 - 3)$

21. $6 \times (9 - 3)$

22. $2 \times (3 + 5 + 8)$

23. $(8 + 5) + (3 + 1)$

24. $4 + (5 + 7) + 2$

25. $2 \times (3 \times 1)$

26. $9 - (7 - 3) - 2$

27. $(8 \times 2) - (3 \times 4)$

28. $3 \times (7 + 4) \times 5$

29. $23 + (15 - 6) + 10$

30. $(18 \div 9) + (63 \div 7)$

VOCABULARY POWER

REVIEW

parentheses [pə•ren′thə•sēz] *noun*
In mathematics, parentheses are used to separate an expression within an expression, as in $3 \times (5 + 9)$. In written language, parentheses can be used to separate a word or phrase within a sentence. Give examples of parentheses in written language.

 www.harcourtschool.com/mathglossary

PREVIEW

numerical expression

variable

algebraic expression

evaluate

equation

solution

Commutative Property

Associative Property

Distributive Property

Identity Property of Addition

Identity Property of Multiplication

compensation

exponent

base

order of operations

algebraic operating system (AOS)

ALGEBRA
Expressions

Learn how to identify, write, and evaluate expressions involving whole numbers.

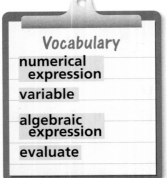

Vocabulary

numerical expression

variable

algebraic expression

evaluate

QUICK REVIEW

1. $23 + 14$ **2.** $67 - 40$ **3.** 15×6 **4.** $180 \div 30$ **5.** 25×8

In a basketball game, a team scored 27 points in the first half and 38 points in the second half. To represent the total points, you could use a numerical expression. A **numerical expression** is a mathematical phrase that includes only numbers and operation symbols.

$$27 + 38 \leftarrow \text{total points}$$

Here are other examples of numerical expressions.

$60 + 25$ $42 \div 7$ $16 - 3$ 51×36 $30 + 12 + 41$

If you didn't know how many points the team scored in the second half, you could use a variable to represent the points. A **variable** is a letter or symbol that can stand for one or more numbers. An expression that includes a variable is called an **algebraic expression**.

$27 + p \leftarrow$ *Use p to represent points scored in second half.*

Here are other examples of algebraic expressions.

$5 + n$ $7 \times a$ $k - 3$ $y \div 2$ $6 \times 5 \times b$

In algebraic expressions, there are many ways to show multiplication.

$7 \times a$ can be written as $a \times 7$, $7a$, $7(a)$, or $7 \cdot a$.

Word expressions can be translated into numerical or algebraic expressions.

EXAMPLE 1

Write a numerical or algebraic expression for the word expression.

A. three dollars less than five dollars $5 - 3$

B. two times a distance, d $2 \times d$, $2(d)$, $2d$, or $2 \cdot d$

To **evaluate** a numerical expression, you find its value. To evaluate an algebraic expression, replace the variable with a number and then find the value.

EXAMPLE 2

Evaluate each expression.

A. $a + 150$, for $a = 18$

$a + 150$	*Replace a*
$18 + 150$	*with 18.*
168	*Add.*

B. $b \div 10 \times 3$, for $b = 120$

$b \div 10 \times 3$	*Replace b with*
$120 \div 10 \times 3$	*120.*
12×3	*Divide and*
36	*then multiply.*

Think and ▶
Discuss

Look back at the lesson to answer each question.

1. **Explain** the difference between a numerical expression and an algebraic expression. Give some examples of each.

2. **Show** four different ways to write an algebraic expression for the product of the number 10 and the variable g.

Guided ▶
Practice

Write a numerical or algebraic expression for the word expression.

3. forty-six less than one hundred twenty-five

4. one hundred seven more than y

5. y divided by fifteen

Evaluate each expression.

6. 21×15

7. $100 - g$, for $g = 54$

8. $s \div 8$, for $s = 720$

PRACTICE AND PROBLEM SOLVING

Independent ▶
Practice

Write a numerical or algebraic expression for the word expression.

9. twenty-five $20 bills

10. q more than two hundred fifteen

11. seventy-six decreased by k

12. x divided by fourteen

Evaluate each expression.

13. 15×31

14. $3{,}021 + 915$

15. $10{,}340 - 1{,}340$

16. $k - 65$, for $k = 95$

17. $\frac{d}{7} \times 2$, for $d = 490$

18. $100b$, for $b = 54$

19. cd, for $c = 5$ and $d = 200$

20. $m \div n$, for $m = 1{,}230$ and $n = 410$

Problem Solving ▶
Applications

21. Let n represent the number of free throws Nathan made. Bryan made 12 more free throws than Nathan. Write an algebraic expression to show how many free throws Bryan made.

22.  **Write About It** Explain how to evaluate an algebraic expression when you know the value of each variable. Give an example.

23. **REASONING** Tiffany, Deidre, Luisa, Kendall, and Ann Marie are runners. Kendall can outrun Luisa and Tiffany, but Deidre can outrun Kendall. Luisa can outrun Ann Marie, but Deidre can outrun Luisa. Which one of the girls is the fastest runner?

MIXED REVIEW AND TEST PREP

24. 530×42 (p. 24)

25. $3{,}870 \div 18$ (p. 24)

26. $1{,}234 + 453$ (p. 22)

27. $8{,}000 - 357$ (p. 22)

⭐ 28. **TEST PREP** Christina bought 3 pens and 1 notebook for $5.85. A pen cost $1.20. How much did the notebook cost?

    A $1.20   **B** $1.25   **C** $1.85   **D** $2.25

EXTRA PRACTICE page 54, Set A

ALGEBRA
Mental Math and Equations

Learn how to use mental math to solve equations.

Vocabulary

equation
solution

QUICK REVIEW

Evaluate each expression.

1. 25×8 **2.** $80 + d$, for $d = 37$

3. $g \div 8$, for $g = 72$ **4.** $450 - 225$

5. Find the missing factor. $\blacksquare \times 8 = 24$

An **equation** is a statement showing that two quantities are equal. These are equations:

$$6 + 7 = 13 \qquad 24 \div 3 = 8 \qquad k - 3 = 1 \qquad 2d = 18 \qquad a + b = 11$$

If an equation contains a variable, you can solve the equation by finding the value of the variable that makes the equation true. That value is the **solution**.

EXAMPLE 1

Remember that a variable is a letter or symbol that stands for one or more numbers.

Which of the numbers 8, 9, and 10 is a solution of the equation $12p = 108$?

Replace p with 8.	*Replace p with 9.*	*Replace p with 10.*
$12(8) \overset{?}{=} 108$	$12(9) \overset{?}{=} 108$	$12(10) \overset{?}{=} 108$
$96 = 108$ *false*	$108 = 108$ *true*	$120 = 108$ *false*

The solution is 9 because $12(9) = 108$.

• Which of the numbers 4, 5, and 6 is a solution of the equation $222 \div n = 37$?

Some equations with variables can be solved by using mental math. Think of the value of the variable that makes the equation true. Then check your answer.

EXAMPLE 2

The Statue of Liberty's hand is about 16 ft long. The index finger is 8 ft long. What is the length of the palm of her hand? Solve the equation $16 = c + 8$ by using mental math.

$16 = c + 8$ *What number added to 8 gives 16?*
$\;8 = c$ *The solution is 8.*

Check:
$16 = 8 + 8$ *Replace c with 8.*
$16 = 16$ *8 + 8 is equal to 16.*

• Solve the equation $m - 7 = 56$ by using mental math.

Think and ▶
Discuss

Look back at the lesson to answer each question.

1. **Explain** whether 4 is a solution of the equation $x + 3 = 9$. If it is not, find the solution.

2. **Give** an example of an equation with a solution of 5.

Guided ▶
Practice

Determine which of the given values is the solution of the equation.

3. $f - 7 = 13$; $f = 19, 20,$ or 21 4. $t + 9 = 20$; $t = 10, 11,$ or 12

Solve each equation by using mental math.

5. $27 = x - 3$ 6. $\dfrac{h}{9} = 3$ 7. $4 \times k = 60$

PRACTICE AND PROBLEM SOLVING

Independent ▶
Practice

Determine which of the given values is the solution of the equation.

8. $3h = 39$; $h = 11, 12,$ or 13 9. $17 - x = 12$; $x = 5, 6,$ or 7

10. $48 + s = 57$; $s = 8, 9,$ or 10 11. $3 = 54 \div k$; $k = 16, 17,$ or 18

Solve each equation by using mental math.

12. $p - 7 = 17$ 13. $9m = 81$ 14. $13 + r = 30$

15. $x - 16 = 4$ 16. $h \div 8 = 7$ 17. $14 = k - 15$

18. $87 = e \div 10$ 19. $12 \times v = 240$ 20. $t \div 6 = 125$

21. $12 + 4 + d = 25$ 22. $3 \times 4 = c - 8$ 23. $p + 14 = 32 - 12$

Problem Solving ▶
Applications

24. The equation $w + 12 = 40$ describes the number of men and women riding the bus to a convention. If w is the number of women riding the bus, how many men are riding the bus?

25. Mr. Murakami teaches 5 classes of 25 students each. One hundred of his students are sixth graders. How many are not sixth graders?

26. **?** **What's the Question?** A roller coaster has 7 cars. Fifty-six people can ride the roller coaster at one time. The answer is 8.

MIXED REVIEW AND TEST PREP

27. Evaluate $a + 14$ for $a = 27$. (p. 36)

28. $525 \div 25$ (p. 24)

29. Find $4,310 - 1,900 + 3,450 - 870$. (p. 22)

30. Find the greatest common factor of 15 and 35.

⭐ 31. **TEST PREP** Andre left the house at 8:45 A.M. He arrived home $4\frac{1}{2}$ hours later. At what time did Andre arrive home?

     A 12:15 P.M.   **B** 12:45 A.M.   **C** 12:45 P.M.   **D** 1:15 P.M.

EXTRA PRACTICE page 54, Set B

ALGEBRA
Properties

Learn about the different properties of addition and multiplication.

Vocabulary

Commutative Property

Associative Property

Distributive Property

Identity Property of Addition

Identity Property of Multiplication

QUICK REVIEW

1. 4×25 **2.** 35×1 **3.** $19.6 + 0$

4. $8 \times (9 + 1)$ **5.** $4 \times (5 \times 2)$

The examples below explain how the properties of addition and multiplication can help you compute mentally.

The **Commutative Property** states that if the order of addends or factors is changed, the sum or product stays the same.

COMMUTATIVE PROPERTY	
Addition	$6 + 2 = 2 + 6 = 8$
Multiplication	$9 \times 3 = 3 \times 9 = 27$

The **Associative Property** states that whatever way addends are grouped or factors are grouped does not change their sum or product.

ASSOCIATIVE PROPERTY	
Addition	$(8 + 5) + 4 = 8 + (5 + 4) = 17$
Multiplication	$(6 \times 7) \times 2 = 6 \times (7 \times 2) = 84$

The **Distributive Property** states that multiplying a sum by a number is the same as multiplying each addend by the number and then adding the products.

DISTRIBUTIVE PROPERTY
$4 \times (7 + 3) = (4 \times 7) + (4 \times 3) = 40$

The **Identity Property of Addition** states that the sum of zero and any number is that number. The **Identity Property of Multiplication** states that the product of 1 and any number is that number.

IDENTITY PROPERTIES	
Identity Property of Addition	$2 + 0 = 2$ and $0 + 2 = 2$
Identity Property of Multiplication	$8 \times 1 = 8$ and $1 \times 8 = 8$

EXAMPLE

Name the property shown.

A. $14 \times (3 + 2) = (14 \times 3) + (14 \times 2)$ *Distributive Property*

B. $42 + 0 = 42$ *Identity Property of Addition*

C. $45 + 73 = 73 + 45$ *Commutative Property*

D. $(28 \times 3) \times 12 = 28 \times (3 \times 12)$ *Associative Property*

E. $17 \times 1 = 17$ *Identity Property of Multiplication*

Think and ▶
Discuss

Look back at the lesson to answer each question.

1. **Explain** how you can use the Distributive Property to find the value of $6 \times (10 + 3)$.

2. **Tell** which property helps you find the value of k.
$(37 \times 23) \times 21 = 37 \times (k \times 21)$

Guided ▶
Practice

Name the property shown.

3. $53 \times 27 = 27 \times 53$

4. $60 + 0 = 60$

5. $7 \times (9 + 6) = (7 \times 9) + (7 \times 6)$

6. $(8 + 21) + 5 = 8 + (21 + 5)$

PRACTICE AND PROBLEM SOLVING

Independent ▶
Practice

Name the property shown.

7. $(11 \times 6) \times 3 = 11 \times (6 \times 3)$

8. $34 \times 1 = 34$

9. $14 + 20 = 20 + 14$

10. $29 + 0 = 29$

11. $8 \times (9 + 7) = (8 \times 9) + (8 \times 7)$

12. $7 + (16 + 4) = (7 + 16) + 4$

13. $3 \times (5 + 8) = (3 \times 5) + (3 \times 8)$

14. $(4 \times 7) \times 15 = 4 \times (7 \times 15)$

15. $75 + 0 = 75$

16. $20 + 51 = 51 + 20$

Find the value of n. Name the property used.

17. $4 \times (9 + 3) = (4 \times n) + (4 \times 3)$

18. $63 \times 47 = n \times 63$

19. $11 + (37 + 8) = (11 + n) + 8$

20. $18 + n = 18$

21. $n \times 1 = 52$

22. $(9 \times 10) \times 7 = 9 \times (10 \times n)$

Problem Solving ▶
Applications

23. Pete bought 6 tickets to a tennis match, each priced at $14. To find the total cost, he added the product 6×10 to the product 6×4, for a total of $84. Which property did he use?

24. Jason said, "$(20 - 10) - 5 = 20 - (10 - 5)$, so the Associative Property works for subtraction." Do you agree? Explain.

25. **REASONING** What if you forgot the value of 8×7? How could you use the Distributive Property to find 8×7?

MIXED REVIEW AND TEST PREP

26. Solve. $12 \times n = 360$ (p. 38)

27. Write the value of the 5 in 453,607,916. (p. 16)

28. Solve. 208×36 (p. 24)

29. Solve. $3,000 - 853$ (p. 22)

⭐**30. TEST PREP** Which is the best estimate for $4,763 \div 59$? (p. 18)

A 70 **B** 80 **C** 90 **D** 100

EXTRA PRACTICE page 54, Set C

41

MENTAL MATH
Use the Properties

Learn how to use properties and mental math to find sums, differences, products, and quotients.

Vocabulary

compensation

Use the table to find how many bones the spine, head, and shoulders have in all. Mentally find the sum by first reordering using the Commutative Property.

$26 + 28 + 4 = 26 + 4 + 28$ *Commutative Property*

$\qquad\qquad = 30 + 28$ *Use mental math.*
$\qquad\qquad = 58$

Mentally find the sum by regrouping using the Associative Property.

$(26 + 28) + 4 = 26 + (28 + 4)$ *Associative Property*

$\qquad\qquad = 26 + 32$ *Use mental math.*
$\qquad\qquad = 58$

BONES IN THE HUMAN BODY	
Part	Number of Bones
Head	28
Spine	26
Throat	1
Chest	25
Shoulders	4
Arms	6
Hands	54
Legs	10
Feet	52

So, the spine, head, and shoulders have a total of 58 bones.

You can use the Distributive Property to mentally solve a problem.

EXAMPLE 1

How many bones are in 5 models of the human spine?
$5 \times 26 = 5 \times (20 + 6)$ *Break 26 into parts.*

$\qquad = (5 \times 20) + (5 \times 6)$ *Use the Distributive Property. Multiply mentally.*

$\qquad = 100 + 30$ *Add the products.*
$\qquad = 130$

So, there are 130 bones in 5 models.

You can also use the Commutative and Associative Properties to try to make partial products that end in 0.

EXAMPLE 2

Use mental math to find the value.

Commutative Property
$6 \times 7 \times 5 = 6 \times 5 \times 7$
$\qquad\qquad = 30 \times 7$
$\qquad\qquad = 210$

Associative Property
$(9 \times 25) \times 2 = 9 \times (25 \times 2)$
$\qquad\qquad = 9 \times 50$
$\qquad\qquad = 450$

A strategy you can use for some addition and subtraction problems is **compensation**. For addition, change one number to a multiple of 10 and then adjust the other number to keep the balance.

<table>
<tr><td>

EXAMPLE 3

</td><td>

Mr. Forge and his friends play basketball for an hour on Fridays and Saturdays. On Friday they scored a total of 44 points, and on Saturday they scored 57 points. Use compensation to find the total points scored for both days.

$44 + 57 = (44 + 6) + (57 - 6)$ *Add 6 to 44 and subtract 6 from 57.*

$= 50 + 51$ *Use mental math to add.*

$= 101$

So, the total points scored is 101.

</td></tr>
</table>

When you use compensation to subtract, you have to do the same thing to each number. Since it's easy to subtract numbers ending in 0, try to make the second number a multiple of 10.

EXAMPLE 4

Use compensation to find $128 - 56$.

$128 - 56 = (128 + 4) - (56 + 4)$ *Add 4 to 128 and to 56 before subtracting.*

$= 132 - 60$

$= 72$

So, the difference is 72.

You can sometimes divide mentally by breaking a number into smaller parts that are each divisible by the divisor.

EXAMPLE 5

Use mental math to find $396 \div 4$.

$396 = 360 + 36$ *Break 396 into parts.*

$360 \div 4 = 90$ and $36 \div 4 = 9$ *Divide each part by 4 mentally.*

$90 + 9 = 99$ *Add the parts of the quotient.*

So, $396 \div 4 = 99$.

• Tell another way to break 396 into two parts to divide by 4.

Math Idea ▶ Using the number properties and other mental math strategies will help you add, subtract, multiply, and divide mentally.

CHECK FOR UNDERSTANDING

Think and Discuss ▶ **Look back at the lesson to answer each question.**

1. **Explain** how using the Associative Property in Example 2 made the problem easier to solve.

2. **Explain** two ways to use compensation to find $349 + 138$ mentally.

Use mental math to find the value.

3. 12×17 **4.** $45 + 9 + 15$ **5.** $124 + 17 + 16$ **6.** 9×36

7. $(6 + 37) + 13$ **8.** $2 \times 9 \times 50$ **9.** 5×29 **10.** 11×43

11. $39 + 16$ **12.** $83 + 38$ **13.** $426 \div 3$ **14.** $16 + 35$

15. $279 \div 3$ **16.** $137 - 51$ **17.** $65 - 22$ **18.** $567 \div 7$

PRACTICE AND PROBLEM SOLVING

Independent ▶
Practice

Use mental math to find the value.

19. 24×7 **20.** $73 - 27$ **21.** 45×11 **22.** 12×35

23. $87 + 98$ **24.** $(12 + 23) + 8$ **25.** 4×27 **26.** $18 + 26$

27. 4×53 **28.** $64 - 29$ **29.** $24 + 32 + 16$ **30.** 19×14

31. $126 + 118$ **32.** $293 - 137$ **33.** $765 \div 9$

34. $32 + 36$ **35.** $19 + 26$ **36.** $4 \times 6 \times 50$

37. $25 \times 30 \times 2$ **38.** $172 \div 4$ **39.** $1,526 - 498$

40. $40 \times 15 \times 2$ **41.** $(4 \times 33) + (4 \times 7)$ **42.** $(6 \times 24) + (6 \times 6)$

43. $192 \div n$, for $n = 3$ **44.** $c \times 9 \times 5$, for $c = 8$

45. $p \div 12$, for $p = 624$ **46.** $a + 19 + 32$, for $a = 18$

Name each missing reason.

47. $80 \times 3 = (8 \times 10) \times 3$ 80 means 8×10.

$\qquad = 8 \times (10 \times 3)$ Associative Property

$\qquad = 8 \times (3 \times 10)$ ___?___

$\qquad = (8 \times 3) \times 10$ ___?___

$\qquad = 24 \times 10$ ___?___

$\qquad = 240$ ___?___

48. What if the product of three whole numbers is 210? Without using 1 as a factor, what are the possible choices for the numbers?

Problem Solving ▶
Applications

Use Data   **For 49–51, use the data below.**

49. Use mental math to find how many CDs were bought in all. Explain how you got your answer.

50. If Nick and Selena each gave 12 CDs to Brenda, how many would Brenda have then?

51. How many CDs would Brenda, Selena, Ricardo, and Nick each have if they shared their CDs equally?

CDs Bought
Brenda 12
Selena 17
Nick 25
Ricardo 18

52. Vocabulary Power The prefix *re-* in *regroup* means "again." How does this help you understand the meaning of *reorder*?

53. Ann needs 250 signatures on a petition. On Monday she got 23 signatures, on Tuesday she got 3 times as many as on Monday, and on Wednesday and Thursday she got 45 each. How many more signatures does she need?

54. Jocelyn has $253.47. Her aunt gives her $87.95 more. Jocelyn buys a pair of shoes for $39.99, three T-shirts for $7.77 each, and two pairs of jeans for $60.22 each. Use estimation to find about how much money Jocelyn has left.

55. **Write About It** Explain how to use compensation to add two numbers. Give an appropriate example to support your explanation.

MIXED REVIEW AND TEST PREP

56. Use mental math to solve. $a \div 7 = 21$ (p. 38)

57. Multiply. 732×46 (p. 24)   **58.** Divide. $64,270 \div 35$ (p. 24)

59. TEST PREP Rob changes 4 quarts of oil in his car every 3,000 miles. How many quarts of oil will Rob have used after driving 9,000 miles? (p. 24)

A 3   **B** 9   **C** 12   **D** 36

60. TEST PREP Joe bought 3 basketballs for $22.99 each and a net for $5.99. Which numerical expression can be used to find the total cost of the basketballs and net? (p. 36)

F $3 \times (22.99 + 5.99)$ **H** $(3 \times 5.99) + 22.99$

G $(3 \times 22.99) + 5.99$ **J** $(3 + 22.99) + 5.99$

PROBLEM SOLVING

MATH FUN Practice using mental math strategies to solve this puzzle.

1. Copy the diagram. Place the values of the expressions below in the circles so that every sum of three numbers in a line is the same.

$84 \div 2$
$36 + 8$
$28 + 16 + 2$
$3 \times 8 \times 2$ $8 + 14 + 32$
$28 + 22$ $448 \div 8$
4×13 $4 + 38 + 16$

2. Use mental math. What is the sum of each row of three numbers?

Exponents

Learn how to represent numbers by using exponents.

Vocabulary

exponent

base

Remember that when you multiply two or more numbers to get a product, the numbers multiplied are called factors.

$8 \times 3 \times 4 = 96$

The numbers 8, 3, and 4 are factors of 96.

Large numbers can be hard to understand. Some football stadiums can seat over 100,000 people. On the right are four ways to write 100,000 using smaller numbers.

$10 \times 10,000$
$10 \times 10 \times 1,000$
$10 \times 10 \times 10 \times 100$
$10 \times 10 \times 10 \times 10 \times 10$

Another way to write 100,000 is by using an exponent. An **exponent** shows how many times a number called the **base** is used as a factor.

$$\overset{\text{exponent}}{\underset{\text{base}}{10^5}} = \underbrace{10 \times 10 \times 10 \times 10 \times 10}_{\text{equal factors}} = 100,000$$

EXPONENT FORM	READ	VALUE
10^1	The first power of ten	10
$10^2 = 10 \times 10$	Ten squared, or the second power of ten	100
$10^3 = 10 \times 10 \times 10$	Ten cubed, or the third power of ten	1,000

EXAMPLE 1

Find the values of 2^4, 4^2, and 6^3.

$2^4 = 2 \times 2 \times 2 \times 2$
$\quad = 16$
2 is a factor four times.

$4^2 = 4 \times 4$
$\quad = 16$
4 is a factor two times.

$6^3 = 6 \times 6 \times 6$
$\quad = 216$
6 is a factor three times.

Note: The first power of any number equals that number.

$6^1 = 6 \qquad 9^1 = 9 \qquad 10^1 = 10$

The zero power of any number, except zero, is defined to be 1.

$6^0 = 1 \qquad 9^0 = 1 \qquad 10^0 = 1$

EXAMPLE 2

Write 125 using an exponent and the base 5.

$125 = 5 \times 25 = 5 \times 5 \times 5$ *Find the equal factors.*
$\quad\ = 5^3$ *Write using the base and the exponent.*

So, $125 = 5^3$.

Think and ▶ **Look back at the lesson to answer each question.**
Discuss

1. **Tell** how many zeros there are in the standard form of 10^7.

2. **Explain** how to write $6 \times 6 \times 6 \times 6$ using an exponent.

Guided ▶ **Write the equal factors. Then find the value.**
Practice

3. 2^3 **4.** 5^2 **5.** 3^4 **6.** 9^3 **7.** 1^4

PRACTICE AND PROBLEM SOLVING

Independent ▶ **Write the equal factors. Then find the value.**
Practice

8. 4^5 **9.** 7^3 **10.** 1^{12} **11.** 5^3 **12.** 2^5

13. 34^2 **14.** 13^2 **15.** 10^8 **16.** 20^2 **17.** 2^{10}

18. 10^4 **19.** 3^0 **20.** 15^2 **21.** 25^1 **22.** 90^2

Write in exponent form.

23. $12 \times 12 \times 12$ **24.** $1 \times 1 \times 1 \times 1 \times 1$ **25.** $4 \times 4 \times 4 \times 4$

26. $2 \times 2 \times 2 \times 2 \times 2$ **27.** $n \times n$ **28.** $y \times y \times y \times y$

Express with an exponent and the given base.

29. 64, base 8 **30.** 216, base 6 **31.** 10,000; base 10

32. Write 64 using a base of 8, a base of 4, and a base of 2.

Problem Solving ▶ **33. Use Data** In which year shown
Applications did Kansas first have a population
greater than 8^7? Explain.

34. Ben saves movie ticket stubs.
He puts them in albums with
2^4 pages. Each page holds 3^2
stubs. How many albums
does he need for 720 stubs?

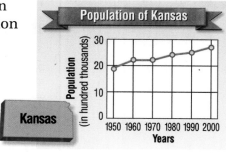

35. **(?) What's the Question?** Scott has 3^2 video games and Aaron
has 2^3 games. The answer is 1.

MIXED REVIEW AND TEST PREP

36. Solve the equation by using mental math. $n \div 3 = 93$. (p. 38)

37. Round 45,621 to the nearest thousand. (p. 18)

38. $943,012 - 57,806$ (p. 22) **39.** $32,047 \div 43$ (p. 24)

40. TEST PREP Which expression is not equivalent to $(3 + 5) \times 2$? (p. 36)

A $(5 + 3) \times 2$ **B** $3 \times 2 + 5 \times 2$ **C** $3 + 5 \times 2$ **D** 8×2

EXTRA PRACTICE page 54, Set E

Order of Operations

Learn how to use the order of operations.

You need a calculator.

QUICK REVIEW

1. $16 \div 24$ **2.** $(24 \div 6) \div 2$

3. 14×10 **4.** $(75 - 21) + 8$

5. $4 \times (6 + 2)$

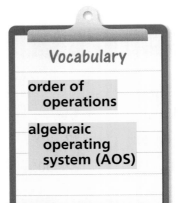

Vocabulary

order of
  operations

algebraic
  operating
  system (AOS)

For many of the things you do every day, you must complete steps in a certain order. For example, when using a phone to call a friend, you first pick up or turn on the phone, then press the number keys, and then listen for the connection to be made.

In mathematics, when evaluating expressions that contain more than one operation, you follow rules called the **order of operations**.

Order of Operations

1. Perform operations in parentheses.

2. Clear exponents.

3. Multiply and divide from left to right.

4. Add and subtract from left to right.

EXAMPLE 1

Tell the operations used to evaluate the expression.

$35 \div 7 + 5 \times 3^2$	*Clear the exponent.*
$35 \div 7 + 5 \times 9$	*Divide.*
$5 + 5 \times 9$	*Multiply.*
$5 + 45$	*Add.*
50	

• List in order the operations to find the value of
  $3 + 5^2 \times 2 \div 10 - 4$.

EXAMPLE 2

Find the value of the expression $285 + 93 \div (3 - 2) \times 3 \times 4^2$.

$285 + 93 \div (3 - 2) \times 3 \times 4^2$	*Operate inside parentheses.*
$285 + 93 \div 1 \times 3 \times 4^2$	*Clear the exponent.*
$285 + 93 \div 1 \times 3 \times 16$	*Divide.*
$285 + 93 \times 3 \times 16$	*Multiply twice.*
$285 + 4{,}464$	*Add.*
$4{,}749$	

• Evaluate the expression $5 + (7 - 4)^2 - 8 \div 2$.

You can use a calculator to evaluate expressions with more than one operation. Some calculators use an **algebraic operating system (AOS)**, which automatically follows the order of operations.

Activity

- Use your calculator to find the value of $8 \div 2 + 6 \times 3 - 4$.

- Following the order of operations, use paper and pencil to find the value of $8 \div 2 + 6 \times 3 - 4$.

- Exchange papers with a classmate, and check each other's work.

- How does the calculator value for $8 \div 2 + 6 \times 3 - 4$ compare with the value you got by using paper and pencil? Does your calculator use an AOS?

- To find the value of an expression with a calculator that does not use an AOS, follow the order of operations or use the memory keys.

- Follow the order of operations to find the value of the expression $2 + 6 \times 3^2 - 4$.

3 2 6 2 4

```
3^2 X 6 + 2 - 4 =
              52
```

- Use the memory keys to find the value of the expression $9^2 + 6 \div 2 \times 4$.

9 2   6 2 4

```
 6 ÷ 2 X 4 + 81 =
              93
```

EXAMPLE 3

Use a calculator to evaluate the expressions.

A. $12 + 8 \times 4^2$

12 8 4 2

```
12 + 8 X 4^2 =
           140
```

B. $9 + (6 - 2) \times 5$

9   6 2 × 5 Enter

```
9 + (6 - 2) X 5 =
              29
```

C. $18 \div (6 - 4) + 5$

18 ÷  6 − 4  + 5 Enter

```
18 ÷ (6 - 4) + 5 =
               14
```

When evaluating algebraic expressions, use the order of operations.

EXAMPLE 4

Evaluate the expression $16 - n^2 - (9 - 7) \times y$, for $n = 2$ and $y = 4$.

$16 - n^2 - (9 - 7) \times y$	*Replace n with 2 and y with 4.*
$16 - 2^2 - (9 - 7) \times 4$	*Operate inside parentheses.*
$16 - 2^2 - 2 \times 4$	*Clear the exponent.*
$16 - 4 - 2 \times 4$	*Multiply.*
$16 - 4 - 8$	*Subtract twice.*
4	

CHECK FOR UNDERSTANDING

Think and Discuss

Look back at the lesson to answer each question.

1. **Show** where to insert parentheses to make this equation true.
   $420 - 100 \div 40 = 8$

2. **Tell** which operation you would do last to evaluate the expression $7 + 8 - 2^3 \div 4$.

Guided Practice

Evaluate the expression.

3. $30 - 15 \div 3$ **4.** $5^2 - (40 \div 4) \div 2$ **5.** $5^2 + 10^2 \div 25 - 1$

PRACTICE AND PROBLEM SOLVING

Independent Practice

Evaluate the expression.

6. $45 \div 15 + 2 \times 3$
7. $7 \times 2^2 + 6 - 9$

8. $3 + 4 \times 250$
9. $12 + (36 \div 4)^2 - 25$

10. $2^6 - (27 - 8) + (5^2 - 21)$
11. $(43 + 57) \times (9 - 6)^0$

12. $4^4 - (5^3 - 7^2) + (3^3 - 25)^3$
13. $(6^2 + 3^2)^2 \div 5 \times 3 + 3$

14. $(24 + 1^8) \times (7 - 5)^3$
15. $(7 \times 4)^2 - (34 + 1^8) \times 2^3$

TECHNOLOGY LINK

More Practice:
**Harcourt Mega Math
Ice Station Exploration,**
Arctic Algebra, Level X

Use a calculator to evaluate the expressions.

16. $23 + (12 \times 6) - 2$
17. $13 + 5 - 3 \times (21 \div 7)$

18. $17 + 8 - 2^3 \div 4$
19. $8^3 + 20 \div (12 - 8)$

ALGEBRA Evaluate the expression for $a = 4$ and $b = 7$.

20. $21 \div b + 8$
21. $a \times 31 - 8^2$

22. $(8 - a) \div 2 + 7$
23. $b^2 \div 7 \times (6 + 5)$

24. $(a^2 + b^2) \times 4$
25. $(b^2 - a^2) \div 3$

Problem Solving Applications

For 26–27, write and evaluate an expression to solve.

26. Heather mailed 3 packages that cost $2.50 each and 2 packages that cost $1.50 each. How much did she spend on postage?

27. Minh bought a watermelon for $3.25 and 3 cantaloupes for $1.29 each. He gave the clerk $20. How much change did he get in return?

28. ≣**FAST FACT** • ART The Muny, located in St. Louis, Missouri, is the largest outdoor theater in the United States and can seat $6^5 + 3{,}024$ people. The Old Mill Outdoor Theatre in Branson, Missouri, can seat 1,100 people. Write an expression using parentheses to find how many more people the Muny can seat than the Old Mill Outdoor Theatre.

29. (?) **What's the Error?** Joe and Brett found the value of $2 + 6 \times 3^2 - 4$. Joe said the answer is 68 and Brett said the answer is 52. Decide who made the error and describe what the error is.

30. The Island Theater holds 236 people. It was filled to capacity for each of its 43 shows last week. This week 8,299 people attended shows at the theater. How many people attended shows at the Island Theater during these two weeks?

MIXED REVIEW AND TEST PREP

31. What are the equal factors and the value for 7^3? (p. 46)

32. Use mental math to find the value. 34×6 (p. 42)

33. Subtract. $2{,}500 - 1{,}646$ (p. 22)

34. Divide. $163 \div 5$ (p. 24)

35. **TEST PREP** Ricky has a total of 64 pennies and quarters in a jar. He has 34 more pennies than quarters. How much money does Ricky have in the jar? (p. 28)

A $4.24   **C** $5.24

B $4.40   **D** $8.80

PROBLEM SOLVING LiNKUP to Careers

Computer Programmer Computers perform operations one at a time, just like people. The difference is that computers can perform millions of operations per second. Computer programmers sometimes use *expression trees* to help them know the order in which computers will perform operations. An expression tree is used to represent an algebraic or arithmetic expression.

Expression: $5 \times (n + 8)$

Expression tree: **Step 1**   *Start with the operation that is performed first.*

        Step 2   *Add the next operation above the first operation.*

Step 1:
```
    +
   / \
  n   8
```

Step 2:
```
    ×
   / \
  5   +
     / \
    n   8
```

Write an expression tree for each expression.

1. $4 \times (p + 7)$ **2.** $10 \div (n + 5)$ **3.** $(y + m) - 5$ **4.** $h \div (3 - b)$ **5.** $9 + (6 \times c)$

EXTRA PRACTICE page 54, Set F

PROBLEM SOLVING SKILL
Multistep Problems

Analyze
Choose
Solve
Check

*L*earn how to solve multistep problems.

Tickets for the All-City Youth Symphony cost $12 for adults and $5 for students. Three-hundred eighty adult tickets were sold. The remaining tickets were purchased by students. The theater has 36 rows with 25 seats in each row. If the concert was a sell-out, how much money was earned from the sale of tickets?

ALL-CITY
YOUTH SYMPHONY
8 P.M. SATURDAY

This problem involves multiple steps. To solve a multistep problem, break it down into single steps.

Step 1 Find the total amount earned from adult tickets.

$380 \times \$12$　　　*Multiply the number of adult tickets*
$380 \times 12 = 4{,}560$　　*sold by the cost of one adult ticket.*

So, the total earned from adult tickets sold was $4,560.

Step 2 Find the number of student tickets sold.

$(36 \times 25) - 380$　　*Find the number of seats in the*
$900 - 380$　　　　　*theater. Then subtract the number of*
520　　　　　　　*adult tickets sold.*

So, 520 student tickets were sold.

Step 3 Find the total amount earned from student tickets.

$520 \times \$5$　　　　*Multiply the number of student tickets*
$520 \times 5 = 2{,}600$　　*sold by the cost of one student ticket.*

So, the total earned from student tickets sold was $2,600.

Step 4 Find the amount of money earned from the sale of all tickets.

$\$4{,}560 + \$2{,}600$　　　*Add the total amounts earned from*
$4{,}560 + 2{,}600 = 7{,}160$　*adult and student tickets.*

So, $7,160 was earned from the sale of tickets.

Talk About It ▶ • **What if** all but 50 of the remaining seats were sold to students? Explain the steps you would use to solve the problem.

Solve by breaking down each problem into single steps.

1. Lynette saves $40 per week for her vacation. Her goal is to save $1,200. If she has been saving for 18 wk, how many more weeks must she save in order to meet her goal?

2. Pencils are on sale at Office Emporium for $0.99 per dozen. Ms. Klein buys 8 pencils for each of her 96 students. How much will she spend on pencils?

3. One week Beth worked 38 hr at $7.75 per hour. The next week she worked 36 hr at $9 per hour. How much more did she earn the second week than she earned the first week?

   A $16.75   **C** $30.00

   B $29.50   **D** $74.00

4. Harvey drove for 7 hr at an average speed of 54 mi per hour. His car averaged 28 mi per gallon of gas. If gas costs $1.24 per gallon, how much did he pay for gas to drive the 7 hr?

   F $14.78   **H** $34.72

   G $16.74   **J** $66.96

5. Ed wants to buy 3 boxes of cereal at $2.99 each, 2 melons at $1.29 each, and 5 cans of juice at $0.79 each. Ed has $12.80. How much more money does he need to buy all of the items?

6. At the Discount Book Barn, books cost $5.00 and magazines cost $1.50. José bought some books and magazines for $21. How many of each did he buy?

7. **Use Data** Use the graph below. The highest waterfall in the world is Angel Falls, in Venezuela. About how much higher is Angel Falls than Ribbon Falls?

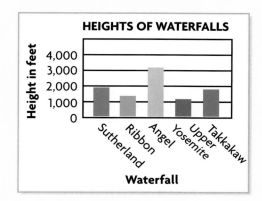

8. Tim has saved $1,475 to make a down payment on a new car. He wants to save a total of three times that amount plus $275. How much money does Tim want to save for a down payment?

9. Ron and his two cousins own videotapes. Ron has twice as many as his older cousin, who has 27 videotapes. Ron has three times as many as his younger cousin. How many videotapes do they have in all?

10. Harry hammered nails into a board to make a circular pegboard. The nails were the same distance apart, and the sixth nail was directly opposite the eighteenth nail. How many nails formed the circle?

11. **Write About It** Explain the steps you would follow to solve the problem. Fencing material costs $8 per foot. One gallon of paint covers 14 ft of fencing and sells for $12 per gallon. If the fencing material costs $448, how much will the paint cost in order to cover the entire fence?

Set A (pp. 36–37)

Write a numerical or algebraic expression for the word expression.

1. nine dollars less than twelve dollars

2. thirteen more than a number, x

3. twenty-two dogs times two bowls

4. fifty-two divided by two

Evaluate each expression.

5. $8 \times a$, for $a = 35$

6. $p - 38$, for $p = 97$

7. $175 \div k$, for $k = 5$

8. $96 + m$, for $m = 48$

Set B (pp. 38–39)

Determine which of the given values is the solution of the equation.

1. $5w = 70$; $w = 12, 13$, or 14

2. $16 - a = 7$; $a = 8, 9$, or 10

3. $48 \div x = 8$; $x = 6, 7$, or 8

Solve each equation by using mental math.

4. $23 + c = 28$

5. $k \div 9 = 5$

6. $q - 25 = 25$

7. $c \times 6 = 426$

Set C (pp. 40–41)

Name the property shown.

1. $(4 + 34) + 6 = 4 + (34 + 6)$

2. $61 \times 1 = 61$

3. $24 \times 51 = 51 \times 24$

4. $6 \times (4 + 3) = (6 \times 4) + (6 \times 3)$

Set D (pp. 42–45)

Use mental math to find the value.

1. $26 + (4 + 18)$

2. $6 \times 4 \times 5$

3. $28 + 9 + 41$

4. $83 - 36$

5. $4 + 19 + 26$

6. 38×6

7. $47 - 29$

8. $7 + 22 + 13$

Set E (pp. 46–47)

Write the equal factors. Then find the value.

1. 10^4

2. 5^6

3. 2^3

4. 3^2

5. 7^4

Set F (pp. 48–51)

Evaluate the expression.

1. $7 + (2 \times 2)^4 - 9 \times 9$

2. $90 \times 5 - 4 \times (18 \div 6)$

3. $3^2 \times (4 + 5)^2 - 36$

4. $15^2 \div (4^2 + 9) + 8^1$

1. **VOCABULARY** A letter or symbol that can stand for one or more numbers is a(n) __?__ . (p. 36)

2. **VOCABULARY** A statement showing that two quantities are equal is a(n) __?__ . (p. 38)

3. **VOCABULARY** To find the value of an expression that has more than one operation, you need to use the __?__ . (p. 48)

Evaluate each expression for $a = 63$, $b = 150$, $c = 7$. (pp. 36–37)

4. $a + 305$
5. $b - 36$
6. $300 \div b$
7. $3c$
8. $a \div 9$

9. $215 - b$
10. $112 \div c$
11. $a \times 5$
12. $2a + 4$
13. $a + b$

Solve each equation by using mental math. (pp. 38–39)

14. $3m = 27$
15. $14 = q + 6$
16. $20 = y - 9$
17. $w \div 50 = 5$
18. $74 + a = 85$

19. $n \div 9 = 23$
20. $36 = n - 10$
21. $a + 18 = 21$
22. $4x = 52$
23. $60 \div n = 12$

Use mental math to find the value. (pp. 42–45)

24. $19 + 43$
25. $76 - 37$
26. $32 + (48 + 83)$

27. 26×12
28. $5,986 \times 1$
29. $4 \times 6 \times 25$

30. $40 \times 25 \times 2$
31. $117 + 128$
32. $193 - 137$

Write the equal factors. Then find the value. (pp. 46–47)

33. 6^2
34. 9^2
35. 3^5
36. 5^4

37. 10^6
38. 7^0
39. 25^1
40. 4^3

Evaluate the expression. (pp. 48–51)

41. $4 \times 5 - 6 \times 3$
42. $(12 \times 7) + 9^2$

43. $13 + 4 \times (20 + 35)$
44. $4^3 - 4 \times 12$

45. $36 \div (24 - 18) + 9$
46. $45 - (12 \times 3) \div 6$

47. $16 \times 9 \div 2^3$
48. $(100 - 28) \div 3^2$

Solve.

49. Doreen has $40.00. She wants to buy 3 pairs of socks for $2.75 each, gloves for $9.99, and 2 T-shirts for $8.79 each. How much money will she have left? (pp. 52–53)

50. Each of three pyramids of Egypt is made up of about 2.5 million large stones. Is the total number of stones greater than or less than 10^8? (pp. 46–47)

NUMBER SENSE, CONCEPTS, AND OPERATIONS

1. The tallest structure in the United States is a TV tower in Blanchard, North Dakota. It is 2,063 feet in height. Which of the following is equivalent to 2,063?

   A 200 + 60 + 3

   B 2,000 + 60 + 3

   C 2,000 + 600 + 3

   D 2,000 + 600 + 30

2. The number of days it takes the planet Venus to travel once around the Sun can be written as $1 + 2^5 \times 7$. How many days does $1 + 2^5 \times 7$ represent?

   F 71 days   **H** 225 days

   G 77 days   **J** 231 days

3. The circle graph shows how Dan spends his allowance.

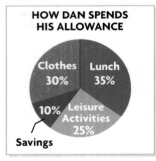

HOW DAN SPENDS HIS ALLOWANCE

Clothes 30%
Lunch 35%
10% Savings
Leisure Activities 25%

   On which item does he spend $\frac{1}{4}$ of his allowance?

   A lunch   **C** clothes

   B leisure activities   **D** savings

4. **Explain It** Latrell has $50 to spend. He wants to buy a shirt for $24.99 and two sports caps for $9.95 each. Decide whether Latrell needs an **estimate** or an **exact answer** to determine if he has enough money. Explain your reasoning.

 MEASUREMENT

5. The diameter of a quarter is 24 millimeters. Which equation can be used to find the circumference of a quarter?

24 mm

   F $C = \pi \times 24$

   G $C = 24 \div \pi$

   H $C = \pi \div 24$

   J $C = 2 \times \pi \times 24$

6. Which rectangle has a perimeter twice as long as the perimeter of rectangle *ABCD*?

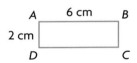

A   6 cm   B
2 cm
D   C

   A
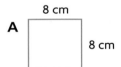
   8 cm
   8 cm

   B

   10 cm
   4 cm

   C
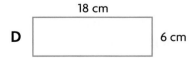
   12 cm
   2 cm

   D
   18 cm
   6 cm

7. **Explain It** Here are the wingspans of three birds: kestrel—21 inches, falcon—1 yard, hawk—2 feet. Explain how you could decide which wingspan is **greatest**. Then order the wingspans from **least** to **greatest**.

wingspan

ALGEBRAIC THINKING

 DATA ANALYSIS AND PROBABILITY

8. Mona plans to save twice as much money each week as she had in her account the week before. She saved $1 the first week. Which of the following shows her total savings after the first four weeks?

> **TIP** **Decide on a plan.** See item 8. Find Mona's savings the second week and her total savings after two weeks. Use the same plan for Weeks 3 and 4.

F $8

G $27

H $10

J $64

9. Look at the table below.

x	y
1	5
2	7
3	9
4	11
5	

Which of the following is the value of y when x = 5?

A 6

B 12

C 13

D 17

10. **Explain It** The temperature in Chicago is 5 degrees cooler than the temperature in Cleveland. The temperature in Chicago is 68 degrees Fahrenheit. Explain how you can write and solve an equation to find the temperature in Cleveland.

11. For a science project, Luis measured the number of hours it took 14 types of wildflower seeds to sprout. Here is his data:

79	84	92	79	87	94	85
92	89	78	85	79	95	88

Which table correctly organizes the data?

F

SPROUTING TIMES	
Time (in hours)	Frequency
70–80	4
80–85	3
90–95	3
95–100	1

G

SPROUTING TIMES	
Time (in hours)	Frequency
76–80	3
81–85	4
86–90	4
91–95	3

H

SPROUTING TIMES	
Time (in hours)	Frequency
76–80	4
80–85	3
85–90	3
90–95	4

J

SPROUTING TIMES	
Time (in hours)	Frequency
76–80	4
81–85	3
86–90	3
91–95	4

12. **Explain It** There are 30 marbles in a bag. Half are red and 5 are yellow. The rest of the marbles are blue. If you choose a marble at random, what is the probability that it will be blue? Explain your reasoning.

CHAPTER 3

Decimal Concepts

≡FAST FACT • SOCIAL STUDIES In 2000, Oklahoma ranked second in the U.S. for growing winter wheat and twentieth for growing corn. Wheat and corn are important crops in the United States. They are used in cereals, breads, pastas, and snacks.

PROBLEM SOLVING Which ingredients of the party mix occur in almost equal amounts?

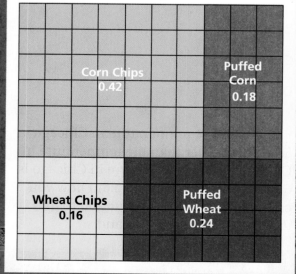

Party Mix Ingredients

Corn Chips
0.42

Puffed Corn
0.18

Wheat Chips
0.16

Puffed Wheat
0.24

Check What You Know

Use this page to help you review and remember important skills needed for Chapter 3.

☑ Represent Decimals

Write the decimal that is modeled.

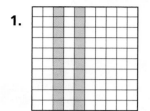  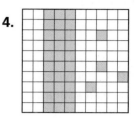

1. 2. 3. 4.

☑ Compare Whole Numbers

Compare the numbers. Write <, >, or = for ●.

5. 143 ● 140 **6.** 808 ● 880 **7.** 716 ● 716 **8.** 691 ● 961

9. 4,062 ● 4,206 **10.** 383 ● 383 **11.** 6,098 ● 6,908 **12.** 48,001 ● 5,586

☑ Round Decimals

Round to the nearest whole number.

13. 3.64 **14.** 1.49 **15.** 18.70 **16.** 95.51

Round to the nearest tenth.

17. 69.64 **18.** 26.37 **19.** 52.489 **20.** 26.397

Round to the nearest hundredth.

21. 5.582 **22.** 4.026 **23.** 75.093 **24.** 35.697

VOCABULARY POWER

REVIEW

PREVIEW

percent

decimal [de′sə•məl] *noun*

The word *decimal* comes from the Latin word *decimus*, meaning "tenth." How does this help you know the relationship between the values of the different decimal places?

 www.harcourtschool.com/mathglossary

Represent, Compare, and Order Decimals

Learn how to use place value to express, compare, and order decimals.

QUICK REVIEW

Compare the numbers. Write <, >, or = for ●.

1. 124 ● 134   **2.** 143 ● 134   **3.** 909 ● 990

4. 987 ● 1,004   **5.** 2,047 ● 2,047

Remember that when reading a number with a decimal point, read the decimal point as "and." Read 8.2 as "eight and two tenths."

Genna read that it costs $0.329 to heat the water to take a 7.5-min shower.

Place value helps you understand numbers. The digits and the position of each digit determine a number's value. Read each number on the place-value chart. These numbers are part of the decimal system. Notice that 3 has a value of 3 tenths, 3 tens, or 3 hundred-thousandths, depending on its position in the number.

	Ten Thousands	Thousands	Hundreds	Tens	Ones	Tenths	Hundredths	Thousandths	Ten-Thousandths	Hundred-Thousandths	Millionths
PLACE VALUE											
0.329					0	3	2	9			
32.4				3	2	4					
8.00023					8	0	0	0	2	3	

When you read and write numbers, you are using place value.

EXAMPLE 1

A. Standard form: 0.329
Expanded form: 0.3 + 0.02 + 0.009
Word form: *three hundred twenty-nine thousandths*

B. Standard form: 32.4
Expanded form: 30 + 2 + 0.4
Word form: *thirty-two and four tenths*

C. Standard form: 8.00023
Expanded form: 8 + 0.0002 + 0.00003
Word form: *eight and twenty-three hundred-thousandths*

Math **I**dea ▶ Knowing the place value of digits will help you read, write, and correctly calculate numbers, including decimal numbers.

Mark notices that one jar of cinnamon contains 2.6 oz and another contains 2.3 oz. He wants to buy the jar with the greater amount of cinnamon.

You can use a number line to compare 2.6 and 2.3.

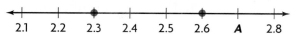

| | | | | | | | |
|2.1|2.2|2.3|2.4|2.5|2.6|**A**|2.8|

Since 2.6 is to the right of 2.3 on the number line, 2.6 is greater than 2.3.

$$2.6 > 2.3$$
↓
greater than

Since 2.3 is to the left of 2.6 on the number line, 2.3 is less than 2.6.

$$2.3 < 2.6$$
↓
less than

So, the 2.6-oz jar has more cinnamon.

- Which number does *A* represent on the number line? Explain how you know if it is greater than or less than 2.2.

You can also use place value to compare decimal numbers.

EXAMPLE 2

Compare 7.28 and 7.2. Use < or >.

Start at the left.

7.28 7.2 *Compare the ones digits. They are the same.*

7.28 7.2 *Compare the tenths digits. They are the same.*

7.28 7.20 *Add a zero so both numbers have the same number of places. Compare the hundredths digits. 8 is greater than 0.*

So, 7.28 > 7.2, and 7.2 < 7.28.

- Which is greater, 7.2 or 7.08? Explain.

Remember that you can add a zero to the right of the digits to the right of the decimal point without changing the value of the decimal.
7.2 = 7.20
2 tenths has the same value as 20 hundredths.

You can use place value to order two or more decimal numbers.

EXAMPLE 3

The prices for the same kind of CD player in four different stores are $132.95, $132.50, $130.25, and $135.25. Order the prices of the CD players from least to greatest.

Compare every possible pair of numbers.

$132.95 > $132.50 $132.95 > $130.25 $132.95 < $135.25

$132.50 > $130.25 $132.50 < $135.25 $130.25 < $135.25

So, the prices in order from least to greatest are $130.25, $132.50, $132.95, $135.25.

Think and ▶
Discuss

Look back at the lesson to answer each question.

1. **Name** the number that is 4 hundredths greater than 2.0369.

2. **Tell** how you would name the place immediately to the right of the millionths.

Guided ▶
Practice

Read the number. Write the value of the blue digit.

3. 15,425.007   4. 2,654,000.25   5. 550.76

Write the number in expanded form.

6. 0.605   7. 0.00103   8. 12.0089   9. 342.046

Compare the numbers. Write <, >, or = for ●.

10. 1.15 ● 1.14   11. 92.3 ● 92.30   12. 0.82 ● 0.84

Write the numbers in order from least to greatest.

13. 1.361, 1.351, 1.363   14. 125.3, 124.32, 125.33

Independent ▶
Practice

Read the number. Write the value of the blue digit.

15. 5.0547   16. 827.142   17. 345.79456

Write the number in expanded form.

18. 46.00105   19. 0.0362   20. 1,500.1   21. 2.456

Compare the numbers. Write <, >, or = for ●.

22. 99.06 ● 99.6   23. 133.3 ● 133.23   24. 707.07 ● 707.07

25. 32.630 ● 32.63   26. 457.3685 ● 457.5683   27. 49.302 ● 49.203

28. 1 + 0.1 + 0.05 ● 1 + 0.1 + 0.04

29. 5 + 0.2 + 0.003 ● 5 + 0.3 + 0.02

Write the numbers in order from least to greatest.

30. 1.41, 1.21, 1.412, 1.12   31. 1.45, 1.05, 0.405, 1.25, 1.125

32. 35.2, 35.72, 35.171, 35.7   33. 9.82, 9.082, 8.91, 9.285, 9.85

Write the numbers in order from greatest to least.

34. 5.004, 5.040, 5.4   35. 125.33, 125.3, 125.35, 125.4

36. $3\frac{1}{10}$, 3.001, $3\frac{1}{100}$, 3   37. 14.01, $14\frac{1}{10}$, 41.01, $14\frac{3}{100}$

TECHNOLOGY LINK

More Practice:
Harcourt Mega Math
Fraction Action,
Number Line Mine,
Level Q

38. A movie studio announced that the box office sales for its new release reached nine million, four hundred fifty-six thousand, three hundred two dollars in the first week. Write ten times that amount in standard and word forms.

39. **Vocabulary Power** As a noun, *form* can mean "the method of expression." Find the meaning of *form* when it is used as a verb.

40. ❓ **What's the Error?** Jon says 8.01 and 8.10 are equal because each number has the same digits. Explain his error.

Use Data For 41–42, use the graph at the right.

41. Estimate the total amount of rainfall during one year in Seattle.

42. Gene would like to visit Seattle to do some outdoor sightseeing. He would like to visit when the normal amount of rainfall is below 2 inches. When might be the best time for Gene to visit?

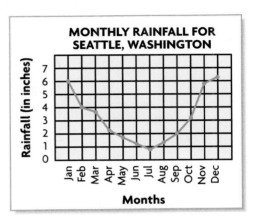

MONTHLY RAINFALL FOR
SEATTLE, WASHINGTON

MIXED REVIEW AND TEST PREP

43. $12 + 3^3 \times 8$ (p. 48)   **44.** 234×38 (p. 24)   **45.** Evaluate $406 \div c$, for $c = 14$. (p. 36)

46. **TEST PREP** Which shows the value of 4^4? (p. 46)

   A 16   **B** 124   **C** 256   **D** 2,414

47. **TEST PREP** If you do homework for 35 to 45 min a day, which is a reasonable estimate of the number of hours you do homework for 8 days? (p. 18)

   F less than 2 hr   **H** between 6 and 8 hr
   G between 4 and 6 hr   **J** more than 8 hr

PROBLEM SOLVING

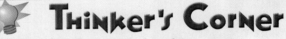

Thinker's Corner

Spin a Decimal Practice comparing and ordering decimals as you play this game.

Materials: a spinner numbered 0–9, a place-value chart

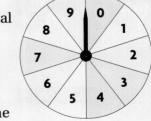

- In a small group, decide whether the player with the greatest decimal or least decimal will win. Taking turns, spin the pointer six times. After each spin, write the digit in the space of your choice on your place-value chart. Once you have written it on your chart, the digit cannot be moved or erased.

- Take turns reading your six-digit numbers aloud. The player with the greatest or the least decimal wins the round and receives a point.

- Continue playing until a player has five points.

EXTRA PRACTICE page 70, Set A

PROBLEM SOLVING STRATEGY
Make a Table

Learn how to solve problems by organizing data in a table.

Andrew chooses new in-line skates from the models below.

RC-204 $99.95; PRX-100 $78.50; D-500 $99.99; OP-1000 $78.99; ZZ-2 $91.50; ZA-45 $99.25

Andrew wants to buy the second most expensive model. His parents want him to buy the second least expensive model. Which models are these? What is the difference in price of the two models?

Analyze

What are you asked to find?

What information is given?

Choose

What strategy will you use?

You can use the strategy *make a table* to show the prices of the in-line skates in order from least to greatest.

Solve

How will you solve the problem?

Compare the prices and order them in a table. Then find the second most expensive model, the second least expensive model, and the difference in their prices.

$78.50 < $78.99 < $91.50 < $99.25 < $99.95 < $99.99

MODEL	PRICE	
PRX-100	$78.50	
OP-1000	$78.99	← *second least expensive*
ZZ-2	$91.50	
ZA-45	$99.25	
RC-204	$99.95	← *second most expensive*
D-500	$99.99	

Subtract: $99.95 − $78.99 = $20.96

So, the difference in price of models RC-204 and OP-1000 is $20.96.

Check

How can you check your answer?

What if Andrew chose model ZZ-2? How much more would he spend than if he bought model OP-1000?

Solve the problem by making a table.

Below are the fractions of games won by 8 baseball teams.

Hawks	0.495	Bulldogs	0.560
Tigers	0.595	Lions	0.360
Angels	0.520	Flames	0.545
Dolphins	0.395	Giants	0.530

1. Which team is in second place?

   A Tigers   **B** Flames   **C** Bulldogs   **D** Angels

2. How many teams are behind the Giants?

   F 2   **G** 3   **H** 4   **J** 5

Use Data For 3–4, reorder the data in the table at the right from greatest to least.

3. Which appliance uses the greatest amount of electricity?

4. Which appliance uses the least amount of electricity?

Electricity Used By Appliances

Appliance	Electricity (In Kilowatts)
Refrigerator	0.6
Air conditioner	1.5
Color TV	0.33
Iron	1.2
Coffeepot	0.9
Toaster	1.2

MIXED STRATEGY PRACTICE

5. A calculator, pen, and notebook cost $14.00 altogether. The calculator costs $9.00 more than the pen and $8.50 more than the notebook. How much does each item cost?

6. Kelly left the house with $16.00. She had $4.50 left after buying a movie ticket for $6.75, buying two snacks for $1.75 each, and paying for a bus ride. How much did she pay for the bus ride?

7. Carlene makes greeting cards. It costs $0.20 to make each card. She then sells them for $0.75 each. How many cards does she need to sell in order to make a profit of $33.00?

8. Frank walks 5 blocks to school for every 3 blocks Robert walks. They walk a total of 24 blocks. How many blocks from school does Robert live?

9. In a survey, teens prefer the Boomer portable stereo over the Blaster, but not as much as the Soundmaster. The Tekesound was preferred above all the others. Which portable stereo was least preferred?

10. **? What's the Question?** Glen read 69 pages each day for 6 days. He then read 23 pages each day for 4 days. The answer is about 500.

Estimate with Decimals

Learn how to estimate decimal sums, differences, products, and quotients.

You can estimate sums, differences, products, and quotients of decimals. To estimate with decimal numbers, use the same methods you use to estimate with whole numbers.

EXAMPLE 1

A long-distance phone company charges the rates shown at the right for calls from the United States. DeAnn made one-minute calls to India, Jordan, and Pakistan. About how much did the three calls cost?

Estimate $1.79 + $1.87 + $2.17.

$1.79   *The three addends*
$1.87   *cluster around $2.00.*
+$2.17   *So, multiply $2.00 by 3.*

3 × $2.00 = $6.00 *Multiply.*

So, the three calls cost about $6.00.

WIRED WORLD PHONE COMPANY	
Country	**Rate per Minute**
Argentina	$0.39
China	$0.49
France	$0.13
Germany	$0.09
India	$1.79
Ireland	$0.15
Jordan	$1.87
Pakistan	$2.17

EXAMPLE 2

Remember that the symbol ≈ means "is approximately equal to."

Estimate.

A. 36.4 × 18.25

Round to the nearest ten.

$$
\begin{array}{r} 36.4 \\ \times 18.25 \end{array} \rightarrow \begin{array}{r} 40 \\ \times 20 \\ \hline 800 \end{array}
$$

So, 36.4 × 18.25 ≈ 800.

B. 162.8 ÷ 8.16

Use compatible numbers.

$$
8.16\overline{)162.8} \rightarrow 8\overline{)160} \;\; {}^{20}
$$

So, 162.8 ÷ 8.16 ≈ 20.

CHECK FOR UNDERSTANDING

Think and ▶ Discuss

Look back at the lesson to answer each question.

1. Tell how you could estimate the sum of 4.79, 18.99, and 3.09.

2. Explain how to use compatible numbers to estimate 423.2 ÷ 2.7.

Estimate.

3. $18.7 + 23.1$ **4.** $123.76 \div 9$ **5.** $185.32 - 101.99$

6. 39.83×36 **7.** $67.8 + 66.1 + 71.7$ **8.** 817.3×11

PRACTICE AND PROBLEM SOLVING

Estimate.

9. $6.7 + 9.4 + 15.82$ **10.** 12.2×8.3 **11.** $82.5 \div 9.3$

12. $\$266.08 - \$97.30$ **13.** $9.8 + 38.2$ **14.** 31.5×2.8

15. 6.8×18.2 **16.** $103.018 - 45.022$ **17.** 56.20×30.7

18. 689.89
$\underline{-\quad 98.5}$
     19. $1,038.54$
$\underline{\times\quad 26.12}$
     20. $234.91 \div 5.79$

21. $\$7,805.90$
$\underline{+\quad 9,158.43}$
     22. $81.5 \times 23.1 \div 3.9$ **23.** $18.2 \times (7.2 - 4.9)$

Estimate to compare. Write $<$ or $>$ for ●.

24. 4.32×8.56 ● 40 **25.** 25 ● $81.27 \div 4.1$ **26.** $34.6 - 12.4$ ● 20

Use Data For 27–29, the table shows the types of waste that make up a typical 100 pounds of garbage in the United States.

27. About how many pounds of newspapers and other paper are included in every 300 pounds of garbage thrown away?

28. About how many more pounds of food waste than glass are thrown away for every 500 pounds of garbage?

What We Throw Away

Type of Garbage	Weight (in lb)
Food Waste	8.6
Yard Waste	17.4
Newspapers	7.9
Other Paper	30.8
Metals	9.2
Glass	5.2
Other	20.9

29. ✎ **Write a problem** involving estimation. Use the data about yard waste, other paper, and metals shown in the table.

MIXED REVIEW AND TEST PREP

30. Write the value of the digit 8 in the number 342.285. (p. 60)

31. Write 2.523, 2.325, 2.532, and 2.235 in order from least to greatest. (p. 60)

32. $20,817 - 19,805$ (p. 22)

33. $25,801 \div 23$ (p. 24)

⭐ **34. TEST PREP** Evaluate $a \times 32$ for $a = 426$. (p. 36)

    A 472   **B** 2,130   **C** 13,522   **D** 13,632

Decimals and Percents

Learn how to write a decimal as a percent and a percent as a decimal.

QUICK REVIEW

1. 2,457 + 4,541   2. 3,470 − 350   3. 6 × 5

4. 50 ÷ 5   5. Write the decimal for $\frac{2}{100}$.

The graph at the right shows the responses to a question about what people in the United States like to eat for breakfast.

Percent means "per hundred" or "hundredths." The symbol used to write a percent is %.

40 percent: $40\% = \frac{40}{100}$

So, 40 out of 100 have toast or a roll.

26 percent: $26\% = \frac{26}{100}$

So, 26 out of 100 have cold cereal.

BREAKFAST FOODS

26% 40%

cold cereal

34%

toast, roll

eggs, meat

Activity

You need: two 10 × 10 grids (decimal squares)

- On one grid, shade complete squares to make the first letter of your first name. On the other grid, shade complete squares to make the first letter of your last name. Make each letter as large as possible. Some examples are shown below.

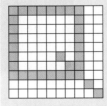 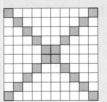 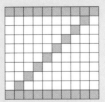

- Since 32 out of 100 squares are shaded for the letter Q, you can write 0.32 or 32%. What decimals and percents can be written for the squares shaded for X and Z?

- Count the number of complete squares you shaded on each of your grids. What percent of the squares are shaded?

You can think about place value when you change decimals to percents or percents to decimals.

Remember that when you read a decimal, you name the place with the least value. For 0.93, the place with the least value is hundredths. The number is read as "93 hundredths."

EXAMPLES

A. Write 0.08 as a percent.
0.08 is 8 hundredths.
So, 0.08 = 8%.

B. Write 32% as a decimal.
32% is 32 hundredths.
So, 32% = 0.32.

Think and Discuss ▶ **Look back at the lesson to answer the question.**

1. Explain how to write 0.6 as a percent.

Guided Practice ▶ **Write the decimal and percent for the shaded part.**

2. 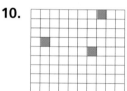   3. 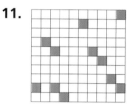   4.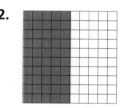

Write the corresponding decimal or percent.

5. 70%   **6.** 0.20   **7.** 0.03   **8.** 84%   **9.** 50%

PRACTICE AND PROBLEM SOLVING

Independent Practice ▶ **Write the decimal and percent for the shaded part.**

Favorite Types of Music	
Alternative	21
Rhythm and Blues	14
Rap	21
Rock	20
Other or none	24

10.   11.   12.

Write the corresponding decimal or percent.

13. 62%   **14.** 0.05   **15.** 28%   **16.** 45%   **17.** 53%

18. 0.63   **19.** 0.85   **20.** 33%   **21.** 0.4   **22.** 7%

Problem Solving Applications ▶ **23. Use Data** The table shows how 100 teens responded to a survey. Write a decimal and a percent to show the number of teens who did not choose Alternative music.

24. What percent shows how many more students chose Rap and Rock music than Rhythm and Blues?

25. ≡**FAST FACT** • SOCIAL STUDIES In 2001, a survey of U.S. teens showed that 79% listen to music when they do chores and 33% listen when eating a meal at home. Write the corresponding decimal for each percent.

MIXED REVIEW AND TEST PREP

26. Order 27.8, 27.5, 27.82 from least to greatest. (p. 60)

27. Evaluate. $35 + 17 \times 3^2 - 16$ (p. 48)   **28.** 168×92 (p. 24)   **29.** $3{,}470 \div 42$ (p. 24)

30. TEST PREP Which shows the sum $34{,}904 + 15{,}456 + 6{,}943$? (p. 22)

A 55,920   **B** 57,303   **C** 68,870   **D** 72,780

EXTRA PRACTICE page 70, Set C

Set A (pp. 60–63)

Write the value of the blue digit.

1. 6.12053   **2.** 0.0231   **3.** 8.7   **4.** 0.849

Write the number in expanded form.

5. 0.00309   **6.** 5.015   **7.** 3.032

8. 20.0518   **9.** 200.05   **10.** 5.16

Compare the numbers. Write <, >, or = for ●.

11. 5.099 ● 5.999   **12.** 226.5 ● 226.4   **13.** 251.36 ● 241.36

14. 18.3 ● 18.30   **15.** 4.18 ● 4.28   **16.** 49.089 ● 49.098

Write the numbers in order from least to greatest.

17. 82.16, 82, 82.15   **18.** 141.14, 114.41, 141.41   **19.** 5.09, 5.49, 5.23

Set B (pp. 66–67)

Estimate.

1. 3.7
     3.15
   +2.98

2. 62.8
   ×   6

3. 109.7
   − 53.622

4. 788.3
   ×   92

5. 5.92
     3.15
   +4.07

6. 21.513
   × 9.8

7. 5.816
     3.215
   +1.6

8. 465.09
   − 73.46

9. 728 ÷ 8.1   **10.** 8.1 − 2.456   **11.** 20.8 ÷ 7   **12.** 123.95 ÷ 61

Set C (pp. 68–69)

Write the decimal and percent for the shaded part.

1.   **2.**   **3.**

Write the corresponding decimal or percent.

4. 60%   **5.** 0.9   **6.** 39%   **7.** 0.04   **8.** 0.46

9. 18%   **10.** 0.41   **11.** 0.38   **12.** 7%   **13.** 90%

1. VOCABULARY A word that means "per hundred" is ___?___ . (p. 68)

Write the value of the blue digit. (pp. 60–63)

2. 3.2497

3. 14.5805

4. 0.09003

5. 628.0402

6. 1.81738

7. 78.05124

Write the numbers in order from least to greatest. (pp. 60–63)

8. 2.365, 2.305, 2.3, 2.35, 2.035

9. 125.3, 124.32, 125.33, 12.245, 120.4

Estimate. (pp. 66–67)

10. 27.6 + 135.2

11. 4.8 × 2.3

12. 30.7 − 6.25

13. 89.75 ÷ 8

14. 8.45 + 8.99 + 9.2

15. 219.48 − 107.43

16. 416.2 × 31

17. 40.02 ÷ 6.3

Write the decimal and percent for the shaded part. (pp. 68–69)

18.

19.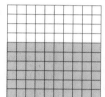

20.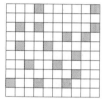

Write the corresponding decimal or percent. (pp. 68–69)

21. 74%

22. 0.07

23. 39%

24. 0.61

25. 0.6

26. 3%

27. 0.04

28. 84%

Solve.

29. The county library charges a fine of $0.10 a day for overdue books. The university library charges a fine of $0.50 for the first day and $0.05 for each additional day. On what day would overdue books have the same fine at both libraries? (pp. 64–65)

30. Planes leave Washington, D.C., for New York City every 45 min. The first plane leaves at 5:45 A.M. What is the departure time closest to 4:30 P.M.? (pp. 64–65)

31. Donna is on the decoration committee. She spent $15.90 on streamers, $12.15 on balloons, $6.84 on tape, $19.98 on banner paper, and $13.22 on banner paint. What is a reasonable estimate of the amount she spent? (pp. 66–67)

32. Frank earns $6.25 per hr. One week he worked 19 hr. About how much did Frank earn that week? (pp. 66–67)

33. Kirk has to list 165.3, 164.36, 165.33, 16.345, and 160.4 in order from greatest to least. Which number should he list third? (pp. 60–63)

 **NUMBER SENSE, CONCEPTS, AND OPERATIONS**

1. Stacy bought one liter of orange juice. The label says that one liter is equal to one and fifty-seven thousandths quarts. Which of the following is the number of quarts written in standard form?

A 0.1057   **C** 1.057

B 0.157   **D** 1.57

2. In 2001, there were 1.0015 times as many women and girls aged 0–64 in the United States as there were men and boys. Which of the following is 1.0015 written in expanded form?

F $1 + 0.0001 + 0.05$

G $1 + 0.001 + 0.0005$

H $1 + 0.001 + 0.5$

J $1 + 0.0015$

3. Stu, Randy, Todd, and Julio bought copies of the same video game at different stores. The table shows the price each person paid.

PRICES PAID FOR VIDEO GAMES	
Person	**Game Price**
Stu	$49.22
Randy	$48.78
Todd	$49.30
Julio	$48.87

Which of the following shows the names in order from the person who paid the **least** to the person who paid the **most**?

A Todd, Stu, Julio, Randy

B Todd, Julio, Stu, Randy

C Randy, Julio, Stu, Todd

D Randy, Julio, Todd, Stu

4. Explain It About 5% of the Earth's crust is iron. Explain how to write 5% as a decimal.

 **MEASUREMENT**

5. The table below shows four students' estimates of the mass of a textbook.

MASS OF A TEXTBOOK	
Student	**Estimate (in kilograms)**
Sara	1.5
Carrie	1.9
Alvin	2.4
Seth	2.0

Seth's estimate is closest to the actual mass. Which could be the actual mass?

F 1.6 kilograms   **H** 2.1 kilograms

G 1.8 kilograms   **J** 2.3 kilograms

6. The winning running high jump at the 2000 Olympics was 2.35 meters. Which is equivalent to 2.35 meters?

A 23.5 centimeters

B 235 centimeters

C 0.235 kilometers

D 23.5 kilometers

7. The figure below shows the size and shape of Molly's bedroom floor. She paid $6.95 per square foot to carpet the entire floor. How much did the carpet cost?

15.5 feet

12 feet

F $1,292.70   **H** $430.90

G $1,251.00   **J** $186.00

8. Explain It The figure shows a portion of a railing along the side of a stairway. What is the unknown angle measure? Explain your reasoning.

9. Sheila works part-time at her brother's store. She recorded the number of hours, h, she worked and the amount of money, m, she made working five days.

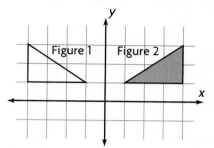 **TIP Eliminate choices.** See item 9. Replace the unknown with answer choice A. Does the result follow the pattern? If not, eliminate A and repeat using the other answer choices until you find the correct missing value.

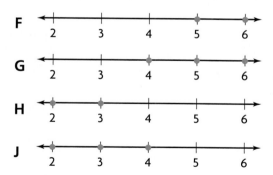

h	4	3	■	2	6
m	$24	$18	$30	$12	$36

What is the value of h when $m = \$30$?

A 5   **C** 18

B 9   **D** 30

10. For a scavenger hunt, no team may have more than 4 members or fewer than 2 members. Which number line shows how many members can be on a team?

F
2 3 4 5 6

G
2 3 4 5 6

H
2 3 4 5 6

J
2 3 4 5 6

11. Explain It At a roller rink, 126 skaters are using in-line skates. That is three times the number of skaters using roller skates. If r represents the number of roller skaters, what equation can you write to find the number of skaters using roller skates? Explain how to determine whether the solution to the equation is 32, 42, or 52.

12. Which statement about the transformation of Figure 1 to Figure 2 on the coordinate plane below is true?

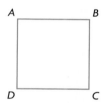

A Figure 2 is a translation of Figure 1.

B Figure 1 is a rotation of Figure 2.

C Figure 2 is a reflection of Figure 1.

D Figure 2 is a rotation of Figure 1.

13. Vince uses square $ABCD$, a piece of cardboard 8 inches on all sides, for a craft project. What is the area of the square?

A ___ B
| |
D ___ C

F 8 square inches

G 16 square inches

H 32 square inches

J 64 square inches

14. Explain It Tell whether the circles are congruent, similar, or both. Explain your reasoning.

Figure 1   Figure 2

≡FAST FACT • SOCIAL STUDIES
More than 400 boys and girls, from ages 9 to 16, participated in the 2001 All American Soap Box Derby in Akron, Ohio. There are three divisions of the competition: stock car, super stock, and masters.

PROBLEM SOLVING The graph shows some qualifying times in the super stock division of the derby. Which heat had the fastest time? How much faster was it than the slowest time?

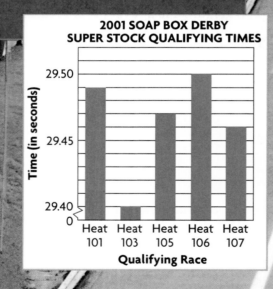

2001 SOAP BOX DERBY SUPER STOCK QUALIFYING TIMES

Time (in seconds) / Qualifying Race

Check What You Know

Use this page to help you review and remember important skills needed for Chapter 4.

 Whole-Number Operations

Add or subtract.

1. $7 + 28 + 12$

2. $45 - 15$

3. $63 - 19$

4. $19 + 41 + 27 + 23$

5. $34 - 17 - 7$

6. $27 + 56 + 100$

7. $143 + 79$

8. $213 - 88$

Multiply.

9. $\begin{array}{r} 63 \\ \times\ 4 \\ \hline \end{array}$

10. $\begin{array}{r} 49 \\ \times\ 9 \\ \hline \end{array}$

11. $\begin{array}{r} 19 \\ \times 76 \\ \hline \end{array}$

12. $\begin{array}{r} 88 \\ \times 32 \\ \hline \end{array}$

13. $\begin{array}{r} 80 \\ \times 50 \\ \hline \end{array}$

14. $\begin{array}{r} 75 \\ \times 11 \\ \hline \end{array}$

15. $\begin{array}{r} 200 \\ \times\ 15 \\ \hline \end{array}$

16. $\begin{array}{r} 340 \\ \times\ 20 \\ \hline \end{array}$

Divide.

17. $4\overline{)96}$

18. $5\overline{)127}$

19. $9\overline{)423}$

20. $7\overline{)760}$

21. $32\overline{)448}$

22. $20\overline{)3,660}$

23. $37\overline{)1,073}$

24. $23\overline{)4,715}$

 Multiply Decimals by 10, 100, and 1,000

Multiply.

25. 4.3×10

26. $9.61 \times 1,000$

27. 100×8.4

28. $25.397 \times 1,000$

29. 194.05×100

30. 10×408.08

VOCABULARY POWER

REVIEW

point [point] *noun*

The word *point* has more than one meaning in mathematics. One meaning is the decimal point, "a symbol used in decimal numbers." How is the word *point* used in geometry?

 www.harcourtschool.com/mathglossary

Add and Subtract Decimals

Learn how to add and subtract decimals.

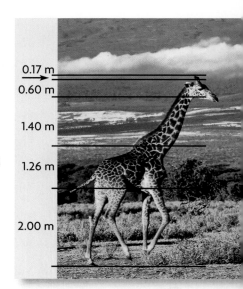

0.17 m
0.60 m
1.40 m
1.26 m
2.00 m

The tallest known mammal was a 6.1-m giraffe named George. Born in Kenya, George spent most of his life in the Chester Zoo in England.

To find the height of the giraffe shown, you must add five partial heights.

Math Idea ▶ When you add or subtract decimals, align the decimal points first and then add or subtract the digits, one place at a time.

2.00	*Align the decimal points.*
1.26	
1.40	
0.60	
+0.17	*Place the decimal point.*
5.43	*Then add.*

So, the total height is 5.43 m.

You can use estimation to check an answer for reasonableness.

EXAMPLE 1

Jamie has $85.75. Running shoes cost $68.45. How much money will Jamie have left after buying the running shoes?

Estimate.

$85.75   → $86   *Round to the nearest dollar.*
− 68.45   − 68
                 $18

Find the answer.

$85.75
− 68.45   *Align the decimal points.*
$17.30   *Place the decimal point. Then subtract.*

Use your estimate to check the reasonableness of the answer. Compare the two. Since $17.30 is close to the estimate of $18, the answer is reasonable.

So, Jamie will have $17.30 left.

Some decimal numbers that you add or subtract do not have the same number of decimal places. The samples below show how Courtney and Jamie found 17.06 + 5.493. Think about which sum is reasonable.

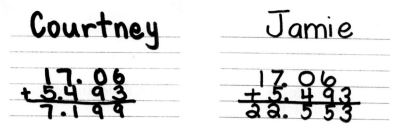

Courtney

17.06
+ 5.493
7.199

Jamie

17.06
+ 5.493
22.553

Use estimation: 17.06 + 5.493 → 17 + 5 = 22

Jamie's sum is reasonable. Courtney forgot to align the decimal points before adding.

Remember that you can add zeros to the right of a decimal without changing its value. Align the decimal points, then use zeros to make all decimals have the same number of decimal places.

EXAMPLE 2

Add. 3.45 + 7 + 0.835
Estimate.

3.45		3	*Round to the nearest whole number.*
7	→	7	
+0.835		+1	
		11	

Find the answer.

3.45		3.450	*Align the decimal points.*
7	or	7.000	*Use zeros as placeholders.*
+0.835		+0.835	
		11.285	*Place the decimal point. Add.*

Compare the answer to your estimate. 11.285 is close to the estimate of 11. The answer is reasonable.

So, 3.45 + 7 + 0.835 = 11.285.

EXAMPLE 3

Find the difference. 351.4 − 65.25
Estimate.

351.4	→	350	
− 65.25		− 70	*Round to the nearest ten.*
		280	

Find the answer.

351.4		351.40	*Align the decimal points.*
− 65.25	or	− 65.25	*Use a zero as a placeholder.*
		286.15	*Place the decimal point. Subtract.*

Compare the answer to your estimate. 286.15 is close to the estimate of 280. The answer is reasonable.

So, 351.4 − 65.25 = 286.15.

Think and Discuss ▸ Look back at the lesson to answer each question.

1. **Explain** why it is important to align the decimal points when you add or subtract.

2. **Explain** the steps you would use to find $67 - 34.58$.

Guided Practice ▸ Add or subtract. Estimate to check.

3. $\begin{array}{r} \$6.18 \\ -\ 5.55 \\ \hline \end{array}$

4. $\begin{array}{r} 0.45 \\ 0.5 \\ +1.349 \\ \hline \end{array}$

5. $\begin{array}{r} 6 \\ 5.43 \\ 1.4 \\ +5.755 \\ \hline \end{array}$

6. $\begin{array}{r} 10.72 \\ -\ 1.3 \\ \hline \end{array}$

7. $3.2 + 2.68 + 15.043$

8. $142.108 - 63.8$

Copy the problem. Place the decimal point correctly in the answer.

9. $37.5 - 0.19 = 3731$

10. $0.431 + 1.549 + 2.017 = 3997$

11. $6 + 118.59 + 0.35 = 12494$

12. $9.7 - 3.01 = 669$

Independent Practice ▸ Add or subtract. Estimate to check.

13. $\begin{array}{r} 50.28 \\ +37.52 \\ \hline \end{array}$

14. $\begin{array}{r} 153.95 \\ +434.16 \\ \hline \end{array}$

15. $\begin{array}{r} 805.41 \\ +633.25 \\ \hline \end{array}$

16. $\begin{array}{r} 31.62 \\ -\ 5.8 \\ \hline \end{array}$

17. $3.2 - 2.6$

18. $735.1 + 37 + 105.73$

19. $370.92 - 83.247$

20. $275.2 - 86.05$

21. $123.1 + 140 + 225.45$

22. $\$8 + \$215.49 + \$0.75$

23. $620.87 - 91.386$

24. $56.60 - 8.476$

Copy the problem. Place the decimal point correctly in the answer.

25. $23.64 + 233.5 = 25714$

26. $\$25.67 + \$7.16 + \$0.35 = \$3318$

27. $11.2 - 1.78 = 942$

28. $4.98 - 3.235 = 1745$

Estimate to determine if the given sum is reasonable.
Write *yes* or *no*.

29. $14.78 + 122.4 = 137.18$

30. $\$32.76 + \$8.09 + \$0.49 = \$41.34$

31. $58.02 - 9.473 = 3.671$

32. $427.7 - 39.27 = 388.43$

ALGEBRA Evaluate each expression for $d = 4.3$.

33. $d - 3.05$

34. $1 + d + 0.7$

35. $8 + d$

36. $37.60 - d$

37. $d - 2.084$

38. $(d + 16.05) - 4.5$

TECHNOLOGY LINK

More Practice:
**Harcourt Mega Math
The Number Games,**
Tiny's Think Tank,
Level L

**Harcourt Mega Math
The Number Games,**
Buggy Bargains,
Level I

39. Jake's batting average is .325. Last year it was .235. What is the difference between his average last year and this year?

40. Karen has saved $15.75, $18.36, $9.07, and $20.37 to buy a camera. How much more does she need to save to buy a camera that costs $165.45?

41. Estimate 30.53 + 95.7 + 75.12. Is the sum more than or less than your estimate? Explain how you know.

42. 📖 **Write About It** Why is it important to estimate the answer when you add and subtract decimals?

43. Four clubs collected 3,905; 3,950; 3,590; and 3,509 lb of paper. Order the four weights of paper. Then find the difference between the least and the greatest weights of paper collected.

MIXED REVIEW AND TEST PREP

44. Write 0.05 as a percent. (p. 68)

45. Write the decimal for 46%. (p. 68)

46. Evaluate $a \div c$ for $a = 4,602$ and $c = 37$. (p. 36)

47. TEST PREP Which shows the value of 7^4? (p. 46)

   A 283   **B** 343   **C** 2,381   **D** 2,401

48. TEST PREP Tanya bought milk for $2.09, two loaves of bread for $1.05 each, cheese for $4.50, and three bottles of juice for $3.00 each. How much did Tanya pay for the items? (p. 22)

   F $12.04   **G** $12.64   **H** $17.69   **J** $23.04

PROBLEM SOLVING LiNKUp to Science

Cytologist Cytologists are scientists who specialize in the study of the tiny cells that make up every living thing. While cells vary widely in size, most plant and animal cells are so small that they can be seen only with a microscope. Cytologists often must use decimals when measuring the sizes of cells and their structures, as in these examples:

Average plant cell	0.000035 meter
Small bacterium	0.0000002 meter
Cell wall or membrane	0.0000000075 meter

• Use your school library to find the sizes of blood cells, skin cells, and nerve cells in the human body. How much larger or smaller is each of these cell types than the average plant cell?

Multiply Decimals

Learn how to multiply decimals.

You need colored pencils and decimal squares.

1.   42
    × 7

2.   83
    × 4

3.   52
    × 6

4.   93
    × 5

5. 36 × 4

You can use a model to find the product of a decimal number and a whole number.

M A T H LAB

Activity

- To find 3 × 0.14, shade 0.14, or 14 small squares, three separate times. Use a different color and shade a different group of 14 small squares each time.

- Count the number of shaded squares. What is 3 × 0.14?

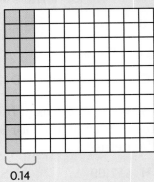

0.14

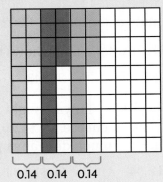

0.14 0.14 0.14

- Use a decimal square to find 5 × 0.17.

- Describe how you shaded your decimal square.

- What is 5 × 0.17?

Sometimes, when the factors are greater, as in 9 × 1.12, you can compute the product without using decimal squares.

EXAMPLE 1

Ed buys 9 sports cards at $1.12 each. How much does he spend?

Multiply. $1.12 × 9

Estimate to know where the decimal point is placed in the answer.

$1.12 × 9 → $1 × 9 = $9

Find the answer.

        $1.12   *Multiply as with whole numbers.*
      ×   9   *Since the estimate is $9, place the*
       $10.08   *decimal point after the 10.*

So, Ed pays $10.08 for sports cards.

Multiply a Decimal by a Decimal

You can use a decimal square or paper and pencil to find the product of two decimals.

EXAMPLE 2

Multiply. 0.2 × 0.6

Shade 6 columns blue for 0.6.

Shade 2 rows yellow for 0.2.

The green area in which the shading overlaps shows the product, or 0.2 of 0.6.

So, 0.2 × 0.6 = 0.12.

Place the decimal point in a product by estimating or by adding the number of decimal places in the factors.

$$
\begin{array}{r}
0.2 \quad \leftarrow \text{1 decimal place} \\
\times 0.6 \quad \leftarrow \text{1 decimal place} \\
\hline
0.12 \quad \leftarrow \text{1 + 1, or 2 decimal places}
\end{array}
$$

EXAMPLE 3

Mr. Ponti works 37.5 hr per week. He earns $8.70 an hour. How much does he earn in a week?

Multiply. $8.70 × 37.5

Estimate. $8.70 × 37.5 → $9 × 40 = $360

Find the answer.

$$
\begin{array}{r}
\$8.70 \quad \leftarrow \text{2 decimal places} \\
\times \ 37.5 \quad \leftarrow \text{1 decimal place} \\
\hline
4350 \\
6090 \\
+2610 \\
\hline
326.250 \quad \leftarrow \text{3 decimal places}
\end{array}
$$

Multiply as with whole numbers.
Place the decimal point in the product.

Since the estimate is $360, the answer is reasonable.

So, Mr. Ponti earns $326.25.

When you multiply decimals, you sometimes have to insert zeros in the answer.

EXAMPLE 4

Multiply. 0.037 × 0.062

$$
\begin{array}{r}
0.037 \quad \leftarrow \text{3 decimal places} \\
\times 0.062 \quad \leftarrow \text{3 decimal places} \\
\hline
74 \\
+222 \\
\hline
0.002294
\end{array}
$$

Multiply as with whole numbers.
Place the decimal point in the product.
The answer must have 6 decimal places, so place 2 zeros to the left of the first 2.

So, 0.037 × 0.062 = 0.002294.

81

This example shows a way to use the Distributive Property.

EXAMPLE 5

Multiply. 9 × 12.8

Estimate. 9 × 12.8 → 9 × 13 = 117

Find the answer.

9 × 12.8 = (9 × 12) + (9 × 0.8)   *Use the Distributive Property.*

       = 108 + 7.2   *Use the number of decimal places*
       = 115.2   *in the factor to locate the*
                            decimal point in the product.

Since the estimate is 117, the answer is reasonable.

So, 9 × 12.8 = 115.2.

CHECK FOR UNDERSTANDING

Think and Discuss ▸ Look back at the lesson to answer the question.

1. **Explain** how you would place the decimal point in the product 0.27 × 0.476.

Guided Practice ▸ Use the decimal square shown to help you multiply.

2.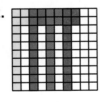

4 × 0.12

3.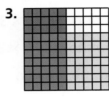

0.7 × 0.5

4.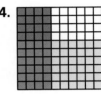

0.6 × 0.4

Copy the problem. Place the decimal point in the product.

5. 3.6 × 7 = 252

6. 2.1 × 8.1 = 1701

7. 4.4 × 5.2 = 2288

8. 9 × 5.4 = 486

9. 0.7 × 4.1 = 287

10. 2.2 × 0.55 = 1210

Multiply. Estimate to check.

11. 0.42 × 2.9

12. 1.25 × 0.4

13. 3.23 × 8

PRACTICE AND PROBLEM SOLVING

Independent Practice ▸ Use the decimal square shown to help you multiply.

14.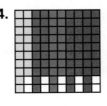

5 × 0.18

15.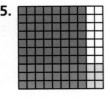

0.3 × 0.8

16.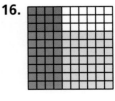

0.7 × 0.4

TECHNOLOGY LINK

More Practice:
**Harcourt Mega Math
The Number Games,**
Tiny's Think Tank,
Level R

Copy the problem. Place the decimal point in the product.

17. $3.7 \times 8.2 = 3034$ **18.** $0.87 \times 0.2 = 174$ **19.** $1.3 \times 0.91 = 1183$

20. $6.37 \times 2.91 = 185367$ **21.** $20.4 \times 9.52 = 194208$

22. $7.32 \times 3 = 2196$ **23.** $0.82 \times 0.5 = 410$ **24.** $32.5 \times 0.06 = 1950$

Multiply. Estimate to check.

25. 3×4.6 **26.** 9×2.5 **27.** 7.3×5

28. 8.2×5 **29.** 1.2×4.1 **30.** 0.9×6.3

31. 0.2×0.4 **32.** 6.3×0.9 **33.** 0.21×2.1

34. 6.15×2.4 **35.** 4.08×1.35 **36.** 6.21×0.95

37. 24.63×1.09 **38.** 20.003×5.01 **39.** 0.102×2.09

40. 108.001×0.37 **41.** 108.9×0.006 **42.** $1,200.5 \times 0.2$

**Problem Solving ▶
Applications**

43. Doug buys 2.25 lb of apples and 0.75 lb of walnuts. Apples are $1.60 per pound and walnuts are $4.95 per pound. How much will the apples and walnuts cost in all?

44. Keith has a wall that is 5.2 m wide. He has 3 bookcases that are each 1.9 m wide. Is there enough room for all of the bookcases to be placed against the wall? Explain.

45. ✎ **Write a problem** that uses multiplication of two decimals to find the answer. The product must have four decimal places.

46. Use Data Look at the graph at the right. Rochelle had to earn 200 points in the first four rounds to advance in a competition. Rochelle says that she did advance. Is this a reasonable statement? Explain.

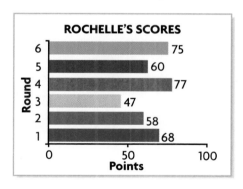

ROCHELLE'S SCORES

Round / Points
6 — 75
5 — 60
4 — 77
3 — 47
2 — 58
1 — 68

MIXED REVIEW AND TEST PREP

47. Add. $46.2 + 3.45 + 16$ (p. 76)

48. Subtract. $604.5 - 76.38$ (p. 76)

49. Evaluate the expression $a \div c$ for $a = 14,067$ and $c = 47$. (p. 36)

50. TEST PREP Which shows the value of m when $8 = m \div 9$? (p. 42)

 A 70 **B** 72 **C** 720 **D** 7,200

51. TEST PREP Which is the best estimate for $21,563 \div 43$? (p. 18)

 F 500 **G** 700 **H** 5,000 **J** 7,000

EXTRA PRACTICE page 96, Set B

Explore Division of Decimals

Explore how to use a model to divide decimals.

You need decimal squares, colored pencils, scissors.

Remember

1 tenth (0.1) = 1 column

1 hundredth (0.01) = 1 small square

QUICK REVIEW

1. $6\overline{)372}$ 2. $8\overline{)427}$ 3. $5\overline{)524}$

4. $4\overline{)123}$ 5. $252 \div 6$

You can shade and cut apart decimal squares to divide a decimal by a whole number.

Activity 1

Find 3.66 ÷ 3.

• Shade 3.66 decimal squares.

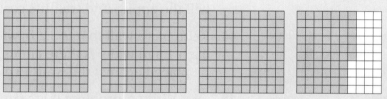

• Divide the shaded wholes into 3 equal groups. Divide the 66 hundredths into 3 equal groups.

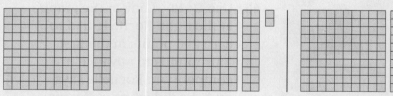

• What decimal names each group? What is the quotient?

• Use decimal squares to find 1.32 ÷ 4.

Think and Discuss

• Find 366 ÷ 3. How is the quotient the same as for 3.66 ÷ 3? How is it different?

• Find 132 ÷ 4. How is the quotient the same as for 1.32 ÷ 4? How is it different?

Practice

Use decimal squares to find the quotient.

1. 4.04 ÷ 4

2. 3.25 ÷ 5

3. 1.35 ÷ 3

You can shade and cut apart decimal squares to divide a decimal by
a decimal.

Activity 2

Find 3.6 ÷ 1.2.

- Shade 3.6 decimal squares.

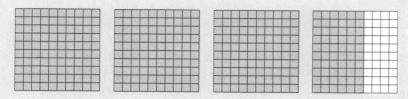

- Cut apart the 6 tenths.

- Divide the shaded squares and shaded tenths into equal groups
  of 1.2. How many groups of 1.2 are in 3.6? What is the quotient?

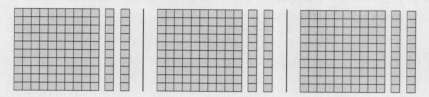

- Use decimal squares to find 3.2 ÷ 1.6.

- How many groups of 1.6 are in 3.2?

Think and Discuss

- Find 36 ÷ 12. How is the quotient the same as for 3.6 ÷ 1.2?
  How is the problem different from 3.6 ÷ 1.2?

- You know that 3.6 ÷ 12 = 0.3 and 3.6 ÷ 1.2 = 3. What do you
  think 3.6 ÷ 0.12 equals?

Practice
Use decimal squares to find the quotient.

1. 7.8 ÷ 1.3
2. 5.6 ÷ 0.8
3. 1.56 ÷ 0.52
4. 5.5 ÷ 1.1

5. Tell which division
problem is shown by
the model at the right.
Explain.

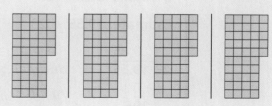

MIXED REVIEW AND TEST PREP

6. Multiply. 64.7 × 3.6 (p. 80)

7. Write the decimal for 57%. (p. 68)

8. Write the value of 3^4. (p. 46)

9. Divide. 3,759 ÷ 42 (p. 24)

⭐**10.** **TEST PREP** Evaluate the expression. 12 × 25 ÷ (12 + 18) (p. 48)

    A 8   **B** 10   **C** 43   **D** 300

Divide Decimals by Whole Numbers

Learn how to divide a decimal by a whole number.

1. $8\overline{)373}$ 2. $6\overline{)205}$ 3. $19\overline{)836}$ 4. $27\overline{)434}$ 5. $294 \div 14$

Bristlecone pines may live to be 4,000 years old.

Scientists learn about ancient climates by measuring the growth rings of old trees. The width of one tree increased 14.85 mm in 5 years. What was the tree's average growth in width per year?

Divide. $14.85 \div 5$

Use compatible numbers to estimate. $14.85 \div 5 \rightarrow 15 \div 5 = 3$

Find the answer. Dividing a decimal by a whole number is like dividing whole numbers.

Remember that compatible numbers are numbers that divide without a remainder, are close to the actual numbers, and are easy to compute mentally.

$$\begin{array}{r} 2.97 \\ 5\overline{)14.85} \\ -10\downarrow \\ \hline 48 \\ -45\downarrow \\ \hline 35 \\ -35 \\ \hline 0 \end{array}$$

Place a decimal point above the decimal point in the dividend.

Divide.

Since the estimate is 3, the answer is reasonable. So, the width of the tree grew an average of 2.97 mm per year.

Sometimes you have to place a zero in the quotient when the dividend is less than the divisor.

EXAMPLE

Mrs. Harmon spends $19.55 to buy 23 booklets about trees. If each booklet costs the same amount, what is the cost for one booklet?

Divide. $19.55 \div 23$

Estimate. $19.55 \div 23 \rightarrow 20 \div 20 = 1$

$$\begin{array}{r} 0.85 \\ 23\overline{)19.55} \\ -0\downarrow \\ \hline 195 \\ -184\downarrow \\ \hline 115 \\ -115 \\ \hline 0 \end{array}$$

Place a decimal point above the decimal point in the dividend.

Divide. Since 19 is less than 23, place a 0 in the ones place in the quotient.

Since the estimate is 1, the answer is reasonable. So, one booklet costs $0.85.

Think and ▶ Discuss

Look back at the lesson to answer each question.

1. **Explain** where to place the decimal point in the quotient when a decimal is divided by a whole number.

2. **Estimate** the average growth per year of a tree's width if it grew 26.94 mm in 9 years.

Guided ▶ Practice

Divide. Estimate to check.

3. $7.88 \div 4$ **4.** $7\overline{)254.8}$ **5.** $\$33.66 \div 11$

PRACTICE AND PROBLEM SOLVING

Independent ▶ Practice

Divide. Estimate to check.

6. $16.8 \div 6$ **7.** $6\overline{)903.6}$ **8.** $201.6 \div 9$

9. $9\overline{)21.15}$ **10.** $3\overline{)\$170.43}$ **11.** $8\overline{)440.8}$

12. $7\overline{)117.6}$ **13.** $137.1 \div 15$ **14.** $\$510.72 \div 42$

15. $5.7 \div 19$ **16.** $448.56 \div 89$ **17.** $26\overline{)\$2,109.12}$

Problem Solving ▶ Applications

18. The bristlecone pine is the world's oldest tree and can be found in the Bristlecone Pine Forest in Nevada. Some of the bristlecone pines have a circumference of 11.2 m, 10.9 m, 9.5 m, and 9.6 m. What is the average circumference of these four trees?

19. Mrs. Harmon and her 23 students each paid $5.75 for admission to the science museum. The cost of renting a bus to go to the museum was $202.80. If the students and Mrs. Harmon shared the total cost of the trip equally, how much did each person pay?

20. A box of 24 rolls of film costs $83.52. A single roll costs $3.79. What is the savings on each roll if you buy a box of 24 rolls?

21. **ALGEBRA** If $n \div 4 = 3.2$, what is the value of $n \div 2$?

22. **Vocabulary Power** The word *compatible* means "capable of operating together; agreeable." How does this definition help you understand the meaning of *compatible numbers*?

TECHNOLOGY LINK

More Practice:
**Harcourt Mega Math
The Number Games,**
Tiny's Think Tank,
Level S

**Harcourt Mega Math
The Number Games,**
Buggy Bargains,
Levels O, P

MIXED REVIEW AND TEST PREP

23. Multiply. 4.59×1.7 (p. 80)

24. Write the corresponding percent for 0.3. (p. 68)

25. Evaluate. $12 + 18 \div 6 - 5$ (p. 48)

26. Evaluate $20n$ for $n = 25$. (p. 36)

27. **TEST PREP** Which expression is equivalent to $3 \times 3 \times 3 \times 3 \times 3$? (p. 46)

A 3×5 **B** 3^5 **C** 5^3 **D** 9^4

EXTRA PRACTICE page 96, Set C

Divide Decimals by Decimals

Learn how to divide a decimal by a decimal.

QUICK REVIEW

1. $2.5 \div 5$ **2.** $3.6 \div 9$ **3.** $0.15 \div 3$ **4.** $15.6 \div 10$ **5.** $43.2 \div 100$

You can use patterns to help you divide a decimal by a decimal.

Activity

• Use a calculator to find the first three quotients in each set.

• Look for a pattern. Try to predict the last quotient in each set.

Set A	Set B
$0.48 \div 0.03 = \blacksquare$	$0.621 \div 0.023 = \blacksquare$
$4.8 \div 0.3 = \blacksquare$	$6.21 \div 0.23 = \blacksquare$
$48 \div 3 = \blacksquare$	$62.1 \div 2.3 = \blacksquare$
$480 \div 30 = \blacksquare$	$621 \div 23 = \blacksquare$

• Describe the pattern that helped you predict the last quotient in each set.

• Look at $4.8 \div 0.3$. Multiply both numbers by 10. How do the quotients for $4.8 \div 0.3$ and $48 \div 3$ compare? How does multiplying the divisor and the dividend by 10 affect the quotient?

To divide a decimal by a decimal, first multiply the divisor and the dividend by a power of 10 to change the divisor to a whole number.

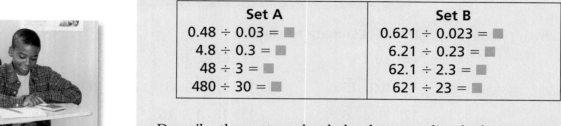

$$0.7\overline{)62.44} \quad \rightarrow \quad 7\overline{)624.4}$$

THINK: $0.7 \times 10 = 7$

$62.44 \times 10 = 624.4$

EXAMPLE 1

Divide. $22.8 \div 0.8$

$0.8\overline{)22.8}$ *Make the divisor a whole number by multiplying the divisor and dividend by 10.*

$8\overline{)228}$ *$0.8 \times 10 = 8$ $22.8 \times 10 = 228$*

$$\begin{array}{r} 28.5 \\ 8\overline{)228.0} \\ -16 \\ \hline 68 \\ -64 \\ \hline 40 \\ -40 \\ \hline 0 \end{array}$$

Place the decimal point in the quotient. Divide.

Since there is a remainder, place a zero in the tenths place in the dividend, and continue to divide.

So, $22.8 \div 0.8 = 28.5$.

EXAMPLE 2

A carat is a unit used to measure the weight of diamonds. The diamonds in a ring weigh a total of 0.35 carats. Each diamond weighs 0.07 carats. How many diamonds are there in the ring?

Divide. $0.07\overline{)0.35}$

$0.0\underset{\smile}{7}\overline{)0.3\underset{\smile}{5}}$ *Make the divisor a whole number by multiplying the divisor and dividend by 100.*

$\begin{array}{r} 5 \\ 7\overline{)35} \\ -35 \\ \hline 0 \end{array}$ *0.07 × 100 = 7   0.35 × 100 = 35*
Divide.

You can use this key sequence on a calculator.

0.35 ÷ 0.07 Enter = $\boxed{0.\ 35 \div 0.\ 07 = 5}$

So, there are 5 diamonds in the ring.

Sometimes there aren't enough places in the dividend to move the decimal to the right.

EXAMPLE 3

Divide. 158.4 ÷ 0.12

$0.1\underset{\smile}{2}\overline{)158.4\underset{\smile}{0}}$ *Make the divisor a whole number by multiplying the divisor and dividend by 100.*

$\begin{array}{r} 1,320 \\ 12\overline{)15,840} \\ -12 \\ \hline 38 \\ -36 \\ \hline 24 \\ -24 \\ \hline 00 \end{array}$

0.12 × 100 = 12   158.4 × 100 = 15,840
Write a zero in the dividend.
Divide.

Since the remainder is zero, the quotient is a whole number. You do not need to put the decimal point in the answer.

You can use this key sequence on a calculator.

158.4 ÷ 0.12 Enter = $\boxed{\begin{array}{r}158.\ 4 \div 0.\ 12 = \\ 1320\end{array}}$

So, 158.4 ÷ 0.12 = 1,320.

CHECK FOR UNDERSTANDING

Think and ▶
Discuss

Look back at the lesson to answer each question.

1. **Explain** how to change the divisor and the dividend before you solve the problem 55.8 ÷ 0.18.

2. Compare the quotients $4.5 \div 1.5$ and $45 \div 15$.

Guided ▶
Practice
Rewrite the problem so that the divisor is a whole number.

3. $9.6 \div 1.6$ **4.** $73.6 \div 0.5$ **5.** $48.24 \div 2.4$

Copy the problem. Place the decimal point in the quotient.

6. $28.50 \div 2.50 = 1140$ **7.** $34.178 \div 2.3 = 1486$ **8.** $62.44 \div 7 = 892$

Divide. Estimate to check.

9. $15.33 \div 2.1$ **10.** $5.82 \div 9.7$ **11.** $0.55\overline{)2.42}$

PRACTICE AND PROBLEM SOLVING

Independent ▶
Practice
Rewrite the problem so that the divisor is a whole number.

12. $48.4 \div 0.4$ **13.** $8.19 \div 0.09$ **14.** $3.7 \div 2.1$

15. $2.39 \div 0.05$ **16.** $45.218 \div 0.23$ **17.** $233.58 \div 10.2$

Copy the problem. Place the decimal point in the quotient.

18. $3.258 \div 0.3 = 1086$ **19.** $53.07 \div 8.7 = 61$ **20.** $1.02 \div 0.2 = 51$

21. $84.87 \div 12.3 = 69$ **22.** $274.89 \div 1.5 = 18326$

Divide. Estimate to check.

23. $1.26 \div 0.2$ **24.** $13.2 \div 0.06$ **25.** $42.5 \div 0.05$

26. $0.9 \div 0.3$ **27.** $1.8 \div 0.6$ **28.** $0.75 \div 0.25$

29. $1.08 \div 0.27$ **30.** $1.49 \div 0.02$ **31.** $0.45 \div 0.3$

32. $2.9\overline{)20.88}$ **33.** $0.78\overline{)0.234}$ **34.** $4.3\overline{)271.76}$

35. $0.38\overline{)13.3}$ **36.** $12.72 \div 0.8$ **37.** $8.2\overline{)469.86}$

38. $100.86 \div 12.3$ **39.** $6.41\overline{)135.892}$ **40.** $8.256 \div 25.8$

Problem Solving ▶
Applications
41. ▆**FAST FACT** • **SCIENCE** The largest diamond ever found, weighing about 3,105.8 carats, was discovered in South Africa in 1905. The diamond was cut into pieces, each weighing about 29.3 carats. Into how many pieces was the original diamond cut?

Use Data   **For 42–43, use the data below.**

42. Use your calculator to find which of the gems sold for the greatest price per carat.

43. About how many times as much as the emerald does the sapphire weigh?

HIGHEST PRICES PAID FOR GEMS		
Type	Price (million $)	Weight (carats)
emerald	2.1	19.77
ruby	4.6	32.08
sapphire	2.8	62.02

44. Connie helped her mother pay for gas for the car. The total cost of the gas was $20.55 for 13.7 gal. How much did Connie pay her mother for 6 gal?

45. Chris wants to try out for the after-school track team. To make the team, he must average no more than 24.75 sec per lap around the track. He runs 4.5 laps in 110.25 sec. What is Chris's average time per lap? Explain how you know whether he makes the team.

46. Emily rents 5 DVD movies for $28.75. Is the price for one movie closer to $5 or to $6? Explain.

47. Jonelle saves $4.95 every week to buy a video that costs $29.70. She has already saved $9. For how many more weeks does she need to save money to have enough to buy the video?

48. **What's the Error?** Michael divided 4.25 by 0.25 and got a quotient of 0.17. Explain the error. What is the correct quotient?

49. Andrew reads 22 pages the first day. He plans to increase the number of pages he reads by 4 a day until he finishes the book. How many pages will he read on the third day?

MIXED REVIEW AND TEST PREP

50. Multiply. 2.051 × 8.6 (p. 80)

51. Is 208.6 greater than or less than 206.605? (p. 60)

52. Use mental math to find 210 ÷ 42. (p. 36)

53. TEST PREP Which shows the value of r when $18 + r = 52$? (p. 42)

    A 34   **B** 30   **C** 24   **D** 14

54. TEST PREP Jocelyn works 12 hours per week. She earns $7.25 an hour. How much does she earn in 4 weeks? (p. 80)

    F $87   **G** $174   **H** $290   **J** $348

PROBLEM SOLVING 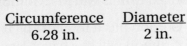 THiNKer's CorNer

REASONING The ancient Greeks discovered that there is one particular number that can be used to relate the dimensions of any circle. They called this particular number π (pi) and found that it is the same number regardless of the size of the circle.

- Determine the approximate value of π by dividing the distance around each circle described below (the circumference) by the distance across that circle (the diameter). Is the answer the same for each?

		Circumference	Diameter
1.	Circle 1	6.28 in.	2 in.
2.	Circle 2	9.42 in.	3 in.

EXTRA PRACTICE page 96, Set D

PROBLEM SOLVING SKILL
Interpret the Remainder

Analyze
Choose
Solve
Check

Learn how to interpret the remainder in a division problem.

The sixth-grade class at Hightown Middle School has an annual class picnic. With the help of some students, Ms. Gordon is planning for the picnic this year.

Ms. Gordon needs 163 boxed drinks for lunch. A package holds 6 boxes. How many packages of drinks will Ms. Gordon need to buy?	$\begin{array}{r} 27\ r1 \\ 6\overline{)163} \\ -12 \\ \hline 43 \\ -42 \\ \hline 1 \end{array}$	Since 27 packages hold only 162 total boxes, increase the quotient by 1. So, Ms. Gordon needs to buy 28 packages of drinks.

Ms. Gordon has 158 ft of ribbon to use for games. She will cut the ribbon into 8-ft lengths. How many 8-ft lengths of ribbon will Ms. Gordon have?	$\begin{array}{r} 19\ r6 \\ 8\overline{)158} \\ -8 \\ \hline 78 \\ -72 \\ \hline 6 \end{array}$	The remainder is not enough for another 8-ft length of ribbon. Drop the remainder. So, Ms. Gordon will have 19 lengths of ribbon.

Students collected 158 prizes. The prizes were put in packages of 5 each. The remaining prizes were given to another class in the school. How many prizes were given to the other class?	$\begin{array}{r} 31\ r3 \\ 5\overline{)158} \\ -15 \\ \hline 8 \\ -5 \\ \hline 3 \end{array}$	The remainder is your answer. So, 3 prizes were given to the other class.

Talk About It ▶

- What does the remainder in the first problem mean?

- **What if** Ms. Gordon buys 28 packages of boxed drinks? How many extra boxed drinks will Ms. Gordon buy?

- **What if** Ms. Gordon has a total of 165 ft of ribbon? How many 8-ft lengths of ribbon will she have? How long will the remaining ribbon be?

PROBLEM SOLVING PRACTICE

Solve the problem by interpreting the remainder.

A total of 39 students and adults tour the science museum to see an exhibit about the shaping of the Earth's surface. The tour director can take a group of up to 5 on each tour. All 39 students and adults need to see the exhibit.

1. How many complete groups of 5 people can the tour director take?

   A 5 groups   **B** 6 groups   **C** 7 groups   **D** 8 groups

2. What is the least number of tours the director will have to give to accommodate all 39 students and adults?

   F 6 tours   **G** 7 tours   **H** 8 tours   **J** 9 tours

3. James has $4.39 to buy magnets at the science museum. Each magnet costs $0.95. He wants to buy as many magnets as he can. How many magnets can James buy?

4. Sharon bought a package of 15 postcards at the museum. She gave the same number of postcards to each of her 4 teachers and kept the ones left over. How many postcards could Sharon have kept?

MIXED APPLICATIONS

5. A train that is scheduled to arrive at 5:15 P.M. arrives 20 minutes late. If the train left at 9:30 A.M., how long was the trip?

6. A total of 51 students and teachers are using cars to go on a field trip. Six people can ride in each car. How many cars are needed for the field trip?

7. Mark estimates that he needs 1 minute to solve a short homework problem and 5 minutes for each long problem. If he has 13 short and 4 long problems, how long should his homework take?

8. Tina makes bracelets for her friends. She uses 3 red beads for every 7 yellow beads to make a pattern. For one bracelet, she uses a total of 50 beads. How many of each color does she use?

9. A board game has 3 times as many red playing pieces as blue. It has 5 times as many green pieces as blue. There are 12 blue pieces. How many playing pieces are there in all?

10. Edgar has twice as many library books as his brother. If Edgar has 10 books in all, how many library books must he return to have the same number as his brother?

11. **? What's the Question?** Use the table at the right. Each presidential term in office is 4 years. The answer is that he served more than one term but fewer than two.

United States Presidents	
President	**Years in Office**
John Kennedy	1961–1963
Richard Nixon	1969–1974
Jimmy Carter	1977–1981
George H.W. Bush	1989–1993
Bill Clinton	1993–2001

ALGEBRA
Decimal Expressions and Equations

Learn how to evaluate expressions and solve equations with decimals.

QUICK REVIEW

Solve by using mental math.

1. $s + 14 = 36$ **2.** $18 \div p = 9$

3. $57 - d = 42$ **4.** $w \div 7 = 7$

5. $a \times 8 = 24$

Different groups of friends eat lunch at a café. The cost of the lunch is $6.45 per person. Write an expression to find the total cost of a lunch for a group of friends.

Let a be the number of friends buying lunch.

$a \times 6.45$, or $6.45a$ *Write the algebraic expression.*

The number of friends varies. What is the total cost for 7 friends?

$a \times 6.45$ *Write the algebraic expression.*

7×6.45 *Replace a with 7.*

45.15 *Multiply.*

So, the total cost is $45.15.

- Evaluate the expression $w \div 3 + 9.3$ for $w = 4.8$.

You solved equations with whole numbers by using mental math. You can use the same methods to solve some equations with decimals.

EXAMPLE

Solve the equation $h \div 6 = 0.6$ by using mental math.

$h \div 6 = 0.6$ *What number divided by 6 = 0.6?*

$h = 3.6$ THINK: *6 × 0.6 = 3.6.*

$h \div 6 = 0.6$ *Check your answer. Replace h with 3.6.*

$3.6 \div 6 = 0.6$

$0.6 = 0.6$

So, $h = 3.6$.

- Solve. $t + 4.24 = 9.48$

Think and ▶
Discuss

Look back at the lesson to answer each question.

1. **What if** 12 friends went to lunch at the café? Use a variable to show how you would find the total cost of the lunch.

2. **Explain** how you would solve the equation $3.2 = a \div 2$.

Guided ▶
Practice

Evaluate each expression.

3. $a + 3.4$
   for $a = 8.3$

4. $1.6 \div b$
   for $b = 0.4$

5. $9.16 - a$
   for $a = 4.08$

Solve each equation by using mental math.

6. $\frac{4.8}{k} = 8$

7. $m - 12.7 = 6.3$

8. $3t = 21.9$

Independent ▶
Practice

Evaluate each expression.

9. $2h$
   for $h = 2.3$

10. $9.6 \div a$
    for $a = 3$

11. $j + 7.1$
    for $j = 6.9$

12. $4.17 - c$
    for $c = 1.09$

13. $m \div 6 + 3.6$
    for $m = 1.8$

14. $g + h - 3.2$
    for $g = 4.1$ and
    $h = 2.3$

Solve each equation by using mental math.

15. $r + 8.1 = 15.8$

16. $1.7 = \frac{d}{4}$

17. $4a = 32.8$

18. $x - 2.4 = 8.6$

19. $p + 11.1 = 28.7$

20. $3.2r = 7.1 + 5.7$

Problem Solving ▶
Applications

21. Let n represent the number of miles Jeremy rides his bicycle to attend 6 baseball practices. Write an expression to show how far he travels for one practice. Evaluate the expression for $n = 28.8$ mi.

22. (?) **What's the Error?** Explain the error at the right. Give the correct solution.

$$24.8 + x = 30$$
$$x = 54.8$$

23. David jogs 3 mi each weekday and 7 mi each Saturday. Ray jogs 18 mi each week. How much farther does David jog in a week?

MIXED REVIEW AND TEST PREP

24. $4.38 \div 7.5$ (p. 88)

25. $18 \div 6 + (16 \times 3) - 14$ (p. 48)

26. $6,045 - 973$ (p. 22)

27. Order from least to greatest. 3.58, 3.08, 3.85, 3.508 (p. 60)

⭐ 28. **TEST PREP** The sum of two numbers is 35. Their difference is less than 10. Which is not a possible pair? (p. 28)

A 15, 20   **B** 17, 18   **C** 10, 25   **D** 22, 13

EXTRA PRACTICE page 96, Set E

Set A (pp. 76–79)

Add or subtract. Estimate to check.

1. $12.8 - 4.1$

2. $\$21.85 + \$17.48$

3. $17.3 - 16.5$

4. $8.36 + 5.216 + 0.09$

5. $8 + 7.317 + 3.06$

6. $5.08 - 2.261$

Set B (pp. 80–83)

Multiply. Estimate to check.

1. 21.3×18.4

2. 7.03×7.05

3. 9.2×2.13

4. 37.5×10.26

5. 6.42×9.1

6. 0.05×2.9

7. 19.3×2.41

8. 2.39×7.6

9. 2×6.005

Set C (pp. 86–87)

Divide. Estimate to check.

1. $80.1 \div 9$

2. $90.30 \div 6$

3. $8\overline{)16.56}$

4. $7\overline{)37.8}$

5. $44.28 \div 54$

6. $11\overline{)109.01}$

7. $90\overline{)10.80}$

8. $60\overline{)12.60}$

Set D (pp. 88–91)

Rewrite the problem so that the divisor is a whole number.

1. $16.92 \div 0.12$

2. $661.44 \div 31.2$

3. $20.2 \div 0.53$

Divide. Estimate to check.

4. $4.48 \div 2.8$

5. $28.68 \div 1.2$

6. $9.87 \div 0.2$

7. $14.16 \div 4.8$

8. $9.72 \div 1.2$

9. $25.56 \div 0.004$

10. $20.801 \div 6.1$

11. $80.4 \div 4.8$

Set E (pp. 94–95)

Evaluate each expression.

1. $8m$ for $m = 4.2$

2. $6.3 + 5.04 + k$ for $k = 8.4$

3. $(3.4 - c) + 63$ for $c = 2.47$

Solve each equation by using mental math.

4. $p + 2.8 = 7.9$

5. $\dfrac{k}{3} = 5.6$

6. $a - 17.1 = 9.5$

7. $6s = 7.2$

8. $x + 22.6 = 30.8$

9. $15n = 4.5$

Add or subtract. Estimate to check. (pp. 76–79)

1.   3.9
         4
       +5.91

2.   7.6
       −0.95

3.   3.02
         0.17
       +4.338

4. $19.3 - 2.56$

5. $0.126 + 5.3 + 3.04$

6. $245 - 39.05$

Multiply. Estimate to check. (pp. 80–83)

7.   8.3
       ×12.9

8.   7.82
       × 4.5

9.   53.6
       ×1.23

Divide. Estimate to check. (pp. 86–87; 88–91)

10. $14\overline{)3.5}$

11. $37\overline{)5.92}$

12. $45\overline{)1.08}$

13. $25\overline{)8.5}$

14. $22.8 \div 0.3$

15. $9.72 \div 2.7$

16. $33.33 \div 1.1$

17. $6.9 \div 0.3$

Evaluate each expression. (pp. 94–95)

18. $(2.3 + c) + 1.7$ for $c = 8$

19. $3 \times d + b$ for $d = 1.7$ and $b = 5.4$

20. $c \div 2 - a$ for $c = 8$ and $a = 2.3$

21. $(5.4 - a) + d$ for $a = 2.3$ and $d = 1.7$

22. $(d + c) - 5$ for $d = 1.7$ and $c = 8$

23. $(a + d) \div 4$ for $a = 2.3$ and $d = 1.7$

Solve each equation by using mental math. (pp. 94–95)

24. $c + 14.07 = 32.97$

25. $6a = 24.78$

26. $8d = 6.4$

27. $7.14 - g = 3.24$

28. $2.4 + f = 4.76$

29. $4y = 29.6$

30. $1.86 \div r = 6.2$

31. $t + 3.6 = 4.5 + 3.3$

Solve. (pp. 92–93)

32. There are 9 golf balls in a box. How many boxes does Hector need if he wants to give away 500 golf balls as souvenirs?

33. On Tuesday, Sabrina gets an invitation to a party that is in 20 days. She can go to the party if it does not fall on the weekend. Can she go to the party? Explain.

NUMBER SENSE, CONCEPTS, AND OPERATIONS

1. Point *K* on the number line shows the average part of a year that it rains or snows in Knoxville, Tennessee. Which number corresponds to point *K*?

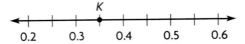

   A 0.035

   B 0.05

   C 0.35

   D 0.5

2. The graph below shows membership in the Westside Middle School Chess Club. Which decimal is equivalent to the percent of girls in the club?

   F 4.5   **H** 0.405

   G 0.45   **J** 0.045

3. Hector bought two shirts at $24.95 each and one cap for $10.95. He gave the clerk $70.00. How much change did Hector receive?

   A $34.10   **C** $10.15

   B $23.15   **D** $9.15

4. **Explain It** The weights of three items that Barb wants to mail are 0.40 kilogram, 0.97 kilogram, and 0.60 kilogram. Explain how Barb can use mental math to find the total weight of the three items.

 ALGEBRAIC THINKING

5. Jan is 62 inches tall. She is 2.75 inches taller than Phil. Phil is *p* inches tall. Which of the following equations could you use to find how tall Phil is?

   F $2.75 + p = 62$ **H** $p + 62 = 2.75$

   G $2.75 + 62 = p$ **J** $p - 2.75 = 62$

6. Marti made a table to show the relationship between the given number of bicycles, *x*, and the total number of wheels on the bicycles, *y*.

x	1	2	3
y	2	4	6

   Which of the following graphs shows the relationship?

   A
   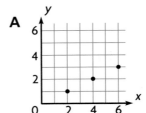

   C
   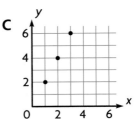

   B
   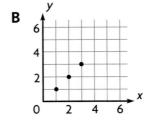

   D
   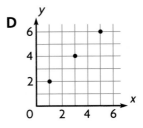

7. **Explain It** The figure below is a regular pentagon. The length of each side is *s*. Write a formula for *P*, the perimeter of the pentagon. Explain why your formula works.

DATA ANALYSIS AND PROBABILITY

 GEOMETRY AND SPATIAL SENSE

8. Vince recorded the temperature for four hours. The graph below shows the change in temperature for four hours.

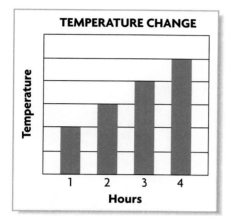

During the four hours, the temperature changed from 20 degrees to 50 degrees. The vertical axis is missing the scale for the temperature. Which of the following would be the **best** units for this scale?

F 5° intervals from 0°–30°

G 10° intervals from 0°–60°

H 20° intervals from 30°–110°

J 25° intervals from 0°–50°

9. Marco's scores on four science tests are shown below. What is his mean score?

   93   90   93   92

A 92

B 93

C 94

D 95

10. Explain It Becky and Val want to compare their math scores by displaying them on the same graph. What type of graph will **best** display the comparison of their math scores? Explain.

11. Each clue on the Math Club's Puzzle Trail leads to the next clue. Clue 8 reads: "Clue 9 is beneath the solid figure that isn't a prism." Which of the following will Clue 9 be beneath?

F 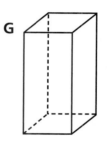   H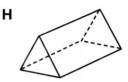

G 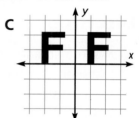   J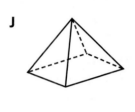

12. Which coordinate plane shows the second figure as a rotation of the first?

A 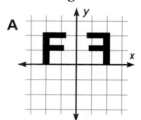   C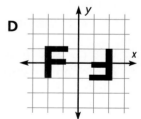

B 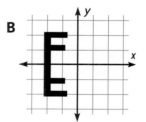   D

13. Explain It Mark has two similar posters on his wall. Are the posters congruent? Explain.

TIP **Look for important words.** See item 13. The words *similar* and *congruent* are important. Think of how similar and congruent figures are alike and different.

Projects
Bi-Folder

IT'S IN THE BAG!

Name the Game

PROJECT Make a game to practice number sense and operation skills.

Materials

- A pizza box or any game-size box
- Construction paper
- Markers
- Brass fastener
- Glue
- Scissors
- Large paper clip
- Scrap paper and pencil

Directions

1. Make a spinner from construction paper and the brass fastener. Use the paper clip as the pointer by attaching it to the fastener. Use a marker to show places on the inside of the box lid for playing cards. Write the directions for your game on construction paper. Glue the game parts to the inside of the box lid. (Picture A)

2. Use construction paper and markers to make the gameboard. Glue it to the inside of the box bottom. (Picture B)

3. Use construction paper and markers to make playing cards. Write a problem on each card. The problems are for the players to solve as they spin the pointer and move around the gameboard. (Picture C)

4. Provide an answer key for the problems on the playing cards.

5. Write the name of your game on the lid of the box. Then use markers to decorate the game box.

Learn how to write numbers by using scientific notation.

820,000 pounds lifting off!

The weight of one type of passenger jet is about 820,000 lb. This number, 820,000, is written using *standard notation*.

You can also write the weight using **scientific notation**. Scientific notation is a shorthand method for writing large numbers.

A number written in scientific notation has two parts separated by a multiplication symbol.

$$8.2 \times 10^5$$

The first part is a number that is at least 1 but less than 10.   The second part is a power of 10.

To write the number 820,000 in scientific notation:
Count the number of places the decimal point must be moved to the left to form a number that is at least 1 but less than 10.

$$820,000 \rightarrow 8.2$$

5 places

Since the decimal point moved 5 places, the power of 10 is 5.

$$820,000 = 8.2 \times 10^5$$

The airplane's weight written in scientific notation is 8.2×10^5 lb. This is how some calculators display 8.2×10^5.

EXAMPLE

About 32,500,000 passengers used Newark International Airport in 1998. Write the number of passengers in scientific notation.

$$32,500,000 \rightarrow 3.25 \times 10^7$$

7 places

The number of passengers was about 3.25×10^7.

TALK ABOUT IT

- Is 1.2×10^9 greater than 9.98×10^8? Explain.

- Show how to write 782.5×10^8 in scientific notation.

- What number is shown in the calculator display?

TRY IT

Write the number in scientific notation.

1. 602,000   2. 8,540   3. 5,010,000   4. 26,200,000

VOCABULARY

1. An expression that includes a variable is a(n) __?__ expression. (p. 36)

2. When you __?__ a decimal by a power of 10, the decimal point moves one place to the right for each factor of 10. (p. 101)

EXAMPLES

EXERCISES

Chapter 1

• **Add and subtract whole numbers.**
(pp. 22–23)

```
  3,921           3,000
     68          −1,650
+   205           1,350
  4,194
```

Find the sum or difference.

3. $756 + 902$
4. $4,293 + 256 + 19$
5. $3,511 − 1,345$
6. $729 + 8 + 3,996$
7. $16,092 − 5,618$
8. $25,080 − 19,387$

• **Multiply and divide whole numbers.**
(pp. 24–27)

```
    273              203 r16
  × 86           41)8,339
  1 638            −8 2
+21 84              13
 23,478            − 0
                   139
                  −123
                    16
```

Multiply or divide.

9. 57×38
10. 430×17
11. 276×809

12. $489 ÷ 26$
13. $9,671 ÷ 42$
14. $9,538 ÷ 19$

Chapter 2

• **Use mental math to solve equations.**
(pp. 38–39)

Solve. $w ÷ 6 = 7$ THINK: *What number divided by 6 equals 7?*

$w = 42$ *42 ÷ 6 = 7*

Solve each equation by using mental math.

15. $b + 5 = 12$
16. $a − 3 = 5$
17. $3y = 18$
18. $k ÷ 5 = 4$

• **Use the order of operations to evaluate expressions.** (pp. 48–51)

Evaluate. $25 ÷ 5 + (8 − 4)^2 × 3$

$25 ÷ 5 + (4)^2 × 3$ *Operate in parentheses.*
$25 ÷ 5 + 16 × 3$ *Clear exponents.*
$5 + 16 × 3$ *Divide.*
$5 + 48$ *Multiply.*
53 *Add.*

Evaluate the expression.

19. $3 × 6 + 7^2 − 9$
20. $(8 + 7) ÷ 3 + (5 − 3)^3$
21. $(15 − 3 × 4) + 8 ÷ 2$
22. $9^2 − 20 × 2 + 5$
23. $32 + (8^2 − 50) × 2$
24. $16 ÷ 2^3 + 4 × 3$

Chapter 3

- **Compare and order decimals.** (pp. 60–63)

  Compare 2.8 and 2.83.

2.8	2.83	*Start at the left.*
2.8	2.83	← *same number of ones*
2.8	2.83	← *same number of tenths*
2.80	2.83	*Add a zero to compare.*

  2.8 < 2.83, or 2.83 > 2.8

Compare the numbers. Write <, > or = for ●.

25. 3.72 ● 3.7   **26.** 5.02 ● 5.021

Write the numbers in order from least to greatest. Use <.

27. 1.67, 1.76, 1.607, 1.706, 1.076

28. 0.0014, 0.4001, 0.0401, 0.0041, 0.014

- **Write decimals as percents and percents as decimals.** (pp. 68–69)

  Write 0.05 as a percent.
  0.05 is 5 hundredths.
  So, 0.05 is 5%.

Write the corresponding decimal or percent.

29. 0.28   **30.** 7%

31. 47%   **32.** 0.6

Chapter 4

- **Add and subtract decimals.** (pp. 76–79)

  Find the difference. $8.2 - 6.391$

8.200	*Align the decimal points.*
−6.391	*Use zeros as placeholders.*
1.809	*Place the decimal point. Subtract.*

Add or subtract.

33. 29.6 + 0.935   **34.** 26.53 + 5.238

35. 76.03 − 58.94   **36.** 347.31 − 48.896

- **Multiply and divide decimals.** (pp. 80–91)

  Find the quotient. $2.46 \div 0.6$

4.1	
0.6)2.46	*Make the divisor a*
−2 4	*whole number.*
06	$0.6 \times 10 = 6$
−6	$2.46 \times 10 = 24.6$
0	*Divide.*

Multiply or divide.

37. 75.8 × 6   **38.** 4.83 × 0.9

39. 3.92 × 0.58   **40.** 68.49 × 3.6

41. 36.48 ÷ 12   **42.** 43.5 ÷ 0.3

43. 59.04 ÷ 4.8   **44.** 8.094 ÷ 0.95

- **Evaluate expressions with decimals.** (pp. 94–95)

  Evaluate $r + s + 3$ for $r = 6.9$ and $s = 4.8$.

$r + s + 3$	*Replace r with 6.9 and s*
	with 4.8.
6.9 + 4.8 + 3 = 14.7	

Evaluate each expression for $c = 2.5$, $d = 3.2$, and $f = 4.1$.

45. $(c \times 3) + d$ **46.** $(10 - d) + f$

47. $\frac{d}{8}$ **48.** $f - c + d$

PROBLEM SOLVING APPLICATIONS

49. Jake has half as many pennies as his sister has. Together their pennies are worth 72 cents. How many pennies does Jake have? (p. 28)

50. Movie tickets cost $3.75 each for the matinee. How many tickets can Ms. Hamil buy with $20? How much money will she have left over? (p. 52)

Performance Assessment

TASK A • Programming Problem

As part of a larger computer program you are building, you need to make a module that will evaluate any numerical expression the user puts into it.

- Write down the steps the computer must go through to evaluate any expression that is put into it.

- Make up your own numerical expression that includes at least three different operations and has part of the expression in parentheses. Explain the steps the computer will go through to evaluate it.

- Tell how the computer will evaluate the following expression:
  $3 \times 0.2 + 9 \div 0.3 - (4^2 - 2^3)$

TASK B • Pizza Party

Peggy is giving a pizza party to celebrate her birthday. To plan it she needs some information about the pizzas she can order.

Pizza Diameter	Number of Slices	Cost per Pizza
12 inches	4	$7
14 inches	6	$9
16 inches	8	$11

- Suppose Peggy has $30 to spend on the pizzas. What are some different ways to spend the money? Make a list. Which way gets her closest to spending all of the $30? What combination of pizzas should she buy to get the greatest number of slices?

Next, she'll have to decide how many friends she can invite.

- How many slices do you think each friend will eat? Find a way for Peggy to order exactly enough pizzas so that each friend gets the same number of slices and none are left over. Describe what you would do. Remember to stay within the budget.

Use a Spreadsheet to Find
Sums and Differences

The table below shows the money Evan earned by working in his parents' store last year. Evan uses a spreadsheet to find the total amount he earned.

Month	Amount	Month	Amount	Month	Amount
January	$35.75	May	$55.50	September	$57.77
February	$30.95	June	$66.85	October	$42.95
March	$41.25	July	$64.60	November	$78.25
April	$48.75	August	$69.00	December	$85.15

- Open the spreadsheet. Enter the months into Column A and the amounts into Column B.

- Click cell B13. On the toolbar find and click Σ and then press *Enter*. If your toolbar doesn't have that icon, click f_x, highlight *SUM*, and click *OK*.

- Type B1:B12. This tells the spreadsheet to add cells B1 through B12. Then press *Enter*.
So, Evan earned a total of $676.77 last year.

How much more did Evan earn in June than in May?

- Click an empty cell. For example, click C6. Type =.

- Click cell B6. Type −. Click cell B5. Then press *Enter*.
So, Evan earned $11.35 more in June than in May.

	A	B	C
1	January	$35.75	
2	February	$30.95	
3	March	$41.25	
4	April	$48.75	
5	May	$55.50	
6	June	$66.85	
7	July	$64.60	
8	August	$69.00	
9	September	$57.77	
10	October	$42.95	
11	November	$78.25	
12	December	$85.15	
13		$676.77	
14			

	A	B	C	D
1	January	$35.75		
2	February	$30.95		
3	March	$41.25		
4	April	$48.75		
5	May	$55.50		
6	June	$66.85	$11.35	
7	July	$64.60		
8	August	$69.00		
9	September	$57.77		
10	October	$42.95		
11	November	$78.25		
12	December	$85.15		
13		$676.77		
14				

Practice and Problem Solving

Make a spreadsheet to find the sum and difference.

1. Eric earned $119.53 in May, $104.15 in June, $99.78 in July, $123.83 in August, and $141.55 in September. What is the total amount he earned? How much more did he earn in September than in July?

2. Nieko earned $45.18 in January, $39.25 in February, $72.59 in March, and $55.92 in April. What is the total amount she earned? How much more did she earn in March than in April?

3. **REASONING** Explain the steps you follow to add and subtract numbers on a spreadsheet.

GO ON-LINE

Multimedia Math Glossary www.harcourtschool.com/mathglossary

Vocabulary Power Look up *clustering* in the Multimedia Math Glossary. Write a problem that can be answered using the example shown in the glossary.

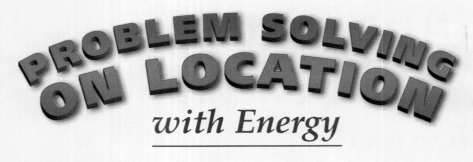

PROBLEM SOLVING ON LOCATION
with Energy

Wind Energy

Wind energy has been used for centuries to pump water, to grind grain, and to power sailboats. Today, many communities use windmills called wind turbines to generate electricity. Several important wind turbine projects are located in Minnesota.

Use Data **For 1–8, use the table.**

1. Order the locations from greatest number of turbines to least.

2. How many more turbines are there at Lake Benton I than at Lake Benton II?

Wind Turbines in Minnesota	
Location	**Number of Turbines**
Lakota Ridge	15
Lake Benton I	143
Lake Benton II	138

3. There are about 50 times as many wind turbines in California as there are at the three sites in Minnesota combined. About how many wind turbines are there in California?

4. How many times as many turbines are there at Lake Benton II as there are at Lakota Ridge? Write your answer as a fraction in simplest form and as a mixed number.

Electricity is measured in kilowatt-hours (kWh). The turbines at Lakota Ridge generate 30 million kWh per year. The turbines at Lake Benton II generate 355 million kWh per year.

5. About how many kWh are generated each day at Lake Benton II?

6. About how many kWh are generated each year by each turbine at Lake Benton II?

7. About how many kWh are generated each year by each turbine at Lakota Ridge?

8. About how many kWh are generated each day at Lakota Ridge?

Solar Energy

Each day huge amounts of free energy strike the Earth in the form of radiation from the sun. This *solar* energy can be converted to heat and electricity for human use. Solar energy, like wind power, is a *renewable* resource.

Reilly Elementary School is one of several schools in Chicago that use solar energy. These schools are part of the Million Solar Roofs program. By using the sun's energy, the schools can provide for some or all of their heating needs. This reduces their dependence on oil, coal, and other *nonrenewable* resources.

1. The solar project at Reilly Elementary School installed 120 solar power units at a total cost of $500,000. What was the average cost of a solar power unit, rounded to the nearest hundred dollars?

2. Out of every dollar spent for the Reilly solar units, the Chicago school system paid 10 cents. If the total cost was $500,000, how much money did the Chicago school system provide?

Use Data   For 3–5, use the table.

3. A quadrillion is a million billion. What is the amount for fossil fuels written in standard form?

U.S. Energy Consumption by Energy Source	
Source	**Amount (in quadrillion btu)**
Fossil Fuels	80
Nuclear Power	7
Renewable Sources	7

4. Write an equation you can use to find how much more energy is consumed from fossil fuels than from renewable sources. Then solve the equation.

5. Suppose the United States set a goal of using renewable energy sources for half of its energy use. By how many btu would the nation's current renewable sources have to increase?

These wind turbines are located at Lake Benton, Minnesota. When the blades spin, they drive generators, which in turn produce electricity.

CHAPTER 5

Collect and Organize Data

Hubbard Glacier
in Alaska

≣FAST FACT • SCIENCE About 70% of Earth's surface is covered with water. However, most of that water is salt water, which is unusable for drinking, watering crops, or manufacturing.

PROBLEM SOLVING What information about Earth's water supply can you find in the graph?

WATER ON THE EARTH

 Fresh Water

 Ice

Salt Water

If you could put all the water on Earth into 100 buckets, 97 buckets would hold the salt water of the oceans and seas, and 2 buckets would hold the frozen fresh water of glaciers and icecaps. Only 1 bucket would hold liquid fresh water.

Check What You Know

Use this page to help you review and remember important skills needed for Chapter 5.

✓ Reading a Table

STUDENTS' FAVORITE SPORTS				
	Gymnastics	**Basketball**	**Baseball**	**Football**
Boys	4	29	16	13
Girls	17	14	9	12

Use the data in the table above to answer the questions.

1. How many boys like baseball the best?

2. How many more girls than boys like gymnastics the best?

3. Which sport was selected by more boys than any other?

4. How many girls like gymnastics or football the best?

5. How many students were surveyed?

✓ Mean, Median, and Mode

Find the mean for each set of data.

6. 8, 6, 11, 7, 6, 10

7. 83, 74, 91, 78, 90, 88

8. $7, $16, $10, $18, $9

9. 103, 130, 114, 121

10. 214, 203, 274, 302, 255, 288

11. 1,100; 1,251; 1,090

Find the median and the mode for each set of data.

12. 16, 32, 24, 10, 48, 32, 28

13. 10, 15, 7, 8, 12, 13, 13, 15, 21

14. $8, $13, $14, $9, $11

15. 121, 108, 116, 108, 110

16. 150, 92, 131, 150, 109, 98

17. 905; 840; 1,102; 995

VOCABULARY POWER

REVIEW

median [mē′dē•ən] *noun*

Median comes from the Latin word *medianus*, which means "middle." Use this meaning to give a mathematical definition and a nonmathematical definition of *median*.

 www.harcourtschool.com/mathglossary

PREVIEW

survey

population

sample

random sample

unbiased sample

biased sample

biased question

cumulative frequency

relative frequency

Samples

Learn how to identify populations and random samples.

QUICK REVIEW

1. 240
    +360

2. 94
    −60

3. 60
    ×20

4. 30)‾270

5. 10)‾850

Vocabulary

survey
population
sample
random sample

A **survey** is a method of gathering information about a group. Surveys are usually made up of questions or other items that require responses.

You can survey the **population**, the entire group of individuals or objects, such as all teenagers. Or, if the population is large, you can survey a part of the group, called a **sample**.

Sample   All Teenagers

EXAMPLE 1

Suppose Jenna wants to find out the favorite game among students in her math class. Describe the population. Should Jenna survey the population or use a sample? Explain.

The population consists of all the students in Jenna's math class. Jenna should survey the population since it is small.

• **What if** the population is changed to all of the 1,800 students in Jenna's school?

A **random sample** is a sample in which each individual or object in the given population has an equal chance of being selected.

EXAMPLE 2

Beth wants to find out the favorite song of students at Roosevelt Middle School. Tell whether each sample below is random. Explain.

A. 100 students at a school dance

B. 100 students whose names are selected, without looking, from a box containing all student names

Sample A is not random because some students at Beth's school probably don't go to school dances, so they would not have a chance of being selected. Sample B is random because each student has an equal chance of being selected.

Math Idea ▶ It is important to select a sample that is representative of the population. For example, if the population includes men and women, then the sample should include both men and women. Selecting a random sample from the correct population is one way to make sure the sample is representative.

Think and ▶
Discuss

Look back at the lesson to answer the question.

1. **Explain** why a sample is often used rather than a population when conducting a survey.

Guided ▶
Practice

Tell whether you would survey the population or use a sample. Explain.

2. You want to find out where the students in your class want to go for a field trip.

Tell whether a random sample was chosen. Explain.

3. Ruth wanted to find out the favorite movies of students in her middle school, so she surveyed all students in her math class.

PRACTICE AND PROBLEM SOLVING

Independent ▶
Practice

Tell whether you would survey the population or use a sample. Explain.

4. You want to know the favorite kinds of food of all teens in Miami.

Tell whether a random sample was chosen. Explain.

5. When conducting a survey, Gina put the names of all sixth graders in a hat and selected 50 names without looking.

6. To determine the favorite lunch items of students, a cafeteria worker surveyed students who bought lunch on Friday.

Problem Solving ▶
Applications

7. **Vocabulary Power** Think about what the word *population* means in your social studies book. Explain how that meaning is similar to the meaning described in this lesson.

8. 📖 **Write About It** Choose a topic you could find out about by taking a survey. Then tell how you would choose a random sample.

MIXED REVIEW AND TEST PREP

Evaluate for $a = 3.1$ and $b = 6.2$. (p. 94)

9. $a + b$ 10. $a \times b$ 11. $b \div a$

⭐**12. TEST PREP** Which is the product of 5.25 and 1.9? (p. 80)

    A 9.975   **B** 99.75   **C** 997.5   **D** 9,975

⭐**13. TEST PREP** Martha saved $0.50 one week. Then she saved $0.50 more each week than she had the week before. How many weeks did it take to save a total of $10.50? (p. 76)

    F 5 weeks   **G** 6 weeks   **H** 7 weeks   **J** 8 weeks

EXTRA PRACTICE page 128, Set A

Bias in Surveys

Learn how to determine whether a sample or a question in a survey is biased.

Vocabulary

unbiased sample
biased sample
biased question

Does the earth revolve around the sun or does the sun revolve around the earth? In a recent survey of more than 1,000 adults, 79% knew the correct answer.

When you collect data in a survey, your sample should represent the whole population. All individuals in that population should have equal chances of being selected. If they do, the sample is an **unbiased sample**.

If certain groups from the population are not represented in the sample, then the sample is a **biased sample**. If the sample for the survey described above included only males, it would be biased since the survey was for all adults.

EXAMPLE 1

Latosha wants to find out how many hours Polk Middle School students spend on the Internet. If she surveys students from this school, which samples below will be biased? Explain.

A. 200 randomly selected girls

B. 200 randomly selected athletes

C. 200 randomly selected students

D. students who ride their bikes to school

Samples A, B, and D are biased. Sample A excludes boys, sample B includes only athletes, and sample D excludes students who don't ride their bikes to school.

Sometimes, questions are biased. A **biased question** suggests or leads to a specific response or excludes a certain group.

EXAMPLE 2

Is the following question biased or unbiased?

Do you agree with a well-known movie critic that movies longer than two hours are boring?

This question is biased since it leads you to agree with the movie critic.

CHECK FOR UNDERSTANDING

Think and ▶
Discuss

Look back at the lesson to answer the question.

1. Write the question in Example 2 so that it is not biased.

Guided ▶
Practice

Tell whether the sample is *biased* or *unbiased*. Explain.

The local gym wants to find out how its members feel about the new exercise equipment.

2. 50 randomly selected female members

3. 50 randomly selected members under age 20

4. 50 randomly selected members who used the gym in August

5. 50 randomly selected members

PRACTICE AND PROBLEM SOLVING

Independent ▶
Practice

Tell whether the sample is *biased* or *unbiased*. Explain.

The Middletown Mall is conducting a survey of its shoppers to find out which days they prefer to shop.

6. 400 randomly selected teenage shoppers

7. 400 randomly selected shoppers

8. 400 randomly selected female shoppers

9. shoppers who enter the record store

Determine whether the question is biased. Write *biased* or *unbiased*.

10. What is your favorite sport?

11. Do you agree with the fruit industry president that green apples taste better than red apples?

Problem Solving ▶
Applications

12. **REASONING**   Students at Memorial Middle School are being surveyed to find out their choice of a new school mascot. If 300 students are randomly selected, do equal numbers of boys and girls have to be chosen? Explain.

13. 🖊 **Write About It**   Is this question biased? Explain.
I think pizza is the best choice for lunch, don't you?

MIXED REVIEW AND TEST PREP

14. To find out the favorite book of students at her school, a teacher surveys students in her science classes. Is this a random sample? Explain. (p. 110)

Find the quotient. (p. 88)

15. $3.6 \div 0.9$

16. $1.44 \div 0.12$

17. $270 \div 0.03$

⭐ 18. **TEST PREP**   Replace ● with the missing operation: $3^2 \times (6 \; ● \; 4) = 90$. (p. 48)

A ÷   **B** ×   **C** −   **D** +

Frequency Tables and Line Plots

Learn how to record and organize data collected in a survey.

Vocabulary

cumulative frequency

relative frequency

In 2000, the largest iceberg on record contained enough ice to provide everyone on earth with 4 gallons of water per day for 40 years! Most of an iceberg is below the surface of the water. The data in the table below show the number of icebergs a scientist observed every day for 20 days.

NUMBER OF ICEBERGS OBSERVED				
12	15	11	16	15
16	16	15	13	16
16	14	12	14	16
15	13	15	14	15

You can use a line plot to record data.

EXAMPLE 1

Remember that the range of a set of data is the difference between the greatest number and the least number in the set.

Use the iceberg data above.

A. Make a line plot.

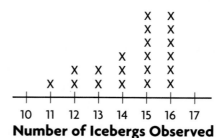

Number of Icebergs Observed

Each X represents the number of icebergs the scientist observed during one day.

B. Find the range.
   $16 - 11 = 5$

So, the range is 5 icebergs.

A line plot helps you see if there are any gaps or extremes in the data. You can also see where data cluster. The line plot in Example 1 shows that the scientist observed 15–16 icebergs per day more often than she observed 11–14 icebergs per day.

Frequency Tables

A frequency table shows the total for each category or group. You can add a cumulative frequency column to the table. **Cumulative frequency** is a running total of the frequencies.

EXAMPLE 2

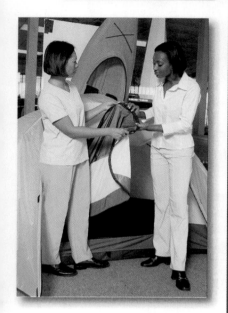

Mrs. Wills recorded the number of tents she sold each week in her sporting goods store. Use the data to make a frequency table. How many tents did Mrs. Wills sell by the end of Week 3?

Tents Sold
Week 1: IIII
Week 2: IIII IIII II
Week 3: IIII II
Week 4: IIII IIII

List the weeks in the first column.
Record the total for each week in the frequency column.
Record the running total in the cumulative frequency column.

TENTS SOLD		
Week	Frequency	Cumulative Frequency
1	5	5
2	12	17
3	7	24
4	10	34

← 5 + 12 = 17
← 17 + 7 = 24
← 24 + 10 = 34

So, Mrs. Wills sold 24 tents by the end of Week 3.

A local mall took a survey to find the number of times people visit the mall in one year. The survey results are shown below.

NUMBER OF TRIPS TO THE MALL									
12	20	5	7	13	11	3	9	19	16
8	17	17	16	1	6	8	5	14	9

EXAMPLE 3

Use the data about the number of trips to the mall to make a cumulative frequency table with 4 intervals.

20 − 1 = 19

Find the range.

Since 20 is above and close to 19, use 20 to make 4 intervals that include 5 consecutive numbers.

Use the range to determine intervals.

Complete the cumulative frequency table.

TRIPS TO THE MALL		
Number of Trips	Frequency	Cumulative Frequency
1-5	4	4
6-10	6	10
11-15	4	14
16-20	6	20

• How many of the people surveyed made 15 or fewer trips to the mall in one year? Explain.

A frequency table can have a column for relative frequency. The **relative frequency** of a given category is the frequency of the category divided by the sum of the frequencies.

EXAMPLE 4

The local mall surveyed 50 teens about the overall quality of food at the mall's food court. Use the data from the survey to make a frequency table. Include a relative frequency column. Write the relative frequency as a decimal and as a percent.

Quality of Food at Food Court	
Quality	Tally
Very Good	JHT JHT III
Good	JHT JHT JHT JHT
Fair	JHT JHT
Poor	JHT II

List each category and record its frequency. Find the relative frequency of each category by dividing the frequency by the sum of the frequencies, 50.

QUALITY OF FOOD AT FOOD COURT		
Quality	**Frequency**	**Relative Frequency**
Very Good	13	13 ÷ 50 = 0.26 or 26%
Good	20	20 ÷ 50 = 0.40 or 40%
Fair	10	10 ÷ 50 = 0.20 or 20%
Poor	7	7 ÷ 50 = 0.14 or 14%

CHECK FOR UNDERSTANDING

Think and Discuss ▸ Look back at the lesson to answer each question.

1. **Name** the intervals you could have in Example 3 if you made 2 intervals. Explain.

2. **Explain** how to find the size of the survey sample by using the frequency table in Example 3.

Guided Practice ▸ For 3–5, use the data in the table.

3. Make a line plot.

4. Find the range.

5. Make a cumulative frequency table with 4 intervals.

AGES OF POP MUSIC LISTENERS						
12	13	17	16	15	13	25
28	27	18	15	12	14	23
13	15	17	13	22	18	15

PRACTICE AND PROBLEM SOLVING

Independent Practice ▸ For 6–8, use the data in the table.

6. Make a line plot.

7. Find the range.

8. Make a cumulative frequency table with 3 intervals.

NUMBER OF KILOMETERS BIKED						
6	11	7	8	8	5	15
14	12	10	18	6	7	9
15	15	8	9	12	17	10

Kim asked people in her neighborhood about their favorite type of movie. Use the data for 9–10.

FAVORITE MOVIES	
Movies	Tally
Drama	~~IIII~~ ~~IIII~~
Action	~~IIII~~ III
Comedy	~~IIII~~ ~~IIII~~ IIII
Mystery	~~IIII~~ III

9. Organize the data into a frequency table. Include a relative frequency column.

10. How many people did Kim survey?

For 11–14, use the data in the box at the right.

11. Make a line plot.

12. Find the range.

13. How many weights would be in each interval if you used the range to make 4 intervals? 6 intervals?

WEIGHTS OF STUDENTS' PET DOGS (LB)					
40	10	22	33	44	40
41	42	12	35	20	10
30	25	20	18	45	35
34	35	40	40	35	38

14. Make a cumulative frequency table using 4 intervals for the weights.

Problem Solving ▶ Applications

15. *REASONING* Survey your classmates about their favorite hobbies. Organize the data in a tally table and a frequency table.

16. Decide on appropriate intervals and make a cumulative frequency table using 6 intervals for the data in the table below.

POUNDS OF VEGETABLES CONSUMED YEARLY											
12	16	18	12	9	21	14	17	18	5	23	25	32
17	16	8	9	22	21	14	18	7	23	24	19	13

17. **? What's the Question?** In a set of data, the greatest value is 54 and the least value is 30. The answer is 24.

MIXED REVIEW AND TEST PREP

Tell whether the question is *biased* or *unbiased*. (p. 112)

18. Do you feel that sixth graders should do two hours of homework each night instead of watching TV?

19. For whom do you intend to vote in the upcoming student government election?

20. Tell if the expression is numerical or algebraic. $a + 3.9$ (p. 36)

⭐21. **TEST PREP** Which is the value of 4^5? (p. 46)

   A 9   **B** 20   **C** 625   **D** 1,024

⭐22. **TEST PREP** Twenty-seven sixth graders read a total of 135 books. If each student reads the same number of books, how many more books must each student read to reach a total of 243 books read? (p. 24)

   F 2 books   **G** 4 books   **H** 50 books   **J** 108 books

Mean, Median, and Mode

Learn how to find the mean, median, and mode of a set of data and decide which best describes the set of data.

QUICK REVIEW

1. 420 ÷ 5   **2.** 392 ÷ 7   **3.** 320 ÷ 8   **4.** 540 ÷ 60   **5.** 720 ÷ 9

The mean, median, and mode can help you describe a set of data.

During 2001 and 2002, amateur rocket builder Ariana Williams set American records for 7- to 13-year-olds in five different rocket events. The winning heights reached by her rockets are shown below. Find the mean, median, and mode for the data.

ROCKET HEIGHTS (m)				
148	91	269	420	50

Mean: $(148 + 91 + 269 + 420 + 50) ÷ 5 = 978 ÷ 5 = 195.6$ m

Median: 50 91 148 269 420; 148 m

Mode: No value occurs more than any other, so there is no mode.

The key sequence below shows how to find the mean of Ariana's rocket heights by using a calculator.

(148 + 91 + 269 + 420 + 50)

÷ 5 = | 195.6 |

Sometimes a line plot can help you find the mode and the median.

EXAMPLE 1

Use the data to make a line plot. Find the mode and the median.

DAILY TEMPERATURES (°F)										
72	82	83	78	81	78	73	74	75	73	76
71	75	80	83	72	72	78	81	79	82	76

```
        X                       X
        X   X       X   X       X           X   X   X
    X   X   X   X   X   X       X   X   X   X   X   X
    +---+---+---+---+---+---+---+---+---+---+---+---+---+---+
    70  71  72  73  74  75  76  77  78  79  80  81  82  83  84
```

Mode: Look on the line plot for the values with the most X's. The modes are 72° and 78° since each occurs 3 times.

Median: Since there are 22 temperatures, the median of 77° is the mean of the 11th and 12th temperatures. $(76 + 78) ÷ 2 = 77$

Math **I**dea ▶ When you want to summarize a set of data as one value, you can use the mean, median, or mode.

EXAMPLE 2

Pedro jogged 6 mi, 5 mi, 2 mi, 2 mi, and 4 mi over 5 days. Which measure is most useful to describe the data?

Mean: (6 + 5 + 2 + 2 + 4) ÷ 5 = 19 ÷ 5 = 3.8 mi

Median: 2 2 4 5 6; 4 mi   **Mode:** 2 mi

The mode, 2, is close to the low end of the data, so the mode is not useful. The mean, 3.8, and the median, 4, are close to most of the data, so the mean or the median is most useful to describe the data.

EXAMPLE 3

The bald eagle, the national bird of the United States, was once endangered. In recent decades, the species has made a dramatic recovery. The map at the right shows the numbers of nests in six zones of Montana. Is the mean or the median more useful to describe the data?

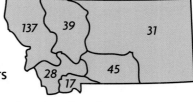

Numbers of nests: 137, 39, 31, 45, 17, 28

Mean: (137 + 39 + 31 + 45 + 17 + 28) ÷ 6 = 297 ÷ 6 = 49.5 nests

Median: 17 28 31 39 45 137 → $\frac{31 + 39}{2}$ = 35 nests

The high value of 137 makes the mean greater than any of the five other values. The median, 35, is closer to most of the data. So, the median is more useful to describe the data.

CHECK FOR UNDERSTANDING

Think and ▶ Discuss

Look back at the lesson to answer the questions.

1. **Explain** how you would find the mean, median, and mode of the membership data below, and find the value of each measure.

   Club memberships: 15, 11, 32, 16, 11

2. **Explain** how the data below are different from the data in Examples 1, 2, and 3. Which measure is most useful to describe the data, the mean, the median, or the mode? Explain your thinking.

   Favorite Pet: cat, dog, bird, cat, dog, dog, cat, fish, hamster

Guided ▶ Practice

For 3–5, use the table below.

Day	Sun	Mon	Tue	Wed	Thu	Fri	Sat
Hours of Sleep	8	6	7	7	4	10	7

3. Find the mean.   4. Find the median.   5. Find the mode.

Find the mean, median, and mode.

6. 22, 24, 22, 29, 33, 14

7. 124, 120, 132, 133, 119, 90, 87

8. Find the mean and median of the data shown below. Then tell which measure is more useful to describe the data. Explain your thinking.

Test Scores: 90, 86, 83, 80, 28, 77, 84, 85, 78, 87

PRACTICE AND PROBLEM SOLVING

Independent ▶ Practice

For 9–11, use the table below.

Game	1	2	3	4	5	6	7	8
Points Scored	10	12	10	17	18	12	20	24

9. Find the mean.   10. Find the median.   11. Find the mode.

Find the mean, median, and mode.

12. 76, 63, 40, 52, 52, 40, 6, 15

13. 365, 180, 360, 720, 59

14. 540, 529, 530, 529, 536

15. 985; 1,050; 970; 1,103

16. Find the mean and median of the data shown below. Then tell which measure is more useful to describe the data. Explain your thinking.

Temperatures (°F): 92, 90, 89, 80, 90, 85, 97

Use the given mean to find the value of n in each data set.

17. 6, 8, 5, 12, n; mean: 8

18. 205, 180, 201, n; mean: 200

Problem Solving ▶ Applications

19. Use the data below to make a line plot. Use your line plot to find the median and the mode. Then use the data to find the mean. Is the mean or the median more useful to describe the data?

YEARLY RAINFALL (IN.)									
47	11	8	14	15	16	13	13	17	22

20. **ALGEBRA** Reggie's average score on five math tests is 92. On the first four tests, Reggie's scores were 88, 97, 93, and 82. What was Reggie's score on the fifth test?

21. **FAST FACT • SPORTS** The first concrete stadium designed for college football was built at Harvard University in 1903. It had 22,000 seats. Find the median number of seats for the stadiums in the table at the right.

COLLEGE FOOTBALL STADIUMS (2002)	
University	**Seats**
Louisiana State University	91,600
University of Florida	83,000
University of Michigan	107,501
University of Notre Dame	80,232

22. Emily scored 75, 85, 35, 85, 70, and 10 on her first six math quizzes. What score does Emily need on her seventh quiz to have a median score of 75?

23. **? What's the Error?** Tim wrote $(7 + 3 + 10 + 4) \div 3 = 8$ to find the mean of 7, 3, 10, and 4. What is his error? What is the correct mean?

24. Joel, Vic, and Liam play soccer, volleyball, or tennis. Each boy plays a different sport. Joel does not play soccer. Liam watched Vic in a volleyball tournament last weekend. Who plays each sport?

MIXED REVIEW AND TEST PREP

For 25–27, use the table. (p. 114)

25. How many joggers are 39 years old or younger?

26. What is the size of the sample?

27. Find the relative frequency for the 40–49 age group. Write the answer as a percent.

AGES OF JOGGERS ON TRAIL		
Age	Frequency	Cumulative Frequency
20–29	10	10
30–39	11	21
40–49	7	28

28. TEST PREP A park has canoes that carry either 3 or 4 persons. There are 5 full canoes carrying a total of 17 people. How many 4-person canoes are there? (p. 28)

A 2   **B** 3   **C** 4   **D** 5

29. TEST PREP Which is greater than 1.540? (p. 60)

F 1.505   **G** 1.510   **H** 1.534   **J** 1.550

PROBLEM SOLVING LiNKUP to Social Studies

World Population The population is growing at different rates around the world. In North America, the population is growing fairly slowly. In Latin America and Africa, the population is growing much more rapidly. The table shows how median ages differ.

Median Ages				
Africa	Asia	Europe	Latin America and Caribbean	North America
18.4 years	26.2 years	37.7 years	24.4 years	35.6 years

1. Explain what it means to say the median age in Asia is 26.2 years.

2. Use < to order the median ages from least to greatest.

Data and Conclusions

Learn how to draw conclusions by analyzing data in tables and graphs.

QUICK REVIEW

1. 250 ÷ 5 2. 540 ÷ 9 3. 560 ÷ 8 4. 420 ÷ 60 5. 350 ÷ 7

Table and graphs are used to record and display data. You can also use them to draw conclusions about the data.

EXAMPLE 1

A theater owner experimented with the prices of tickets at a series of concerts. She wanted to see how ticket price affected income from the concerts. The table and the bar graph show the results of the experiment. Use the table and the graph to draw conclusions.

CONCERT TICKET PRICES	
Concert	Price ($)
1	20
2	16
3	12
4	10
5	8

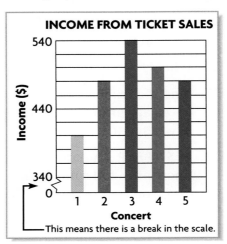

INCOME FROM TICKET SALES

This means there is a break in the scale.

ANALYZE	CONCLUSION
• Look at the table. How did ticket prices change from concert to concert?	• Prices decreased steadily, from $20 for Concert 1 to $8 for Concert 5.
• Look at the table and the graph. Which ticket price resulted in the greatest income?	• The greatest income was $540 at Concert 3, when tickets cost $12.
• Look at the table and the graph. How many people attended Concert 2?	• The ticket price was $16 and the income was $480. The number of people who attended was 480 ÷ 16 = 30.
• What conclusions can the theater owner draw about the relationship between the price of the concert tickets and the income from ticket sales?	• Reducing ticket prices increases the number of people who will buy tickets. When the price falls below $12, however, the total income falls too.

EXAMPLE 2

Random surveys of sixth graders from Florida were taken in 1993 and 2003. In both surveys, students were asked about their favorite type of television program. The results are shown in the graphs below. What conclusions can you draw about sixth-grade students' interest in sitcoms, movies, and dramas?

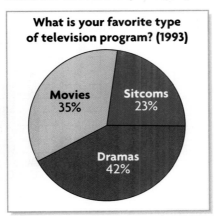

What is your favorite type of television program? (1993)

Movies 35%
Sitcoms 23%
Dramas 42%

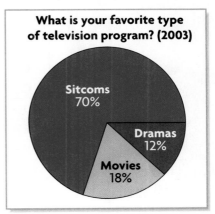

What is your favorite type of television program? (2003)

Sitcoms 70%
Dramas 12%
Movies 18%

Type of Show	Conclusion
Sitcom	Interest in sitcoms increased.
Movie	Interest in movies decreased.
Drama	Interest in dramas decreased.

- Do you think that the conclusions would be the same for seventh graders and eighth graders? Explain.

You can compare the means and medians of similar data sets in order to draw conclusions about the data.

EXAMPLE 3

Two classes took the same math quiz. The chart shows the results. Find the mean and median for each class. Which class did better on the quiz, Mr. Wilson's or Mrs. Brown's?

> **Mr. Wilson's Class**
> 3, 9, 7, 6, 6, 4, 5, 6, 8, 9
>
> **Mrs. Brown's Class**
> 7, 10, 6, 7, 8, 8, 9, 7, 6, 7

Mr. Wilson's Class: mean = 6.3 median = 6
Mrs. Brown's Class: mean = 7.5 median = 7

The mean and median for Mrs. Brown's class are greater than the mean and median for Mr. Wilson's class. So, Mrs. Brown's class did better on the quiz than Mr. Wilson's class.

CHECK FOR UNDERSTANDING

Think and ▶ Discuss

Look back at the lesson to answer each question.

1. **Explain** how a graph can help you draw conclusions about data.

2. **What if**, in Example 1, there had been a sixth concert? If the patterns in ticket prices and income continued, what would be a good estimate for ticket price and income for Concert 6?

Use Data Six teams of students washed cars at a school fund-raiser. A teacher calculated the average time it took for each team to wash one car. For 3–6, use the table and the bar graph, which show the results of the experiment.

CAR WASH TEAMS	
Team	**Number of Students**
A	4
B	5
C	6
D	8
E	10
F	12

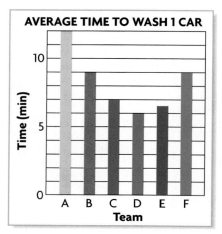

3. Which team had half as many students as Team E?

4. Which team took, on average, 7 minutes to wash one car?

5. Which team washed cars the fastest?

6. What conclusion can the teacher draw about the relationship between the size of a team and the time it took to wash one car?

PRACTICE AND PROBLEM SOLVING

Use Data A gardener conducted an experiment involving six of the same type of plant. He wanted to see how the amount of direct sunlight received each day affected the plants' growth. For 7–9, use the table and the bar graph, which show the results of the experiment.

SUNLIGHT TRIALS	
Plant	**Amount of Sunlight (hr)**
1	2
2	4
3	6
4	8
5	10
6	12

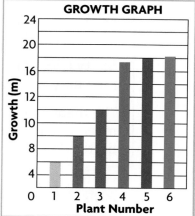

7. Describe how the amount of sunlight received changed from Plant 1 through Plant 6.

8. How many hours of sunlight did the tallest plant receive?

9. What conclusion can the gardener draw about the relationship between the amount of sunlight received and a plant's growth?

10. Two groups of students were surveyed about the number of hours per week that they watch television. Find the mean and median for each group. Compare their values. Which group of students do you think spends less time watching television? Explain.

Group A	Group B
14, 13, 12,	20, 10, 8,
11, 10, 8,	8, 7, 7, 7,
7, 6, 5, 5	6, 6, 5

Problem Solving ▶
Applications

For a survey completed five years ago, middle school students from Memphis were asked, "What is your favorite hobby?"

FAVORITE HOBBIES	
Reading	36%
Crafts	7%
Coin Collecting	2%
Stamp Collecting	2%
Building Models	12%
Trading Cards	39%
Other	2%

Recently, a research company randomly selected 750 current middle school students from Memphis and asked them the same question. The results are shown in the table at the left.

11. For which of the hobbies did interest increase the most? decrease the most?

FAVORITE HOBBIES (5 years ago)

Reading 30%
Crafts 15%
Coin Collecting 10%
Other 7%
Trading Cards 25%
Stamp Collecting 8%
Building Models 5%

12. What conclusion can you draw about student interest in stamp collecting? reading?

13. REASONING Lonnie writes books about hobbies. She wants to write a book with the best chance of attracting middle school students. Which topic listed in the table should she choose? Explain.

14. A target has three circles, one inside of the other. The bull's-eye is 10 points, the middle circle is 6 points, and the outer circle is 4 points. If 3 darts are thrown and only 2 hit the target, what are the possible scores?

MIXED REVIEW AND TEST PREP

Find the mean and median of the data. (p. 118)

15. 2, 4, 4, 3, 6, 8, 1, 6   **16.** 22, 44, 31, 46, 22   **17.** 109, 125, 124, 111, 130

⭐ **18. TEST PREP** Which is the value of the digit 5 in the number 8,050,619? (p. 16)

  A 5,000   **B** 50,000   **C** 500,000   **D** 5,000,000

⭐ **19. TEST PREP** A 6-story school building is 19.2 m high. If each story of the building is the same height, how high is each story? (p. 86)

  F 3.2 m   **G** 5.2 m   **H** 13.2   **J** 115.2 m

EXTRA PRACTICE page 128, Set E

125

Take a Survey

MATH LAB

Explore how to design and take a survey.

QUICK REVIEW

Find the mean.

1. 6, 8, 10   **2.** 20, 32, 41   **3.** 15, 17, 19, 41

4. 25, 25, 25, 25   **5.** 100, 200, 300, 400

You can use what you have learned about collecting and organizing data to take your own survey.

Activity

- Select one of the following topics for a survey.

  a. Favorite ice cream flavor
  b. Number of pets at home
  c. Favorite school subject

- Decide what population you want to survey. Do you want to include all students at your school or just sixth graders?

Remember that an unbiased question is a question that does not lead to a specific response and does not exclude a certain group.

- Write the question for your survey. Make sure the question is unbiased. Try to guess what the responses might be. Explain your guess.

- Make a recording sheet for your data. Here is a sample recording sheet for collecting data.

Person Number	Response
1	
2	
3	
4	

- Survey a random sample of at least 30 students from your chosen population.

- Organize the data from your recording sheet in a frequency table.

- Find the mode of your survey results.

- Draw a graph to display your data.

Think and Discuss

- What conclusions can you draw from your frequency table?

- What conclusions can you draw from your graph? Is there another kind of graph you could use to display the data? Explain.

- If you took another survey using the same question, would you expect your results to be similar?

- Based on your results, is there another question you would like to answer by taking a survey?

- Compare your survey results with those of a classmate who chose the same topic and the same population. Are your results about the same? How do your questions compare?

Practice

1. Write a paragraph describing how you carried out your survey.

2. Rewrite your original question so that it is biased. Explain how your results might be different if you had used the biased question.

3. Design a survey for another of the three given topics. Study the results of your classmates who chose this topic the first time. Then guess what you think the results of your survey will be. Take a survey to see whether your guess is correct.

4. Look in magazines and newspapers. Find a graph or table that is based on a survey. In your own words, describe the population, the sample, the question, and the results.

MIXED REVIEW AND TEST PREP

Two teams of students did an experiment to see which teams' paper airplanes would fly farther. For 5–7, use the results in the table at the right.

DISTANCES FLOWN BY PAPER AIRPLANES (in.)			
Team 1		**Team 2**	
206	245	214	240
304	251	211	258
224	267	302	263

5. Find the mean and median for each team. Which teams' airplanes flew farther? (p. 118)

6. Find the range of the distances for Team 1. (p. 114)

7. Find the range of the distances for Team 2. (p. 114)

8. Name the property shown. $(6 \times 8) \times 12 = 6 \times (8 \times 12)$ (p. 40)

9. **TEST PREP** Lee and Sandra have a total of 210 shells in their collections. Lee has 24 fewer shells than Sandra. How many shells does Sandra have? (p. 28)

   A 93 shells   **B** 105 shells   **C** 117 shells   **D** 141 shells

Set A (pp. 110–111)

Tell whether a random sample was chosen. Explain.

1. The names of club members were placed in a bag. Then Jen selected 30 names without looking.

2. To find out the favorite amusement park of middle school students, a teacher surveyed students at a basketball game.

Set B (pp. 112–113)

A survey is to be conducted about the favorite foods of students at Jefferson Middle School. Tell whether the sampling method is *biased* or *unbiased*.

1. Randomly survey 30 people who get off the school bus one morning.

2. Randomly survey students at Jefferson Middle School.

Set C (pp. 114–117)

Use the table at the right.

1. Copy and complete the table.

2. What is the relative frequency of the 20–29 age group? Write the answer as a percent.

Ages	Tally	Frequency	Cumulative Frequency
10–19	ЖЖ Ж I	■	■
20–29	Ж IIII	■	■
30–39	Ж III	■	■
40–49	Ж	■	■
50–59	III	■	■

Set D (pp. 118–121)

Find the mean, median, and mode.

1. 4, 5, 7, 8, 8

2. 6.1, 8.1, 7.4, 7.2

3. 12, 14, 18, 12, 22

4. 200, 245, 230, 205

Set E (pp. 122–125)

A movie theater owner experimented with the prices of tickets at a series of movies. The table and bar graph show the results of his experiment.

1. How did ticket prices change from movie to movie?

2. What ticket price resulted in the greatest income? Explain.

3. What conclusions can the theater owner draw about the relationship between movie ticket prices and income from ticket sales?

MOVIE TICKETS	
Movie	Price ($)
1	4
2	6
3	8
4	10

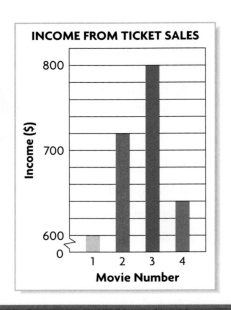

INCOME FROM TICKET SALES

1. **VOCABULARY** In a survey, if certain groups in the population are not represented by the sample, the sample is __?__. (p. 112)

2. **VOCABULARY** A __?__ is a method of gathering information about a group. (p. 110)

3. To find out the favorite season of sixth graders, Anna surveyed students in her science class. Did she choose a random sample? Explain. (pp. 110–111)

Tell whether the sample is biased or unbiased. Explain. (pp. 112–113)

An automobile dealer is conducting a survey of its customers to find out which types of car they like.

4. 100 randomly selected customers

5. 100 randomly selected male customers

For 6–10, use the table at the right. (pp. 114–117)

6. Make a line plot.

7. Find the range.

8. Make a cumulative frequency table with 3 intervals.

9. What is the sample size?

10. Find the relative frequency of each interval.

STUDENTS' HEIGHTS (in inches)									
62	71	63	62	69	70	60	64	66	63
71	62	65	68	63	70	64	62	67	70

Find the mean, median, and mode. (pp. 118–121)

11. 17, 12, 23, 19, 23

12. 89, 95, 87, 91, 95, 89

13. 265, 235, 171, 253

Ten people in Lynn's neighborhood formed a bike club. The table shows the ages of the members. (pp. 118–121)

14. Find the mean.

15. Find the median.

16. Find the mode.

AGES OF MEMBERS OF BIKE CLUB				
13	14	10	11	13
12	13	9	11	10

The graphs at the right show the results of two surveys of sixth graders in New York City about their favorite musical instrument. For 17–20, use the graphs. (pp. 122–125)

17. What conclusion can you draw about student interest in drums?

18. What conclusion can you draw about student interest in violins?

19. What was the favorite musical instrument in 1997? in 2002?

20. For which instrument did interest increase the most? decrease the most?

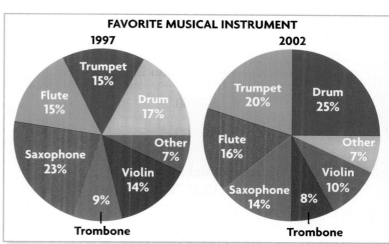

FAVORITE MUSICAL INSTRUMENT
1997 — Trumpet 15%, Drum 17%, Other 7%, Violin 14%, Trombone 9%, Saxophone 23%, Flute 15%
2002 — Trumpet 20%, Drum 25%, Other 7%, Violin 10%, Trombone 8%, Saxophone 14%, Flute 16%

NUMBER SENSE, CONCEPTS, AND OPERATIONS

1. Daily attendances for three days at a state fair were 176,239; 255,464; and 241,950. What was the total attendance?

  A 428,703

  B 497,414

  C 570,103

  D 673,653

2. In New Hampshire's White Mountains, $(3 + 7) \times 4 + 16 \div 2$ peaks rise to elevations greater than 4,000 feet. What is the value of $(3 + 7) \times 4 + 16 \div 2$?

  F 100   **H** 39

  G 48   **J** 28

3. The table below shows the hourly wages for three jobs at Civic Concert Hall.

CIVIC CONCERT HALL WAGES	
Job	**Hourly Wages**
Usher	$6.75
Ticket Salesperson	$7.45
Refreshment Booth Attendant	$6.15

Last week, Lou worked 16 hours as an usher and Jen worked 20 hours as a refreshment booth attendant. How much more money did Jen earn than Lou?

  A $3.80   **C** $24.60

  B $15.00   **D** $36.60

4. Explain It Donnie bought 6 pieces of wood for a total of $13.50. Three of the pieces cost a total of $7.50 and the 3 remaining pieces each cost the same amount. Explain how to find the price of each remaining piece.

MEASUREMENT

5. In $\triangle ABC$ in the flag of Jamaica, $\angle A$ measures 128° and $\angle C$ measures 26°. What is the measure of $\angle B$?

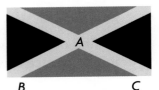

  F 26°

  G 30°

  H 38°

  J 52°

6. The figure below represents Sandy's family room floor.

18 feet

12 feet

> **TIP** **Understand the problem.** See item 6. You need to find a floor with equivalent dimensions. The dimensions given below are in yards and inches. How can you convert from feet to yards and inches?

Which of the following floors has the same dimensions as Sandy's family room?

  A   9 yards / 4 yards

  C   54 yards / 36 yards

  B   6 yards / 4 yards

  D   288 inches / 192 inches

7. Explain It The bus that Jose rides to school weighs about 9.6 tons. Explain how to find the weight of the bus in pounds.

⭐ ALGEBRAIC THINKING

8. A sign in the school auditorium reads, "Maximum number of persons permitted in this auditorium: 240." Which inequality shows this rule?

F $p < 240$ **H** $p \leq 240$

G $p > 240$ **J** $p \geq 240$

9. Frank sewed the pattern below along the border of a tablecloth.

If he continues the pattern, what will the next three figures be?

A

B

C

D

10. Steve was 36 years old 9 years ago. Let y represent Steve's age today. Which equation can be used to find Steve's age?

F $y + 9 = 36$ **H** $36 \div y = 9$

G $y - 9 = 36$ **J** $36 - 9 = y$

11. Explain It A box containing soup cans sits on a balance. Additional cans of soup on each side level the balance, as shown below. How many cans are in the box? Explain your reasoning.

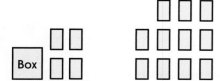

                 ☐ = soup can

⭐ DATA ANALYSIS AND PROBABILITY

12. A local radio station wants to find out which program its listeners like best. Which of the following is an unbiased sample for this survey?

A 100 randomly selected listeners

B 100 randomly selected listeners between the ages of 12 and 21

C 100 randomly selected female listeners

D 100 randomly selected listeners who listen from 9 A.M. to 12 noon

13. Tasha scored the following numbers of points in her last 6 basketball games: 15, 21, 12, 28, 18, 19. What is the median number of points Tasha scored for these 6 games?

F 16.5   **H** 18.5

G 18   **J** 20

14. The cumulative frequency table below shows the ages of members of the Foothills Theater Club.

AGES OF THEATER CLUB MEMBERS		
Age	Frequency	Cumulative Frequency
16–20	5	5
21–25	6	11
26–30	12	33

How many members are 25 years old or younger?

A 33   **C** 12

B 17   **D** 11

15. Explain It Elaine is conducting a survey to determine the favorite type of book of sixth graders at her school. Explain how Elaine can select a random sample.

CHAPTER 6

Graph Data

FAST FACT • SCIENCE There are more than 300 species of sharks. Unlike most fish, sharks lack an air-filled swim bladder to keep them afloat, so sharks sink when they are not swimming. For this reason, most sharks are constantly on the move.

PROBLEM SOLVING About how much heavier is the average tiger shark than the average hammerhead shark? About how many times as great as the weight of the average nurse shark is the weight of the average tiger shark?

AVERAGE WEIGHTS OF SOME SHARK SPECIES

Lemon Shark	🦈
Nurse Shark	🦈 🐟
Tiger Shark	🦈 🦈 🦈 🦈 🦈 🦈 🦈 🦈 🦈 🦈 🦈
Hammerhead Shark	🦈 🦈 🦈 🦈 🦈 🦈 🦈 🦈 🐟

Key: Each 🦈 = 200 lb.

Check What You Know

Use this page to help you review and remember important skills needed for Chapter 6.

 **Read Bar Graphs**

For 1–4, use the bar graph at the right.

1. Name two Great Lakes whose combined area is less than the area of Lake Superior.

2. What is the area of the third-largest Great Lake?

3. How much larger is the area of Lake Michigan than the area of Lake Ontario?

4. Which Great Lake has an area of about 22,000 mi² more than the area of Lake Erie?

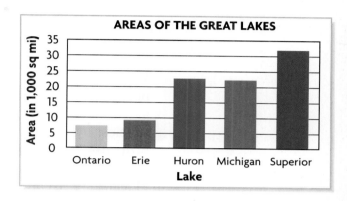

 **Read Stem-and-Leaf Plots**

For 5–11, use the stem-and-leaf plot at the right.

5. What is the score shown by the third stem and fourth leaf?

6. What is the median of Michael's golf scores?

7. What is the range of Michael's golf scores?

8. What is the mode of Michael's golf scores?

9. How many more scores of 90 will Michael need in order to have a mode of 90 for all of his rounds?

10. How many rounds of golf did Michael play?

11. If Michael plays two more rounds and has scores of 86 and 81, what would be the median of the scores?

MICHAEL'S GOLF SCORES

Stems	Leaves
7	6 7 8 9 9
8	0 2 3 5 5 6 8 9
9	0 0 1 2 3 8

VOCABULARY POWER

REVIEW

interval [inʹtər•vəl] *noun*

An interval is the distance between two numbers on the scale of a graph. Look up the definitions of *interpersonal* and *international*. What do these words have in common with *interval*?

 www.harcourtschool.com/mathglossary

PREVIEW

multiple-bar graph

multiple-line graph

stem-and-leaf plot

histogram

box-and-whisker graph

lower extreme

upper extreme

lower quartile

upper quartile

PROBLEM SOLVING STRATEGY
Make a Graph

Learn how to use the strategy *make a graph* to solve problems.

QUICK REVIEW

Find the range.

1. 3, 5, 2, 6, 4   **2.** 3, 0, 3, 1, 2, 4   **3.** 8, 13, 11, 17, 6, 2

4. 58, 23, 37, 68, 41   **5.** 111, 145, 96, 196, 120

Clara is writing a report about penguins. She found the following average heights for some penguin species:
African—70 cm, Chinstrap—68 cm, Emperor—120 cm, Little Blue—40 cm, Macaroni—70 cm.
How can Clara display the data to better understand and compare the heights?

Analyze   What are you asked to find?

What information is given?

Is there information you will not use? If so, what?

Choose   What strategy will you use?

You can use the strategy *make a graph*.

Solve   Which graph can you make?

You can make a bar graph to compare the heights of the penguin species.

The graph shows that Little Blue penguins are the shortest and Emperor penguins are the tallest. African, Chinstrap, and Macaroni penguins are about the same height.

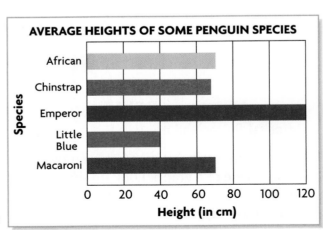

AVERAGE HEIGHTS OF SOME PENGUIN SPECIES

Check   How can you check your results?

PROBLEM SOLVING STRATEGIES

Draw a Diagram or Picture

Make a Model

Predict and Test

Work Backward

Make an Organized List

Find a Pattern

▶ **Make a Table or Graph**

Solve a Simpler Problem

Write an Equation

Use Logical Reasoning

Solve.

Leo surveyed students in his math and science classes to find out their favorite forms of exercise. These are the results.

Girls: aerobics—12, basketball—7, jogging—10, soccer—5

Boys: aerobics—4, basketball—13, jogging—8, soccer—7

1. Use the data above. Make a graph to compare the girls' responses to Leo's survey.

2. Use the data above. Make a graph to compare the boys' responses to Leo's survey.

3. About how many times as tall is the bar for the boys who chose basketball as the bar for the boys who chose aerobics?

    A about 2 times   **C** about 4 times

    B about 3 times   **D** about 5 times

4. Which form of exercise was selected by more girls than any other?

    F aerobics   **H** jogging

    G basketball   **J** soccer

MIXED STRATEGY PRACTICE

5. Julia receives a $50.00 gift certificate to a music store. If she wants to buy three $13.99 CDs and two $7.99 cassettes, how much of her own money will Julia have to add to the $50.00 gift certificate?

6. A basketball team scores 23 points, including six 1-point foul shots. How many 2-point and 3-point baskets could they have made? Make a list of all the possibilities.

7. An automobile club sells books of 10 movie tickets for $45.00. If tickets usually cost $8.75 each, how much do you save on 10 tickets by buying the book?

8. A fence separating two flower gardens is 24 ft long. If there is a post in the ground every 3 ft, how many posts are in the fence?

9. On a wildlife outing, Enrique spots 3 more seagulls than egrets and 5 more egrets than geese. If he spots 8 geese, how many birds does he spot in all?

10. If today is Tuesday, what day of the week will it be 200 days from today?

11. ✎ **Write About It** Explain why it is helpful to make bar graphs using the data from Leo's survey at the top of the page.

Make and Analyze Graphs

Learn how to display and analyze data in bar graphs, line graphs, and circle graphs.

Vocabulary

multiple-bar graph

multiple-line graph

A bar graph is a good way to display data that are grouped in categories. A **multiple-bar graph** shows two or more sets of data for each category. Look at the double-bar graph at the right.

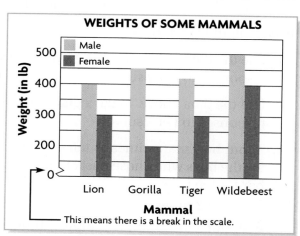

WEIGHTS OF SOME MAMMALS

Male / Female

Weight (in lb) / Mammal: Lion, Gorilla, Tiger, Wildebeest

This means there is a break in the scale.

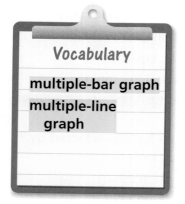

The data in the table below show the number of grams of protein, fat, and carbohydrates in 1 cup of three different foods.

NUTRITIONAL VALUES OF SOME FOODS (1 cup)			
Food	**Plain Macaroni**	**Whole Milk**	**Potato Salad**
Protein	7 g	8 g	7 g
Fat	1 g	8 g	21 g
Carbohydrates	39 g	11 g	28 g

EXAMPLE 1

Use the data in the table above to make a triple-bar graph. Which food has about the same amounts of protein, fat, and carbohydrates?

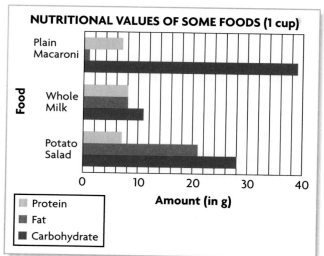

NUTRITIONAL VALUES OF SOME FOODS (1 cup)

Food: Plain Macaroni, Whole Milk, Potato Salad

Amount (in g)

Protein / Fat / Carbohydrate

Determine an appropriate scale.

Use bars of equal width. Use the data to determine the lengths of the bars.

Title the graph and both axes. Include a key.

So, whole milk has about equal amounts of protein, fat, and carbohydrates.

Line Graphs

A line graph is a good way to show data that change over time. The data in the table below show the price of a stock from 1970 to 2000.

STOCK PRICE OF COMPANY A						
Year	1970	1975	1980	1985	1990	1995	2000
Price	$49.25	$51.25	$49.25	$45.50	$45.25	$47.00	$51.75

EXAMPLE 2

Use the data in the table above to make a line graph. During which five-year period was the increase in the stock price the greatest?

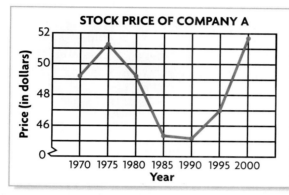

Determine an appropriate scale.

Mark a point for each price, and connect the points.

Title the graph and both axes.

The greatest increase in the stock price was from 1995 to 2000.

A **multiple-line graph** is used to show two or more different sets of data for the same period of time.

MONEY IN SAVINGS ACCOUNTS					
	March	**April**	**May**	**June**	**July**
Bob	$163	$172	$151	$138	$102
Jan	$43	$55	$76	$79	$96

EXAMPLE 3

Use the data in the table above to make a double-line graph. If the trends continue, how would you describe the amount of money that Bob is saving? that Jan is saving?

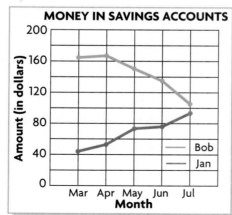

Determine an appropriate scale.

Mark a point for each amount saved for Bob and connect the points.

Mark a point for each amount saved for Jan and connect the points.

Title the graph and both axes. Include a key.

The money in Bob's savings account is decreasing. The money in Jan's savings account is increasing.

A circle graph helps you compare parts of the data to the whole and to other parts.

EXAMPLE 4

In 1987, compact discs (CDs) were new. The circle graph shows the way recorded music was sold in the United States in 1987. About how many cassettes were sold for every CD sold that year?

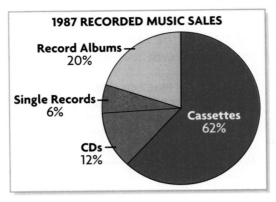

1987 RECORDED MUSIC SALES

Record Albums — 20%

Single Records — 6%

CDs — 12%

Cassettes 62%

Find the parts that represent cassettes and CDs.

Compare the percent of recorded music sold on cassettes to the percent sold on CDs.

Cassettes made up 62% of recorded music sales, while CDs made up 12%. $62 \div 12 \approx 60 \div 12$, or 5.

So, about 5 cassettes were sold for every CD sold.

- By 2000, the percent of recorded music sold in the form of CDs was about 7.5 times as great as it had been in 1987. About what percent of recorded music was sold on CDs in 2000?

CHECK FOR UNDERSTANDING

Think and ▶ Discuss

Look back at the lesson to answer each question.

1. **Explain** why the graphs in Example 1 and Example 3 have a key.

2. **Explain** why a bar graph is an appropriate graph for showing the population of six different cities in your state.

Guided ▶ Practice

Tell if you would use a bar, line, or circle graph to display the data.

3. The average monthly rainfall in your city over two years

4. A family budget divided into types of expenses

PRACTICE AND PROBLEM SOLVING

Independent ▶ Practice

Tell if you would use a bar, line, or circle graph to display the data.

5. The heights of five different students

6. The price of a stock over a period of several months

7. The average monthly temperatures in Orlando, Florida, from July through December are as follows: 82°F, 83°F, 81°F, 75°F, 68°F, and 62°F. Make a line graph for these data. Then describe how the temperature changes over time.

8. Make a triple-bar graph using the data in the table at the right. Compare the number of rainy days in 2000, 2001, and 2002.

9. Make a double-line graph using the data in the table at the right. How would you describe the trends in the prices of the two stocks?

NUMBER OF RAINY DAYS				
	April	**May**	**June**	**July**
2000	12	3	13	5
2001	8	5	9	11
2002	6	7	8	12

AVERAGE STOCK PRICES				
	Sep	**Oct**	**Nov**	**Dec**
Stock A	$26	$29	$32	$27
Stock B	$14	$10	$8	$19

**Problem Solving ▶
Applications**

Use Data **For 10–12, use the double-line graph below.**

10. How do the comedy video rentals compare to the action video rentals?

11. For the months of March and April combined, about how many more comedy rentals were there than action rentals?

12. **REASONING** If the trends continue, what will happen to the number of comedy and action video rentals in July?

Video Rentals

(Double-line graph showing Number of Videos Rented vs. Month, Jan–Jun, with COMEDY and ACTION lines)

Use Data **For 13–14, use the circle graph at left.**

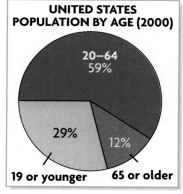

**UNITED STATES
POPULATION BY AGE (2000)**

20–64 59%

29%

12%

19 or younger   65 or older

13. The number of people aged 20–64 is about how many times the number who are 65 or older?

14. **? What's the Error?** Jay looked at the circle graph and said that 59% of the U.S. population is aged 20 or older. What is his error?

15. **FAST FACT • SOCIAL STUDIES** According to the 2000 census, the median age of the 281,421,906 people in the United States is 35.3 years. About how many people are older than 35.3 years?

MIXED REVIEW AND TEST PREP

16. Tell which property helps you find the value of p.
$22 + (45 + 62) = (22 + p) + 62$ (p. 40)

Find the product. (p. 80)

17. 6×0.4

18. 0.8×0.7

⭐ 19. **TEST PREP** Which is 0.27×0.4? (p. 80)

    A 0.108   **B** 0.675   **C** 1.08   **D** 10.8

⭐ 20. **TEST PREP** Find the value of 21^2. (p. 46)

    F 21   **G** 23   **H** 42   **J** 441

EXTRA PRACTICE page 150, Set A

Stem-and-Leaf Plots and Histograms

Learn how to display and analyze data in stem-and-leaf plots and histograms.

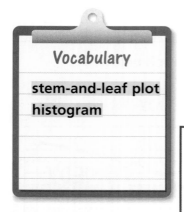

QUICK REVIEW

1. $8.5 + 4.2$
2. $125.80 + 11.20$
3. $10.8 - 8.6$
4. $225.65 - 5.60$
5. $10.2 + 2.4 + 3.1$

You can use a **stem-and-leaf plot** to organize data when you want to see each item in the data. For a stem-and-leaf plot, choose the stems first and then write the leaves.

EXAMPLE 1

The greatest wind speed recorded in New Orleans, Louisiana, is 69 miles per hour. The table lists the greatest wind speeds for 18 other cities in the United States. Make a stem-and-leaf plot for these data.

GREATEST WIND SPEEDS					
73	60	80	54	65	52
59	86	60	76	73	54
75	71	81	66	51	58

51	52	54	54	58	59
60	60	65	66		
71	73	73	75	76	
80	81	86			

First, group the data by the tens digits. Then, order the data from least to greatest.

Greatest Wind Speeds

Stem	Leaves
5	1 2 4 4 8 9
6	0 0 5 6
7	1 3 3 5 6
8	0 1 6

Use the tens digits as stems. Use the ones digits as leaves. Write the leaves in increasing order.

The line 8 | 0 1 6 means 80, 81, and 86.

EXAMPLE 2

Use the data from a domino stacking competition to make a stem-and-leaf plot. Then use the stem-and-leaf plot to help find the mode, the median, and the range.

NUMBER OF DOMINOES STACKED									
97	88	74	96	98	58	68	90	80	90
72	86	69	78	93	84	99	92	85	

Stem	Leaves
5	8
6	8 9
7	2 4 8
8	0 4 5 6 8
9	0 0 2 3 6 7 8 9

90 occurs more than any other number.

There are 19 scores. The median is the 10th score.

Range = 99 − 58

Mode: 90   Median: 86   Range: 41

A **histogram** is a bar graph that shows the frequency, or number of occurrences of data within intervals. The bars in a histogram are connected, rather than separated.

BAR GRAPH

HISTOGRAM

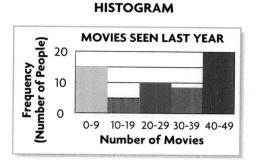

Remember that you can use the range of a set of data to help determine intervals.

This bar graph shows information about individual movie customers. The histogram shows information about groups of movie customers.

EXAMPLE 3

The table below shows the number of sit-ups students in gym class did in one minute. Make a histogram for the data.

NUMBER OF SIT-UPS									
28	19	32	45	44	12	24	32	35	47
55	59	24	25	37	36	38	36	42	41

First, make a frequency table with intervals of 10. Start with 10.

Interval	10–19	20–29	30–39	40–49	50–59
Frequency	2	4	7	5	2

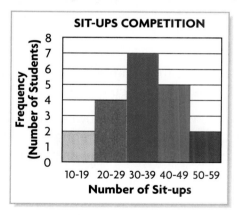

Title the graph and label the scales and axes.

Graph the number of students who did sit-ups within each interval.

• Use the histogram. How many students did at least 40 sit-ups?

CHECK FOR UNDERSTANDING

Think and ▶ Discuss

Look back at the lesson to answer each question.

1. **Explain** how the stem-and-leaf plot in Example 1 is useful in showing the greatest wind speeds for the 18 cities.

2. **Explain** how a histogram differs from a bar graph.

141

3. Make a stem-and-leaf plot of the data 32, 24, 44, 57, 31, 25, 41, 26.

Explain whether a bar graph or a histogram is more appropriate.

4. number of customers at different intervals of time

5. populations of five different states

PRACTICE AND PROBLEM SOLVING

6. Make a stem-and-leaf plot of the data 89, 74, 63, 65, 68, 74, 71, 80.

Explain whether a bar graph or a histogram is more appropriate.

7. heights of the tallest mountains in the United States

8. ages of 75 ice-skating competitors at a competition

Use the data in the table for 9.

9. a. Make a stem-and-leaf plot of the data.

PLANT HEIGHTS IN INCHES					
28	36	25	24	20	32
15	18	28	12	19	26

b. Use the stem-and-leaf plot to help find the median, mode, and range.

c. *REASONING* Can you tell what the mean is for this set of data by looking at the stem-and-leaf plot? Explain.

AGES OF MARIA'S MUSIC CUSTOMERS									
10	25	33	14	54	62	29	44	41	40
11	31	41	24	65	16	39	50	51	55
19	22	17	26	31	42	17	18	42	37

10. Use the data in the table above to make a histogram. Which age group has the most customers? the fewest customers?

11. Vocabulary Power The lowest note on a guitar is produced by a string vibrating with a frequency of 82 times per second. How is the *frequency* of a guitar string like the frequency shown on a histogram?

MIXED REVIEW AND TEST PREP

12. $64{,}989 + 40{,}816$ (p. 22)

13. Write the value of 2^9. (p. 46)

14. Evaluate $3k$ for $k = 6.5$. (p. 94)

15. Write 0.73 as a percent. (p. 68)

⭐**16. TEST PREP** Mt. McKinley has a height of 20,320 ft. Mt. Whitney has a height of 14,494 ft. If Brian climbs both mountains and wants to climb a total of 40,000 ft, how many more feet does he need to climb? (p. 22)

A 34,814 ft   **B** 25,506 ft   **C** 19,680 ft   **D** 5,186 ft

EXTRA PRACTICE page 150, Set B

Explore Box-and-Whisker Graphs

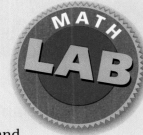

Explore how to make a box-and-whisker graph and understand its parts.

You need at least eleven 3 in. × 5 in. cards, marker.

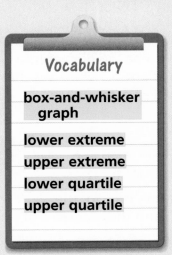

Vocabulary

box-and-whisker graph

lower extreme

upper extreme

lower quartile

upper quartile

A **box-and-whisker graph** shows how far apart and how evenly data are distributed.

Activity

- Write each of the data in the table on a separate card.

NUMBER OF TROPHIES WON									
35	21	24	32	36	20	24	29	27	30

- Order the data from least to greatest. Draw a star on the card with the least value, or **lower extreme**, and the card with the greatest value, or **upper extreme**.

- Find the median of the data. If the median is not one of the numbers already written, write it on a card, put it in the middle of the data, and circle it.

- Find the median of the lower half of the data. This median is called the **lower quartile.** Circle it. Separate the data to the left of the lower quartile from the rest of the data.

- Find the median of the upper half of the data. This median is the **upper quartile.** Circle it. Separate the data to the right of the upper quartile from the rest of the data.

Think and Discuss

- Look at your cards. Into how many parts do the lower quartile, the median, and the upper quartile separate the data?

- What fraction of the data are to the left of the lower quartile? to the right of the upper quartile? What fraction of the data are between the lower quartile and the upper quartile?

You have found all you need to make this box-and-whisker graph.

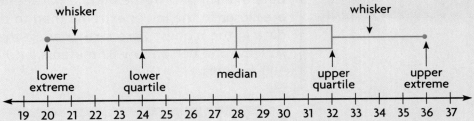

Practice

- Make a box-and-whisker graph of the data.

POINTS SCORED									
10	12	9	22	17	7	14	8	11	19

143

Box-and-Whisker Graphs

Learn how to analyze a box-and-whisker graph.

The only actual data you can identify from the data set in a box-and-whisker graph are the extremes.

EXAMPLE 1

The data in the box-and-whisker graph represent the diameters in kilometers of some asteroids observed by a scientist. What was the diameter of the largest asteroid? of the smallest asteroid?

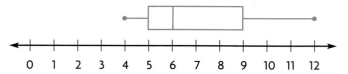

The upper extreme is 12 and the lower extreme is 4. So, the diameter of the largest asteroid was 12 km, and the diameter of the smallest asteroid was 4 km.

• Look again at the graph. Which of the following can you determine—mean, median, mode, range?

EXAMPLE 2

Data about the number of meteors seen during a particular hour at different locations during the 1999 Leonids meteor shower are shown in the box-and-whisker graph. What does the graph show about how the data are distributed?

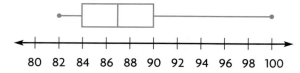

The data in the lowest $\frac{1}{4}$ of the data set are very close together. The data in each part of the middle $\frac{1}{2}$ are somewhat farther apart. They are closer to the lower extreme than to the upper extreme. The data in the highest $\frac{1}{4}$ are farther apart than those in the middle. At least one person saw 82 meteors, and at least one person saw 100 meteors.

CHECK FOR UNDERSTANDING

Think and ▶
Discuss

Look back at the lesson to answer the question.

1. Explain why you can't find the mean and the mode when looking at a box-and-whisker graph.

Guided ▶ Practice

For 2–3, use the box-and-whisker graph.

2. What are the median, lower quartile, and upper quartile?

10 12 14 16 18 20 22

3. What are the lower and upper extremes and the range?

PRACTICE AND PROBLEM SOLVING

Independent ▶ Practice

For 4–5, use the box-and-whisker graph.

4. What are the median, lower quartile, and upper quartile?

56 58 60 62 64 66 68

5. What are the lower and upper extremes and the range?

For 6–8, use the data in the table below.

6. What are the median, lower quartile, and upper quartile?

WEIGHTS OF PANTHERS FOOTBALL PLAYERS					
85	102	89	86	104	92
103	97	91	100	100	93

7. What are the lower and upper extremes and the range?

8. Make a box-and-whisker graph and a histogram. Compare them.

Problem Solving ▶ Applications

The box-and-whisker graph shows data about the numbers of points scored by the basketball team in each game.

9. What are the least and greatest numbers of points?

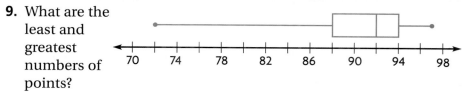

70 74 78 82 86 90 94 98

10. What does the graph show about how the data are distributed?

11. **(?) What's the Question?** Use the box-and-whisker graph for 9–10. The answers are 88 and 94.

MIXED REVIEW AND TEST PREP

12. If you are displaying data about the number of cars that cross an intersection during different intervals of time, is a bar graph or a histogram more appropriate? (p. 140)

13. Sue purchases three items that cost $3.73, $9.21, and $2.99. If she pays with $20.00, how much change will she receive? (p. 76)

Write the value of the blue digit. (p. 60)

14. 9.64

15. 124.024

⭐ **16. TEST PREP** Which is $3 \times 3 \times 3 \times 3$ in exponent form? (p. 46)

A 3×4 **B** 3^2 **C** 3^3 **D** 3^4

EXTRA PRACTICE page 150, Set C

Misleading Graphs

Learn how to analyze data displays and determine how results and conclusions may have been influenced.

Data can be displayed in many different ways. Sometimes, the way a question is asked can influence the results that are displayed.

Rita took a survey asking the following question: Do you agree with me that George Washington was the greatest United States President, or would you choose Thomas Jefferson or Abraham Lincoln?

EXAMPLE 1

The results of Rita's survey are displayed in the bar graph shown at the right. Could the way the question was asked have influenced the results? Explain.

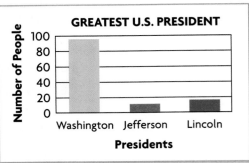

GREATEST U.S. PRESIDENT

Yes. Rita's question is biased, since it leads people to agree with her that George Washington was the greatest U.S. President. As a result, the graph is misleading.

EXAMPLE 2

The results of two other surveys are shown below. Which graph is more likely to come from which question? Explain your reasoning.

Question 1: Would you rather visit the Grand Canyon, Mount Rushmore, or the Statue of Liberty?

Question 2: Would you rather visit the spectacular Grand Canyon, or would you rather visit Mount Rushmore or the Statue of Liberty?

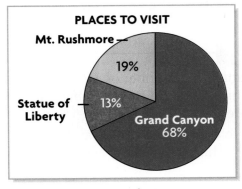

Graph A **Graph B**

Graph A probably goes with Question 2, since the question is biased and leads people to choose the Grand Canyon. Graph B probably goes with Question 1, since that question is not biased.

Graphs can communicate information quickly. That's why they are used by advertisers on television and in magazines and newspapers. Some graphs can be misleading and influence conclusions that are drawn.

EXAMPLE 3

Jon looked at the bar graph below and concluded that the Mississippi River is more than twice as long as the Missouri River. Explain Jon's mistake and tell why his conclusion is wrong.

The bar for the Mississippi is more than twice as long as the bar for the Missouri. However, if you look at the scale, you see that the rivers are about the same length. Because the lower part of the scale is missing, the differences are exaggerated.

When two graphs with different scales show two similar sets of data, comparing the graphs can sometimes be misleading.

EXAMPLE 4

The weekly ticket sales for the Mississippi River tour boat cruise are shown in the graphs below. Deb looked at the graphs and concluded that more tickets were sold in April than in March. Explain Deb's mistake.

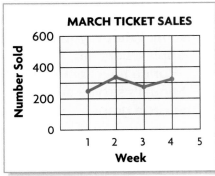

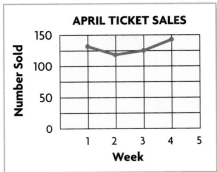

It appears that the April ticket sales were greater than in March since the line for April is higher than the line for March. However, if you look at the scale for each graph, you can see that ticket sales were much greater in March than in April.

CHECK FOR UNDERSTANDING

Think and ▶ Discuss

Look back at the lesson to answer each question.
1. **Explain** how you could rewrite the question in Example 1 so it would not influence the results of the survey.

147

2. Explain how you could change the graph in Example 3 so it is not misleading.

Guided ▶ Practice

Rosa took a survey, asking the following question: Don't you think that the Mustangs are the best baseball team, or would you choose the Wildcats or Cougars? The results of her survey are displayed in the bar graph at the right.

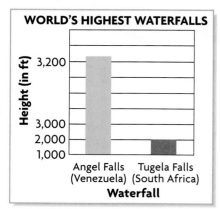

BEST BASEBALL TEAM

3. Could the way the question was asked have influenced the results? Explain.

For 4–6, use the graph at the right. The graph is misleading.

4. About how many times as high is the bar for Angel Falls as the bar for Tugela Falls?

5. Is Angel Falls 6 times as high as Tugela Falls? Explain.

6. How could you change the graph so it is not misleading?

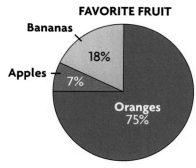

WORLD'S HIGHEST WATERFALLS

Angel Falls

PRACTICE AND PROBLEM SOLVING

Independent ▶ Practice

Miguel took a survey, asking the following question: What is your favorite fruit—apples, bananas, or delicious, juicy Florida navel oranges? The results of Miguel's survey are displayed in the circle graph.

7. Could the way the question was asked have influenced the results? Explain.

FAVORITE FRUIT

For 8–10, use the graph at the right. The graph is misleading.

8. About how many times as high as the bar for Brand A is the bar for Brand B?

9. Does Brand B cost twice as much as Brand A? Explain.

10. How can you change the graph so it is not misleading?

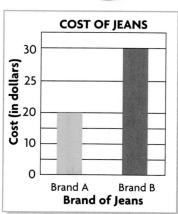

COST OF JEANS

11. Jeff looked at the bar graph at the right and concluded that Indiana has three times the population of Maryland. Explain Jeff's mistake and tell why his conclusion is wrong.

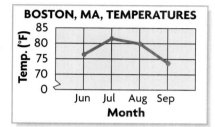

STATE POPULATIONS

12. How could you fix the graph so Jeff would not make a mistake?

13. Lin looked at the graphs below and concluded that from June to September the temperatures in Asheville are about the same as the temperatures in Boston. Explain Lin's mistake.

Boston, Massachusetts

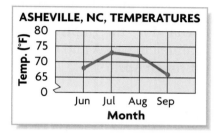

BOSTON, MA, TEMPERATURES

ASHEVILLE, NC, TEMPERATURES

MIXED REVIEW AND TEST PREP

For 14–15, use the box-and-whisker graph. (p. 143)

14. What is the median?

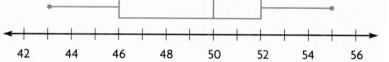

15. What are the least and greatest values?

16. Find the mean of the data set 18, 12, 10, 8, 9, 14, and 6. (p. 118)

⭐17. **TEST PREP** Which is the value of $2n + 3.7$ for $n = 2.9$? (p. 94)

    A 6.6   **B** 9.5   **C** 13.2   **D** 21.46

⭐18. **TEST PREP** Replace ● with the missing operation. $(3 + 24) ● 3 \times 2 - 1 = 17$ (p. 48)

    F ×   **G** ÷   **H** +   **J** −

PROBLEM SOLVING ⎰ LiNKÜP to Reading

Strategy • Classify and Categorize
To classify information means to group together similar information. To categorize the information, label the groups. Paige wants to buy a piece of Indian pottery. She can choose Navajo, Hopi, or Zuni style and select small, medium, or large size. By classifying and categorizing the data, you can see that she has 9 different choices.

Style	Size
Navajo	small, medium, large
Hopi	small, medium, large
Zuni	small, medium, large

• Jerome is buying an Indian drum. He can choose Navajo, Hopi, or Zuni style and select miniature, small, medium, large, or extra-large size. How many choices does he have?

EXTRA PRACTICE page 150, Set D

Set A (pp. 136–139)

For 1–2, use the data in the table at the right.

1. Make a double-bar graph using the data.

2. How does the attendance of males compare to the attendance of females?

For 3–4, use the data in the table at the right.

3. Make a double-line graph using the data.

4. What does the graph show about the average rainfall in City A and City B from January through April?

CLUB MEETING ATTENDANCE				
	Sept	Oct	Nov	Dec
Male	42	31	65	61
Female	56	47	51	60

AVERAGE RAINFALL (IN INCHES)				
	Jan	Feb	Mar	Apr
City A	4	5	3	5
City B	8	12	4	7

Set B (pp. 140–142)

1. Make a stem-and-leaf plot of the data below. Find the mode, median, and range.

2. Use the data in the chart below to make a histogram. Find the number of people who exercise 11 hours or less per month.

14	22	37	41	13	18	22	29	33
36	25	21	30	48	44	19	17	28

NUMBER OF HOURS OF MONTHLY EXERCISE					
0–2	3–5	6–8	9–11	12–15	16–18
12	15	19	22	21	6

Set C (pp. 144–145)

For 1–4, use the box-and-whisker graph. The graph shows the number of tickets sold.

1. What was the greatest number of tickets sold?

2. What is the median?

3. What are the lower and upper quartiles?

4. What is the lower extreme?

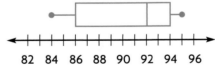

82 84 86 88 90 92 94 96

Set D (pp. 146–149)

For 1–3, use the bar graph at the right.

1. About how many times as high is the bar for Central as the bar for Lee?

2. Has Central won four times as many championships as Lee? Explain.

3. How can you change the graph so it is not misleading?

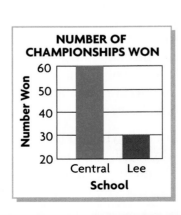

NUMBER OF CHAMPIONSHIPS WON

1. **VOCABULARY** A bar graph that shows frequencies within intervals is a(n) __?__ . (p. 141)

2. **VOCABULARY** A graph that shows how far apart and how evenly data are distributed is a(n) __?__ . (p. 143)

3. What type of graph would best show the highest and lowest temperatures for each of the last four years? (pp. 136–139)

4. What type of graph would best show high and low temperatures for a week? (pp. 136–139)

5. Make a double-line graph with the data at the right. (pp. 136–139)

6. Describe how the stock prices changed from September to January. (pp. 136–139)

END-OF-MONTH STOCK PRICES					
	Sep	**Oct**	**Nov**	**Dec**	**Jan**
Stock A	$80	$74	$45	$50	$52
Stock B	$50	$52	$52	$50	$45

For 7–8, use the table at the right. (pp. 136–139)

7. Make a triple-bar graph.

8. Compare the favorite beverages of students in sixth, seventh, and eighth grade.

FAVORITE BEVERAGE SURVEY				
Grade	**Juice**	**Milk**	**Soft Drink**	**Water**
Sixth	48	52	74	26
Seventh	46	55	59	40
Eighth	52	35	63	50

9. Make a stem-and-leaf plot for the data. (pp. 140–142)

10. Make a histogram for the data. (pp. 140–142)

POINTS SCORED					
33	52	45	47	34	52
34	58	48	52	46	59

HEIGHTS OF BUILDINGS (IN FT)						
20	50	80	20	40	45	85
25	30	80	60	70	75	55

For 11–16, use the following data: 14, 16, 9, 21, 35, 2, 26, 8, 17. (pp.143–145)

11. Find the upper extreme.

12. Find the lower extreme.

13. Find the upper quartile.

14. Find the lower quartile.

15. Find the median.

16. Make a box-and-whisker graph.

For 17–19, use the graph at the right. (pp. 146–149)

17. About how many times as high is the bar for green peppers as the bar for carrots?

18. Were three times as many pounds of green peppers sold as pounds of carrots? Explain.

19. How could you change the graph so that it is not misleading?

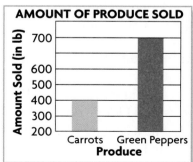

20. In his encyclopedia Sal found these average masses for some penguin species: African—3.5 kg, Chinstrap—5 kg, Emperor— 30 kg, Little Blue—1 kg, Macaroni—4.5 kg. Make a graph to compare the masses of these penguin species. (pp. 134–135)

NUMBER SENSE, CONCEPTS, AND OPERATIONS

1. Manuel lives 1,267 miles from Houston. On a trip from home to Houston, he drove 325 miles each day for 3 days. At the end of the third day, how far was he from Houston?

   A 975 miles

   B 942 miles

   C 425 miles

   D 292 miles

2. The table gives the heights of four house plants in centimeters.

HEIGHTS OF HOUSE PLANTS	
Plant	**Height (in centimeters)**
Silk Oak	90.07
Jade Plant	89.55
Peacock Plant	90.086
Weeping Fig	90.14

   Which list shows the plants' heights in order from **least** to **greatest**?

   F Peacock Plant, Silk Oak, Weeping Fig, Jade Plant

   G Jade Plant, Silk Oak, Peacock Plant, Weeping Fig

   H Peacock Plant, Jade Plant, Weeping Fig, Silk Oak

   J Jade Plant, Peacock Plant, Silk Oak, Weeping Fig

3. **Explain It** Jeff's skiing trip is planned for 6 days and 5 nights. Transportation to the ski resort costs $45.00 round trip and his ski lodge costs $70.00 per night. If he has a budget of $650.00, how much will he have left to spend each day for food and entertainment after he pays for transportation and lodging? Explain your answer.

 MEASUREMENT

4. A facet of a diamond is one of the flat polygon-shaped faces that is cut into the diamond to give it its shape. The figure below shows a quadrilateral-shaped facet with angles measuring 45°, 135°, and 135°. What is the measure of the fourth angle of the facet?

   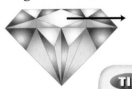
   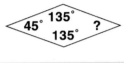

   A 30°

   B 45°

   C 60°

   D 75°

   > **TIP** **Understand the problem.** See item 4. You are given the measures of three angles of the quadrilateral. What do you know about the sum of the angle measures of a quadrilateral?

5. In the diagram of Anna's flower-garden design below, each grid square represents 1 square foot. Which is the **best** estimate for the area of the garden?

   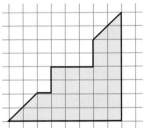

   F 64 square feet

   G 32 square feet

   H 30 square feet

   J 28 square feet

6. **Explain It** Ellen has 3 feet of wire to make bracelets. She wants to make 3 bracelets. She needs 8 inches of wire for each bracelet. Explain how Ellen can ESTIMATE to determine if she has enough wire.

★ ALGEBRAIC THINKING

7. Jon exercised for 10 minutes on Thursday. He plans to exercise 5 minutes more each day than he exercised the day before. Which table shows the number of minutes he will have exercised at the end of each of the first 4 days?

A

Thur	Fri	Sat	Sun
10	15	20	25

B

Thur	Fri	Sat	Sun
10	25	45	70

C

Thur	Fri	Sat	Sun
10	20	30	40

D

Thur	Fri	Sat	Sun
10	25	40	55

8. The table below shows the number of questions each student answered correctly on a science test.

SCIENCE TEST RESULTS			
Karen	Mike	Jacob	Nicole
23	19	27	25

Let q represent how many more questions Nicole answered correctly than Mike. Which equation can you use to find how many more questions Nicole answered correctly than Mike?

F $19 - q = 25$

G $q = 25 + 19$

H $25 = q - 19$

J $19 + q = 25$

9. Explain It Pam sold 5 times as many gallons of yogurt as gallons of ice cream. Explain how you can use an expression to find the number of gallons of yogurt sold if Pam sold 6 gallons of ice cream.

★ DATA ANALYSIS AND PROBABILITY

10. The table below shows the number of radio stations and television stations in three cities in 2002.

RADIO AND TELEVISION STATIONS		
City	Radio Stations	TV Stations
Chicago	44	14
Cleveland	32	7
Denver	43	17

Which type of graph would be **best** to compare the number of radio and TV stations in the three cities?

A line graph

B histogram

C double-bar graph

D stem-and-leaf plot

11. The graph below shows the enrollment of an elementary school every three years from 1990 to 2002.

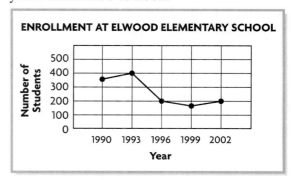

During which 3-year period did the school enrollment decrease the **most**?

F 1990 to 1993   **H** 1996 to 1999

G 1993 to 1996   **J** 1999 to 2002

12. Explain It Find the mean and median of the following backpack prices: $20, $15, $18, $15, $16, $20, $43. Is the mean or median more useful to describe the data? Explain your thinking.

IT'S IN THE BAG!

Graphing Collection Bags

PROJECT Make an accordion-style book to hold different types of graphs.

Materials

- Scissors and tape
- Two 7-in. × 6-in. sheets of colored card stock
- Two brass fasteners
- Hole punch
- One 6-in. ribbon
- Four quart-size plastic bags
- Markers
- Four 5-in. × 6-in. sheets of white paper

Directions

1. Tape the four bags together side to side, leaving a small space between them.

2. Fold the bags accordion style, back and forth. Tape a sheet of colored card stock to the top of the first bag. Label this cover *Statistics and Graphing,* and decorate it. *(Picture A)*

3. Turn the stack of bags over, and tape a sheet of colored card stock to the bottom of the last bag.

4. Punch a hole on the right side of the front cover, and attach a brass fastener. Do the same for the left side of the back cover. Then attach the piece of ribbon to the brass fastener on the back cover. *(Picture B)*

5. On the white sheets of paper, draw four different kinds of graphs that you learned about in Unit 2. Place each of these graphs inside one of the bags. Close the book by attaching the ribbon to the front fastener. *(Picture C)*

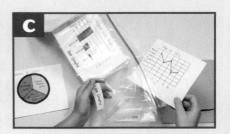

Explore Scatterplots

Do you think there is any relationship between the number of people who paint a large building and the number of hours it takes them to finish?

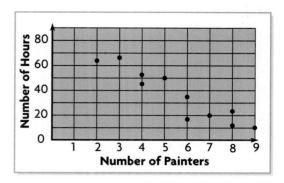

The *scatterplot* displays data for 11 large buildings that were painted. It shows that as the number of painters increased, the time it took them to finish tended to decrease.

A scatterplot shows the relationship between two variables.

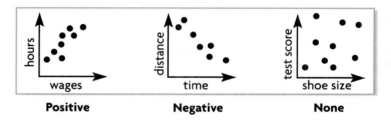

Positive	**Negative**	**None**

When the values of the two variables increase or decrease together, there is a **positive correlation**.

When the values of one variable increase while the others decrease, there is a **negative correlation**.

When the data points show no pattern of increase or decrease, there is **no correlation**.

TALK ABOUT IT

• Tell if the relationship between the speed of a car and the number of hours needed to drive 500 miles has a positive correlation, a negative correlation, or no correlation.

TRY IT

Sketch a scatterplot that could represent the situation. Then identify the type of correlation between the variables.

1. amount of time walking *and* total distance that you walk

2. number of rooms in house *and* street address of house

Write *positive correlation*, *negative correlation*, or *no correlation* to describe the relationship shown in the scatterplot.

3.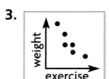

4.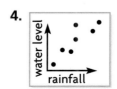

VOCABULARY

1. Everyone in a population has the same chance of being selected in a(n) __?__ . (p. 110)

2. A bar graph that shows the frequency at which data occur within intervals is a(n) __?__ . (p. 141)

3. Certain groups from the population are not represented in the sample if the sample is __?__ . (p. 112)

EXAMPLES

EXERCISES

Chapter 5

• **Tell whether the sample is *biased* or *unbiased*.** (pp. 112–113)

From a computer list of students, each of whom has an equal chance of being selected, 100 students are randomly chosen.

This is an unbiased sample.

The Melville Tourist Bureau is surveying visitors to Melville to learn which local attractions are the most popular. Tell whether the sample is *biased* or *unbiased*.

4. a sample of 100 randomly selected visitors to the Melville Railroad Museum

5. a sample of 150 randomly selected Melville tourists

• **Record and organize data.** (pp. 114–117)

What is the size of the sample?

SCORES ON MATH TEST		
Score Interval	Frequency	Cumulative Frequency
91–100	5	5
81–90	8	13
71–80	6	19
Below 71	5	24

There are 24 people in the sample.

For 6–7, use the following data.

NUMBER OF MOVIES SEEN IN ONE YEAR			
8	12	16	12
9	10	9	8
9	15	20	14
12	7	9	15

6. Make a line plot.

7. Make a cumulative frequency table with five intervals.

• **Find the mean, median, and mode.** (pp. 118–121)

24, 20, 24, 21, 26
Mean: $24 + 20 + 24 + 21 + 26 = 115$;
$\quad 115 \div 5 = 23$

Median: 24

Mode: 24

Find the mean, median, and mode.

8. 2, 7, 9, 4, 6, 8, 6

9. 5.3, 8.8, 4.7, 6.5, 4.7

10. 79, 87, 90, 100, 96, 89, 92, 87

11. Suppose you added the number 10.6 to the data in Exercise 9. Which measure(s) of central tendency would change?

Chapter 6

- **Display data in graphs.** (pp. 136–139)

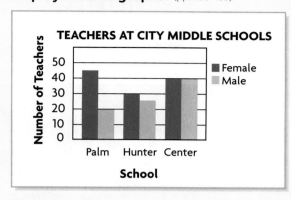

TEACHERS AT CITY MIDDLE SCHOOLS

For 12, use the graph at the left.

12. Which schools have more female teachers than male teachers?

13. Would you use a bar graph, line graph, or circle graph to display a city's temperature readings for 1 month? Explain.

14. Make a double-line graph with the data below.

HIGH AND LOW TEMPERATURES					
	Mon	**Tues**	**Wed**	**Thurs**	**Fri**
Highs	45°	53°	41°	48°	50°
Lows	34°	39°	35°	40°	41°

- **Use stem-and-leaf plots and histograms.** (pp. 140–142)

In a stem-and-leaf plot, the tens digits of the data are stems, and the ones digits are leaves.

Ages

Stem	Leaves
1	1 3 3
2	0 3 5 5
3	7 7 8

Some students are participating in a competition. Their ages are 10, 15, 18, 20, 15, 11, 13, 10, 14, 14, 18, 19, 22, and 21.

15. Use the data to make a stem-and-leaf plot.

16. Use the data to make a histogram.

- **Make a box-and-whisker graph.** (pp. 143–145)

Heights of Students (in cm)

135 168 148 160 159 148 163 165 167

Draw a box-and-whisker graph.

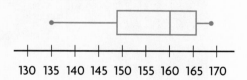

130 135 140 145 150 155 160 165 170

For 17–20, use the table below.

HEIGHTS OF TREES (in ft)								
8	12	6	9	15	9	16	20	24

17. What is the median?

18. What are the lower and upper quartiles?

19. What are the lower and upper extremes?

20. Make a box-and-whisker graph.

PROBLEM SOLVING APPLICATIONS

For 21–26, use the following data. The four shopping malls in Fryburg have the following numbers of stores: Northside Mall, 22; River Mall, 11; Metro Mall, 31; Central Mall, 20.

21. Would a bar graph or line graph be better to display these data? Explain. (pp. 136–139)

22. Make a graph to compare the number of stores in Fryburg's malls. (pp. 134–135)

23. About how many times as many stores are there in the Metro Mall as there are in the River Mall? (pp. 134–135)

24. About how many times as many stores are there in the Northside Mall as there are in the River Mall? (pp. 134–135)

25. Which mall has the greatest number of stores? (pp. 134–135)

26. Which mall has about the same number of stores as the Central Mall? (pp. 134–135)

Performance Assessment

TASK A • Too Much Homework?

For homework, Scott has 3 social studies questions, 3 English questions, 2 science problems, 5 Spanish questions, and 20 math exercises. Scott's friend Beth asks him about how much homework he has in each subject. Would he give the mean, median, or mode of the number of items to make his homework assignment seem as long as possible?

a. Explain your choice. Write down your thinking as you make your decision.

b. Suppose your friend asks you the same question about the homework you really have. How would you respond?

TASK B • Graph Analysis

Elements in the Earth's Crust: Aluminum 8.1%, Calcium 3.6%, Iron 5.0%, Oxygen 46.6%, Silicon 27.7%, All Others 9.0%

a. Organize the data in a table. Use the data to make a graph. Then write a short description of the graph. Include the following:

- What the title and axes represent

- What the parts represent, if it is a circle graph

- What stands out as important or obvious

b. Describe how the data can be used to make a different kind of graph.

c. Write a question that can be answered from either graph.

Use a Spreadsheet to Make Graphs

The table at the right shows the amounts of money earned through different activities at the school carnival. Enter the activities and the amounts earned into a spreadsheet. Then use the spreadsheet to make a bar graph of the data.

CARNIVAL EARNINGS	
Activity	**Amount Earned**
Refreshments	$250
Crafts	$170
Games	$320
Bake Sale	$380

To make a graph using the spreadsheet, first highlight all the activities and amounts you entered. Then click ⬛. This icon opens the chart maker.

Step 1 Choose *Column* to make a vertical bar graph. Then click *Next.*

Step 2 This shows a preview of the graph. Click *Next.*

Step 3 Fill in the labels for the graph.

- Chart title: MONEY EARNED AT SCHOOL CARNIVAL
- Category (X) axis: Activity
- Category (Y) axis: Amount Earned (in dollars) Click *Next.*

Step 4 Click *As object in:* to place the graph on the spreadsheet with the data. You can also click *As new sheet* to place the graph on a new page. Click *Finish* to view the completed graph.

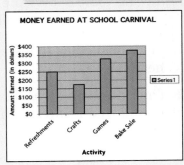

Practice and Problem Solving

1. Use the carnival data to make a horizontal bar graph and a circle graph.

2. Refer to your graphs from Problem 1. Which activity earned the most money? Explain how you know from each graph.

3. *REASONING* Explain why choosing a line graph for the chart type would **not** be appropriate for the carnival data.

4. There are 38 sixth graders, 45 seventh graders, and 29 eighth graders in the school chorus. Make a bar graph and a circle graph of the data.

GO ON-LINE **Multimedia Math Glossary** www.harcourtschool.com/mathglossary
Vocabulary Power Look up *line graph* in the Multimedia Math Glossary.
Use the data in the line graph to make a vertical bar graph.

PROBLEM SOLVING ON LOCATION

In
North Carolina

Cape Lookout Lighthouse

The Cape Lookout Lighthouse is located on the southern end of the Outer Banks, a string of islands along North Carolina's east coast. The lighthouse was built in 1812 and painted with red and white horizontal stripes. It was rebuilt in 1859 and painted with a black-and-white check pattern to help distinguish it from the other lighthouses on the Outer Banks.

Use Data For 1–5, use the table at the right. The table shows the heights of some lighthouses in North Carolina.

1. Find the median of the lighthouse heights.

2. Find the mean of the lighthouse heights. Round your answer to the nearest whole number.

3. Is the mean or median more useful for describing the heights of the lighthouses? Explain.

4. Find the range of the lighthouse heights.

5. Make and label a bar graph to display the heights of the seven lighthouses. Explain how the graph helps you compare the heights of the lighthouses.

6. An Internet survey asks the following question: *What is your favorite North Carolina Lighthouse?* Is the question *biased* or *unbiased*? Explain.

NORTH CAROLINA LIGHTHOUSES	
Lighthouse	**Height (in feet)**
Oak Island	169
Cape Lookout	165
Bald Head Island	90
Bodie Island	150
Ocracoke	76
Cape Hatteras	225
Currituck Beach	162

The signal from the Cape Lookout Lighthouse can be seen from 19 miles away.

Asheville Weather

Asheville, the tenth largest city in North Carolina, is located in the western part of North Carolina. It is surrounded by the Great Smoky Mountains and the Blue Ridge Mountains. With an average temperature of about 56°F, the weather in Asheville is considered mild.

Use Data   For 1–3, use the double-line graph.

1. What does the graph show about the difference between the average high temperature and average low temperature in Asheville from January through December?

2. By about how many degrees does the average low temperature change from January to March?

3. **Stretch Your Thinking**   Find the average high temperatures and average low temperatures of your city from January to December. Make a double-line graph to display your data.

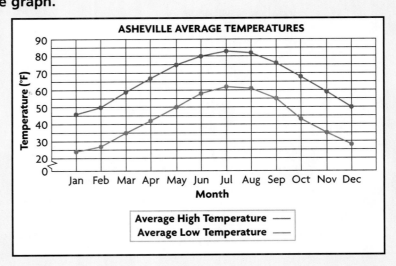

ASHEVILLE AVERAGE TEMPERATURES

Temperature (°F) vs. Month

Average High Temperature —
Average Low Temperature —

Use Data   For 4–5, use the circle graph. The circle graph shows the average percents of clear, cloudy, and partly cloudy days in Asheville each year.

4. The number of cloudy days per year is about how many times the number of clear days?

5. Would you say that clear days and partly cloudy days account for a little less than half or more than half of the days per year? Explain your thinking.

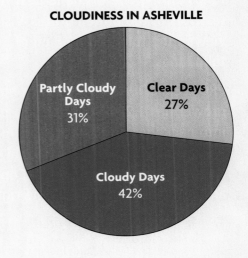

CLOUDINESS IN ASHEVILLE

Partly Cloudy Days 31%
Clear Days 27%
Cloudy Days 42%

FAST FACT • SOCIAL STUDIES

In May 2002, visitors to Holland, Michigan, viewed more than 6 million tulips during one of the largest flower festivals in the United States. Visitors viewed the tulips along 8 mi of tulip lanes.

PROBLEM SOLVING Suppose a bulb grower has 1,200 tulip bulbs to put into packages of 20 each. How many packages could be made? Would there be any bulbs left over? Copy and complete the table at the right.

PACKAGES OF TULIP BULBS

Tulip Bulbs per Package	Complete Package Yes or No?
25	Yes
30	
35	
40	Yes
45	
50	Yes

Check What You Know

Use this page to help you review and remember important skills needed for Chapter 7.

 **Division**

Divide and check.

1. $3\overline{)48}$ 2. $2\overline{)56}$ 3. $4\overline{)72}$ 4. $6\overline{)72}$

5. $6\overline{)21}$ 6. $3\overline{)14}$ 7. $8\overline{)40}$ 8. $9\overline{)39}$

9. $4\overline{)68}$ 10. $7\overline{)91}$ 11. $3\overline{)27}$ 12. $8\overline{)21}$

 Multiples

Write the next three multiples.

13. 4   4, 8, 12, ▪, ▪, ▪   14. 10   10, 20, 30, ▪, ▪, ▪   15. 12   12, 24, 36, ▪, ▪, ▪

16. 8   8, 16, 24, ▪, ▪, ▪   17. 5   5, 10, 15, ▪, ▪, ▪   18. 11   11, 22, 33, ▪, ▪, ▪

Write the first five multiples of each number.

19. 6   20. 22   21. 30

22. 7   23. 9   24. 13

 Factors

Write all of the factors of each number.

25. 8   26. 9   27. 11

28. 18   29. 54   30. 32

VOCABULARY POWER

REVIEW

multiple [mul'tə•pəl] *noun*

In mathematics, a multiple can be the product of a given whole number and another whole number. Which operation in mathematics is related to the word *multiple*?

 www.harcourtschool.com/mathglossary

PREVIEW

prime number
composite number
prime factorization
least common multiple (LCM)
greatest common factor (GCF)

Divisibility

Learn how to tell if a number is divisible by 2, 3, 4, 5, 6, 8, 9, or 10.

Remember that a number is divisible by another number if the remainder is zero.

You can use divisibility rules to help you decide if a number is divisible by another number.

A number is divisible by	Divisible	Not Divisible
2 if the last digit is even (0, 2, 4, 6, or 8).	11,994	2,175
3 if the sum of the digits is divisible by 3.	216	79
4 if the last two digits form a number divisible by 4.	1,024	621
5 if the last digit is 0 or 5.	15,195	10,007
6 if the number is divisible by 2 and 3.	1,332	44
8 if the last three digits form a number divisible by 8.	5,336	3,180
9 if the sum of the digits is divisible by 9.	144	33
10 if the last digit is 0.	2,790	9,325

EXAMPLES

Tell whether each number is divisible by 2, 3, 4, 5, 6, 8, 9, or 10.

A. 610 is divisible by
2; the last digit is even.
5; the last digit is 0 or 5.
10; the last digit is 0.

B. 459 is divisible by
3; the sum of the digits
is divisible by 3.
9; the sum of the digits
is divisible by 9.

Another way to decide whether a number is divisible by 3 is to break it into smaller parts. Tell whether 648 is divisible by 3.

$648 = 6 \times 100 + 4 \times 10 + 8$ *Write 648 in expanded form.*

Since 99 and 9 are divisible by 3, rewrite 100 as 99 + 1 and 10 as 9 + 1.

$648 = 6 \times (99 + 1) + 4 \times (9 + 1) + 8$ *100 = 99 + 1 and 10 = 9 + 1.*
$= (6 \times 99) + (6 \times 1) + (4 \times 9) +$ *Use the Distributive Property.*
$(4 \times 1) + 8$
$= (6 \times 99) + (4 \times 9) + (6 \times 1) +$ *Use the Commutative Property.*
$(4 \times 1) + 8$
$= (6 \times 99) + (4 \times 9) + 6 + 4 + 8$

Since 99 and 9 are divisible by 3, the sum $(6 \times 99) + (4 \times 9)$ is also divisible by 3. Now you only have to check whether the sum of the remaining addends, $6 + 4 + 8$, is divisible by 3.

$6 + 4 + 8 = 18$ *18 is divisible by 3.*

Since $(6 \times 99) + (4 \times 9)$ is divisible by 3, and 18 is divisible by 3, then 648 is divisible by 3.

Think and ▶ Discuss

Look back at the lesson to answer each question.

1. **Compare** the divisibility rules for 3 and 9.

2. **Explain** the advantages of knowing the divisibility rules.

Guided ▶ Practice

Tell whether each number is divisible by 2, 3, 4, 5, 6, 8, 9, or 10.

3. 56   **4.** 200   **5.** 784   **6.** 2,345   **7.** 3,009

PRACTICE AND PROBLEM SOLVING

Independent ▶ Practice

Tell whether each number is divisible by 2, 3, 4, 5, 6, 8, 9, or 10.

8. 75   **9.** 324   **10.** 45   **11.** 812   **12.** 501

13. 615   **14.** 936   **15.** 744   **16.** 5,188   **17.** 4,335

18. 1,407   **19.** 48,006   **20.** 7,064   **21.** 221   **22.** 1,044

For 23–24 write *T* or *F* to tell whether each statement is true or false. If it is false, give an example that shows it is false.

23. All even numbers are divisible by 2.

24. All odd numbers are divisible by 3.

25. Break 753 into smaller parts to explain whether it is divisible by 3.

26. A number is between 80 and 100 and is divisible by both 5 and 6. What is the number?

27. *REASONING*   Find all possible digits for ■ that make 34,■25 divisible by 3.

28. **Vocabulary Power** The number 16 is divisible by 8 since the remainder is zero; $16 \div 8 = 2$ r0. So, 8 is a factor of 16. Use a different example to explain how *divisible* and *factor* are related.

29. Amber charges $8.25 per hour to baby-sit. One Saturday she baby-sat for 3.5 hr in the morning and 2.25 hr in the evening. To the nearest cent, how much did she earn on Saturday?

TECHNOLOGY LINK

More Practice:
**Harcourt Mega Math
Ice Station Exploration,**
Arctic Algebra,
Levels M, N

Problem Solving ▶ Applications

MIXED REVIEW AND TEST PREP

30. What is the lower quartile of the data 24, 26, 28, 29, 30, 32, 34, 36, 37? (p. 143)

31. $36.4 \div 0.28$ (p. 88)

32. Write the percent for 0.05. (p. 68)

33. 858×19 (p. 24)

34. **TEST PREP**   Which is the value of $3^2 + 2 \times 5 - 6$? (p. 48)

    A 13   **B** 24   **C** 34   **D** 49

EXTRA PRACTICE page 176, Set A

Learn how to identify prime and composite numbers.

Vocabulary

prime number

composite number

Prime and Composite Numbers

Write all the factors for each number.

1. 4   **2.** 7   **3.** 9   **4.** 12   **5.** 26

You can use rectangular arrays to show the factors of 12.

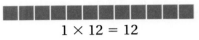
$1 \times 12 = 12$

$2 \times 6 = 12$

$3 \times 4 = 12$

The factors of 12 are 1, 2, 3, 4, 6, and 12.

An array can also be used to show the factors of 17.

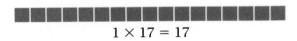
$1 \times 17 = 17$

The factors of 17 are 1 and 17.

All whole numbers greater than 1 are either prime numbers or composite numbers. A **prime number** is a whole number greater than 1 whose only factors are itself and 1. A **composite number** is a whole number greater than 1 that has more than two factors.

Since 12 has six factors, it is a composite number. Since 17 has two factors, it is a prime number. The numbers 0 and 1 are neither prime nor composite.

To know that a whole number is composite, you need to find only one factor which is not 1 or the number itself.

EXAMPLE 1

Tell whether 28 is prime or composite.

$2 \times 14 = 28$ *Use the divisibility rules to try to find a factor other than 1 or 28.*

So, 28 is a composite number.

• Which other divisibility rule could you have used? Explain.

EXAMPLE 2

Tell whether 31 is prime or composite.

$1 \times 31 = 31$ *Use the divisibility rules to try to find a factor other than 1 or 31. There are no factors other than 1 or 31.*

So, 31 is a prime number.

Think and ▶
Discuss

Look back at the lesson to answer each question.

1. **Explain** how you can tell if 19 is a prime or composite number.

2. **Explain** why 2 is the only even prime number.

Guided ▶
Practice

Write *prime* or *composite*.

3. 8	**4.** 15	**5.** 23	**6.** 40
7. 19	**8.** 34	**9.** 45	**10.** 57
11. 60	**12.** 71	**13.** 131	**14.** 147

PRACTICE AND PROBLEM SOLVING

Independent ▶
Practice

Write *prime* or *composite*.

15. 17	**16.** 27	**17.** 29	**18.** 42
19. 26	**20.** 53	**21.** 41	**22.** 63
23. 83	**24.** 94	**25.** 39	**26.** 70
27. 43	**28.** 51	**29.** 121	**30.** 221

Problem Solving ▶
Applications

31. James made a list of the prime numbers less than 50. Which prime number did James put on his list after 37?

32. There are 115 lockers, numbered 1–115, outside Cheryl's classroom. Her locker has a 3-digit prime number on the door. List the possible numbers that could be on Cheryl's locker.

33. Ken used 15 lb of birdseed to fill his bird feeders. Solve $34 = k - 15$ to find the amount of birdseed Ken started with. Is the value of k prime or composite?

34. Kim ran 7 km every day for 6 days. Lori ran 3 km every day for 5 days. Tell whether the total number of kilometers Kim and Lori ran is prime or composite.

MIXED REVIEW AND TEST PREP

35. Tell whether 270 is divisible by 2, 3, 4, 5, 6, 8, 9, or 10. (p. 164)

36. Divide. $0.434 ÷ 0.7$ (p. 88)

37. Subtract. $47.03 - 1.7$ (p. 76)

38. Evaluate the expression.
$7^2 + (8 - 3) × 6$ (p. 48)

⭐ **39. TEST PREP** What is the value of $n + 45.9$ for $n = 3.84$? (p. 94)

A 8.43   **B** 48.74   **C** 49.74   **D** 84.3

Prime Factorization

Learn how to write a composite number as the product of prime numbers.

Write the equal factors for each.

1. 3^2 **2.** 2^4 **3.** 4^3 **4.** 9^2 **5.** 5^4

Vocabulary

prime factorization

A prime number is a whole number greater than 1 that has only two factors. Here are the prime numbers less than 50.

2, 3, 5, 7, 11, 13, 17, 19, 23, 29, 31, 37, 41, 43, 47

A composite number, like 104, has more than two factors. You can write a composite number as the product of prime factors. This is called the **prime factorization** of the number.

You can divide to find the prime factors of a composite number.

EXAMPLE 1

Find the prime factorization of 104.

```
 2|104
 2|52
 2|26
13|13
    1
```
Repeatedly divide by the smallest possible prime factor until the quotient is 1.

$2 \times 2 \times 2 \times 13$ *List the prime numbers you divided by. These are the prime factors.*

So, the prime factorization of 104 is $2 \times 2 \times 2 \times 13$, or $2^3 \times 13$.

Use a factor tree to find the prime factors of a composite number.

EXAMPLE 2

Find the prime factorization of 156.

Choose any two factors of 156. Continue until only prime factors are left.

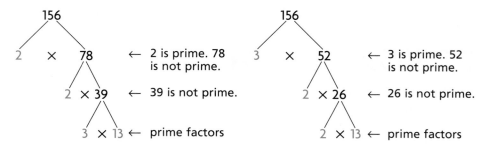

So, the prime factorization of 156 is $2 \times 2 \times 3 \times 13$, or $2^2 \times 3 \times 13$.

Math Idea ▶ Every composite number can be written as a product of two or more prime factors. No matter how you find the prime factors, you will get the same factors, but the order may be different.

**Think and ▶
Discuss**

Look back at the lesson to answer each question.

1. **Tell** what the prime factorization would be in Example 2 if you started with 4 and 39.

2. **Explain** how you know when you have finished the prime factorization of a number.

**Guided ▶
Practice**

Use division or a factor tree to find the prime factorization.

3. 12 **4.** 65 **5.** 16 **6.** 42

TECHNOLOGY LINK

More Practice:
**Harcourt Mega Math
Ice Station Exploration,**
Arctic Algebra,
Levels O, W

Write the prime factorization in exponent form.

7. 21 **8.** 28 **9.** 254 **10.** 908

PRACTICE AND PROBLEM SOLVING

**Independent ▶
Practice**

Use division or a factor tree to find the prime factorization.

11. 128 **12.** 50 **13.** 76 **14.** 108

Write the prime factorization in exponent form.

15. 18 **16.** 302 **17.** 49 **18.** 217

19. 532 **20.** 45 **21.** 746 **22.** 99

Solve for *n* to complete the prime factorization.

23. $2 \times n \times 5 = 20$ **24.** $44 = 2^2 \times n$ **25.** $75 = 3 \times 5 \times n$

**Problem Solving ▶
Applications**

26. *REASONING* A number, *c,* is a prime factor of both 12 and 60. What is *c*?

27. ≡**FAST FACT** • SOCIAL STUDIES The 23-karat gold-leaf dome atop the capitol building in Charleston, West Virginia, is the largest state capitol dome in the United States. The building is 293 ft tall, 5 ft taller than the nation's Capitol. Write in exponent form the prime factorization of the height of the nation's Capitol.

28. ✎ **Write About It** Do the prime factors of a number differ depending on which factors you choose first? Explain.

Capitol building, Charleston, WV

MIXED REVIEW AND TEST PREP

29. Is 3,543 divisible by 2, 3, or 9? (p. 164)

30. Write the percent for 0.6. (p. 68)

31. $18.3 + 22.6 + 17.03 + 21.99$ (p. 76)

32. Find the median for the data 13, 8, 9, 16, 18. (p. 118)

33. **TEST PREP** The prices of five stuffed animals are $4.95, $1.40, $9.25, $5.00, and $3.75. What is the average price of the stuffed animals? (p. 118)

A $24.35 C $4.95

B $6.08 D $4.87

Least Common Multiple and Greatest Common Factor

Learn how to find the LCM and GCF of numbers and use them to solve problems.

Vocabulary

least common multiple (LCM)

greatest common factor (GCF)

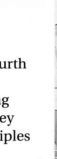

Kirk and Amber volunteer during December. Kirk volunteers every fourth day beginning December 4. Amber volunteers every third day beginning December 3. To find the first day they will volunteer together list the multiples of 4 and 3.

multiples of 4:   4, 8, 12, 16, 20, 24, 28

multiples of 3:   3, 6, 9, 12, 15, 18, 21, 24, 27, 30

The multiples in blue are common multiples. The smallest of the common multiples is the **least common multiple**, or **LCM**.
The LCM of 4 and 3 is 12, the product of the two numbers. So, the first day Kirk and Amber will volunteer together is December 12.

Examples 1 and 2 show two ways to find the LCM.

EXAMPLE 1

One Way   Find the LCM of 12 and 8.

12: 12, 24, 36, 48, 60, 72, 84   *List the first seven multiples.*

 8: 8, 16, 24, 32, 40, 48, 56   *Find the common multiples.*

So, the LCM of 12 and 8 is 24.   *Find the LCM.*

EXAMPLE 2

Another Way   Find the LCM of 6, 9, and 18.

Write the prime factorizations.

$6 = 2 \times 3$ $9 = 3 \times 3 = 3^2$ $18 = 2 \times 3 \times 3 = 2 \times 3^2$

Write a product using each prime factor only once.

$$2 \times 3$$

For each factor, write the greatest exponent used with that factor in any of the prime factorizations. Multiply.

$$2 \times 3^2 = 18$$

So, the LCM of 6, 9, and 18 is 18.

Greatest Common Factor

Factors shared by two or more numbers are called common factors. The greatest of the common factors is called the **greatest common factor**, or **GCF**.

To find the GCF of two or more numbers, list all the factors of each number, find the common factors, and then find the greatest common factor.

45:	1, 3, 5, 9, 15, 45	*The common factors are 1, 3, and 9.*
27:	1, 3, 9, 27	*The GCF of 45 and 27 is 9.*

The GCF can be used to solve problems.

EXAMPLE 3

Carlyn has 12 pens and 36 pencils. She is making packages, all with the same number of pens and the same number of pencils. What is the greatest number of packages she can make without any items left over? How many of each item will be in each package?

You can find the greatest number of packages by finding the GCF of 12 and 36.

12:	1, 2, 3, 4, 6, 12	*List the factors.*
36:	1, 2, 3, 4, 6, 9, 12, 18, 36	*Find the common factors.*
The GCF of 12 and 36 is 12.		*Find the GCF.*

So, Carlyn can make 12 packages without any items left over.

To find the number of each item, divide the number of pens and the number of pencils by the number of packages.

$$\text{Pens: } 12 \div 12 = 1 \qquad \text{Pencils: } 36 \div 12 = 3$$

So, there will be 1 pen and 3 pencils in each package.

To find the GCF of two numbers, you can also use their prime factors. List the prime factors, find the common prime factors, and then find their product.

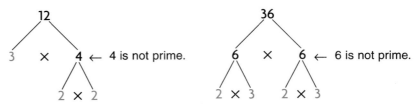

The prime factors of 12 are $2 \times 2 \times 3$.

The prime factors of 36 are $2 \times 2 \times 3 \times 3$.

The common prime factors are 2, 2, and 3.

Find the product of the common factors: $2 \times 2 \times 3$, or $2^2 \times 3 = 12$.

The GCF of 12 and 36 is 12.

EXAMPLE 4

Use prime factors to find the GCF of 48 and 72.

48: $2 \times 2 \times 2 \times 2 \times 3$ *Find the prime factors.*

72: $2 \times 2 \times 2 \times 3 \times 3$

2, 2, 2, and 3   *Find the common prime factors.*

$2 \times 2 \times 2 \times 3 = 24$ *Multiply the common factors.*

So, the GCF of 48 and 72 is 24.

CHECK FOR UNDERSTANDING

Think and Discuss ▸ Look back at the lesson to answer each question.

1. **Explain** why you are able to find the greatest common factor but not the greatest common multiple of two or more numbers.

2. **Tell** the number of pens and pencils there would be in each package in Example 3 if Carlyn made 6 packages.

Guided Practice ▸ List the first five multiples of each number.

3. 3   **4.** 7   **5.** 11   **6.** 15

Find the LCM of each set of numbers.

7. 3, 7   **8.** 2, 3   **9.** 6, 9   **10.** 5, 8, 20

Find the GCF of each set of numbers.

11. 6, 9   **12.** 4, 20   **13.** 9, 24   **14.** 12, 16, 20

PRACTICE AND PROBLEM SOLVING

Independent Practice ▸ List the first five multiples of each number.

15. 4   **16.** 8   **17.** 16   **18.** 55

19. 10   **20.** 27   **21.** 14   **22.** 39

Find the LCM of each set of numbers.

23. 3, 8, 24   **24.** 32, 128   **25.** 12, 20   **26.** 40, 105

27. 24, 30   **28.** 18, 21, 36   **29.** 12, 27   **30.** 48, 116

Find the GCF of each set of numbers.

31. 16, 18   **32.** 15, 18   **33.** 21, 306   **34.** 16, 24, 40

35. 25, 33   **36.** 200, 215   **37.** 24, 32, 40   **38.** 630, 712

Find a pair of numbers for each set of conditions.

39. The LCM is 36. The GCF is 3.

40. The LCM is 24. The GCF is 2.

41. Peter will distribute cereal samples with pamphlets about good nutrition. The samples come in packages of 15. The pamphlets come in packages of 20.

    a. What is the least number of cereal samples and pamphlets needed to have the same number of each?

    b. How many packages of each does he need for that number?

42. Ruth has 36 markers and 48 erasers. She will put them in bags, all with the same number of markers and the same number of erasers. What is the greatest number of bags she can make?

43. **What's the Error?** Jan says the LCM of 10 and 15 is 5. Find her error and the correct answer.

MIXED REVIEW AND TEST PREP

44. Write the prime factorization of 45 in exponent form. (p. 168)

45. Evaluate $a \div c$, for $a = 4{,}602$ and $c = 37$. (p. 36)

46. Find the value of 5^4. (p. 46)

47. **TEST PREP** Which is the exponential notation for $3 \times 3 \times 3 \times 4 \times 4 \times 5 \times 5$? (p. 46)

  A $3 \times 4 \times 5^7$ **B** $3^3 \times 2^4 \times 2^5$ **C** $3^3 \times 4^2 \times 5^2$ **D** $3^3 \times 4^4 \times 5^5$

48. **TEST PREP** Which shows the decimal for 46%? (p. 68)

  F 0.046   **G** 0.46   **H** 4.6   **J** 46

PROBLEM SOLVING ⎯ THINKER'S CORNER

Logical Thinking You have learned how to find the LCM and the GCF of a pair of numbers. The table below can help you understand the relationship between a pair of numbers and its LCM and GCF.

FIRST NUMBER	SECOND NUMBER	PRODUCT OF NUMBERS	GCF	LCM	GCF × LCM
3	7	21	1	21	21
4	6	24	2	12	24
5	10	50	5	10	50
15	25	375	5	75	375
18	27	486	9	54	486

1. Look at 3 and 7 in the first row. When the GCF of two numbers is 1, what is the LCM?

2. Look at 5 and 10 in the third row. When the GCF of two numbers is one of the numbers, what is the LCM?

3. Look at each pair of numbers. What is the relationship between the product of two numbers and the product of their GCF and LCM?

Learn how to solve problems by making an organized list.

PROBLEM SOLVING STRATEGY
Make an Organized List

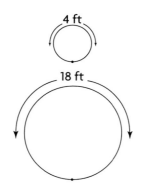

4 ft

18 ft

QUICK REVIEW

Find the LCM of each set of numbers.

1. 3, 9   **2.** 5, 2   **3.** 14, 4

4. 8, 12   **5.** 10, 35

Like many early bicycles, the Boneshaker had different-size wheels. Suppose the circumferences of the wheels were 4 ft and 18 ft. How many revolutions would each wheel make before marks on their rims would both be in the same position again, at the same time?

The Boneshaker was invented in 1865. The wooden wheels made for an uncomfortable ride.

Analyze   What are you asked to find?

What facts are given?

Choose   What strategy will you use?

You can use the strategy *make an organized list*. List the total distance traveled by each wheel for every complete turn.

Solve   How will you solve the problem?

Make a list of multiples of 4 and 18.
  multiples of 4: 4, 8, 12, 16, 20, 24, 28, 32, 36, 40
  multiples of 18: 18, 36, 54

The least common multiple is 36. When the wheels had traveled 36 ft, the marks would both be in the same position again.

36 is the ninth multiple of 4, so the small wheel would make 9 revolutions.

36 is the second multiple of 18, so the large wheel would make 2 revolutions.

Check   How can you check your answer?

What if the smaller wheel had a circumference of 8 ft? How many revolutions would each wheel make before the marks were both in the same position again, at the same time?

Solve the problem by making an organized list.

1. Justin and Amy help with the shopping for their individual families. Justin goes to the store every 3 days and Amy goes every 5 days. They see each other at the store on September 30. On what date will Justin and Amy see each other at the store again?

PROBLEM SOLVING STRATEGIES

Draw a Diagram or Picture
Make a Model
Predict and Test
Work Backward
▶ **Make an Organized List**
Find a Pattern
Make a Table or Graph
Solve a Simpler Problem
Write an Equation
Use Logical Reasoning

For 2–3, use the information below.

Susanna buys one bag with 40 snacks and another with 32. She uses all the snacks to make snack packs for a party. All snack packs must have the same number of each snack.

2. If you make lists to find the greatest number of snack packs Susanna can make, what will you include in the lists?

   A addends   **B** factors   **C** multiples   **D** fractions

3. What is the greatest number of snack packs Susanna can make?

   F 2 packs   **G** 4 packs   **H** 8 packs   **J** 15 packs

MIXED STRATEGY PRACTICE

4. Ray begins an eight-week exercise program. He exercises 30 min during the first week, 45 min the second week, and 60 min the third week. If this pattern continues, how many hours and minutes will Ray exercise the sixth week?

5. DeAnn has a total of 6 ft of yarn to make gifts. She uses 13 in. of yarn for each of the 5 gifts she is making. Find how many inches of yarn DeAnn will have left after making the 5 gifts.

6. A total of 316 middle school teachers are going to a meeting. There are 30 more male teachers than female. How many teachers are male?

7. Christi rides her bicycle 7 blocks south, 3 blocks east, 5 blocks north, and 8 blocks west. How many blocks has she ridden when she crosses her own path?

8. Use the graph at the right. Look at the area in square miles for each lake. How much larger is Lake Michigan than Lake Erie and Lake Ontario together?

9. ? **What's the Question?** Laura wants to buy the same number of plums as apricots. Plums are sold in bags of 4 and apricots are sold in bags of 7. The answer is 28 plums.

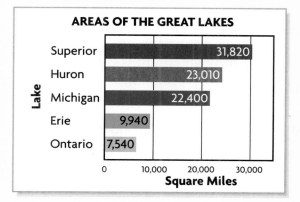

AREAS OF THE GREAT LAKES

Lake	Square Miles
Superior	31,820
Huron	23,010
Michigan	22,400
Erie	9,940
Ontario	7,540

Set A (pp. 164–165)

Tell whether each number is divisible by 2, 3, 4, 5, 6, 8, 9, or 10.

1. 80　　　　**2.** 99　　　　**3.** 105　　　　**4.** 126　　　　**5.** 234

6. 370　　　**7.** 591　　　**8.** 1,620　　　**9.** 3,048　　　**10.** 8,020

Set B (pp. 166–167)

Write *prime* or *composite*.

1. 13　　　　**2.** 42　　　　**3.** 30　　　　**4.** 23　　　　**5.** 34

6. 28　　　　**7.** 31　　　　**8.** 99　　　　**9.** 71　　　　**10.** 106

Set C (pp. 168–169)

Use division or a factor tree to find the prime factorization.

1. 18　　　　**2.** 40　　　　**3.** 36　　　　**4.** 27　　　　**5.** 420

Write the prime factorization in exponent form.

6. 28　　　**7.** 420　　　**8.** 48　　　**9.** 81　　　**10.** 72

11. 80　　　**12.** 144　　　**13.** 121　　　**14.** 168　　　**15.** 1,475

Solve for *n* to complete the prime factorization.

16. $2 \times 5 \times n = 50$　　　　**17.** $2 \times n \times 5 = 30$　　　　**18.** $2 \times 3 \times n = 18$

19. $n \times 3 \times 3 = 27$　　　　**20.** $2 \times 2 \times 2 \times n = 16$　　　　**21.** $n \times 2 \times 3 = 42$

Set D (pp. 170–173)

List the first five multiples of each number.

1. 4　　　　**2.** 9　　　　**3.** 14　　　　**4.** 21

Find the LCM of each set of numbers.

5. 45, 54　　　**6.** 10, 35　　　**7.** 55, 33, 44　　　**8.** 35, 25, 49

9. Jean needs eggs and muffins for the class breakfast. Eggs come in cartons of 12 and muffins come in packages of 8. What is the least number of eggs and muffins she can buy to have equal numbers of them?

Find the GCF of each set of numbers.

10. 12, 108　　　**11.** 148, 84　　　**12.** 132, 108　　　**13.** 56, 280, 400

1. **VOCABULARY**   A composite number written as the product of prime factors is called the ___?___ of the number. (p. 168)

2. **VOCABULARY**   The greatest of the common factors of two or more numbers is the ___?___. (p.171)

Tell whether each number is divisible by 2, 3, 4, 5, 6, 8, 9, or 10. (pp. 164–165)

3. 42	**4.** 64	**5.** 96	**6.** 225
7. 330	**8.** 963	**9.** 450	**10.** 2,385

Write *prime* or *composite*. (pp. 166–167)

11. 23	**12.** 27	**13.** 13	**14.** 40
15. 72	**16.** 89	**17.** 14	**18.** 49
19. 17	**20.** 97	**21.** 46	**22.** 107

Use division or a factor tree to find the prime factorization. Write the prime factorization in exponent form. (pp. 168–169)

23. 9	**24.** 8	**25.** 14	**26.** 18
27. 80	**28.** 12	**29.** 33	**30.** 50
31. 49	**32.** 98	**33.** 504	**34.** 891

Find the LCM and the GCF of each set of numbers. (pp. 170–173)

35. 3, 9	**36.** 2, 6	**37.** 4, 6	**38.** 10, 15
39. 8, 12	**40.** 9, 27	**41.** 15, 25	**42.** 18, 48
43. 56, 98	**44.** 6, 8, 12	**45.** 6, 9, 12	**46.** 8, 16, 20

Solve.

47. A number is between 60 and 70. It is divisible by 3 and 9. What is the number? (pp. 164–165)

48. Meat patties are sold in packages of 12. Buns are sold in packages of 8. What is the least number of meat patties and buns needed to have the same number of each? (pp. 170–173)

49. Cashews are sold in 8-oz jars, almonds in 12-oz jars, and peanuts in 16-oz jars. What is the least number of ounces you can buy of each nut to make mixed nuts with equal amounts of the three nuts and no nuts left over? How many jars of each nut will you need? (pp. 170–173)

50. Alissa jogs in the park every 3 days. Jocelyn jogs in the park once a week on Saturday. If they met in the park on Saturday, April 30, when will they meet in the park again? (pp. 174–175)

NUMBER SENSE, CONCEPTS, AND OPERATIONS

1. The table below shows the number of members in the U.S. House of Representatives from each of four states.

> **TIP** Look for **important words.**
> See item 1. The important word is *prime*. Recall that a prime number is divisible only by itself and 1.

U.S. HOUSE OF REPRESENTATIVES	
State	**Number of Representatives**
Pennsylvania	21
Texas	30
New York	31
California	52

Which state has a number of representatives that is a prime number?

A Pennsylvania **C** New York

B Texas **D** California

2. The athletes attending the Festival of Sports can be divided evenly into basketball teams of 5 players each or into baseball teams of 9 players each. Which of the following could be the number of athletes attending the festival?

F 654 **H** 765

G 665 **J** 790

3. Mr. Hines is the director for a theatrical production. He hires 117 dancers to perform in a show. How many equal groups of 13 dancers can there be?

A 6 **C** 11

B 9 **D** 17

4. Explain It Wendy's car has 6.9 gallons of gas in the tank and can travel 20 miles on 1 gallon of gas. Does she need an estimate or an exact answer to know whether she can drive 150 miles? Explain your reasoning.

MEASUREMENT

5. Jessie wants to make a frame for her 18-inch by 12-inch painting. After finding the perimeter, she notices that she has twice as much framing material as she needs for her frame.

Which of the following paintings can she also make a frame for so that no framing material is left over?

F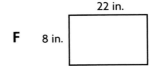
22 in. / 8 in.

G
36 in. / 24 in.

H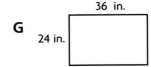
9 in. / 6 in.

J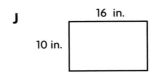
16 in. / 10 in.

6. Mel needs to buy a container of juice for a party. Which of the following measurements is the **greatest** capacity?

A 16 fl oz

B 24 fl oz

C 1.5 pt

D 1 qt

7. Explain It Noel says that the width of a playground is 32 yards. Werner says that the width of the same playground is 96 feet. Is 96 feet greater than, less than, or equal to 32 yards? Explain your reasoning.

8. Cara drove 517 miles in two days. The first day she drove 256 miles. Which equation could you use to find d, the distance she drove the second day?

F $256 - d = 517$

G $256 + d = 517$

H $517 + d = 256$

J $d - 256 = 517$

9. Yen made the table below to show the relationship between the diameter of a circle, x, and its radius, y.

x	2	4	6	8
y	1	2	3	4

Which of the following graphs represents the function shown in Yen's table?

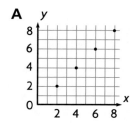

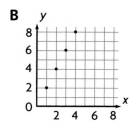

10. Explain It Ali is 15 years old. The equation $s - 4 = 15$ shows how Seth's age, s, is related to Ali's age. What is the relationship between Seth's age and Ali's age?

DATA ANALYSIS AND PROBABILITY

11. Below are the ages of the twenty members of the Big Oak Hiking Club.

10	12	18	20	35
24	22	8	5	15
33	35	18	25	11
32	14	21	4	25

Which frequency table correctly displays the data?

F

AGE OF MEMBERS	
Age	Frequency
0 – 10	5
11 – 20	8
21 – 30	4
31 – 40	5

G

AGE OF MEMBERS	
Age	Frequency
0 – 10	4
10 – 20	7
20 – 30	5
30 – 40	4

H

AGE OF MEMBERS	
Age	Frequency
0 – 10	4
11 – 20	7
21 – 30	5
31 – 40	4

J

AGE OF MEMBERS	
Age	Frequency
0 – 5	2
6 – 10	7
10 – 20	6
20 – 30	6

12. Explain It The masses of some adults, in kilograms, are 88, 94, 91, 84, 79, 100, 92, 90, 87. What is the median mass? Explain how you found your answer.

CHAPTER 8 Fraction Concepts

≡FAST FACT • **SCIENCE** There are more than 30 different species of cats living in forests, grasslands, deserts, and mountains around the world. The body lengths of these cats range from 2 ft to 10 ft. The average bobcat is $3\frac{1}{4}$ ft long while the average jaguar is 6 ft long.

PROBLEM SOLVING Compare the average length of a tiger to that of a lion.

AVERAGE BODY LENGTHS OF CATS

Average Body Length (in feet)

Cheetah	$4\frac{1}{2}$ ft
Snow Leopard	5 ft
Tiger	$9\frac{1}{4}$ ft
Jaguar	6 ft
Lion	$6\frac{1}{2}$ ft
Bobcat	$3\frac{1}{4}$ ft

Type of Cat

Check What You Know

Use this page to help you review and remember important skills needed for Chapter 8.

 Compare and Order Whole Numbers

Write <, >, or = for each 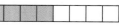.

1. 35,408 ● 35,480
2. 164,279 ● 164,277
3. 30 tens ● 3 hundreds
4. 1,089,315 ● 1,089,351
5. 2,918,808 ● 2,918,880
6. 356,782,436 ● 356,482,438

Order the numbers from greatest to least.

7. 3,400; 3,439; 3,399
8. 61,060; 62,000; 61,600
9. 98,450; 98,405; 98,540

 **Model Fractions**

Write the fraction for the shaded part.

10.
11.
12.
13.

14.
15.
16.
17.

 Model Percents

Write the percent for the shaded part.

18.
19.
20.
21.

VOCABULARY POWER

REVIEW

remainder [ri•mān′dər] *noun*

Remainder means "something left over" as in "Jim ate the remainder of the sandwich." Give an example relating *remainder* to a division problem.

 www.harcourtschool.com/mathglossary

PREVIEW

equivalent fractions
simplest form
mixed number
terminating decimal
repeating decimal

Equivalent Fractions and Simplest Form

Learn how to identify and write equivalent fractions, and how to write fractions in simplest form.

Vocabulary

equivalent fractions

simplest form

Fractions that name the same amount or the same part of a whole are called **equivalent fractions**. The figures show that the fractions $\frac{1}{4}$ and $\frac{2}{8}$ are equivalent, because they name the same part of a whole circle.

There are several ways to find equivalent fractions.

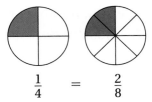

$\frac{1}{4} = \frac{2}{8}$

Read: One fourth equals two eighths.

Activity

You need: fraction bars

Find how many eighths are equivalent to $\frac{1}{2}$.

• Place $\frac{1}{8}$ fraction bars along the $\frac{1}{2}$ bar until the lengths are equal. How many $\frac{1}{8}$ bars are there?

• Complete. $\frac{1}{2} = \frac{\blacksquare}{8}$

• Use fraction bars. How many fourths are equivalent to $\frac{1}{2}$?

• Complete. $\frac{1}{2} = \frac{\blacksquare}{4}$

Another way to find an equivalent fraction is to multiply or divide the numerator and denominator of a fraction by the same number, other than 0 or 1. Doing this does not change the fraction's value, because this is the same as multiplying or dividing by 1.

EXAMPLE 1

Complete. $\frac{2}{4} = \frac{\blacksquare}{12}$

THINK: To get the denominator 12, I need to multiply the denominator 4 by 3. So, to get the missing numerator, I should also multiply the numerator 2 by 3.

$\frac{2 \times \boxed{3}}{4 \times \boxed{3}} = \frac{6}{12}$

$\frac{3}{3} = 1$, so the product is still equal to $\frac{2}{4}$.

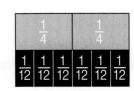

$\frac{2}{4} = \frac{6}{12}$

Read: Two fourths equals six twelfths.

EXAMPLE 2

Complete. $\frac{6}{10} = \frac{\blacksquare}{5}$

THINK: I can get the denominator 5 by dividing the denominator 10 by 2. So, to get the missing numerator, I should also divide the numerator 6 by 2.

$\frac{6 \div \boxed{2}}{10 \div \boxed{2}} = \frac{3}{5}$

$\frac{2}{2} = 1$, so the quotient is still equal to $\frac{6}{10}$.

$\frac{1}{10}$	$\frac{1}{10}$	$\frac{1}{10}$	$\frac{1}{10}$	$\frac{1}{10}$	$\frac{1}{10}$
$\frac{1}{5}$		$\frac{1}{5}$		$\frac{1}{5}$	

$$\frac{6}{10} = \frac{3}{5}$$

Read: Six tenths equals three fifths.

Math **I**dea ▶ When the numerator and denominator of a fraction have no common factors other than 1, the fraction is in **simplest form**.

$\frac{9}{16}$ **is** in simplest form because 9 and 16 have no common factors other than 1.

$\frac{9}{15}$ **is not** in simplest form because 9 and 15 have the common factor 3.

EXAMPLE 3

The sun is much farther from the Earth than the moon is. So, even though the sun is much larger than the moon, the sun's tide-raising force is only $\frac{12}{30}$ of the moon's force. Write $\frac{12}{30}$ in simplest form.

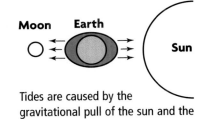

Tides are caused by the gravitational pull of the sun and the moon on Earth's oceans.

The world's highest tides occur in Canada's Bay of Fundy.

12: 1, 2, 3, 4, 6, 12   *Find the common factors of 12 and 30.*
30: 1, 2, 3, 5, 6, 10, 15, 30

$\frac{12}{30} = \frac{12 \div 3}{30 \div 3} = \frac{4}{10}$ *Divide the numerator and denominator by a common factor.*

$\frac{4}{10} = \frac{4 \div 2}{10 \div 2} = \frac{2}{5}$ *Repeat until the fraction is in simplest form.*

So, $\frac{2}{5}$ is the simplest form of $\frac{12}{30}$.

Bay of Fundy during low tide

In Example 3, the numerator and denominator were divided by common factors twice to find the simplest form. You can find it in just one step if you divide by the greatest common factor (GCF).

EXAMPLE 4

Bay of Fundy during high tide

Tides in Seattle, Washington, average only about $\frac{12}{42}$ of tidal heights in Canada's Bay of Fundy. Write $\frac{12}{42}$ in simplest form.

12: 1, 2, 3, 4, 6, 12   *Find the GCF of 12 and 42.*
42: 1, 2, 3, 6, 7, 14, 21, 42
GCF = 6

$\frac{12}{42} = \frac{12 \div 6}{42 \div 6} = \frac{2}{7}$ *Divide the numerator and denominator by the GCF.*

So, $\frac{2}{7}$ is the simplest form of $\frac{12}{42}$.

Think and ▶
Discuss

Look back at the lesson to answer each question.

1. **Explain** what you must do to find a fraction equivalent to $\frac{2}{3}$ if you first multiply the numerator by 5. What is the equivalent fraction?

2. **Explain** how you know that $\frac{5}{12}$ is in simplest form.

Guided ▶
Practice

Complete.

3. $\frac{3}{5} = \frac{\blacksquare}{20}$ 4. $\frac{3}{24} = \frac{\blacksquare}{8}$ 5. $\frac{8}{12} = \frac{\blacksquare}{6}$ 6. $\frac{3}{4} = \frac{\blacksquare}{24}$

7. $\frac{4}{8} = \frac{\blacksquare}{2}$ 8. $\frac{9}{24} = \frac{\blacksquare}{8}$ 9. $\frac{8}{18} = \frac{\blacksquare}{36}$ 10. $\frac{12}{54} = \frac{\blacksquare}{9}$

Write the factors common to the numerator and denominator.

11. $\frac{4}{8}$ 12. $\frac{9}{24}$ 13. $\frac{8}{18}$ 14. $\frac{12}{54}$

Write the fraction in simplest form.

15. $\frac{4}{32}$ 16. $\frac{14}{21}$ 17. $\frac{9}{54}$ 18. $\frac{48}{54}$

19. $\frac{22}{8}$ 20. $\frac{18}{5}$ 21. $\frac{9}{30}$ 22. $\frac{48}{32}$

Independent ▶
Practice

Complete.

23. $\frac{1}{2} = \frac{\blacksquare}{10}$ 24. $\frac{10}{15} = \frac{\blacksquare}{3}$ 25. $\frac{16}{20} = \frac{\blacksquare}{5}$ 26. $\frac{9}{27} = \frac{\blacksquare}{3}$

27. $\frac{2}{12} = \frac{1}{\blacksquare}$ 28. $\frac{\blacksquare}{36} = \frac{2}{9}$ 29. $\frac{21}{24} = \frac{7}{\blacksquare}$ 30. $\frac{40}{\blacksquare} = \frac{5}{8}$

31. $\frac{9}{\blacksquare} = \frac{3}{4}$ 32. $\frac{3}{\blacksquare} = \frac{12}{16}$ 33. $\frac{16}{28} = \frac{4}{\blacksquare}$ 34. $\frac{25}{40} = \frac{\blacksquare}{8}$

Write the factors common to the numerator and denominator.

35. $\frac{1}{7}$ 36. $\frac{9}{30}$ 37. $\frac{6}{27}$ 38. $\frac{9}{63}$

39. $\frac{10}{35}$ 40. $\frac{16}{40}$ 41. $\frac{3}{5}$ 42. $\frac{8}{10}$

Write the fraction in simplest form.

43. $\frac{4}{24}$ 44. $\frac{9}{12}$ 45. $\frac{6}{48}$ 46. $\frac{10}{15}$

47. $\frac{10}{18}$ 48. $\frac{20}{15}$ 49. $\frac{18}{90}$ 50. $\frac{28}{42}$

51. $\frac{22}{33}$ 52. $\frac{24}{30}$ 53. $\frac{60}{42}$ 54. $\frac{24}{28}$

55. $\frac{16}{64}$ 56. $\frac{8}{12}$ 57. $\frac{18}{90}$ 58. $\frac{48}{18}$

59. $\frac{4^2}{32}$ 60. $\frac{3^2}{12}$ 61. $\frac{2^3}{12}$ 62. $\frac{3^2}{6^2}$

TECHNOLOGY LINK

More Practice:
Harcourt Mega Math
Fraction Action,
Fraction Flare-Up,
Levels D, E

Problem Solving ▶ Applications

AMERICAN METEOR SOCIETY FIREBALL REPORT, 2001	
Month	**Number**
July	34
August	58
September	26
October	6
November	6
December	6

63. Use Data Look at the table at the left. A "fireball" is an extremely bright meteor occasionally seen streaking across the night sky. What fraction of the fireballs reported to the American Meteor Society during the last 6 months of 2001 occurred in July?

64. Technology Some calculators have a [Simp] key that can be used to simplify fractions. What fraction would this key sequence give? 10 [n] 15 [d] [Simp] [Enter]

65. **What's the Question?** Esteban has 6 apple muffins, 2 corn muffins, and 4 bran muffins. The answer is $\frac{1}{3}$ of the muffins.

66. 📓 **Write a problem** about everyday life that involves finding the simplest form of a fraction.

MIXED REVIEW AND TEST PREP

Evaluate each expression.

67. $(6 \div 3)^3 + 2^4$ (p. 48)

68. $(6^2 \div 3^2) + 1$ (p. 48)

69. 3.5×0.01 (p. 80)

⭐**70. TEST PREP** 0.5×1.2 (p. 80)

    A 0.06   **B** 0.6   **C** 6   **D** 6.2

⭐**71. TEST PREP** An adult's movie ticket costs \$7.50, and a child's ticket costs \$5.50. Find the total cost for 2 adults and 3 children. (p. 80)

    F \$13.00   **G** \$20.50   **H** \$24.00   **J** \$31.50

PROBLEM SOLVING 💡 THiNKer's CorNer

ALGEBRA You can use what you know about equivalent fractions to solve some types of algebraic equations.

A. $\frac{2}{3} = \frac{x - 5}{27}$

THINK: I need to find a fraction equivalent to $\frac{2}{3}$ that has 27 as its denominator. I'll multiply by 9.

$$\frac{2}{3} = \frac{\blacksquare}{27} \qquad \frac{2 \times 9}{3 \times 9} = \frac{18}{27}$$

So, $x - 5 = 18$. If 5 less than some number is 18, that number must be 23. So, $x = 23$.

B. $\frac{3}{s + 2} = \frac{18}{24}$

THINK: I need to find a fraction equivalent to $\frac{18}{24}$ that has 3 as its numerator. I'll divide by 6.

$$\frac{3}{\blacksquare} = \frac{18}{24} \qquad \frac{3}{4} = \frac{18 \div 6}{24 \div 6}$$

So, $s + 2 = 4$. If some number plus 2 equals 4, that number must be 2. So, $s = 2$.

Solve the equation.

1. $\frac{x + 3}{10} = \frac{1}{2}$

2. $\frac{5}{8} = \frac{c - 5}{40}$

3. $\frac{3}{b - 4} = \frac{9}{15}$

4. $\frac{1}{(2 + y)} = \frac{6}{24}$

5. $\frac{4}{9} = \frac{(w + 4)}{18}$

6. $\frac{(k - 5)}{8} = \frac{12}{32}$

EXTRA PRACTICE page 194, Set A

Mixed Numbers and Fractions

Learn how to write fractions as mixed numbers and mixed numbers as fractions.

QUICK REVIEW

1. $4 \times 7 + 2$ 2. $19 + 11$
3. $2 \times 7 + 5$ 4. $35 + 9$
5. $8 \times 4 + 6$

A total solar eclipse occurs when the moon passes between the sun and the Earth, blocking the sun's light.

Total solar eclipses are rare, with only three visible in most of the U.S. since 1963. Eclipses last different times. In the graph, each quarter-section of a circle represents $\frac{1}{4}$ minute. How long will the 2017 eclipse last? It is represented by 11 sections, or $\frac{11}{4}$ minutes.

The graph shows that 11 sections equal 2 whole minutes plus $\frac{3}{4}$ of another minute. So, $\frac{11}{4} = 2\frac{3}{4}$. The 2017 eclipse will last $2\frac{3}{4}$ minutes.

The fraction $\frac{11}{4}$ has a value greater than 1 because the numerator is greater than the denominator. Sometimes a fraction such as $\frac{11}{4}$ is called an "improper fraction." Any such fraction can be written as a **mixed number**, like $2\frac{3}{4}$.

APPROXIMATE LENGTH OF U.S. TOTAL SOLAR ECLIPSES

1963 ⊕ ◖

1970 ⊕ ⊕ ⊕ ◖

1979 ⊕ ⊕ ⊕

2017 ⊕ ⊕ ⊕ ◔

◸ $= \frac{1}{4}$ minute

Math Idea ▶ A mixed number has a whole-number part that is not 0 and a fraction part.

EXAMPLE 1

The longest total solar eclipse in the next 200 years will take place in 2186. It will last about $\frac{15}{2}$ minutes. Write $\frac{15}{2}$ as a mixed number.

$$\frac{15}{2} \rightarrow \begin{array}{r} 7\frac{1}{2} \\ 2\overline{)15} \\ -14 \\ \hline 1 \end{array}$$

Divide the numerator by the denominator. For the fraction part of the quotient, use the remainder as the numerator and the divisor as the denominator. Write the fraction in simplest form.

So, $\frac{15}{2} = 7\frac{1}{2}$. The 2186 eclipse will last about $7\frac{1}{2}$ minutes.

You can also write a mixed number as a fraction.

EXAMPLE 2

Write the mixed number $3\frac{2}{5}$ as a fraction.

$$3\frac{2}{5} = \frac{3 \times 5}{5} + \frac{2}{5} = \frac{(3 \times 5) + 2}{5} = \frac{17}{5}$$

Multiply the whole number by the denominator. Add the numerator. Use the same denominator.

So, $3\frac{2}{5} = \frac{17}{5}$.

Think and ▶ Discuss

Look back at the lesson to answer the question.

1. **Explain** how you know that a given number is a mixed number.

Write the fraction as a mixed number or a whole number.

2. $\frac{5}{3}$ 3. $\frac{7}{2}$ 4. $\frac{15}{5}$ 5. $\frac{11}{3}$ 6. $\frac{13}{4}$

Guided ▶ Practice

Write the mixed number as a fraction.

7. $1\frac{1}{4}$ 8. $1\frac{3}{5}$ 9. $2\frac{2}{3}$ 10. $3\frac{4}{5}$ 11. $5\frac{2}{7}$

PRACTICE AND PROBLEM SOLVING

Independent ▶ Practice

Write the fraction as a mixed number or a whole number.

12. $\frac{7}{4}$ 13. $\frac{9}{2}$ 14. $\frac{11}{2}$ 15. $\frac{23}{4}$ 16. $\frac{27}{3}$

17. $\frac{31}{6}$ 18. $\frac{18}{11}$ 19. $\frac{90}{7}$ 20. $\frac{104}{13}$ 21. $\frac{150}{9}$

22. $\frac{x}{y}$ for $x = 18$ and $y = 12$ 23. $\frac{a}{b}$ for $a = 55$ and $b = 15$

Write the mixed number as a fraction.

24. $3\frac{2}{3}$ 25. $6\frac{1}{2}$ 26. $5\frac{1}{3}$ 27. $1\frac{9}{10}$ 28. $4\frac{1}{9}$

29. $9\frac{1}{4}$ 30. $2\frac{3}{8}$ 31. $4\frac{9}{11}$ 32. $11\frac{4}{9}$ 33. $18\frac{3}{5}$

Problem Solving ▶

34. **?** **What's the Error?** Marti changed $3\frac{1}{4}$ to $12\frac{1}{4}$. What mistake did she make? What is the correct answer?

35. **Write About It** Can any fraction be written as a mixed number? Explain.

36. **≡FAST FACT • SCIENCE** On February 26, 1998, a total solar eclipse lasted $4\frac{3}{20}$ min. On August 11, 1999, a total solar eclipse lasted $\frac{143}{60}$ min. Which lasted longer? How much longer?

MIXED REVIEW AND TEST PREP

Write the prime factorization of each number. (p.168)

37. 36   38. 42   39. 23

40. Is the following question biased? If so, rewrite it so that it is unbiased: The film *Time Warp* is great, isn't it? (p. 112)

41. **TEST PREP** Noella is hiking a 25-km trail. She has hiked 3.8 km to the first overlook and another 6.5 km to the second overlook. How many kilometers does she have left to hike? (p. 76)

  A 9.3 km   **B** 10.3 km   **C** 14.7 km   **D** 15.7 km

EXTRA PRACTICE page 194, Set B

Compare and Order

Learn how to compare and order fractions and mixed numbers.

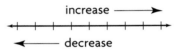

Remember that values increase as you move to the right on a number line. Values decrease as you move left.

increase ⟶

◄—— decrease

QUICK REVIEW

1. $\frac{1}{2} = \frac{\blacksquare}{10}$ 2. $\frac{2}{3} = \frac{\blacksquare}{9}$ 3. $\frac{4}{5} = \frac{\blacksquare}{20}$ 4. $\frac{3}{8} = \frac{\blacksquare}{24}$

5. Write the first four multiples of 12.

If two fractions have the same denominator, the fraction with the greater numerator is greater. So, $\frac{7}{12} > \frac{5}{12}$ because $7 > 5$, and $1\frac{5}{8} > 1\frac{3}{8}$ because $5 > 3$. If two mixed numbers have different whole numbers, the mixed number with the greater whole number is greater. So, $3\frac{3}{8} > 1\frac{7}{8}$ because $3 > 1$.

If fractions or mixed numbers do not have the same denominators, a number line can be used to compare and order them. The number line shows that $\frac{1}{4} < \frac{3}{8} < \frac{1}{2}$. From least to greatest the order is $\frac{1}{4}, \frac{3}{8}, \frac{1}{2}$. The number line also shows that $1\frac{3}{8} < 1\frac{1}{2} < 1\frac{3}{4}$. From least to greatest the order is $1\frac{3}{8}, 1\frac{1}{2}, 1\frac{3}{4}$.

You can also use common multiples to compare and order fractions and mixed numbers.

EXAMPLE

George Washington Carver made over 500 useful agricultural products using peanuts, sweet potatoes, and pecans. About $\frac{7}{10}$ of the products used peanuts, and about $\frac{1}{4}$ used sweet potatoes. Did Carver make more products with sweet potatoes or with peanuts?

To compare $\frac{7}{10}$ and $\frac{1}{4}$, find equivalent fractions with any common denominator.

$\frac{7}{10} = \frac{7 \times 4}{10 \times 4} = \frac{28}{40}$

$\frac{1}{4} = \frac{1 \times 10}{4 \times 10} = \frac{10}{40}$

$\frac{28}{40} > \frac{10}{40}$, so $\frac{7}{10} > \frac{1}{4}$.

Rewrite the fractions, using 40 as the common denominator.

Compare $\frac{28}{40}$ and $\frac{10}{40}$.

So, Carver made more products with peanuts.

• What other denominators could you use?

George Washington Carver, one of America's most honored scientists, was born in 1864.

• Use the least common multiple, LCM, to compare $1\frac{3}{4}$ and $1\frac{3}{8}$.

Think and ▶ Discuss

Look back at the lesson to answer the question.

1. **Explain** how to compare $1\frac{1}{8}$ and $1\frac{5}{8}$.

Guided ▶ Practice

Compare. Write <, >, or = for each ●.

2. $\frac{13}{20}$ ● $\frac{9}{20}$

3. $\frac{1}{4}$ ● $\frac{9}{20}$

4. $\frac{5}{6}$ ● $\frac{2}{3}$

5. $1\frac{3}{8}$ ● $1\frac{6}{16}$

Order from least to greatest.

6. $\frac{3}{4}, \frac{1}{3}, \frac{11}{12}$

7. $\frac{2}{3}, \frac{1}{4}, \frac{6}{12}$

8. $\frac{1}{3}, \frac{5}{12}, \frac{2}{4}$

9. $\frac{5}{6}, \frac{1}{4}, \frac{1}{2}$

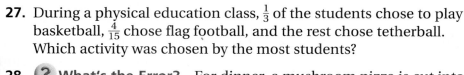

PRACTICE AND PROBLEM SOLVING

Independent ▶ Practice

Compare. Write <, >, or = for each ●.

10. $\frac{6}{7}$ ● $\frac{4}{7}$

11. $\frac{3}{11}$ ● $\frac{4}{11}$

12. $\frac{4}{12}$ ● $\frac{1}{3}$

13. $\frac{17}{20}$ ● $\frac{3}{5}$

14. $\frac{5}{6}$ ● $\frac{15}{18}$

15. $\frac{7}{9}$ ● $\frac{11}{12}$

16. $1\frac{3}{4}$ ● $1\frac{5}{8}$

17. $2\frac{11}{15}$ ● $1\frac{2}{3}$

Order from least to greatest.

18. $\frac{9}{12}, \frac{1}{2}, \frac{2}{6}$

19. $\frac{4}{12}, \frac{4}{6}, \frac{7}{12}$

20. $\frac{7}{12}, \frac{5}{6}, \frac{1}{2}$

21. $\frac{5}{8}, \frac{1}{2}, \frac{3}{4}$

22. $\frac{2}{5}, \frac{3}{10}, \frac{1}{2}$

23. $\frac{11}{16}, \frac{3}{4}, \frac{5}{8}$

24. $\frac{1}{3}, \frac{1}{6}, \frac{1}{2}$

25. $\frac{2}{3}, \frac{2}{9}, \frac{2}{6}$

26. $1\frac{3}{4}, 1\frac{1}{12}, 1\frac{5}{8}$

Problem Solving ▶ Applications

27. During a physical education class, $\frac{1}{3}$ of the students chose to play basketball, $\frac{4}{15}$ chose flag football, and the rest chose tetherball. Which activity was chosen by the most students?

28. **? What's the Error?** For dinner, a mushroom pizza is cut into eighths and a cheese pizza into twelfths. After the meal there are 3 pieces of each left. Pablo tells his mother that the same amount of each pizza is left. What mistake did he make?

29. **REASONING** Write an equivalent fraction for $\frac{8}{23}$ with 16 as the numerator. Compare the equivalent fraction with $\frac{16}{43}$. Explain your reasoning.

MIXED REVIEW AND TEST PREP

Evaluate each expression for $a = 2.3$, $b = 0.7$, and $c = 5.4$. (p. 94)

30. $a - b + c$

31. $(b \times 5) + a$

32. Find the LCM of 8 and 12. (p. 170)

33. Find the GCF of 16 and 40. (p. 170)

34. **TEST PREP** There are 12 cans of soup in 1 case. How many cases should you order if you need 132 cans of soup? (p. 24)

   A 10   **B** 11   **C** 1,200   **D** 1,584

Explore Fractions and Decimals

MATH LAB

Explore how to convert fractions to decimals.

You need graph paper, scissors, colored pencils.

You can use decimal squares to help you convert fractions to decimals.

Activity

• Cut out a 10 × 10 grid from graph paper. Fold it into 2 equal parts. Then use a colored pencil to shade one of the equal parts. What fraction of the grid is shaded?

• How many small squares are in the whole grid? How many of these squares are shaded? What fraction compares these shaded squares to those in the whole grid? What decimal can you write for this fraction?

• How many columns are in the whole grid? How many columns are shaded? What fraction compares the shaded columns to the whole grid? What decimal can you write for this fraction?

• Are the fractions $\frac{1}{2}$, $\frac{5}{10}$, and $\frac{50}{100}$ equivalent? How do you know? What are two ways to write the fraction $\frac{1}{2}$ as a decimal?

• Cut out another 10 × 10 grid. Fold the grid into 5 equal parts and shade one part. How many rows or columns are shaded? How can you write $\frac{1}{5}$ as a decimal?

Think and Discuss

• How can you show tenths in a 10 × 10 grid?

• How can you show hundredths in a 10 × 10 grid?

• What fractions are easiest to write as decimals?

• How is the 10 × 10 grid helpful for writing fractions as decimals?

Practice

Write the fraction as a decimal. Use decimal squares.

1. $\frac{3}{10}$ 2. $\frac{60}{100}$ 3. $\frac{7}{10}$ 4. $\frac{3}{5}$ 5. $\frac{90}{100}$

6. $\frac{2}{10}$ 7. $\frac{2}{5}$ 8. $\frac{6}{10}$ 9. $\frac{85}{100}$ 10. $\frac{4}{5}$

TECHNOLOGY LINK

More Practice:
Harcourt Mega Math Fraction Action,
Number Line Mine,
Level N

Fractions, Decimals, and Percents

Learn how to convert fractions to decimals, decimals to fractions, and fractions to percents.

Remember that *percent* means "out of one hundred." For example, 25% means "25 out of 100."

QUICK REVIEW

1. $24 \div 4$ **2.** $144 \div 6$ **3.** $155 \div 5$ **4.** $137 \div 3$ **5.** $253 \div 7$

You can use place value to write a decimal as a fraction.

0.7 **THINK:** *"seven tenths"*

$0.7 = \frac{7}{10}$

0.29 **THINK:** *"twenty-nine hundredths"*

$0.29 = \frac{29}{100}$

A number line can be used to help you write numbers as fractions, decimals, and percents. The number line shows that $\frac{2}{5} = 0.4 = 40\%$.

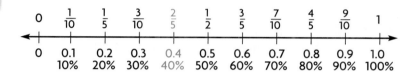

To rewrite a fraction as a decimal, use long division or a calculator.

EXAMPLE 1

A newborn koala is about $\frac{3}{4}$ in. long. Change $\frac{3}{4}$ to a decimal.

Use long division.

$$\begin{array}{r} 0.75 \\ 4)\overline{3.00} \\ -2\,8 \\ \hline 20 \\ -20 \\ \hline 0 \end{array}$$

Divide the numerator by the denominator.

So, $\frac{3}{4} = 0.75$.

Use a calculator.

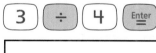

$3 \div 4 = \qquad 0.75$

The decimal 0.75 is an example of a **terminating decimal**. A decimal terminates if you have a remainder of zero when using long division.

The decimal for the fraction $\frac{4}{11}$ does not terminate. When you divide 4 by 11, you never reach a remainder of zero. This decimal is a **repeating decimal** because it has a pattern of repeating remainders after each division step. This pattern causes digits in the quotient to repeat.

$$\begin{array}{r} 0.3636 \\ 11)\overline{4.0000} \\ -3\,3 \\ \hline 70 \\ -66 \\ \hline 40 \\ -33 \\ \hline 70 \\ -66 \\ \hline 4 \end{array}$$

To write a repeating decimal, show the pattern and then three dots, or draw a bar over the repeating digits.

$\frac{4}{11} = 0.363636\ldots \qquad \frac{4}{11} = 0.\overline{36}$

191

To compare a fraction and a decimal, you can first rewrite the fraction as a decimal. Then compare the decimals.

EXAMPLE 2

A newborn panda weighs about $\frac{1}{4}$ lb. A newborn cocker spaniel weighs about 0.4 lb. Which animal weighs less at birth?

Use long division.

$$\begin{array}{r} 0.25 \\ 4\overline{)1.00} \\ -8 \\ \hline 20 \\ -20 \\ \hline 0 \end{array}$$

Divide the numerator by the denominator.

Use a calculator.

$0.25 < 0.4$, so $\frac{1}{4} < 0.4$.

So, a newborn panda weighs less than a newborn cocker spaniel.

To write a fraction as a percent, first convert the fraction to a decimal. Then write the decimal as a percent.

EXAMPLE 3

The barrow ground squirrel of Point Barrow, Alaska, is the world's longest-hibernating animal. The squirrel hibernates $\frac{9}{12}$ of the year. What percent of the year does it hibernate?

$\frac{9}{12} = 0.75$ *Use long division or a calculator to rewrite the fraction as a decimal.*

$0.75 = \frac{75}{100}$ THINK: *75 hundredths. Write the decimal as a fraction.*

$= 75\%$ THINK: *Percent means "out of one hundred." So, 75 hundredths is 75 percent.*

So, the barrow ground squirrel hibernates 75% of the year.

CHECK FOR UNDERSTANDING

Think and Discuss ▶ **Look back at the lesson to answer each question.**

1. **Explain** how to use place value to change 0.026 to a fraction.

2. **Compare** a repeating decimal with a terminating decimal.

Guided Practice ▶ **Write the decimal as a fraction.**

3. 0.7   **4.** 0.39   **5.** 0.105   **6.** 0.007

Write as a decimal. Tell whether the decimal terminates or repeats.

7. $\frac{7}{20}$ **8.** $\frac{2}{3}$ **9.** $\frac{8}{11}$ **10.** $\frac{5}{6}$

Compare. Write $<$, $>$, or $=$ for each ●.

11. 0.62 ● $\frac{1}{2}$ **12.** $\frac{12}{20}$ ● 0.9 **13.** $\frac{1}{8}$ ● 0.125

Write the fraction as a percent.

14. $\frac{7}{10}$ **15.** $\frac{1}{5}$ **16.** $\frac{1}{4}$ **17.** $\frac{40}{100}$

Independent ▸ Practice

Write the decimal as a fraction.

18. 0.4   **19.** 0.06   **20.** 0.35   **21.** 0.61

22. 0.115   **23.** 0.205   **24.** 0.079   **25.** 0.009

Write as a decimal. Tell whether the decimal terminates or repeats.

26. $\frac{1}{5}$ **27.** $\frac{1}{6}$ **28.** $\frac{1}{15}$ **29.** $\frac{5}{8}$

30. $\frac{5}{12}$ **31.** $\frac{1}{9}$ **32.** $\frac{11}{12}$ **33.** $\frac{9}{25}$

34. $\frac{17}{33}$ **35.** $\frac{15}{99}$ **36.** $\frac{1}{7}$ **37.** $\frac{2}{7}$

Compare. Write <, >, or = for each ●.

38. $\frac{1}{10}$ ● 0.04   **39.** 0.15 ● $\frac{3}{20}$ **40.** $\frac{1}{2}$ ● 0.52

41. 0.65 ● $\frac{3}{4}$ **42.** $\frac{1}{20}$ ● 0.1   **43.** 0.58 ● $\frac{7}{12}$

Write the fraction as a percent.

44. $\frac{9}{10}$ **45.** $\frac{3}{4}$ **46.** $\frac{1}{2}$ **47.** $\frac{6}{100}$

48. $\frac{3}{5}$ **49.** $\frac{25}{50}$ **50.** $\frac{3}{2}$ **51.** $\frac{1}{200}$

Problem Solving ▸ Applications

52. The goal of the East Side Animal Shelter is to have 0.8 of its animals adopted. One week, the shelter found homes for 20 of its 24 animals. Did the shelter reach its goal? Explain.

Use Data   **For 53–55, use the table.**

53. Write Brian's math test score as a decimal.

54. Did Juan get a higher score on the math or science test?

55. Which student got a higher score on the math test than on the science test?

STUDENT	MATH SCORE	SCIENCE SCORE
Brian	$\frac{18}{25}$	0.95
Juan	$\frac{21}{25}$	0.85
Sabina	$\frac{17}{25}$	0.75
Megan	$\frac{23}{25}$	0.90

56. Vocabulary Power In mathematics, a decimal *terminates* if the reminder is zero when using long division. Find another meaning of *terminate*. How is it similar to the mathematical meaning?

MIXED REVIEW AND TEST PREP

57. Write $4\frac{1}{2}$ as a fraction. (p. 186)

58. Write $\frac{36}{5}$ as a mixed number. (p. 186)

59. $79.02 - 2.13$ (p. 76)

60. $48.541 + 11$ (p. 76)

61. TEST PREP Tim's mean score on five history tests is 92. His scores on the first four tests are 89, 100, 93, and 90. What is Tim's score on the fifth test? (p. 118)

  A 88   **B** 90   **C** 92   **D** 93

EXTRA PRACTICE page 194, Set D

193

Set A (pp. 182–185)

Write the fraction in simplest form.

1. $\frac{24}{80}$
2. $\frac{14}{63}$
3. $\frac{24}{56}$
4. $\frac{15}{60}$
5. $\frac{16}{40}$
6. $\frac{50}{90}$

Complete.

7. $\frac{9}{12} = \frac{\blacksquare}{4}$

8. $\frac{7}{42} = \frac{\blacksquare}{6}$

9. $\frac{25}{\blacksquare} = \frac{5}{10}$

10. $\frac{3}{7} = \frac{21}{\blacksquare}$

11. $\frac{1}{12} = \frac{\blacksquare}{144}$

12. $\frac{9}{20} = \frac{\blacksquare}{60}$

13. $\frac{5}{\blacksquare} = \frac{15}{27}$

14. $\frac{12}{\blacksquare} = \frac{3}{8}$

Set B (pp. 186–187)

Write the fraction as a mixed number or a whole number.

1. $\frac{7}{3}$
2. $\frac{9}{2}$
3. $\frac{36}{5}$
4. $\frac{72}{8}$
5. $\frac{10}{2}$
6. $\frac{13}{4}$
7. $\frac{36}{6}$
8. $\frac{12}{9}$

Write the mixed number as a fraction.

9. $4\frac{1}{4}$
10. $5\frac{2}{3}$
11. $2\frac{1}{8}$
12. $7\frac{1}{9}$
13. $3\frac{4}{7}$
14. $1\frac{6}{11}$
15. $4\frac{3}{8}$
16. $15\frac{3}{4}$

Set C (pp. 188–189)

Compare. Write $<$, $>$, or $=$ for each ●.

1. $\frac{5}{9}$ ● $\frac{1}{2}$
2. $\frac{3}{8}$ ● $\frac{1}{5}$
3. $\frac{7}{25}$ ● $\frac{3}{5}$
4. $2\frac{3}{5}$ ● $2\frac{12}{20}$

Order from least to greatest.

5. $\frac{1}{3}, \frac{1}{6}, \frac{1}{10}$
6. $\frac{4}{9}, \frac{2}{3}, \frac{3}{8}$
7. $1\frac{1}{9}, 1\frac{3}{4}, 1\frac{5}{12}$

Set D (pp. 191–193)

Write the decimal as a fraction.

1. 0.9
2. 0.081
3. 0.29

Write as a decimal. Tell whether the decimal terminates or repeats.

4. $\frac{3}{8}$
5. $\frac{5}{16}$
6. $\frac{1}{3}$
7. $\frac{7}{9}$

Compare. Write $<$, $>$, or $=$ for each ●.

8. $\frac{3}{10}$ ● 0.03
9. $\frac{2}{3}$ ● 0.7
10. 0.79 ● $\frac{5}{8}$
11. 0.15 ● $\frac{3}{20}$

Write each fraction as a percent.

12. $\frac{6}{25}$
13. $\frac{7}{10}$
14. $\frac{9}{20}$
15. $\frac{4}{5}$

1. **VOCABULARY** When the numerator and denominator of a fraction have no common factors other than 1, the fraction is in __?__. (p. 183)

2. **VOCABULARY** A number that is made up of a whole number and a fraction is called a __?__. (p. 186)

Write the fraction in simplest form. (pp. 182–185)

3. $\frac{6}{12}$

4. $\frac{12}{16}$

5. $\frac{25}{30}$

Complete. (pp. 182–185)

6. $\frac{3}{5} = \frac{\blacksquare}{20}$

7. $\frac{2}{\blacksquare} = \frac{10}{35}$

8. $\frac{24}{32} = \frac{\blacksquare}{8}$

Write the fraction as a mixed number or a whole number. (pp. 186–187)

9. $\frac{7}{3}$

10. $\frac{30}{6}$

11. $\frac{19}{4}$

Write the mixed number as a fraction. (pp. 186–187)

12. $1\frac{5}{6}$

13. $3\frac{1}{3}$

14. $5\frac{7}{8}$

Compare. Write $<$, $>$, or $=$ for each ●. (pp. 188–189)

15. $\frac{7}{8}$ ● $\frac{5}{8}$

16. $\frac{2}{3}$ ● $\frac{8}{12}$

17. $\frac{1}{3}$ ● $\frac{1}{2}$

18. $\frac{1}{2}$ ● $\frac{11}{20}$

19. $3\frac{3}{4}$ ● $3\frac{3}{8}$

20. $2\frac{7}{25}$ ● $2\frac{1}{5}$

Write the decimal as a fraction. (pp. 191–193)

21. 0.27

22. 0.1

23. 0.089

Write as a decimal. Tell whether the decimal terminates or repeats.
(pp. 191–193)

24. $\frac{1}{4}$

25. $\frac{5}{6}$

26. $\frac{7}{20}$

Write the fraction as a percent. (pp. 191–193)

27. $\frac{3}{4}$

28. $\frac{9}{100}$

29. $\frac{11}{25}$

30. In the election for class president, Marcus received $\frac{5}{12}$ of the votes, Denise received $\frac{1}{4}$ of the votes, and Alonzo received $\frac{1}{3}$ of the votes. Who won the election? (pp. 188–189)

31. **Use Data** Use the table to find the fraction of the new November films that are rated PG-13. Write your answer in simplest form. What percent is this? (pp. 182–185)

32. Of all U.S. car tunnels longer than 1 mile, $\frac{3}{8}$ are in Pennsylvania. Change $\frac{3}{8}$ to a decimal. (pp. 191–193)

33. On Library Day, $\frac{13}{20}$ of the students at Pine Street School checked books out of the library. What percent of the students checked out books? (pp. 191–193)

NOVEMBER FILMS	
Rating	**Number**
G	3
PG-13	8
PG	5
R	4

NUMBER SENSE, CONCEPTS, AND OPERATIONS

1. The average high temperature for the month of January in Shreveport, Louisiana, is 56 degrees Fahrenheit. Which of the following shows the prime factorization of 56?

   A $2^2 \times 3$

   B $2^2 \times 7$

   C $2 \times 4 \times 7$

   D $2^3 \times 7$

2. Written in expanded form, the elevation of Colorado's North Maroon Peak is $10{,}000 + 4{,}000 + 10 + 4$. What is the elevation written in standard form?

   F 15,014   H 14,014

   G 14,140   J 5,140

3. The table gives the fraction of all commuters that drive to work alone.

COMMUTERS THAT DRIVE ALONE	
City	**Fraction**
Houston	$\frac{18}{25}$
Jacksonville	$\frac{3}{4}$
Los Angeles	$\frac{13}{20}$
San Diego	$\frac{7}{10}$

   In which city does the **greatest** fraction of commuters drive alone?

   A Houston   C Los Angeles

   B Jacksonville   D San Diego

4. **Explain It** Marlene ran $\frac{1}{3}$ mile. Dan ran $\frac{3}{8}$ mile. How much farther did Dan run than Marlene? Explain how you found the answer.

ALGEBRAIC THINKING

5. Julie painted this pattern in art class.

   If the pattern continues, what are the next three shapes?

   F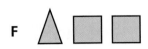

   G

   H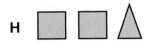

   J

6. Jake and Martie are soccer players. Let n represent the number of hours Jake practiced soccer one month. Martie practiced 6 more hours than twice the number of hours Jake practiced. Which expression shows this relationship?

   A $2n + 6$

   B $2(n + 6)$

   C $6n + 2$

   D $6(n + 2)$

7. **Explain It** The total length of an alligator lizard is its body length plus its tail length. An alligator lizard with a total length of 18 inches has a body length of b inches. Is the tail length $18 - b$ inches or $b - 18$ inches? Explain your answer.

8. The pictograph shows the results of a survey of students and their favorite types of music.

STUDENTS' FAVORITE MUSIC	
Types of Music	**Number of Votes**
Hip Hop	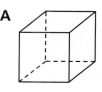
Dance	
Country	
Reggae	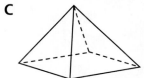

Key: Each ♫ = 5 votes.

How many more votes did the type of music with the most votes receive than the type with the fewest votes?

F   3

G   9

H   15

J   25

9. Tina played 5 games of miniature golf one week. Tina had the following scores for the 5 games: 78, 80, 69, 75, 73. Which of the following is the mean score?

A   75

B   74

C   71

D   50

10. **Explain It** Jack surveyed all the boys in his sixth-grade class to find out what a typical sixth grader does for fun on the weekend. The results showed that they usually played or watched a team sport. Was this an unbiased sample? Explain why or why not.

11. What type of transformation moved the pair of musical notes from position *A* to position *B*?

F   tessellation

G   rotation

H   reflection

J   translation

12. Hallie built a greenhouse with a roof shaped like a rectangular pyramid. Which of the following figures could be the shape of the roof?

> **TIP** **Choose the answer.** See item 12. When the answer choices are pictures, look at each picture alone while you cover the others. Choose the picture that best fits the description given in the problem.

A
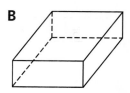

C

B

D

13. **Explain It** The figure shows the approximate dimensions of Philadelphia's Rittenhouse Square. Could the figure be called a rectangle? Explain your answer.

Rittenhouse Square

500 ft

500 ft

CHAPTER 9

Add and Subtract Fractions and Mixed Numbers

≡FAST FACT • SOCIAL STUDIES A Navajo weaver may spend as many as 238 hours to complete a handmade 3 ft × 5 ft rug. Traditional Navajo rugs often have geometric patterns woven into them.

PROBLEM SOLVING One of the patterns from the rug in the picture is shown at the right. What fraction of the small squares in the picture are dark brown border squares? What benchmark fraction is this closest to?

Check What You Know

Use this page to help you review and remember important skills needed for Chapter 9.

✅ Simplify Fractions

Write each fraction in simplest form.

1. $\frac{6}{8}$
2. $\frac{5}{10}$
3. $\frac{4}{12}$
4. $\frac{18}{27}$
5. $\frac{12}{9}$

6. $\frac{16}{20}$
7. $\frac{12}{8}$
8. $\frac{9}{15}$
9. $\frac{10}{20}$
10. $\frac{15}{18}$

11. $\frac{26}{39}$
12. $\frac{12}{16}$
13. $\frac{15}{9}$
14. $\frac{6}{32}$
15. $\frac{17}{51}$

16. $\frac{48}{54}$
17. $\frac{100}{200}$
18. $\frac{25}{10}$
19. $\frac{80}{64}$
20. $\frac{84}{96}$

✅ Add and Subtract Like Fractions

Find the sum or difference. Write each answer in simplest form.

21. $\frac{1}{3} + \frac{1}{3}$
22. $\frac{3}{5} + \frac{1}{5}$
23. $\frac{3}{8} + \frac{1}{8}$
24. $\frac{5}{6} + \frac{1}{6}$
25. $\frac{1}{9} + \frac{2}{9}$

26. $\frac{3}{4} - \frac{1}{4}$
27. $\frac{5}{8} - \frac{3}{8}$
28. $\frac{2}{3} - \frac{1}{3}$
29. $\frac{4}{5} - \frac{2}{5}$
30. $\frac{6}{7} - \frac{2}{7}$

31. $\frac{3}{6} + \frac{2}{6}$
32. $\frac{7}{8} - \frac{1}{8}$
33. $\frac{3}{4} + \frac{1}{4}$
34. $\frac{7}{8} - \frac{3}{8}$
35. $\frac{3}{10} + \frac{1}{10}$

36. $\frac{4}{9} - \frac{2}{9}$
37. $\frac{1}{12} + \frac{7}{12}$
38. $\frac{13}{14} - \frac{3}{14}$
39. $\frac{1}{15} + \frac{8}{15}$
40. $\frac{8}{21} - \frac{5}{21}$

VOCABULARY POWER

REVIEW

equivalent [ē•kwiv′ə•lənt] *adj*

The prefix *equi-* means "equal" or "equally." *Equivalent* means "having the same value." What does this meaning tell you about two quantities that are equivalent?

PREVIEW

unlike fractions

least common denominator (LCD)

 www.harcourtschool.com/mathglossary

Estimate Sums and Differences

Learn how to estimate sums and differences of fractions and mixed numbers.

Estimate the sum or difference.

| 1. | 823
+116 | 2. | 364
−232 | 3. | 736
−381 | 4. | 589
+ 42 | 5. | 6,755
− 482 |

You can decide whether a fraction is closest to 0, $\frac{1}{2}$, or 1.

One Way Use a number line.

Look at the number line below. Is $\frac{3}{8}$ closest to 0, $\frac{1}{2}$, or 1?

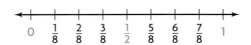

$\frac{3}{8}$ is closest to $\frac{1}{2}$.

Another Way Compare the numerator to the denominator.

| $\frac{1}{8}$ | $\frac{1}{6}$ | $\frac{2}{9}$ | | $\frac{4}{9}$ | $\frac{5}{8}$ | $\frac{2}{3}$ | | $\frac{7}{9}$ | $\frac{5}{6}$ | $\frac{7}{8}$ |

The numerators are much less than half the denominators. So, the fractions are close to 0.

The numerators are about one half the denominators. So, the fractions are close to $\frac{1}{2}$.

The numerators are about the same as the denominators. So, the fractions are close to 1.

Sometimes when you add and subtract fractions, you do not need an exact answer.

EXAMPLE 1

The Pacific Crest Trail runs from Mexico to Canada, a distance of 1,680 miles. The Tanner family is hiking the 848-mile portion from Ashland, Oregon, to Stehekin, Washington. The family hiked $\frac{3}{10}$ of this portion in June. Then they hiked another $\frac{3}{8}$ in July. About how much of the trail through Oregon and Washington did the Tanners hike in June and July?

Estimate $\frac{3}{10} + \frac{3}{8}$.

$$\frac{3}{10} \rightarrow \frac{1}{2}$$
$$+\frac{3}{8} \rightarrow +\frac{1}{2}$$
$$\overline{\phantom{+\frac{3}{8}} 1}$$

$\frac{3}{10}$ is between 0 and $\frac{1}{2}$, but closer to $\frac{1}{2}$.

$\frac{3}{8}$ is between 0 and $\frac{1}{2}$, but closer to $\frac{1}{2}$.

The sum is greater than $\frac{1}{2}$, but less than 1.

So, the Tanners hiked more than $\frac{1}{2}$ of the trail, but not all of it.

EXAMPLE 2

Estimate $\frac{7}{8} - \frac{5}{6}$.

$\frac{7}{8} \rightarrow 1$ $\frac{7}{8}$ is between $\frac{1}{2}$ and 1, but closer to 1.

$-\frac{5}{6} \rightarrow -1$ $\frac{5}{6}$ is between $\frac{1}{2}$ and 1, but closer to 1.

$\overline{0}$ Subtract.

The fractions are close to each other, and their difference is close to 0.

Remember that a mixed number is a whole number and a fraction combined. $4\frac{2}{5}$ is a mixed number.

Look at the number line below. Is $3\frac{5}{8}$ in. closest to 3 in., $3\frac{1}{2}$ in., or 4 in.?

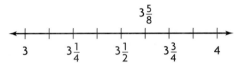

$3\frac{5}{8}$ in. is closest to $3\frac{1}{2}$ in.

To estimate sums and differences of mixed numbers, compare each mixed number to the nearest whole number or the nearest $\frac{1}{2}$.

EXAMPLE 3

Bianca's goal is to jog 15 miles a week. So far this week she has jogged $2\frac{5}{6}$ mi and $3\frac{1}{10}$ mi. About how many more miles must she jog to meet her goal?

Estimate $15 - \left(2\frac{5}{6} + 3\frac{1}{10}\right)$.

$15 - \left(2\frac{5}{6} + 3\frac{1}{10}\right)$ $2\frac{5}{6}$ is close to 3, and $3\frac{1}{10}$ is close to 3.

$ \downarrow \downarrow$

$15 - (3 \ + 3)$ Add.

$15 - 6 = 9$ Subtract.

So, Bianca needs to jog about 9 more miles to meet her goal.

You can find a range to estimate a sum or difference.

EXAMPLE 4

Estimate $5\frac{3}{4} - 4\frac{7}{8}$.

Since $5\frac{3}{4}$ is halfway between $5\frac{1}{2}$ and 6, find two estimates.

$5\frac{3}{4} - 4\frac{7}{8}$ $5\frac{3}{4}$ is close to 6, and $4\frac{7}{8}$ is close to 5. $5\frac{3}{4} - 4\frac{7}{8}$ $5\frac{3}{4}$ is close to $5\frac{1}{2}$, and $4\frac{7}{8}$ is close to 5.

$\downarrow \quad \downarrow$ *AND* $\downarrow \quad \downarrow$

$6 - 5 = 1$ Subtract. $5\frac{1}{2} - 5 = \frac{1}{2}$ Subtract.

The range is $\frac{1}{2}$ to 1. A good estimate of $5\frac{3}{4} - 4\frac{7}{8}$ would be $\frac{3}{4}$, which is halfway between $\frac{1}{2}$ and 1.

Think and ▶
Discuss

Look back at the lesson to answer each question.

1. **Explain** how to round fractions less than 1.

2. **Compare** the numerator and denominator of several fractions greater than $\frac{1}{2}$. What do you notice about the relationship between the numerator and denominator?

Guided ▶
Practice

Use the number line to tell whether the fraction is closest to 0, $\frac{1}{2}$, or 1. Write *close to 0, close to $\frac{1}{2}$,* or *close to 1.*

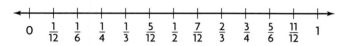

3. $\frac{11}{12}$ 4. $\frac{1}{12}$ 5. $\frac{1}{3}$ 6. $\frac{2}{3}$

Estimate the sum or difference.

7. $\frac{3}{5} + \frac{6}{7}$ 8. $\frac{10}{12} - \frac{4}{5}$ 9. $\frac{7}{8} - \frac{4}{9}$ 10. $\frac{5}{16} + \frac{4}{9}$

11. $4\frac{3}{8} + 2\frac{3}{4}$ 12. $3\frac{2}{16} - \frac{8}{15}$ 13. $4\frac{11}{12} - 3\frac{1}{5}$ 14. $6\frac{7}{8} + 5\frac{5}{9}$

Independent ▶
Practice

Use the number line to tell whether the fraction is closest to 0, $\frac{1}{2}$, or 1. Write *close to 0, close to $\frac{1}{2}$,* or *close to 1.*

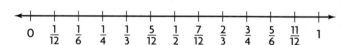

15. $\frac{5}{6}$ 16. $\frac{5}{12}$ 17. $\frac{1}{6}$ 18. $\frac{7}{12}$

Estimate the sum or difference.

19. $\frac{8}{10} + \frac{2}{3}$ 20. $2\frac{1}{4} + 1\frac{1}{8}$ 21. $\frac{15}{16} - \frac{6}{10}$ 22. $7\frac{9}{16} - 4\frac{2}{9}$

23. $12\frac{1}{12} + 4\frac{4}{5}$ 24. $\frac{18}{20} - \frac{3}{50}$ 25. $4\frac{3}{8} - 1\frac{1}{3}$ 26. $\frac{3}{5} + \frac{6}{7}$

27. $\frac{5}{9} - \frac{1}{2}$ 28. $\frac{1}{12} + 1\frac{3}{10}$ 29. $9\frac{7}{12} - 5\frac{1}{5}$ 30. $\frac{13}{15} + \frac{8}{9} + \frac{1}{7}$

Use a range to estimate each sum or difference.

31. $6\frac{1}{4} + 2\frac{5}{6}$ 32. $5\frac{7}{10} - 2\frac{1}{4}$ 33. $8\frac{3}{4} - 4\frac{1}{8}$

34. $3\frac{1}{4} - 1\frac{1}{8}$ 35. $1\frac{3}{4} + 3\frac{4}{5}$ 36. $4\frac{1}{9} + 5\frac{3}{4}$

37. Estimate the sum. $3\frac{1}{5} + 2\frac{1}{3} + 1\frac{11}{12}$

38. Estimate the difference between 8 and $2\frac{7}{18}$.

39. About how much more is $8\frac{7}{10}$ feet than $2\frac{3}{8}$ feet?

40. Estimate the sum of $2\frac{1}{8}$, $7\frac{7}{9}$, $1\frac{7}{8}$, and $8\frac{1}{4}$.

41. Estimate the sum of 8.5, $5\frac{1}{4}$, $4\frac{2}{3}$, and 6.75.

42. Estimate the difference between $15\frac{3}{5}$ and $4\frac{2}{9}$.

43. Estimate the sum of $18\frac{3}{10}$, $5\frac{7}{8}$, $2\frac{1}{4}$, and $3\frac{4}{5}$.

44. About how much more is $24\frac{1}{3}$ yd than $11\frac{5}{6}$ yd?

Problem Solving ▶
Applications

Use Data The table shows data on the longest ski trails at five different mountains in the United States. For 45–46, use the table.

45. Estimate the mean length of the ski trails. Which trail's length is closest to the estimate?

46. Find the median of the trail lengths.

Ski Trails	
Mountain	**Longest Ski Trail (mi)**
Beaver Creek, CO	$2\frac{3}{4}$
Killington, VT	$10\frac{1}{5}$
Mammoth, CA	$2\frac{1}{2}$
Taos, NM	$5\frac{1}{4}$
Sugar Mountain, NC	$1\frac{1}{2}$

47. Leo needs $\frac{3}{4}$ yd of blue fabric, $\frac{7}{10}$ yd of purple fabric, and $\frac{1}{5}$ yd of white fabric for a sewing project. About how much fabric does he need for the sewing project?

48. 📖 **Write a problem** about everyday life at home that can be solved by estimating a sum or difference of fractions. Exchange with a classmate and solve.

49. Vocabulary Power The root word *nomen* in the words *nominate* and *denominator* means "to name." How does this meaning help you understand the meaning of *denominator*?

MIXED REVIEW AND TEST PREP

Write the fraction or decimal as a percent. (p. 191)

50. $\frac{3}{4}$ **51.** 0.45

52. A survey question reads "Is blue your favorite color?" Is the question biased or unbiased? (p. 112)

⭐ **53. TEST PREP** The band members are setting up chairs for a concert in the school auditorium. They can put 25 chairs in each row. How many rows will they need to seat 350 people? (p. 24)

A 10   **B** 14   **C** 18   **D** 25

⭐ **54. TEST PREP** Find the GCF for 80, 96, and 112. (p.170)

F 6   **G** 8   **H** 14   **J** 16

EXTRA PRACTICE page 220, Set A

Model Addition and Subtraction

Explore how to use fraction bars to add and subtract fractions with unlike denominators.

You need fraction bars.

Vocabulary

unlike fractions

QUICK REVIEW

Find the LCM for each set of numbers.

1. 2, 8   **2.** 6, 9

3. 4, 15   **4.** 4, 10

5. 2, 3, 10

Fractions with the same denominator, such as $\frac{5}{9}$ and $\frac{4}{9}$, are called like fractions. Fractions with different denominators are called **unlike fractions**. You can use fraction bars to rename the denominators before adding.

Activity 1

Find $\frac{1}{6} + \frac{1}{3}$.

- Use fraction bars to show both fractions.

- Which fraction bars fit exactly across $\frac{1}{6}$ and $\frac{1}{3}$?

- What is $\frac{1}{6} + \frac{1}{3}$?

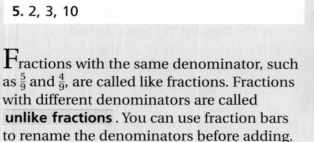

$$\frac{1}{6} = \frac{2}{12} \qquad \frac{1}{3} = \frac{4}{12}$$

Think and Discuss

- Look at the model for $\frac{1}{6} + \frac{1}{3}$. What do you know about $\frac{1}{6}$ and $\frac{2}{12}$? about $\frac{1}{3}$ and $\frac{4}{12}$?

- How are the denominators of $\frac{1}{6}$, $\frac{1}{3}$, and $\frac{1}{12}$ related? (HINT: Think about common multiples.)

Practice

Use fraction bars to find the sum. Draw a diagram of your model.

1. $\frac{1}{4} + \frac{1}{2}$ **2.** $\frac{1}{2} + \frac{1}{3}$ **3.** $\frac{1}{2} + \frac{2}{5}$ **4.** $\frac{2}{3} + \frac{1}{6}$

5. $\frac{1}{3} + \frac{1}{4}$ **6.** $\frac{3}{8} + \frac{1}{4}$ **7.** $\frac{1}{6} + \frac{1}{2}$ **8.** $\frac{3}{8} + \frac{1}{2}$

9. $\frac{1}{5} + \frac{1}{2}$ **10.** $\frac{3}{4} + \frac{1}{6}$ **11.** $\frac{1}{3} + \frac{1}{6}$ **12.** $\frac{5}{8} + \frac{1}{4}$

Fraction bars also can be used to subtract unlike fractions.

Activity 2

Find $\frac{1}{2} - \frac{1}{5}$.

- Use fraction bars to show $\frac{1}{2}$ and $\frac{1}{5}$.

- Which fraction bars fit exactly across $\frac{1}{2}$ and $\frac{1}{5}$?

- Compare $\frac{5}{10}$ and $\frac{2}{10}$. How much more is $\frac{5}{10}$ than $\frac{2}{10}$?

- What is $\frac{5}{10} - \frac{2}{10}$? What is $\frac{1}{2} - \frac{1}{5}$?

Think and Discuss

- How are the denominators of $\frac{1}{2}$, $\frac{1}{5}$, and $\frac{1}{10}$ related?

- Look at the model of $\frac{3}{4} - \frac{1}{3}$. Which fraction bars will fit exactly across $\frac{3}{4}$ and $\frac{1}{3}$? Explain.

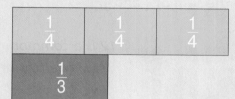

- Which fraction bars will fit exactly across $\frac{1}{2} - \frac{1}{4}$?

Practice

Use fraction bars to subtract. Draw a diagram of your model.

1. $\frac{3}{4} - \frac{1}{3}$ 2. $\frac{2}{5} - \frac{1}{10}$ 3. $\frac{1}{3} - \frac{1}{4}$ 4. $\frac{1}{2} - \frac{1}{3}$

5. $\frac{1}{2} - \frac{2}{5}$ 6. $\frac{1}{2} - \frac{5}{12}$ 7. $\frac{1}{4} - \frac{1}{6}$ 8. $\frac{3}{5} - \frac{1}{10}$

9. $\frac{1}{4} - \frac{1}{8}$ 10. $\frac{1}{2} - \frac{1}{4}$ 11. $\frac{5}{6} - \frac{1}{3}$ 12. $\frac{7}{8} - \frac{3}{4}$

MIXED REVIEW AND TEST PREP

Compare. Write $<$, $>$, or $=$ for each ●. (p. 191)

13. $\frac{3}{8}$ ● 0.375   **14.** 0.15 ● $\frac{1}{4}$ **15.** 0.6 ● $\frac{11}{20}$

16. Multiply. 9.25×3.2 (p. 80)

17. TEST PREP   Of the 80 people at the Moorer family reunion, there are 8 fewer females than males. How many males are at the reunion? (p. 28)

   A 32   **B** 36   **C** 40   **D** 44

Add and Subtract Fractions

Learn how to add and subtract fractions.

Solve. Write your answer in simplest form.

1. $\frac{1}{7} + \frac{5}{7}$ 2. $\frac{5}{6} - \frac{1}{6}$ 3. $\frac{7}{16} - \frac{5}{16}$ 4. $\frac{4}{12} + \frac{8}{12}$ 5. $\frac{8}{9} - \frac{3}{9}$

Vocabulary

least common denominator (LCD)

You can use a diagram to add and subtract fractions. To help you, think about common denominators and equivalent fractions.

EXAMPLE 1

Kayla is making two recipes. One recipe calls for $\frac{1}{4}$ c raisins, and the other recipe calls for $\frac{1}{3}$ c raisins. How many total cups of raisins does Kayla need?

Complete the diagram to find the sum of $\frac{1}{4}$ and $\frac{1}{3}$.

$\frac{1}{4}$	$\frac{1}{3}$
?	

$\frac{1}{4}$	$\frac{1}{3}$
$\frac{1}{12}$ $\frac{1}{12}$ $\frac{1}{12}$	$\frac{1}{12}$ $\frac{1}{12}$ $\frac{1}{12}$ $\frac{1}{12}$

12 is a common multiple of 4 and 3. Draw twelfths under $\frac{1}{4}$ and $\frac{1}{3}$.
THINK: $\frac{1}{4} = \frac{3}{12}$ and $\frac{1}{3} = \frac{4}{12}$.

So, Kayla needs $\frac{7}{12}$ c of raisins.

Math **I**dea ▶ To add fractions without using diagrams, you can write equivalent fractions by using a common denominator or the **least common denominator (LCD)**. The LCD is the LCM of the denominators.

EXAMPLE 2

Find $\frac{1}{2} + \frac{3}{5}$.

Estimate. Each fraction is close to $\frac{1}{2}$, so the sum is about 1.

$$\frac{1}{2} = \frac{1 \times 5}{2 \times 5} = \frac{5}{10}$$
$$+\frac{3}{5} = +\frac{3 \times 2}{5 \times 2} = +\frac{6}{10}$$

The LCM of 2 and 5 is 10, so the LCD of $\frac{1}{2}$ and $\frac{3}{5}$ is 10. Multiply to write equivalent fractions using the LCD.

$$\frac{1}{2} = \frac{5}{10}$$
$$+\frac{3}{5} = +\frac{6}{10}$$

Add the numerators. Write the sum over the denominator.

$$\frac{11}{10}, \text{ or } 1\frac{1}{10}$$

Write the answer as a fraction or as a mixed number.

Compare the answer to your estimate. Since $1\frac{1}{10}$ is close to the estimate of 1, the answer is reasonable. So, $\frac{1}{2} + \frac{3}{5} = 1\frac{1}{10}$.

• How does the sum compare to the addends? Explain.

You can use a similar method to subtract unlike fractions.

EXAMPLE 3

Kayla is preparing a pasta dish for a small dinner party. Kayla has grated $\frac{1}{2}$ c of mozzarella cheese. The recipe calls for $\frac{2}{3}$ c of grated mozzarella cheese. How much more mozzarella cheese does Kayla need to grate?

Find $\frac{2}{3} - \frac{1}{2}$.

Estimate. $\frac{2}{3}$ is a little more than $\frac{1}{2}$, so the difference is close to 0.

$$\frac{2}{3} = \frac{2 \times 2}{3 \times 2} = \frac{4}{6}$$ *The LCD of $\frac{2}{3}$ and $\frac{1}{2}$ is 6.*

$$-\frac{1}{2} = -\frac{1 \times 3}{2 \times 3} = -\frac{3}{6}$$ *Multiply to find the equivalent fractions using the LCD.*

$$\frac{2}{3} = \frac{4}{6}$$
$$-\frac{1}{2} = -\frac{3}{6}$$
$$\frac{1}{6}$$

Subtract the numerators. Write the difference over the denominator.

Compare the answer to your estimate. Since $\frac{1}{6}$ is close to the estimate of 0, the answer is reasonable.

So, Kayla needs to grate $\frac{1}{6}$ c more cheese.

EXAMPLE 4

A. $$\frac{5}{6} = \frac{5 \times 9}{6 \times 9} = \frac{45}{54}$$

$$-\frac{7}{9} = -\frac{7 \times 6}{9 \times 6} = -\frac{42}{54}$$
$$\frac{3}{54} = \frac{1}{18}$$

B. $$\frac{5}{12} = \frac{5}{12}$$

$$-\frac{1}{4} = -\frac{1 \times 3}{4 \times 3} = -\frac{3}{12}$$
$$\frac{2}{12} = \frac{1}{6}$$

CHECK FOR UNDERSTANDING

Think and Discuss ▶ **Look back at the lesson to answer each question.**

1. **Tell** how much more cheese Kayla would need to grate if she had grated $\frac{1}{4}$ c of cheese.

2. **Explain** how to solve Example 4A using the LCD.

Guided Practice ▶ **Use a common denominator to rewrite the problem using equivalent fractions.**

3. $\frac{7}{10} + \frac{1}{5}$

4. $\frac{1}{3} + \frac{1}{8}$

5. $\frac{4}{5} - \frac{1}{3}$

Write the sum or difference in simplest form. Estimate to check.

6. $\frac{1}{5} + \frac{3}{5}$ **7.** $\frac{7}{9} - \frac{4}{9}$ **8.** $\frac{7}{9} - \frac{1}{6}$ **9.** $\frac{2}{3} + \frac{3}{4}$

10. $\frac{3}{4} - \frac{3}{8}$ **11.** $\frac{2}{5} - \frac{1}{3}$ **12.** $\frac{2}{5} + \frac{2}{4}$ **13.** $\frac{4}{9} + \frac{1}{3}$

PRACTICE AND PROBLEM SOLVING

Independent ▶ Practice

TECHNOLOGY LINK

More Practice:
Harcourt Mega Math
Fraction Action,
Fraction Flare-Up,
Level K

Use a common denominator to rewrite the problem using equivalent fractions.

14. $\frac{9}{10} - \frac{1}{5}$ **15.** $\frac{6}{7} - \frac{3}{4}$ **16.** $\frac{1}{4} + \frac{5}{8}$

Write the sum or difference in simplest form. Estimate to check.

17. $\frac{1}{6} + \frac{2}{3}$ **18.** $\frac{4}{7} - \frac{1}{7}$ **19.** $\frac{1}{2} + \frac{3}{10}$ **20.** $\frac{1}{3} - \frac{1}{4}$

21. $\frac{5}{7} - \frac{1}{2}$ **22.** $\frac{1}{3} + \frac{2}{3}$ **23.** $\frac{6}{10} - \frac{4}{10}$ **24.** $\frac{3}{8} + \frac{1}{3}$

25. $\frac{3}{4} + \frac{5}{8}$ **26.** $\frac{7}{12} + \frac{2}{3}$ **27.** $1 - \frac{3}{8}$ **28.** $\frac{1}{2} - \frac{2}{5}$

29. $\frac{4}{5} - \frac{1}{3}$ **30.** $\frac{1}{4} + \frac{2}{3}$ **31.** $\frac{5}{9} - \frac{1}{3}$ **32.** $\frac{3}{8} + \frac{3}{20}$

33. Find the sum of $\frac{1}{8}$, $\frac{3}{8}$, and $\frac{2}{8}$.   **34.** Find $\frac{1}{2} + \frac{2}{3} + \frac{1}{6}$.

35. Find $\frac{3}{4} + 0.5 + 0.75$.   **36.** Find $0.6 - \frac{3}{8}$.

37. How much longer than $\frac{1}{4}$ mile is $\frac{2}{3}$ mile?

Solve each equation mentally. Write the answer in simplest form.

38. $p + \frac{1}{4} = \frac{3}{4}$ **39.** $r = \frac{5}{12} + \frac{7}{12}$ **40.** $\frac{4}{5} - q = \frac{2}{5}$

41. $c = \frac{7}{10} - \frac{1}{10}$ **42.** $\frac{3}{7} + s = \frac{5}{7}$ **43.** $m - \frac{1}{6} = \frac{5}{6}$

Problem Solving ▶ Applications

Use Data For 44–46, use the recipe at the right.

44. Keisha has $\frac{7}{8}$ c of orange juice. How much orange juice does she have left to drink after she doubles the recipe for fruit cups?

45. How many total teaspoons of vanilla and orange extract does she need to make the fruit cups?

46. Keisha used $\frac{1}{4}$ tsp of orange extract. By how much did she exceed the amount of orange extract in the recipe?

Fruit Cups

2 cups of orange sections
1 cup blueberries
$\frac{1}{4}$ cup orange juice
1 tbsp sugar
1 tsp lemon juice
$\frac{1}{2}$ tsp vanilla extract
$\frac{1}{8}$ tsp orange extract

47. Each week, Reina spends $\frac{2}{3}$ of her allowance on school lunches and saves $\frac{1}{5}$ of it. What fraction of her allowance is left? Which operation(s) did you use? Why?

48. ? **What's the Question?** In Mrs. Lucero's class, $\frac{1}{10}$ of the students are wearing blue shirts and $\frac{3}{5}$ of the students are wearing white shirts. The answer is $\frac{3}{10}$ of the class.

49. *REASONING* John is thinking of two numbers. Each number is between 21 and 30. The GCF of the numbers is 4. What are the numbers?

50. One cup of whole milk contains 166 calories and one cup of skim milk contains 88 calories. How many more calories are there in 4 cups of whole milk than in 1 quart of skim milk?

MIXED REVIEW AND TEST PREP

For 51–52, write in simplest form. (p.182)

51. $\frac{36}{81}$ **52.** $\frac{95}{200}$ **53.** Subtract. $8,145 - 752$ (p. 22)

54. TEST PREP What is the prime factorization in exponent form for 135? (p. 168)

  A 3×5 **B** $5^2 \times 3$ **C** $3^3 \times 5$ **D** $3^2 \times 5$

55. TEST PREP Eric skated 500 meters in 37.14 seconds. Andre skated the same distance in 37.139 seconds, and Al in 37.12 seconds. What is the correct order of their times in seconds, from fastest to slowest times? (p. 60)

  F 37.14, 37.139, 37.12   **H** 37.12, 37.139, 37.14

  G 37.12, 37.14, 37.139   **J** 37.139, 37.12, 37.14

PROBLEM SOLVING Thinker's Corner

DOMINO FRACTIONS
Materials: set of dominoes

Dominoes have been played for centuries throughout the world. The Chinese played with them in the 12th century, and a set was even found in a tomb from Ancient Egypt. To play this domino game, think of each of the 15 dominoes shown above as a fraction. If a domino shows 2 circles and 4 circles, the fraction is $\frac{2}{4}$. Play with a partner to combine 5 dominoes at a time to form a fraction sum of $2\frac{1}{2}$. Then break the 15 dominoes into 3 sets of 5, each of which has a sum of $2\frac{1}{2}$.

EXTRA PRACTICE page 220, Set B

209

Add and Subtract Mixed Numbers

Learn how to add and subtract mixed numbers.

A flock of birds is migrating from Canada to Florida for the winter. One day the birds fly $2\frac{3}{4}$ hours before stopping to rest. Then they fly $1\frac{1}{6}$ more hours. For how long do the birds fly?

One Way　You can draw a diagram.

EXAMPLE 1

Remember that to write a fraction as a mixed number, you divide the numerator by the denominator.

$$\frac{13}{3} \rightarrow 3\overline{)13} \begin{array}{r} 4 \\ -12 \\ \hline 1 \end{array}$$

$$\frac{13}{3} = 4\frac{1}{3}$$

Show $2\frac{3}{4} + 1\frac{1}{6}$.

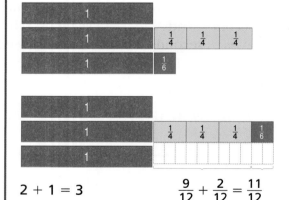

$2 + 1 = 3$　　$\frac{9}{12} + \frac{2}{12} = \frac{11}{12}$

Combine whole numbers. Combine fractions. Draw equivalent fractions with the LCD, 12.

Add fractions. Add whole numbers.

So, the birds fly for $3\frac{11}{12}$ hours.

Another Way　You can use a common denominator to write equivalent fractions.

EXAMPLE 2

Find $4\frac{2}{3} + 5\frac{4}{5}$.

$$\begin{array}{r} 4\frac{2}{3} = 4\frac{10}{15} \\ +5\frac{4}{5} = +5\frac{12}{15} \\ \hline 9\frac{22}{15} = 9 + 1\frac{7}{15} = 10\frac{7}{15} \end{array}$$

Write equivalent fractions, using the LCD, 15.
Add fractions. Add whole numbers.
Rename the fraction as a mixed number. Rewrite the sum.

So, $4\frac{2}{3} + 5\frac{4}{5} = 10\frac{7}{15}$.

Subtract Mixed Numbers

One Way   You can use diagrams to subtract mixed numbers.

EXAMPLE 3

Find $1\frac{1}{2} - 1\frac{1}{10}$.

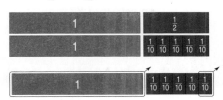

Draw $1\frac{1}{2}$.
Find the LCD for $\frac{1}{2}$ and $\frac{1}{10}$.
Change the half to tenths.

Subtract $1\frac{1}{10}$ from $1\frac{5}{10}$.

So, $1\frac{1}{2} - 1\frac{1}{10} = \frac{4}{10}$, or $\frac{2}{5}$.

• Draw a diagram to find $2\frac{1}{2} - 1\frac{1}{3}$.

Another Way   When you subtract mixed numbers with unlike fractions, use a common denominator to write equivalent fractions.

EXAMPLE 4

The rusty-spotted cat, the smallest meat-eating wild feline, lives in southern India and Sri Lanka. An adult has a head-and-body length of $13\frac{2}{5}$ in. to $18\frac{9}{10}$ in. Find the difference between the greatest and least lengths.

Find $18\frac{9}{10} - 13\frac{2}{5}$.

Estimate. $18\frac{9}{10}$ is close to 19 and $13\frac{2}{5}$ is close to 13. So, the difference is about $19 - 13$, or 6.

$$18\frac{9}{10} = \quad 18\frac{9}{10}$$

Write equivalent fractions, using the LCD, 10.

$$-13\frac{2}{5} = -13\frac{4}{10}$$

Subtract the fractions.

$$5\frac{5}{10} = 5\frac{1}{2}$$

Subtract the whole numbers.

The answer is reasonable because it is close to the estimate of 6. So, the difference between the greatest and least lengths is $5\frac{1}{2}$ in.

• How does the difference compare to the minuend, or the number being subtracted from? Explain.

CHECK FOR UNDERSTANDING

Think and Discuss ▶ Look back at the lesson to answer each question.

1. **Explain** why you must find equivalent fractions to add $1\frac{1}{5} + 1\frac{1}{2}$.

2. **Explain** how you know that $6\frac{1}{2} - 4\frac{1}{4}$ is more than 2.

Guided Practice ▶ Draw a diagram to find each sum or difference. Write the answer in simplest form.

3. $2\frac{3}{5} + 1\frac{1}{5}$ 4. $1\frac{1}{4} + 2\frac{2}{3}$ 5. $2\frac{4}{5} - 1\frac{1}{2}$

211

Write the sum or difference in simplest form.
Estimate to check.

6. $1\frac{1}{8} + 1\frac{5}{8}$ **7.** $2\frac{1}{4} + 4\frac{1}{3}$ **8.** $5\frac{3}{8} - 1\frac{1}{4}$

9. $4\frac{1}{3} - 3\frac{1}{6}$ **10.** $3\frac{3}{4} + 4\frac{5}{12}$ **11.** $6\frac{5}{6} - 5\frac{7}{9}$

PRACTICE AND PROBLEM SOLVING

Independent ▶ Practice

Draw a diagram to find each sum or difference. Write the answer in simplest form.

12. $1\frac{5}{12} + 1\frac{1}{4}$ **13.** $1\frac{1}{3} + 1\frac{1}{6}$ **14.** $4\frac{1}{2} - 2\frac{2}{5}$

Write the sum or difference in simplest form.
Estimate to check.

15. $4\frac{1}{2} + 3\frac{4}{5}$ **16.** $4\frac{1}{3} - 2\frac{1}{4}$ **17.** $5\frac{5}{6} + 4\frac{2}{9}$

TECHNOLOGY LINK
More Practice:
Harcourt Mega Math
The Number Game,
Tiny's Think Tank,
Level W

18. $3\frac{1}{4} - 1\frac{1}{6}$ **19.** $7\frac{1}{2} - 3\frac{2}{5}$ **20.** $3\frac{2}{7} + 8\frac{1}{3}$

21. $7\frac{3}{4} + 3\frac{2}{5}$ **22.** $5\frac{5}{6} - 2\frac{7}{9}$ **23.** $4\frac{5}{7} + 3\frac{1}{2}$

24. How much greater is $5\frac{3}{4}$ than 3?

25. What is the sum of $25\frac{3}{8}$ and $2\frac{3}{4}$?

26. What is the sum of $4\frac{5}{8}$ and 7.8?

Find the missing number and identify which property of addition you used.

27. $3\frac{7}{8} + \blacksquare = 2\frac{1}{4} + 3\frac{7}{8}$ **28.** $3\frac{3}{4} + 0 = \blacksquare$ **29.** $\left(\frac{2}{3} + 1\frac{5}{6}\right) + \frac{1}{6} = \frac{2}{3} + \left(\blacksquare + \frac{1}{6}\right)$

Problem Solving ▶ Applications

Use Data The graph shows the head-and-body lengths of five small mammals. For 30–31, use the graph.

30. How much longer is the harvest mouse than the Kitti's hognosed bat?

31. The masked shrew is $1\frac{2}{3}$ in. long. Is it longer or shorter than the little brown bat? How much? Which operation did you use? Why?

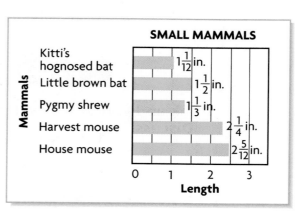

SMALL MAMMALS

Mammals	Length
Kitti's hognosed bat	$1\frac{1}{12}$ in.
Little brown bat	$1\frac{1}{2}$ in.
Pygmy shrew	$1\frac{1}{3}$ in.
Harvest mouse	$2\frac{1}{4}$ in.
House mouse	$2\frac{5}{12}$ in.

32. On its way to the shore, a sea turtle traveled $4\frac{1}{4}$ hr the first day. The second day, the turtle traveled $3\frac{1}{2}$ hr. How many hours did the sea turtle travel in the two days?

33. Mrs. Myers used $1\frac{1}{2}$ c of flour to make muffins, $4\frac{1}{4}$ c to make bread, and $\frac{3}{4}$ c to make gravy. If she had $9\frac{3}{4}$ c before she started the meal, how much flour does Mrs. Myers have left?

34. **?** **What's the Error?** DeAnn added $3\frac{1}{4}$ and $2\frac{2}{3}$ and got $5\frac{3}{12}$. Explain the error. What is the correct sum?

35. Betty, Jim, Manuel, and Rosa won the first four prizes in a design contest. Jim won second prize. Manuel did not win third prize. Rosa won fourth prize. What prize did Betty win?

36. Alexis needs a new blender. She found the same blender on sale at five different stores. The prices are $22.95, $21.85, $22.05, $20.95, and $21.99. Order the prices from least to greatest.

MIXED REVIEW AND TEST PREP

37. Find the sum of $\frac{2}{3}$ and $\frac{2}{5}$. (p. 206)

38. Subtract. $425.2 - 51.05$ (p. 76)

39. Order $\frac{1}{2}$, $\frac{4}{5}$, and $\frac{2}{3}$ from greatest to least. (p. 188)

40. TEST PREP Find the value of $(6 + 4)^2 \div 5$. (p. 48)

   A 4   **B** 4.4   **C** 9.2   **D** 20

41. TEST PREP Which is the solution of $x + 3 = 10$? (p. 38)

   F $x = 3$ **G** $x = 7$ **H** $x = 10$ **J** $x = 13$

PROBLEM SOLVING **LiNKUP** to Reading

Strategy • Choose Relevant Information
Sometimes a word problem contains more information than you need. You must decide which information is relevant, or needed to solve the problem.

The koala of eastern Australia feeds mostly on eucalyptus leaves. It nibbles on about 6 of the 500 species of eucalyptus per day and selects certain trees and leaves over others to find the $1\frac{1}{4}$ pounds of food that it needs. Suppose the koala finds only $1\frac{1}{8}$ pounds of food by the end of the day. How many more pounds of eucalyptus leaves does the koala need?

1. What does the problem ask you to find?

2. Identify relevant information.

3. What information is not relevant?

4. Solve the problem.

EXTRA PRACTICE page 220, Set C

Subtract Mixed Numbers

Learn how to subtract mixed numbers involving renaming.

QUICK REVIEW

Write the number that makes the fraction equivalent to $\frac{1}{2}$.

1. $\frac{\blacksquare}{8}$ 2. $\frac{\blacksquare}{6}$ 3. $\frac{\blacksquare}{20}$ 4. $\frac{\blacksquare}{14}$ 5. $\frac{\blacksquare}{100}$

Sometimes you need to rename mixed numbers before you can subtract.

Activity 1

You need: fraction bars

Find $2\frac{1}{5} - 1\frac{4}{5}$.

• Use fraction bars to model $2\frac{1}{5}$.

| 1 | 1 | $\frac{1}{5}$ | $\leftarrow 2\frac{1}{5}$ |

• Here is another way to model $2\frac{1}{5}$.

| 1 | $\frac{1}{5}$ | $\frac{1}{5}$ | $\frac{1}{5}$ | $\frac{1}{5}$ | $\frac{1}{5}$ | $\frac{1}{5}$ | $\leftarrow 1\frac{6}{5}$ |

• From which model can you subtract $1\frac{4}{5}$?

• Subtract $1\frac{4}{5}$ from $1\frac{6}{5}$. What is $2\frac{1}{5} - 1\frac{4}{5}$?

EXAMPLE 1

The normal rainfall in January in New Orleans, LA, is $5\frac{1}{10}$ in. In Jacksonville, FL, the normal amount for the month is $3\frac{3}{10}$ in. How much greater is the normal January rainfall in New Orleans than in Jacksonville?

Find $5\frac{1}{10} - 3\frac{3}{10}$.

Estimate. $5\frac{1}{10}$ is close to 5, and $3\frac{3}{10}$ is close to 3. So, the difference is about $5 - 3$, or 2.

$$
\begin{aligned}
5\frac{1}{10} &= 4\frac{11}{10} \\
-3\frac{3}{10} &= -3\frac{3}{10} \\
\hline
&\quad 1\frac{8}{10} = 1\frac{4}{5}
\end{aligned}
$$

Since $\frac{3}{10} > \frac{1}{10}$, rename $5\frac{1}{10}$.

$5\frac{1}{10} = 4 + \frac{10}{10} + \frac{1}{10} = 4\frac{11}{10}$

Subtract the fractions. Subtract the whole numbers. Simplify.

The answer is reasonable because it is close to the estimate of 2 in. So, the normal January rainfall is $1\frac{4}{5}$ in. greater in New Orleans than in Jacksonville.

When you subtract mixed numbers, you can use a common denominator to rename the mixed number before subtracting.

Activity 2

You need: fraction bars

Find $2\frac{1}{6} - 1\frac{5}{12}$.

- Use fraction bars to model $2\frac{1}{6}$.

| 1 | 1 | $\frac{1}{6}$ | ← $2\frac{1}{6}$

- Since you are subtracting twelfths, think of the LCD for $\frac{1}{6}$ and $\frac{5}{12}$. Change the sixths to twelfths.

| 1 | 1 | $\frac{1}{12}$ $\frac{1}{12}$ | ← $2\frac{2}{12}$

- Can you subtract $1\frac{5}{12}$ from either of these models?
- Here is another way to model $2\frac{2}{12}$.

| 1 | $\frac{1}{12}$ $\frac{1}{12}$ $\frac{1}{12}$ $\frac{1}{12}$ $\frac{1}{12}$ $\frac{1}{12}$ $\frac{1}{12}$ $\frac{1}{12}$ $\frac{1}{12}$ $\frac{1}{12}$ $\frac{1}{12}$ $\frac{1}{12}$ $\frac{1}{12}$ $\frac{1}{12}$ | ← $1\frac{14}{12}$

- Subtract $1\frac{5}{12}$ from $1\frac{14}{12}$. What is $2\frac{1}{6} - 1\frac{5}{12}$?

A blizzard brought record temperatures, wind, and snow to many areas in the southern and eastern United States.

EXAMPLE 2

How much more snow did Mount LeConte receive than Birmingham received?

Find $4\frac{1}{3} - 1\frac{5}{12}$.

Estimate. $4\frac{1}{3}$ is close to $4\frac{1}{2}$, and $1\frac{5}{12}$ is close to $1\frac{1}{2}$. So, the difference is about $4\frac{1}{2} - 1\frac{1}{2}$, or 3.

SNOWFALL AMOUNTS	
Location	**Snow (ft)**
Birmingham, AL	$1\frac{5}{12}$
Asheville, NC	$1\frac{7}{12}$
Syracuse, NY	$3\frac{7}{12}$
Mount LeConte, TN	$4\frac{1}{3}$

Subtract.

$$\begin{aligned} 4\frac{1}{3} &= 4\frac{4}{12} \\ -1\frac{5}{12} &= -1\frac{5}{12} \end{aligned}$$

The LCD of $\frac{1}{3}$ and $\frac{5}{12}$ is 12.
Write equivalent fractions, using the LCD, 12.

$$\begin{aligned} 4\frac{1}{3} &= 4\frac{4}{12} = 3\frac{16}{12} \\ -1\frac{5}{12} &= -1\frac{5}{12} = -1\frac{5}{12} \\ & \qquad\qquad\qquad 2\frac{11}{12} \end{aligned}$$

Since $\frac{5}{12}$ is greater than $\frac{4}{12}$, rename $4\frac{4}{12}$.
$4\frac{4}{12} = 3 + \frac{12}{12} + \frac{4}{12} = 3\frac{16}{12}$.
Subtract the fractions.
Subtract the whole numbers.

The answer is reasonable because it is close to the estimate of 3 ft. So, Mount LeConte received $2\frac{11}{12}$ ft more snow than Birmingham.

Sometimes you need to subtract a mixed number from a whole number.

EXAMPLE 3

Jake is running in a 5-km race. So far he has run $1\frac{4}{5}$ km. How far does he have to go?

Find the difference. $5 - 1\frac{4}{5}$

$$5 = 4\frac{5}{5}$$ *Since you are subtracting fifths, rename 5 as $4\frac{5}{5}$.*

$$\frac{-1\frac{4}{5} = -1\frac{4}{5}}{3\frac{1}{5}}$$ *Subtract the fractions.*
Subtract the whole numbers.

So, Jake has $3\frac{1}{5}$ km to go.

CHECK FOR UNDERSTANDING

Think and ▶ **Look back at the lesson to answer each question.**
Discuss

1. **Explain** how to rename $3\frac{1}{3}$ so you could subtract $1\frac{2}{3}$.

2. **What if** you wanted to find $4\frac{5}{12} - 2\frac{3}{8}$? What equivalent fractions would you write using a common denominator?

Guided ▶ **Write the difference in simplest form. Estimate to check.**
Practice

3. $4\frac{1}{3} - 2\frac{1}{4}$ **4.** $6 - 2\frac{2}{3}$ **5.** $7\frac{3}{10} - 3\frac{2}{5}$

6. $6\frac{1}{5} - 3\frac{7}{10}$ **7.** $8 - 4\frac{8}{9}$ **8.** $16\frac{3}{8} - 7\frac{1}{2}$

PRACTICE AND PROBLEM SOLVING

Independent ▶ **Write the difference in simplest form. Estimate to check.**
Practice

9. $3\frac{1}{3} - 1\frac{2}{3}$ **10.** $3\frac{3}{8} - \frac{3}{4}$ **11.** $3\frac{1}{9} - 1\frac{2}{3}$

12. $2\frac{3}{8} - 1\frac{1}{2}$ **13.** $1\frac{1}{2} - \frac{4}{5}$ **14.** $3\frac{1}{5} - 1\frac{3}{10}$

15. $2\frac{2}{3} - 1\frac{3}{4}$ **16.** $3\frac{1}{12} - 2\frac{5}{6}$ **17.** $1\frac{3}{4} - \frac{7}{8}$

18. $3 - 1\frac{1}{4}$ **19.** $5\frac{1}{2} - 3\frac{7}{10}$ **20.** $12\frac{1}{9} - 7\frac{1}{3}$

21. $4\frac{1}{4} - 2\frac{2}{5}$ **22.** $8 - 5\frac{2}{3}$ **23.** $7\frac{5}{9} - 2\frac{5}{6}$

24. $11\frac{1}{4} - 9\frac{7}{8}$ **25.** $5.25 - 2\frac{3}{8}$ **26.** $6.2 - 3\frac{1}{2}$

Evaluate each expression for $j = 5\frac{1}{2}$, $k = 4\frac{3}{5}$, and $m = 2\frac{7}{10}$.

27. $j - k$ **28.** $j - m$ **29.** $k - m$

30. Whit usually drives $4\frac{7}{8}$ mi on the expressway to work. Sometimes traffic is bad due to weather conditions and he takes another route which is $5\frac{3}{4}$ mi long. How much shorter is his usual route?

31. **≡FAST FACT • SCIENCE** The greatest wind speed ever recorded, 231 mi per hr, was measured at the top of Mount Washington, New Hampshire, in 1934. Quarter horses have been timed running at $47\frac{1}{2}$ mi per hr. How much faster was the greatest wind speed than the speed of quarter horses?

32. Write About It Why do you write equivalent fractions before you rename? Can you rename before you write equivalent fractions?

33. **Number Sense** Prime numbers that differ by 2, such as 3 and 5, or 59 and 61, are called twin primes. Write two other pairs of twin primes between 1 and 50.

MIXED REVIEW AND TEST PREP

34. Tell which are equivalent numbers.
$\frac{11}{3}$, $7\frac{1}{3}$, $6\frac{1}{3}$, $\frac{22}{3}$ (p. 182)

35. Find the sum of $1\frac{1}{3}$ and $2\frac{1}{6}$. (p. 210)

36. Find the median for the data. 30, 36, 39, 38, 36, 33 (p. 118)

37. **TEST PREP** Tyra earns $5.50 per hour working part-time. Last week she worked 3 hr on Tuesday and twice as long on Saturday. How much did she earn last week? (p. 80)

A $33.00   **B** $44.00   **C** $49.50   **D** $55.50

38. **TEST PREP** Alexander buys 3 boxes of computer paper for $10.79 per box, including tax. How much change will he get from $50? (p. 80)

F $39.21   **G** $32.37   **H** $17.63   **J** $11.00

PROBLEM SOLVING LINKUP to Social Studies

Floods In April 2001, the upper Mississippi River rose to its highest levels since 1965. As a result, many cities along that part of the Mississippi River were flooded.

The map at the right shows the river's maximum height above its banks, in feet, for five cities. For each pair of cities below, find the difference in maximum heights.

1. Wabasha and Alma

2. Winona and La Crosse

3. McGregor and Wabasha

The Mississippi River Flood of 2001
Height Above Flood Stage (in ft.)

Wabasha, MN $6\frac{11}{50}$

Alma, WI $2\frac{2}{5}$

Winona, MN $7\frac{2}{25}$

La Crosse, WI $4\frac{41}{100}$

McGregor, IA $7\frac{3}{4}$

PROBLEM SOLVING STRATEGY
Draw a Diagram

Learn how to use the strategy *draw a diagram* to solve problems.

A taxicab travels $1\frac{1}{3}$ mi west, 4 mi north, $8\frac{1}{4}$ mi east, $1\frac{1}{3}$ mi south, and then 10 mi west. What is the least number of miles the taxicab will travel to return to the starting place?

Analyze

What are you asked to find?

What information is given?

Is there numerical information you will not use? If so, what?

Choose

What strategy will you use?

You can draw a diagram that shows the taxicab's route.

Draw a diagram and label the distances and locations.

Solve

How will you solve the problem?

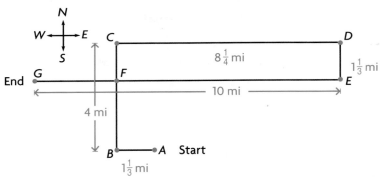

To return to the starting place, the taxicab must go from point G to point A.

Find the distance from point G to point F. $10 - 8\frac{1}{4} = 1\frac{3}{4}$

Find the distance from point F to point B. $4 - 1\frac{1}{3} = 2\frac{2}{3}$

Find the distance from point B to point A. $1\frac{1}{3}$

Add the distances. Use the common denominator 12 to write equivalent fractions.

$$1\frac{3}{4} + 2\frac{2}{3} + 1\frac{1}{3} = 1\frac{9}{12} + 2\frac{8}{12} + 1\frac{4}{12} = 4\frac{21}{12} = 5\frac{9}{12} = 5\frac{3}{4}$$

So, the taxicab will travel $5\frac{3}{4}$ mi to return to the starting place.

Check

How can you check to see if your answer is reasonable?

PROBLEM SOLVING PRACTICE

Solve by drawing a diagram.

1. A tour bus travels $7\frac{1}{2}$ mi south, $3\frac{1}{3}$ mi east, $4\frac{1}{3}$ mi north, and $11\frac{1}{2}$ mi west. How far has the tour bus traveled when it crosses its own path?

2. Tanisha needs a fence that is 33 ft long to separate her two gardens. If she puts one post in the ground every $5\frac{1}{2}$ ft, how many posts will Tanisha need for the fence?

For 3–4, use the information below.

Carla drives south $2\frac{1}{2}$ mi from her home. Next, she drives east $\frac{1}{3}$ mi. Then, she drives south 3 mi.

3. How many total miles does Carla drive from her home?

   A 5 mi   **C** $5\frac{5}{6}$ mi

   B $5\frac{1}{5}$ mi   **D** 6 mi

4. In which directions must Carla drive to return home?

   F east and north   **H** west and north

   G east and south   **J** west and south

PROBLEM SOLVING STRATEGIES

▶ **Draw a Diagram or Picture**

Make a Model

Predict and Test

Work Backward

Make an Organized List

Find a Pattern

Make a Table or Graph

Solve a Simpler Problem

Write an Equation

Use Logical Reasoning

MIXED STRATEGY PRACTICE

5. A display in a store has 24 cans in the bottom row, 21 in the second row, and 18 in the third row. If the pattern continues, how many cans are in the fifth row?

6. Tickets to see an Irish dance group cost $52 and $28. Mario bought 7 tickets for his family and paid a total of $316. How many tickets at each price did he buy?

7. Ms. Lopez travels north from home to pick up Maria at school. Then she travels $3\frac{1}{2}$ mi east to pick up Marcos and $4\frac{1}{4}$ mi south to pick up Carter. If Ms. Lopez has driven a total of $12\frac{1}{2}$ mi, what is the distance from home to Maria's school?

8. Tim has a job in the city. He has to commute $6\frac{1}{2}$ km to work. The bus he takes to work travels about $3\frac{1}{4}$ km in 10 minutes. About how much time does Tim spend on the bus going to and from work?

9. In a recent contest, Gary scored more points than Catherine, who scored more points than Clara. Christopher scored more points than Clara but fewer than Gary. Who had the most points?

10. Use the table below. What is Joshua's total bill if he rented 3 videos and kept them for 6 days?

11. ✎ **Write a problem** that can be solved by using the strategy *draw a diagram*. Explain the steps you would use to solve the problem, and draw the diagram.

Video Rental Prices	
1 movie for 1 day	$2.99
Each additional day	$0.99
5 additional days	$3.79

Set A (pp. 200–203)

Estimate the sum or difference.

1. $\frac{4}{7} - \frac{3}{8}$
2. $3\frac{7}{9} + 1\frac{10}{11}$
3. $5\frac{4}{5} - 3\frac{1}{2}$
4. $\frac{8}{9} + \frac{3}{5}$

5. $\frac{4}{9} + \frac{2}{3}$
6. $\frac{8}{9} - \frac{5}{7}$
7. $\frac{4}{9} - \frac{1}{6}$
8. $3\frac{10}{13} + 4\frac{1}{9}$

9. $\frac{3}{7} + \frac{1}{9}$
10. $5\frac{3}{4} - 1\frac{1}{8}$
11. $\frac{5}{9} - \frac{3}{7}$
12. $8\frac{7}{8} + 5\frac{1}{2}$

13. Shawna practiced the tuba for $\frac{5}{6}$ hr on Monday, $\frac{1}{3}$ hr on Wednesday, and $\frac{1}{4}$ hr on Friday. About how many hours did Shawna practice last week?

Set B (pp. 206–209)

Write the sum or difference in simplest form. Estimate to check.

1. $\frac{3}{4} + \frac{1}{2}$
2. $\frac{4}{7} - \frac{1}{3}$
3. $\frac{1}{6} + \frac{5}{18}$
4. $\frac{9}{10} - \frac{2}{5}$

5. $\frac{5}{6} + \frac{1}{4}$
6. $\frac{6}{20} + \frac{3}{5}$
7. $\frac{5}{9} - \frac{1}{2}$
8. $\frac{7}{8} - \frac{1}{16}$

9. $\frac{3}{5} - \frac{1}{9}$
10. $\frac{5}{20} + \frac{11}{20}$
11. $\frac{11}{12} - \frac{1}{6}$
12. $\frac{1}{10} + \frac{3}{8}$

13. Rico read $\frac{1}{5}$ of a book on Saturday and $\frac{1}{3}$ of the same book on Sunday. What portion of the book does he have left to read?

Set C (pp. 210–213)

Draw a diagram to find each sum or difference. Write the answer in simplest form.

1. $2\frac{3}{8} + 1\frac{1}{4}$
2. $2\frac{1}{3} - 1\frac{1}{6}$
3. $1\frac{1}{5} + 1\frac{7}{10}$
4. $3\frac{1}{3} - 1\frac{3}{4}$

Write the sum or difference in simplest form. Estimate to check.

5. $4\frac{5}{12} - 2\frac{1}{6}$
6. $5\frac{2}{5} - 3\frac{3}{10}$
7. $2\frac{1}{9} + 1\frac{2}{5}$
8. $4\frac{2}{3} + 6\frac{1}{6}$

9. Stefan bought $1\frac{1}{2}$ lb of potato salad, $2\frac{1}{4}$ lb of coleslaw, and $4\frac{3}{4}$ lb of chicken at a deli. What is the total weight of his purchase?

Set D (pp. 214–217)

Write the difference in simplest form. Estimate to check.

1. $4\frac{5}{9} - 3\frac{2}{9}$
2. $5\frac{1}{3} - 4\frac{1}{9}$
3. $6\frac{1}{4} - 3\frac{3}{4}$
4. $6\frac{1}{3} - 4\frac{7}{9}$

5. $4 - 1\frac{3}{7}$
6. $5\frac{3}{10} - \frac{2}{5}$
7. $7\frac{1}{6} - \frac{1}{2}$
8. $4\frac{1}{4} - 1\frac{5}{8}$

9. Mr. Norman had $51\frac{1}{3}$ ft of plastic pipe. He installed $25\frac{3}{4}$ ft in the bathroom. How much pipe does he have left?

Estimate the sum or difference. (pp. 200–203)

1. $\frac{7}{12} + \frac{1}{4}$

2. $\frac{4}{5} - \frac{2}{7}$

3. $\frac{4}{5} + \frac{3}{8}$

4. $4\frac{2}{9} - \frac{1}{7}$

5. $\frac{9}{20} + 1\frac{4}{5}$

6. $6\frac{1}{4} + 3\frac{2}{9}$

Write the sum or difference in simplest form.
Estimate to check. (pp. 206–209)

7. $\frac{1}{2} + \frac{1}{3}$

8. $\frac{3}{4} + \frac{1}{6}$

9. $\frac{2}{5} + \frac{2}{4}$

10. $\frac{5}{6} + \frac{2}{3}$

11. $\frac{1}{3} + \frac{5}{6}$

12. $\frac{3}{8} + \frac{3}{4}$

13. $\frac{3}{4} - \frac{1}{3}$

14. $\frac{7}{8} - \frac{1}{4}$

15. $\frac{5}{6} - \frac{2}{9}$

16. $\frac{7}{8} - \frac{5}{6}$

17. $\frac{7}{12} - \frac{5}{12}$

18. $\frac{3}{5} - \frac{1}{4}$

Draw a diagram to find each sum or difference. Write the answer in simplest form. (pp. 210–213)

19. $2\frac{3}{8} + 1\frac{1}{4}$

20. $6\frac{2}{3} - 3\frac{1}{4}$

21. $5\frac{2}{5} - 3\frac{3}{10}$

Write the sum or difference in simplest form.
Estimate to check. (pp. 210–213, 214–217)

22. $1\frac{1}{6} + 3\frac{2}{3}$

23. $2\frac{3}{4} + 3\frac{1}{8}$

24. $1\frac{1}{2} + 2\frac{1}{4}$

25. $1\frac{1}{5} + 1\frac{3}{10}$

26. $7\frac{3}{4} - 5\frac{1}{3}$

27. $8\frac{1}{3} - 3\frac{1}{8}$

28. $3\frac{1}{4} - 2\frac{1}{2}$

29. $4\frac{1}{2} - 1\frac{2}{3}$

30. $7\frac{1}{5} - 5\frac{4}{9}$

Solve. (pp. 218–219)

31. A minibus leaves the garage and travels $9\frac{5}{6}$ mi north to pick up Tanya. Then it travels $3\frac{1}{6}$ mi west to pick up Luis, $4\frac{1}{4}$ mi south to pick up Alissa, and $4\frac{5}{12}$ mi east to the school. What is the least number of miles the minibus will travel to return from the school back to the garage?

32. Satoko has a board that is 9 ft long. She needs to cut the board into $2\frac{1}{4}$-ft sections. How many cuts will she have to make?

33. Del drives $3\frac{1}{4}$ mi north from his home. Next, he drives west $\frac{3}{4}$ mi. Then, he drives north $\frac{1}{2}$ mi. In which directions must Del drive to return home?

NUMBER SENSE, CONCEPTS, AND OPERATIONS

1. On Monday Mr. Wilson's class spent $\frac{1}{3}$ of the day on math and $\frac{1}{5}$ of the day on spelling. What fraction of the day did the class spend on other subjects?

   A $\frac{1}{15}$

   B $\frac{7}{15}$

   C $\frac{8}{15}$

   D $\frac{3}{4}$

2. The circle graph shows how students at Hall Middle School travel to school.

   HOW STUDENTS TRAVEL TO SCHOOL

   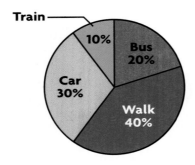

   Train — 10%
   Bus 20%
   Car 30%
   Walk 40%

   What fraction of the students either take a bus or walk to school?

   F $\frac{1}{5}$

   G $\frac{1}{4}$

   H $\frac{2}{5}$

   J $\frac{3}{5}$

   > **TIP** **Get the information you need.** See item 2. Use the circle graph to find the percents you need.

3. **Explain It** Of all the water on Earth, 1% is fresh water found in lakes and rivers, and $\frac{1}{50}$ is fresh water in the form of ice. Is the greater amount of fresh water found in lakes and rivers or in the form of ice? Explain your reasoning.

 MEASUREMENT

4. The area of Pioneer Park is about 8 square miles. Which figure on the grid below shows approximately the same number of square miles as Pioneer Park?

   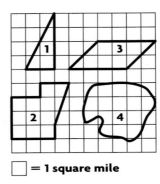

   $\square$ = 1 square mile

   A Figure 1

   B Figure 2

   C Figure 3

   D Figure 4

5. An office building is 80 feet tall by 60 feet wide. A scale model of the building is 9 inches wide. Which of the following is the height of the scale model of the building?

   F 44 inches

   G 26 inches

   H 10 inches

   J 12 inches

6. **Explain It** Eric drinks between 10 and 12 ounces of water four times a day. Does he drink more than, less than, or exactly one quart of water each day? Explain your answer.

★ ALGEBRAIC THINKING

7. Brittany wants to see if there is a relationship between the temperatures on a Celsius thermometer and a Fahrenheit thermometer. She made the table below showing Celsius temperatures and the equivalent Fahrenheit temperatures.

Celsius (°C)	0	5	10	15	20	25
Fahrenheit (°F)	32	41	50	59	68	▪

What is the Fahrenheit temperature when the Celsius temperature is 25°?

A 88°F

B 86°F

C 78°F

D 77°F

8. Kyle is filling his 5-gallon tropical fish tank with water. Let g = the number of gallons of water in the tank. Which number sentence shows the possible amounts of water in the tank at any given time during the process?

F $g = 5$

G $g > 5$

H $g \geq 5$

J $g \leq 5$

9. Explain It The figures below follow a rule to form a pattern. Describe a possible rule. Draw the figure that should come next in the pattern. Explain why you chose that figure.

★ DATA ANALYSIS AND PROBABILITY

10. Jonah recorded the morning temperatures at hourly intervals.

Hour	6	7	8	9	10
Temperature	45	49	54	59	68

He wants to display the data in a graph. Which type of graph will **best** display the change in data?

A a line graph

B a pictograph

C a stem-and-leaf plot

D a histogram

11. Karl has the coins shown below in his pocket. If he reaches into his pocket and randomly selects a coin, what is the probability that it will be a dime?

F $\frac{2}{3}$

G $\frac{2}{5}$

H $\frac{1}{3}$

J $\frac{1}{4}$

12. Explain It Denise has a game spinner that is divided into six equal sections. Three sections are yellow, one section is red, and two sections are green. What is the probability that the pointer lands on green? Explain your reasoning.

10 Multiply and Divide Fractions and Mixed Numbers

≡FAST FACT • SOCIAL STUDIES The downhill mountain-bike course at Sugar Mountain in North Carolina is 1 mi long and has a vertical drop of more than 800 ft. As riders near the finish line, they may be traveling at more than 40 mi per hr.

PROBLEM SOLVING Use the graph to estimate the difference between the winning time and David's time.

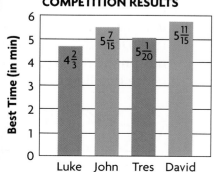

2001 DOWNHILL MOUNTAIN BIKE COMPETITION RESULTS

Best Time (in min)

Luke $4\frac{2}{3}$

John $5\frac{7}{15}$

Tres $5\frac{1}{20}$

David $5\frac{11}{15}$

Junior Olympic Boys

Check What You Know

Use this page to help you review and remember important skills needed for Chapter 10.

✓ Round Fractions

Write whether the fraction is closest to 0, $\frac{1}{2}$, or 1.

1. $\frac{2}{9}$ **2.** $\frac{7}{8}$ **3.** $\frac{7}{15}$ **4.** $\frac{5}{8}$ **5.** $\frac{1}{4}$

6. $\frac{2}{15}$ **7.** $\frac{3}{8}$ **8.** $\frac{5}{6}$ **9.** $\frac{1}{3}$ **10.** $\frac{10}{11}$

11. $\frac{11}{20}$ **12.** $\frac{7}{12}$ **13.** $\frac{1}{6}$ **14.** $\frac{4}{7}$ **15.** $\frac{2}{6}$

✓ Mental Math and Equations

Use mental math to solve.

16. $9.3 + x = 12.5$ **17.** $4c = 128$ **18.** $x - 160 = 520$ **19.** $5.11 = 5.28 - x$

20. $0.12 = \frac{x}{0.6}$ **21.** $35 - t = 21$ **22.** $6y = 0.24$ **23.** $r + 3.7 = 6.3$

✓ Fractions and Mixed Numbers

Write each fraction as a mixed number.

24. $\frac{18}{5}$ **25.** $\frac{7}{6}$ **26.** $\frac{16}{15}$ **27.** $\frac{4}{3}$ **28.** $\frac{21}{8}$

Write each mixed number as a fraction.

29. $1\frac{5}{8}$ **30.** $7\frac{1}{2}$ **31.** $3\frac{2}{3}$ **32.** $2\frac{4}{5}$ **33.** $4\frac{3}{7}$

VOCABULARY POWER

REVIEW

inverse [in′vərs] *noun*

The word *inverse* means "the direct opposite; reverse." In mathematics, subtraction is the *inverse* of addition, since $4 + 8 = 12$ and $12 - 8 = 4$. Give an example of how division is the inverse of multiplication.

PREVIEW

reciprocal

 www.harcourtschool.com/mathglossary

Estimate Products and Quotients

Learn how to estimate products and quotients of fractions and mixed numbers.

In a landfill, bulldozers spread and compact the garbage into 10-foot layers. Every layer is covered with clean soil.

It is estimated that each person in the United States produces $4\frac{2}{5}$ pounds of garbage a day. If the population of the United States was $299\frac{7}{10}$ million, about how many pounds of garbage would be produced every day?

Remember when rounding fractions to round to 0, $\frac{1}{2}$, or 1. When rounding mixed numbers, round to the nearest whole numbers.

One way to estimate the answer is to round the mixed numbers to the nearest whole numbers.

Estimate. $4\frac{2}{5} \times 299\frac{7}{10}$

$$4\frac{2}{5} \times 299\frac{7}{10}$$ *Round to the nearest whole numbers.*

$\downarrow$ $\downarrow$ **THINK:** *$\frac{2}{5}$ rounds to 0, and $\frac{7}{10}$ rounds to 1.*

$4 \times 300 = 1{,}200$ *Multiply.*

So, about 1,200 million pounds would be produced.

You can also estimate by averaging two estimates.

EXAMPLE

Estimate. $8 \div \frac{3}{4}$

Since $\frac{3}{4}$ is halfway between $\frac{1}{2}$ and 1, find the two estimates and then find their average.

$8 \div \frac{3}{4} \rightarrow 8 \div 1 = 8$ *Round up.*

$8 \div \frac{3}{4} \rightarrow 8 \div \frac{1}{2} = 16$ *Round down.*

$8 + 16 = 24;\ 24 \div 2 = 12$ *Find the average.*

So, $8 \div \frac{3}{4}$ is about 12.

You can use compatible numbers to estimate a product or quotient.

Estimate. $23\frac{3}{4} \div 4\frac{1}{2} \rightarrow 25 \div 5 = 5$ *Use compatible numbers.*

So, $23\frac{3}{4} \div 4\frac{1}{2}$ is about 5.

**Think and ▶
Discuss**

Look back at the lesson to answer each question.

1. What if each person in the United States produced $2\frac{1}{5}$ lb of garbage? About how many pounds of garbage would be produced?

2. **Tell** what compatible numbers you could use to find $75\frac{3}{5} \div 12\frac{7}{8}$.

**Guided ▶
Practice**

Estimate each product or quotient.

3. $\frac{7}{8} \times \frac{7}{16}$

4. $10\frac{8}{11} \div 2\frac{1}{5}$

5. $78\frac{3}{7} \div 4\frac{1}{6}$

6. $\frac{3}{5} \times 38$

7. $1\frac{3}{4} \times 35$

8. $21\frac{3}{8} \div 17\frac{1}{3}$

9. $58\frac{3}{4} \times 1\frac{5}{6}$

10. $98\frac{7}{8} \div 23\frac{1}{5}$

PRACTICE AND PROBLEM SOLVING

**Independent ▶
Practice**

Estimate each product or quotient.

11. $\frac{7}{9} \times \frac{1}{3}$

12. $10\frac{8}{9} \times \frac{5}{6}$

13. $\frac{5}{6} \div \frac{11}{12}$

14. $67\frac{9}{12} \div 2\frac{7}{10}$

15. $24\frac{9}{10} \div 6\frac{2}{3}$

16. $36\frac{5}{8} \div 13\frac{3}{5}$

17. $67\frac{2}{3} \div 23\frac{1}{8}$

18. $97\frac{2}{9} \div 52\frac{5}{8}$

19. $3\frac{11}{12} \times 4\frac{4}{5}$

20. $12\frac{5}{24} \div \frac{5}{12}$

21. $\frac{5}{9} \times \frac{7}{12}$

22. $\frac{2}{5} \div \frac{10}{21}$

**Problem Solving ▶
Applications**

Estimate to compare. Write $<$ or $>$ for each ●.

23. $4\frac{1}{6} \times 3\frac{2}{3}$ ● $7\frac{5}{8} \div 2\frac{1}{3}$

24. $7\frac{2}{3} \div 5$ ● $2\frac{4}{8} \times 3\frac{1}{8}$

25. Cal runs $5\frac{3}{10}$ miles in $33\frac{4}{5}$ minutes. About how many minutes does it take for Cal to run one mile?

26. ✎ **Write About It** Explain how you would estimate a quotient of mixed numbers.

27. Doris collected newspapers in her neighborhood for six days. The first day she collected 1 kg. On the second day, she had a total of 2.5 kg, and on the third day she had a total of 4 kg. If this pattern continues, how many kilograms of newspapers will she have at the end of 6 days?

MIXED REVIEW AND TEST PREP

28. Write $\frac{7}{20}$ as a percent. (p. 191)

29. $5\frac{7}{9} - 2\frac{1}{3}$ (p. 210)

30. Find the mean, median, and mode for the data.
27, 48, 83, 76, 48, 27 (p. 118)

31. Evaluate the expression $m - 4^2$ for $m = 3^3$. (p. 36)

⭐ 32. **TEST PREP** How much greater is the LCM of 18 and 24 than the LCM of 12 and 8? (p.170)

A 2   **B** 8   **C** 48   **D** 128

EXTRA PRACTICE page 244, Set A

Multiply Fractions

Learn how to multiply fractions.

Carolyn asked $\frac{3}{4}$ of her classmates what time they leave for school in the morning. Of those she asked, $\frac{1}{2}$ leave at 7:00 A.M. What fractional part of the classmates she asked told her that they leave for school at 7:00 A.M.?

One way to find the fractional part of a fraction is to make a model.

Find $\frac{1}{2}$ of $\frac{3}{4}$, or $\frac{1}{2} \times \frac{3}{4}$.

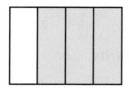

Fold a piece of paper into 4 equal parts.

Shade 3 parts to show $\frac{3}{4}$.

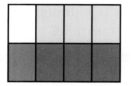

Fold the paper in half. Shade $\frac{1}{2}$ of the paper.

Of the $2 \times 4 = 8$ parts, $1 \times 3 = 3$ are shaded twice, so $\frac{3}{8}$ of the paper is shaded twice. These parts represent $\frac{1}{2} \times \frac{3}{4}$.

$$\frac{1}{2} \times \frac{3}{4} = \frac{3}{8}$$

So, $\frac{3}{8}$ of the students asked said they leave for school at 7:00 A.M.

• Make a model to find $\frac{1}{3} \times \frac{3}{4}$.

• For both models, compare the numerator and denominator of the products with the numerators and denominators of the factors. What relationship do you see?

You can see this relationship in the solution to the problem.

$$\frac{\text{numerator} \times \text{numerator}}{\text{denominator} \times \text{denominator}} = \frac{\text{numerator}}{\text{denominator}}$$

↑   ↑   ↑

factor   factor   product

You can use this relationship to multiply fractions without making a model.

EXAMPLE 1

Remember that to write a fraction in simplest form, divide the numerator and the denominator by a common factor.

Find $\frac{1}{3} \times \frac{3}{7}$. Write the product in simplest form.

$$\frac{1}{3} \times \frac{3}{7} = \frac{1 \times 3}{3 \times 7} = \frac{3}{21}$$
Multiply the numerators.
Multiply the denominators.

$$= \frac{3 \div 3}{21 \div 3}$$
Divide the numerator and the denominator by the common factor, 3.

$$= \frac{1}{7}$$
Write the product in simplest form.

So, $\frac{1}{3} \times \frac{3}{7} = \frac{1}{7}$.

- Explain why the product, $\frac{1}{7}$, is less than the factor $\frac{3}{7}$.

You can also multiply a whole number and a fraction without making a model.

EXAMPLE 2

Ms. Jones's car is being repaired after being in an accident. Her daughter Cindy will have to walk a total of $\frac{9}{10}$ mi to and from school every day for 11 days. How far will Cindy walk in all?

Find $11 \times \frac{9}{10}$.

Estimate. $11 \times 1 = 11$

$$11 \times \frac{9}{10} = \frac{11}{1} \times \frac{9}{10}$$
Write the whole number as a fraction.

$$= \frac{11 \times 9}{1 \times 10}$$
Multiply the numerators.
Multiply the denominators.

$$= \frac{99}{10}, \text{ or } 9\frac{9}{10}$$
Write the answer as a fraction or as a mixed number in simplest form.

Compare the product to your estimate. $9\frac{9}{10}$ is close to the estimate of 11. The product is reasonable.

So, Cindy will walk $9\frac{9}{10}$ mi.

- **What if** Cindy walked to school for 21 days? How far would Cindy walk in all?

When a numerator and a denominator have a common factor, you can simplify before you multiply.

EXAMPLE 3

Cheryl has $\frac{3}{4}$ of a box of snacks left from a school party. She gives $\frac{2}{5}$ of the snacks to the people in the school office. What part of the box of snacks does she give the people in the office?

Find $\frac{2}{5} \times \frac{3}{4}$.

Estimate. $\frac{1}{2} \times 1 = \frac{1}{2}$

$\frac{2}{5} \times \frac{3}{4}$ ← The GCF of 2 and 4 is 2.

Look for a numerator and denominator with common factors. Find the GCF.

$\frac{\overset{1}{2}}{5} \times \frac{3}{\underset{2}{4}}$ ← $2 \div 2 = 1$
← $4 \div 2 = 2$

Divide the numerator and denominator by the GCF, 2.

$\frac{\overset{1}{2}}{5} \times \frac{3}{\underset{2}{4}} = \frac{1 \times 3}{5 \times 2} = \frac{3}{10}$

Multiply.

So, Cheryl gives away $\frac{3}{10}$ of the box of snacks.

• What is $\frac{1}{8} \times \frac{6}{7}$? Simplify the fractions before you multiply.

EXAMPLE 4

Find $\frac{8}{9} \times \frac{3}{4}$. Simplify the fractions before you multiply.

$\frac{8}{9} \times \frac{3}{4}$ ← The GCF of 8 and 4 is 4.
← The GCF of 3 and 9 is 3.

$\frac{\overset{2}{8}}{\underset{3}{9}} \times \frac{\overset{1}{3}}{\underset{1}{4}} = \frac{2 \times 1}{3 \times 1} = \frac{2}{3}$

Divide the numerators and denominators by the GCFs, 3 and 4. Multiply.

So, $\frac{8}{9} \times \frac{3}{4} = \frac{2}{3}$.

CHECK FOR UNDERSTANDING

Think and Discuss Look back at the lesson to answer each question.

1. **Explain** how to make a model to show $\frac{1}{3} \times \frac{3}{8}$.

2. **Explain** how you can rewrite a whole number before you multiply it by a fraction.

Guided Practice Make a model to find the product.

3. $\frac{3}{4} \times \frac{1}{2}$ 4. $\frac{1}{3} \times \frac{5}{8}$ 5. $\frac{2}{5} \times \frac{1}{2}$ 6. $\frac{1}{3} \times \frac{1}{2}$

Find the product. Write it in simplest form.

7. $\frac{3}{4} \times \frac{2}{5}$ 8. $\frac{2}{5} \times \frac{7}{8}$ 9. $\frac{1}{8} \times \frac{4}{9}$ 10. $\frac{2}{3} \times 16$

11. $\frac{2}{3} \times 4$ 12. $9 \times \frac{2}{3}$ 13. $\frac{5}{6} \times \frac{2}{3}$ 14. $\frac{3}{5} \times \frac{5}{6}$

PRACTICE AND PROBLEM SOLVING

Independent ▶ Practice

Make a model to find the product.

15. $\frac{3}{4} \times \frac{1}{4}$ 16. $\frac{3}{4} \times \frac{2}{3}$ 17. $\frac{1}{8} \times \frac{1}{2}$ 18. $3 \times \frac{1}{4}$

Find the product. Write it in simplest form.

19. $\frac{1}{3} \times \frac{2}{3}$ 20. $\frac{3}{4} \times \frac{1}{3}$ 21. $\frac{1}{5} \times \frac{2}{3}$ 22. $\frac{1}{4} \times \frac{2}{7}$

23. $\frac{4}{5} \times \frac{7}{8}$ 24. $\frac{2}{9} \times \frac{3}{4}$ 25. $\frac{1}{8} \times \frac{4}{5}$ 26. $\frac{5}{9} \times \frac{3}{10}$

27. $\frac{4}{9} \times \frac{3}{5}$ 28. $\frac{2}{3} \times 21$ 29. $24 \times \frac{1}{12}$ 30. $\frac{1}{8} \times 16$

TECHNOLOGY LINK

More Practice: **Harcourt Mega Math Fraction Action,** *Fraction Flare-Up,* Level O

Compare. Write <, >, or = for ●.

31. $\frac{2}{9} \times \frac{3}{10}$ ● $\frac{2}{9}$ 32. $\frac{5}{6} \times 5$ ● $\frac{5}{6}$ 33. $8 \times \frac{1}{9}$ ● 8

Problem Solving ▶ Applications

34. Sandra takes $\frac{1}{2}$ hr to walk to school. She spends $\frac{1}{2}$ of that time walking down her street. What part of an hour does Sandra spend walking down her street? How many minutes is this?

35. There are 144 registered voters in Booker County. In the last election, $\frac{1}{4}$ of them did not vote. How many voters did vote?

36. **❓ What's the Question?**   Natalie runs $\frac{2}{3}$ the distance her brother runs in one week. Her brother runs 15 miles one week. The answer is 10 miles.

37. **REASONING**   Scott chose a number, added 2, multiplied the sum by 4, and divided the product by 8. The final number was 4. What number had Scott chosen?

MIXED REVIEW AND TEST PREP

38. $3\frac{2}{3} + 2\frac{1}{7}$ (p. 210)   39. Solve. $5b = 60.45$ (p. 94)   40. 267.45×2.8 (p. 80)

⭐ 41. **TEST PREP**   Gene's goal is to work $23\frac{1}{2}$ hr a week. So far he has worked $4\frac{1}{4}$ hr, $3\frac{3}{4}$ hr, $1\frac{1}{2}$ hr, and $7\frac{3}{4}$ hr. How many hours does Gene need to work to reach his goal? (p. 214)

   A $17\frac{1}{4}$ hr   **B** $15\frac{1}{2}$ hr   **C** $6\frac{1}{4}$ hr   **D** $5\frac{1}{2}$ hr

⭐ 42. **TEST PREP**   Which shows the GCF for 130 and 75? (p. 170)

   F 3   **G** 4   **H** 5   **J** 6

EXTRA PRACTICE page 244, Set B

Multiply Mixed Numbers

Learn how to multiply mixed numbers.

Write the missing numerator.

1. $1\frac{2}{3} = \frac{\blacksquare}{3}$ 2. $6\frac{3}{5} = \frac{\blacksquare}{5}$

3. $7\frac{3}{7} = \frac{\blacksquare}{7}$ 4. $9\frac{3}{8} = \frac{\blacksquare}{8}$

5. $3\frac{2}{5} = \frac{\blacksquare}{5}$

Remember that you can write a mixed number as a fraction.

$$2\frac{3}{4} = \frac{(2 \times 4) + 3}{4}$$

$$= \frac{11}{4}$$

Ann and Sheri are training for a bicycle race. On one day, Ann rides $3\frac{1}{5}$ mi. Sheri rides $2\frac{1}{2}$ times as far as Ann. How many miles does Sheri ride?

Find $2\frac{1}{2} \times 3\frac{1}{5}$.   Estimate. $3 \times 3 = 9$

$2\frac{1}{2} \times 3\frac{1}{5} = \frac{5}{2} \times \frac{16}{5}$ *Write the mixed numbers as fractions.*

$= \frac{\overset{1}{\cancel{5}}}{\underset{1}{\cancel{2}}} \times \frac{\overset{8}{\cancel{16}}}{\underset{1}{\cancel{5}}}$ *Simplify the fractions. Multiply.*

$= \frac{8}{1}$, or 8 *Write the answer in simplest form or as a whole or mixed number.*

So, Sheri rides 8 mi. The answer is reasonable since it is close to the estimate of 9 mi.

You can use the Distributive Property to multiply a whole number by a mixed number.

EXAMPLE

Multiply. $5 \times 2\frac{3}{8}$

$5 \times 2\frac{3}{8} = 5 \times \left(2 + \frac{3}{8}\right)$

$= (5 \times 2) + \left(5 \times \frac{3}{8}\right)$ *Use the Distributive Property.*

$= (5 \times 2) + \left(\frac{5}{1} \times \frac{3}{8}\right)$ *Write the whole number as a fraction. Find 5×2 and $\frac{5}{1} \times \frac{3}{8}$.*

$= 10 + \frac{15}{8}$

$= 10 + 1\frac{7}{8} = 11\frac{7}{8}$ *Write the fraction as a mixed number. Find the sum.*

So, $5 \times 2\frac{3}{8} = 11\frac{7}{8}$.

Think and ▶
Discuss

Look back at the lesson to answer each question.

1. **Explain** how to use the Distributive Property to find $3 \times 4\frac{2}{3}$.

2. **Explain** whether the product of two mixed numbers is greater than or less than each factor. Give two examples.

Guided ▶
Practice

Find the product. Write it in simplest form.

3. $\frac{3}{4} \times 1\frac{1}{2}$ 4. $\frac{1}{2} \times 2\frac{1}{3}$ 5. $1\frac{1}{2} \times 1\frac{1}{2}$ 6. $1\frac{2}{5} \times 2\frac{1}{4}$

Use the Distributive Property to multiply.

7. $6\frac{1}{8} \times 3$ 8. $3 \times 9\frac{4}{5}$ 9. $1\frac{1}{8} \times 2$ 10. $6 \times 4\frac{1}{4}$

PRACTICE AND PROBLEM SOLVING

Independent ▶
Practice

Find the product. Write it in simplest form.

11. $4\frac{2}{3} \times 1\frac{3}{4}$ 12. $1\frac{3}{8} \times 4\frac{2}{3}$ 13. $5\frac{1}{2} \times 6$ 14. $2 \times 3\frac{1}{7}$

15. $4\frac{1}{6} \times 3\frac{3}{5}$ 16. $1\frac{3}{4} \times 3$ 17. $10\frac{1}{5} \times 8\frac{1}{3}$ 18. $5 \times 1\frac{5}{6}$

Use the Distributive Property to multiply.

19. $3 \times 2\frac{2}{5}$ 20. $4 \times 8\frac{5}{6}$ 21. $3\frac{3}{4} \times 6$ 22. $1\frac{1}{2} \times 12$

Compare. Write <, >, or = for each ●.

23. $3\frac{1}{3} \times 2\frac{1}{7}$ ● $3\frac{1}{4} \times 5$ 24. $7 \times 7\frac{3}{7}$ ● $6\frac{3}{4} \times 4\frac{4}{5}$

Problem Solving ▶
Applications

25. Mr. Jackson rides his bicycle $1\frac{2}{3}$ mi every day. His wife rides $1\frac{1}{4}$ times as far as he does. How many miles does Mrs. Jackson ride her bicycle?

26. John works part time for $6.50 an hour. He works $3\frac{1}{2}$ hr each on Monday, Tuesday, and Thursday afternoons. How much does he earn those three days?

27. ✏️ **Write About It** Without multiplying, tell whether the product $\frac{2}{3} \times \frac{3}{4}$ is a fraction, a whole number, or a mixed number.

MIXED REVIEW AND TEST PREP

28. $\frac{4}{9} \times \frac{2}{3}$ (p. 228)   29. $8\frac{3}{4} - 2\frac{2}{5}$ (p. 210)   30. Simplify. $\frac{27}{45}$ (p. 182)   31. $414,089 - 62,036$ (p. 22)

⭐ 32. **TEST PREP** Which is the mean of the data? (p. 118)

90, 94, 65, 90, 84, 94, 85

A 29   **B** 86   **C** 90   **D** 94

Divide Fractions

 M A T H LAB

Explore how to model division of fractions.

You need fraction circles.

1. $3 \times \frac{1}{3}$ **2.** $\frac{1}{4} \times 4$ **3.** $7 \times \frac{3}{2}$

4. $2 \times \frac{8}{12}$ **5.** $\frac{2}{5} \times \frac{5}{2}$

Using models will help you understand division of fractions.

Activity 1

A. Use fraction circles to find $4 \div \frac{1}{3}$, or the number of thirds in 4 wholes.

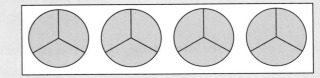

- Trace 4 whole circles on your paper.

- Model $4 \div \frac{1}{3}$ by tracing $\frac{1}{3}$-circle pieces on the 4 circles.

One whole equals three thirds.

- How many thirds are in 4 wholes? What is $4 \div \frac{1}{3}$?

B. Use fraction circles to find $\frac{1}{3} \div \frac{1}{6}$, or the number of sixths in $\frac{1}{3}$.

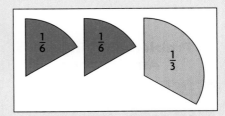

- Place as many $\frac{1}{6}$ pieces as you can on the $\frac{1}{3}$ piece.

- How many sixths are in $\frac{1}{3}$? What is $\frac{1}{3} \div \frac{1}{6}$?

Think and Discuss

- If $4 \div \frac{1}{3} = 12$, tell what $8 \div \frac{1}{3}$ must be.

- If $2 \div \frac{1}{6} = 12$, tell what $8 \div \frac{1}{6}$ must be.

Practice

Use fraction circles to model each problem. Draw a diagram of your model.

1. $3 \div \frac{1}{3}$ **2.** $4 \div \frac{1}{4}$ **3.** $\frac{1}{2} \div \frac{1}{8}$ **4.** $\frac{3}{4} \div \frac{1}{8}$

Two numbers are **reciprocals** if their product is 1.

$$\frac{1}{2} \times 2 = 1 \qquad \frac{3}{4} \times \frac{4}{3} = 1 \qquad 6 \times \frac{1}{6} = 1$$

$$\uparrow \quad \uparrow \qquad\qquad \uparrow \quad \uparrow \qquad\qquad \uparrow \quad \uparrow$$

reciprocals   reciprocals   reciprocals

TECHNOLOGY LINK

More Practice:
**Harcourt Mega Math
Fraction Action,**
Fraction Flare-Up,
Level P

By using inverse operations, you can write related number sentences.

$$1 \div \frac{1}{2} = 2 \qquad 1 \div \frac{3}{4} = \frac{4}{3} \qquad 1 \div 6 = \frac{1}{6}$$

$$1 \div 2 = \frac{1}{2} \qquad 1 \div \frac{4}{3} = \frac{3}{4} \qquad 1 \div \frac{1}{6} = 6$$

You can use reciprocals and inverse operations when you divide.

Activity 2

- Study these problems.

Find $6 \div \frac{1}{2}$.

$1 \div \frac{1}{2} = 2$ *Think of the reciprocal of $\frac{1}{2}$.*

Since $1 \div \frac{1}{2} = 1 \times 2$, $6 \div \frac{1}{2} = 6 \times 2$.

So, $6 \div \frac{1}{2} = 6 \times 2 = 12$.

Find $\frac{3}{4} \div \frac{1}{3}$.

$1 \div \frac{1}{3} = 3$ *Think of the reciprocal of $\frac{1}{3}$.*

Since $1 \div \frac{1}{3} = 1 \times 3$, $\frac{3}{4} \div \frac{1}{3} = \frac{3}{4} \times 3$.

So, $\frac{3}{4} \div \frac{1}{3} = \frac{3}{4} \times 3 = \frac{9}{4}$, or $2\frac{1}{4}$.

Think and Discuss

- When you divide 1 by a number, what is the quotient?

- If $1 \div \frac{1}{3} = 3$, then what is $2 \div \frac{1}{3}$? What is $5 \div \frac{1}{3}$?

- If $1 \div \frac{2}{5} = \frac{5}{2}$, then what is $2 \div \frac{2}{5}$? What is $\frac{1}{2} \div \frac{2}{5}$?

Practice

Find the value of *n*.

1. If $1 \div \frac{1}{2} = 2$, then $2 \div \frac{1}{2} = n$.

2. If $1 \div \frac{4}{5} = \frac{5}{4}$, then $4 \div \frac{4}{5} = n$.

3. If $1 \div \frac{2}{3} = \frac{3}{2}$, then $\frac{1}{2} \div \frac{2}{3} = n$.

4. If $1 \div \frac{3}{5} = \frac{5}{3}$, then $\frac{3}{4} \div \frac{3}{5} = n$.

Find the quotient.

5. $6 \div \frac{3}{4}$ 6. $4 \div \frac{1}{2}$ 7. $\frac{1}{2} \div \frac{1}{3}$ 8. $\frac{2}{3} \div \frac{1}{8}$

MIXED REVIEW AND TEST PREP

9. $2\frac{4}{5} \times 3\frac{3}{8}$ (p. 232)

10. Complete. $\frac{3}{8} = \frac{\blacksquare}{24}$ (p. 182)

11. Compare 606.64 and 606.074.
Use $<$, $>$, or $=$. (p. 60)

12. $46.08 - 19.204$ (p. 76)

13. **TEST PREP** How many times as great is the GCF of 15 and 18 than the GCF of 25 and 33? (p. 170)

     A 2   **B** 3   **C** 5   **D** 6

Divide Fractions and Mixed Numbers

Learn how to divide with fractions and mixed numbers.

QUICK REVIEW

Write each mixed number as a fraction.

1. $2\frac{1}{3}$
2. $1\frac{3}{8}$
3. $4\frac{1}{2}$
4. $3\frac{9}{10}$
5. $6\frac{2}{3}$

Stacey is bringing juice to be served after the school council meeting. Stacey said she would bring enough juice for everyone at the meeting to have a glass. Each glass holds $\frac{1}{5}$ liter. How many glasses can be served if Stacey brings 8 liters of juice?

Find $8 \div \frac{1}{5}$.

Math Idea ▶ When you divide by a fraction, multiply by the reciprocal to find the quotient.

Rewrite the division problem as a multiplication problem by using the reciprocal.

$8 \div \frac{1}{5} = \frac{8}{1} \div \frac{1}{5}$ *Write the whole number as a fraction.*

$= \frac{8}{1} \times \frac{5}{1}$ *Use the reciprocal of the divisor to write a multiplication problem.*

$= \frac{8}{1} \times \frac{5}{1} = \frac{40}{1}$, or 40   *Multiply.*

So, 8 liters can fill 40 glasses.

Multiply by the reciprocal of the divisor when you divide fractions and mixed numbers.

EXAMPLE 1

Find $\frac{2}{3} \div \frac{4}{7}$.

$\frac{2}{3} \div \frac{4}{7} = \frac{2}{3} \times \frac{7}{4}$ *Use the reciprocal of the divisor to write a multiplication problem.*

$= \frac{\overset{1}{\cancel{2}}}{3} \times \frac{7}{\underset{2}{\cancel{4}}}$ *Divide the numerator and denominator by the GCF, 2.*

$= \frac{7}{6}$, or $1\frac{1}{6}$ *Multiply.*

So, $\frac{2}{3} \div \frac{4}{7} = 1\frac{1}{6}$.

EXAMPLE 2

Each member of the school council will write his or her name on a strip of paper at the meeting. Jeremy has pieces of paper $5\frac{1}{4}$ in. long. Each strip of paper should be $1\frac{3}{4}$ in. How many strips can Jeremy cut from the length of one piece of paper?

Find $5\frac{1}{4} \div 1\frac{3}{4}$.

Estimate. $5 \div 2 = 2\frac{1}{2}$

$5\frac{1}{4} \div 1\frac{3}{4} = \frac{21}{4} \div \frac{7}{4}$ *Write the mixed numbers as fractions.*

$= \frac{21}{4} \times \frac{4}{7}$ *Use the reciprocal of the divisor to write a multiplication problem.*

$= \frac{\overset{3}{\cancel{21}}}{\underset{1}{\cancel{4}}} \times \frac{\overset{1}{\cancel{4}}}{\underset{1}{\cancel{7}}}$ *Simplify and multiply.*

$= \frac{3}{1}$, or 3

Compare the product to your estimate. 3 is close to the estimate of $2\frac{1}{2}$. The product is reasonable.

So, Jeremy can cut 3 strips from each piece of paper.

• Explain how to find $2\frac{3}{4} \div 1\frac{2}{5}$.

Sometimes you can use mental math to divide whole numbers and fractions.

EXAMPLE 3

Use mental math to solve.

A. $9 \div \frac{1}{2}$ **THINK:** $9 \times 2 = 18$.   *Dividing by $\frac{1}{2}$ is the same as multiplying by 2.*

So, $9 \div \frac{1}{2} = 18$.   *There are 18 halves in 9.*

B. $13 \div \frac{1}{3}$ **THINK:** $13 \times 3 = 39$.   *Dividing by $\frac{1}{3}$ is the same as multiplying by 3.*

So, $13 \div \frac{1}{3} = 39$.   *There are 39 thirds in 13.*

C. $20 \div \frac{2}{5}$ **THINK:** $20 \times 5 = 100$.   *Dividing by $\frac{2}{5}$ is the same as multiplying by $\frac{5}{2}$.*
                $100 \div 2 = 50$.

So, $20 \div \frac{2}{5} = 50$.

• Use mental math to find $15 \div \frac{1}{6}$.

Think and ▶
Discuss

Look back at the lesson to answer each question.

1. **Explain** what the reciprocal of a number is. Give an example.

2. **Give** an example of a fraction or mixed-number division problem in which the quotient is greater than the dividend.

Guided ▶
Practice

Write the reciprocal of the number.

3. $\frac{2}{3}$　　　　4. $\frac{3}{4}$　　　　5. 7　　　　6. $2\frac{3}{8}$　　　　7. $4\frac{1}{3}$

Find the quotient. Write it in simplest form.

8. $\frac{1}{3} \div \frac{1}{2}$　　　9. $\frac{1}{5} \div \frac{1}{4}$　　　10. $\frac{1}{4} \div \frac{1}{2}$　　　11. $\frac{1}{8} \div 3$

12. $4 \div \frac{2}{3}$　　　13. $3\frac{3}{5} \div 1\frac{1}{5}$　　　14. $2\frac{3}{5} \div 4$　　　15. $3\frac{1}{4} \div 2\frac{2}{3}$

Independent ▶
Practice

Write the reciprocal of the number.

16. $\frac{5}{8}$　　　17. 10　　　18. $\frac{1}{6}$　　　19. $\frac{2}{9}$　　　20. $3\frac{1}{2}$

21. $\frac{15}{7}$　　　22. $\frac{1}{5}$　　　23. 9　　　24. $1\frac{5}{6}$　　　25. $2\frac{3}{5}$

Find the quotient. Write it in simplest form.

26. $\frac{3}{8} \div \frac{1}{2}$　　　27. $\frac{2}{3} \div \frac{4}{7}$　　　28. $\frac{7}{8} \div \frac{1}{3}$　　　29. $8 \div \frac{6}{7}$

30. $12 \div \frac{3}{5}$　　　31. $\frac{3}{4} \div \frac{1}{3}$　　　32. $\frac{4}{9} \div \frac{3}{5}$　　　33. $4 \div \frac{4}{5}$

34. $3\frac{2}{5} \div 1\frac{1}{5}$　　　35. $3\frac{4}{5} \div \frac{3}{4}$　　　36. $4\frac{1}{2} \div \frac{1}{4}$　　　37. $4\frac{1}{5} \div 2\frac{3}{5}$

Use mental math to find each quotient.

38. $10 \div \frac{1}{2}$　　　39. $11 \div \frac{1}{4}$　　　40. $6 \div \frac{1}{4}$　　　41. $8 \div \frac{1}{4}$

42. $3 \div \frac{1}{6}$　　　43. $9 \div \frac{1}{9}$　　　44. $7 \div \frac{1}{2}$　　　45. $12 \div \frac{2}{3}$

ALGEBRA Evaluate the expression.

46. $4 \div a$ for $a = \frac{2}{3}$　　　　　　　47. $b \div 2\frac{1}{3}$ for $b = 5\frac{1}{2}$

48. $1\frac{4}{5} \div a$ for $a = 2\frac{3}{5}$　　　　　49. $c \div 7\frac{4}{5}$ for $c = 2\frac{1}{6}$

50. $b \div 7$ for $b = \frac{1}{5}$　　　　　　　51. $3\frac{1}{5} \div b$ for $b = 4$

52. Vocabulary Power In a division problem, the *divisor* is the number you divide by. What is the dividend?

53. Katie bought 2-lb, 7-lb, and 3-lb packages of ground turkey. How many $\frac{1}{4}$-lb turkey burgers can she make?

54. In a $\frac{1}{4}$-mi relay, each runner on a team runs $\frac{1}{16}$ mi. How many runners are in the relay?

55. Gerald has $8\frac{3}{4}$ yd of fabric to make costumes for the school play. Each costume requires $1\frac{1}{4}$ yd of fabric. How many costumes can Gerald make with the fabric that he has?

56. **?** **What's the Error?** Jamie worked the problem below. What mistake did Jamie make? What is the correct answer in simplest form?

$$3\frac{1}{3} \div 2\frac{2}{9} = \frac{10}{3} \div \frac{20}{9} = \frac{3}{10} \times \frac{20}{9} = \frac{2}{3}$$

57. Jacki wants to buy a blouse for $12.95, a T-shirt for $15.95, a book for $10.50, and two pens for $3.75 each. What is the total cost?

MIXED REVIEW AND TEST PREP

58. $3\frac{1}{3} \times 2\frac{2}{5}$ (p. 232)   **59.** $10\frac{1}{2} + 2\frac{7}{8}$ (p. 210)   **60.** Evaluate $5.2x$ for $x = 3.41$. (p. 94)

61. TEST PREP Which is the sum for $234,607 + 84,395$? (p. 22)

   A 218,002   **B** 218,992   **C** 318,902   **D** 319,002

62. TEST PREP Which shows $4\frac{3}{8}$ as a fraction? (p. 186)

   F $\frac{11}{8}$ **G** $\frac{15}{8}$ **H** $\frac{35}{8}$ **J** $\frac{39}{8}$

PROBLEM SOLVING LiNKUP to Careers

Architecture Horace King was born in South Carolina in 1807. As an adult, he built more than 100 covered bridges in Georgia and nearby states. A bridge builder must first plan on paper a structure that will support heavy loads and withstand forces of nature. The mathematics that a bridge builder uses must be exact and correct at all times.

• The panels used on a covered bridge are $\frac{3}{4}$ ft wide. How many panels are needed to cover a side of a bridge that is 90 ft long?

PROBLEM SOLVING SKILL
Choose the Operation

Analyze
Choose
Solve
Check

Learn how to choose the operation needed to solve a problem.

Use the chart to help you decide how the numbers in a problem are related.

Then choose the operation needed to solve each problem.

ADD	• Joining groups of different sizes
SUBTRACT	• Taking away or comparing groups
MULTIPLY	• Joining equal-sized groups
DIVIDE	• Separating into equal-sized groups • Finding out how many in each group

Read each problem and decide how you would solve it.

A. In one week, José drove $3\frac{1}{4}$ mi to play practice, $3\frac{1}{4}$ mi to the hardware store to buy supplies, and $7\frac{4}{5}$ mi to Jim's house to work on the costumes for the play. How many miles did he drive in all?	**B.** Carla bought 6 yd of terry cloth to make collars for some of the costumes for the play. Each collar takes $\frac{2}{3}$ yd of fabric. How many collars can Carla make?
C. Leanne makes props for the school play. She uses $4\frac{1}{8}$ lb of clay to make each vase and $2\frac{3}{4}$ lb to make each bowl. How much more clay does Leanne use to make one vase than one bowl?	**D.** Sean bought $12\frac{2}{3}$ yd of pine lumber for $6 per yd to build some scenery for the school play. How much money did he spend?

• What operation would you use to solve each problem?

• Which problems could you solve by using a combination of operations?

• How did the chart above help you decide which operation to use for each problem?

• Solve each problem.

Solve. Name the operations used.

1. It takes Karen $5\frac{1}{2}$ min to walk to the community center. It takes Jackie $7\frac{1}{3}$ min. How much longer does it take Jackie?

2. Rob makes candles that weigh $1\frac{3}{16}$ lb each. How much do 24 of them weigh?

3. Katie decorates travel bags. Each bag requires $1\frac{1}{3}$ yd of trim around the top and 1 yd of trim on the handle.

   a. Which operations could you use to find how much trim is needed for a number of bags?

   b. How much trim would it take to make 4 bags?

       A subtraction and division

       B addition and multiplication

       C division and multiplication

       D addition and division

       F 8 yd

       G $8\frac{1}{3}$ yd

       H 9 yd

       J $9\frac{1}{3}$ yd

MIXED APPLICATIONS

4. Marcie has 18 oz of dough left in a container. She needs $3\frac{3}{5}$ oz of dough to make one decoration.

   a. Write the expression you would use to find the number of decorations she can make. Solve the problem.

   b. How many ounces of dough are left in the container if she makes 4 decorations?

Use Data For 5–8, use the map.

5. Darrin hiked the shortest route from the trailhead to Hart Mountain in $7\frac{3}{4}$ hr. What is the average number of miles he hiked in 1 hr?

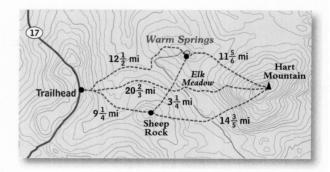

6. How much shorter was the trail that Darrin took than the trail through Warm Springs?

7. Elk Meadow is halfway along the trail from the trailhead to Hart Mountain. How far is it from the trailhead to Elk Meadow?

8. Sharlene left the trailhead at 8:30 A.M. for a daylong hike. She returned to the trailhead $7\frac{1}{2}$ hr after she left. What time did she return?

9. ✏️ **Write About It** Explain how you decide what operation to use when solving a problem.

Choose the Method

Learn how to choose the method to solve problems.

QUICK REVIEW

Solve. Write the answer in simplest form.

1. $\frac{4}{9} + \frac{1}{9}$ 2. $\frac{13}{16} - \frac{5}{16}$ 3. $\frac{2}{3} \times \frac{4}{5}$ 4. $\frac{5}{8} \div \frac{9}{8}$ 5. $2\frac{2}{7} \div 3\frac{4}{7}$

To solve some fraction problems, you can use mental math. For other problems you may choose to use paper and pencil or a calculator.

Carrie wants to put a border around two sides of her rectangular shaped garden. She has a 20-ft piece of lumber that will be cut into $\frac{2}{3}$-ft pieces. How many $\frac{2}{3}$-ft pieces can she cut from the lumber?

Use Mental Math

Divide: $20 \div \frac{2}{3}$.

THINK: $20 \times \frac{3}{2}$ *Dividing by $\frac{2}{3}$ is the same as multiplying by $\frac{3}{2}$.*

$20 \times 3 = 60$

$60 \div 2 = 30$

So, 30 pieces can be cut from the lumber.

Carrie has $15\frac{3}{4}$ lb of decorative rock to put in the garden. She has $3\frac{1}{2}$ times as many pounds of mulch. How many pounds of mulch does Carrie have?

Use Paper and Pencil

Multiply: $15\frac{3}{4} \times 3\frac{1}{2}$.

$15\frac{3}{4} \times 3\frac{1}{2} = \frac{63}{4} \times \frac{7}{2}$ *Write the mixed numbers as fractions.*

$= \frac{63}{4} \times \frac{7}{2}$ *Multiply.*

$= \frac{441}{8} = 55\frac{1}{8}$ *Write the fraction as a mixed number.*

Use a Calculator

Multiply: $15\frac{3}{4} \times 3\frac{1}{2}$.

15 3 4   3 1 2 Enter

$15\frac{3}{4} \times 3\frac{1}{2} = \quad 55\frac{1}{8}$

So, Carrie has $55\frac{1}{8}$ lb of mulch.

**Think and ▶
Discuss**

Look back at the lesson to answer the question.

1. Tell which method you would use to find $\frac{4}{15} \times \frac{7}{15}$.

**Guided ▶
Practice**

Solve. Choose mental math, paper and pencil, or a calculator.

2. $\frac{3}{5} \times \frac{1}{5}$

3. $\frac{4}{5} \times \frac{5}{12}$

4. $\frac{5}{11} \div \frac{3}{11}$

5. $30 \div \frac{2}{3}$

6. $2\frac{2}{3} \div 1\frac{1}{4}$

7. $5\frac{7}{8} \times 3\frac{1}{8}$

**Independent ▶
Practice**

Solve. Choose mental math, paper and pencil, or a calculator.

8. $\frac{5}{8} \times \frac{5}{8}$

9. $\frac{3}{7} \div \frac{1}{7}$

10. $\frac{8}{9} \times \frac{5}{12}$

11. $25 \div \frac{1}{5}$

12. $2\frac{1}{2} \times 1\frac{1}{5}$

13. $5\frac{4}{7} \div 1\frac{1}{12}$

14. $9\frac{1}{3} \times 1\frac{1}{14}$

15. $4\frac{5}{8} \div \frac{5}{8}$

16. $2\frac{2}{5} \div 1\frac{1}{5}$

**Problem Solving ▶
Applications**

17. **FAST FACT • SCIENCE**   About $\frac{3}{4}$ of all commercially grown tomatoes are made into juice, canned tomatoes, sauces, pastes, and ketchup. How much of 12,000 lb of tomatoes would be used in this way?

18. A group of neighbors each have a vegetable garden in their yard. Each neighbor worked $2\frac{1}{3}$ hr in their garden on Tuesday. Together they worked $9\frac{1}{3}$ hr. How many people are in the group of neighbors?

19. In one year, Carrie uses $3\frac{1}{4}$ bags of fertilizer in her vegetable garden. Each bag of fertilizer weighs $8\frac{1}{2}$ lb. How many pounds of fertilizer does Carrie use?

20. Gavin purchased three types of meat at the deli totaling 5 lb. He bought $1\frac{1}{2}$ lb of bologna and $2\frac{1}{4}$ lb of ham. How much of the other type of meat did Gavin purchase?

21. ✏️ **Write About It**   Write a word problem using $2\frac{1}{4}$ divided by $\frac{1}{2}$ and solve.

MIXED REVIEW AND TEST PREP

22. Divide. $3 \div 1\frac{2}{3}$ (p. 236)

23. Subtract. $8\frac{1}{4} - 5\frac{2}{5}$ (p. 210)

24. What is the LCM of 8 and 24? (p. 170)

25. Divide. $58.32 \div 0.03$ (p. 88)

⭐ 26. **TEST PREP**   What is the value of $8 + 7 \times 6 - 5$? (p. 48)

   A 15   **B** 45   **C** 85   **D** 90

Set A (pp. 226–227)

Estimate each product or quotient.

1. $\frac{8}{9} \times \frac{3}{5}$

2. $\frac{1}{6} \times \frac{4}{9}$

3. $5\frac{1}{2} \div \frac{5}{6}$

4. $\frac{7}{9} \div \frac{3}{4}$

5. $3\frac{1}{3} \times 5\frac{1}{5}$

6. $8\frac{3}{5} \div 2\frac{3}{4}$

7. $9\frac{7}{8} \times 10\frac{1}{2}$

8. $18\frac{3}{4} \div 5\frac{1}{8}$

9. Liz is making cookies to give to some new neighbors. The recipe calls for $1\frac{3}{4}$ cups of flour. About how much flour does Liz need if she makes $2\frac{1}{2}$ times the recipe?

Set B (pp. 228–231)

Find the product. Write it in simplest form.

1. $\frac{2}{4} \times \frac{3}{4}$

2. $\frac{2}{5} \times \frac{1}{4}$

3. $\frac{3}{8} \times \frac{3}{5}$

4. $3 \times \frac{7}{8}$

5. $\frac{2}{7} \times 8$

6. $\frac{5}{6} \times \frac{3}{8}$

7. $\frac{5}{9} \times \frac{1}{5}$

8. $\frac{1}{9} \times \frac{3}{4}$

9. To make a dye for art class, Jan needs $\frac{1}{4}$ tsp of red coloring and $\frac{1}{2}$ that amount of green coloring. How much green coloring does Jan need to make the dye?

Set C (pp. 232–233)

Find the product. Write it in simplest form.

1. $2\frac{2}{3} \times 2\frac{1}{4}$

2. $2\frac{1}{2} \times \frac{1}{5}$

3. $\frac{1}{5} \times 2\frac{2}{8}$

4. $3\frac{1}{6} \times 5\frac{1}{4}$

5. $2\frac{3}{4} \times \frac{5}{6}$

6. $2\frac{2}{7} \times \frac{2}{5}$

7. $3\frac{2}{3} \times 2\frac{3}{5}$

8. $6\frac{8}{9} \times 2\frac{3}{7}$

Set D (pp. 236–239)

Find the quotient. Write it in simplest form.

1. $\frac{2}{9} \div \frac{8}{18}$

2. $\frac{3}{8} \div 2\frac{1}{4}$

3. $2 \div 2\frac{2}{3}$

4. $1\frac{11}{12} \div 1\frac{5}{6}$

5. $\frac{3}{4} \div \frac{1}{8}$

6. $\frac{5}{6} \div 1\frac{2}{3}$

7. $3\frac{3}{4} \div 2\frac{7}{12}$

8. $\frac{5}{7} \div \frac{10}{11}$

Set E (pp. 242–243)

Solve. Choose mental math, paper and pencil, or a calculator.

1. $3 \div \frac{1}{2}$

2. $\frac{5}{6} \div \frac{1}{6}$

3. $3\frac{1}{2} \times 2\frac{1}{2}$

4. $3\frac{5}{8} \div 1\frac{1}{4}$

5. $2\frac{5}{6} \times 1\frac{2}{3}$

6. $4\frac{1}{2} \div 3\frac{3}{5}$

7. Ken has $4\frac{1}{2}$ lb of diced ham to make salads. If he uses $\frac{3}{8}$ lb of ham in each salad, how many salads can he make?

1. **VOCABULARY**   Two numbers are ___?___ if their product is 1. (pp. 235)

Estimate each product or quotient. (pp. 226–227)

2. $\frac{2}{9} \times \frac{1}{6}$
3. $\frac{7}{8} \div \frac{11}{12}$
4. $\frac{7}{15} \div \frac{8}{9}$
5. $\frac{3}{4} \times \frac{5}{6}$

6. $\frac{5}{8} \times \frac{1}{5}$
7. $\frac{5}{7} \div \frac{5}{9}$
8. $31\frac{3}{8} \div 4\frac{1}{2}$
9. $2\frac{4}{5} \times 3\frac{3}{10}$

10. $4\frac{2}{15} \times 5\frac{1}{3}$
11. $5\frac{1}{4} \div 3\frac{2}{5}$
12. $2\frac{5}{8} \times 4\frac{2}{3}$
13. $3\frac{1}{3} \div \frac{5}{6}$

Find the product. Write it in simplest form. (pp. 228–233)

14. $\frac{1}{6} \times \frac{3}{5}$
15. $\frac{2}{3} \times \frac{4}{5}$
16. $16 \times \frac{5}{12}$
17. $\frac{3}{8} \times 10$

18. $1\frac{1}{2} \times \frac{3}{4}$
19. $4\frac{1}{2} \times 2\frac{1}{3}$
20. $1\frac{1}{2} \times \frac{2}{3}$
21. $2\frac{1}{3} \times 3\frac{1}{5}$

22. $2\frac{5}{8} \times 4\frac{2}{3}$
23. $5\frac{1}{4} \times 3\frac{2}{5}$
24. $4\frac{1}{3} \times 6\frac{3}{4}$
25. $1\frac{5}{7} \times 3\frac{1}{3}$

Find the quotient. Write it in simplest form. (pp. 236–239)

26. $\frac{2}{3} \div \frac{3}{5}$
27. $\frac{3}{4} \div \frac{1}{3}$
28. $3\frac{1}{3} \div 2\frac{4}{5}$
29. $9\frac{1}{2} \div 1\frac{3}{8}$

30. $8 \div \frac{3}{4}$
31. $\frac{4}{5} \div 4$
32. $2\frac{3}{5} \div 4\frac{1}{5}$
33. $\frac{5}{8} \div 10$

34. $\frac{3}{10} \div 4$
35. $\frac{5}{8} \div 2\frac{1}{2}$
36. $3\frac{1}{3} \div \frac{2}{3}$
37. $2\frac{2}{3} \div 1\frac{1}{6}$

Solve. Choose mental math, paper and pencil, or a calculator. (pp. 242–243)

38. $\frac{2}{5} \times \frac{4}{5}$
39. $40 \div \frac{1}{5}$
40. $\frac{7}{8} \div \frac{3}{4}$
41. $\frac{4}{5} \times \frac{3}{8}$

42. $2\frac{1}{8} \times 6\frac{2}{3}$
43. $3\frac{1}{10} \div 1\frac{1}{2}$
44. $2\frac{1}{2} \times \frac{1}{2}$
45. $2\frac{2}{3} \div 2\frac{1}{2}$

Solve.

46. Mike rides his bicycle $6\frac{1}{2}$ min to school. Cami rides her bicycle $1\frac{1}{2}$ times as long. How long does it take Cami to ride to school? (pp. 228–233)

47. Eric practiced $\frac{3}{4}$ hr on Monday and $\frac{2}{5}$ hr on Saturday. How much longer did Eric practice on Monday? (pp. 240–241)

48. A race course is $\frac{3}{4}$ mi long. Racers want to run three equal sprints. How far apart should the markers be for the sprints? (pp. 236–239)

49. Sara has $\frac{5}{6}$ yd of ribbon and Mark has $\frac{3}{4}$ yd of ribbon. How much ribbon do Sara and Mark have altogether? (pp. 240–241)

50. The sum of Kiesha's and Brent's heights is $127\frac{1}{4}$ in. Kiesha's height is $64\frac{1}{2}$ in. What is Brent's height? (pp. 240–241)

NUMBER SENSE, CONCEPTS, AND OPERATIONS

1. Darlene rode her bicycle $1\frac{2}{5}$ miles on Tuesday, $2\frac{1}{4}$ miles on Thursday, and $\frac{4}{5}$ mile on Saturday. Which of the following is a reasonable estimate of the total distance Darlene rode her bicycle?

   A 3 miles

   B $4\frac{1}{2}$ miles

   C $5\frac{1}{2}$ miles

   D $6\frac{1}{2}$ miles

2. Each member of a group of students took $\frac{1}{8}$ hour to present an oral report. The group needed $\frac{1}{2}$ hour to present all of its reports. How many students were in the group?

   F 2

   G 4

   H 6

   J 8

3. Mrs. Gregg bought $2\frac{1}{2}$ pounds of beans, $2\frac{3}{4}$ pounds of fruit salad, and $1\frac{5}{8}$ pounds of pasta salad. Which of the following shows how much more fruit salad she bought than pasta salad?

   A $\frac{3}{4}$ pound

   B 1 pound

   C $1\frac{1}{8}$ pounds

   D 2 pounds

4. **Explain It** Ted drove $4\frac{1}{8}$ hours at an average speed of $58\frac{3}{5}$ miles per hour. Explain whether 250 miles is a reasonable estimate of the distance Ted drove.

★ **MEASUREMENT**

5. The map below shows where the Hoya family traveled on vacation.

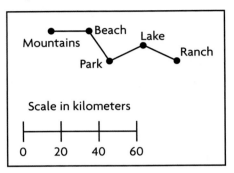

   Based on the scale provided, which of the following is the **best** approximate distance the Hoyas traveled between the lake and the beach?

   F 12.5 kilometers   **H** 40 kilometers

   G 25 kilometers   **J** 75 kilometers

6. The figure below shows a map of the Big Triangle Ranch.

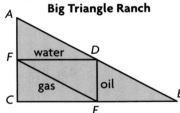

   Points D, E, and F are the midpoints of the three sides of $\triangle ABC$. The water line, oil pipeline, and gas line divide the ranch into four congruent triangles. Rectangle $FDEC$ is what fraction of the area of the ranch?

   A $\frac{3}{4}$ **C** $\frac{1}{3}$

   B $\frac{1}{2}$ **D** $\frac{1}{4}$

7. **Explain It** Amber will rollerblade 547.5 meters on Monday and 3.5 kilometers on Tuesday. How many meters will Amber rollerblade in all? Explain your answer.

ALGEBRAIC THINKING

8. Which of the following algebraic expressions represents "29.1 times a number, n"?

F $29.1 - n$

G $29.1 + n$

H $n \div 29.1$

J $29.1 \times n$

9. Eric read 20 pages of his book on Monday. Each day he plans to read 4 more pages than he read the day before. Which of the following shows how many pages he will read each day for the next four days?

A 4, 8, 12, 16

B 20, 24, 28, 32

C 24, 28, 32, 36

D 44, 72, 104, 140

10. Wyoming averages about 5 people per square mile. Let a equal the number of square miles. Which equation could you use to find the number of square miles in Wyoming on which about 25 people live?

F $5 \times 25 = a$ **H** $\frac{a}{5} = 25$

G $5a = 25$ **J** $25a = 5$

11. Explain It What does the equation below mean? Explain the steps you can use to solve it. Then solve.

$s + 1.1 = 5.9$

> **TIP** **Check your work.** See item 11. Is your answer correct? To find out, replace the variable in the equation with your answer and see whether the equation is true.

GEOMETRY AND SPATIAL SENSE

12. Jerianne drew the map grid below of her neighborhood.

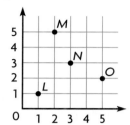

Which of the following names the location of the ordered pair (2,5)?

A L

B M

C N

D O

13. Bob drew the two figures shown below. What appears to be true about the figures?

F They are congruent.

G They are similar.

H They are hexagons.

J They are octagons.

14. Explain It Paula used prism-shaped bricks like the one shown below to make a patio. How many faces, vertices, and edges does each brick have? Explain your answer.

IT'S IN THE BAG!

Keys to Math

PROJECT Make a key chain to practice your divisibility rules.

Materials

- One piece of cardstock
- 10 pieces of white paper
- Color cardstock
- Metal ring
- Scissors
- Stapler
- Markers
- Hole punch
- Key pattern

Directions

1. Start a book by folding the cardstock in half. Center the white papers on the opened cover. Staple the papers together in the fold. (*Picture A*)

2. Write *PRACTICE PAGES* on the cover. Punch a hole in the top left corner of the book, and attach the book to the metal ring. Open the book and on the first page, write *TELL WHAT EACH NUMBER IS DIVISIBLE BY*.

3. Use the key pattern and cardstock to make nine keys. On one key, write the title *KEYS TO DIVISIBILITY*. Write one of the divisibility rules from page 164 on each of the remaining eight keys. Punch a hole in each of the keys, and attach them to the metal ring. (*Picture B*)

4. Write one of the following numbers on each page of the book: 75; 615; 1,407; 324; 936; 48,006; 45; 744; 7,064; 812; 5,188; 12,111; 501. (*Picture C*)

5. Use the rules to practice finding whether the numbers in the practice book are divisible by 2, 3, 4, 5, 6, 8, 9, or 10.

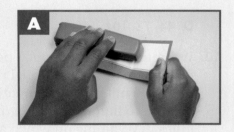

A

B

C

Challenge

Mixed Numbers and Time

Learn how to write times as mixed numbers, and how to add and subtract times.

The ticket agent at the airport told Mario that his flight from Portland, OR, to St. Paul, MN, would take "about $4\frac{1}{2}$ hours." The agent expressed the time as a mixed number.

To write a time period as a mixed number, use the fact that there are 60 minutes in 1 hour.

EXAMPLE 1

Mario's flight from Portland to St. Paul took 4 hours 24 minutes. Write the time as a mixed number.

$24 \text{ min} = 24 \times \frac{1}{60} \text{ hr} = \frac{24}{60} \text{ hr}$ — *Think: 60 min = 1 hr. So, 1 min = $\frac{1}{60}$ hr.*

$= \frac{2}{5} \text{ hr}$ — *Write the fraction in simplest form.*

$4 \text{ hr } 24 \text{ min} = 4\frac{2}{5} \text{ hr}$ — *Write the time.*

So, Mario's flight took $4\frac{2}{5}$ hr.

To add or subtract times, use the same methods you use to add or subtract mixed numbers.

EXAMPLE 2

Solve.

A. $\quad 2 \text{ hr } 18 \text{ min}$
$\quad\underline{+\ 3 \text{ hr } 52 \text{ min}}$
$\quad\ \ 5 \text{ hr } 70 \text{ min}$

$= 5 \text{ hr} + (60 + 10) \text{ min}$
$= 5 \text{ hr} + 1 \text{ hr} + \frac{10}{60} \text{ hr}$
$= 6 \text{ hr} + \frac{1}{6} \text{ hr}$
$= 6\frac{1}{6} \text{ hr}$

B. $\quad 8 \text{ hr } 14 \text{ min} \ \rightarrow \ 7 \text{ hr } (60 + 14) \text{ min}$
$\quad\underline{-3 \text{ hr } 20 \text{ min}} \ \rightarrow \ \underline{-3 \text{ hr } 20 \text{ min}}$

$\quad\quad\quad\quad\quad\quad\quad 7 \text{ hr } 74 \text{ min}$
$\quad\quad\quad\quad\quad\underline{-3 \text{ hr } 20 \text{ min}}$
$\quad\quad\quad\quad\quad\ \ 4 \text{ hr } 54 \text{ min}$

$= 4 \text{ hr} + \frac{54}{60} \text{ hr}$
$= 4\frac{9}{10} \text{ hr}$

TALK ABOUT IT

• Tell how you would write the time 7 hours 35 minutes as a mixed number.

TRY IT

Write as a fraction or mixed number.

1. 1 hr 30 min   **2.** 4 hr 55 min   **3.** 1 hr 19 min

4. 28 min   **5.** 45 min   **6.** 3 hr 42 min

Solve. Write as a mixed number.

7. 5 hr 12 min + 8 hr 18 min   **8.** 6 hr 10 min − 4 hr 20 min

VOCABULARY

1. The largest of the common factors of two numbers is the __?__ . (p. 170)

2. To add unlike fractions, you can write equivalent fractions by using the __?__ . (p. 206)

EXAMPLES	EXERCISES

Chapter 7

- **Write whether a number is prime or composite.** (pp. 166–167)

  Tell whether 27 is prime or composite.

  $3 \times 9 = 27$

  So, 27 is a composite number.

  Use the divisibility rules to see if you can find a factor other than 1 or 27.

Write *prime* or *composite*.

3. 16   4. 37   5. 19

6. 57   7. 45   8. 63

9. 105   10. 151   11. 193

- **Write the prime factorization of a number.** (pp. 168–169)

  Find the prime factorization of 150.

  $2 \times 3 \times 5^2$

Write the prime factorization in exponent form.

12. 52   13. 125   14. 180

15. 27   16. 100   17. 72

- **Find the GCF and LCM of two or more numbers.** (pp. 170–173)

  Find the LCM of 9 and 15.

  9: 9, 18, 27, 36, 45 *Find multiples of 9*
  15: 15, 30, 45   *and 15.*
  LCM = 45   *Find the LCM.*

Find the GCF of each set of numbers.

18. 15, 30   19. 9, 12   20. 8, 16, 12

Find the LCM of each set of numbers.

21. 6, 10   22. 6, 8   23. 5, 9, 12

Chapter 8

- **Write fractions in simplest form.** (pp. 182–185)

  Write $\frac{18}{30}$ in simplest form.

  $\frac{18}{30} = \frac{18 \div 6}{30 \div 6} = \frac{3}{5}$ *Divide by the GCF.*

Write the fraction in simplest form.

24. $\frac{8}{12}$ 25. $\frac{15}{20}$ 26. $\frac{40}{50}$

27. $\frac{36}{48}$ 28. $\frac{18}{21}$ 29. $\frac{90}{40}$

- **Write mixed numbers as fractions and fractions as mixed numbers.** (pp. 186–187)

  Write $3\frac{5}{6}$ as a fraction.

  $3\frac{5}{6} = \frac{(3 \times 6)}{6} + \frac{5}{6} = \frac{23}{6}$

Write the mixed number as a fraction.

30. $4\frac{2}{3}$ 31. $2\frac{8}{9}$ 32. $8\frac{1}{2}$

Write the fraction as a mixed number.

33. $\frac{17}{2}$ 34. $\frac{40}{7}$ 35. $\frac{33}{4}$

- **Convert among fractions, decimals, and percents.** (pp. 191–193)

  Write $\frac{1}{8}$ as a percent.

  $\frac{1}{8} = 1 \div 8 = 0.125$ *Change $\frac{1}{8}$ to a decimal.*

  $0.125 = 12.5\%$

  So, $\frac{1}{8} = 12.5\%$.

Write the decimal as a fraction.

36. 0.75   **37.** 0.6   **38.** 0.43

Write the fraction as a percent.

39. $\frac{5}{8}$ **40.** $\frac{2}{5}$ **41.** $\frac{5}{2}$

Chapter 9

- **Add and subtract fractions and mixed numbers.** (pp. 206–217)

  Subtract. $4\frac{1}{4} - 2\frac{2}{3}$

  $$4\frac{1}{4} = 4\frac{3}{12} = 3\frac{15}{12}$$
  $$-2\frac{2}{3} = -2\frac{8}{12} = -2\frac{8}{12}$$
  $$\overline{} \quad \overline{} \quad \overline{1\frac{7}{12}}$$

  Write equivalent fractions. Rename as needed.

  Subtract fractions. Subtract whole numbers.

Write the sum or difference in simplest form. Estimate to check.

42. $\frac{3}{4} + \frac{1}{3}$ **43.** $\frac{3}{5} + \frac{1}{2}$

44. $\frac{9}{10} - \frac{3}{5}$ **45.** $\frac{5}{6} - \frac{1}{4}$

46. $2\frac{3}{8} + 3\frac{3}{4}$ **47.** $4\frac{3}{5} + 2\frac{1}{3}$

48. $4\frac{1}{3} - 1\frac{5}{6}$ **49.** $5\frac{1}{8} - 3\frac{2}{3}$

Chapter 10

- **Multiply and divide fractions and mixed numbers.** (pp. 228–239)

  Divide. $3\frac{3}{4} \div 4\frac{1}{2}$

  $3\frac{3}{4} \div 4\frac{1}{2} = \frac{15}{4} \div \frac{9}{2}$ *Write mixed numbers as fractions.*

  $= \frac{15}{4} \times \frac{2}{9}$ *Multiply by the reciprocal.*

  $= \frac{5}{6}$

Find the product or quotient. Write it in simplest form.

50. $\frac{1}{3} \times \frac{2}{5}$ **51.** $\frac{5}{8} \times \frac{7}{10}$

52. $\frac{5}{9} \div \frac{1}{3}$ **53.** $9 \div \frac{4}{5}$

54. $3\frac{3}{4} \times 3\frac{1}{3}$ **55.** $3\frac{1}{8} \times 1\frac{1}{5}$

56. $1\frac{2}{3} \div 3\frac{5}{6}$ **57.** $1\frac{7}{9} \div 2\frac{2}{5}$

PROBLEM SOLVING APPLICATIONS

58. Katelynn has two sheets of paper $8\frac{1}{2}$ in. by 11 in. She cuts out a 3-in. square from the center top edge of one of the sheets. Which has the greater perimeter, the sheet with the square cut out or the uncut sheet? How much greater? (pp. 218–219)

59. Juan goes to the fruit market every 6 days. Anita goes to the market every 4 days. They meet at the market on August 31. When will they meet at the market again? (pp. 174–175)

60. In one week, Emilio rode his bicycle $1\frac{3}{4}$ mi to his grandmother's house, $2\frac{1}{2}$ mi to his friend's house, and $3\frac{1}{2}$ mi to the park. How many miles did Emilio ride his bicycle in all? (pp. 240–241)

TASK A • Fraction Fun

Margo finds the product of $3\frac{1}{2}$ and $8\frac{2}{3}$ by writing each as a fraction and multiplying numerators and denominators. Chen said he can find the product by using the Distributive Property. Here's how he starts:

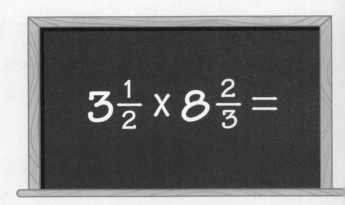

$$3\frac{1}{2} \times 8\frac{2}{3} = (3 + \frac{1}{2}) \times (8 + \frac{2}{3})$$

$$= 3 \times (8 + \frac{2}{3}) + \frac{1}{2} \times (8 + \frac{2}{3})$$

a. Finish Chen's solution to find the answer.

b. Use Margo's method to find $3\frac{1}{2} \times 8\frac{2}{3}$. Do you get the same answer as with Chen's method?

c. Tom said he thinks $(3 + \frac{1}{2}) \times (8 + \frac{2}{3}) = 3 \times 8 + \frac{1}{2} \times \frac{2}{3}$. Is he correct? Explain.

TASK B • Pen Pal

Assume that you have a pen pal and are going to start writing. This is your first letter. Write a short paragraph describing yourself and your activities. Include the following in the paragraph:

a. How you divide your time during a typical week

b. How your school day is divided by classes and other activities

c. What you like to do after school

As you write your letter, use fractions or decimals to name parts of classes, hours, days, or weeks. Each time you use a fraction, write the equivalent decimal in parentheses next to it. Do the reverse each time you use a decimal.

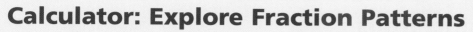

Calculator: Explore Fraction Patterns

You can use a calculator to find patterns in the following problems and their products.

$$\frac{1}{2} \times \frac{2}{3} \qquad \frac{2}{3} \times \frac{3}{4} \qquad \frac{3}{4} \times \frac{4}{5} \qquad \frac{4}{5} \times \frac{5}{6}$$

One pattern in the factors of each problem is that the denominator of the first fraction is the numerator of the second fraction.

Use a calculator to multiply the fractions, and see if there is a pattern in the products.

Use the key sequence below to find $\frac{1}{2} \times \frac{2}{3}$. Do not simplify.

 1 2 2 3 Enter

$$\begin{array}{c} \frac{N}{D} \rightarrow \frac{n}{d} \\ \frac{1}{2} \times \frac{2}{3} = \qquad \qquad \frac{2}{6} \end{array}$$

Use a calculator to find each product. Do not simplify.

$$\frac{1}{2} \times \frac{2}{3} = \frac{2}{6} \qquad \frac{2}{3} \times \frac{3}{4} = \blacksquare \qquad \frac{3}{4} \times \frac{4}{5} = \blacksquare \qquad \frac{4}{5} \times \frac{5}{6} = \blacksquare$$

• What pattern do you see in the products?

• If you continue the pattern, will the products increase or decrease?

Practice and Problem Solving

1. Use your pattern to predict the next three products. Explain how you made your prediction.

2. Write the next 3 multiplication problems. Then use a calculator to find the products. Do not simplify the products. How do they compare with your prediction?

3. **STRETCH YOUR THINKING** Use a calculator to find the following products: $\frac{1}{3} \times \frac{3}{4}$, $\frac{1}{3} \times \frac{3}{5}$, $\frac{1}{3} \times \frac{3}{6}$, and $\frac{1}{3} \times \frac{3}{7}$. Write each product in simplest form. Is there a pattern to the products? Explain.

Multimedia Math Glossary www.harcourtschool.com/mathglossary

Vocabulary Power Look up *prime factorization* in the Multimedia Math Glossary. Use a factor tree to write the prime factorization of 256.

PROBLEM SOLVING ON LOCATION
In Tennessee

Hiking Trails

Tennessee has more than 40 state parks, with a wide range of activities available at each one. The table below shows information about hiking trails at Dunbar Cave State Natural Area and Cedars of Lebanon State Park.

Use Data   For 1–4, use the table.

1. How many times as great is the length of Recovery Trail as the length of Short Loop trail?

2. Suppose you hike all three trails at Dunbar. How many miles will you hike in all? Explain.

3. How much longer is the longest trail at Cedars than the longest trail at Dunbar?

4. Over two weeks, Yvette hiked four of the trails. She hiked a total of $8\frac{3}{10}$ mi. On which trails did she hike?

HIKING TRAILS	
Park/Trail	**Length (in mi)**
Dunbar/Lake Trail	$\frac{2}{3}$
Dunbar/Short Loop	$\frac{4}{5}$
Dunbar/Recovery Trail	$1\frac{7}{10}$
Cedars/Cedar Forest Trail	2
Cedars/Dixon Merrit Trail	$\frac{1}{2}$
Cedars/Hidden Springs Trail	5

5. In Cedars of Lebanon State Park, a total of 900 acres is used for recreational activities. This represents $\frac{1}{10}$ of the total area of the park. The rest of the park is operated by the state forestry division as a state forest. How many acres are **not** used for recreation? Explain.

6. **Stretch Your Thinking**   The expected winter low temperature in Cedars of Lebanon State Park is 35°F. This is $\frac{7}{18}$ of the expected summer high temperature. What is the expected high temperature during the summer? Explain.

Many state parks in Tennessee have at least one hiking trail. The trails range from easy, for casual walkers, to rugged, for serious backpackers.

The Nashville Parthenon is a model of a building that was built over 2,000 years ago.

The Parthenon

Nashville's Parthenon and statue of Athena are full-scale replicas of those in ancient Greece. Nashville's Parthenon was originally built in 1897 for Tennessee's Centennial Exposition. It was restored between 1991 and 2001. Today, the Parthenon acts as the city of Nashville's art museum. The table below shows data about the Parthenon and the statue of Athena with Nike.

Use Data   For 1–4, use the table and photographs.

1. The length of the front of the Parthenon is about 1.6 times the height. To the nearest foot, what is the length of the front of the building? Explain.

2. The Parthenon is 228 ft in length. The length of the treasury room is what fraction of the length of the Parthenon?

3. Explain how you know that your answer for Exercise 2 is written in simplest form.

4. In Athena's right hand stands a statue of Nike. Round the heights of Athena's statue and Nike's statue to the nearest foot. The height of the statue of Nike is about what fraction of the height of the statue of Athena?

5. ✍ **Write a problem** using data from the table in which the solution is a fraction.

6. **Stretch Your Thinking**   When you face the longer side of the Parthenon, you see 17 columns. When you face the shorter side, you see 8 columns. How many columns are found around the outside of the building? Explain.

MEASUREMENTS OF THE PARTHENON	
Part of the Building	**Measurement**
Height of building	65 ft
Length of the temple room	93 ft
Length of the treasury room	44 ft
Height of Athena's statue	$41\frac{5}{6}$ ft
Height of Nike's statue	$6\frac{1}{3}$ ft

CHAPTER 11

Algebra: Expressions

≡FAST FACT • SCIENCE The wildlife in Kruger National Park in South Africa includes more than 800 species of mammals, birds, reptiles, and amphibians. Many types of plants are also contained within the park's 7,523 square miles.

PROBLEM SOLVING Suppose there are *n* leopards in Kruger National Park. Write an expression with *n* to show how many leopards and lions live in the park.

ESTIMATED NUMBERS OF ANIMALS IN KRUGER NATIONAL PARK

Type of Animal	Number of Animals
Lions	2,500
Elephants	10,000
Buffalo	21,000
Crocodiles	3,000
Antelope	

0, 10,000, 20,000, 30,000, 40,000, 50,000, 60,000, 70,000, 80,000, 90,000, 100,000

Number of Animals

Check What You Know

Use this page to help you review and remember important skills needed for Chapter 11.

 Exponents

Find the value.

1. 4^3
2. 2^5
3. 3^4
4. 5^3
5. 3^3
6. 2^4
7. 8^2
8. 9^2
9. 2^8
10. 7^2
11. 1^{12}
12. 6^0

 Order of Operations

Evaluate each expression.

13. $6 + 3 \cdot 5$
14. $3^2 + 4^2$
15. $(5 + 2) \cdot 6$
16. $(8 + 4) - (3 + 2)$
17. $24 \div (8 - 5)$
18. $\frac{(15 - 7)}{8} \cdot 2$
19. $\frac{(5 + 9)}{7} + 4^2$
20. $5^2 - (4 - 2)$
21. $3^2 \div (5 - 3)$
22. $24 - 8 \div 2$
23. $2^3 \cdot (15 - 8)$
24. $8^2 \div (9 + 7)$
25. $3^2 + 4 - (2 + 1)$
26. $20 - 5 \cdot 3 + 16$
27. $3^3 \div (13 - 4) + 8$

 Expressions

Evaluate each expression.

28. 321×29
29. $k - 42$ for $k = 98$
30. $21.5 + x$ for $x = 8.2$
31. $100y$ for $y = 15$
32. ab for $a = 19$ and $b = 7$
33. $\frac{m}{9}$ for $m = 153$

VOCABULARY POWER

REVIEW

expression [ik•spre′shən] *noun*

Many math vocabulary words have meanings outside the context of mathematics. Write mathematical and nonmathematical definitions for *expression*.

PREVIEW

terms
like terms
square
square root

 www.harcourtschool.com/mathglossary

Write Expressions

Learn how to write algebraic expressions.

Remember that $a \times b$ can be written as $a \cdot b$ or ab.

John mows lawns to earn spending money. He charges a flat rate of $15.75 for each lawn plus $2.00 for every hour it takes him to mow, trim, and edge the lawn. To find the total amount of money he earns, John uses the algebraic expression below.

$15.75 for each lawn	**plus**	**$2.00 for every hr**
↓	↓	↓
15.75	+	$2 \cdot h$
		↑
		number of hours

Word expressions can be written as algebraic expressions.

EXAMPLE 1

Write an algebraic expression for the word expression.

the cost, c, increased by $15	$c + 15$
q divided by 8, added to the product of t and r	$tr + \dfrac{q}{8}$
5.6 less than $\frac{4}{5}m$	$\frac{4}{5}m - 5.6$
the sum of $\frac{1}{2}a$, $\frac{1}{6}b$, and $\frac{1}{4}c$	$\frac{1}{2}a + \frac{1}{6}b + \frac{1}{4}c$

You can also write word expressions for numerical and algebraic expressions.

EXAMPLE 2

Write a word expression for the numerical or algebraic expression.

a. $15 + 4.5$ the sum of 15 and 4.5

b. $\frac{2}{3}m + 8$ 8 more than $\frac{2}{3}m$

c. $xy - \dfrac{z}{5}$ the product of x and y decreased by z divided by 5

• If x represents Kim's allowance and y represents Pat's allowance, what does $x + y$ represent?

Think and ▶ Discuss

Look back at the lesson to answer the question.

1. Give another word expression for Example 2b.

Guided ▶ Practice

Write an algebraic expression for the word expression.

2. 7 more than $\frac{3}{8}y$

3. y divided by 1.5

Write a word expression for each.

4. $19 + 8.7$

5. $19x - 54$

6. $p \cdot q \cdot r$

PRACTICE AND PROBLEM SOLVING

Independent ▶ Practice

Write an algebraic expression for the word expression.

7. 2.9 more than 3 times c

8. d divided by 8, less $\frac{1}{3}$

9. the product of h, $4j$, and k

10. 2 less than a, divided by 3.5

11. the difference between $6.3p$ and $5m$

12. $\frac{1}{2}$ multiplied by the sum of $2m$ and $4n$

Write a word expression for each.

13. $42 + 2.5$

14. $8c - \frac{5}{6}$

15. $4.5 \cdot a \cdot b$

16. $yz + \frac{1}{2}x$

17. $a + b + c$

18. $98 \div 4.1y$

Problem Solving ▶ Applications

19. **What if** John charged a flat rate of \$14.25 per lawn and \$3.50 for each hour he mows, trims, and edges? What expression could he use to find the total amount he charges?

20. José is taller than his nephew. If a represents José's height and b is his nephew's height, what does $a - b$ represent?

21. Jill's niece is 2 inches taller than twice her nephew's height. What algebraic expression could you write for her niece's height?

22. **FAST FACT** • SCIENCE The record height for a person is 107 in. If h represents your height in inches, what does $107 - h$ represent?

23. Write a problem in which you have to write an algebraic expression using the variable x.

MIXED REVIEW AND TEST PREP

24. $\frac{1}{3} \times \frac{2}{5}$ (p. 228)

25. $\frac{3}{5} \div \frac{4}{7}$ (p. 236)

26. $5\frac{1}{2} \div 2\frac{1}{4}$ (p. 236)

27. Find a pair of numbers that have an LCM of 24 and a GCF of 2. (p. 170)

28. **TEST PREP** Use mental math to tell which is the solution for $x + 2.5 = 10.5$. (p. 94)

   A $x = 13$ **B** $x = 8.5$ **C** $x = 8$ **D** $x = 2.5$

Evaluate Expressions

Learn how to evaluate algebraic expressions.

QUICK REVIEW

Evaluate for x = 3 and y = 4.
  1. $x + y$ **2.** $2x + y$ **3.** $2x + 2y$ **4.** $2x - y$ **5.** $3x - 2y$

Vocabulary

terms

like terms

Ricardo runs the concession stand at school. To find the profit, he uses the algebraic expression $s - c - a$ where s is the amount of sales, c is the cost of food products, and a is advertising costs.

EXAMPLE 1

During the month of November, Ricardo spent $327 on food products and $50 on advertising for the concession stand. The amount of sales was $405. How much money did the concession stand make during November?

Use the algebraic expression $s - c - a$.

$s - c - a$	*Replace s with 405, c with 327, and a with 50.*
$405 - 327 - 50$	*Subtract.*
$78 - 50$	*Subtract.*
28	

So, the concession stand made $28 during November.

Algebraic expressions can be evaluated for different values of the variables.

EXAMPLE 2

Remember that the order of operations is:
1. Operate inside parentheses.
2. Clear exponents.
3. Multiply and divide from left to right.
4. Add and subtract from left to right.

Evaluate $4x + 7$ for $x = 3, 2, 1,$ and $0.$

$x = 3$		$x = 2$	
$4x + 7$	*Replace x with 3.*	$4x + 7$	*Replace x with 2.*
$4 \cdot 3 + 7$	*Multiply.*	$4 \cdot 2 + 7$	*Multiply.*
$12 + 7$	*Add.*	$8 + 7$	*Add.*
19		15	
So, for $x = 3, 4x + 7 = 19.$		So, for $x = 2, 4x + 7 = 15.$	

$x = 1$		$x = 0$	
$4x + 7$	*Replace x with 1.*	$4x + 7$	*Replace x with 0.*
$4 \cdot 1 + 7$	*Multiply.*	$4 \cdot 0 + 7$	*Multiply.*
$4 + 7$	*Add.*	$0 + 7$	*Add.*
11		7	
So, for $x = 1, 4x + 7 = 11.$		So, for $x = 0, 4x + 7 = 7.$	

Some algebraic expressions are more complicated. To evaluate them, replace each variable with its given value. Then follow the order of operations.

EXAMPLE 3

Evaluate $2(a + b)^2 \div c$ for $a = 5$, $b = 4$, and $c = 3$.

$2(a + b)^2 \div c$	*Replace a, b, and c with their given values.*
$2(5 + 4)^2 \div 3$	*Operate inside parentheses.*
$2 \cdot 9^2 \div 3$	*Clear the exponent.*
$2 \cdot 81 \div 3$	*Multiply.*
$162 \div 3$	*Divide.*
54	

So, for $a = 5$, $b = 4$, and $c = 3$, the expression $2(a + b)^2 \div c = 54$.

The parts of an algebraic expression that are separated by an addition or subtraction sign are called **terms**. Before you evaluate some algebraic expressions, you can simplify them by combining like terms. **Like terms** have the same variable raised to the same power.

ALGEBRAIC EXPRESSION	LIKE TERMS
$6x + 5x + 17$	$6x$ and $5x$
$42 + 13y^2 - 10y^2$	$13y^2$ and $10y^2$

To make an algebraic expression simpler, combine like terms by adding or subtracting like terms.

ALGEBRAIC EXPRESSION	SIMPLIFIED
$6x + 5x + 17$	$11x + 17$
$42 + 13y^2 - 10y^2$	$42 + 3y^2$

EXAMPLE 4

Simplify $5x + (7 + 3x)$ by combining like terms. Then evaluate the expression for $x = 2$.

$5x + (7 + 3x)$	$= 5x + (3x + 7)$	*Commutative Property.*
	$= (5x + 3x) + 7$	*Associative Property.*
	$= 8x + 7$	*Simplify by combining 5x and 3x.*
	$= 8 \cdot 2 + 7$	*Replace x with 2 and multiply.*
	$= 16 + 7$	*Add.*
	$= 23$	

So, for $x = 2$, $5x + (7 + 3x) = 23$.

You can use the Distributive Property to solve some problems mentally.

EXAMPLE 5

Evaluate pq for $p = 8$ and $q = 57$.

pq
$8 \cdot 57$ *Replace p with 8 and q with 57.*
$8(50 + 7)$ *Think of 57 as 50 + 7. Then*
$8 \cdot 50 + 8 \cdot 7$ *use the Distributive Property*
$400 + 56$ *and mental math.*
456

CHECK FOR UNDERSTANDING

Think and ▶
Discuss

Look back at the lesson to answer each question.

1. **Explain** why it can help to simplify an algebraic expression before evaluating it.

2. **Show** that evaluating the following expression before you simplify gives the same result as evaluating it after you simplify.
   $4x + 6x + 17$ for $x = 2$

Guided ▶
Practice

Evaluate the expression for $x = 3, 2, 1,$ and 0.

3. $6 + 5x$ **4.** $2x + 3$ **5.** $14 + 8x$

6. $6x + (9 - 4)$ **7.** $x^2 + 3$ **8.** $\dfrac{24}{3x + 2}$

Simplify the expression. Then evaluate the expression for the given value of the variable.

9. $4x + 3x - 8$ for $x = 3$ **10.** $15y - 11y + 10$ for $y = 3$

PRACTICE AND PROBLEM SOLVING

Independent ▶
Practice

Evaluate the expression for $x = 1, 2, 3,$ and 4.

11. $12 - 3x$ **12.** $0.25x + 4$ **13.** $21 - \frac{1}{2}x$

14. $x^2 + 4$ **15.** $\dfrac{12}{x} + 7$ **16.** $\dfrac{48}{2x + 4}$

TECHNOLOGY LINK

More Practice:
Harcourt Mega Math
Ice Station Exploration,
Arctic Algebra, Level I

Simplify the expression if you can. Then evaluate the expression for the given value of the variable.

17. $3x + 9x - 4$ for $x = 4$ **18.** $22y - 19y + 17$ for $y = 9$

19. $356 + 13a - 7a$ for
        $a = 20$ **20.** $10x + 6x - 59 + 8y$ for $x = 12$
                                         and $y = 8$

Evaluate the expression for the given values of the variables.

21. $2a^2 + bc$ for $a = 7,$ **22.** $\frac{1}{2}x - 2y + z$ for $x = 20, y = 4,$
        $b = 25,$ and $c = 4$ and $z = 10$

Name a property you could use to help evaluate the expression. Then evaluate the expression.

23. $x + y + z$ for $x = 17$, $y = 58$, and $z = 2$

24. ab for $a = 3$ and $b = 87$

Find a value of x for which the expressions are equal.

25. $5x$; $x + 8$

26. $x - 3$; $17 - x$

27. $2x + 1$; $3x$

Problem Solving ▶ Applications

28. To determine if there is enough money in her checking account to write the last check, Julie uses the expression $a + d - c$, where a is the starting amount, d is the total of the deposits made, and c is the total of her checks. Does Julie have enough money in her checking account if she started with $339?

Deposits	Checks
$72	$177
$18	$53
$28	$70
$14	$48
	$122

29. **(?) What's the Error?** Rick evaluates $x + xy$ for $x = 3$ and $y = 4$. He says the answer is 24. Find his error and the correct answer.

30. **Vocabulary Power** *Value* can be defined as the worth of something. How does this relate to the value of a variable in an expression?

MIXED REVIEW AND TEST PREP

31. Write an algebraic expression for 3 more than twice x. (p. 258)

32. $\frac{1}{3} + \frac{1}{5} + \frac{3}{10}$ (p. 206)

33. $\frac{3}{4} + \frac{1}{2} + 0.75$ (p. 206)

34. TEST PREP Solve using mental math. $3a = 6.3$ (p. 94)

A $a = 18.9$ **B** $a = 6.3$ **C** $a = 3$ **D** $a = 2.1$

35. TEST PREP A satellite mission cost $4,500 per second. Find the cost from 19 seconds after launch until 49 seconds after launch. (p. 24)

F $150   **G** $36,000   **H** $81,000   **J** $135,000

PROBLEM SOLVING LiNKUP to Reading

Strategy • Use Graphic Aids Sometimes a graphic aid, such as a table, can help you to see the solution to a problem. Chad is ordering CDs from a catalog. Each CD costs $11 and there is a $7 charge for shipping no matter how many CDs are ordered. If Chad has $57 to spend, what is the maximum number of CDs he can order?

Use the expression $11 \cdot x + 7$ and an input/output table.

So, Chad can order a maximum of 4 CDs.

- Suppose Chad had $90, each CD cost $13, and the shipping cost $5. What is the maximum number of CDs he could order?

INPUT (CDs)	RULE 11 · x + 7	OUTPUT (COST)
1	11 · 1 + 7	$18
2	11 · 2 + 7	$29
3	11 · 3 + 7	$40
4	11 · 4 + 7	$51
5	11 · 5 + 7	$62

EXTRA PRACTICE page 268, Set B

263

Squares and Square Roots

Explore how to use a model to find squares and square roots.

You need square tiles.

Vocabulary

square

square root

QUICK REVIEW

QUICK REVIEW

Find the value.

1. 10^2 2. 15^2 3. 3^3
4. 4^3 5. 5^3

A **square** is the product of a number and itself. The square of 4 is 16 since $4 \cdot 4 = 16$. A square can be expressed with the exponent 2. You read 4^2 as "4 squared." Use square arrays to model square numbers.

Activity 1

• Make a square array with 4 square tiles on each side. How many tiles did you use?

• Make a square array with 5 square tiles on each side.

• Make a square array with 6 square tiles on each side.

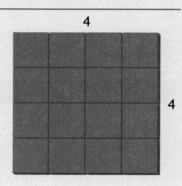

Think and Discuss

• How many tiles are in the array with 5 tiles on each side? Complete: $5^2 = $ ■.

• How many tiles are in the array with 6 tiles on each side? Complete: $6^2 = $ ■.

• Without making an array, tell how many tiles are in these: a 7×7 array, an 8×8 array, a 9×9 array, and a 10×10 array.

• Suppose you have a square with n tiles on each side. How many tiles would be in the array?

Practice

Use square tiles to find each square.

1. 2^2 2. 3^2 3. 7^2

You can also use a calculator to find squares.

16 [x²] [256   ]   *To find 16^2, enter the value of the base, 16. Then press [x²].*

So, $16^2 = 256$.

4. Use a calculator to find 17^2, 25^2, and 51^2.

When you find the two equal factors of a number, you are finding the **square root** of the number. The symbol for a positive square root is $\sqrt{}$.

Since $5^2 = 25$, $\sqrt{25} = 5$. You read $\sqrt{25}$ as "the square root of 25."

Activity 2

You can think about the sides of a square array to help you find the square root of a number.

- Make a square array with 9 square tiles. How many tiles are on each side of your square array? What is $\sqrt{9}$?

- How many tiles are on each side of a square array with 16 tiles? What is $\sqrt{16}$?

Think and Discuss

- How many tiles do you think would be on each side of a square array with 225 square tiles? 400 square tiles? Explain.

- Can you form a square with 10 square tiles? 12 square tiles? Explain.

You can use a calculator to find square roots.

289 SHIFT √ | 17 |

So, $\sqrt{289}$ is 17.

Enter the number, 289. Then press SHIFT *and* √ .

Practice

Find the square root.

1. $\sqrt{64}$ 2. $\sqrt{144}$ 3. $\sqrt{196}$

4. $\sqrt{441}$ 5. $\sqrt{484}$ 6. $\sqrt{1{,}764}$

7. If $9 \cdot 9 = 81$, then $\sqrt{\blacksquare} = \blacksquare$.

MIXED REVIEW AND TEST PREP

8. Evaluate $3xy + z$ for $x = 2$, $y = 3$, and $z = 4$. (p. 260)

9. Simplify and evaluate $5a + 7a + 35$ for $a = 7$. (p. 260)

10. Write an algebraic expression for $\frac{1}{2}$ more than twice k. (p. 258)

11. Compare. Write $<$ or $>$ for $\bullet$. $\frac{3}{5}$ $\bullet$ $\frac{5}{9}$ (p. 188)

☆ 12. **TEST PREP** Replace $\bullet$ with the correct operation sign.

$2^4 \cdot (5 - 3) \, \bullet \, (6 - 2) = 36$ (p. 48)

    A $+$ **B** $-$ **C** $\times$ **D** $\div$

Expressions with Squares and Square Roots

Learn how to evaluate expressions with squares and square roots.

$\mathbf{Y}$ou can evaluate expressions containing squares and square roots by using the order of operations. Evaluate square roots at the same time you evaluate exponents.

EXAMPLE 1

Mayla Sue wants to plant a square garden whose area is 64 ft^2. How much fencing should she buy to enclose her garden?

Since the garden is square, the length of one side is $\sqrt{64}$.

$\sqrt{64} = 8$ *Evaluate $\sqrt{64}$. $\sqrt{64} = 8$ since $8 \cdot 8 = 64$.*

So, the length of one side is 8 ft. The formula for the perimeter of a square is $P = 4s$. Evaluate for $s = 8$.

$P = 4s = 4 \cdot 8$ *Replace s with 8. Then multiply.*

$P = 32$

So, she should buy 32 ft of fencing to enclose her garden.

EXAMPLE 2

Evaluate $18 - (\sqrt{100} + 2^2)$.

$18 - (\sqrt{100} + 2^2)$ *Evaluate $\sqrt{100}$ and 2^2.*

$18 - (10 + 4)$ *Operate inside parentheses.*

$18 - 14$ *Subtract.*

4 So, $18 - (\sqrt{100} + 2^2) = 4$.

EXAMPLE 3

Evaluate $(\sqrt{x} - 2)^2 + 8$ for $x = 25$.

$(\sqrt{x} - 2)^2 + 8$ *Substitute 25 for x.*

$(\sqrt{25} - 2)^2 + 8$ *Evaluate $\sqrt{25}$ inside the parentheses.*

$(5 - 2)^2 + 8$ *Operate inside parentheses.*

$3^2 + 8$ *Clear the exponent.*

$9 + 8$ *Add.*

17 So, for $x = 25$, the expression $(\sqrt{x} - 2)^2 + 8 = 17$.

Think and Discuss ▶ **Look back at the lesson to answer the question.**

1. **Explain** how to evaluate the expression $\sqrt{36} \cdot (7 - 5)$. Then evaluate.

Guided Practice ▶ **Evaluate the expression.**

2. $\sqrt{25} + 8^2 + 42$

3. $10 + \sqrt{36} - 4^2$

4. $\sqrt{100} \cdot \sqrt{225}$

5. $45 \div \sqrt{81} \cdot 7 + 59$

PRACTICE AND PROBLEM SOLVING

Independent Practice ▶ **Evaluate the expression.**

6. $\sqrt{4} + 5^2 + 22$

7. $246 + \sqrt{16} - 10^2$

8. $25(\sqrt{49} - 1)$

9. $88 \div \sqrt{121} \cdot 3$

Evaluate the expression for the given value of the variable.

10. $\sqrt{a^2}$ for $a = 3$

11. $\sqrt{a^2}$ for $a = 9$

12. $(5^2 + \sqrt{p}) \div 4$ for $p = 225$

13. $\sqrt{a^2 + b^2}$ for $a = 3$ and $b = 4$

14. $(\sqrt{a} + \sqrt{b})^2$ for $a = 9$ and $b = 16$

Compare for $a = 5$, $b = 20$, and $c = 16$. Use $<$, $>$, or $=$.

15. $a^2 + 10 \ \bullet \ 10a^2$

16. $\sqrt{ab} \ \bullet \ c$

Problem Solving Applications ▶

17. **REASONING** Insert one square root symbol so the value of the expression $25 + 64 + 16 \cdot 81$ is 233.

18. A square flower garden and a sidewalk around the garden have an area of 400 ft^2. The sidewalk has a width of 3 ft. What is the length of one side of the flower garden?

19. ? **What's the Question?** The expression is $\sqrt{x} + 2$. The answer is 7.

MIXED REVIEW AND TEST PREP

Evaluate the expression for $x = 1, 2, 3$, and 4. (p. 260)

20. $4x + 2$

21. $20 - 5x$

22. $\frac{12}{x} - 2$

23. Find $5\frac{2}{3} \div 2\frac{1}{3}$. (p. 236)

⭐ 24. **TEST PREP** A bag held $6\frac{3}{4}$ c of flour. Bill took out $2\frac{1}{2}$ c. He had too much, so he put back $\frac{3}{4}$ c. How much flour was left in the bag? (p. 210)

    A $3\frac{1}{2}$ c   **B** 5 c   **C** $8\frac{1}{2}$ c   **D** 10 c

EXTRA PRACTICE page 268, Set C

Set A (pp. 258–259)

Write an algebraic expression for the word expression.

1. 9 less than y

2. 13 more than a number, x

3. $\frac{3}{4}$ increased by y

4. 7 more than the quotient of 52 and k

5. Fred has 32 more than twice the number of baseball cards that José has. Write an algebraic expression for the number of baseball cards Fred has.

Write a word expression for each.

6. $9^2 + a$

7. $7x + 12$

8. $24 - \frac{1}{5}c$

9. $y + \frac{1}{2}x$

Set B (pp. 260–263)

Evaluate the expression for the given values of the variables.

1. $x - 6$ for $x = 12$

2. $y + 13$ for $y = 25$

3. $42 - k$ for $k = 30$

4. $38 + p$ for $p = 22$

5. $a^2 - 25$ for $a = 9$

6. $x^3 - 19$ for $x = 3$

7. $3(a + b)^2 - c$ for $a = 3$, $b = 5$, and $c = 8$

8. $6xyz$ for $x = 4$, $y = 3$, and $z = 6$

9. $3pq + r$ for $p = 2$, $q = 8$, and $r = 15$

Evaluate the expression for $x = 2, 3, 4,$ and 5.

10. $7x + 12$

11. $4x + 10$

12. $3x - 6$

13. $9x - 4$

14. $\frac{60}{x} - 12$

15. $\frac{60}{x} + 14$

Simplify the expression if you can. Then evaluate the expression for the given value of the variable.

16. $5x + 3x + 12$ for $x = 4$

17. $2y + 7y - 25$ for $y = 20$

18. $42z - 30z - 20$ for $z = 2$

Set C (pp. 266–267)

Evaluate the expression.

1. $\sqrt{100} - 2 + 6$

2. $3 \times (9^2 - 41)$

3. $4 \times \sqrt{25} - 3 \times 2$

4. $\sqrt{36} \cdot \sqrt{36}$

5. $530 \times (\sqrt{4} - 2)^2$

6. $8 + \sqrt{49} - 3^2$

Evaluate the expression for $a = 16, b = 3,$ and $c = 6$.

7. $a + (b + c)^2$

8. $\frac{c}{b} + \sqrt{a}$

9. $\sqrt{a + b + c}$

1. **VOCABULARY** When you find the two equal factors of a number, you are finding the __?__ of the number. (p. 265)

2. **VOCABULARY** The parts of an algebraic expression that are separated by an addition or subtraction sign are __?__. (p. 261)

Write an algebraic expression for the word expression. (pp. 258–259)

3. the product of 2, 7, and b

4. the quotient of s and 1.6

5. 15 more than twice p

6. $\frac{1}{2}$ less than the product of 6 and r

7. the sum of $4a$ and $5b$

8. the product of $2q$ and r

Evaluate the expression for $y = 5$. (pp. 260–263)

9. $4y + 12$

10. $y^3 + 12$

11. $4 + 2y$

12. $5 + 3y$

13. $\frac{10}{y} - 1$

14. $10 + 3y$

Evaluate the expression for $a = 4$, $b = 3$, and $c = 5$. (pp. 260–263)

15. $3b + (c - a)$

16. $12 - a + c$

17. $28 + (c + 2)^2$

18. $18c + \frac{8b}{a}$

19. $(3c - a)^2 - b$

20. $578 \div (a + 2bc)^2$

Simplify the expression if you can. Then evaluate the expression for the given value of the variable. (pp. 260–263)

21. $6x - 2x$, $x = 2$

22. $3x + 2x + 6$, $x = 1$

23. $10x - 2x$, $x = 10$

Evaluate the expression. (pp. 266–267)

24. $\sqrt{49} - 2 + 5$

25. $3 \times (6^2 - 16)$

26. $4 \times \sqrt{81} - 3 \times 6$

27. $\sqrt{25} \cdot \sqrt{16}$

28. $124 \times (\sqrt{64} - 6)$

29. $10 + \sqrt{100} - 4^2$

Evaluate the expression for the given value of the variable. (pp. 266–267)

30. $14 - \sqrt{c}$ for $c = 49$

31. $5^2 - \sqrt{d}$ for $d = 121$

32. A cashier uses the expression $d + s - c$ to check the amount of money in her cash drawer, where d is the initial amount in the drawer, s is the amount of cash that customers pay, and c is the amount of change that customers receive. Suppose the initial amount is $125.00, customers pay $15.00, $18.25, and $24.00, and the amount of change returned is $1.50 and $1.95. How much money is in the cashier's drawer? (pp. 260–263)

33. Write an expression for the perimeter of the rectangle. Then evaluate the expression to find the perimeter when $a = 4$ cm and $b = 7$ cm. (pp. 260–263)

a

b

★ NUMBER SENSE, CONCEPTS, AND OPERATIONS

1. The 391-kilometer subway in London, England, is the world's longest subway. The table below lists four other major subway systems of the world. The fractions give the approximate lengths of the systems compared to the length of the London subway. Which of the four is the shortest?

SUBWAY SYSTEMS				
City	Moscow	Tokyo	Mexico City	New York
Length	$\frac{1}{2}$	$\frac{11}{25}$	$\frac{9}{20}$	$\frac{4}{5}$

   A Moscow   **C** Mexico City

   B Tokyo   **D** New York

2. Violins, violas, cellos, and double basses are the four types of stringed instruments in an orchestra. The expression $10 + 2 \times 5^2$ gives the number of stringed instruments in an orchestra. Which of the following is equivalent to $10 + 2 \times 5^2$?

   F 30   **H** 110

   G 60   **J** 300

3. A store sells pens for $0.80 each and pencils for $0.55 each. José bought 5 pens and 5 pencils. Which of the following expressions gives the total cost?

   A $5 \times 0.80 + 0.55$

   B $5 + (0.80 \times 0.55)$

   C $5 \times (0.80 \times 0.55)$

   D $5 \times (0.80 + 0.55)$

4. Explain It At Park Clean-Up Day, 58 volunteers collected 4,175 pounds of trash. What is a reasonable estimate of the average amount collected by each person? Explain how you made your estimate.

★ DATA ANALYSIS AND PROBABILITY

5. The graph shows the membership in four sixth-grade clubs. How many more students are in the Science Club than in the Chess Club?

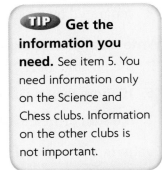
TIP **Get the information you need.** See item 5. You need information only on the Science and Chess clubs. Information on the other clubs is not important.

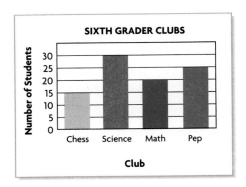

   F 2

   G 15

   H 20

   J 30

6. Explain It The table shows the results of a survey of 50 randomly chosen students. Each was asked, "What is your favorite day of the week?"

FAVORITE DAY OF THE WEEK	
Day	Number Choosing
Friday	15
Saturday	28
Sunday	7

If 450 students were surveyed, predict how many would choose Friday as their favorite day. Explain your reasoning.

⭐ ALGEBRAIC THINKING

7. Let x represent the number of hours that Teresa watched television last week. Teresa's brother watched four hours less than twice the number of hours that Teresa watched. Which expression gives the number of hours that her brother watched?

A $2x - 4$

B $4x - 2$

C $2(x - 4)$

D $\frac{1}{2}x - 4$

8. The number of cupcakes that Joey orders for a party depends on how many people will attend the party.

CUPCAKE ORDERS				
Number of People	2	4	6	8
Number of Cupcakes	3	6	9	12

If the pattern continues, how many cupcakes will Joey order for 12 people?

F 12

G 15

H 18

J 20

9. A sign on a bus reads: "No more than 32 passengers may ride this bus." Which inequality shows this rule?

A $x < 32$

B $x \leq 32$

C $x > 32$

D $x \geq 32$

10. Explain It Justin purchased some tropical fish. Write an expression for the total cost of the fish. Use f for the number of tropical fish, d for the cost per fish, and t for the tax. Explain how you determined the expression.

⭐ GEOMETRY AND SPATIAL SENSE

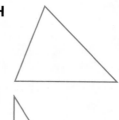

11. A tent manufacturer surveyed 400 possible customers to find out which tent shape they preferred. More than half chose "equilateral triangle." Which of the following shapes was chosen by more than 200 people?

F H

G J

12. Shawn was looking at the figures shown below. Which of the following is the **best** description of the two figures?

A The figures are similar.

B The figures are congruent.

C The figures are both similar and congruent.

D The figures are neither similar nor congruent.

13. Explain It Vickie drew a block letter of her initial, plus two lines that she said were lines of symmetry. Her drawing is shown below. Are both of the lines she drew lines of symmetry? Explain your answer.

CHAPTER 12

Algebra: Addition and Subtraction Equations

≡FAST FACT • SOCIAL STUDIES The youth division of the National Wheelchair Basketball Association has 36 teams from 23 states and Canada. The Turnstone Flyers of Fort Wayne, Indiana, have been ranked as high as eleventh in the country after only 5 years of playing as a team.

PROBLEM SOLVING During 8 games, the Flyers scored a total of 333 points. The graph shows their points in 7 of these games. Write and solve an equation to find the number of points the Flyers scored in Game 8.

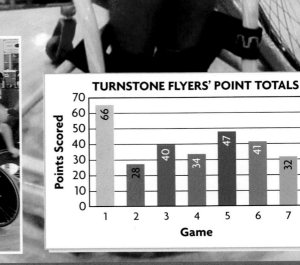

TURNSTONE FLYERS' POINT TOTALS

Check What You Know

Use this page to help you review and remember important skills needed for Chapter 12.

✔ Mental Math and Equations

Solve each equation by using mental math.

1. $x + 3 = 5$
2. $q + 2 = 6$
3. $z - 1 = 4$
4. $c - 3 = 7$
5. $x + 8 = 12$
6. $y + 10 = 15$
7. $m - 6 = 12$
8. $n - 4 = 20$
9. $k - 10 = 8$
10. $10 = r + 4$
11. $7 = s + 5$
12. $3 = e - 6$
13. $5 = t - 4$
14. $20 = 10 + q$
15. $17 = 5 + r$

✔ Words for Operations

Write an algebraic expression for the word expression.

16. the sum of p and 12
17. the product of 3 and x
18. the difference of 30 and k
19. b divided by 4
20. 15 times y
21. m decreased by 4
22. n reduced by 72
23. 234 increased by z
24. 8 more than $\frac{2}{3}y$

Write a word expression for the algebraic expression.

25. $x + 5$
26. $5y$
27. $z - 4$
28. $a \div 5$
29. $12 \div b$
30. $18 - c$
31. $9p$
32. $8 + q$
33. $r + s$

VOCABULARY POWER

REVIEW

variable [vâr′ē•ə•bəl] *noun*

In algebra, a variable is a letter or symbol that can stand for one or more numbers. Use a dictionary to find other meanings of *variable*. How are these meanings similar to the algebraic meaning?

PREVIEW

Subtraction Property of Equality

Addition Property of Equality

 www.harcourtschool.com/mathglossary

Words and Equations

Learn how to translate words into numbers, variables, and operations.

Mt. McKinley in Alaska is the highest point in the United States.

Remember that an equation is a statement showing that two quantities are equal.

You can translate word expressions into equations by translating words into numbers, variables, and operations.

The peak of Mt. Mitchell, in North Carolina, has an altitude of 2,037 m. It is the highest summit east of the Mississippi River. The altitude of Mt. McKinley, in Alaska, is 4,158 m greater than the altitude of Mt. Mitchell.

EXAMPLE 1

Write an equation to find the altitude of Mt. McKinley.

Choose a variable. Let a represent the altitude of Mt. McKinley. Then translate the words into an equation.

altitude of Mt. McKinley	is	4,158 m	greater than	altitude of Mt. Mitchell
↓	↓	↓	↓	↓
a	$=$	4,158	$+$	2,037

So, the equation is $a = 4{,}158 + 2{,}037$.

• Write an equation to show that the altitude of Mt. Hood, in Oregon, is 2,768 m less than the altitude of Mt. McKinley, which is 6,195 m.

Equations can also include subtraction, multiplication, and division.

EXAMPLE 2

Write an equation for the following word sentence: The number of hours worked, less $3\frac{1}{2}$ hr, is $15\frac{1}{4}$ hr.

Choose a variable. Let h represent the number of hours worked.

number of hours worked	less	$3\frac{1}{2}$ hr	is	$15\frac{1}{4}$ hr	
↓	↓	↓	↓	↓	*Translate the sentence*
h	$-$	$3\frac{1}{2}$	$=$	$15\frac{1}{4}$	*into an equation.*

So, the equation is $h - 3\frac{1}{2} = 15\frac{1}{4}$.

• Write a word sentence for the equation $4x = 24$.

Think and ▶ Discuss

Look back at the lesson to answer each question.

1. **Explain** what the variable represents when you translate a word sentence into an algebraic equation.

Guided ▶ Practice

Write an equation for the word sentence.

2. 7 more than a number is 20.

3. 9 fewer than a number is $17\frac{5}{8}$.

4. 5 times the number of marbles is 35.

5. The quotient of 567 points and the number of test scores is 81.

PRACTICE AND PROBLEM SOLVING

Independent ▶ Practice

Write an equation for the word sentence.

6. 14 is 12 more than a number.

7. 8.09 less than a number equals 44.2.

8. A number divided by $2\frac{3}{4}$ is $\frac{5}{6}$.

9. 16 times a number is 144.

Write a word sentence for each equation.

10. $x + 5 = 7$

11. $7y = 56$

Problem Solving ▶ Applications

12. ≡**FAST FACT** • SCIENCE The diameter of Saturn is 72,000 miles. This is about 9 times as great as the diameter of Earth. Write an equation that describes this relationship.

13. Translate the following sentence into an equation: 2 is 10 less than a number. Could 12 be the number? Explain.

14. ✎ **Write a problem** using facts found in your science book. Then translate the problem into an equation.

15. **Number Sense** Picnic forks come in packs of 20, and picnic knives come in packs of 32. What is the least number of packs of each that you could buy to have the same number of forks and knives?

MIXED REVIEW AND TEST PREP

Simplify the expression. Then evaluate the expression for the given value of the variable. (p. 260)

16. $5x + 3x - 15$ for $x = 2$

17. $10y - 8y + 22$ for $y = 6$

18. $25 + 22z - 13z$ for $z = 8$

19. Find the quotient $4\frac{2}{3} \div 1\frac{1}{2}$. (p. 236)

★20. **TEST PREP** How much greater is $5\frac{4}{5}$ than $2\frac{5}{6}$? (p. 214)

A $2\frac{29}{30}$ B $3\frac{29}{30}$ C $7\frac{9}{11}$ D $8\frac{7}{30}$

Model and Solve One-Step Equations

Explore how to model the solutions to one-step equations.

You need algebra tiles, or green paper rectangles and yellow squares.

Math Idea ▶

Activity

• Model an equation by using algebra tiles. Use a green rectangle to represent the variable. Use a yellow square to represent 1. Model and solve the equation $x + 3 = 4$.

$$x \quad + \quad 3 \quad = \quad 4 \qquad \leftarrow x + 3 = 4$$

• To solve an equation, you must get the variable alone on one side. To do this, take away 3 ones from each side.

• Taking 3 ones from each side of the equation leaves the variable alone on one side. The equation is now solved.

$$x \quad = \quad 1$$

The green rectangle is alone on one side of the equation.

The value of the variable that makes the equation true is called the solution of the equation.

Think and Discuss

• What is the solution of the equation $x + 3 = 4$?

• How can you tell this from the model?

• What operation did you model in the second step?

• What would you do to solve the equation $x + 8 = 11$?

Practice

Solve each equation by using algebra tiles. Draw a picture of your model.

1. $x + 2 = 6$ **2.** $5 = x + 3$ **3.** $x + 1 = 8$ **4.** $x + 4 = 9$

5. $x + 1 = 4$ **6.** $x + 4 = 7$ **7.** $6 = x + 5$ **8.** $x + 2 = 7$

Solve Addition Equations

Learn how to solve addition equations.

QUICK REVIEW

1. $9.7 - 4.3$ 2. $5.8 - 2.7$

3. $12.9 - 4.2$ 4. $9\frac{3}{4} - 4\frac{1}{4}$

5. $10 - 3.7$

Vocabulary

Subtraction Property of Equality

Ralf Laue of Leipzig, Germany, set a world record for the most dominoes stacked. He stacked 555 dominoes on a single supporting domino.

How many more dominoes would you need to stack to match the world record if you have already stacked 123? One way to solve the problem is by representing it with an equation.

dominoes left to stack		dominoes stacked		total
↓		↓		↓
d	$+$	123	$=$	555

Addition and subtraction are inverse operations. To solve the addition equation, you will use the inverse operation, subtraction, to get the variable alone on one side of the equation. The Subtraction Property of Equality justifies that step.

Subtraction Property of Equality

If you subtract the same number from both sides of an equation, the two sides remain equal.

$5 = 5$
$5 - 2 = 5 - 2$
$3 = 3$

EXAMPLE 1

Solve the equation $d + 123 = 555$ to find the number of additional dominoes you need to stack. Check your solution.

$d + 123 = 555$	*Write the equation.*
$d + 123 - 123 = 555 - 123$	*Use the Subtraction Property of Equality.*
$d + 0 = 432$	*Use the Identity Property.*
$d = 432$	
$d + 123 = 555$	*Check your solution.*
$432 + 123 \stackrel{?}{=} 555$	*Replace d with 432.*
$555 = 555 \checkmark$	*The solution checks.*

Remember that the Identity Property of Addition states: For all numbers a, $a + 0 = a$.

So, you must stack 432 more dominoes to match the world record.

You can sometimes use the Commutative Property of Addition to help solve equations. Remember that equations can include decimals and fractions.

EXAMPLE 2

Solve and check. $8.4 + x = 12.7$

$$8.4 + x = 12.7$$ *Use the Commutative Property of Addition.*

$$x + 8.4 = 12.7$$

$$x + 8.4 - 8.4 = 12.7 - 8.4$$ *Use the Subtraction Property of Equality.*

$$x + 0 = 4.3$$ *Use the Identity Property.*

$$x = 4.3$$

$$8.4 + x = 12.7$$ *Check your solution.*

$$8.4 + 4.3 \stackrel{?}{=} 12.7$$ *Replace x with 4.3.*

$$12.7 = 12.7 ✓$$ *The solution checks.*

So, $x = 4.3$.

• Solve. $1.4 + x = 8$

TECHNOLOGY LINK

More Practice:
**Harcourt Mega Math
Ice Station Exploration,**
Arctic Algebra, Level Y

Sometimes the variable will be on the right side of the equation.

EXAMPLE 3

Solve and check. $14 = k + 8\frac{2}{3}$

$$14 = k + 8\frac{2}{3}$$

$$14 - 8\frac{2}{3} = k + 8\frac{2}{3} - 8\frac{2}{3}$$ *Use the Subtraction Property of Equality.*

$$5\frac{1}{3} = k + 0$$ *Use the Identity Property.*

$$5\frac{1}{3} = k$$

$$14 = k + 8\frac{2}{3}$$ *Check your solution.*

$$14 \stackrel{?}{=} 5\frac{1}{3} + 8\frac{2}{3}$$ *Replace k with $5\frac{1}{3}$.*

$$14 = 14 ✓$$ *The solution checks.*

So, $k = 5\frac{1}{3}$.

• Solve. $6\frac{5}{6} = 3\frac{1}{4} + y$

CHECK FOR UNDERSTANDING

Think and Discuss ▶ **Look back at the lesson to answer each question.**

1. **Explain** why the choice of a variable does not affect the solution of the equation.

2. **Describe** how to solve an addition equation.

Solve and check.

3. $x + 10 = 17$ **4.** $3 + b = 9$ **5.** $5.2 = c + 2.5$

6. $y + 1.2 = 18$ **7.** $21 = m + 5\frac{3}{4}$ **8.** $7\frac{1}{5} + d = 22$

PRACTICE AND PROBLEM SOLVING

Independent ▶
Practice

Solve and check.

9. $x + 4 = 12$ **10.** $29 = a + 17$ **11.** $9 + k = 32$

12. $z + 6.3 = 11.7$ **13.** $4.2 = b + 1.3$ **14.** $14.9 = 12.5 + c$

15. $y + 9\frac{1}{4} = 18$ **16.** $16 = 3\frac{2}{5} + s$ **17.** $12 = t + 4 + 3$

Problem Solving ▶
Applications

For 18–19, choose a variable, write an equation, and solve it.

18. What if you stack 221 dominoes? How many more would you have to stack to match the world record?

19. Geometry The perimeter of the triangle at the right is 29 cm. Find the unknown length.

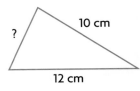
10 cm
?
12 cm

20. **What's the Question?** Jay opened a savings account with a deposit of $124.50. Later he made two equal deposits and his account balance was $350.30. The answer is $112.90.

MIXED REVIEW AND TEST PREP

For 21–22, write an equation for the word sentence. (p. 274)

21. 11 is 8 more than a number.

22. 3.65 less than a number is 12.2.

23. Evaluate. $\sqrt{64} - 4 + 9$ (p. 266)

24. Evaluate. $25 + \sqrt{81} - 4^2$ (p. 266)

⭐ **25. TEST PREP** Evaluate $3(a - b)^2 \cdot c$ for $a = 3$, $b = 1$, and $c = 2$. (p. 260)

A 72   **B** 24   **C** 16   **D** 12

PROBLEM SOLVING 💡 Thinker's Corner

Equation Relation Solve the equations below. What is the relationship among the solutions of the blue equations? Which one of the green equations should be blue?

$x + 5 = 12$	$59 = a + 17$	$b + 19 = 22$
$10 = s + 2$	$b + 15 = 43$	$95 = a + 25$
$r + 6 = 29$	$78 = m + 1$	$c + 4 = 48$
$79 = p + 23$	$x + 12 = 103$	$105 = t + 42$

EXTRA PRACTICE page 284, Set B

Solve Subtraction Equations

Learn how to solve subtraction equations.

QUICK REVIEW

1. $3.7 + 9.2$ 2. $8.2 + 10.3$

3. $1.9 + 8.2$ 4. $2\frac{1}{8} + 3\frac{5}{8}$

5. $25.1 + 18.7$

Vocabulary

Addition Property of Equality

Tamika was practicing the trick of catching dimes stacked on her elbow. On her first try, she caught 13 dimes. How many dimes were originally stacked on her elbow if 11 fell to the floor?

One way to solve this problem is by writing and solving an equation. Let d represent the number of dimes originally stacked on Tamika's elbow.

dimes on elbow		dimes caught		dimes on floor
↓		↓		↓
d	$-$	13	$=$	11

Addition and subtraction are inverse operations. To solve the subtraction equation, use the inverse operation, addition, to get the variable alone on one side of the equation. The Addition Property of Equality justifies that step.

Addition Property of Equality	$5 = 5$
If you add the same number to both sides of an equation, the two sides remain equal.	$5 + 2 = 5 + 2$
	$7 = 7$

EXAMPLE

TECHNOLOGY LINK

More Practice:
Harcourt Mega Math
Ice Station Exploration,
Arctic Algebra, Level Z

Solve the equation $d - 13 = 11$ to find the number of dimes originally stacked on Tamika's elbow. Check your solution.

$$d - 13 = 11 \qquad \textit{Write the equation.}$$
$$d - 13 + 13 = 11 + 13 \qquad \textit{Use the Addition Property of Equality.}$$
$$d - 0 = 24 \qquad \textit{Use the Identity Property.}$$
$$d = 24$$

$$d - 13 = 11 \qquad \textit{Check your solution.}$$
$$24 - 13 \stackrel{?}{=} 11 \qquad \textit{Replace d with 24.}$$
$$11 = 11 \checkmark \qquad \textit{The solution checks.}$$

So, Tamika had 24 dimes stacked on her elbow.

• Solve. $k - 4.7 = 5.8$

Think and Discuss ▶ Look back at the lesson to answer the question.

1. **Explain** how you know what number to add to both sides of a subtraction equation.

Guided Practice ▶ Solve and check.

2. $x - 8 = 15$ 3. $b - 23 = 29$ 4. $7.9 = c - 3.4$

5. $y - 1.2 = 22$ 6. $7\frac{1}{8} = m - 4\frac{3}{4}$ 7. $d - 8\frac{4}{5} = 25\frac{2}{3}$

PRACTICE AND PROBLEM SOLVING

Independent Practice ▶ Solve and check.

8. $x - 6 = 10$ 9. $29 = a - 4$ 10. $k - 5 = 2$

11. $z - 5.8 = 11.2$ 12. $7.2 = b - 1.9$ 13. $14.5 = c - 8.8$

14. $y - 9\frac{1}{4} = 18$ 15. $17\frac{2}{3} = s - 5\frac{1}{4}$ 16. $8 = t - 5$

17. $2.8 = m - 8.3$ 18. $h - 11 = 3$ 19. $f - \frac{3}{8} = \frac{5}{12}$

Problem Solving Applications ▶ For 20–21, choose a variable, write an equation, and solve it.

20. **What if** Tamika had caught 17 dimes but 2 dimes fell on the floor? How many dimes would she have had stacked on her elbow?

21. **Use Data** Look at the graph. Juanita withdrew money from her savings account for back-to-school shopping. She has $527 left in her savings account. How much did she have in her account before she withdrew the money?

JUANITA'S BACK-TO-SCHOOL SHOPPING

$40 School Supplies
$90 New Bicycle
$110 New Clothes

22. ❓ **What's the Error?** Frank said the solution of the equation $x - 7 = 10$ is $x = 3$. Find his error and then solve the equation.

23. **Vocabulary Power** When you solve a problem, you find its solution. In your own words, explain what a solution to an equation is.

MIXED REVIEW AND TEST PREP

For 24–26, solve and check. (p. 277)

24. $x + 3 = 9$ 25. $5.6 = b + 1.2$ 26. $5\frac{1}{4} = 3 + p$

27. Evaluate $2x + 5$ for $x = 2$, 1, and 0. (p. 260)

⭐ 28. **TEST PREP** Which is an algebraic expression for the word expression below? (p. 258)

8.5 more than 3 times a

A $8.5 + 3 + a$ **B** $8.5 \times 3 \times a$ **C** $3a - 8.5$ **D** $3a + 8.5$

EXTRA PRACTICE page 284, Set C

PROBLEM SOLVING STRATEGY
Write an Equation

Learn how to solve problems by writing and using an equation.

Kevin formed a number pattern by choosing two numbers and then adding them together to get the next number in the pattern. He started with the numbers 4 and 9. The beginning of his pattern is shown below.

4, 9, 13, 22, 35,...

4 + 9
9 + 13
13 + 22

Kevin started with 4 and 9. Next he added 4 + 9 to get 13, 9 + 13 to get 22, and 13 + 22 to get 35.

Two successive numbers in the pattern are 390 and 631. Find the number that comes before 390.

Analyze What are you asked to find?

What information are you given?

Is there information you will not use? If so, what?

Choose What strategy will you use?

Use the strategy *write an equation* to find the number that comes before 390.

Solve How will you solve the problem?

Use variables and an equation.

Let *a*, *b*, and *c* represent three successive numbers in the pattern. Write an equation using *a*, *b*, and *c*. Use the equation to find *a*, when $b = 390$ and $c = 631$.

$$a + b = c$$
$$a + 390 = 631$$
$$a + 390 - 390 = 631 - 390$$
$$a + 0 = 241$$
$$a = 241$$

So, 241 comes before 390.

Check How can you check your answer?

What if you had to find the number between 631 and 1,652 in the pattern? Show the equation you would use and its solution.

PROBLEM SOLVING PRACTICE

For 1–2, use the information below. Solve by writing an equation.

Mr. Hayes starts with the numbers 8 and 11. His class adds them to get the next number, 19. Then they add 11 and 19 to get the next number, 30. The class continues to extend the number pattern.

1. In the pattern, the number 335 comes after 207. Find the number that comes before 207.

2. In the pattern, what is the number that comes between 542 and 1,419?

For 3–4, use the information below.

Rebecca notices that there are a dozen apples left in a bowl. She and her friends have eaten 9 of the apples.

3. Which of the equations could you use to find the number of apples that were originally in the bowl?

A $a + 12 = 9$ **C** $a + 9 = 12$

B $a - 9 = 12$ **D** $a = 12 - 9$

4. How many apples were originally in the bowl?

F 3   **H** 12

G 9   **J** 21

PROBLEM SOLVING STRATEGIES

Draw a Diagram or Picture
Make a Model
Predict and Test
Make an Organized List
Work Backward
Find a Pattern
Make a Table or Graph
Solve a Simpler Problem
▶ **Write an Equation**
Use Logical Reasoning

MIXED STRATEGY PRACTICE

Use Data For 5–6, use the table.

5. Predict the sales for Day 6 if the pattern continues in the same way.

6. Find the increase in sales from Day 4 to Day 8 if the pattern continues.

SALES PER DAY				
Day 1	**Day 2**	**Day 3**	**Day 4**	**Day 5**
$95	$115	$140	$170	$205

7. In how many different ways can the four letters in the word MATH be arranged? List all of the different ways.

8. Jackson is thinking of two powers of 4. Their difference is 252. What are the two powers of 4?

9. In the example on page 282, it says that two successive numbers in the given pattern are 390 and 631. Is this correct? Is 1,652 also a number in the pattern? Explain.

10. At 5:00 P.M. in the city of Centerville the temperature was 72°F. It fell at a steady rate. At 8:00 P.M. it was 54°F. If the pattern continues, what will the temperature be at 9:00 P.M.?

11. A farmer paid $40,000 for 25 acres of farmland. The farmer wants to buy 15 acres more at the same price per acre. How much will the 15 acres cost?

12. ✎ **Write a problem** that involves solving an equation about the ages of Julio and his mother. Julio is 23 yr younger than his mother.

Set A (pp. 274–275)

Write an equation for the word sentence.

1. $\frac{2}{3}$ of a number is 12.

2. 1.6 more than a number is 5.

3. $1\frac{1}{2}$ less than a number is 6.

4. A number divided by 6 is 30.

5. 9 times a number is 53.

6. 1.5 increased by a number is 4.2.

7. $3\frac{1}{2}$ decreased by a number is $\frac{1}{2}$.

8. The quotient of a number and 3.3 is 99.

9. The sum of 11.2 and a number is 65.07.

10. 64 divided by a number is 3.2.

11. Leroy sold 250 boxes of apples during a fund-raiser. This was 5 times as many apples as Mary sold. Write an equation that represents the situation.

12. Reggie has 243 baseball cards in his collection that he plans to give to three of his friends. He will give each of his three friends the same number of cards. Write an equation that represents this situation.

Set B (pp. 277–279)

Solve and check.

1. $x + 6 = 15$

2. $15 = a + 2$

3. $7 + 4 + k = 25$

4. $z + 2.7 = 19.6$

5. $5.7 = b + 1.2 + 1.6$

6. $24.8 = 17.2 + c$

7. $y + 8\frac{2}{3} = 16$

8. $13\frac{1}{4} = 4\frac{4}{5} + s$

9. $13\frac{3}{8} = t + 7\frac{5}{6}$

10. $13.2 = x + 7.12$

11. $t + 7\frac{1}{3} = 10\frac{1}{12}$

12. $4.06 + r = 13.56$

13. A carpenter cut a 72-in. board into 3 pieces. One of the pieces is 24 in. long and the other is 12 in. long. How long is the third piece?

14. Jennifer has to hang 75 flyers to advertise the school dance. She has already hung 37 flyers. How many more flyers does she have to hang?

Set C (pp. 280–281)

Solve and check.

1. $x - 7 = 11$

2. $31 = a - 7$

3. $k - 10 = 42$

4. $z - 3.9 = 15.8$

5. $6.5 = b - 21.3$

6. $56.7 = c - 19.8$

7. $y - 5\frac{5}{6} = 13$

8. $22\frac{1}{3} = s - 4\frac{3}{4}$

9. $8\frac{3}{5} = t - 4\frac{5}{7}$

10. $a - 27 = 18$

11. $60.3 = b - 8.07$

12. $4\frac{7}{9} = x - 1\frac{2}{3}$

13. Bret withdrew $175 from his checking account so he could go shopping for the new school year. His new balance was $234. How much was in the account before the withdrawal?

14. Kendra sold 39 of the coins that were in her coin collection. She now has 142 coins left in her collection. How many coins were originally in her collection?

1. **VOCABULARY**   If you subtract the same number from both sides of an equation, you are using the __?__ Property of Equality. (p. 277)

2. **VOCABULARY**   Subtraction is the __?__ of addition. (p. 277)

3. **VOCABULARY**   If you add the same number to both sides of an equation, you are using the __?__ Property of Equality. (p. 280)

Write an equation for the word sentence. (pp. 274–275)

4. 72 is 15 more than a number.

5. 8.6 decreased by a number is 9.

6. 18 times a number is 45.

7. A number divided by $\frac{3}{8}$ is 16.

8. The product of $1\frac{3}{4}$ and a number is $21\frac{3}{5}$.

9. A number increased by 17 is 24.

10. 72 less than a number is 125.

11. The quotient of a number and 8 is 17.

Solve and check. (pp. 277–281)

12. $x + 7 = 10$

13. $9 + y = 19$

14. $x - 6 = 3$

15. $3.78 = c - 2.33$

16. $9 + 12 + n = 52$

17. $x + 3\frac{1}{3} = 4\frac{2}{3}$

18. $3.4 + x = 19.5$

19. $1.9 = k - 1.2$

20. $y - 3\frac{1}{9} = 11\frac{5}{9}$

21. $d - 23 = 18$

22. $42\frac{1}{5} + v = 51\frac{2}{3}$

23. $x - 33.7 = 10.9$

24. $w + 9\frac{3}{8} = 11\frac{2}{3}$

25. $2.3 + x = 5.4$

26. $q - 9.1 = 1.37$

27. $3\frac{1}{4} = x - 2\frac{1}{3}$

28. $17.5 = 2.7 + x$

29. $\frac{3}{5} + y = \frac{9}{10}$

For 30–33, choose a variable, write an equation, and solve it.

30. After soccer practice Li saw that there were 14 bottles of water left. During the practice the team had consumed 18 bottles. How many bottles had there been at the start of practice? (pp. 280–281)

31. Mirabelle has collected $37.50 so far for her favorite charity. The most she had collected in the past was $55.75. How much more does she need to collect to equal her record? (pp. 277–279)

32. A triangle has a perimeter of 42 in. The lengths of two sides of the triangle are 13 in. and 16 in. Find the length of the third side of the triangle. (pp. 277–279)

33. Keisha formed a number pattern by choosing two numbers and then adding them together to get the next number. She started with the numbers 8 and 9. Two successive numbers in the pattern are 181 and 293. Find the number that comes before 181. (pp. 282–283)

NUMBER SENSE, CONCEPTS, AND OPERATIONS

1. In the 2000 Presidential election, George Bush and Al Gore each received about 48% of the votes. What fraction of the votes did each of them receive?

> **TIP** **Eliminate choices.** See item 1. Decide which choices are not reasonable. Since 48% is slightly less than half, eliminate answers that are much less than half, or more than half.

A $\frac{2}{5}$

B $\frac{12}{25}$

C $\frac{11}{20}$

D $\frac{3}{5}$

2. The table below gives the weights of four large animals. How many polar bears would it take to have a total weight greater than one African elephant?

ANIMAL WEIGHTS	
Species	**Weight (in lb)**
African Elephant	14,432
Hippopotamus	5,512
Polar Bear	1,323

F 13   **H** 11

G 12   **J** 10

3. The atomic number of a chemical element is the number of protons in one atom of the element. The atomic number of californium is 98. Which is the prime factorization of 98?

A 49×3 **C** $7^2 \times 3$

B 49×2 **D** $7^2 \times 2$

4. Explain It A farmer packed 341 eggs into cartons that each hold a dozen eggs. Were any eggs left over after the last full carton was packed? How do you know?

 MEASUREMENT

5. A letter-size sheet of paper measures $8\frac{1}{2}$ inches by 11 inches. A legal-size sheet of paper measures $8\frac{1}{2}$ inches by 14 inches. How much greater is the perimeter of a legal-size sheet than that of a letter-size sheet?

F 12 inches   **H** 3 inches

G 6 inches   **J** $1\frac{1}{2}$ inches

6. A carpenter attached a brace at the base of a bookshelf to give it added support. The brace is shaped like a triangle. One of its angles is a right angle. One angle measures 42°. What type of angle is the third angle?

A straight   **C** right

B obtuse   **D** acute

7. At the post office, Tim bought a sheet of stamps measuring 4.5 inches by 3 inches. It was divided into stamps each measuring 1.5 inches by 1 inch and selling for 75¢. How much did the entire sheet of stamps cost?

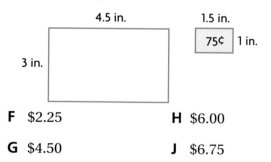

F $2.25   **H** $6.00

G $4.50   **J** $6.75

8. Explain It Gina combined 11 cups of water and 1 cup of grape juice concentrate to make grape juice. How many quarts of grape juice did she make? Explain your reasoning.

ALGEBRAIC THINKING

9. There are 14 more counties in South Dakota than there are in North Dakota. If *n* represents the number of counties in North Dakota, which expression represents the number of counties in South Dakota?

A 14*n*

B *n* + 14

C *n* – 14

D 14 – *n*

10. The graph shows the number of movie tickets that were sold on each of four days.

On Friday, the number of tickets sold was 32 fewer than the combined number sold on Monday and Wednesday. How many tickets were sold on Friday?

F 201

G 208

H 233

J 297

11. Explain It Emma is using a pattern for the stars she is sewing on a T-shirt. The first four rows are shown below. How many stars should she use in Row 5? Explain your reasoning.

GEOMETRY AND SPATIAL SENSE

12. The flag of the Solomon Islands has two congruent triangles on it separated by a yellow diagonal.

Which pair of line segments are congruent?

A $\overline{AB}$ and $\overline{DE}$

B $\overline{AB}$ and $\overline{DF}$

C $\overline{AB}$ and $\overline{AD}$

D $\overline{AB}$ and $\overline{EF}$

13. The figure below will be used as a pattern to cut congruent triangles for a quilt.

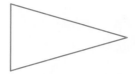

Which of the figures below appears to be congruent to the triangle above?

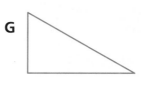

14. Explain It The logo for the Peppy Corporation is the combination of the letter P and its reflection across a vertical line. Sketch the logo. Explain why you drew the logo the way you did.

CHAPTER 13

Algebra: Multiplication and Division Equations

≡FAST FACT • SOCIAL STUDIES Washington, D.C., has over 80 taxicab companies employing more than 6,200 drivers. Within the city of Washington, taxi charges are based on a zone system. In other cities, taxi charges are based on a starting fare and a metered mileage charge.

PROBLEM SOLVING Suppose it costs $2.50 when you get into a cab. Added to that is a mileage charge of $1.50 per mile. You can use the equation $m = 1.50x$ to find the mileage charge, m, for any number of miles, x. What is the total charge for a 2-mile trip? How would you find the number of miles traveled if the total charge is $7.75? Find the number of miles.

TAXI CHARGES		
City	Starting Fare	Per-Mile Rate
Chicago, IL	$1.90	$1.60
New Orleans, LA	$2.50	$1.60
New York, NY	$2.00	$1.50
Miami, FL	$1.50	$2.00
Charlotte, NC	$1.80	$0.30

Check What You Know

Use this page to help you review and remember important skills needed for Chapter 13.

☑ Words and Equations

Write an equation for the word expression.

1. 18 is 6 more than a number.

2. 12.5 less than a number equals 23.7.

3. A number divided by 2 is $\frac{2}{3}$.

4. 6 times a number is 90.

5. Twice a number is 47.

6. The quotient of a number and 3 is 24.

7. 5 more than a number is 15.

8. 7 fewer than a number is $3\frac{1}{3}$.

9. A number divided by 3 is 42.

10. The product of a number and 5 is 120.

11. A number increased by 8 is 17.

12. A number multiplied by 7 is 84.

☑ Evaluate Expressions

Evaluate the expressions for the given values of the variables.

13. $2x$ for $x = 7$

14. $3a + 7$ for $a = 5$

15. $5t - 13$ for $t = 12$

16. pq for $p = 5$ and $q = 14$

17. $4mn$ for $m = 5$ and $n = 7$

18. $8ab$ for $a = 5$ and $b = 3$

19. $\frac{1}{2}x$ for $x = 18$

20. $\frac{2}{3}k$ for $k = 24$

21. $\frac{z}{4}$ for $z = 100$

22. $\frac{5}{9}f$ for $f = 27$

23. $\frac{9}{5}c$ for $c = 10$

24. $\frac{9}{5}c + 32$ for $c = 0$

25. $\frac{9}{5}c + 32$ for $c = 10$

26. $\frac{9}{5}c + 32$ for $c = 20$

27. $\frac{9}{5}c + 32$ for $c = 30$

VOCABULARY POWER

REVIEW

formula [fôr′myə•lə] *noun*

Formula can be defined as "a rule written using symbols." Many kinds of formulas are used in mathematics, including some that are related to measurement, geometry, probability, and algebra. Write two formulas that you know, using variables. Then write the formulas in words.

PREVIEW

Division Property of Equality

Multiplication Property of Equality

inequality

 www.harcourtschool.com/mathglossary

Model Multiplication Equations

MATH LAB

Explore how to model the solutions of multiplication equations.

You need algebra tiles or paper rectangles and squares.

You can use algebra tiles to model solving multiplication equations.

Activity

- A green rectangle represents a variable, and a yellow square represents the value 1. Here is a model of the multiplication equation $3y = 12$. To represent $3y$, use 3 green rectangles.

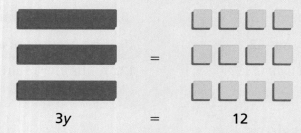

$$3y \qquad = \qquad 12$$

- Divide each side of the model into 3 equal groups.

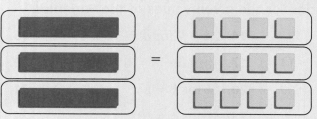

- Look at one group on each side. What is in each pair? What equation does this model?

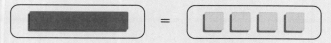

Think and Discuss

- What is the solution of the equation $3y = 12$?

- What operation did you model in the second step? How does this operation relate to multiplication?

- **REASONING** How do you think you would solve an algebraic equation involving division?

Practice

Use algebra tiles to model and solve each equation. Draw a picture of your model.

1. $2c = 8$ **2.** $3a = 9$ **3.** $4b = 8$ **4.** $15 = 5y$

Solve Multiplication and Division Equations

Learn how to solve multiplication and division equations.

Vocabulary

Division Property of Equality

Multiplication Property of Equality

Over a period of 7 days, a koala can sleep as many as 154 hr. Excluding animals that hibernate, the koala averages the most hours of sleep per day of any animal. Write and solve an equation to find the average number of hours per day a koala sleeps.

Choose a variable to represent the average number of hours per day that a koala sleeps. Then write an equation.

$$\begin{array}{ccccc} \text{number} & & \text{average daily} & & \text{total hours} \\ \text{of days} & \times & \text{hours of sleep} & = & \text{of sleep} \\ \downarrow & & \downarrow & & \downarrow \\ 7 & \times & h & = & 154 \end{array}$$

Remember that division can be written as a fraction.

$$2 \div 3 = \frac{2}{3}$$

$$x \div 3 = \frac{x}{3}$$

Multiplication and division are inverse operations. To solve the multiplication equation, use the inverse operation, division, so that the variable is alone on one side of the equation. The Division Property of Equality explains that step.

Division Property of Equality	$10 = 10$
If you divide both sides of an equation by the same nonzero number, the two sides remain equal.	$\frac{10}{2} = \frac{10}{2}$ $5 = 5$

EXAMPLE 1

Solve and check the equation $7h = 154$.

$$7h = 154 \qquad \textit{Write the equation.}$$

$$\frac{7h}{7} = \frac{154}{7} \qquad \textit{Use the Division Property of Equality.}$$

$$1 \times h = 22 \qquad \textit{7 \div 7 = 1; 154 \div 7 = 22}$$

$$h = 22 \qquad \textit{Use the Identity Property.}$$

$$7h = 154 \qquad \textit{Check your solution.}$$

$$7 \times 22 \stackrel{?}{=} 154 \qquad \textit{Replace h with 22.}$$

$$154 = 154 \checkmark \qquad \textit{The solution checks.}$$

So, a koala sleeps an average of 22 hr a day.

You can solve equations with fractions.

EXAMPLE 2

TECHNOLOGY LINK

More Practice: **Harcourt Mega Math Ice Station Exploration,** *Arctic Algebra*, Levels AA and BB

Solve and check. $16 = \frac{2}{3}y$

$$16 = \frac{2}{3}y \qquad \text{\textit{Write the equation.}}$$

$$\frac{16}{\frac{2}{3}} = \frac{\frac{2}{3}y}{\frac{2}{3}} \qquad \text{\textit{Use the Division Property of Equality.}}$$

$$16 \div \frac{2}{3} = 1 \times y \qquad \frac{2}{3} \div \frac{2}{3} = 1$$

$$16 \cdot \frac{3}{2} = y \qquad \text{\textit{Multiply by the reciprocal. Use the Identity Property.}}$$

$$24 = y$$

$$16 = \frac{2}{3}y \qquad \text{\textit{Check your solution.}}$$

$$16 \stackrel{?}{=} \frac{2}{3} \cdot 24 \qquad \text{\textit{Replace y with 24.}}$$

$$16 = 16 \checkmark \qquad \text{\textit{The solution checks.}}$$

So, $y = 24$.

• Solve and check. $\frac{1}{4}x = 22$

To solve a division equation, use the inverse operation, multiplication, and the Multiplication Property of Equality.

Multiplication Property of Equality	$10 = 10$
If you multiply both sides of an equation by the same number, the two sides remain equal.	$5 \times 10 = 5 \times 10$ $50 = 50$

EXAMPLE 3

Solve and check. $\frac{a}{5} = 14$

$$\frac{a}{5} = 14 \qquad \text{\textit{Write the equation.}}$$

$$5 \cdot \frac{a}{5} = 5 \cdot 14 \qquad \text{\textit{Use the Multiplication Property of Equality.}}$$

$$\frac{5}{1} \cdot \frac{a}{5} = 70$$

$$\frac{5a}{5} = 70$$

$$a = 70 \qquad 5 \div 5 = 1 \text{ and } 1a = a$$

$$\frac{a}{5} = 14 \qquad \text{\textit{Check your solution.}}$$

$$\frac{70}{5} \stackrel{?}{=} 14 \qquad \text{\textit{Replace a with 70.}}$$

$$14 = 14 \checkmark \qquad \text{\textit{The solution checks.}}$$

So, $a = 70$.

• Solve and check. $9 = \frac{c}{12}$

Think and ▶
Discuss
Look back at the lesson to answer the question.

1. **Explain** how you solve multiplication and division equations and how you solve addition and subtraction equations.

Guided ▶
Practice
Solve and check.

2. $\frac{x}{3} = 8$ 3. $4x = 28$ 4. $45 = \frac{1}{2}x$ 5. $1.8 = \frac{y}{4}$

PRACTICE AND PROBLEM SOLVING

Independent ▶
Practice
Solve and check.

6. $3x = 6$ 7. $8k = 48$ 8. $\frac{y}{5} = 7$ 9. $\frac{a}{6} = 3$

10. $4 = \frac{m}{3}$ 11. $48 = 3p$ 12. $15 = \frac{s}{5}$ 13. $60 = 12n$

14. $\frac{1}{4}d = 60$ 15. $4.12 = \frac{a}{4}$ 16. $24 = \frac{4}{5}b$ 17. $2.1 = \frac{w}{1.3}$

Solve and check.

18. $\frac{8}{15} = \frac{c}{45}$ 19. $\frac{a}{4} = 2\frac{1}{2}$ 20. $\frac{3}{5}m = 2\frac{2}{5}$

Problem Solving ▶
Applications

21. Larry divided his marbles equally among 3 friends. Each friend got 14 marbles. Write and solve an equation to find how many marbles Larry had originally.

22. Chris uses the equation $s = \$6.25h$ to find his salary. Write a possible word sentence for the equation. Then solve for h if $s = \$137.50$.

23. Write and solve a multiplication equation to find the width of a rectangle with an area of 0.45 cm^2 and a length of 0.9 cm.

24. **? What's the Error?** Mike's steps to solve the equation $2x = 12$ are shown at the right. Find his error and give the correct solution.

$$2x = 12$$
$$2x - 2 = 12 - 2$$
$$x = 10$$

MIXED REVIEW AND TEST PREP

Solve and check. (p. 280)

25. $x - 5 = 17$ 26. $6 = y - 10$ 27. $15 = z - 3$

28. Evaluate the expression $\sqrt{121} - 3^2 + 12$. (p. 266)

⭐29. **TEST PREP** The low temperatures in Anchorage for five days were 4°F, 6°F, 4°F, 2°F, and 14°F. How much greater is the average low temperature with 14°F, than without? (p. 122)

A 14°F   **B** 6°F   **C** 4°F   **D** 2°F

EXTRA PRACTICE page 304, Set A   **293**

Use Formulas

Learn how to use formulas to solve problems.

QUICK REVIEW

Solve.

1. $4x = 12$ **2.** $5k = 45$

3. $64 = 8p$ **4.** $84 = 7m$

5. $36 = 9a$

The Verrazano-Narrows Bridge in New York is the longest bridge in the United States. The bridge is 13,700 feet long. Elena walked across the bridge at an average speed of 264 ft per min. How long did it take her to walk across the bridge?

If you know two of the three parts of the formula *distance = rate · time*, or $d = rt$, you can solve for the third part.

EXAMPLE 1

Find how long it took Elena to walk across the Verrazano-Narrows Bridge.

$d = rt$	*Write the formula.*
$13{,}700 = 264t$	*Replace d with 13,700 and r with 264.*
$\dfrac{13{,}700}{264} = \dfrac{264t}{264}$	*Solve the equation.*
$51\frac{59}{66} = t$	

So, it took $51\frac{59}{66}$ min, or about 52 min, for Elena to walk across the Verrazano-Narrows Bridge.

• Suppose Elena walked at an average speed of 250 ft per min. How long would it take her to cross the bridge?

You can solve for the distance if you know the rate and the time.

EXAMPLE 2

How far would Elena travel if she drove her car at an average speed of 57 mi per hr for $3\frac{1}{2}$ hr?

$d = rt$	*Write the formula.*
$d = 57 \cdot 3\frac{1}{2}$	*Replace r with 57 and t with $3\frac{1}{2}$.*
$d = 199\frac{1}{2}$	*Multiply.*

So, Elena would travel $199\frac{1}{2}$ mi.

You can solve for the rate if you know the distance and the time.

EXAMPLE 3

Suppose Elena took 5 hr to drive 306.5 mi. What was Elena's average speed?

$d = rt$ — *Write the formula.*

$306.5 = r \cdot 5$ — *Replace d with 306.5 and t with 5.*

$\dfrac{306.5}{5} = \dfrac{5r}{5}$ — *Solve the equation.*

$61.3 = r$

So, Elena's average speed was 61.3 mi per hr.

Cleveland is located in the northeast corner of Ohio near Lake Erie. The monthly normal temperature for November in Cleveland is about 10°C. You may be more familiar with the Fahrenheit temperature scale. To convert from degrees Celsius to degrees Fahrenheit, use the formula below.

$$F = \left(\frac{9}{5} \cdot C\right) + 32$$

EXAMPLE 4

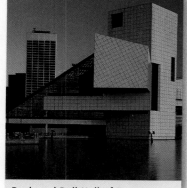

Rock and Roll Hall of Fame
Cleveland, Ohio

Find the monthly normal temperature for November in Cleveland in degrees Fahrenheit (°F). Write your answer as a decimal.

$F = \left(\frac{9}{5} \cdot C\right) + 32$ — *Write the formula.*

$F = \left(\frac{9}{5} \cdot 10\right) + 32$ — *Replace C with 10. Operate inside parentheses.*

$F = 18 + 32$ — *Add.*

$F = 50$

So, the monthly normal temperature for November is about 50°F.

To convert from degrees Fahrenheit to degrees Celsius, use the formula below.

$$C = \frac{5}{9} \cdot (F - 32)$$

EXAMPLE 5

The monthly normal temperature in Cleveland for June is 78°F. Find the temperature in degrees Celsius (°C). Write your answer as a decimal and round to the nearest tenth of a degree.

$C = \frac{5}{9} \cdot (F - 32)$ — *Write the formula.*

$C = \frac{5}{9} \cdot (78 - 32)$ — *Replace F with 78. Operate inside parentheses.*

$C = \frac{5}{9} \cdot 46$ — *Multiply.*

$C = 25\frac{5}{9} \approx 25.6$

So, the monthly normal temperature for June is about 25.6°C.

Think and ▶
Discuss

Look back at the lesson to answer the questions.

1. **Explain** how you know the unit of time in Example 1 is minutes.

2. **Explain** how you know the unit of length in Example 2 is miles.

3. **Tell** what a comfortable room temperature would be in degrees Celsius.

Guided ▶
Practice

Use the formula $d = rt$ to complete.

4. $d = \blacksquare$ ft
   $r = 22$ ft per min
   $t = 4$ min

5. $d = 100$ mi
   $r = \blacksquare$ mi per hr
   $t = 5$ hr

6. $d = 300$ mi
   $r = 50$ mi per hr
   $t = \blacksquare$ hr

Convert the temperature to degrees Fahrenheit. Write your answer as a decimal.

7. $10°C$ 8. $20°C$ 9. $30°C$ 10. $40°C$ 11. $5°C$

Convert the temperature to degrees Celsius. Write your answer as a decimal and round to the nearest tenth of a degree.

12. $85°F$ 13. $57°F$ 14. $212°F$ 15. $100°F$ 16. $32°F$

Independent ▶
Practice

Use the formula $d = rt$ to complete.

17. $d = \blacksquare$ ft
    $r = 8$ ft per sec
    $t = 4.6$ sec

18. $d = 44$ km
    $r = \blacksquare$ km per hr
    $t = 2.2$ hr

19. $d = 162.5$ mi
    $r = 65$ mi per hr
    $t = \blacksquare$ hr

Convert the temperature to degrees Fahrenheit. Write your answer as a decimal.

20. $50°C$ 21. $37°C$ 22. $100°C$ 23. $95°C$ 24. $32°C$

Convert the temperature to degrees Celsius. Write your answer as a decimal and round to the nearest tenth of a degree.

25. $32°F$ 26. $104°F$ 27. $47°F$ 28. $72°F$ 29. $94°F$

Solve.

30. Rita drove for $3\frac{1}{2}$ hours at a rate of 40 mi per hr. How far did Rita travel?

31. A train traveled 350 mi in 4 hours. Find the train's average rate of speed.

32. A hot air balloon climbed 4,200 ft in 14 min. Find the balloon's average climbing rate.

Problem Solving ▶ Applications

33. **FAST FACT** • SCIENCE   In order to remain in orbit, the space shuttle must reach speeds of about 17,500 mi per hr. Suppose the space shuttle travels 52,650 mi in 3 hr. Is the space shuttle traveling fast enough to remain in orbit? Explain.

Use Data   This summer, Jorge is traveling to Canada and Jacque is traveling to North Carolina. For 34–35, use the data in the table below.

34. The formula $F \approx 2C + 30$ estimates the conversion from °C to °F. Estimate the normal July temperature for Toronto and Vancouver in °F.

NORMAL JULY TEMPERATURES	
Toronto, Canada	27°C
Vancouver, Canada	22°C
Asheville, NC	73°F
Raleigh, NC	78°F

35. The formula $C \approx \frac{1}{2}(F - 30)$ estimates the conversion from °F to °C. Estimate the normal July temperature for Asheville and Raleigh in °C.

36. ✎ **Write a problem** that you must use $d = rt$ to solve.

MIXED REVIEW AND TEST PREP

Solve and check. (p. 291)

37. $3x = 15$

38. $42 = 7y$

39. $\frac{z}{8} = 3$

⭐**40. TEST PREP**   Which equation shows 18 is 6 more than a number, x? (p. 274)

   A $18 + 6 = x$ **B** $18 + x = 6$ **C** $18 = x + 6$ **D** $18 = x - 6$

⭐**41. TEST PREP**   Simplify $2x + 4x - 12$ by combining like terms. Then evaluate the expression for $x = 4$. (p. 260)

   F 4   **G** 10   **H** 12   **J** 36

PROBLEM SOLVING LINKUP to Careers

Mathematician   Evelyn Boyd Granville is a mathematician who has needed formulas throughout her career. When the United States space program was brand new, Dr. Granville worked on Project Mercury and Project Apollo, calculating orbits and programming computers. She has also worked with students from kindergarten through college.

• The distance to the moon is approximately 239,000 miles. Suppose a space craft took 6 days to reach the moon. What was its average speed in miles per hour?

EXTRA PRACTICE page 304, Set B

PROBLEM SOLVING STRATEGY
Work Backward

Learn how to use the strategy *work backward* to solve problems.

Felipe's parents paid $155 to rent a game room for his birthday party. The rates for renting the game room were $75 for the first hour and then $20 for each additional half hour. For how long did Felipe's parents rent the game room?

Analyze   What are you asked to find?

What information is given?

Is there information you will not use? If so, what?

Choose   What strategy will you use?

You can use inverse operations and the *work backward* strategy to solve the problem.

Solve   How will you solve the problem?
The cost of renting the game room was calculated in this way:

number of additional half hours		cost for additional half hours		cost for first hour		total cost of renting game room
	×		+		=	
■	×	$20	+	$75	=	$155

You can work backward by reversing the operations and the order.

($155	−	$75)	÷	$20	=	4

first hour + additional half hours = total time
1 hour + 4 half hours = 1 hour + 2 hours = 3 hours

So, Felipe's parents rented the game room for 3 hours.

Check   How can you check your answer?

What if Felipe's parents had paid $175 to rent the game room? For how long would they have rented the game room?

PROBLEM SOLVING STRATEGIES

Draw a Diagram or Picture

Make a Model

Predict and Test

► **Work Backward**

Make an Organized List

Find a Pattern

Make a Table or Graph

Solve a Simpler Problem

Write an Equation

Use Logical Reasoning

Solve the problem by working backward.

1. The local cab company charges $1.25 for the first mile traveled and then $0.35 for each additional mile. Natalie spent $7.20 on a ride in a cab. How many miles did Natalie travel?

2. Abby buys three CDs in a set for $29.98. She saves $6.44 by buying the set instead of buying the individual CDs. If each CD costs the same amount, how much does each of the three CDs cost when purchased separately?

MIXED STRATEGY PRACTICE

For 3–5, use this information.

There are 141 students on the field trip to the Space Museum. It takes 3 full buses to transport the students. The buses are all identical. There will be 51 more students on the next field trip.

3. Which expression could you use to help find the number of buses needed for the next field trip if b is the number of students per bus?

   A $141 - (b + 51)$ **C** $(141 + 51) \div b$
   B $51b + 3$ **D** $141 + 51 - b$

4. Which of the equations below could you use to find b, the number of students per bus?

   F $\frac{50}{b} = 3$ **H** $\frac{b}{50} = 141$
   G $50 + b = 141$ **J** $3b = 141$

5. Mr. Washington is in charge of ordering the buses for the next field trip. How many buses does he need to order to transport all of the students for the next field trip?

6. Jana has 89 CDs in her CD collection. She wants to take all of them with her on vacation. A CD carrying case holds 25 CDs. How many carrying cases does Jana need to carry all 89 CDs?

7. Elliot has nickels and dimes in his pocket. He has twice as many dimes as nickels. If the total value of the coins in his pocket is $1.00, how many of each coin does he have?

8. Amanda is making a small quilt that is 36 in. by 54 in. She wants to add a 3-in. border of trim. She has 10 ft of the trim. How much more trim does she need?

9. Half of the computer club members use $\frac{3}{8}$ of the computer stations in the technology lab. What is the least number of students that could be in the computer club?

10. ❓ **What's the Question?** Sean has a balance of $183 in his checking account. Last week he wrote a check for $25 and one for $217. The answer is $425.

Inequalities

Vocabulary

inequality

Remember that you can use these symbols when you compare numbers:

= is equal to
≠ is not equal to
< is less than
> is greater than
≤ is less than or equal to
≥ is greater than or equal to

QUICK REVIEW

Use < or > to compare.

1. $6 + 9 \bullet 13$ 2. $30 \div 3 \bullet 13$
3. $2 \times 6 \bullet 9$ 4. $15 \bullet 25 - 9$
5. $68 \div 4 \bullet 16$

An equation or equality is an algebraic sentence that contains the symbol =. An **inequality** is an algebraic sentence that contains the symbol <, >, ≤, ≥, or ≠.

These are inequalities:

$n > 5$ $x + 3 < 7$ $4y \geq 32$

Jonathan wants to know if his brother, Jackson, is tall enough to go with him on a carnival ride. The sign says your height must be greater than or equal to 48 in.

This information can also be expressed as an inequality. Here, the variable h represents height in inches.

$$h \geq 48$$

This inequality has many solutions. You can show the solutions of $h \geq 48$ on a number line.

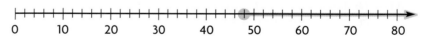

The blue line shows that all values greater than 48 are included. The blue arrow means they continue beyond 80. The filled-in blue circle means that 48 is also included. This number line starts at zero since you cannot have heights that are negative. Remember that negative numbers are less than zero.

EXAMPLE 1

Graph the inequality $x < 3$ on a number line.

With no restrictions on the variable, the solutions are all numbers, positive, zero, or negative, that are less than 3.

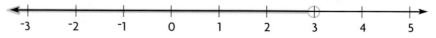

The circle at 3 is not filled in because 3 is not a solution. Only the numbers less than 3 are solutions.

• Is ⁻2 a solution of $x < 3$?

An equation is solved when the variable is alone on one side of the equation. You solve inequalities in much the same way.

Activity 1

You need: algebra tiles

Solve $x + 3 < 7$.

- Model the inequality by using algebra tiles. A green rectangle represents the variable. A yellow square represents 1.

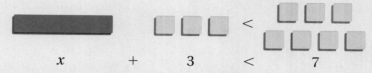

$$x \qquad + \qquad 3 \qquad < \qquad 7$$

- To solve the inequality, remove enough tiles from both sides so that the green tile, the variable, is alone on one side.

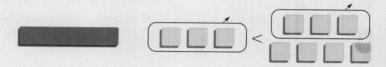

- Taking three ones from each side of the inequality leaves the variable alone on one side. The inequality is now solved.

$$x \qquad < \qquad 4$$

The green rectangle is alone on one side of the inequality.

Addition and subtraction are inverse operations. Use subtraction to solve an addition inequality. Use addition to solve a subtraction inequality. The Addition and Subtraction Properties of Equality can be used for inequalities.

| EXAMPLE 2 |

Solve and graph the inequality $y - 15 \geq 11$ on a number line.

$$y - 15 \geq 11 \qquad \textit{Write the inequality.}$$
$$y - 15 + 15 \geq 11 + 15 \qquad \textit{Add 15 to both sides.}$$
$$y \geq 26$$

$$y - 15 \geq 11 \qquad \textit{Check your solution.}$$
$$30 - 15 \geq 11 \qquad \textit{Use a number greater than 26 for y. Try 30.}$$
$$15 \geq 11 \quad \checkmark \qquad \textit{The solution checks. So, 30 is part of the solution and must be included on the graph.}$$

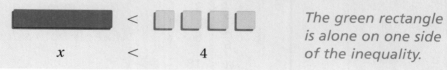

- How would the graph of the solution change if the inequality were $y - 15 > 11$?

Math Idea ▶ When you add or subtract the same number from both sides of an inequality, you get another inequality with the same solution. When you multiply or divide both sides of an inequality by the same *positive* number, you get another inequality with the same solution.

EXAMPLE 3

Solve and graph the inequality $3z > 42$ on a number line.

$3z > 42$	*Write the inequality.*
$\frac{3z}{3} > \frac{42}{3}$	*Divide both sides by 3.*
$z > 14$	

$3z > 42$	*Check your solution.*
$3 \times 15 > 42$	*Use a number greater than 14 for z. Try 15.*
$45 > 42$ ✓	*The solution checks. So, 15 is part of the solution and must be included on the graph.*

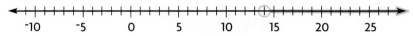

EXAMPLE 4

Solve and graph the inequality $\frac{w}{6} < 3$ on a number line.

$\frac{w}{6} < 3$	*Write the inequality.*
$6 \times \frac{w}{6} < 6 \times 3$	*Multiply both sides by 6.*
$w < 18$	

$\frac{w}{6} < 3$	*Check your solution.*
$\frac{12}{6} < 3$	*Use a number less than 18 for w. Try 12.*
$2 < 3$ ✓	*The solution checks. So, 12 is part of the solution and must be included on the graph.*

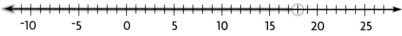

- List all the multiples of 3 that are less than 18 and part of the solution to $\frac{w}{6} < 3$.

CHECK FOR UNDERSTANDING

Think and Discuss ▶ Look back at the lesson to answer these questions.

1. **Explain** how to solve an addition inequality.

2. **Tell** whether or not the circle at ⁻3 should be filled in on the number line graph for $x \geq {}^{-}3$.

Guided Practice ▶ Solve and graph the inequality on a number line.

3. $x + 3 < 8$ 4. $y - 16 \geq 3$ 5. $4z > 56$

Independent ▶
Practice

Solve and graph the inequality on a number line.

6. $2 + a > 8$ **7.** $b + 5 \le 8$ **8.** $5c < 50$

9. $x - 2 > 4$ **10.** $2y \ge 16$ **11.** $z + 3 \ge 3$

12. $n - 1 < 12$ **13.** $\frac{m}{2} > 1$ **14.** $\frac{p}{5} \le 20$

Write an inequality for the word sentence.

15. The value for x is less than or equal to 2.

16. The value for y is greater than $^{-}10$.

17. The width, w, plus 2 is 8 or more.

18. The height, h, is at least 54.

Problem Solving ▶
Applications

19. Measurement A certain fishing line is sold for weights up to and including 12 lb. Write an inequality that represents the weights that will not break the line.

20. Trout less than 10 in. long must be thrown back. Write an inequality that represents the lengths that may be kept.

Use Data   **For 21–22, use the data in the table.**

21. Write an inequality relating a, the altitude of any U.S. location other than Mount McKinley, to Mount McKinley's altitude.

UNITED STATES SUPERLATIVES	
Highest Point	**Lowest Point**
Mount McKinley, AK	Death Valley, CA
Altitude: 20,320 ft	Altitude: $^{-}$282 ft

22. Write an inequality relating a, the altitude of any U.S. location, to Death Valley's altitude.

23. Vocabulary Power Look up *equality* in the dictionary. How does the definition of *equality* help you understand inequalities in mathematics?

24. **?** **What's the Error?** Tyra wrote the solutions of the inequality $\frac{a}{4} < 8$ as $a < 2$. What did she do? What is the correct answer?

MIXED REVIEW AND TEST PREP

25. Pat bought 31 ribbons and 1 bow. The total cost was $28.18. The bow cost $0.59. If each ribbon cost the same, what was the cost for one ribbon? (p. 86)

26. Write $\frac{3}{8}$ as a percent. (p. 191)   **27.** Write 125% as a decimal. (p. 68)

★ 28. TEST PREP Which is the prime factorization of 108, written in exponent form? (p. 168)

  A 4×27 **B** $2^3 \times 3^2$ **C** 4×3^3 **D** $2^2 \times 3^3$

★ 29. TEST PREP For the expression $2x + 4$, which value of x gives 6? (p. 260)

  F $x = 0$ **G** $x = 1$ **H** $x = 5$ **J** $x = 10$

EXTRA PRACTICE page 304, Set C

Set A (pp. 291–293)

Solve and check.

1. $3x = 12$

2. $7k = 56$

3. $\frac{p}{16} = 3$

4. $\frac{a}{14} = 2$

5. $27 = 3x$

6. $8.8 = 2.2n$

7. $4x = 24$

8. $8x = 32$

9. $9 = \frac{p}{3}$

For 10, write and solve an equation to answer the question.

10. Celia divided all of her baseball cards equally among 4 friends. Each friend got 23 baseball cards. How many baseball cards did Celia have originally?

Set B (pp. 294–297)

Use the formula $d = rt$ to complete.

1. $d = \blacksquare$ mi
$r = 35$ mi per hr
$t = 4$ hr

2. $d = 1{,}600$ km
$r = \blacksquare$ km per min
$t = 400$ min

3. $d = 2{,}100$ km
$r = 70$ km per sec
$t = \blacksquare$ sec

Convert the temperature to degrees Fahrenheit. Write your answer as a decimal.

4. 40°C

5. 2.3°C

6. 14°C

7. 20°C

Convert the temperature to degrees Celsius. Write your answer as a decimal and round to the nearest tenth of a degree.

8. 42°F

9. 47°F

10. 79°F

11. 100°F

12. The Concorde jet has a cruising speed of 1,354 mi per hr. Suppose the Concorde maintained this speed for $3\frac{1}{2}$ hr. How far would the Concorde travel?

Set C (pp. 300–303)

Solve and graph the inequality on a number line.

1. $a + 6 > 19$

2. $c + 8 \leq 41$

3. $6b < 90$

4. $x - 7 > 51$

5. $3y \geq 42$

6. $z + 3 \geq 12$

7. $n - 17 < 32$

8. $\frac{a}{5} \geq 13$

9. $\frac{r}{4} < 11$

Write an inequality for the word sentence.

10. The value of q is greater than or equal to 7.

11. The value for m is less than 12.

12. The height, h, minus 7 is 22 or less.

13. The weight, w, is at least 2,000.

1. **VOCABULARY**   The property which states that if you divide both sides of an equation by the same nonzero number, the two sides remain equal is the __?__. (p. 291)

2. **VOCABULARY**   The property which states that if you multiply both sides of an equation by the same number, the two sides remain equal is the __?__. (p. 292)

Solve and check. (pp. 291–293)

3. $6x = 24$

4. $28 = 4a$

5. $\frac{y}{7} = 11$

6. $1.9 = \frac{a}{12}$

7. $1.1n = 55$

8. $\frac{x}{5} = 3$

9. $9y = 72$

10. $6 = \frac{x}{3}$

Use the formula $d = rt$ to complete. (pp. 294–297)

11. $d = 1{,}485$ mi
    $r = 55$ mi per hr
    $t = \blacksquare$ hr

12. $d = 220$ km
    $r = \blacksquare$ km per hr
    $t = \frac{1}{2}$ hr

13. $d = \blacksquare$ ft
    $r = 10$ ft per sec
    $t = 36$ sec

14. $d = 3{,}570$ ft
    $r = 140$ ft per min
    $t = \blacksquare$ min

15. $d = 1{,}625$ mi
    $r = \blacksquare$ mi per hr
    $t = 25$ hr

16. $d = \blacksquare$ m
    $r = 32$ m per sec
    $t = 9.6$ sec

17. $d = 273.42$ km
    $r = 18.6$ km per hr
    $t = \blacksquare$ hr

18. $d = 157.5$ in.
    $r = \blacksquare$ in. per min
    $t = 42$ min

Convert the temperature to degrees Fahrenheit. Write your answer as a decimal. (pp. 294–297)

19. 12°C

20. 25°C

21. 2°C

22. 41°C

Convert the temperature to degrees Celsius. Write your answer as a decimal and round to the nearest tenth of a degree. (pp. 294–297)

23. 59°F

24. 89°F

25. 72°F

26. 38°F

Solve and graph the inequality on a number line. (pp. 300–303)

27. $x + 12 > 62$

28. $y - 14 \leq 31$

29. $7z \geq 56$

30. $\frac{a}{20} > 3$

Solve.

31. The maximum speed of the X-15A-2 jet is 4,534 mi per hr. How long would it take this jet to travel the 2,787 mi from Los Angeles to New York if it is traveling at its maximum speed? Round your answer to the nearest tenth. (pp. 294–297)

32. André paid $14.35 for a cab ride. The rate for riding in the cab was $1.75 for the first mile and then $0.35 for each additional mile. How many miles long was André's cab ride? (pp. 298–299)

33. Two days ago, Raul had a certain amount of money in his wallet. He then added $2 to his wallet. Yesterday, he was paid for his chores, and the amount of money in his wallet tripled. He now has $18 in his wallet. How much was originally in his wallet? (pp. 298–299)

★ NUMBER SENSE, CONCEPTS, AND OPERATIONS

1. Hot Springs National Park, located in Hot Springs, Arkansas, has an area of 5,549 acres. Dry Tortugas National Park, west of Key West, Florida, has an area 1,888 acres less than 12 times the area of Hot Springs National Park. Which is the area of Dry Tortugas National Park?

A 68,476 acres   **C** 65,300 acres

B 66,588 acres   **D** 64,700 acres

2. Two-fifths of the tiles in the rectangular lobby at the County Art Museum are blue. There are a total of 90 tiles in the lobby. How many of the tiles are blue?

F 25

G 36

H 54

J 90

3. Earth has 1 moon. The planet Jupiter has $5^2 + (3^3 - 26) \times 3$ moons. How many moons does Jupiter have?

A 13 moons

B 28 moons

C 29 moons

D 78 moons

> **TIP** **Decide on a plan.** See item 3. Use the order of operations.
> 1. Operate in parentheses.
> 2. Clear exponents.
> 3. Multiply and divide.
> 4. Add and Subtract.

4. Explain It Allan has been reading a book. He said that since he has read $\frac{3}{4}$ of the book, he only has 28 more pages to read. His book has a total of 112 pages. Is his statement correct? Explain why or why not.

★ ALGEBRAIC THINKING

5. A bathtub has 40 gallons of water in it. Juanita lets the water drain out of the tub. Which inequality best describes the amount of water in the tub at any given time? Let t represent the amount of water in the tub.

F $t \le 40$ **H** $t < 40$

G $t \ge 40$ **J** $t > 40$

6. Austin and his two sisters paid $84 for a portable CD player for their mother's birthday present. Each child paid the same amount. Which of the following shows the correct equation for finding the amount each child paid?

A $2x = \$84$ **C** $\frac{x}{2} = \$84$

B $3x = \$84$ **D** $\frac{x}{3} = \$84$

7. A scientist recorded the number of cells she observed each hour for four hours.

NUMBER OF CELLS OBSERVED				
Hour	1	2	3	4
Number	1	2	4	8

If this pattern continues, how many cells will she observe the fifth hour?

F 128

G 64

H 32

J 16

8. Explain It In 1964, Robert Hayes won an Olympic gold medal for the United States. He ran the 100-meter dash in 10 seconds. Explain how to use the formula $d = rt$ to find Hayes's average rate of speed for the race. What was his rate?

9. The table below lists the numbers of quarters per state that Marsha has in her coin bank.

STATE QUARTER COLLECTION	
State	**Number**
New York	8
North Carolina	15
Tennessee	4
Indiana	3

If Marsha randomly selects one quarter out of the bank, what is the probability it will be a Tennessee quarter?

A $\frac{2}{15}$ **C** $\frac{1}{10}$

B $\frac{2}{13}$ **D** $\frac{1}{2}$

10. Ruby wants to wear a different outfit each day. Each outfit is made of a shirt and a pair of pants. Using the shirts and pants shown below, how many different outfits does she have to choose from?

F 3

G 4

H 7

J 12

11. Explain It Emily surveyed 30 students to find how many cousins they had. She is making a line plot with the data. Explain how she can find the mode of her data when she has completed the plot.

12. Franco is designing a single tile shape that he can use to tessellate his kitchen counter. Which of the following shapes can he use?

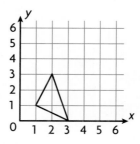

13. A triangle is shown on the coordinate plane below. Which are the new coordinates of the triangle if it is translated 3 units to the right and 2 units up?

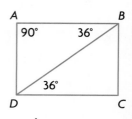

F (3,3), (4,5), (5,2)

G (4,4), (5,6), (6,3)

H (3,4), (5,5), (2,6)

J (4,3), (5,5), (6,2)

14. Explain It The figure shows $\overline{BD}$, the diagonal support for a highway billboard. Are $\overline{AD}$ and $\overline{DC}$ parallel, perpendicular, or neither? Explain your reasoning.

≡FAST FACT • ART The Fibonacci Fountain, located in Bowie, Maryland, is made from over 45 tons of granite. The design of the fountain is based on the famous Fibonacci sequence (1, 1, 2, 3, 5, 8, . . .).

PROBLEM SOLVING Numbers from the sequence also appear in nature. Look at the chart. The total number of stems the plant has each month shows the Fibonacci sequence. If the pattern continues, how many stems will it have on August 1?

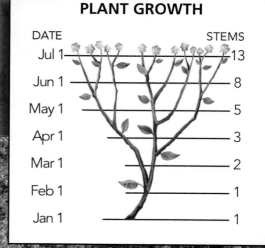

PLANT GROWTH

DATE	STEMS
Jul 1	13
Jun 1	8
May 1	5
Apr 1	3
Mar 1	2
Feb 1	1
Jan 1	1

Check What You Know

Use this page to help you review and remember important skills needed for Chapter 14.

 Input/Output Tables

Copy and complete each table.

1.

INPUT	OUTPUT
x	$x - 6$
16	▣
27	▣

2.

INPUT	OUTPUT
y	$y + 14.7$
12	▣
12.5	▣

3.

INPUT	OUTPUT
w	$w \div 4$
100	▣
102	▣

4.

INPUT	OUTPUT
a	$a \times 15$
10	▣
23	▣

5.

INPUT	OUTPUT
z	$3z$
3	▣
5	▣

6.

INPUT	OUTPUT
b	$10b$
25	▣
30	▣

7.

INPUT	OUTPUT
k	$2k + 4$
8	▣
10	▣

8.

INPUT	OUTPUT
c	$4c - 8$
6	▣
7	▣

 Number Patterns

Write a rule for each pattern and predict the next number.

9.

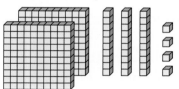 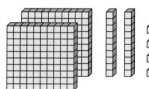 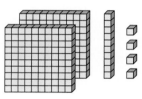

10. 4, 6, 8, 10, 12

11. 95, 90, 85, 80

12. 98, 96, 94, 92

13. 10, 18, 26, 34

14. 125, 150, 175

15. 500, 490, 480

16. 280, 260, 240

17. 25, 75, 125

VOCABULARY POWER

REVIEW

pattern [pat′ərn] *noun*

In mathematics, a pattern can be an arrangement of objects or numbers, such as 2, 4, 6, 8, 10. List some examples of patterns you have seen outside of mathematics. How are the patterns you listed similar to number patterns?

PREVIEW

triangular number
sequence
term
function
fractal
iteration

 www.harcourtschool.com/mathglossary

PROBLEM SOLVING STRATEGY
Find a Pattern

Learn to solve problems by using the strategy *find a pattern*.

The members of a professional skydiving team make formations in the air by holding on to each other. After one second, one person begins a formation. At three seconds, three others join with the first person. At five seconds, five more people join. At seven seconds, seven more join the group. If this pattern continues, how many people will be in the group after eleven seconds?

Analyze

What are you asked to find?

What information are you given?

Is there information you will not use? If so, what?

Choose

What strategy will you use?

You can use the strategy *find a pattern*.

Solve

How will you solve the problem?

Find patterns for skydivers added and total skydivers.

Skydivers added

1, 3, 5, 7, . . .

Pattern: consecutive odd numbers

Total skydivers

1, 4, 9, 16, . . .

Pattern: squares of consecutive numbers

Show the patterns in a table to find the number of skydivers in the formation after eleven seconds.

Time	1 sec	3 sec	5 sec	7 sec	9 sec	11 sec
Skydivers added	1	3	5	7	9	11
Total skydivers	1	4	9	16	25	36

So, there are 36 skydivers at 11 seconds.

Check

How can you check your answer?

What if there are 81 skydivers? At how many seconds are there 81?

PROBLEM SOLVING PRACTICE

PROBLEM SOLVING STRATEGIES

Draw a Diagram or Picture
Make a Model
Predict and Test
Work Backward
Make an Organized List
▶ **Find a Pattern**
Make a Table or Graph
Solve a Simpler Problem
Write an Equation
Use Logical Reasoning

Solve the problem by finding a pattern.

1. Alex is beginning a new physical training program. He will do 7 push-ups the first day, 12 push-ups the second day, and 17 push-ups the third day, and will continue until he does 42 push-ups in one day. If this pattern continues, on which day will Alex do 42 push-ups?

2. The school choir learns songs for a competition to be held in 7 weeks. The choir knows 5 songs after the first week, 8 after the second week, and 11 after the third week. If this pattern continues, how many songs will the choir know after 7 weeks?

For 3–4, use this information.

The air temperature decreases 8°C for every 1,500-m gain in altitude.

3. Which algebraic expression can be used to find the temperatures if the starting temperature is 20°C and n is the number of 1,500-m gains in altitude?

   A $20 - 8n$ **C** $20 + n$

   B $20 + 8n$ **D** $20 - n$

4. It was 20°C when Rachel began her ascent in a hot-air balloon. How many meters had the balloon gone up when the temperature was 4°C?

   F 3 m   **H** 4,500 m

   G 3,000 m   **J** 6,000 m

MIXED STRATEGY PRACTICE

5. Paul bought previously viewed videos for $119.50. He paid $12.50 each for some and $8.00 each for others. He bought fewer than 8 videos at each price. How many videos did Paul buy for $12.50?

6. Jill can buy party favors at $1.10 each or for $10 a dozen. She wants to buy two dozen. How much does she save when buying them by the dozen instead of buying one at a time?

7. Light poles along a highway are placed at regular intervals. The distance from the first pole to the sixth pole is 300 ft. What is the distance from the twentieth pole to the thirty-first pole?

8. A card collection was divided among Michelle and her three brothers. Armand received $\frac{1}{3}$ of the cards, Ben received $\frac{1}{4}$ of the cards, and Denis received $\frac{1}{6}$ of the cards. Michelle received 345 cards. How many cards were in the collection before it was divided?

9. Sandy has to be at the airport for a 5:20 P.M. flight. She wants to arrive 1 hr 15 min early. If it takes 50 min to drive to the airport, when should she leave?

10. **? What's the Question?** Anne bought 28 fish. She bought 3 times as many goldfish as angelfish. The answer is 7.

Patterns in Sequences

Learn how to recognize, describe, and extend patterns in sequences.

Vocabulary

triangular number

sequence

term

Mr. Fabano designed patterns for the members of his marching band to make when they perform. His patterns, shown below, are triangular arrays.

A number that can be represented by a triangular array is a **triangular number**.

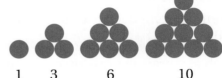

triangular arrays →
triangular numbers →   1   3   6   10

The pattern of triangular numbers above can be written in a number sequence. A **sequence** is an ordered set of numbers. Each number in the sequence is called a **term**.

To get the next term in the triangular number sequence, you add 1 more than was added previously. Use this rule to find the next term in the sequence.

sequence →   1   3   6   10   ■
                  +2 +3 +4 +5

Since $10 + 5 = 15$, the next triangular number is 15.

Math Idea ▶ A sequence can have a repeating pattern of addition, subtraction, multiplication, division, or any combination of these operations.

EXAMPLE 1

Identify a pattern in the sequence $1, 5\frac{1}{2}, 10, 14\frac{1}{2}, 19, \ldots$ and write the rule. Using your rule, find the next three terms in the sequence.

1       $5\frac{1}{2}$ 10 $14\frac{1}{2}$ 19
   $+4\frac{1}{2}$ $+4\frac{1}{2}$ $+4\frac{1}{2}$ $+4\frac{1}{2}$

Look for a pattern. Compare each term with the next.

A rule is to add $4\frac{1}{2}$ to each term to get the next term.

$19 + 4\frac{1}{2} = 23\frac{1}{2}$ $23\frac{1}{2} + 4\frac{1}{2} = 28$ $28 + 4\frac{1}{2} = 32\frac{1}{2}$

So, $23\frac{1}{2}$, 28, and $32\frac{1}{2}$ are the next three terms.

• What is the tenth term of the sequence in Example 1?

Sequences that show a decreasing pattern often involve subtraction or division.

EXAMPLE 2

Find the next three possible terms in the sequence.

3,645; 1,215; 405; 135; . . .

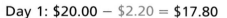

3,645   1,215   405   135   *Look for a pattern. Compare*
                                     each term with the next.

        ÷3   ÷3   ÷3

A rule is to divide each term by 3 to get the next term.

135 ÷ 3 = 45   *Start with 135 and divide by 3.*

45 ÷ 3 = 15

15 ÷ 3 = 5

So, 45, 15, and 5 are the next three terms.

You can use a rule to write a sequence.

EXAMPLE 3

James has $20.00. He spends $2.20 every day on his school lunch. Write a sequence to show how James will spend his $20.00. How much money will James have left after three days?

Start: $20.00
Rule: Subtract $2.20 from each term.

Day 1: $20.00 − $2.20 = $17.80   *Subtract $2.20 from each term*
Day 2: $17.80 − $2.20 = $15.60   *to find the next term.*
Day 3: $15.60 − $2.20 = $13.40

$20.00, $17.80, $15.60, $13.40, . . .   *Write the terms as a sequence.*

So, James will have $13.40 left after three days.

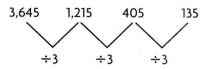

• **What if** James continues this pattern? How many more school lunches can he buy with the money left after three days?

CHECK FOR UNDERSTANDING

Think and ▶
Discuss

Look back at the lesson to answer each question.

1. **Write** a rule to make the following sequence. Then find the next three terms. 8, 32, 128, 512, . . .

2. **Tell** whether the sequence 1,200; 240; 48; . . . is increasing or decreasing.

Guided ▶
Practice

Write a rule for each sequence. Then find the sixth term.

3. 5, 20, 35, 50, . . .   4. 0.001, 0.01, 0.1, 1, . . .

TECHNOLOGY LINK

More Practice:
**Harcourt Mega Math
The Number Games,**
Tiny's Think Tank,
Levels T and V

Find the next three possible terms in each sequence.

5. 10, 21, 32, 43, . . .   **6.** 0.2, 2, 20, 200, . . .

PRACTICE AND PROBLEM SOLVING

**Independent ▶
Practice**

Write a rule for each sequence. Then find the sixth term.

7. 648, 216, 72, 24, . . .   **8.** 17.5, 16.3, 15.1, 13.9, . . .

9. 7, 7.89, 8.78, 9.67, . . .   **10.** 12, 30, 75, $187\frac{1}{2}$, . . .

Find the next three possible terms in each sequence.

11. 35, 65, 125, 215, . . .   **12.** 400, 200, 100, 50, . . .

13. 91, 90, 88, 85, . . .   **14.** 4, 40, 400, 4,000, . . .

Use the rule to write a sequence.

15. Start with 9; add 3.7.   **16.** Start with 5; multiply by 6.

**Problem Solving ▶
Applications**

17. Mr. Amano started a coin collection. He started his collection with 29 coins and then set a goal to add a certain number of coins each year. The sequence 29, 41, 53, 65, . . . shows the pattern of the number of coins in his collection. Write the rule for the pattern and find the number of coins in his collection in the sixth year.

18. **FAST FACT** • SCIENCE The Fibonacci Sequence, 1, 1, 2, 3, 5, 8, 13, . . . can be seen in the spirals of pine cones and in the patterns of seeds on flower heads. Write a rule for the pattern, and list the first 15 terms in the sequence. As it continues, what other patterns do you find?

19. Write a problem involving a number sequence that starts with $\frac{1}{2}$ and uses multiplication to get the next number. Explain your rule.

20. **Vocabulary Power** Write a mathematical and nonmathematical definition for *rule*. Give an example of each.

MIXED REVIEW AND TEST PREP

21. Solve the inequality $x - 4 > 2$ and graph its solutions. (p. 300)

22. What is the length of a side of the square at the right? (p. 266)

23. Evaluate $3 \times (7 + 4) \times 2^3$. (p. 48)

24. Solve. $\frac{h}{1.5} = 30$ (p. 291)

★25. **TEST PREP** Six soccer teams compete in the regional play-offs. Each team plays each of the other teams once. How many games are played in the play-offs? (p. 174)

   A 6   **B** 12   **C** 15   **D** 30

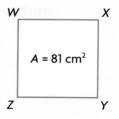

W   X

A = 81 cm²

Z   Y

Number Patterns and Functions

Learn how to write an equation to represent a function.

Vocabulary

function

Evaluate each expression.

1. $a + 3.2$ for $a = 5.4$ 2. $5.6 - r$ for $r = 1.2$
3. $0.25 \times m$ for $m = 4$ 4. $q \div 0.3$ for $q = 9$
5. $y - 16$ for $y = 25.2$

Delia earns $5.25 per hour. She wants to buy a camera that costs $125. How many hours will Delia have to work to earn $125?

Use the pattern below.

HOURS WORKED	MONEY EARNED
1	$5.25
2	$10.50
3	$15.75
4	$21.00
5	$26.25

The pattern shows that for the first five hours, as the number of hours increases by 1, the money earned increases by $5.25.

Delia used the pattern to write an equation in which h equals the number of hours worked and m equals the amount of money earned. She can use the equation to find how many hours she needs to work to earn $125.

$$m = 5.25h$$

$$125 = 5.25h \qquad \textit{Replace m with 125.}$$

$$\frac{125}{5.25} = \frac{5.25h}{5.25} \qquad \textit{Solve the equation.}$$

$$23.81 \approx h$$

So, Delia needs to work about 24 hr.

Math **I**dea ▶ A **function** is a relationship between two quantities in which one quantity depends uniquely on the other. Every input has exactly one output. Delia's equation is a function because the amount of money she earns, m, depends on the number of hours, h, that she works.

You can use a function table or an equation to represent some functions.

EXAMPLE 1

Mrs. Nien told her students that she used a pattern to determine the different sizes of paper to cut for them to use in class. The sizes, in inches, are shown below. Look for a pattern. Then write an equation to find the length when the width is 10 in.

width, w	3	4	5	6	7
length, l	7	9	11	13	15

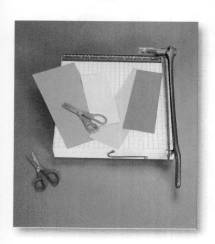

Compare the length and the width.
The length is 1 in. more than 2 times the width.   ← pattern

$l = 2w + 1$ *Write the equation.*

Use the equation to find the length when the width is 10 in.

$l = (2 \times 10) + 1$ *Replace w with 10.*

$l = 20 + 1$

$l = 21$

So, the length is 21 in. when the width is 10 in.

• In Example 1, the value of l depends on what other value?

You can use an equation to find missing terms in a function table.

EXAMPLE 2

Write an equation to describe the function. Then use it to find the missing term.

x	1	2	3	4	5	6
y	1	4	9	16	25	■

THINK: Since each y-value is greater than the corresponding x-value, use either addition or multiplication. What number is each x-value multiplied by to get the y-value?

Each x-value is multiplied by itself.   ← pattern

The equation is $y = x^2$.

$y = x^2$

$y = 6^2$ *Replace x with 6.*

$y = 36$ ← $6^2 = 6 \times 6$

So, the missing term is 36.

• Find y when $x = 13$.

Think and ▶
Discuss

Look back at the lesson to answer each question.

1. **Explain** how, in Example 1, you would find the value of w if you knew $l = 21$.

2. **Write** an equation for this function: the amount earned is $6 times the number of hours worked.

Guided ▶
Practice

Write an equation to represent a function that matches the data.

3.

a	10	9	8	7	6
b	4	3	2	1	0

4.

x	0	1	2	3	4
y	0	12	24	36	48

PRACTICE AND PROBLEM SOLVING

Independent ▶
Practice

Write an equation to represent a function that matches the data.

5.

c	1	2	3	4	5
d	2.1	3.1	4.1	5.1	6.1

6.

m	1	4	9	16	25
n	1	2	3	4	5

7.

w	1.2	1.3	1.4	1.5	1.6
l	4.8	5.2	5.6	6.0	6.4

8.

x	5	4	3	2	1
y	9	7	5	3	1

Write an equation to represent a function that matches the data. Then use it to find the missing term.

9.

k	24	34	44	54
g	12	17	22	■

10.

s	11	14	17	20
r	22	■	28	31

11.

c	16	24	32	36
d	4	6	■	9

12.

a	42	48	52	56
b	14	■	$17\frac{1}{3}$	$18\frac{2}{3}$

Problem Solving ▶
Applications

13. Write an equation for each function. Tell what each variable you use represents.

   a. The length of a rectangle is 5 times its width.

   b. Distance is the product of the rate of travel and the time traveled.

   c. The cost of shipping a package is $1.25 per pound.

   d. The cost of riding in a cab is $3.00 plus $0.75 per mile.

14. Felicity wants to purchase a CD player for $115.99. She earns $5.25 per hour baby-sitting. Write an equation and find how many hours Felicity needs to baby-sit to buy the CD player.

15. **REASONING** In a function, every input has exactly one output. In the equation $y = 2x + 5$, x is the input and y is the output. Does the equation $y = 2x + 5$ represent a function? Explain.

16. Different sizes of signs are shown below. Look for a pattern. Then write an equation to find the height when the width is 13 ft.

width, w	1	3	5	7	9
height, h	5	11	17	23	29

17. Tasha sells homemade bookmarks for 75¢ each. Her sales for each of seven weeks are shown below. Write an equation to represent the function, and complete the table.

n	8	15	22	29	36	43	50
t	$6	$11.25	$16.50	$21.75	$27	$32.25	▪

Use Data **For 18–19, use the graph of Vincent's budget.**

18. Vincent saved $380 to spend on his vacation. How much did he plan to pay for meals and entertainment?

19. How much money did Vincent plan to spend on souvenirs and entrance fees?

VACATION BUDGET

Meals and entertainment 45% — Entrance fees 25% — Souvenirs 30%

MIXED REVIEW AND TEST PREP

20. Using a rule, name the next three terms. 0.82, 0.75, 0.68, 0.61, . . . (p. 312)

21. $\frac{12}{13} + 1\frac{1}{8}$ (p. 210)

22. $(324 \div 12) + 4^3$ (p. 48)

23. TEST PREP Oranges are 5 for $1.80. How much will 2 dozen oranges cost? (p. 24)

A $1.92   **B** $3.20   **C** $4.32   **D** $8.64

24. TEST PREP Which shows $\sqrt{25} + 13$? (p. 266)

F 38   **G** 18   **H** 12   **J** 8

PROBLEM SOLVING Thinker's Corner

Algebra The binary, or base-two, number system uses only the digits 0 and 1.

DECIMAL	0	1	2	3	4	5	6	7	8	9	10
BINARY	0	1	10	11	100	101	110	111	1000	1001	1010

In the decimal system, each place value is *ten* times the place value to the right. In the binary system, each place value is *twice* the place to the right. You can use powers of 2 to find the decimal equivalent of a binary number.

$$10100_{two} = (1 \times 2^4) + (0 \times 2^3) + (1 \times 2^2) + (0 \times 2^1) + (0 \times 2^0)$$
$$= (1 \times 16) + (0 \times 8) + (1 \times 4) + (0 \times 2) + (0 \times 1)$$
$$= 16 + 0 + 4 + 0 + 0$$
$$= 20$$

Find the decimal equivalent of each binary number.

1. 1111_{two} **2.** 10001_{two} **3.** 11000_{two} **4.** 11111_{two}

EXTRA PRACTICE page 322, Set B

Geometric Patterns

Learn how to recognize, describe, and extend patterns of geometric figures.

Vocabulary

fractal

iteration

Ayita is making a wall hanging using a geometric figure. Patterns of geometric figures are based on the shape, color, size, position, or number of the figures. The pattern below is what Ayita started with for her wall hanging.

Notice that the size of the figure increases twice before the pattern repeats. The next figure in the pattern might be the large figure again.

EXAMPLE 1

Ayita used this pattern for another craft project she made. Look for a possible pattern. Draw the next three possible figures.

Look for a possible pattern. The circles, alternating between two and one, move clockwise around the inside of the figure.

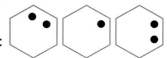

So, the next three figures might be:

EXAMPLE 2

Look for a possible pattern. Draw the next possible figure.

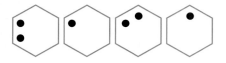

Look for a possible pattern. The figures are flipped horizontally about a vertical axis. The top left square and then the bottom left square are changed.

So, the next figure might be:

You can also find patterns in three-dimensional figures.

EXAMPLE 3

Mr. Gallo is displaying boxes in his store. Look for a pattern. Draw what the next two displays might look like.

A new layer is added to the bottom. A pattern for the total number of boxes in the bottom layer is 1, 3, 6,...

So, these might be the next two displays:

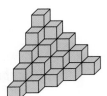 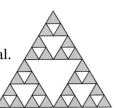

Some geometric figures contain a repeating pattern of smaller and smaller parts. This can be described as a fractal. A **fractal** has an endlessly repeating pattern containing shapes that are like the whole but of different sizes throughout. Note the repeating pattern in this figure.

You can build fractals from two-dimensional figures by repeating a process over and over again. This is called iterating. An **iteration** is a step in the process of iterating.

EXAMPLE 4

Build two stages of a developing fractal from a square by repeating this iteration process two times. Find the number of shaded squares that would be in Stage 3.

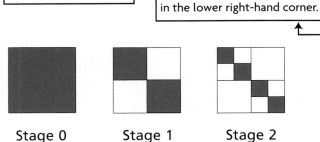

| Draw a shaded square. | → | Reduce the entire figure to one-half in length and width. Place one copy in the upper left-hand corner and one in the lower right-hand corner. |

Look for a pattern. Stage 0 has 1 shaded square, Stage 1 has 2, and Stage 2 has 4.

Stage 0   Stage 1   Stage 2

The pattern of shaded squares is 1, 2, 4, ...

So, 8 smaller squares would be shaded in Stage 3.

CHECK FOR UNDERSTANDING

Think and ▶ Discuss

Look back at the lesson to answer the question.

1. **Draw** a geometric pattern that uses a triangle.

Guided ▸ Practice Draw the next three possible figures in the pattern.

2.

3.

PRACTICE AND PROBLEM SOLVING

Independent ▸ Practice Draw the next three possible figures in the pattern.

TECHNOLOGY LINK

More Practice:
**Harcourt Mega Math
The Number Games,**
Tiny's Think Tank,
Level U

4.

5.

6.

7.

For 8–9, use the figures at the right.

8. The iterative process is (1) reduce the figure to one-third in length and width and (2) place five copies in the corners and center. How many yellow squares would be in Stage 3?

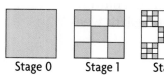

Stage 0   Stage 1   Stage 2

9. Use exponents to describe the pattern for the number of yellow squares at each stage.

Problem Solving ▸ Applications

10. Ayita saves part of the money made by selling her wall hangings. She saves $55 of the $450 she gets for the first hanging. She will increase the amount saved by $4 each time she sells a hanging. Write the pattern of amounts. For which hanging will she save $75?

11. The figure at the right was made with rectangular prisms. The top level has 1 prism, the next level has 4 prisms, and the bottom has 9 prisms. How many prisms might be in the next two levels added at the bottom?

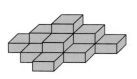

12. ✎ **Write a problem** using a geometric pattern in your school. Describe it in words and with a drawing.

MIXED REVIEW AND TEST PREP

13. For $y = 6x + 3$, find the values of y for $x = 0, 1,$ and 2. (p. 315)

14. Compare. Write $<$ or $>$ for ●.
$\frac{1}{2}$ ● 0.60 (p. 191)

15. Write the prime factorization for 65. (p. 168)

16. Evaluate $3x + 9x - 36$ for $x = 5$. (p. 260)

★**17. TEST PREP** Which is the GCF of 54 and the number that is the LCM of 3, 5, 9, and 15? (p. 170)

A 6   **C** 18
B 9   **D** 45

Set A (pp. 312–314)

Write a rule for each sequence. Then find the sixth term.

1. 2, 6, 18, 54, . . .

2. $\frac{1}{10}, \frac{1}{5}, \frac{3}{10}, \frac{2}{5}, \cdots$

3. 5, 20, 35, 50, . . .

4. 440, 44, 4.4, 0.44, . . .

Find the next three possible terms in each sequence.

5. $\frac{2}{5}, \frac{4}{5}, 1\frac{1}{5}, \ldots$

6. 2.3, 3.9, 5.5, . . .

7. 7, 17, 37, 67, . . .

8. 27, 9, 3, 1, . . .

9. Vittorio practices 6 weeks for the skateboard championship. The first 4 weeks he practices $9\frac{1}{2}$ hr, $11\frac{1}{4}$ hr, 13 hr, and $14\frac{3}{4}$ hr. If this pattern continues, how many hours will Vittorio practice the sixth week?

Set B (pp. 315–318)

Write an equation to represent a function that matches the data.

1.

x	0	1	2	3	4
y	3	4	5	6	7

2.

x	10	9	8	7	6
y	6	5	4	3	2

3.

x	0	1	2	3	4
y	0	8	16	24	32

4.

x	30	27	24	21	18
y	10	9	8	7	6

Set C (pp. 319–321)

Draw the next two possible figures in the pattern.

1.

2.

3.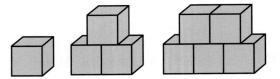

4.

1. **VOCABULARY** A relationship in which one quantity depends uniquely on another is a(n) __?__ . (p. 315)

2. **VOCABULARY** An ordered set of numbers is called a(n) __?__ . (p. 312)

3. **VOCABULARY** Each number in a sequence is called a(n) __?__ . (p. 312)

Write a rule for each sequence. Then find the sixth term. (pp. 312–314)

4. 220, 22, 2.2, . . .

5. 3, 9, 27, . . .

6. 100, 99.1, 98.2, . . .

7. $4, 3\frac{2}{3}, 3\frac{1}{3}, \ldots$

8. 243, 81, 27, . . .

9. $\frac{7}{8}, 3\frac{1}{8}, 5\frac{3}{8}, \ldots$

Find the next three possible terms in each sequence. (pp. 312–314)

10. $7, 5\frac{3}{4}, 4\frac{1}{2}, \ldots$

11. 90, 79, 68, . . .

12. 9, 15, 21, . . .

13. 3, 6, 12, . . .

14. 32, 16, 8, . . .

15. 5, 17, 29, . . .

Write an equation to represent a function that matches the data. (pp. 315–318)

16.

x	9	8	7	6	5
y	6	5	4	3	2

17.

x	10	11	12	13	14
y	17	18	19	20	21

18.

x	4	3	2	1	0
y	40	30	20	10	0

19.

x	64	56	48	40	32
y	8	7	6	5	4

Draw the next two possible figures in the pattern. (pp. 319–321)

20.

21.

22.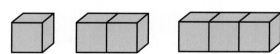

23.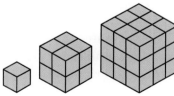

Solve. (pp. 310–311)

24. Ms. Wong received 110 orders the first month, 125 the second month, and 140 the third month. If this pattern continues, how many orders will she receive the sixth month?

25. The temperature was 21°F at 6 P.M. At 7 P.M. it was 18°F, and at 8 P.M. it was 15°F. If this pattern continues, what will the temperature be at midnight?

★ ALGEBRAIC THINKING

1. Lavonne earns $1 on Monday. Each day from Tuesday through Friday, she earns double the amount she earned the previous day. How much will she have earned in total by the end of the day on Friday?

   TIP Decide on a plan. See item 1. Start with what you know (Lavonne's Monday earnings). Write the amounts she earns Tuesday through Friday. Then solve the problem.

   A $16   **C** $31

   B $30   **D** $63

2. The cost of a rental car in dollars, d, can be found using the formula $d = 20 + 0.3m + 2g$, where d is the cost, m is the number of miles driven, and g is the number of gallons of gas needed to fill the tank.

   Albert rented a car for one day and drove 50 miles. When he returned the car, he needed 3 gallons of gas to fill the tank. How much did the car rental cost?

   F $176   **H** $35

   G $41   **J** $25

3. Jackie's age is 3 years greater than the sum of Kendra's age, k, and twice Gary's age, g. Which expression represents Jackie's age?

   A $k + g - 3$ **C** $2k + g + 3$

   B $k + g + 3$ **D** $k + 2g + 3$

4. **Explain It** Kelly bought 5 dictionaries for a total of $30. Each dictionary cost the same. Write an equation that could be used to find the cost of 1 dictionary. Explain why your equation makes sense.

★ DATA ANALYSIS AND PROBABILITY

5. During five months, Reggie earned $245, $320, $175, $399, and $280. What is the mean amount Reggie earned per month during the five months?

   F $280.00   **H** $354.75

   G $283.80   **J** $1,419.00

6. Hurricanes are rated from Category 1, the weakest, to Category 5, the strongest. The categories of the ten most expensive hurricanes ever to have hit the United States are 4, 4, 3, 3, 3, 1, 3, 2, 1, and 5. What is the mode of the data?

   A 2.9   **C** 4

   B 3   **D** 5

7. The owner of a music shop made a line graph to show the number of CDs sold during a 4-week period. Which trend does the graph show?

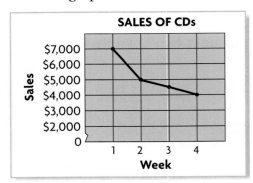

   F Sales are increasing.

   G Sales are not changing.

   H Sales are decreasing.

   J No trend is shown.

8. **Explain It** Ray surveyed students to find their favorite school subjects. Which type of graph should he use to display his data? Explain your choice.

9. From 1986 to 2001, the Minnesota Twins won $\frac{2}{15}$ of the American League baseball pennants, the New York Yankees won $\frac{1}{3}$, the Oakland A's won 0.2, and the Boston Red Sox won $0.0\overline{6}$. Which team won the most American League baseball pennants?

   A Minnesota

   B New York

   C Oakland

   D Boston

10. Lila cut a rectangular piece of fabric into 12 equal squares. She used three of the squares, or $\frac{1}{4}$ of all the squares, to sew patches on her jeans. What percent of all the squares did she use?

   F 25%   H 40%

   G 30%   J 70%

11. Elliott collects minerals for a hobby. The masses, in grams, of five malachite samples that he found are listed below. Which is the **best** estimate of the total masses of the five samples?

   22.38 g, 28.60 g, 32.12 g, 28.52 g, 30.21 g

   A 140 grams

   B 175 grams

   C 200 grams

   D 250 grams

12. **Explain It** Hallie jogged $6\frac{1}{2}$ miles four days in a row. Explain how you could use the Distributive Property to find the total distance that she jogged.

13. The teratoron, an extinct South American bird, had the greatest wingspan of any bird. The teratoron's wingspan is estimated at 300 inches. What is the estimation of the wingspan in feet?

   F $8\frac{1}{3}$ feet

   G   20 feet

   H   25 feet

   J   3,600 feet

14. The kite shown is formed from equilateral $\triangle ABD$ at the top, and isosceles $\triangle CBD$ at the bottom. The perimeter of $\triangle CBD$ is 60 inches. $\overline{BC}$ and $\overline{DC}$ both measure 24 inches. What is the perimeter of $\triangle ABD$?

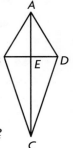

   A 12 inches

   B 24 inches

   C 30 inches

   D 36 inches

15. Mount Everest, the world's tallest mountain, is 8.85 kilometers in height. How tall is Mount Everest in meters?

   F   0.00885 meters

   G   88.5 meters

   H   885 meters

   J   8,850 meters

16. **Explain It** Science textbooks are $1\frac{1}{2}$ inches thick. They are packed in boxes with two stacks in each box. Boxes are 15 inches tall. How many textbooks can one box hold? Explain your reasoning.

IT'S IN THE BAG!

Can-Do Algebra

PROJECT Make a container to help you solve equations.

Materials

- Three-sided can or other container with plastic top
- Construction paper
- Markers
- Glue
- Ten 3-in. by 5-in. index cards
- Scissors

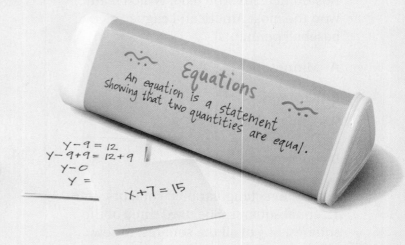

Equations
An equation is a statement showing that two quantities are equal.

$Y - 9 = 12$
$Y - 9 + 9 = 12 + 9$
$Y - 0$
$Y =$

$X + 7 = 15$

Directions

1. Cover a three-sided can or other container with construction paper. *(Picture A)*

2. Write the Addition Property of Equality, the Subtraction Property of Equality, and the definition of an equation on the sides of the can. *(Picture B)*

3. Cut ten index cards in half across the longer side of the cards.

4. Write an equation on one side of each of the cards. On the other side, write the steps you would use to solve the equation, and write the solution. *(Picture C)*

5. Store the cards inside the can.

A

B

C

Solving Two-Step Equations

Learn how to use models to solve two-step equations.

You need algebra tiles

Some equations involve more than one step. You can use models to solve two-step equations.

- Use algebra tiles or paper rectangles and squares to model $2x + 2 = 6$. Use a rectangle to represent the variable x, and use a square to represent 1.

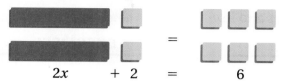

$$2x \quad + \ 2 \quad = \quad 6$$

- To solve the equation, arrange the model so that a rectangle is alone on one side. First, remove two squares from each side.

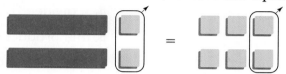

- The model now shows $2x = 4$.

- Separate the model into two equal groups on each side.

- Look at one group on each side. What is in each pair? What is the solution to the equation?

TALK ABOUT IT

- What operation did you model when you formed two equal groups on each side?

TRY IT

1. Copy the model below. What equation does it represent? Use the model to solve the equation.

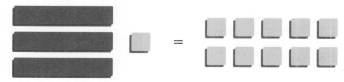

Use a model to solve each equation.

2. $2b + 5 = 9$ **3.** $4y + 2 = 10$ **4.** $3x + 2 = 14$ **5.** $4n + 1 = 5$

VOCABULARY

1. The parts of an algebraic expression that are separated by an addition or subtraction sign are called ___?___. (p. 261)

2. The terms $3x^2$ and $2x^2$ have the same variable raised to the same power. They are called ___?___ terms. (p. 261)

3. The product of a number and itself is a ___?___. (p. 264)

EXAMPLES	EXERCISES

Chapter 11

- **Write numerical and algebraic expressions.** (pp. 258–259)

  Write an algebraic expression for the word expression.

  3.8 less than a $a - 3.8$

  the sum of twice b and 5 $2b + 5$

Write an algebraic expression for the word expression.

4. c divided by 2.6

5. the product of h and $\frac{3}{4}$

6. the difference between b and 45

- **Evaluate numerical and algebraic expressions.** (pp. 260–263, 266–267)

  Evaluate $12 + 8x$ for $x = 4$.

  $12 + 8 \times 4$ *Replace x with 4.*

  $12 + 32$ *Multiply.*

  44 *Add.*

For 7–11, evaluate the expression for $x = 3$ and $y = 9$.

7. $6x - 8$

8. $4x + 2x + 9$

9. $12x - 7x + 15$

10. $4x^2 + xy$

11. $\sqrt{144} - 3^2 + 35y$

12. Evaluate $a - c + b$ for $a = 12.5$, $b = 7.8$, and $c = 12$.

Chapter 12

- **Write word sentences as equations.** (pp. 274–275)

  Forty is fifteen more than a number.

  $\downarrow$ $\downarrow$ $\downarrow$ $\downarrow$ $\downarrow$

  40   =   15   + n

  Equation: $40 = 15 + n$

Write an equation for the word sentence.

13. 9 is six less than a number.

14. A number divided by 2.5 is fifteen.

15. A number times $\frac{2}{3}$ is eighteen.

- **Solve addition and subtraction equations.** (pp. 277–279, 280–281)

  $x + 6.4 = 9.8$

  $x + 6.4 - 6.4 = 9.8 - 6.4$ *Use the Subtraction Property of Equality.*

  $x = 3.4$

Solve and check.

16. $6 + m = 24$

17. $r + 3\frac{2}{3} = 4$

18. $p + 5.8 = 13$

19. $15.1 = w + 3.89$

20. $m - 8 = 1$

21. $r - 1\frac{1}{2} = 3\frac{1}{4}$

22. $0.6 = p - 1.4$

23. $5 = w - 9$

Chapter 13

- **Solve multiplication and division equations.** (pp. 291–293)

$$\frac{m}{6} = 4.8$$

$$6 \cdot \frac{m}{6} = 4.8 \cdot 6 \quad \textit{Use the Multiplication Property of Equality.}$$

$$m = 28.8$$

Solve and check.

24. $18 = \frac{3}{4}c$

25. $7.2t = 14.4$

26. $6z = 96$

27. $\frac{n}{8} = 3.4$

28. $2x = 36$

29. $\frac{k}{1.2} = 5$

- **Use formulas.** (pp. 294–297)

Use the formula $d = rt$ to complete.

rate = 54 miles per hour
time = 5 hours   distance = ■ mi

$$d = rt$$

$$d = 54 \times 5 \quad \textit{Replace r with 54 and t with 5.}$$

$$d = 270 \quad \textit{Multiply.}$$

The distance is 270 miles.

Use the formula $A = lw$ to complete.

30. length = 8.6 in., width = 3 in., area = ■

31. area = 420 in.^{2}, length = 70 in., width = ■

Use the formula $P = 2l + 2w$ to complete.

32. length = $9\frac{1}{2}$ ft, width = $4\frac{1}{2}$ ft, perimeter = ■ ft

33. perimeter = 34 cm, length = 12 cm, width = ■ cm

Chapter 14

- **Write an equation to represent a function.** (pp. 315–318)

x	15	18	21	24
y	12	15	18	21

The x-values are 3 more than the y-values, so the equation is $y = x - 3$.

Write an equation to represent a function that matches the data.

34.
x	15	16	17	18
y	10	11	12	13

35.
x	72	64	56	48
y	9	8	7	6

- **Extend geometric patterns.** (pp. 319–321)

What is the next possible figure in the pattern?

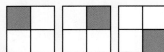

The shaded square moves clockwise 90° in these figures. So, the next figure has the shaded square in the bottom left.

Draw the next two possible figures in the pattern.

36.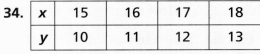

37.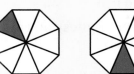

PROBLEM SOLVING APPLICATIONS

Solve. (pp. 298–299)

38. Val took half of the tennis balls from a box. Greg took half of what was left. Kendra took the remaining 5 balls. How many tennis balls were in the box to begin with?

39. Andrew is thinking of a number between 1 and 10. If he multiplies the number by 4 and then subtracts 5, the result is 31. What is the number?

Performance Assessment

TASK A • Horse Sense

Alex wants to buy a saddle for his horse. The saddle costs $300. He has $87.25 saved. In addition to keeping his horse at the stable for free, Alex earns $5.25 an hour grooming horses and cleaning out all the stables. He wants to know how many hours he will have to work before he can buy the saddle.

Alex writes this equation to find the amount of money, m, that he needs to buy the saddle.

$$m + \$87.25 = \$300$$

a. Explain how to use the inverse operation to solve for m. Then solve.

b. Alex wrote this expression to figure his earnings: $\$5.25 + h$. What mistake did he make?

c. How could you find the number of hours Alex needs to work to buy the saddle? How many hours does he need to work?

d. Alex has the chance to work at the stable shop. He can work there 2 hours for every 5 hours he works in the stable. Working in the stable shop pays $9.00 per hour. If Alex decides to do this, how many hours must he work at each job to earn enough to pay for the saddle? Explain your reasoning.

TASK B • On the Road

Materials: maps, mileage charts

Plan a trip to a city in the United States that is at least 200 miles away from where you live.

a. Choose two different routes you can take. Figure out how many miles each route is.

b. Show how you would use the distance formula to find the number of hours of driving it would take to reach the city at 55 miles per hour on each of the routes.

c. How long would it take to drive to that city at a rate of 65 miles per hour?

d. Suppose the speed limit on the longer route is 55 miles per hour and the speed limit on the shorter route is 40 miles per hour. Which route will get you to the city faster?

Use a Spreadsheet to
Complete Function Tables

The input/output table shown here gives values of the algebraic expression $b \times 7 + 2$. Each output is the value of the expression for a given input value of the variable. You can use a spreadsheet to complete input/output tables.

Tosha orders books online. Each book costs $7. A shipping charge of $2 is added to each book order. How much would it cost to order 1 book? to order 2, 3, 4, 5, or 6 books?

Write an expression. Then use a spreadsheet to evaluate the expression.

$$b \times 7 + 2 \qquad \leftarrow b = \text{number of books}$$

- Enter the number of books into Column A.

- Enter the expression into cell B1. Type =.
  Click in cell A1. Type *7 + 2. Press *Enter*.

- Highlight cells B1–B6. Click on *Edit* and choose *Fill Down*.

- The values in Column B are the costs of buying from 1 to 6 books.

So, it would cost $9, $16, $23, $30, $37, and $44 to order 1, 2, 3, 4, 5, and 6 books.

Expression: $b \times 7 + 2$	
Input (b)	**Output**
1	$1 \times 7 + 2 = 9$
2	$2 \times 7 + 2 = 16$
3	$3 \times 7 + 2 = 23$
4	$4 \times 7 + 2 = 30$
5	$5 \times 7 + 2 = 37$
6	$6 \times 7 + 2 = 44$

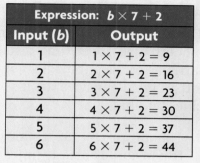

Practice and Problem Solving

Use a spreadsheet to complete the table for the expression.

1.

$x + 8 \times 2 - 3$	
Input (x)	Output
4	
5	
6	
7	

2.

$y \times 3 + 12$	
Input (y)	Output
15	
16	
17	
18	

3.

$2 \times z + 3 \times z$	
Input (z)	Output
11	
12	
13	
14	

4. STRETCH YOUR THINKING Write a rule for a function table. Then use a spreadsheet to complete the function table for 20 values.

GO ON-LINE

Multimedia Math Glossary www.harcourtschool.com/mathglossary

Vocabulary Power Look up *square* and *square root* in the Multimedia Math Glossary. Write a description of the relationship between square and square root.

PROBLEM SOLVING ON LOCATION

In Pennsylvania

The First Superhighway

The Pennsylvania Turnpike was the first highway designed for modern high-speed long-distance travel. Completed in 1940, the turnpike crossed the Allegheny Mountains between Harrisburg and Pittsburgh, Pennsylvania. It shortened travel time between those two cities by 3 hr.

1. The turnpike is 132 ft wide on the section called the Southwestern Expansion. That is $1\frac{5}{6}$ times the road's width on the portion called the Northeastern Extension. Write an equation you can use to find the width of the Northeastern Extension. Then solve the equation.

2. Originally 160 mi long, the Pennsylvania Turnpike has since been lengthened to 514 mi. Write an equation you can use to find how much longer the highway is today than it was in 1940. Then solve the equation.

Use Data For 3–5, use the figure, which shows distances on a section of the Pennsylvania Turnpike.

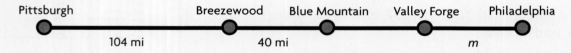

Pittsburgh ——— 104 mi ——— Breezewood ——— 40 mi ——— Blue Mountain ——— Valley Forge ——— m ——— Philadelphia

It is 100 mi farther from Blue Mountain to Valley Forge than it is from Valley Forge to Philadelphia. (Note: Diagram not drawn to scale.)

3. Use the variable m to write an expression for the distance from Blue Mountain to Valley Forge.

4. Write and simplify an expression for the distance from Pittsburgh to Philadelphia.

5. It is 24 miles from Valley Forge to Philadelphia. How far is it from Pittsburgh to Philadelphia?

Fifteen thousand workers from 18 states labored for 2 years to build the Pennsylvania Turnpike.

The First Oil Well

Pennsylvania was the birthplace not only of America's modern highway system, but of its oil industry too. In 1859, Edwin L. Drake drilled the world's first oil well, beside Oil Creek, near Titusville, Pennsylvania.

At the Drake Well Museum, you can see a replica of the first oil well and learn about the early petroleum industry.

Before Drake drilled his well, small amounts of oil seeped from the ground near Oil Creek. Drake's well produced about 210 times as much oil each day as could be collected above ground.

1. Let *A* represent the amount of oil that could be collected above ground each day. Write an expression for the daily amount produced by Drake's well.

2. About 5 gallons of oil could be collected above ground each day. Use the expression you wrote to find the daily production of Drake's well.

3. There are 42 gallons in 1 barrel of oil. Find the daily production of Drake's well in barrels.

4. In 1859, oil sold for about $\sqrt{400}$ dollars per barrel. Find the value of one day's production of oil at Drake's well.

The surface of the ground at Drake's well is located at an altitude of 1,200 ft above sea level.

5. To reach oil, Drake first drilled through gravel to an altitude of 1,168 ft above sea level. Then he drilled through shale an additional 37.5 ft. What was the total depth below ground level at which Drake struck oil?

6. A few months later, Drake drilled a second well nearby. It was 63 ft deeper than 6 times the depth of the first well. Let *d* represent the depth of the first well. Write an expression for the depth of the second well.

7. How deep was Drake's second well?

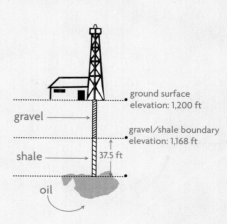

ground surface
elevation: 1,200 ft

gravel

gravel/shale boundary
elevation: 1,168 ft

shale   37.5 ft

oil

15 Geometric Figures

≡FAST FACT • ART Frank Lloyd Wright designed more than 800 buildings, of which about 400 were actually built. His buildings often had large walls, terraces, and roof overhangs that reached out into the landscape. Wright built this house between 1936 and 1939. He named it Fallingwater.

PROBLEM SOLVING What types of angles do you see in the decks that hang over the waterfalls?

TYPES OF ANGLES	
Name	**Figure**
acute	
right	
obtuse	
straight	

Check What You Know

Use this page to help you review and remember important skills needed for Chapter 15.

✅ Classify Angles

Classify each angle by stating whether it is *acute, obtuse, right,* or *straight.*

1.

2.

3.

4.

5.

6.

7.

8.

✅ Name Angles

Name the angle formed by the blue rays.

9.

10.

11.

12.

13.

14.

15.

16.

VOCABULARY POWER

REVIEW

angle [ang′gəl] *noun*

Angle and *ankle* both come from the Latin word *angulus.* Explain how an angle and an ankle are similar.

PREVIEW

line segment

ray

vertex

vertical angles

adjacent angles

complementary angles

supplementary angles

parallel lines

perpendicular lines

transversal

interior angles

exterior angles

Points, Lines, and Planes

Learn how to describe figures by using the terms of geometry.

QUICK REVIEW
1. $3x = 36$ 2. $5y = 30$ 3. $9b = 36$ 4. $56 = 8d$ 5. $24 = 10k$

Points, lines, and planes are the building blocks of geometry.

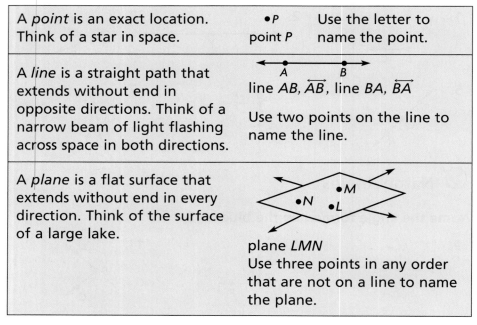

A *point* is an exact location. Think of a star in space.	•P Use the letter to point *P* name the point.
A *line* is a straight path that extends without end in opposite directions. Think of a narrow beam of light flashing across space in both directions.	line *AB*, $\overleftrightarrow{AB}$, line *BA*, $\overleftrightarrow{BA}$ Use two points on the line to name the line.
A *plane* is a flat surface that extends without end in every direction. Think of the surface of a large lake.	plane *LMN* Use three points in any order that are not on a line to name the plane.

Line segments and rays are parts of a line.

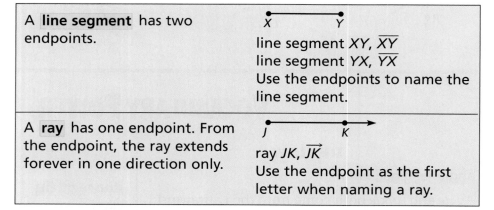

A **line segment** has two endpoints.	line segment *XY*, $\overline{XY}$ line segment *YX*, $\overline{YX}$ Use the endpoints to name the line segment.
A **ray** has one endpoint. From the endpoint, the ray extends forever in one direction only.	ray *JK*, $\overrightarrow{JK}$ Use the endpoint as the first letter when naming a ray.

Vocabulary

line segment

ray

Remember that symbols can be used to name lines, line segments, and rays.

• line *BC*: $\overleftrightarrow{BC}$
• line segment *BC*: $\overline{BC}$
• ray *BC*: $\overrightarrow{BC}$

You see models of points, lines, and planes every day. Specks of dust on a window model points. Flagpoles and pencils model line segments. Table tops and ceilings of rooms model planes.

Lines extend without end. So, real-world objects like goal "lines" and boundary "lines" are really just parts of lines. For the same reason, the sides of a skyscraper or of a gemstone are just portions of planes.

CHECK FOR UNDERSTANDING

Think and Discuss ▶ Look back at the lesson to answer the question.

1. Name the geometric figure modeled by each of the following: a page of a book; a single dot, or "pixel," on a computer screen; the path of a passenger jet across the sky.

Guided Practice ▶ Name the geometric figure.

2.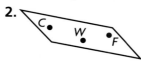

3. •R

4.

PRACTICE AND PROBLEM SOLVING

Independent Practice ▶ Name the geometric figure.

5. C •

6.

7.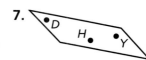

8. M●———●N

9. X• Y

10.  G H

For 11–14, use the figure at the right.

11. Name three different line segments.

12. Name four different rays.

13. Give six names for the line. **14.** Give another name for ray *RQ*.

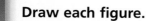

Problem Solving Applications ▶ Name the geometric figure formed by the intersection of each pair of figures.

15. two lines   16. two planes   17. line and plane

Draw each figure.

18. ray *CD*   19. point *P*

20. line *JK*   21. line segment *EF*

22. 📓 **Write About It** Can a line segment be part of a ray? Explain.

MIXED REVIEW AND TEST PREP

23. For $n = pq$, find n when $p = 24$ and $q = 4$. (p. 260)

24. Order from least to greatest: 0.4, 3, 1.19, 0.085 (p. 60)

25. Evaluate. $\sqrt{225} - 2^3$ (p. 266)

26. Solve. $5.2 = k - 3.7$ (p. 280)

⭐ 27. **TEST PREP** Tim has two apples that weigh $\frac{3}{16}$ lb and $\frac{1}{4}$ lb. How much less than a pound of apples does Tim have? (p. 206)

A $\frac{1}{6}$ lb   **B** $\frac{1}{16}$ lb   **C** $\frac{9}{16}$ lb   **D** $\frac{1}{4}$ lb

Angles

Explore how to name, measure, and draw angles.

You need protractor, straightedge, paper, scissors.

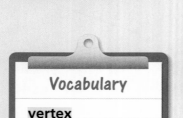

Vocabulary

vertex

QUICK REVIEW

1. $5x = 90$ 2. $6y = 3.6$ 3. $\frac{1}{4}b = 8$

4. $26 = 4d$ 5. $\frac{2}{3} = 2k$

An angle is formed by two rays with a common endpoint, called the **vertex** . The vertex is the key to naming an angle. You can name an angle by using the letter of its vertex alone. You can also use the letter of a point on each side, along with the letter of the vertex, to name the angle. The middle letter should always be for the vertex.

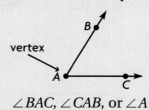

∠*BAC*, ∠*CAB*, or ∠*A*

An angle is measured in degrees. One degree measures $\frac{1}{360}$ of a circle. The number of degrees determines the type of angle.

An acute angle measures less than 90°.	
A right angle measures 90°.	
An obtuse angle measures more than 90° but less than 180°.	
A straight angle measures 180°.	

Activity 1

You can measure an angle by using a protractor.

- On a sheet of paper, draw an angle that looks approximately like ∠*XYZ*.

- Place the center point of the protractor on the vertex of the angle.

- Place the base of the protractor along ray *YZ*.

- Read the scale that starts with 0 at ray *YZ*. The measure of ∠*XYZ* above is 75°. This can be written as m∠*XYZ* = 75°.

Activity 2

You can also use a protractor to draw angles of a given measure.

- Draw a ray on a sheet of paper.

- Place the center point of the protractor on the endpoint of the ray. Align the protractor so that the ray passes through 0°.

- Draw an angle of 150° by making a mark on the paper above 150 on the scale you are using.

- Use your straightedge to draw a ray to complete the angle.

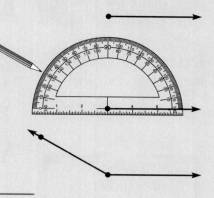

Activity 3

To estimate the size of an angle, you can compare it to a right angle.

- Fold a sheet of paper twice to make a right angle.

- Draw an acute angle and an obtuse angle on a sheet of paper.

- Compare their measures to the right angle you made, and estimate how many degrees they each contain. Measure the angles to check your estimates.

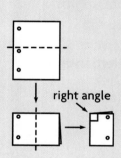

Think and Discuss

- What kind of angle did you draw in Activity 1?

- The protractor has two scales, a top scale and a bottom scale. How can you decide which scale to use?

Practice

Trace the angle. Then measure it and tell what kind of angle it is.

1.   2.    3.

Draw an angle with the given measure.

4. 48°   5. 180°   6. 154°   7. 90°   8. 45°

Estimate the measure. Then trace the angle and use a protractor to check your estimate.

9.   10.   11.

MIXED REVIEW AND TEST PREP

12. Name the geometric figure. (p. 336)

    E   F

13. Solve. $96 = 12b$ (p. 291)

14. Find the product. $\$31.82 \times 4$ (p. 80)

15. How much greater is $\frac{4}{5} \div 3$ than $\frac{4}{5} \div 6$? (p. 236)

16. **TEST PREP** Find the mean, median, and mode: 50, 52, 56, 51, 50, 53. (p. 118)

    A 51.5, 50, 52   **B** 50, 52, 51.5   **C** 52, 51.5, 50   **D** 51.5, 52, 50

339

Angle Relationships

Learn how to understand relationships of angles.

Vocabulary

vertical angles
congruent
adjacent angles
complementary angles
supplementary angles

Angle relationships play an important role in many sports and games. Miniature-golf players must understand angles to know where to aim the ball. In the miniature-golf hole shown, $m\angle 1 = m\angle 2$, $m\angle 3 = m\angle 4$, and $m\angle 5 = m\angle 6$.

Certain angle pairs are given special names in geometry.

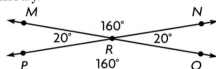

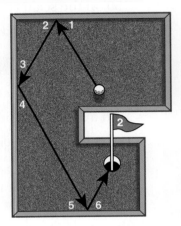

Vertical angles are formed opposite each other when two lines intersect. Vertical angles have the same measure. Angles with the same measure are said to be **congruent**.

$\angle MRP$ and $\angle NRQ$ are vertical angles.

$\angle MRN$ and $\angle PRQ$ are vertical angles.

Adjacent angles are side-by-side and have a common vertex and ray.

$\angle MRN$ and $\angle NRQ$ are adjacent angles.

EXAMPLE 1

Identify the type of angle pair shown.

a.

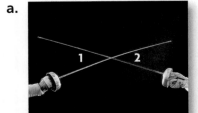

b.

$\angle 1$ and $\angle 2$ are opposite each other and are formed by two intersecting lines. They are vertical angles.

$\angle 3$ and $\angle 4$ are side-by-side and have a common vertex and ray. They are adjacent angles.

• If $\angle 1$ measures 40° in Example 1, what does $\angle 2$ measure?

Complementary and Supplementary Angles

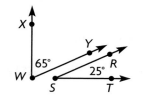
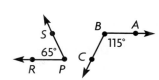

Two angles are complementary if the sum of their measures is 90°.
65° + 25° = 90°   ∠XWY and ∠RST are **complementary angles**.

Two angles are supplementary if the sum of their measures is 180°.
65° + 115° = 180°   ∠RPS and ∠ABC are **supplementary angles**.

In some cases you can use the definitions of complementary and supplementary angles to find the measures of angles.

EXAMPLE 2

The two adjacent angles are complementary. Find the unknown measure.

75° + ■ = 90°   *The sum of the measures is 90°.*

90° − 75° = ■   *Subtract to find the unknown measure.*

90° − 75° = 15°

So, the unknown angle measure is 15°.

EXAMPLE 3

The angles are supplementary. Find the unknown measure.

80° + ■ = 180°   *The sum of the measures is 180°.*

180° − 80° = ■   *Subtract to find the unknown measure.*

180° − 80° = 100°

So, the unknown angle measure is 100°.

When an object bounces off a surface, it always rebounds at the same angle. In the figure, ∠SWQ and ∠TWR have the same measure.

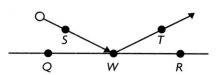

EXAMPLE 4

A hockey puck hits $\overline{BD}$, the wall of an ice rink, at an angle of 35°. $\overline{AC}$ is drawn so that ∠BCA and ∠DCA are right angles. Find the measures of ∠1 and ∠3.

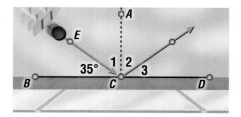

The puck rebounds at the same angle, so the measure of ∠3 is 35°.

∠1 and ∠ECB form a right angle, so they are complementary.
m∠1 + 35° = 90°
90° − 35° = 55°, so the measure of ∠1 is 55°.

Think and
Discuss ▶

Look back at the lesson to answer each question.

1. **Describe** vertical, adjacent, complementary, and supplementary angles.

2. **Explain** how you can find the measure of an angle complementary to a given angle; an angle supplementary to a given angle.

Guided ▶
Practice

For 3–6, use the figure at the right.

3. Name two pairs of vertical angles.

4. Name two pairs of adjacent angles.

5. Name a pair of complementary angles.

6. Name two pairs of supplementary angles.

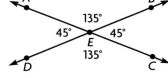

Find the unknown angle measure. Explain your answer.

7.

8.

9.

Independent ▶
Practice

For 10–13, use the figure at the right.

10. Name two angles adjacent to ∠AOB.

11. Name the angle vertical to ∠AOB.

12. Name the angle complementary to ∠AOB.

13. Name two angles supplementary to ∠BOC.

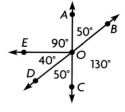

Find the unknown angle measure. Explain your answer.

14.

15.

16.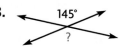

17.

18.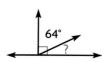

19.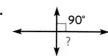

Tell if the angles are *vertical, adjacent, complementary, supplementary,* or *none of these.*

20. ∠TUV and ∠XUY

21. ∠XUY and ∠TUY

22. ∠VUW and ∠TUV

23. ∠XUW and ∠TUV

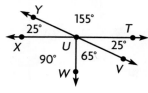

Problem Solving ▶
Applications

For 24–26, use the figure at the right. Trace the figure. Find the measures of the numbered angles.

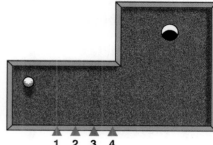

24. Name each pair of vertical angles. Tell how you know the angles are vertical.

25. Name each pair of adjacent angles. Tell how you know the angles are adjacent.

26. Name each pair of complementary angles and supplementary angles. Tell how you know the angles are complementary or supplementary.

27. Which number should you aim at to hit the golf ball into the hole in one bounce? Use a protractor to decide. Explain your reasoning.

28. *REASONING* Two angles are each complementary to the same angle. What can you conclude about them?

29. Draw a figure that has at least one pair of each type of angle: vertical, adjacent, complementary, and supplementary. Name each pair of angles.

30. (?) **What's the Question?** Eva drew angles for a project. She drew 6 angles every 2 minutes. The answer is 21 angles.

MIXED REVIEW AND TEST PREP

31. Name the geometric figure. (p. 336)

32. Find the distance, d, for $r = 12.6$ ft per sec and $t = 22.5$ sec. (p. 294)

33. Evaluate. $80 - \sqrt{144} \times 3$ (p. 266)

34. TEST PREP Find $5,500 \div 25$. (p. 24)

   A 200   **B** 200 r5   **C** 220   **D** 2,200

35. TEST PREP John bought 3 sweaters for $49, $29.95, and $36.75. How much change did he get from $120? (p. 76)

   F $4.30   **G** $4.75   **H** $5.15   **J** $6.00

PROBLEM SOLVING   LiNKŮP to Art

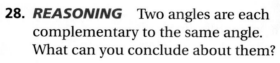

Design Kuba cloth is made by the Kuba people of Zaire, Africa. The cloth is made from the fiber of the raffia palm. Originally, Kuba cloth was meant to be worn, but people now collect and display it because of its artistic beauty.

• Describe how the design shown involves vertical angles.

EXTRA PRACTICE page 348, Set B

Lines and Angles

Learn how to classify pairs of lines and pairs of angles.

Vocabulary

parallel lines
intersecting lines
perpendicular
  lines
skew lines
transversal
interior angles
exterior angles
alternate
  interior angles
alternate
  exterior angles
corresponding
  angles

The chart shows some of the ways lines can relate to one another.

Parallel lines are lines in a plane that are always the same distance apart. They never intersect and have no common points.	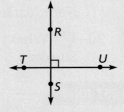	Line *AB* is parallel to line *ML*. $\overrightarrow{AB} \parallel \overrightarrow{ML}$ (∥ means "is parallel to.")
Intersecting lines cross at exactly one point.	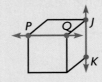	Line *EF* intersects line *CD* at point *H*.
Perpendicular lines intersect to form 90° angles, or right angles.	(diagram: R, T, U, S)	Line *RS* is perpendicular to line *TU*. $\overrightarrow{RS} \perp \overrightarrow{TU}$ (⊥ means "is perpendicular to.")
Skew lines are lines that are not in the same plane, are not parallel, and do not intersect.	(diagram: P, Q, J, K)	Line *JK* and line *PQ* are a pair of skew lines.

Line segments can also be parallel, intersecting, or perpendicular.

EXAMPLE 1

The map shows a section of New York City. Describe each relationship as parallel, intersecting, or perpendicular.

a. streets to streets
   Streets are parallel to each other.

b. avenues to avenues
   Avenues are parallel to each other.

c. streets to avenues
   Streets are perpendicular to avenues and intersect avenues.

d. Broadway to streets and avenues
   Broadway intersects streets and avenues.

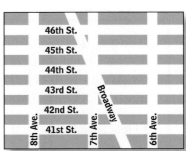

A **transversal** is a line that crosses two or more lines. In many cases, those lines are parallel. In the figure at the right, $\overleftrightarrow{AB}$ is a transversal. The angles in the green section are between line m and line n and are called **interior angles**. The angles in the blue section are outside of the lines and are called **exterior angles**.

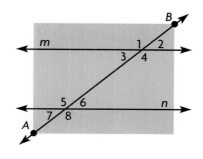

Interior Angles	$\angle 3, \angle 4, \angle 5, \angle 6$
Exterior Angles	$\angle 1, \angle 2, \angle 7, \angle 8$

Opposite sides of a transversal are called alternate sides and help form pairs of **alternate interior angles** and pairs of **alternate exterior angles**.

Pairs of Alternate Interior Angles	$\angle 3$ and $\angle 6$, $\angle 4$ and $\angle 5$
Pairs of Alternate Exterior Angles	$\angle 1$ and $\angle 8$, $\angle 2$ and $\angle 7$

Corresponding angles are angles that appear in the same positions in relation to a transversal and two lines. Each of the figures at the right shows a pair of corresponding angles. Both angles in each pair are on the same side of a transversal, and both are either above or below one of the lines.

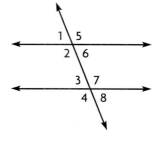

EXAMPLE 2

Use the figure at the right. Name all the pairs of the given type of angles.

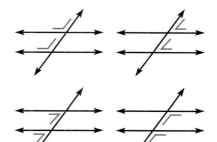

a. alternate interior angles
$\angle 2$ and $\angle 7$, $\angle 3$ and $\angle 6$

b. alternate exterior angles
$\angle 1$ and $\angle 8$, $\angle 5$ and $\angle 4$

c. corresponding angles
$\angle 1$ and $\angle 3$, $\angle 2$ and $\angle 4$, $\angle 5$ and $\angle 7$, $\angle 6$ and $\angle 8$

CHECK FOR UNDERSTANDING

Think and ▶ Discuss

Look back at the lesson to answer each question.

1. **Explain** why skew lines can never be parallel lines.

2. **Draw** line AB parallel to line CD. Draw line EF perpendicular to line AB. Describe the relationship between line CD and line EF.

345

Classify the lines as parallel, perpendicular, or intersecting. Use the symbol ∥ or ⊥ when appropriate.

3.

4.

5.

6.

For 7–9, use the figure at the right.

7. Name all the pairs of alternate interior angles.

8. Name all the pairs of alternate exterior angles.

9. Name all the pairs of corresponding angles.

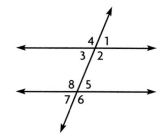

PRACTICE AND PROBLEM SOLVING

Independent ▶ Practice

Classify the lines as parallel, perpendicular, or intersecting. Use the symbol ∥ or ⊥ when appropriate.

10.

11.

12.

13.

For 14–16, use the figure at the right.

14. Name and measure all the pairs of alternate interior angles. What do you notice about the angle measures?

15. Name and measure all the pairs of alternate exterior angles. What do you notice about the angle measures?

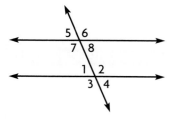

16. Name and measure all the pairs of corresponding angles. What do you notice about the angle measures?

The lines in the figure at the right intersect to form a cube.

17. Name all the lines that are parallel to $\overleftrightarrow{AC}$.

18. Name three pairs of skew lines.

19. Name all the lines that are perpendicular to and intersect $\overleftrightarrow{BD}$.

20. Are $\overleftrightarrow{CD}$ and $\overleftrightarrow{GH}$ skew lines? Explain.

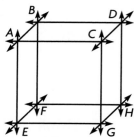

For 21–22, write *true* or *false* for each statement.

21. A set of railroad tracks models parallel lines.

22. Corresponding angles are on alternate sides of the transversal.

23. Vocabulary Power The word *transversal* begins with the prefix *trans-*. Look up the definitions of words that begin with *trans-*. What do these words have in common?

24. The figure at the right shows part of the New York City map from page 344. Name each of the following.

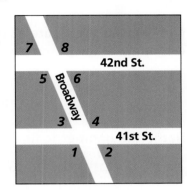

    a. a transversal

    b. parallel lines

    c. alternate interior angles

    d. alternate exterior angles

    e. corresponding angles

25. **≡FAST FACT • ART** More than 14,000 miles of wire were used for the suspension cables on the Brooklyn Bridge. What types of lines are modeled by the cables in the photo of the Brooklyn Bridge, at the left?

The Brooklyn Bridge

For 26–27, use this information. Main Street is a straight street. It intersects 3rd, 4th, and 5th Streets, which are parallel to each other. Pine and Oak Streets are perpendicular to 5th Street.

26. Draw a map showing the six streets.

27. Suppose that Pine and Oak Streets are perpendicular to Main Street rather than to 5th Street. Draw a map showing the streets.

28. ❓ **What's the Error?** Allen said that all perpendicular lines are intersecting lines and all intersecting lines are perpendicular. What is wrong with his statement?

29. Rachel wants to join a health club for 2 years. Club A charges $400 per year and Club B charges $36.25 per month. How much money will Rachel save if she joins Club A?

MIXED REVIEW AND TEST PREP

30. Find the sum. $3\frac{5}{8} + 5\frac{3}{8}$ (p. 210)

31. Which is greater, $\frac{5}{12}$ or $\frac{1}{3}$? (p. 188)

32. Suppose it took Carly 4.5 hours to drive 266.4 mi. What was Carly's average speed? (p. 294)

33. TEST PREP Find the unknown angle measure in the figure at the right. (p. 340)

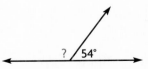

    A 144°   **B** 126°   **C** 90°   **D** 36°

34. TEST PREP Protractors sell for $0.09 each. How many more protractors can you buy for $9.00 than for $7.20? (p. 88)

    F 0.01   **G** 10   **H** 20   **J** 30

EXTRA PRACTICE page 348, Set C

Set A (pp. 336–337)

R · S · T · W ·

For 1–4, use the figure at the right. Tell how many of each you can name. Then name them.

1. points   **2.** line segments

3. rays   **4.** lines

Name the geometric figure.

5.  D H

6. · S · G Z

7. C ———— K

8. · F

Set B (pp. 340–343)

Tell if the angles are *vertical, adjacent, complementary, supplementary,* or *none of these.*

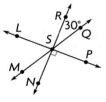

1. ∠EFA and ∠DFE

2. ∠AFB and ∠CFD

3. ∠EFA and ∠CFD   **4.** ∠AFB and ∠BFC

Find the unknown angle measure.

5. ? 20°

6. 45° ?

7. 35° ?

8. 75° ?

Find the measure of each angle.

9. ∠QSP   **10.** ∠LSR   **11.** ∠QSN

12. ∠RSP   **13.** ∠MSN   **14.** ∠RSN

R 30° Q L S P M N

Set C (pp. 344–347)

Use the figure.

A G 1 2 B F E 3 4 C D

1. Name all the lines that are parallel to $\overleftrightarrow{BE}$.

2. Name a line that is perpendicular to and intersects $\overleftrightarrow{BE}$.

3. Name all the lines that are perpendicular to $\overleftrightarrow{AD}$.

4. Name a line that is parallel to $\overleftrightarrow{AC}$.

5. Which angle corresponds to ∠2?

1. **VOCABULARY**   A(n) __?__ is part of a line and has two endpoints. (p. 336)

2. **VOCABULARY**   __?__ angles are opposite angles formed when two lines intersect. (p. 340)

3. **VOCABULARY**   __?__ angles are two angles whose sum is 180°. (p. 341)

4. **VOCABULARY**   Lines that intersect to form right angles are called __?__ . (p. 344)

Name the geometric figure. (pp. 336–337)

5.  F •————————→ G   6. C •——————• D   7. ←•————————•→ A ... B

5. F •————→• G   6. C •————• D   7. A ←————→ B

Tell whether the angle is *acute*, *right*, *obtuse*, or *straight*. (pp. 338–339)

8. 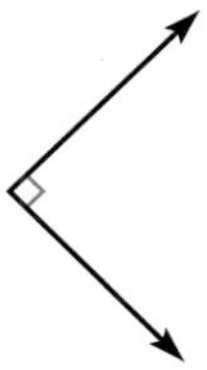   9. 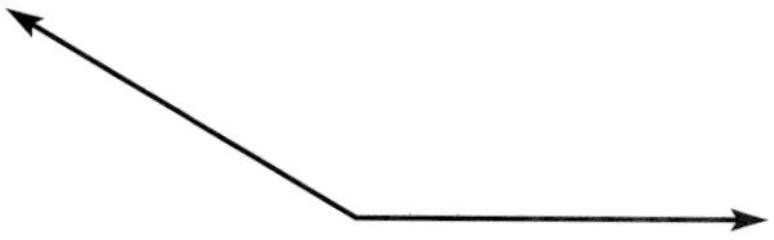   10. 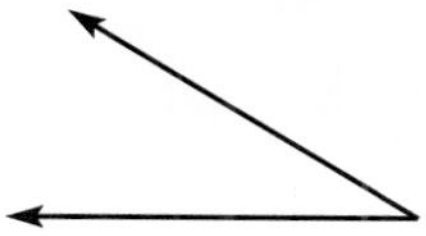   11.

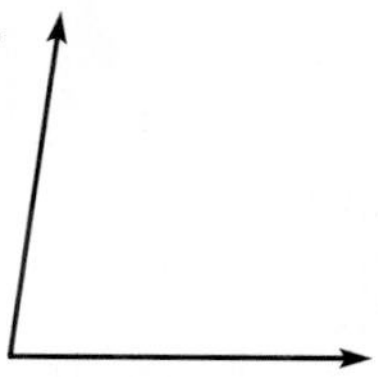

Use the figure to find the measure of each angle. (pp. 340–343)

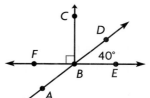

12. ∠ABF   13. ∠ABE

14. ∠CBD   15. ∠CBF

16. ∠FBE   17. ∠FBD

For 18–21, use the figure at the right. The lines intersect to form a cube. (pp. 344–347)

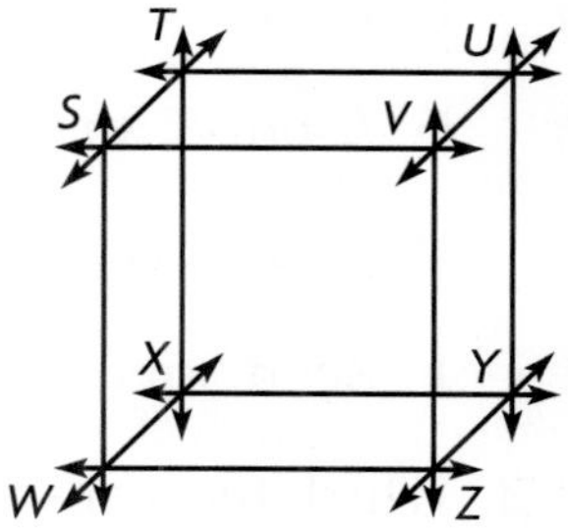

18. $\overleftrightarrow{WZ} \parallel$ __?__   19. $\overleftrightarrow{TX}$ and __?__ are skew lines.

20. $\overleftrightarrow{SW} \perp$ __?__   21. $\overleftrightarrow{UY} \parallel$ __?__

22. Complete: If two angles are complementary, both angles must be __?__ (acute, right, obtuse, straight). (p. 341)

23. Complete: If two lines are perpendicular, then they are also __?__ (parallel, intersecting). (pp. 344–347)

24. Two streets intersect and form a 38° angle. Find the unknown angle measure. (pp. 340–343)

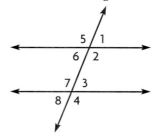

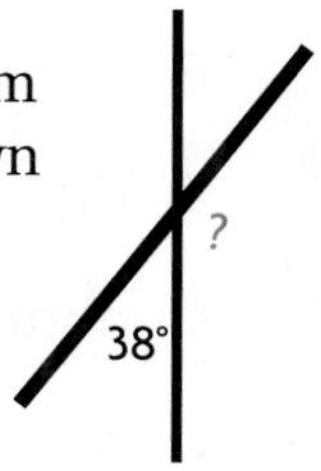

25. Use the figure at the right. Name all the pairs of alternate interior angles, alternate exterior angles, and corresponding angles. (pp. 344–347)

349

★ **GEOMETRY AND SPATIAL SENSE**

★ **ALGEBRAIC THINKING**

1. The map shows a portion of Blain's neighborhood. Angle X is which of the following types of angles?

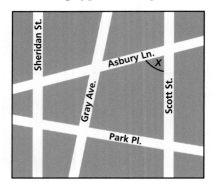

A acute

B obtuse

C right

D straight

2. Look at the map in Problem 1. Which of the following is parallel to Sheridan Street?

F Gray Avenue

G Asbury Lane

H Park Place

J Scott Street

3. Which term describes an angle that measures 110 degrees?

A acute

B right

C obtuse

D straight

4. Explain It Draw two parallelograms and measure the angles. Describe the relationships among the angles in a parallelogram.

5. Paula made 190 tote bags. She sold 115 of them at a craft fair for a total of $2,070. Which equation can be used to find the price, p, for which she sold each tote bag?

> **TIP Eliminate choices.** See item 5. Determine the information in the problem that is not needed. Look for answers that might contain that information and determine if you can eliminate them.

F $190 \times 115 = p$

G $190 \times p = 115$

H $190 \times p = \$2,070$

J $115 \times p = \$2,070$

6. Three families are going to the community play. They will divide the cost of the tickets evenly. They need to buy six adult tickets at $12 each and seven children's tickets at $9 each. Which equation can be used to find the amount, a, that each family will have to pay?

A $a = \dfrac{(7 \times 9) + (6 \times 12)}{3}$

B $a = \dfrac{12 + 9}{3}$

C $a = 3(12 + 9)$

D $a = (7 \times 9) + (6 + 12)$

7. Explain It The weight of an object on Earth is 6 times the weight of the same object on the moon. Suppose an astronaut weighs 150 pounds on Earth. What is the weight of the same astronaut on the moon? Explain your reasoning.

8. The school orchestra rehearsed for $2\frac{1}{2}$ hours on Thursday and $3\frac{1}{2}$ hours on Friday. How long did the orchestra rehearse in all?

F   5 hours

G $5\frac{1}{2}$ hours

H   6 hours

J $6\frac{1}{2}$ hours

9. The table below shows the times for four runners in the 100-yard dash.

TIMES FOR THE 100-YARD DASH	
Student	**Time (seconds)**
Inez	11.24
Trevor	10.46
Kelly	10.9
Justin	11.3

Which of the following lists the names in order from the runner with the fastest time to the runner with the slowest time?

A   Kelly, Trevor, Justin, Inez

B   Inez, Justin, Trevor, Kelly

C   Trevor, Kelly, Inez, Justin

D   Justin, Inez, Kelly, Trevor

10. Explain It Trudy spent $\frac{3}{4}$ hour practicing the piano, $\frac{2}{3}$ hour mowing the lawn, and $\frac{5}{6}$ hour doing homework. On which task did she spend the most time? Explain how you found the answer.

11. Mark is building a bird feeder. He must drill a hole $1\frac{1}{4}$ inches from the left end of the piece of wood shown below.

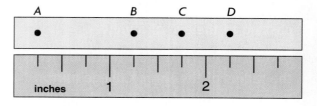

Which of the following shows the point where Mark will drill the hole?

F   point A

G   point B

H   point C

J   point D

12. Fran has a large garbage bag full of glass bottles and cans that she wants to weigh. Which of the following is the best estimate for the weight of the bag?

A   25 grams

B   25 ounces

C   25 pounds

D   25 tons

13. Explain It Sal estimates that she needs 135 inches of fringe for a sewing project. The fringe she wants is sold only by the yard. How many yards must she buy in order to have enough fringe for her sewing project? Explain your reasoning.

CHAPTER 16 Plane Figures

≡FAST FACT • SCIENCE A 32-inch-diameter mirror in a reflecting telescope collects about 26,000 times as much light as the human eye. Light from a star or planet reflects off the circular mirror before passing to the eye of a viewer.

PROBLEM SOLVING How much longer is the radius of the Three College mirror than the radius of the McMath mirror?

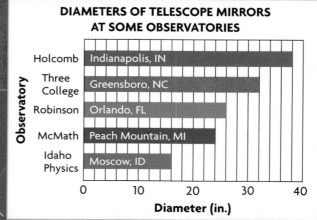

DIAMETERS OF TELESCOPE MIRRORS AT SOME OBSERVATORIES

Observatory	Location
Holcomb	Indianapolis, IN
Three College	Greensboro, NC
Robinson	Orlando, FL
McMath	Peach Mountain, MI
Idaho Physics	Moscow, ID

Diameter (in.)

Check What You Know

Use this page to help you review and remember important skills needed for Chapter 16.

✔ Identify Polygons

Name each polygon.

1.

2.

3.

4.

5.

6.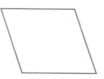

7.

8.

9.

10.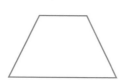

11.

12.

✔ Evaluate Expressions

Evaluate each expression.

13. $60 - (16 + 24)$ **14.** $80 - (20 + 20)$ **15.** $(75 - 20) + 38$

16. $(78 - 10) + 50$ **17.** $90 - (35 - 21)$ **18.** $90 - (40 - 10)$

19. $(105 - 34) - 15$ **20.** $120 - (30 + 45)$ **21.** $(140 - 35) - 27$

22. $180 - (80 + 5)$ **23.** $(250 - 60) + 40$ **24.** $300 - (24 - 18)$

VOCABULARY POWER

REVIEW

quadrilateral [kwä•drə•la'tə•rəl] *noun*

A quadrilateral is a closed plane figure formed by four straight sides that are connected line segments. A square is one type of quadrilateral. Name and draw another type of quadrilateral.

 www.harcourtschool.com/mathglossary

PREVIEW

polygon	equilateral triangle
vertex	isosceles triangle
decagon	scalene triangle
acute triangle	regular polygon
obtuse triangle	radius
right triangle	diameter
n-gon	chord

Polygons

Learn how to name and classify polygons.

Vocabulary

polygon

vertex

n-gon

decagon

QUICK REVIEW

Name the geometric figure.

1.  2.   3.   4.   5.

vertex

A **polygon** is a closed plane figure with straight sides that are connected line segments. Each point where two sides meet is a **vertex**. A polygon has the same number of sides, angles, and vertices.

Here are the steps Sally follows when drawing the polygon above.

A polygon can have 3 or more sides. The table gives the specific names for certain polygons with relatively few sides. A polygon with n sides is called an **n-gon**.

- How many sides does a 12-gon have?

- How many sides does a 20-gon have?

POLYGONS	
Type	**Sides, Angles, and Vertices**
triangle	3
quadrilateral	4
pentagon	5
hexagon	6
octagon	8
decagon	10
n-gon	n

EXAMPLE 1

How many total sides are there in four hexagons and three 15-gons?
hexagon: 6 sides   15-gon: 15 sides
$(4 \times 6) + (3 \times 15) = 24 + 45 = 69$

So, there are 69 total sides in four hexagons and three 15-gons.

Simple geometric designs often contain many different polygons. You can name a polygon by using the letters of its vertices.

EXAMPLE 2

Use the design below. Name and classify a polygon with the given number of sides. More than one answer may be possible.

a. 5 sides   *BCEFP* is a pentagon.

b. 6 sides   *BCEGJL* is a hexagon.

c. 7 sides   *BCEFHJL* is a 7-gon.

d. 8 sides   *BCEFHIKL* is an octagon.

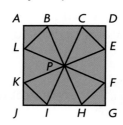

Think and ▶
Discuss

Look back at the lesson to answer the question.

1. **Explain** how you can identify a polygon.

Guided ▶
Practice

For 2–5, use the figure at the right.

2. Name two pentagons.

3. Name three quadrilaterals.

4. Classify the polygon named *FGP*.

5. Name the two 7-gons in the figure.

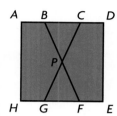

Independent ▶
Practice

For 6–10, use the figure at the right.

6. Name two triangles.

7. Name three hexagons.

8. Name two pentagons.

9. Classify the polygon named *QRSUVCA*.

10. How many quadrilaterals are in the figure?

Problem Solving ▶
Applications

11. Seth draws three pentagons, four octagons, and two 12-gons. How many sides are there in all?

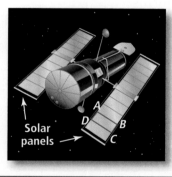

Solar panels ➔

12. **FAST FACT • SCIENCE** Each solar panel on the Hubble Space Telescope produces 1,200 watts of electric energy. Classify polygon *ABCD*, and estimate how many 40-watt bulbs it is capable of lighting.

13. *REASONING* Liz drew three polygons. None of the polygons have the same number of sides. When she counted all the vertices, she got 12. What polygons did she draw?

MIXED REVIEW AND TEST PREP

14. Two angles are complementary. If one angle measures 55°, what does the other angle measure? (p. 340)

15. Solve. $8 + y > 17$ (p. 300)

16. Divide. $6 \div 1\frac{1}{5}$ (p. 236)

17. Write the numbers in order from least to greatest: 65,185,347; 65,158,647; 65,185,437. (p. 16)

⭐ **18. TEST PREP** Replace ● with the missing operation. $2^3 \times (9 ● 4) = 40$ (p. 48)

    A +   **B** −   **C** ×   **D** ÷

EXTRA PRACTICE page 370, Set A

Triangles

Learn how to classify triangles and solve problems involving the angle measures of triangles.

Vocabulary

acute triangle

obtuse triangle

right triangle

equilateral triangle

isosceles triangle

scalene triangle

A triangle can be classified by the angles it contains. An **acute triangle** contains only acute angles. An **obtuse triangle** contains one obtuse angle. A **right triangle** contains one right angle.

acute triangle   obtuse triangle   right triangle

You can use what you know about rectangles to find the sum of the measures of the angles of a right triangle.

Each angle of a rectangle measures 90°. So, the sum of the angles of a rectangle is 4 × 90°, or 360°. If a diagonal is drawn, two congruent right triangles are formed. Since the two triangles are congruent, the sum of the angles in each of these right triangles is 360° ÷ 2, or 180°.

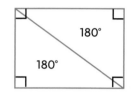

For triangles other than right triangles, look at △ABC. A line segment drawn from C to $\overline{AB}$ forms right triangles ADC and BDC as shown.

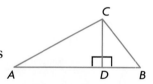

The sum of the angles in both right triangles ADC and BDC is 180°, so the total measure of all the angles in both triangles combined is 360°. If the sum of the two right angles is subtracted, then 180° remains. The 180° comes from the measures of ∠CAB, ∠ABC, and ∠BCA, the three angles of △ABC. So, the sum of the angles of △ABC must be 180°.

Math **I**dea ▶ The sum of the measures of the angles of a triangle is 180°. To decide whether a triangle is acute, obtuse, or right, you need to know the measures of its angles.

EXAMPLE 1

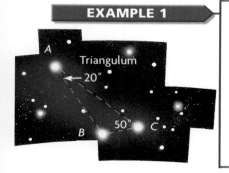

Three stars form a triangle known as Triangulum, with two angles measuring 20° and 50°. Classify the triangle.

To classify the triangle, find the measure of ∠B in the figure.

180° − (20° + 50°) = 180° − 70°   *Subtract the sum of the known*
= 110°   *angle measures from 180°.*

So, the measure of ∠B is 110°. Because △ABC contains one obtuse angle, Triangulum forms an obtuse triangle.

A triangle can also be classified by the lengths of its sides. Sides with the same length are congruent. An **equilateral triangle** has three congruent sides. An **isosceles triangle** has exactly two congruent sides. A **scalene triangle** has no congruent sides.

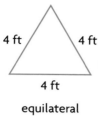
equilateral

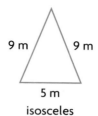
isosceles

scalene

EXAMPLE 2

Juan made a sketch of one of the triangles shown on the dome at the right. Classify the triangle by the lengths of its sides.

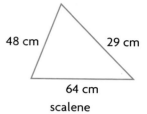

All three sides are congruent, so △*ABC* is an equilateral triangle.

You can classify triangles by both sides and angles.

EXAMPLE 3

Polygon *ABCD* is a square. Name all the triangles in the figure, and classify them by their sides and angles.

△*ABD* is an isosceles right triangle.
△*BCP* is a scalene acute triangle.
△*PCD* is a scalene obtuse triangle.
△*BCD* is an isosceles right triangle.

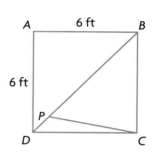

CHECK FOR UNDERSTANDING

Think and ▶ Discuss

Look back at the lesson to answer each question.

1. **Explain** why a triangle cannot have two obtuse angles.

2. **Draw** an example of each: isosceles acute triangle; scalene right triangle; isosceles obtuse triangle.

Guided ▶ Practice

Find the measure of ∠*B* and classify △*ABC* by its angles.

3.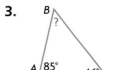

4.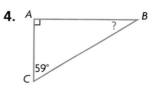

5.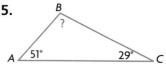

Classify each triangle by the lengths of its sides.

6.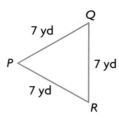
7 yd

7 yd

7 yd

P

Q

R

7.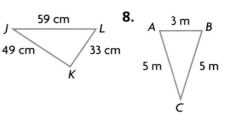
59 cm

49 cm

33 cm

J

L

K

8.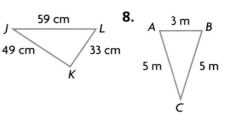
3 m

5 m

5 m

A

B

C

PRACTICE AND PROBLEM SOLVING

Independent ▶ Practice

Find the measure of ∠B **and classify** △ABC **by its angles.**

9.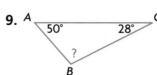
A

50°

28°

?

B

C

10.
B

?

70°

49°

A

C

11.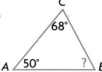
C

68°

50°

?

A

B

Classify each triangle by the lengths of its sides.

12.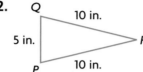
Q

10 in.

5 in.

R

P

10 in.

13.
N

5 ft

P

4 ft

7 ft

M

14.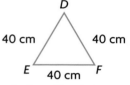
D

40 cm

40 cm

E

40 cm

F

TECHNOLOGY LINK

More Practice:
Harcourt Mega Math
Ice Station Exploration,
Polar Planes, Level F

For 15–16, name all the triangles in the figure, and classify them by their sides and angles.

15.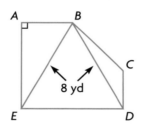
A

B

C

8 yd

E

D

16.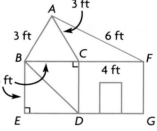
A

3 ft

3 ft

6 ft

B

C

F

3 ft

4 ft

E

D

G

Problem Solving ▶ Applications

17. In a video game, a moving ball always bounces off an edge at the same angle at which it hit the edge. Find the measure of the unknown angle.

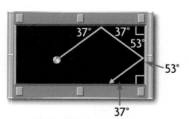
37°

37°

53°

53°

37°

a.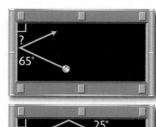
?

65°

b.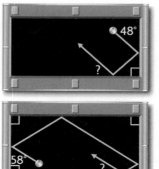
48°

?

c.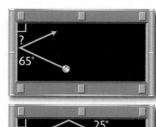
25°

?

d.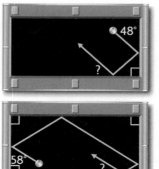
58°

?

18. The three main stars that are in the constellation known as Leo Minor seem to form an isosceles triangle, with congruent base angles. The third angle in the triangle measures 144°. Find the measure of each base angle.

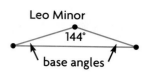
Leo Minor
144°
base angles

19. REASONING How many total degrees are in the angles of a quadrilateral? (**Hint:** Divide it into two triangles.)

For 20–21, use the figure at the right.

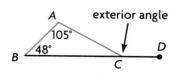
A
exterior angle
105°
48°
B
C
D

20. If you extend a side of a triangle, you form an *exterior angle.* In the figure, ∠ACD is an exterior angle of △ABC. Find the measure of ∠ACD.

21. **What's the Question?** The answer is ∠BCA and ∠ACD.

MIXED REVIEW AND TEST PREP

22. Classify the lines. (p. 344)

23. Which is greatest, 0.03, 0.009, or 0.107? (p. 60)

24. What is the median of the values 24, 17, 39, 19, and 21? (p. 118)

25. TEST PREP Which is the value of x in the expression $\frac{6}{x} = \frac{18}{12}$? (p. 182)

  A $x = 2$ **B** $x = 4$ **C** $x = 9$ **D** $x = 24$

26. TEST PREP Miguel wants to record a TV movie that begins at 9:40 P.M. and ends at 12:10 A.M. How long does the movie last? (p. 240)

  F 9 hr 30 min   **G** 3 hr 50 min   **H** 2 hr 30 min   **J** 2 hr 10 min

---

PROBLEM SOLVING ⟨ 💡 ThiNKer'ſ CorNer

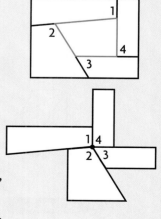

Figure It Out With a partner, draw a triangle, a quadrilateral, a pentagon, and a hexagon on separate sheets of paper. In each polygon, make the sides different lengths.

For each figure you draw, extend each side from one of its endpoints to the edge of the paper, as shown for the quadrilateral at the right. The angles you form outside the polygon are exterior angles.

For each figure, cut the paper along all the line segments and arrange the exterior angles around a common point.

1. Tell the sum of the measures of the exterior angles for the triangle, the quadrilateral, the pentagon, and the hexagon.

2. What can you guess about the sum of the measures of the exterior angles of a polygon? Explain how you came up with your guess.

EXTRA PRACTICE page 370, Set B

PROBLEM SOLVING STRATEGY
Find a Pattern

Learn how to use the strategy *find a pattern* to solve problems.

Vocabulary

regular polygon

QUICK REVIEW

QUICK REVIEW

1. 1×80
2. 2×100
3. 3×150
4. 4×110
5. 5×120

Mrs. Jones is building a deck in the shape of a regular octagon. A **regular polygon** is a polygon in which all sides are congruent and all angles are congruent. So, a regular octagon has 8 congruent sides and 8 congruent angles. What is the measure of each angle of the regular octagon?

Analyze   What are you asked to find?

What information is given?

Choose   What strategy will you use?

Look for a pattern in the sums of the measures of the angles of polygons that have fewer sides than an octagon.

Solve   How will you solve the problem?

Draw polygons that have fewer sides than an octagon. Divide each into triangles. Make a table to record your data and help you look for a pattern.

triangle

quadrilateral

pentagon

hexagon

POLYGON	SIDES	TRIANGLES	SUM OF ANGLE MEASURES
Triangle	3	1	180°
Quadrilateral	4	2	2 x 180° = 360°
Pentagon	5	3	3 x 180° = 540°
Hexagon	6	4	4 x 180° = 720°

The number of triangles is always 2 fewer than the number of sides. So, an octagon can be divided into $8 - 2 = 6$ triangles.

$$6 \times 180° = 1,080°$$

The sum of the angle measures of an octagon is 1,080°. To find the measure of each angle in a regular octagon, divide the sum by 8.

$$1,080° \div 8 = 135°$$

Check   How can you check your answer?

What if Mrs. Jones wants to build a deck in the shape of a decagon? What would be the measure of each angle?

PROBLEM SOLVING PRACTICE

PROBLEM SOLVING STRATEGIES

Draw a Diagram or Picture

Make a Model

Predict and Test

Work Backward

Make an Organized List

▶ **Find a Pattern**

Make a Table or Graph

Solve a Simpler Problem

Write an Equation

Use Logical Reasoning

Solve the problem by finding a possible pattern.

1. Connect the vertices of a square, and a regular pentagon, hexagon, and 7-gon. The square and regular pentagon are shown. Count the number of lines drawn for each figure. Predict how many lines will be drawn for regular polygons with 8, 9, and 10 sides.

2. There were 10 players in the checkers tournament. If each player shook the hand of every other player 1 time, how many handshakes were there?

Edmund is making a design for a quilt using blue and white squares.

3. How many squares will there be in the eighth row?

   A 8   **B** 9   **C** 15   **D** 17

4. After he has 8 rows, how many squares will he have used in all?

   F 8   **G** 16   **H** 36   **J** 64

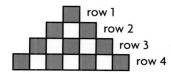

MIXED STRATEGY PRACTICE

5. Silvia, David, and Rhoda have blue, green, and brown eyes, though not necessarily in that order. Silvia's eyes are the color of the sky. Rhoda does not have brown eyes. Give the color of each person's eyes.

6. This week Cheryl earned $23 more than last week. Last week she earned $225. She plans to spend $\frac{3}{8}$ of this week's earnings, put half in her checking account, and save the rest. How much will she save?

Use Data   **For 7–8, use the table.**

7. Estimate the amount the Alpha Corporation earns from publishing if its total revenues are $11.6 billion.

8. Draw a circle graph to show the sources of revenue for the Alpha Corporation. Then use the graph to find two revenue sources that together produce more than half of the company's revenues.

SOURCES OF REVENUE FOR ALPHA CORPORATION	
Publishing	35%
Movies and TV	28%
Broadcasting and Cable	20%
Other	17%

9. Julia noted that her car's mileage gauge read 12,445 mi at the start of a trip. At the end of the trip, the gauge read 12,830 mi. If she used 16 gal of gas on the trip, about how many miles per gallon did she get?

10. ✏️ **Write a problem** that can be solved by finding a pattern. Exchange with a classmate and solve. Explain your solution.

LESSON 16.4

Quadrilaterals

Learn how to identify, classify, and compare quadrilaterals.

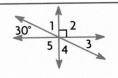

QUICK REVIEW

Find each angle measure.
1. ∠1 2. ∠2 3. ∠3
4. ∠4 5. ∠5

Remember that a quadrilateral is a polygon with four sides, four vertices, and four angles.

These two figures are quadrilaterals:

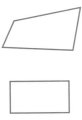

Five types of quadrilaterals are especially important. Their names and properties are listed below. Note: The same marking on two sides or more of a figure indicates that those sides are congruent.

QUADRILATERAL	FIGURE	PROPERTIES
parallelogram		opposite sides parallel and congruent
rectangle		parallelogram with four right angles
rhombus		parallelogram with four congruent sides
square		rectangle with four congruent sides
trapezoid		quadrilateral with exactly two parallel sides

Notice that rectangles and rhombuses are types of parallelograms.

Rectangle:

Parallelogram with **four right angles**

Rhombus:

Parallelogram with **four congruent sides**

A square is both a type of rectangle and a type of rhombus.

Square:

Rectangle with **four congruent sides**

Square:

Rhombus with **four right angles**

The figure at the right has four sides, so it is a quadrilateral. A more *exact* name for the figure, however, is *rectangle*, because the name *rectangle* describes the figure's properties more completely than the name *quadrilateral* does.

Quadrilateral: 4 sides
Rectangle: parallelogram with 4 right angles

EXAMPLE 1

Give the most exact name for the figure.

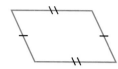

The figure is a rhombus.

The figure is a square.

The figure is a parallelogram.

- Why wouldn't it be more exact to name the figure above at the far right a rhombus or a rectangle?

Statements about geometric figures are often given in "If … then" form.

- *If* a polygon has five sides, *then* it is a pentagon.

- *If* a figure is a triangle, *then* the sum of the measures of its angles is 180°.

You can use what you know about quadrilaterals to write "If … then" statements about quadrilaterals.

EXAMPLE 2

Complete the statement, giving the most exact name for the figure: If a rhombus is also a rectangle, then the rhombus is a ___?___ .

THINK: A rhombus has four congruent sides and opposite sides parallel. If it is also a rectangle, then it has four right angles, which makes it a square.

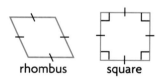

rhombus   square

In the activity below, you will name quadrilaterals by using their properties.

Activity

A   B   C   D

- List the properties of each figure above.

- Give the most exact name for each figure.

363

Think and ▶
Discuss

Look back at the lesson to answer each question.

1. **Compare** and **contrast** a rectangle and a rhombus.

2. **Explain** how to determine if a quadrilateral is a trapezoid.

Guided ▶
Practice

Give the most exact name for the figure.

3.

4.

5.

Complete the statement, giving the most exact name for the figure.

6. If the opposite sides of a quadrilateral are parallel, then the quadrilateral is a ___?___ .

7. If a parallelogram has four right angles, then it is a ___?___ .

8. If a rectangle has four congruent sides, then it is a ___?___ .

PRACTICE AND PROBLEM SOLVING

Independent ▶
Practice

Give the most exact name for the figure.

9.

10.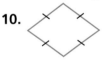

11.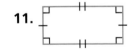

12.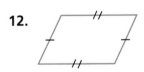

13.

14.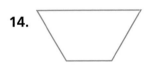

Complete the statement, giving the most exact name for the figure.

15. If a parallelogram has four congruent sides, then it is a ___?___ .

16. If a polygon has five sides, then it is a ___?___ .

17. If a quadrilateral has four congruent sides and four congruent angles, then the quadrilateral is a ___?___ .

18. If exactly two sides of a quadrilateral are parallel, then it is a ___?___ .

19. If a polygon has four sides, then it is a ___?___ .

TECHNOLOGY LINK

More Practice:
**Harcourt Mega Math
Ice Station Exploration,**
Polar Planes, Level G

In 20–22, portions of quadrilaterals are hidden from view. Name some possible quadrilaterals each figure could be.

20.   21.   22.

23. A rectangular picture frame is 4 inches wider than it is tall. The total length of the four sides of the frame is 52 inches. What are the dimensions of the frame?

24. Kaya cut two square frames from a 90-in. length of aluminum. If each side of one frame was 16 in. long, how long was each side of the second frame?

For 25–26, use the figure at the right.

25. **?** **What's the Error?** Elton says that the quadrilateral cannot be a trapezoid because it has two right angles. What is wrong with his statement?

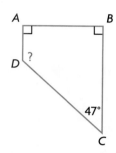

26. Find the measure of ∠*ADC*.

MIXED REVIEW AND TEST PREP

27. Two angles in a triangle each measure 48°. Find the measure of the third angle. (p. 356)

28. ∠*M* is complementary to a 75° angle. What is the measure of ∠*M*? (p. 340)

29. Write 8% as a decimal. (p. 68)

⭐**30. TEST PREP** Which is the greatest common factor of 18 and 24? (p. 170)

    A 2   **B** 3   **C** 6   **D** 72

⭐**31. TEST PREP** Which number is *not* prime? (p. 166)

    F 29   **G** 41   **H** 77   **J** 83

PROBLEM SOLVING   LINKUP to Reading

Strategy • Make Generalizations Sometimes you need to *make generalizations* to solve a problem. When you generalize, you make a statement that is true about a whole group of similar situations or objects.

Use the Venn diagram to make generalizations about quadrilaterals.

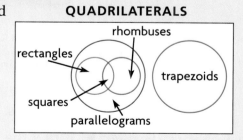

QUADRILATERALS

Complete. Write *always*, *sometimes*, or *never*.

1. A square is __?__ a parallelogram.

2. A trapezoid is __?__ a rectangle.

3. A rhombus is __?__ a trapezoid.

4. A rectangle is __?__ a square.

(EXTRA PRACTICE) page 370, Set C

Draw Plane Figures

Learn how to draw plane geometric figures.

Remember that an isosceles triangle has two congruent sides.

QUICK REVIEW

Write *acute*, *right*, *obtuse*, or *straight* for each angle measure.

1. 135°   **2.** 180°   **3.** 10°   **4.** 55.7°   **5.** 90°

You can use the properties of geometric figures to draw plane figures on dot paper.

EXAMPLES

A. Draw a right isosceles triangle.

Use square dot paper to draw figures with right angles.

THINK: *The triangle must have one right angle.*

The triangle also must have two congruent sides.

B. Draw a pentagon with two right angles.

THINK: *The figure must have two right angles.*

The figure also must have five sides.

C. Draw a rhombus with no right angles.

Use isometric dot paper to draw figures with congruent sides and no right angles.

CHECK FOR UNDERSTANDING

Think and ▶ Discuss

Look back at the lesson to answer each question.

1. **Explain** how you could draw a trapezoid on dot paper.

2. **Tell** whether you could draw an isosceles triangle with two obtuse angles. Explain.

Guided ▶ Practice

Draw the figure. Use square dot paper or isometric dot paper.

3. a scalene triangle   **4.** an equilateral triangle   **5.** a hexagon with no congruent sides

Independent ▶ Practice

Draw the figure. Use square dot paper or isometric dot paper.

6. an acute isosceles triangle

7. an obtuse scalene triangle

8. an octagon with 2 right angles

9. a quadrilateral with no congruent sides or parallel sides

10. a quadrilateral with 4 right angles

11. a pentagon with no congruent sides

Complete the sentence by using *must*, *can*, or *cannot*.

12. A rhombus __?__ have all sides congruent.

13. A right triangle __?__ have two right angles.

14. A trapezoid __?__ have all sides congruent.

15. A scalene triangle __?__ be obtuse.

Problem Solving ▶ Applications

16. Anita drew a quadrilateral. Then she drew a line segment connecting one pair of opposite corners. She saw that she had divided the quadrilateral into two isosceles right triangles. Classify the quadrilateral she began with.

17. Vocabulary Power Both *octo* and *octa* mean "eight." Write two words that begin with *octo* and two words that begin with *octa*.

18. On a separate sheet of paper, draw an equilateral triangle with sides 4 in. long. Cut out the triangle. Then cut from each corner of the triangle an equilateral triangle with sides 1 in. long. What is the perimeter of the figure that remains?

19. ❓ **What's the Error?** Victor said he drew a triangle with one acute, one right, and one obtuse angle. Explain his mistake.

20. Ted drew three sides of a quadrilateral as shown at the right. If he wants a third angle to be 90°, what will be the measure of the fourth angle?

21. Name a parallelogram with four right angles. (p. 362)

22. Name the figure. (p. 336)

23. Evaluate the expression. (p. 266)
$8^2 + \sqrt{100} - 7$

24. 3.6×0.25 (p. 80)

25. TEST PREP A box with a height of $1\frac{9}{16}$ ft is shelved on top of a box with a height of $2\frac{1}{2}$ ft. The distance between shelves is 5 ft. How far is it from the top of the upper box to the shelf above? (p. 210)

A $1\frac{15}{16}$ ft **B** $1\frac{4}{9}$ ft **C** $1\frac{3}{16}$ ft **D** $\frac{15}{16}$ ft

EXTRA PRACTICE page 370, Set D

367

Circles

Learn how to identify and draw parts of circles.

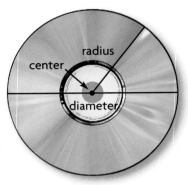

radius = 6.25 cm
diameter = 12.5 cm

Vocabulary

radius

diameter

chord

A compact disc (CD) is shaped like a *circle*. A circle is the set of all points a given distance from a point called the center. At the edge of the CD, every point on the circle is 6.25 cm from the center.

A line segment with one endpoint at the center of a circle and the other endpoint on the circle is a **radius** (plural, *radii*). A line segment that passes through the center of a circle and has both endpoints on the circle is a **diameter**. The length of a diameter is always twice the length of a radius.

CD radius = 6.25 cm   CD diameter = 2 × 6.25 = 12.5 cm

A circle can be named by its center. Like a polygon, a circle is a plane figure. A circle is not made up of line segments, so it is not a polygon.

EXAMPLE

Name the center, the circle, a diameter, and three radii of the circle.

O is the center. The circle is circle O. $\overline{AB}$ is a diameter. $\overline{OA}$, $\overline{OB}$, and $\overline{OC}$ are radii.

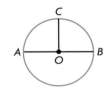

Line segments, called chords, can be formed on a circle. A **chord** is a line segment with its endpoints on a circle.

chord AB

Activity

You need: compass, straightedge

- Draw and label a circle with center P.

- Draw and label diameter ST and radius PV.

- Draw and label chord SU.

- Is the diameter that you drew also a chord? Explain.

- What is the relationship between the length of $\overline{PT}$ and the length of $\overline{PV}$?

Think and ▶ Look back at the lesson to answer each question.
Discuss

1. **Explain** how you can find the radius of a circle if you know the diameter.

2. **Draw** a circle and a chord that has the longest possible length that can be drawn on the circle.

Guided ▶ For 3–6, use the circle at the right.
Practice Name the given parts of the circle.

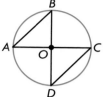

3. center 4. chords

5. radii 6. diameters

Independent ▶ For 7–10, use the circle at the right.
Practice Name the given parts of the circle.

7. center 8. chords

9. radii 10. diameter

11. Draw circle *M*. Label diameter *EF*, radius *MG*, and chord *FH*.

Problem Solving ▶ 12. **REASONING** What happens to the length of a radius as the size
Applications of a circle increases?

Use Data For 13–14, use the table.

13. Find the lengths of the radii of the LP, the 45, and the 78.

14. About how much longer will it take an LP to revolve (spin) 1,000 times than it will take a CD?

15. ✎ **Write About It** The radius of a circle is 6 cm long. Chord *AB* is 8 cm long. Explain why $\overline{AB}$ cannot be a diameter.

TYPES OF RECORDING DISCS		
Disc	Diameter	Revolutions Per Minute
CD	12.5 cm	200
LP	12 in.	$33\frac{1}{3}$
45	$6\frac{7}{8}$ in.	45
78	10 in.	78

MIXED REVIEW AND TEST PREP

16. Give the most exact name for the figure. (p. 362)

17. Find the unknown angle measure. (p. 340)

18. Evaluate. $18 - 9 \div 3 + 5$ (p. 48)

19. What is the LCM of 15 and 20? (p. 170)

⭐20. **TEST PREP** Find $24 \div \frac{3}{4}$. (p. 236)

A 16 **B** 18 **C** 32 **D** 36

EXTRA PRACTICE page 370, Set E

Set A (pp. 354–355)

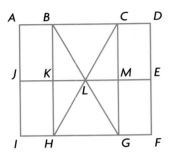

For 1–4, use the figure.

1. Name six triangles.

2. Name a hexagon.

3. Classify the polygon named *DCLGF*.

4. Classify the polygon named *ABLCDFI*.

5. How many total sides are there in three octagons and two 14-gons?

Set B (pp. 356–359)

Find the measure of the unknown angle, and classify the triangle by its angles.

1.

2.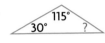

3.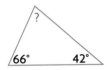

4.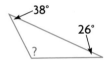

Set C (pp. 362–365)

Give the most exact name for the figure.

1.

2.

3.

4.

Set D (pp. 366–367)

Draw the figure. Use square dot paper or isometric dot paper.

1. a rectangle

2. a trapezoid

3. a scalene right triangle

4. a pentagon with no congruent sides

5. an equilateral triangle

6. a rhombus

Set E (pp. 368–369)

Name the given parts of the circle.

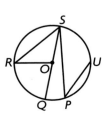

1. center

2. chords

3. radii

4. diameter

1. **VOCABULARY**   A triangle containing one obtuse angle is a(n) ___?___ triangle. (p. 356)

2. **VOCABULARY**   A triangle containing one right angle is a(n) ___?___ triangle. (p. 356)

3. **VOCABULARY**   Any line segment with endpoints on a circle is called a(n) ___?___ . (p. 368)

For 4–8, use the figure at the right. (pp. 354–355)

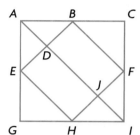

4. Name two quadrilaterals.

5. Name a pentagon.

6. Classify the polygon named *DAB*.

7. Classify the polygon named *BCFHGE*.

8. Classify the polygon named *ABFJIHED*.

Find the measure of the unknown angle, and classify the triangle by its angles. (pp. 356–359)

9.

10.

11.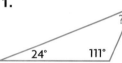

12.

Give the most exact name for the figure. (pp. 362–365)

13.

14.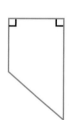

15.

16.

Draw the figure. Use square dot paper or isometric dot paper. (pp. 366–367)

17. an isosceles right triangle

18. a trapezoid with two right angles

19. a rhombus

Name the given parts of the circle. (pp. 368–369)

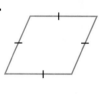

20. center

21. chords

22. radii

23. diameters

24. Jamie decorated her bike wheels by stringing ribbons between the ends of spokes. Classify △ *ABO*. (*O* is the center.) (pp. 356–359)

25. The figure shows a roof with vertical support $\overline{BD}$. Find the measure of the top roof angle, ∠*ABC*. (pp. 356–359)

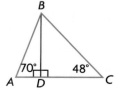

NUMBER SENSE, CONCEPTS, AND OPERATIONS

1. Lake Huron is the second largest lake in the United States. Written in expanded form, its area is $20,000 + 3,000 + 10$ square miles. Which of the following shows the area in standard form?

    A 23,100

    B 23,010

    C 20,310

    D 2,310

2. The table below shows what fractional part of a library book each of four students read in one week.

PART OF BOOK READ IN ONE WEEK	
Student	**Fractional Part**
Beth	$\frac{2}{3}$
Kendra	$\frac{7}{12}$
Barry	$\frac{3}{4}$
Sean	$\frac{4}{12}$

    Which of the following orders the names of the students from the least part of a book read to the greatest part of a book read?

    F Beth, Barry, Kendra, Sean

    G Beth, Kendra, Barry, Sean

    H Kendra, Barry, Sean, Beth

    J Sean, Kendra, Beth, Barry

3. **Explain It** David had $5\frac{1}{4}$ cups of flour. He used $1\frac{3}{8}$ cups in a recipe. How much flour is left? Explain your reasoning.

★ **ALGEBRAIC THINKING**

4. Tickets to the Classic Car Show cost $2. There is also a $1 service charge no matter how many tickets you buy. The table below shows the relationship between x, the number of tickets purchased, and y, the total cost of the tickets.

x	5	7	9	11
y	11	15	19	23

    Which of the following **best** describes the relationship between x and y?

    A $y = 2x + 1$

    B $y = 6 + x$

    C $y = (3 \times x) - 4$

    D $y = x + 4$

5. The cost of a meal was shared equally among 7 friends. If m represents the cost of the meal, which expression represents the amount each friend paid?

    F $\frac{7}{m}$

    G $m + 7$

    H $7 - m$

    J $\frac{m}{7}$

6. **Explain It** In the 400-meter relay race, four runners each run 100 meters, one after the other. The record time for completing the race is 37.4 seconds. Write an equation to find the average time for each of the four runners in the record-setting race. Explain how to solve the equation.

7. The pictograph below shows the results of the election for class president.

CLASS ELECTION RESULTS	
Student	**Number of Votes**
Alicia	⌧ ⌧ ⌧
Martin	⌧ ⌧ ⌧
Miguel	⌧ ⌧ ⌧ ⌧
Brittany	⌧ ⌧

Key: Each ⌧ = 3 votes.

How many more votes did the winner receive than the student who came in fourth place?

A 2

B 3

C 6

D 9

8. Dawn is playing a game with a spinner that is divided into 12 equal sections. The sections are numbered 1–12. Which of the following shows the probability of Dawn spinning a number greater than 8?

F $\frac{1}{3}$

G $\frac{5}{12}$

H $\frac{1}{2}$

J $\frac{3}{4}$

9. Explain It Thomas walked every day for ten days. The numbers of miles he walked are 5, 4, 3, 6, 4, 7, 5, 3, 4, and 6. To the nearest tenth of a mile, what was the mean distance Thomas walked? Explain how you found the answer.

10. A diameter of a bicycle wheel has its endpoints at points M and N. The center of the wheel is point P. Which term describes $\overline{MP}$?

A diameter

B radius

C circumference

D arc

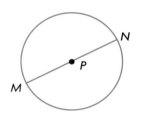

11. The logo for the Three Kids Company includes an isosceles right triangle. Which figure below could be part of the company's logo?

> **TIP** Look for important words.
> See item 11. The key words are *isosceles right triangle*. Recall the definition of each word. Then look for a figure that fits all the definitions.

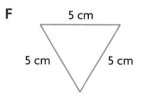

F (triangle, 5 cm, 5 cm, 5 cm)

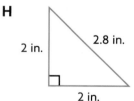

G (triangle, 3 cm, 4 cm, 5 cm)

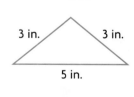

H (triangle, 2 in., 2 in., 2.8 in.)

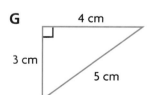

J (triangle, 3 in., 3 in., 5 in.)

12. Explain It Which design below can NOT be used as a tessellation for a quilt pattern? Explain your choice.

Figure 1   Figure 2

CHAPTER 17

Congruence and Similarity

OUTLINES OF NESTING DOLLS

≡**FAST FACT** • ART Nesting boxes were first created more than 900 years ago in China. The word *nesting* is used to describe objects that fit inside each other. About 100 years ago, Russian artists started making nesting dolls.

PROBLEM SOLVING Are the dolls shown on the grid congruent? Are they similar?

Check What You Know

Use this page to help you review and remember important skills needed for Chapter 17.

✓ Congruent Figures

Tell whether the figures appear to be congruent or not. Write *yes* or *no*.

1.

2.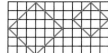

3.

4.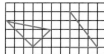

5.

6.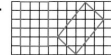

7.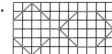

8.

✓ Classify Lines

Classify each pair of lines as parallel, perpendicular, or intersecting. There may be two ways to classify a pair.

9.

10.

11.

12.

13.

14.

15.

16.

VOCABULARY POWER

REVIEW

measure [mezh′ər] *verb, noun*

The word *measure* can be used as a verb or as a noun. Used as a verb, *measure* means "to find the length or weight of an object." Give an example of the use of *measure* as a noun.

 www.harcourtschool.com/mathglossary

PREVIEW

congruent ≅
bisect
midpoint
perpendicular bisector
similar figures

Congruent Segments and Angles

QUICK REVIEW

Draw an angle with the measure indicated.

1. 90°   **2.** 120°   **3.** 165°   **4.** 25°   **5.** 47°

Vocabulary

congruent ≅

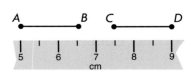

Line segments that have the same length are said to be **congruent**. Use the symbol ≅ to show that two segments are congruent. In the figure, $\overline{AB}$ and $\overline{CD}$ are each 1.5 cm long, so $\overline{AB} \cong \overline{CD}$.

If you have a ruler, you can use it to see whether two line segments are congruent. As you'll see in the following activity, you can also use a compass to test for congruence.

Activity

You need: compass

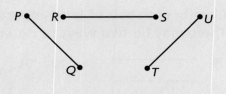

- Trace $\overline{PQ}$, $\overline{RS}$, and $\overline{TU}$ on your paper. Place the compass point on point P. Open the compass to the length of $\overline{PQ}$.

- Use the compass to compare the length of $\overline{PQ}$ with the lengths of $\overline{RS}$ and $\overline{TU}$.

- Which segment is congruent to $\overline{PQ}$? Use the symbol ≅ to show the congruence.

Use a compass and a straightedge to construct congruent line segments.

EXAMPLE 1

Trace $\overline{EF}$. Then construct a line segment congruent to $\overline{EF}$.

Draw a ray that is longer than $\overline{EF}$. Label the endpoint H.

Place the compass point on point E. Open the compass to the length of $\overline{EF}$. Use the same compass opening. Place the compass point on H. Draw an arc that intersects the ray. Label the intersection point M.

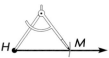

So, $\overline{HM} \cong \overline{EF}$.

Congruent Angles

Like line segments, angles can be congruent. Two angles are congruent if they have the same measure in degrees.

When a beam of light hits a mirror, the angle at which it arrives—the *angle of incidence*—is congruent to the angle at which it reflects off the mirror—the *angle of reflection*. In the figure, $\angle ABD \cong \angle DBC$. Both angles measure 28°.

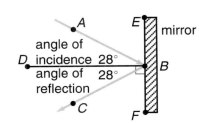

- Do you think $\angle EBA \cong \angle FBC$? Explain.

Use a compass and a straightedge to construct congruent angles.

Congruent angles often appear on buildings.

EXAMPLE 2

Trace $\angle B$. Then construct an angle congruent to $\angle B$.

Draw a ray with endpoint M.

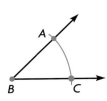

Place the compass point on B, and draw an arc through $\angle B$. Label the points of intersection A and C.

Place the compass point on M. Draw the same arc through the ray. Label the point of intersection P.

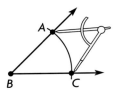

Use the compass to measure the distance between A and C.

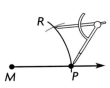

Use the same compass opening to locate point R.

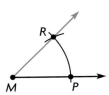

Draw $\overrightarrow{MR}$.

So, $\angle RMP \cong \angle ABC$.

377

Think and ▶
Discuss

Look back at the lesson to answer each question.

1. **Explain** how you know that in the last step in Example 1, *M* is the same distance from *H* as *F* is from *E*.

2. **Give** some examples of congruent line segments in your classroom.

Guided ▶
Practice

Use a compass to decide which two line segments in each group are congruent.

3.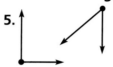

4.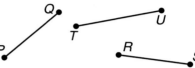

Find the measure of each angle, using a protractor. Then tell whether the angles in each pair are congruent. Write *yes* or *no*.

5.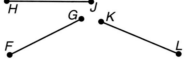

6.

7.

Independent ▶
Practice

Use a compass to decide which two line segments in each group are congruent.

8.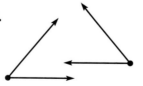

9.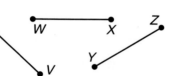

Find the measure of each angle, using a protractor. Then tell whether the angles in each pair are congruent. Write *yes* or *no*.

10.

11.

12.

Use a compass and a straightedge to construct a line segment congruent to the given segment.

13.

14.

15.

Use a compass and a straightedge to construct an angle congruent to the given angle.

16.

17.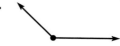

18.

**Problem Solving ▶
Applications**

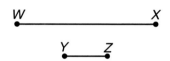

19. Construct an angle with a measure equal to the measure of ∠ABC plus the measure of ∠DEF.

20. Construct a line segment with a length equal to the length of $\overline{WX}$ minus the length of $\overline{YZ}$.

21. A beam of light from point A strikes Mirror 1 at point B. The angle of incidence is 24°. The beam then strikes Mirror 2 at point C. Find the measure of ∠ECD.

22. ✎ **Write About It** Explain how you could use a compass to find a point on $\overline{ML}$ that is the same distance from M as P is from N.

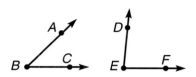

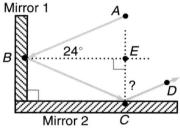

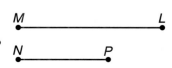

MIXED REVIEW AND TEST PREP

23. $1\frac{1}{4} \div 1\frac{1}{8}$ (p. 236)

24. Complete. $\frac{8}{12} = \frac{\blacksquare}{18}$ (p. 182)

25. Solve. $15 = \frac{1}{2}x$ (p. 291)

26. TEST PREP Find the sum. $3\frac{2}{3} + 1\frac{5}{6}$ (p. 210)

A $4\frac{7}{9}$ **B** $5\frac{1}{2}$ **C** $5\frac{8}{12}$ **D** $7\frac{11}{12}$

27. TEST PREP Ben's car travels 16 miles per gallon of gasoline. Ben used 9 gal of gasoline while driving. How far did he drive? (p. 24)

F 25 mi **G** 100 mi **H** 144 mi **J** 154 mi

PROBLEM SOLVING

ThiNKer's CorNer

GEOMETRIC GEOGRAPHY Find geometric figures in maps.

Materials: ruler

Most states have borders that twist and turn. But some states have borders that model line segments. Use the map shown at the right to answer the questions.

1. Describe where these four states have borders that appear to model line segments.

2. Does any state have two borders that are almost congruent?

3. Why do you think the border between Iowa and Illinois and between Missouri and Illinois twists and turns?

EXTRA PRACTICE page 388, Set A

379

Bisect Line Segments and Angles

Learn how to bisect line segments and angles by using a compass and straightedge.

QUICK REVIEW

1. 18 ÷ 2   **2.** 60 ÷ 2   **3.** 28 ÷ 2

4. 100 ÷ 2   **5.** 46 ÷ 2

When you **bisect** a line segment, you divide it into two congruent parts. The **midpoint** of a line segment is the point halfway between the endpoints of the segment. The midpoint bisects the line segment.

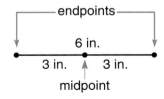

Use a compass and a straightedge to draw a line that intersects a line segment at its midpoint to form a 90° angle. This line is called the **perpendicular bisector**.

Activity

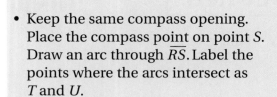

You need: compass, straightedge

- Draw a line segment. Label the endpoints *R* and *S*.

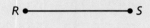

- Place the compass point on point *R*. Open the compass to more than half the distance from *R* to *S*. Draw an arc through $\overline{RS}$.

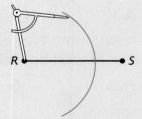

- Keep the same compass opening. Place the compass point on point *S*. Draw an arc through $\overline{RS}$. Label the points where the arcs intersect as *T* and *U*.

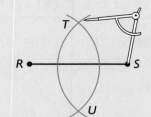

- Use a straightedge to draw a line through *T* and *U*. Use *P* to label the point where $\overline{TU}$ intersects $\overline{RS}$.

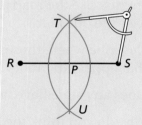

- $\overline{TU}$ is the perpendicular bisector of $\overline{RS}$. Point *P* is the midpoint of $\overline{RS}$. Therefore, $\overline{RP} \cong \overline{PS}$.

Bisecting Angles

When you bisect an angle, you divide it into two congruent angles. In the figure, $\overrightarrow{NR}$ bisects $\angle MNP$, so $\angle MNR \cong \angle RNP$.

You can use a compass and a straightedge to bisect an angle.

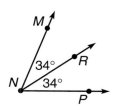

EXAMPLE

Trace $\angle K$. Then bisect the angle.

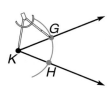

Place the compass point on point K. Draw an arc that intersects both sides of $\angle K$. Label the intersection points of the angle and the arc G and H.

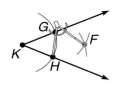

With the compass point on point G, draw an arc in the middle of the angle. Keep the same compass opening. Repeat, placing the compass point on point H. Label the point where the arcs intersect point F.

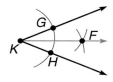

Draw $\overrightarrow{KF}$.

$\overrightarrow{KF}$ is the bisector of $\angle GKH$. So, $\angle GKF \cong \angle FKH$.

CHECK FOR UNDERSTANDING

Think and ▶ Discuss

Look back at the lesson to answer each question.

1. **Tell** how many congruent angles are formed when you bisect an angle. How many congruent line segments are formed when you bisect a line segment?

2. **Explain** how bisecting an angle is like bisecting a line segment.

Guided ▶ Practice

If a line segment of the given length is bisected, how long will each of the smaller segments be?

3. 38 in.   4. 112 cm   5. 0.3 m   6. 713.6 mm

If an angle of the given measure is bisected, how many degrees will there be in each of the smaller angles that are formed?

7. 52°   8. 79°   9. 8.1°   10. 119.1°

Trace the figure. Then bisect it.

11.
A •————————• B

12.
Y •—— X ↗
    Z →

381

Independent ▶ Practice

If a line segment of the given length is bisected, how long will each of the smaller segments be?

13. 17 ft   **14.** 2.01 m   **15.** 99.35 cm   **16.** 411 yd

If an angle of the given measure is bisected, how many degrees will there be in each of the smaller angles that are formed?

17. 65°   **18.** 51°   **19.** 142.6°   **20.** 179.5°

Trace the figure. Then bisect it.

21.

22.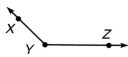

23.

24.

25.

26.

Problem Solving ▶ Applications

27. Trace the square. Use a compass and a straightedge to find the midpoint of each side, then connect the midpoints. What figure is formed?

28. With a compass, draw a large circle on a sheet of paper. Use a straightedge to draw a scalene triangle so that each side touches the circle at a single point. Now bisect each angle of the triangle. What is special about the point where the three bisectors intersect?

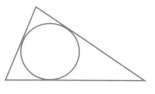

29. The measures of two angles of a triangle are 61° and 43°. If the third angle is bisected, what is the measure of each of the angles that are formed?

30. **?** **What's the Question?** The original angle measures 80°. The answer is 40°.

MIXED REVIEW AND TEST PREP

31. ∠A ≅ ∠R and ∠V ≅ ∠R. If ∠V measures 60°, what is the measure of ∠A? (p. 377)

32. What are the measures of two angles that are congruent and supplementary? (p. 340)

33. Write 0.48 as a fraction in simplest form. (p. 191)

34. 0.82 ÷ 0.4 (p. 88)

35. **TEST PREP** Ellen has 15 more than twice as many silver dollars as Sheri has. If Ellen has 75 silver dollars, which equation could you use to find the number of silver dollars that Sheri has? (p. 274)

   A $b + 15 = 75$ **B** $75 = b - 15$ **C** $2 \times b = 75$ **D** $2b + 15 = 75$

EXTRA PRACTICE page 388, Set B

Construct Parallel Lines

Explore how to construct parallel lines by using a compass and a straightedge.

You need compass, straightedge.

Parallel lines are lines that never intersect, no matter how far they extend in a plane. You can use a compass and a straightedge to construct parallel lines.

Activity

• Draw a line. Draw a point, *P,* that is not on the line. Draw another line that goes through point *P* and intersects the original line. Label the point of intersection *W*.

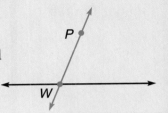

• Construct congruent angles.

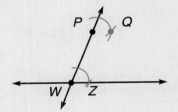

• Draw $\overrightarrow{PQ}$. $\overrightarrow{PQ}$ is a line parallel to $\overleftrightarrow{WZ}$.

$\overrightarrow{PQ} \parallel \overleftrightarrow{WZ}$

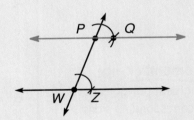

Think and Discuss

• Describe two examples of parallel lines in your classroom.

• What type of figure could you draw with two sets of parallel lines?

Practice

1. Draw a line. Have another student construct a line parallel to it.

2. Use a compass and a straightedge to construct a parallelogram.

LESSON 17.4 Similar and Congruent Figures

Learn how to identify and construct similar and congruent figures.

Vocabulary

similar figures

Remember that congruent polygons have all corresponding sides congruent and all corresponding angles congruent.

QUICK REVIEW

If a line segment of the given length is bisected, how long will each of the smaller segments be?

1. 10 cm   **2.** 17 in.   **3.** 4 yd   **4.** 5 ft   **5.** 26 in.

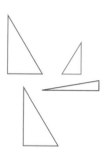

Figures that have the same shape are **similar figures**. The red, blue and green triangles all have the same shape, so they are similar. The purple triangle has a different shape, so it is not similar to the others.

Congruent figures have the same shape and the same size. The red and green triangles are both congruent and similar, because they have the same shape and the same size.

Math Idea ▶ Figures can be congruent, similar, both, or neither. All congruent figures are similar, but similar figures do not have to be congruent.

EXAMPLE 1

Decide whether the figures in each pair appear to be similar, or congruent. If the figures appear not to be similar, write *neither*.

A

same shape, not same size
The figures are similar. You can use the symbol ~ to show that figures are similar.

ABCD ~ HJKL   *Read: ABCD is similar to HJKL.*

B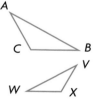

same shape, not same size
The figures are similar.

△*ABC* ~ △*VWX*

C

same shape, same size
The figures are congruent, and so they are also similar.

MNPL ≅ *YZWX*

D

not same shape, not same size
The figures are neither similar nor congruent.

Activity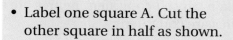

You need: 2 congruent paper squares, ruler, scissors

- Label one square A. Cut the other square in half as shown.

- Label one new piece B. Cut the other piece in half as shown.

- Label one new piece C. Cut the other piece in half. Label the two new pieces D and E.

- Look at A, B, C, D, and E. Which are congruent? Which are similar?

- Name six pairs of pieces that are neither congruent or similar.

You can draw a figure similar to a given figure by doubling the dimensions of the given figure.

Jackie is using her computer to draw similar figures. Rectangle *ABCD* measures 2 in. by 3 in. She rotated the figure $\frac{1}{4}$ turn and doubled the dimensions to draw rectangle *PQRS*.

When you double the dimensions, the size changes but not the shape. So, the two rectangles are similar.

$ABCD \sim PQRS$

You can also draw a similar figure by tripling the dimensions of the given figure.

EXAMPLE 2

Draw a triangle similar to △*MKV* by doubling the dimensions of △*MKV*.

Draw another similar triangle by tripling the dimensions of △*MKV*.

$$\triangle ABC \sim \triangle MKV$$

$$\triangle DEF \sim \triangle MKV$$

- Is △*ABC* similar to △*DEF*?

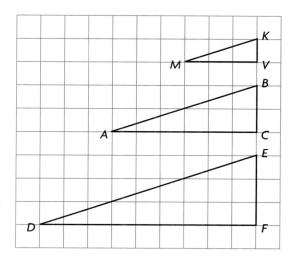

385

**Think and ▶
Discuss**

Look back at the lesson to answer each question.

1. **Explain** why all congruent figures are similar but not all similar figures are congruent.

2. **Explain** why two polygons that are similar to a third polygon must be similar to each other.

**Guided ▶
Practice**

Use ~ or ≅ to compare the figures if they appear to be similar or congruent. If the figures appear not to be similar or congruent, write *neither*.

3.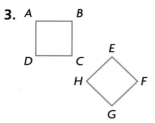

4.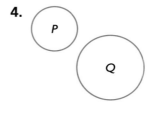

5.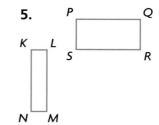

**Independent ▶
Practice**

Use ~ or ≅ to compare the figures if they appear to be similar or congruent. If the figures appear not to be similar or congruent, write *neither*.

6.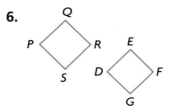

7.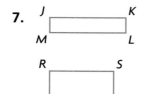

8.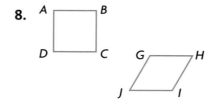

9.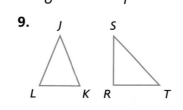

10.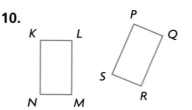

11.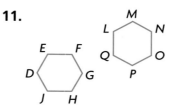

TECHNOLOGY LINK

More Practice:
**Harcourt Mega Math
Ice Station Exploration,**
Polar Planes, Level I

12. Draw a 2-in. by 3-in. rectangle. Draw another with the dimensions doubled. Are the two rectangles congruent? similar?

For 13–14, draw the figures.

13. two congruent triangles

14. two triangles that are similar but not congruent

Problem Solving ▶
Applications

15. Jackie printed the word MATH in 12-point Helvetica type and in 18-point Helvetica type. Do the two words appear to be similar, congruent, or neither?

12-point   18-point
MATH   **MATH**

16. **≡FAST FACT • SOCIAL STUDIES** United States flags come in different sizes, but the length is always 1.9 times the height. One U.S. flag has a height of 3 ft. Another flag has a height of 6 ft. Are the flags similar? Explain.

17. **Vocabulary Power** Figures with two *dimensions* have length and width. Draw a rectangle and then measure and label each dimension with inches. Draw a similar rectangle by halving the dimensions.

18. Kevin is taking a drafting class. He draws a 6-in. by 4-in. rectangle. Kevin then draws another rectangle with the dimensions tripled. What are the dimensions of the new rectangle? Are the two rectangles congruent? Are they similar?

19. The 4-in. by 6-in. print at the right was made from a photo slide that measured 24 mm by 36 mm. Are the images congruent? Are the images similar?

4-in. by 6-in. print

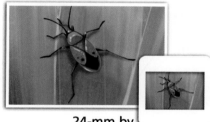

24-mm by 36-mm slide

For 20–22, use the figure at the right.
Points *D*, *E*, and *F* are midpoints of the three sides of equilateral triangle *ABC*.

20. Which triangles in the figure are similar?

21. Which triangles are also congruent?

22. Name all the trapezoids in the figure. Are they all similar? Are they all congruent?

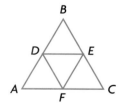

MIXED REVIEW AND TEST PREP

23. Subtract. $3^2 - 2^3$ (p. 266)

24. Multiply. 30.2×0.75 (p. 80)

25. Write $\frac{27}{4}$ as a mixed number. (p. 186)

⭐26. **TEST PREP** The cafeteria buys packs of peanuts for $0.19 each and sells them for $0.50. How many packs must be sold to earn at least $10 more than the cost of the packs? (p. 88)

A 20   **B** 33   **C** 53   **D** 120

⭐27. **TEST PREP** Which type of triangle has no congruent sides? (p. 356)

F scalene   **G** equilateral   **H** isosceles   **J** isosceles right

EXTRA PRACTICE page 388, Set C

387

Set A (pp. 376–379)

Use a compass to decide which two line segments in each group are congruent.

1.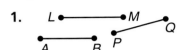

2.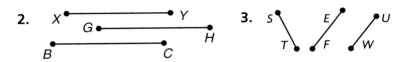

3.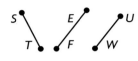

Find the measure of each angle, using a protractor. Then tell whether the angles in each pair are congruent. Write *yes* or *no*.

4.

5.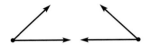

6.

Use a compass and a straightedge to construct a figure congruent to the given figure.

7.

8.

9.

10.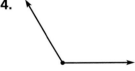

11.

12.

Set B (pp. 380–382)

Trace the figure. Then bisect it.

1.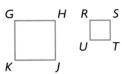

2.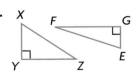

3.

4.

5.

6.

Set C (pp. 384–387)

Use ~ or ≅ to compare the figures if they appear to be similar or congruent. If the figures appear not to be similar or congruent, write *neither*.

1. G   H   R   S
   K   J   U   T

2. X   F   G
   Y   Z   E

3. L   M

1. **VOCABULARY** When you divide an angle into two equal parts, you __?__ the angle. (p. 380)

2. **VOCABULARY** The point halfway between the endpoints of a segment is the __?__ of the segment. (p. 380)

3. **VOCABULARY** Figures that have the same shape but not necessarily the same size are __?__ . (p. 384)

Use a compass to decide which two line segments in each group are congruent. (pp. 376–379)

4.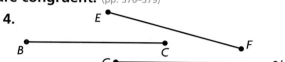

5.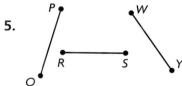

Find the measure of each angle, using a protractor. Then tell whether the angles in each pair are congruent. Write *yes* or *no*. (pp. 376–379)

6.

7.

For 8–14, use a compass and a straightedge.

8. Construct two lines that are parallel. (p. 383)

9. Draw a line segment. Construct a line segment congruent to it. (pp. 376–379)

10. Draw an angle. Construct an angle congruent to it. (pp. 376–379)

Trace the figure. Then bisect it. (pp. 380–382)

11.

12.

13.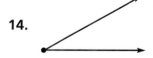

14.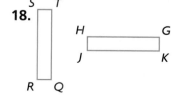

Use ∼ or ≅ to compare the figures if they appear to be similar or congruent. If the figures appear not to be similar or congruent, write *neither*. (pp. 384–387)

15.

16.

17.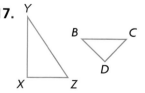

18.

19. The perimeter of a triangle is 54 cm. Two of the sides measure 17 cm and 19 cm. If the third side is bisected, what is the measure of each of the new line segments formed? (pp. 380–382)

20. If ∠*DEF* is congruent to ∠*ABC*, and ∠*GHI* is congruent to ∠*DEF,* what can you conclude about ∠*ABC* and ∠*GHI*?

(pp. 376–379)

NUMBER SENSE, CONCEPTS, AND OPERATIONS

1. The table shows the wages of four workers at a pet store.

PET STORE WAGES	
Job	Wage (per hour)
Inventory Manager	$6.85
Cashier	$6.25
Manager	$10.25
Pet Caretaker	$8.75

On Wednesday, only the manager and pet caretaker worked. What are the total combined wages for the manager and pet caretaker for an 8-hour day?

A $82   **C** $152

B $132   **D** $182

2. Lisa has a 25-foot roll of ribbon. She needs $1\frac{1}{2}$ feet of ribbon for each gift bow she will make. How many bows can she make from the roll of ribbon?

F 15   **H** 17

G 16   **J** 18

3. The Dames Point Bridge in Jacksonville, Florida, is 396 meters long. Which of the following shows only numbers that 396 is divisible by?

A 2, 3, 4, 6, 8, and 9

B 2, 3, 4, 6, and 9

C 2, 3, 5, and 6

D 2, 3, 4, 6, 9, and 10

4. Explain It What is the prime factorization of 180? Explain how you found the answer.

 **MEASUREMENT**

5. What is the wingspan, or width from one wingtip to the other, of the butterfly below to the **nearest** centimeter?

centimeters

F 2 centimeters   **H** 3.5 centimeters

G 3 centimeters   **J** 4 centimeters

6. The local weather station keeps a record of daily temperatures. One day's high temperature is shown on the thermometer at the right. Which was that day's high temperature?

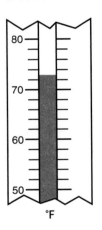

A 70°F   **C** 72°F

B 71°F   **D** 73°F

7. Explain It Jake is measuring the angle in the drawing below. What is the measure of the angle? Explain your answer.

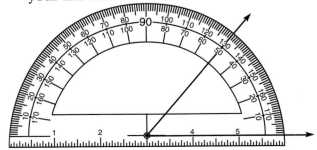

DATA ANALYSIS AND PROBABILITY

8. Mrs. Lewis collected data on the mean number of girls and boys in the 4th, 5th, and 6th grade classes. The table below shows the data.

MEAN NUMBER OF STUDENTS PER CLASS			
Grade	4th	5th	6th
Girls	12	16	10
Boys	14	14	12

Which type of graph would be **best** for displaying the data?

F a stem-and-leaf plot

G a circle graph

H a double-bar graph

J a box-and-whisker plot

9. The frequency table shows the weights of dogs available for adoption at the Best Friend Animal Shelter.

WEIGHTS OF DOGS		
Weight (pounds)	Frequency	Cumulative Frequency
4–12	5	5
13–21	6	11
22–30	12	23
31–39	7	30
40 or more	10	40

Sherrie wants to adopt a dog that weighs more than 12 pounds but less than 31 pounds. How many dogs does she have to choose from?

A 12   **C** 23

B 18   **D** 30

10. Explain It The owner of Freeway Motors wants to find the mean price of the cars sold the previous year. Explain how the owner can do this.

GEOMETRY AND SPATIAL SENSE

11. James decorated his room with figures that were both similar and congruent.

> **TIP** Look for **important words.** See item 11. Note the word *both* in the directions for finding the answer. The figures must be congruent.

Which of the following shows the figures that James could have used?

F

G

H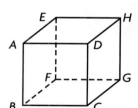

J

12. In the cube at the right, which line segments are parallel?

A $\overline{EH}$ and $\overline{BC}$

B $\overline{AB}$ and $\overline{AD}$

C $\overline{FG}$ and $\overline{AE}$

D $\overline{BF}$ and $\overline{HG}$

13. Explain It The projection arms in Acme overhead projectors form 149° angles as shown. Explain how you could check the angle for the correct measurement before the projector is sold.

18 Geometry and Motion

⫸FAST FACT • SCIENCE There are at least 1,800 species of starfish. Starfish come in different colors and many have line symmetry.

PROBLEM SOLVING In your classroom, look for an object that is shaped like one of the polygons in the line plot. Sketch the object and show its lines of symmetry.

NUMBER OF LINES OF SYMMETRY FOR REGULAR POLYGONS

Check What You Know

Use this page to help you review and remember important skills needed for Chapter 18.

✅ Slides, Flips, and Turns

Write *slide*, *flip*, or *turn* to describe the motion.

1.

2.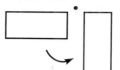

3.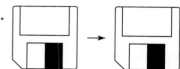

4.

5.

6.

✅ Line Symmetry

Trace the figure. Draw the lines of symmetry.

7.

8.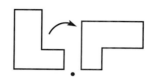

9.

10.

11.

12.

13.

14.

VOCABULARY POWER

REVIEW

congruent [kən•grōō′ənt] *adjective*

Congruent figures have the same size and shape. Draw a picture of congruent figures to show your understanding.

PREVIEW

transformation line symmetry

translation   line of symmetry

rotation   rotational

reflection   symmetry

tessellation   point of rotation

 www.harcourtschool.com/mathglossary

ON-LINE

Transformations of Plane Figures

Learn how to use translations, rotations, and reflections to transform geometric shapes.

Vocabulary

transformation

translation

rotation

reflection

Estimate the measure of each angle.

1. 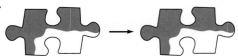 2. 3.

4. 5.

A movement of a figure without changing the size or shape of the figure is a rigid **transformation**. Since the size and shape do not change, the original figure and the transformation are always congruent.

A **translation** is the movement of a figure along a straight line.

Only the location of the figure changes with translation.

Turning a figure around a point is called a **rotation**.

Both the position and the location of the figure can change.

A point of rotation can be on or outside a figure.

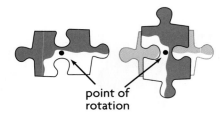

point of rotation

Flipping a figure over a line is called a **reflection** about that line.

Both the position and the location of the figure change with reflection.

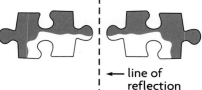

← line of reflection

EXAMPLE 1

Draw a 90° clockwise rotation of the figure around the given point of rotation.

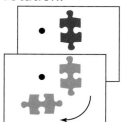

Trace the figure and the point of rotation.

Place your pencil on the point of rotation.

Rotate the figure clockwise 90°.

Trace the figure in its new location.

• How would the rotation look if you turned the figure 180°?

EXAMPLE 2

Draw a horizontal reflection and a vertical reflection of the shape of the state of Florida.

Trace the figure and the vertical line of reflection.

Reflect the figure horizontally over the line. This is a horizontal reflection.

Trace the figure in its new location.

Use the same process for a horizontal line of reflection.

Reflect the figure vertically over the line. This is a vertical reflection.

Trace the figure in its new location.

• Rotate the original state shape 90° clockwise about a point in its upper left corner.

CHECK FOR UNDERSTANDING

Think and ▶ Discuss

Look back at the lesson to answer each question.

1. **Explain** why a rigid transformation is always congruent to the original figure.

2. **Describe** how the new position of a figure that has been rotated 360° compares with its original position.

Guided ▶ Practice

Tell which type or types of transformation the second figure is of the first figure. Write *translation, rotation,* or *reflection*.

3.   4.   5.   6.

Tell what moves were made to transform each figure into its next positions.

7.    8.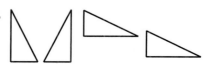

Independent ▶ Practice

Tell which type or types of transformation the second figure is of the first figure. Write *translation*, *rotation*, or *reflection*.

9.
10.
11.
12.

Tell what moves were made to transform each figure into its next positions.

13.
14.

Trace each figure. Draw a 90° clockwise rotation around the given point followed by a horizontal reflection and a vertical translation.

15.
16.
17.
18.

Problem Solving ▶ Applications

19. Kathy is working on a design for a logo. She drew a profile of an eagle and wants to have two eagles facing each other. What transformation should she do to the profile?

20. The mirror image of the word AMBULANCE is written on the front of ambulances so that it can be read in a car's rearview mirror. Identify the transformation and write the word as it appears on the front of the ambulance.

21. **REASONING** Draw a figure that looks the same when transformed by rotation and by reflection. Describe the location of the point of rotation and the line of reflection.

22. **≡FAST FACT • SCIENCE** The record low temperature in Hawaii is 12°F, and the record high temperature is 100°F. What is the range of these temperatures?

MIXED REVIEW AND TEST PREP

23. Draw the next three figures in the geometric pattern at the right. (p. 319)

24. Evaluate $9y - 8$ for $y = 1, 2, 3,$ and 4. (p. 260)

25. Write 342,006,509 in expanded form. (p. 16)

26. Write the decimal for 45%. (p. 68)

⭐ 27. **TEST PREP** Mike, Lily, and Sue shared a pizza that had 8 slices. There are $1\frac{1}{2}$ slices left. Mike had 2 slices, and Lily had $2\frac{1}{2}$ slices. How many slices did Sue have? (p. 210)

 A $1\frac{1}{2}$ slices   **B** 2 slices   **C** $2\frac{1}{4}$ slices   **D** $2\frac{1}{2}$ slices

EXTRA PRACTICE page 406, Set A

Tessellations

Learn how to use polygons to make tessellations and how to make figures for tessellations.

QUICK REVIEW

Tell which type of transformation the second figure is of the first figure.

1. A^A   2. A A   3. A   4. A   5. A

Vocabulary

tessellation

A repeating arrangement of shapes that completely covers a portion of a plane, with no gaps and no overlaps, is called a **tessellation**. Although most tessellations are made by humans, a few occur in nature.

The tessellation of hexagons shown below models a honeycomb.

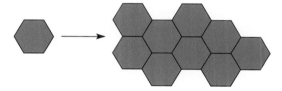

• Can a tessellation be formed by using a square?

In addition to being made from polygons, tessellations can be made from figures that are not polygons.

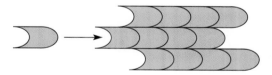

Activity 1

You need: pattern blocks, colored pencils or markers

Make a tessellation.

• Choose a pattern block to use for your tessellation shape.

• Design your tessellation. Remember that the shapes must fit together without overlapping or leaving gaps.

• Record your tessellation. Color it to make a pleasing design.

397

Math Idea ▶ Using regular polygons that can form tessellations, you can make other shapes that tessellate the plane.

Activity 2

You need: paper, scissors, and tape

Make a tessellation shape.

• Cut out a square that is 2 in. × 2 in.

• Use scissors to cut out a part of the square on one side.

• Translate the cutout part of the square to the opposite side of the square. Then tape it.

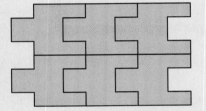

• Trace the new shape to form at least two rows of a tessellation. You can rotate, translate, or reflect the shape.

• **What if,** after you cut out part of a square, you didn't tape the cutout to the opposite side? Could the shape tessellate the plane? Explain.

CHECK FOR UNDERSTANDING

Think and ▶
Discuss

Look back at the lesson to answer each question.

1. **Explain** how you know when a pattern of shapes forms a tessellation.

2. **Give an example** of a shape that does not form a tessellation.

Guided ▶
Practice

Trace and cut out several of each polygon. Tell whether the polygon can be used to form a tessellation. Write *yes* or *no*.

3.   4.   5.   6.

Make the tessellation shape described by each pattern. Then form two rows of a tessellation by using transformations.

TECHNOLOGY LINK

More Practice:
Harcourt Mega Math
Ice Station Exploration,
Polar Planes, Level O

7.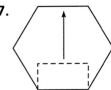

8.

9.

PRACTICE AND PROBLEM SOLVING

Independent ▶
Practice

Trace and cut out several of each shape. Tell whether the shape can be used to form a tessellation. Write *yes* or *no*.

10.

11.

12.

13.

Make the tessellation shape described by each pattern. Then form two rows of a tessellation by using transformations.

14.

15.

16.

17.

Problem Solving ▶
Applications

18. Cut out a regular hexagon, and then change it by cutting out a part on one side. Translate the cutout part to the opposite side of the hexagon. Does this new shape form a tessellation?

19. ✏️ **Write About It** Explain why you can translate a cutout from the side of a regular hexagon to the opposite side when you want to make a tessellation pattern.

20. Vocabulary Power A polygon is a closed plane figure with straight sides that are line segments. Explain why a circle is not a polygon.

MIXED REVIEW AND TEST PREP

21. Tell which type of transformation the second figure is of the first figure. (p. 394)

22. $25 \div 5 + (7 - 3)^2$ (p. 48)

23. $\frac{3}{4} + \frac{1}{6}$ (p. 206)   **24.** Solve. $x - 8 = 40$ (p. 280)

⭐**25. TEST PREP** Susan has run for five days. The distances of her runs were 4.5 mi, 3 mi, 4 mi, 3.5 mi, and 5 mi. How many miles will she have to run the sixth day for her mean distance to be 4.5 mi? (p. 118)

A 3.5 mi   **B** 4 mi   **C** 7 mi   **D** 27 mi

EXTRA PRACTICE page 406, Set B

PROBLEM SOLVING STRATEGY
Make a Model

Learn how to solve problems that involve transformations by making a model.

 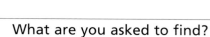

Robert divided a square grid into two separate polygons as shown at the right. Are the blue and yellow polygons congruent?

Analyze

What are you asked to find?

What information are you given?

Is there information you will not use? If so, what?

Choose

What strategy will you use?

You can use the strategy *make a model*.

Solve

How will you solve the problem?

Trace, color, and cut out a copy of the blue polygon. Then transform (reflect, rotate, or translate) the blue polygon and compare it to the yellow polygon.

You can rotate the blue polygon 180° clockwise about the point marked by the pencil. The copy of the blue polygon matches the yellow polygon exactly, so the polygons are congruent.

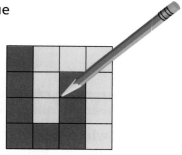

Check

How can you check your answer?

What if Robert wants to use the figure at the right to cover the top of a table? Will this figure tessellate a plane? Make a model to test your ideas.

PROBLEM SOLVING PRACTICE

PROBLEM SOLVING STRATEGIES

Draw a Diagram or Picture

▶ **Make a Model**

Predict and Test

Work Backward

Make an Organized List

Find a Pattern

Make a Table or Graph

Solve a Simpler Problem

Write an Equation

Use Logical Reasoning

Solve the problem by making a model.

1. What transformation can you perform to show that the figures at the right are congruent?

2. Are the polygons shown at the right congruent? Explain.

Three holes are drilled into a wall in a straight line. Hole 2 is between hole 1 and hole 3. The distance between hole 1 and hole 3 is 18 cm. The distance between hole 1 and hole 2 is $\frac{1}{3}$ the distance between hole 1 and hole 3.

3. What is the distance between hole 1 and hole 2?

   A 5 cm   **C** 9 cm

   B 6 cm   **D** 12 cm

4. What is the distance between hole 2 and hole 3?

   F 5 cm   **H** 9 cm

   G 6 cm   **J** 12 cm

MIXED STRATEGY PRACTICE

Use Data For 5–6, use the table.

5. Find the median temperature.

6. Make a stem-and-leaf plot of the temperature data.

HIGH TEMPERATURES IN MIAMI						
Mon	Tue	Wed	Thurs	Fri	Sat	Sun
100	91	93	95	89	89	94

7. Shelley wants to make a quilt out of tessellating shapes. Which of the following shapes can she use?

   a.   **b.**

8. Ed had $40 when he went to the mall. He spent $24.88 on a shirt and $8.42 on a CD. Estimate how much he had left for lunch.

9. Bernie, Nash, Lisa, and Gerta are standing in the lunch line. Bernie is not first in line. Lisa has at least two people ahead of her in line. Nash is third. Give the order of the four in line.

10. A palindrome is a number that is the same backward and forward, such as 1,221. Find a three-digit palindrome in which the product of the digits is divisible by 35.

11. Victor's store had 3,500 CDs at the beginning of the month. He put aside $\frac{1}{7}$ of them and sold $\frac{1}{2}$ of the remaining CDs. How many CDs did he sell?

12. ✎ **Write a problem** that involves transformations and can be solved by making a model. Exchange problems with a classmate and solve.

Symmetry

Learn how to identify line symmetry and rotational symmetry.

Vocabulary

line symmetry

line of symmetry

rotational symmetry

point of rotation

QUICK REVIEW

Give the degree equivalent of each fractional portion of a full rotation.

1. $\frac{1}{4}$ 2. $\frac{1}{2}$ 3. $\frac{1}{8}$ 4. $\frac{3}{5}$ 5. $\frac{2}{3}$

Symmetry can be found all around us, both in nature and in manufactured objects. This Oregon Swallowtail butterfly has symmetry because each wing looks like a reflection of the other.

A figure has **line symmetry** if it can be folded or reflected so that the two parts of the figure match, or are congruent. The line across which the figure is symmetric is known as the **line of symmetry**.

Activity 1

You need: paper, scissors, dark crayon

• Fold the paper in half. Use the crayon to write your name in cursive along the fold line.

• Fold the paper along the fold line so your name is inside. Use the handle of the scissors to make a rubbing of your name.

• Unfold the paper. Your name appears on the other half of the paper. Your design has line symmetry.

• Where is the line of symmetry in the design you made from your name?

• How many lines of symmetry does the design have?

Some figures have several lines of symmetry.

EXAMPLE 1

Find all the lines of symmetry in the regular hexagon.

Trace the figure and cut it out.

Fold it in half in different ways.

If the halves match, then the fold is a line of symmetry.
Count the different lines of symmetry.

Remember that regular polygons have all sides congruent and all angles congruent.

The figure has six lines of symmetry.

• Do all hexagons have six lines of symmetry? Explain.

Letters and whole words can have lines of symmetry.

EXAMPLE 2

Do the words DECIDED and MUM have line symmetry?

Copy each word.

Draw the dashed lines as shown.

Each word can be folded so that the two halves match.

So, the words have line symmetry.

A figure has **rotational symmetry** if it can be rotated less than 360° around its center point, or **point of rotation**, and still look exactly the same as the original figure.

MATH LAB

Activity 2

You need: 4-in.-square paper, scissors

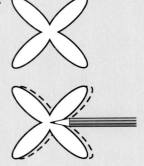

- Fold the square of paper in half and then in half again.

- Draw a petal shape on the folded paper, and cut it out so that the center is connected.

- Trace your flower on a piece of paper.

- Match the cutout flower with its tracing. Place the point of your pencil at the center of the cutout.

- Rotate the flower, using the point of the pencil as the point of rotation, until it matches the tracing again. The figure you made has rotational symmetry.

- What part of a turn brings the figure back to its original position?

EXAMPLE 3

Does the figure of the starfish below have rotational symmetry? If it does, what are the fraction and the angle measure of each turn?

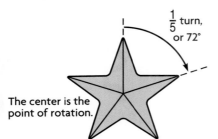

$\frac{1}{5}$ turn, or 72°

The center is the point of rotation.

Trace the figure.

Place your pencil point at the point of rotation.

Rotate the figure until it looks like the original figure.

Use a protractor to measure the degree and fraction of rotation.

The figure has $\frac{1}{5}$-turn, or 72°, rotational symmetry.

- Does the starfish figure above also have line symmetry?

CHECK FOR UNDERSTANDING

Think and ▶ Discuss

Look back at the lesson to answer each question.

1. **Explain** the difference between line symmetry and rotational symmetry.

2. **Draw** a pentagon that has fewer than five lines of symmetry.

Guided ▶ Practice

Trace the figure. Tell if the figure has line symmetry. If so, draw the lines of symmetry.

3.   4.   5.   6.

Trace the figure. Complete the other half of the figure.

7.   8.   9.   10.

Tell whether each figure has rotational symmetry, and, if so, identify the symmetry as a fraction of a turn and in degrees.

11.   12.   13.   14.

PRACTICE AND PROBLEM SOLVING

Independent ▶ Practice

Trace the figure. Tell if the figure has line symmetry. If so, draw the lines of symmetry.

15.   16.   17.   18.

Trace the figure. Complete the other half of the figure.

19.   20.   21.   22.

23.   24.   25.   26.

Tell whether each figure has rotational symmetry, and, if so, identify the symmetry as a fraction of a turn and in degrees.

27. **28.** **29.** **30.**

Problem Solving ▶ Applications

31. Philip has a square cake. He cuts it along all the lines of symmetry of the square. Will all the pieces be congruent? Will Philip be able to give each of his 10 friends a piece of cake? Explain.

32. *REASONING* Does a circle have line symmetry? rotational symmetry? Explain.

33. (?) What's the Error? Nick says that all figures have rotational symmetry, because when you rotate any figure 360° it matches up. What's his error?

MIXED REVIEW AND TEST PREP

Tell which type or types of transformation the second figure is of the first figure. (p. 394)

34.  **35.**   **36.**

⭐**37. TEST PREP** Which shows the prime factorization of 36? (p. 168)

   A $3 \times 2 \times 2$ **B** $3 \times 3 \times 3$ **C** $3^2 \times 2$ **D** $2^2 \times 3^2$

⭐**38. TEST PREP** Don drove 148 miles. Ed drove twice as many miles. How many miles did they travel altogether? (p. 52)

   F 444 miles   **G** 296 miles   **H** 222 miles   **J** 148 miles

---

PROBLEM SOLVING | LiNKUP to Reading

Strategy • Choose Important Information A word problem may contain more information than is needed. You must decide what information you need to solve the problem.

Susan visited her cousin in Guatemala and brought back fabric to make a quilt that will be 3 ft long and 2 ft wide. She has cotton pieces that are 4 in. on a side, cotton-blend pieces that are 3 in. on a side, and wool pieces that are 6 in. on a side. How many squares will she need for a wool quilt?

1. What does the problem ask you to find?

2. What information is needed to solve the problem?

3. Tell the important information in this problem. Then solve.
Pauline will fold two pieces of paper along each of their lines of symmetry one time. One is a square measuring 3 in. on a side, and one is a rectangle measuring 4 in. by 8 in. How many folds must she make in all?

EXTRA PRACTICE page 406, Set C

Set A (pp. 394–396)

Tell which type or types of transformation the second figure is of the first figure. Write *translation*, *rotation*, or *reflection*.

1.
2.
3.
4.

5. Eric starts a math test with his paper face down. What type of transformation can he use so that his paper is face up?

Set B (pp. 397–399)

Trace and cut out several of each shape. Tell whether the shape can be used to form a tessellation. Write *yes* or *no*.

1.
2.
3.
4.

5. Jill wants to make a design using one of these shapes: octagon, circle, or equilateral triangle. She wants the design to tessellate a plane. Which shape can she use?

Set C (pp. 402–405)

Trace the figure. Tell if the figure has line symmetry. If so, draw the lines of symmetry.

1.
2.
3.
4.

Tell whether each figure has rotational symmetry, and, if so, identify the symmetry as a fraction of a turn and in degrees.

5.
6.
7.
8.

9. Dale made a garden in the shape of an equilateral triangle. Then he used all possible lines of symmetry to separate the garden into sections. If he plants 3 rosebushes in each section, how many will he need in all?

1. **VOCABULARY**   A movement of a plane or solid figure without changing the figure's size or shape is a rigid ___?___ . (p. 394)

2. **VOCABULARY**   A repeating arrangement of shapes that completely covers a portion of a plane with no overlaps or gaps is called a ___?___ . (p. 397)

3. **VOCABULARY**   A line across which a figure is symmetric is known as a ___?___ . (p. 402)

Tell which type or types of transformation the second figure is of the first figure. Write *translation*, *rotation*, or *reflection*. (pp. 394–396)

4.

5.

6.

7.

Trace and cut out several of each polygon. Tell whether the polygon can be used to form a tessellation. Write *yes* or *no*. (pp. 397–399)

8.

9.

10.

11.

Make the tessellation shape described by each pattern. Then form two rows of a tessellation by using transformations. (pp. 397–399)

12.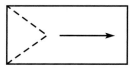

13.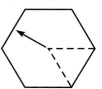

14.

15.

Trace the figure. Tell if the figure has line symmetry. If so, draw the lines of symmetry. (pp. 402–405)

16.

17.

18.

19.

Tell whether each figure has rotational symmetry, and, if so, identify the symmetry as a fraction of a turn and in degrees. (pp. 402–405)

20.

21.

22.

23.

24. Richard builds a wall 6 full bricks wide, starting and ending every other layer with a half of a brick. The figure shows the first 3 layers of the wall. How many full bricks and how many half bricks does he need for 8 layers? (pp. 400–401)

25. There are 6 shelves that are 18 inches apart, and the bottom shelf is 24 inches from the floor. How far from the floor is the top shelf? (pp. 400–401)

MEASUREMENT

 ALGEBRAIC THINKING

1. Gabrielle earns extra money selling vegetables. Her vegetable garden is 15 feet wide by 24 feet long. Which of the following shows the area of the vegetable garden?

 A 560 square feet

 B 360 square feet

 C 340 square feet

 D 144 square feet

2. Based on the scale provided, what is the approximate distance from Hampton to Shelville to Margate?

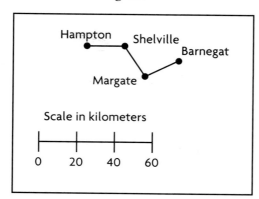

 F 10 kilometers

 G 20 kilometers

 H 40 kilometers

 J 80 kilometers

3. Which of the following is the **best** estimate of the height of a classroom door?

 A 8 miles **C** 8 feet

 B 8 yards **D** 8 inches

4. **Explain It** A movie begins at 2:15 P.M. and ends at 4:10 P.M. How long does the movie last? Explain your answer.

5. Randy is using the following pattern to make decorations to sell at a crafts fair.

 If the pattern continues, which of the following figures will come next?

 F   **H**

 G   **J**

6. Bruce makes phone calls for his club. The table below shows the relationship between x, the number of calls he makes, and y, the length of time it takes to make the calls.

 > **TIP** **Get the information you need.** See item 6. First, identify the pattern. How does y change as x increases by 1? When you see the pattern, apply it to find y when x is 6.

x	2	3	4	5	6
y	5	7	9	11	■

 How long will it take him to make 6 calls?

 A 3 minutes **C** 15 minutes

 B 13 minutes **D** 16 minutes

7. **Explain It** Elise works $7\frac{1}{2}$ hours each day. She is paid d dollars per hour. Write an expression to show her earnings for one day. Then evaluate the expression for $d = \$8.40$. Explain your reasoning.

8. Vivian repairs computers at her company. She said the P4 Computer had 25% fewer repairs during a five-month period than the T6 Computer had during the same five months. The graph below shows the number of repairs for both computers over the last five months.

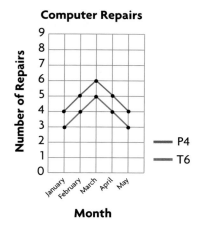

Computer Repairs

Which of the following statements **best** describes the data shown on the graph?

F The P4 did have fewer repairs.

G The P4 had fewer repairs but not 25% fewer.

H The T6 had fewer repairs than the P4.

J Both computers had the same number of repairs.

9. The mean of 5 numbers is 25.6. Which of the following is the sum of the numbers?

A 128   **C** 306

B 261   **D** 1,280

10. **Explain It** Jon had these scores for five rounds of golf: 78, 85, 72, 75, 73. After the sixth round, the range of his scores was 15. What scores might he have gotten on his sixth round? Explain your reasoning.

11. Roy used a regular polygon to make a tessellation. Which of the following figures was NOT the polygon he used?

F 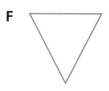   **H**

G    **J**

12. Annie, Bob, Heidi, and Dedee printed their names in block capital letters. Three of the names have line symmetry. Which name does NOT have line symmetry?

A ANNIE

B BOB

C HEIDI

D DEDEE

13. Which type of transformation of Figure 1 is shown by Figure 2 below?

Figure 1   Figure 2

F translation   **H** reflection

G rotation   **J** symmetry

14. **Explain It** Two different rectangular gardens have a perimeter of 24 feet. Are the gardens similar or congruent? Explain.

IT'S IN THE BAG!

Gift Bag Geometry Journal

PROJECT Make a journal of geometry questions and answers.

Materials

- One medium-size gift bag
- Six sheets of white paper
- Markers
- Scissors
- Stapler
- Glue
- One sheet of colored paper

Directions

1. Cut the bottom and sides off the bag, leaving the handles in place. Staple the left edges of the white papers in between the remaining front and back pieces of the gift bag. (*Picture A*)

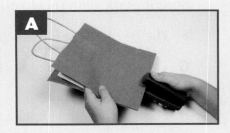

2. Glue the colored paper onto the front cover, and label it *GEOMETRY JOURNAL*. Then decorate the cover. (*Picture B*)

3. Write 10–12 questions about the geometry topics that you studied in Unit 5. Write two questions on each page of your journal. Include questions that require you to provide an explanation for your answer. For example, *Can two lines be both parallel and intersecting? Explain your answer*. (*Picture C*)

4. Write an answer for each question in your journal.

Stretching Figures

Learn how to stretch a geometric figure.

Melissa is making a small quilt. She found a pattern for a star in a quilting book. She will cut out the stars she makes and sew them onto the quilt.

Here are the coordinates of the pattern:
(3,7), (4,4), (6,4), (4,3), (5,1), (3,2), (1,1), (2,3), (0,4), (2,4)

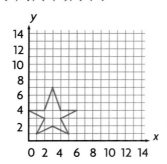

Melissa would like the sides of the pattern to be longer, so she decides to enlarge, or stretch, them by doubling the coordinates.

When she doubles the coordinates, she gets: (6,14), (8,8), (12,8), (8,6), (10,2), (6,4), (2,2), (4,6), (0,8), (4,8)

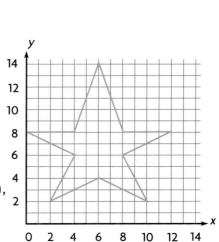

TALK ABOUT IT

What if Melissa wants to make stars of different sizes on her quilt? What coordinates should she use to draw a star if she wants the sides of the star to be five times as long as the original pattern?

TRY IT

Use the figure shown at the right. Give the new coordinates and draw the stretched figure.

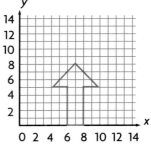

1. Stretch the figure so the sides are twice as long.

2. Stretch the figure so the sides are five times as long.

3. Stretch the figure by doubling only the *x*-coordinates.

4. Stretch the figure by doubling only the *y*-coordinates.

VOCABULARY

1. Two angles whose measures have a sum of 180° are __?__ . (p. 341)

2. A line segment that has both endpoints on a circle and that passes through the center of the circle is a __?__ . (p. 368)

3. A movement of a figure along a straight line is called a __?__ . (p. 394)

4. Figures that have the same shape are called __?__ . (p. 384)

EXAMPLES

EXERCISES

Chapter 15

- **Identify and classify angles.** (pp. 338–339)

  Tell if the angle is *acute, right,* or *obtuse.*

  The angle is acute since its measure is less than 90°.

Tell if each angle is *acute, right,* or *obtuse.*

5.

6.

7.

8.

- **Identify angle relationships.** (pp. 340–343)

  Find the measure of ∠*BOF*.

  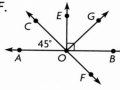

  ∠*BOF* and ∠*COA* are vertical angles and are congruent. So, the measure of ∠*BOF* is 45°.

Find the measure of each angle.

9. ∠*XTY*

10. ∠*ZTR*

11. ∠*YTZ*

12. ∠*RTV*

13. ∠*VTZ*

14. ∠*XTR*

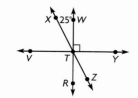

Chapter 16

- **Classify triangles.** (pp. 356–359)

  Find the measure of the unknown angle, and classify the triangle by its angles.

  $180° - (60° + 60°) =$
  $180° - 120° = 60°$

  The measure of the angle is 60°.

  The triangle is an acute triangle.

Find the measure of the unknown angle, and classify the triangle by its angles.

15.

16.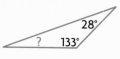

17.

18.

- **Classify quadrilaterals.** (pp. 362–365)

Give the most exact name for the figure.

Opposite sides are congruent and parallel. There are 4 right angles. So, the figure is a square.

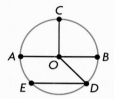

Give the most exact name for the figure.

19.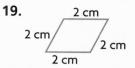

20.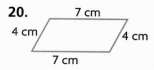

- **Identify parts of a circle.** (pp. 368–369)

$\overline{AB}$ is a diameter.

$\overline{OC}$ is a radius.

$\overline{DE}$ is a chord.

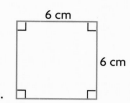

Name the given parts of the circle.

21. chord

22. diameter

23. radius

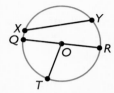

Chapter 17

- **Identify similar and congruent figures.** (pp. 384–387)

Similar figures have the same shape.

Congruent figures have the same shape and the same size.

Use ∼ or ≅ to compare the figures if they appear to be similar or congruent. Write *neither* if the figures appear not to be similar or congruent.

24.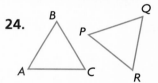

25.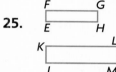

Chapter 18

- **Use translations, rotations, and reflections to transform geometric shapes.** (pp. 394–396)

A *translation* moves a figure along a straight line.

A *rotation* turns a figure around a point.

A *reflection* flips a figure over a line.

Tell which type of transformation the second figure is of the first figure. Write *translation*, *rotation*, or *reflection*.

26.

27.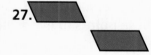

28.

29.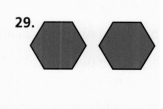

PROBLEM SOLVING APPLICATIONS

30. Eight players were in a tennis match. Each player had to play every other player. How many matches did they play altogether? (pp. 360–361)

31. Juan made a model of an octagonal prism. How many vertices and how many edges did his model have? (pp. 360–361)

Performance Assessment

TASK A • On the Border

Materials: poster board, markers, ruler, compass, straightedge

Mrs. Hansen needs a new border to decorate the walls of her math classroom. She wants student volunteers to make designs on 1-foot by 3-foot pieces of poster board. Each design must show the following:

- at least three different polygons
- similar and congruent figures
- at least two different transformations

a. Make a design for the border. Describe the figures in your design.

b. Identify the figures in your design that are similar and the figures that are congruent. Explain how you know.

c. What transformations does your design show?

TASK B • Lines and Angles

Materials: square sheet of paper, straightedge, protractor, colored pencils

Begin with a square sheet of paper. Label the vertices *A*, *B*, *C*, and *D*, as shown in the picture at the right. Then fold the square in half and in half again. Open the square and label the middle points *E*, *F*, *G*, and *H*. Label the center *O*. Draw lines from each of these points to every other labeled point, as shown.

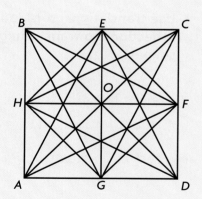

a. Use letters to name a rectangle, a square, and a rhombus that you see in the figure. Add letters to the drawing if needed.

b. Name two vertical angles. Measure your angles to check.

c. Name two complementary angles and two supplementary angles.

d. Use letters to name parallel lines, perpendicular lines, and intersecting lines.

e. Find a quadrilateral and a trapezoid in the drawing. Color the quadrilateral blue and the trapezoid red. Color an acute triangle green, an obtuse triangle yellow, and a right triangle orange.

Technology Linkup

Lines, Angles, and Plane Figures

You can use the drawing toolbar of a word processor to draw line segments, angles, and plane figures.

Open the drawing toolbar. Different icons help you draw many different kinds of figures, such as lines, rays, angles, circles, and polygons.

- To draw an angle, click the black arrow icon on the toolbar. Move the cursor to the place on the page where you want to draw the angle. Click and drag the mouse to draw a ray.

- Click the black arrow icon again. Set the crossbar on the endpoint of the first ray. Click and drag to complete the angle.

- Click on one of the rays. Click and drag the arrow of the ray to change the size of the angle.

- To draw a circle, click the *AutoShapes* icon. Highlight *Basic Shapes* and click the oval icon. Go to the place on the page where you want to draw the circle. Holding down the shift key, click and drag to insert a circle.

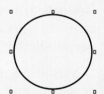

- To draw the diameter, click the circle to select it. Then click on the line icon. Set the crossbar on one of the small squares on the circumference of the circle. Click and drag a line segment to the square on the opposite side of the circle.

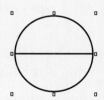

Practice and Problem Solving

Use drawing tools to draw each geometric figure.

1. line segment
2. obtuse angle
3. right angle
4. circle with chord
5. perpendicular lines
6. intersecting lines
7. parallel lines
8. acute triangle
9. right triangle
10. trapezoid
11. circle with radius
12. obtuse triangle

13. **Write About It** Choose one of the figures in Exercises 1–12. Describe how to use drawing tools to draw the figure.

Multimedia Math Glossary www.harcourtschool.com/mathglossary
Vocabulary Power Look up *plane figure* in the Multimedia Math Glossary. Name and describe each of the plane figures shown in the glossary.

PROBLEM SOLVING ON LOCATION
In Louisiana

The Lake Pontchartrain Causeway

Lake Pontchartrain is the largest lake in Louisiana. The bridge above Lake Pontchartrain, named the Lake Pontchartrain Causeway, is about 24 miles long, making it the world's longest bridge over water. The Causeway actually consists of two bridges, also called spans. One span is for northbound traffic and the other is for southbound traffic. The spans are connected by seven "crossovers" which allow drivers moving in each direction to change direction.

For 1–4, use the drawing below, which shows a small section of the Lake Pontchartrain Causeway including two of its crossovers.

1. Describe the relationship between the two spans of the Causeway as parallel, perpendicular, intersecting, or skew.

2. Describe the relationship between a crossover and each span.

3. What types of angles are shown in the drawing?

4. Each span of the Lake Pontchartrain Causeway is 28 feet wide, and the spans are 80 feet apart. What is the total width of the Causeway?

5. Measurements taken at the north end of Lake Pontchartrain show that the water level has been rising about 0.45 cm per year since 1931. By about how much did the water level rise from 1950 to 2000?

6. ✏️ **Write About It** Find a photo of a bridge in your state. Identify and describe any lines, angles, and other plane figures that you see in the photo.

The Lake Pontchartrain Causeway

The Louisiana Superdome opened on August 3, 1975.

Louisiana Superdome

The Louisiana Superdome is a huge indoor arena located in New Orleans. Many events, such as college and professional basketball and football games, concerts, and circuses, take place there each year. The Superdome had 87,500 people at a concert in 1981 and holds the world record for attendance at an indoor concert.

Use Data   For 1–4, use the diagram below. The diagram shows a cross section of the Louisiana Superdome. Six sections representing six different seating types are shown in color in the diagram.

1. What geometric term can be used to describe all six sections?

2. What geometric figure is represented by the Terrace section?

3. What is the most exact name for the geometric figure represented by the Plaza section?

4. **Stretch Your Thinking** An isosceles trapezoid is a trapezoid whose two non-parallel sides are congruent. Which of the seating sections in the Superdome appears to have the shape of an isosceles trapezoid?

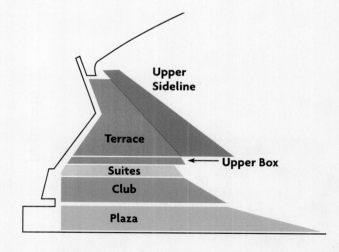

5. The Superdome contains 400 miles of electrical wiring and fiber optic lines. How many feet of electrical wiring and fiber optic lines does the arena contain?

6. The diameter of the Superdome's circular dome is 680 ft long. What is the length of the radius of the dome?

19 Units of Measure

≣FAST FACT • SOCIAL STUDIES
Of the two waterfalls that make up Niagara Falls, American Falls is 9 ft higher than Horseshoe Falls.

PROBLEM SOLVING The graph shows the heights of some other waterfalls in North America. How many yards higher is Takakkaw Falls than American Falls?

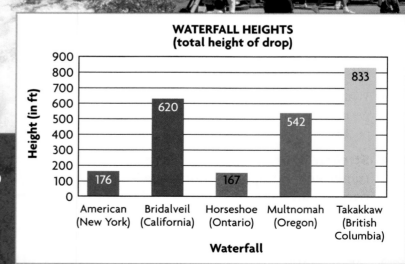

WATERFALL HEIGHTS
(total height of drop)

Height (in ft)

Waterfall	Height
American (New York)	176
Bridalveil (California)	620
Horseshoe (Ontario)	167
Multnomah (Oregon)	542
Takakkaw (British Columbia)	833

Check What You Know

Use this page to help you review and remember important skills needed for Chapter 19.

 Customary Conversions

Complete.

1. 1 ft = ▪ in.
2. 1 gal = ▪ qt
3. 1 yd = ▪ ft
4. 1 qt = ▪ c
5. 36 in. = ▪ 1 ft
6. 8 qt = ▪ gal
7. 6 ft = ▪ yd
8. 12 c = ▪ qt

 Multiply by 10, 100, and 1,000

Use mental math to complete.

9. $1 \times 0.2 = 0.2$
   $10 \times 0.2 = 2$
   $100 \times 0.2 = 20$
   $1,000 \times 0.2 = $ ▪

10. $1 \times 3.64 = 3.64$
    $10 \times 3.64 = 36.4$
    $100 \times 3.64 = 364$
    $1,000 \times 3.64 = $ ▪

11. $1 \times 0.527 = 0.527$
    $10 \times 0.527 = 5.27$
    $100 \times 0.527 = $ ▪
    $1,000 \times 0.527 = $ ▪

12. $1 \times 0.28 = 0.28$
    $10 \times 0.28 = $ ▪
    $100 \times 0.28 = $ ▪
    $1,000 \times 0.28 = $ ▪

Multiply each number by 10, by 100, and by 1,000.

13. 0.7
14. 0.61
15. 0.008
16. 0.026
17. 0.3289
18. 3.98
19. 45.69
20. 2.0703

 Compare Numbers

Compare. Write < or > for each ●.

21. 1.01 ● 1.1
22. $1\frac{1}{4}$ ● $1\frac{1}{2}$
23. 87 ● 85
24. 576 ● 479
25. 0.7 ● 0.35
26. 9.23 ● 9.31
27. 0 ● $\frac{1}{16}$
28. 2,108 ● 2,110
29. 3.1 ● 2.9
30. $\frac{7}{8}$ ● $\frac{3}{4}$
31. 10.1 ● 9.09
32. 0.5 ● 0.06

Vocabulary Power

REVIEW

centimeter [sen′tə•mē•tər] *noun*

A centimeter is a measure of length that is equal to $\frac{1}{100}$ of a meter. Other words that begin with *cent* include *century*, *centennial*, and *centipede*. What do these words have in common with the word *centimeter*?

PREVIEW

precision

 www.harcourtschool.com/mathglossary

Customary Measurements

Learn how to convert between customary units of measure.

The Davis Cup is a prized trophy presented to the nation whose team wins against other nations in a tournament. The trophy was donated in 1900 by American player Dwight F. Davis. Tournament matches are played on a rectangular tennis court that measures 12 yd wide and 26 yd long. How many feet long is the tennis court?

The Davis Cup is 13 in. high and 18 in. across the top.

You can use the rules below to convert between customary units of length.

Math Idea ▶ To convert from a larger unit to a smaller unit, multiply. To convert from a smaller unit to a larger unit, divide.

26 yd = ■ ft

number of	×	number of feet	=	total
yards		in 1 yard		feet
↓		↓		↓
26	×	3	=	78

Since a yard is a larger unit than a foot, and 1 yd = 3 ft, multiply by 3.

So, the tennis court is 78 ft long.

• How many feet wide is the tennis court?

You can also use the rules above to convert between customary units of weight and between customary units of capacity.

EXAMPLE 1

In a powerlifting competition held over 2 days, Chris lifted a total of 992,288 lb. How many tons is 992,288 lb?

992,288 lb = ■ T

992,288 ÷ 2,000 = 496.144

Since a pound is a smaller unit than a ton, and 1 T = 2,000 lb, divide by 2,000.

So, Chris lifted 496.144 T, or about 496 T.

• How many tons is 630,932 lb?

EXAMPLE 2

At a tennis match, there are 20 gal of water in a cooler. There are 32 players at the match. If each player gets the same amount of water, how many quarts are available to each player?

20 gal = ■ qt   *Since a gallon is a larger unit than a quart,*
20 × 4 = 80   *and 1 gal = 4 qt, multiply by 4.*

80 ÷ 32 = $2\frac{1}{2}$ *Divide the total number of quarts by the number of players.*

So, there are $2\frac{1}{2}$ qt of water available to each player.

The same rules apply for converting between different units of time.

EXAMPLE 3

Over 792 days, Canadian Rick Hansen traveled 24,901 mi in his wheelchair, a trip equal to the distance around the Earth at the equator.

A. How many weeks did it take Rick to travel 24,901 mi?

792 days = ■ wk   *Since a day is a smaller unit than a*
792 ÷ 7 = $113\frac{1}{7}$ *week, and 1 wk = 7 days, divide by 7.*

So, it took Rick $113\frac{1}{7}$ wk to travel 24,901 mi.

B. How many hours did it take Rick to travel 24,901 mi?

792 days = ■ hr   *Since a day is a larger unit than an hour,*
792 × 24 = 19,008   *and 1 day = 24 hr, multiply by 24.*

So, it took Rick 19,008 hr to travel 24,901 mi.

• How many minutes did it take Rick to travel 24,901 mi? How many seconds?

CHECK FOR UNDERSTANDING

Think and Discuss ▶ **Look back at the lesson to answer each question.**

1. **Tell** whether you would multiply or divide when converting inches to yards.

2. **Explain** how to convert pounds to ounces.

3. **Explain** whether or not the number of cups of water needed to fill a tub is greater than or less than the number of pints.

Guided Practice ▶ **Convert to the given unit.**

4. 2 qt = ■ pt   **5.** 84 in. = ■ ft   **6.** 8 lb = ■ oz

421

PRACTICE AND PROBLEM SOLVING

Independent ▶
Practice

Convert to the given unit.

7. 10 c = ■ fl oz   **8.** 36 ft = ■ yd   **9.** 8 days = ■ hr

10. 8 oz = ■ lb   **11.** 3.5 T = ■ lb   **12.** 54 in. = ■ yd

13. 20 pt = ■ fl oz   **14.** 15 gal = ■ qt   **15.** 34 pt = ■ qt

16. 36 oz = ■ lb   **17.** 27 c = ■ qt   **18.** 39 in. = ■ ft

19. 48 hr = ■ min   **20.** 24 wk = ■ days   **21.** 93 min = ■ sec

Compare. Write <, >, or = for each ●.

22. 31 ft ● 16 yd   **23.** 144 hr ● 6 days   **24.** 77 fl oz ● 9 c

25. 4 mi ● 7,100 yd   **26.** 12,000 lb ● 5 T   **27.** 41 wk ● 294 days

Problem Solving ▶
Applications

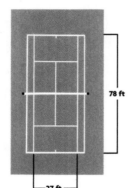
78 ft
27 ft

28. The width of the singles half-court section on a tennis court is $13\frac{1}{2}$ ft. How many yards wide is the singles half-court section?

29. What are the dimensions of a singles tennis court in yards?

30. What are the dimensions of a singles tennis court in inches?

31. ≡**FAST FACT** • SOCIAL STUDIES In 2001, for the first time in U.S. Open Tennis Tournament history, two sisters played against each other for the championship. It took Venus Williams 4,140 sec to defeat her sister Serena Williams in the championship match. How many minutes did the championship match take?

32. Juan says that each guest will drink $2\frac{1}{2}$ c of punch. How many gallons of punch will Juan need for 80 guests to each have $2\frac{1}{2}$ c?

33. *REASONING* If 20 mubs = 5 bliks, which is heavier, a mub or a blik? Explain.

34. ❓ **What's the Error?** A sign on a bridge says, "Weight limit 12,000 lb." Eric's truck weighs 12 tons. He says he will be able to drive across the bridge. What's his error? How many pounds does his truck weigh?

MIXED REVIEW AND TEST PREP

35. Write $\frac{4}{5}$ as a percent. (p. 191)

36. $3\frac{2}{5} \div 2\frac{3}{4}$ (p. 236)

37. $\frac{5}{9} - \frac{1}{2}$ (p. 206)

38. $0.218 + 2.143$ (p. 76)

⭐**39. TEST PREP** Martha had 132 trading cards. She gave $\frac{1}{4}$ to her sister and $\frac{1}{3}$ to her brother. How many trading cards does she have left? (p. 228)

A 33   **B** 44   **C** 55   **D** 77

EXTRA PRACTICE page 436, Set A

Metric Measurements

Learn how to convert between metric units of measure.

Remember

kilo- (k) = 1,000
hecto- (h) = 100
deka- (da) = 10
deci- (d) = 0.1
centi- (c) = 0.01
milli- (m) = 0.001

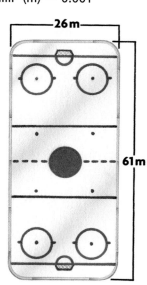

The Stanley Cup is the oldest trophy competed for by professional ice hockey teams in North America. The trophy was donated in 1892 by Sir Frederick Arthur, Lord Stanley of Preston. Ice hockey games are played on an ice rink 61 meters long and 26 meters wide. How many kilometers long is the ice rink?

The original Stanley Cup is displayed in the Hockey Hall of Fame in Toronto, Canada.

One Way You can use the same rules for converting between customary units of length to convert between metric units of length.

To convert from a larger unit to a smaller unit, multiply.
To convert from a smaller unit to a larger unit, divide.

61 m = ■ km

number of ÷ meters	number of meters in 1 kilometer	= total kilometers
↓	↓	↓
61 ÷	1,000	= 0.061

Since a meter is a smaller unit than a kilometer, and 1 km = 1,000 m, divide by 1,000.

So, the ice rink is 0.061 km long.

• How many kilometers wide is the ice rink?

You can also use the rules to convert between metric units of mass and between metric units of capacity.

EXAMPLE 1

It takes about 30.2 kiloliters of water to make the ice for the ice rink. How many liters of water does it take to make the ice?

30.2 kL = ■ L
30.2 × 1,000 = 30,200

Since a kiloliter is a larger unit than a liter, and 1 kL = 1,000 L, multiply by 1,000.

So, it takes 30,200 L of water.

• How many kiloliters are in 1,800 L?

Another Way You can quickly convert between metric units of measure by using the relationship between the units.

Activity

- Look at the chart below. The value of each unit is 10 times the value of the next smaller unit.

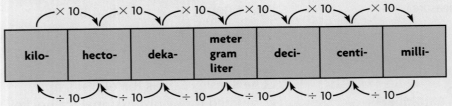

| kilo- | hecto- | deka- | meter gram liter | deci- | centi- | milli- |

To change kilometers to meters, you would multiply by 1,000 ($10 \times 10 \times 10$), or move the decimal three places to the right.

- Convert 10 km to meters. How many places and in what direction did the decimal point move?

- Convert 35.2 mL to deciliters. How many places and in what direction did the decimal point move?

- Describe how you could use the chart to convert between metric units of measure.

Remember that you can quickly find the product or quotient when multiplying or dividing with powers of 10 by moving the decimal point to the right or left.

$$100 \times 3.257 = 325.7$$
$$729.8 \div 1,000 = 0.7298$$

EXAMPLE 2

A hockey puck has a mass of about 164.4 g. Use the chart to find the approximate mass of a hockey puck in kilograms and milligrams.

164.4 g = 0.1644 kg   *Kilograms are 3 places to the left of grams. Move the decimal point 3 places to the left. This is the same as dividing by 1,000.*

164.4 g = 164,400 mg   *Milligrams are 3 places to the right of grams. Move the decimal point 3 places to the right. This is the same as multiplying by 1,000.*

So, a hockey puck weighs about 0.1644 kg, or about 164,400 mg.

CHECK FOR UNDERSTANDING

Think and ▶ Discuss

Look back at the lesson to answer each question.

1. **Tell** what you would multiply or divide by to convert one metric measurement to another.

2. **Explain** how to convert liters to milliliters.

3. **Tell** whether 50 mg is heavier or lighter than 50 cg.

Convert to the given unit.

4. 5 m = ▣ km **5.** 35 cm = ▣ mm **6.** 9 L = ▣ mL

7. 2 g = ▣ kg **8.** 4.2 kg = ▣ cg **9.** 0.76 kL = ▣ L

PRACTICE AND PROBLEM SOLVING

Independent ▶
Practice

Convert to the given unit.

10. 200 kL = ▣ L **11.** 40 dm = ▣ cm **12.** 500 m = ▣ km

13. 10 g = ▣ kg **14.** 1,200 m = ▣ km **15.** 12 mm = ▣ m

16. 440 g = ▣ mg **17.** 9 L = ▣ mL **18.** 18 kL = ▣ L

19. 0.34 m = ▣ km **20.** 425,000 mg = ▣ g **21.** 320 mm = ▣ cm

22. 0.25 hg = ▣ mg **23.** 0.006 km = ▣ mm **24.** 54 L = ▣ mL

TECHNOLOGY LINK

More Practice:
**Harcourt Mega Math
The Number Games,**
Tiny's Think Tank,
Level Q

Compare. Write $<$, $>$, or $=$ for each ⬤.

25. 40 m ⬤ 400 cm **26.** 200 kL ⬤ 2,000,000 L **27.** 10 g ⬤ 0.01 kg

28. 3 g ⬤ 2,500 mg **29.** 54,000 mm ⬤ 6 km **30.** 2,500 cL ⬤ 3 L

Problem Solving ▶
Applications

31. Karen carries her hockey equipment in her gym bag when she goes to practice. When the bag is empty its mass is 2,000 g. What is the mass of the empty bag in kilograms?

32. ❓**What's the Question?** Marie needs 2,500 mL of soup for a dinner party. The answer is 2.5 L.

33. Two angles of △*ABC* measure 25° and 37°. Two angles of △*DEF* measure 41° and 23°. Which triangle has the third angle with the greater measure?

34. Lucy made her favorite punch for a party. She mixed 3,000 mL of soda, 1,000 mL of lemonade, 1,250 mL of pineapple juice, and 1,500 mL of cranberry juice. How many liters of punch did she make?

35. *REASONING* Shawna bought a 3-m length of tissue paper to use for an art project. She used a piece 200 cm long. What fraction of the paper is left over?

MIXED REVIEW AND TEST PREP

36. 8 days = ▣ hours (p. 420)

37. Write $\frac{2}{5}$ as a percent. (p. 191)

38. Solve. $8.2x = 131.2$ (p. 291)

39. Solve. $x = \sqrt{81} - 4$ (p. 266)

⭐ **40. TEST PREP** Mina spends $7.60 for $9\frac{1}{2}$ lb of apples. What is the cost per pound? (p. 236)

A $0.80 **B** $0.84 **C** $0.95 **D** $1.29

Relate Customary and Metric

Learn how to estimate conversions between metric and customary units of measure.

QUICK REVIEW

Convert to the given unit.

1. 10 c = ■ fl oz   2. 5 years = ■ mo   3. 60 in. = ■ ft
4. 9 L = ■ kL   5. 4 g = ■ mg

Niagara Falls consists of two waterfalls, the Horseshoe Falls and the American Falls. While Catherine is visiting the Horseshoe Falls, she does some sightseeing in Ontario, Canada. She reads that the Horseshoe Falls is about 3 m deep at the center. Catherine wants to estimate how many feet deep the Horseshoe Falls is at the center.

Use the table below to estimate conversions between customary and metric units of measure.

APPROXIMATE CUSTOMARY AND METRIC CONVERSIONS			
1 in. ≈ 2.5 cm	1 mi ≈ 1.6 km	1 kg ≈ 2.2 lb	1 fl oz ≈ 30 mL
1 ft ≈ 30 cm	1 m ≈ 39 in.	1 oz ≈ 30 g	1 L ≈ 1 qt

300 ÷ 30 = 10   *Since 3 m = 300 cm, and 1 ft ≈ 30 cm, divide 300 by 30.*

So, the Horseshoe Falls is about 10 ft deep at the center.

EXAMPLE 1

Catherine buys a bottle of juice that contains 360 mL. About how many fluid ounces does the bottle of juice contain?

360 ÷ 30 = 12   *Since 1 fl oz ≈ 30 mL, divide 360 by 30.*

So, the bottle of juice contains about 12 fl oz.

• Suppose Catherine bought a 2-L bottle of juice. About how many quarts were in the bottle of juice?

EXAMPLE 2

The total vertical drop of the American Falls is about 56 m. About how many inches is the vertical drop?

56 × 39 = 2,184, or about 2,200   *Since 1 m ≈ 39 in., multiply 56 by 39.*

So, the American Falls has a vertical drop of about 2,200 in.

Think and ▶ Discuss

Look back at the lesson to answer each question.

1. Tell whether 1 mi is longer or shorter than 1 km. Explain.

2. Explain how you would estimate the number of miles in 40 km.

Guided ▶ Practice

Estimate the conversion.

3. 2 in. ≈ ■ cm
4. 15 mi ≈ ■ km
5. 60 g ≈ ■ oz

6. 3 L ≈ ■ qt
7. 3 m ≈ ■ in.
8. 10 cm ≈ ■ in.

PRACTICE AND PROBLEM SOLVING

Independent ▶ Practice

Estimate the conversion.

9. 16 km ≈ ■ mi
10. 3 fl oz ≈ ■ mL
11. 2 kg ≈ ■ lb

12. 90 cm ≈ ■ ft
13. 3 in. ≈ ■ cm
14. $2\frac{1}{2}$ qt ≈ ■ L

15. 120 mL ≈ ■ fl oz
16. 6.6 lb ≈ ■ kg
17. 2 m ≈ ■ in.

18. $3\frac{1}{2}$ oz ≈ ■ g
19. $4\frac{2}{3}$ ft ≈ ■ cm
20. $7\frac{1}{2}$ mi ≈ ■ km

Compare. Write < or > for each ●.

21. 15 cm ● 4 in.
22. 120 g ● 10 oz
23. 11 lb ● 3 kg

Problem Solving ▶ Applications

24. The water passing over the American Falls cuts away the rock beneath the falls at the rate of about 4 in. every 10 yr. Estimate the number of centimeters of rock that is cut away every 10 yr.

25. *REASONING* Pete took photos of Niagara Falls using film that was 35 mm wide. About how wide was the film in inches?

26. *REASONING* Ramona saw a road sign near the Canadian border stating that the speed limit was 80 km per hour. Estimate the speed limit in miles per hour.

27. **Vocabulary Power** Customary measures are based on how people used to measure. A yard was the distance from the end of the nose to the tip of the middle finger of an outstretched arm. Why do you think the system is called customary?

MIXED REVIEW AND TEST PREP

28. Convert 9 L to kiloliters. (p. 423)

29. Convert 6 mi to feet. (p. 420)

30. Write a rule for the sequence. (p. 312)

2, 4, 8, 16, . . .

31. Simplify $\frac{21}{18}$. (p. 182)

32. TEST PREP Find the unknown angle measure in the figure at the right. (p. 340)

165°
?

A 180°   **B** 165°   **C** 90°   **D** 15°

EXTRA PRACTICE page 436, Set C

Appropriate Tools and Units

Learn how to measure to a given degree of precision by using the appropriate mathematical tools and units of measure.

Vocabulary

precision

Which number is greater?

1. $\frac{1}{8}, \frac{1}{4}$ 2. $\frac{5}{16}, \frac{3}{4}$ 3. $\frac{7}{8}, \frac{6}{40}$ 4. 0.2, 0.02   5. 1.4, 1.41

When Doris runs to train for the track and field competition, she measures her time to the nearest second. When she runs in the competition, the time is measured to the nearest hundredth of a second. Doris's time is measured more precisely when hundredths of seconds are used instead of seconds.

The **precision** of a measurement is related to the unit of measure you use. The smaller the unit of measure used, the more precise the measurement is.

Math Idea ▶ Metric and customary units are used to measure length, capacity, temperature, and weight (or mass). When you measure quantities, the measurement you get is an approximation.

Activity

You need: 2 different-size bags of rice; quart, pint, and cup measuring tools

Copy the table and record your findings.

	CUP	PINT	QUART
LARGER BAG			
SMALLER BAG			

Work with a partner, and begin with the larger bag of rice.

- Use the quart measure. Record the amount of rice you have to the nearest quart.

- Use the pint measure. Record the amount of rice you have to the nearest pint.

- Use the one-cup measure. Record the amount of rice you have to the nearest cup.

- Repeat the activity with the smaller bag of rice.

Think and Discuss
- Which measurement for each bag of rice is most precise? Why?

- How could you get a more precise measurement?

Measured to the nearest centimeter, this segment is about 4 cm.

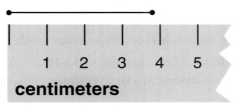

You can measure the length of the same line segment more precisely with a ruler that is divided into millimeters.

A more precise measurement of the length is 38 mm.

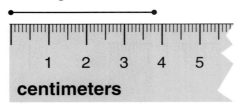

EXAMPLE 1

Measure the segment to the nearest $\frac{1}{4}$ in., $\frac{1}{8}$ in., and $\frac{1}{16}$ in. Which measurement is most precise?

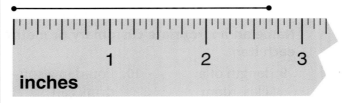

To the nearest $\frac{1}{4}$ in., the line segment is $2\frac{3}{4}$ in. long.

To the nearest $\frac{1}{8}$ in., the line segment is $2\frac{5}{8}$ in. long.

To the nearest $\frac{1}{16}$ in., the line segment is $2\frac{11}{16}$ in. long.

So, $2\frac{11}{16}$ in. is most precise.

When you measure an object, you must decide which unit of measurement is most appropriate. If you wanted to measure the amount of water in a bathtub, for example, you would use liters or gallons. It would not be as appropriate to use milliliters or cups.

EXAMPLE 2

What is an appropriate unit of measure for each item?

A. The mass of two small apples *gram* or *kilogram* Gram is more appropriate.	B. The amount of punch per serving *quart* or *cup* Cup is more appropriate.
C. The length of your fingernail *millimeter* or *centimeter* Millimeter is more appropriate.	D. The weight of a math book *ounce* or *pound* Pound is more appropriate.

Think and ▶ Discuss

Look back at the lesson to answer each question.

1. **Explain** whether the mass of a textbook is more precise measured to the nearest gram or kilogram.

2. **Give** a more precise measurement for a room that is about 12 ft long.

Guided ▶ Practice

Measure the line segment to the given length.

3. nearest centimeter; nearest millimeter

4. nearest inch; nearest half inch

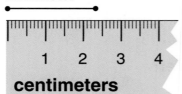

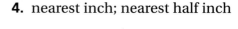
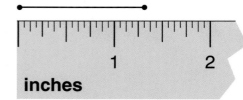

Tell which measurement is more precise.

5. 7 ft or 85 in.   6. $1\frac{1}{2}$ c or 2 pt   7. 4 lb or 65 oz   8. 6 cm or 61 mm

Name an appropriate customary or metric unit of measure for each item.

9. length of a classroom

10. liquid in a soft-drink can

11. mass or weight of a new pencil

Independent ▶ Practice

Measure the line segment to the given length.

12. nearest centimeter; nearest millimeter

13. nearest half inch; nearest quarter inch

14. nearest centimeter; nearest millimeter

15. nearest quarter inch; nearest eighth inch

Tell which measurement is more precise.

16. 71 mm or 7 cm   17. 3 yd or 8 ft   18. 3 pt or 5 c   19. $\frac{1}{2}$ lb or 9 oz

Name an appropriate customary or metric unit of measure for each item.

20. weight or mass of a chair

21. thickness of a magazine

22. distance from one city to another

Compare. Write <, >, or = for each ●.

23. 8 qt ● 16 pt   24. 9,000 lb ● 6 T   25. 739 mL ● 0.739 L

26. Chris said the county repaired 2,650 yd of highway in her town. Her brother said the county repaired 1.5 mi of highway. Which measurement is more precise?

27. Which is more precise, measuring to the nearest half centimeter or to the nearest millimeter? Explain.

28. ✍ **Write About It** Explain the most precise metric unit of measurement you might use to measure the length and width of a small photograph.

Use Data **For 29–30, use the table.**

29. ⒶⒷⒸ**ALGEBRA** The length of the Golden Gate Bridge is how many times as great as the length of the Peace Bridge? Write an expression to find this. Do the same to compare the Golden Gate Bridge to the Brooklyn Bridge.

BRIDGES	
Bridge	**Length in feet**
Golden Gate	8,981
Brooklyn Bridge	3,460
Peace Bridge	5,800

30. What is the length of the Golden Gate Bridge in miles?

MIXED REVIEW AND TEST PREP

31. 10 mi ≈ ▮ km (p. 426)   **32.** 3 in. ≈ ▮ cm (p. 426)   **33.** 4 kg ≈ ▮ lb (p. 426)

34. TEST PREP Kim has to allow 45 min to practice her cello before she leaves for soccer practice. She also wants to study for 1 hr 10 min and spend 25 min eating breakfast and getting dressed. If she has to leave for soccer practice at 1 P.M., what time should she get up? (p. 420)

    A 9:40 A.M.   **B** 10:40 A.M.   **C** 11:00 A.M.   **D** 10:40 P.M.

35. TEST PREP Which is the solution of the inequality $x + 5 < 7$? (p. 300)

    F $x < 2$ **G** $x > 2$ **H** $x < 7$ **J** $x > 7$

PROBLEM SOLVING ⎯ 💡 THiNKER's CorNer

WHAT'S THE UNIT? Choose the appropriate unit of measure from the column on the right. Write the letters in the order shown below the blanks to learn the name of a customary measure that is equal to 4 pecks.

    1. Volume of gasoline   **B** mile

    2. Length of a football field   **E** yard

    3. Distance from Chicago to New York   **H** gram

    4. Weight of a hummingbird   **L** gallon

    5. Weight of a herd of elephants   **S** pound

    6. Weight of a pork roast   **U** ton

    ___   ___   ___   ___   ___   ___
    3   5   6   4   2   1

Compare Measurements

Explore how to measure objects and compare the measurements.

You need pen, pencil, eraser, chalk, two different sized containers, customary and metric ruler, spring scale, balance, customary and metric measuring cup, rice

QUICK REVIEW

Compare. Write $<$ or $>$ for each ⬤.

1. 8 ⬤ 7
2. 3.70 ⬤ 3.61
3. 0.7 ⬤ 0.09
4. $2\frac{1}{4}$ ⬤ $2\frac{1}{8}$
5. $5\frac{5}{16}$ ⬤ $5\frac{3}{8}$

You can use a ruler, scale, and measuring cup to measure the length, weight, and capacity of objects in customary units.

Activity 1

- Copy the table. Estimate the lengths of the pen and pencil to the nearest $\frac{1}{2}$ inch, the weights of the eraser and chalk to the nearest ounce, and the capacity of each of the two containers to the nearest cup. Record your estimates in the table.

MEASUREMENTS		
Object	Estimate	Actual
Pen		
Pencil		
Eraser		
Chalk		
Container 1		
Container 2		

- Measure the lengths of the pen and pencil to the nearest $\frac{1}{8}$ inch. Record your results in the table. Use $<$ or $>$ to compare the lengths.

- Use the spring scale to measure the weights of the eraser and chalk to the nearest ounce. Record your results in the table. Use $<$ or $>$ to compare the weights.

- Fill both containers with rice. Measure the capacity of each of the two containers to the nearest $\frac{1}{8}$ cup. Record your results in the table. Use $<$ or $>$ to compare the capacities.

Think and Discuss

- How did your estimates of length, weight, and capacity compare to the measurements?

Practice

1. Estimate and measure the weights of two objects in your classroom using customary units. Use $<$ or $>$ to compare the measured weights. How did your estimates compare to the measurements?

2. Estimate and measure the lengths of two objects in your classroom using customary units. Use $<$ or $>$ to compare the measured lengths. How did your estimates compare to the measurements?

You can also use a ruler, balance, and measuring cup to measure the length, mass, and capacity of objects in metric units.

Activity 2

- Copy the table. Estimate the lengths of the pen and pencil to the nearest centimeter, the masses of the eraser and chalk to the nearest gram, and the capacity of each of the two containers to the nearest milliliter. Record your estimates in the table.

MEASUREMENTS		
Object	Estimate	Actual
Pen		
Pencil		
Eraser		
Chalk		
Container 1		
Container 2		

- Measure the lengths of the pen and pencil to the nearest millimeter. Record your results in the table. Use < or > to compare the lengths.

- Measure the masses of the eraser and chalk to the nearest gram. Record your results in the table. Use < or > to compare the masses.

- Fill both containers with rice. Measure the capacity of each of the two containers to the nearest milliliter. Record your results in the table. Use < or > to compare the capacities.

Remember that 1 cm is about the width of a finger, 1 gram has about the same mass as a paper clip, and 1 mL will fill a hollow centimeter cube.

Think and Discuss

- How did your estimates compare to the measurements?

- Would you use a ruler, balance, or measuring cup to measure the mass of a book? the capacity of a bottle?

Practice

1. Estimate and measure the masses of two objects in your classroom using metric units. Use < or > to compare the masses. How did your estimates compare to the measurements?

2. Estimate and measure the capacities of two objects in your classroom using metric units. Use < or > to compare the capacities. How did your estimates compare to the measurements?

MIXED REVIEW AND TEST PREP

Estimate the conversion. (p. 426)

1. 3 in. ≈ ▇ cm   2. 120 g ≈ ▇ oz   3. 8 L ≈ ▇ qt

4. **TEST PREP** Which pair of lines are parallel lines? (p. 344)

   A $\overleftrightarrow{AB}, \overleftrightarrow{BC}$ B $\overleftrightarrow{AB}, \overleftrightarrow{CD}$ C $\overleftrightarrow{AB}, \overleftrightarrow{DH}$ D $\overleftrightarrow{AB}, \overleftrightarrow{BF}$

5. **TEST PREP** Which pair of lines are skew lines? (p. 344)

   F $\overleftrightarrow{AB}, \overleftrightarrow{BC}$ G $\overleftrightarrow{AB}, \overleftrightarrow{CD}$ H $\overleftrightarrow{AB}, \overleftrightarrow{DH}$ J $\overleftrightarrow{AB}, \overleftrightarrow{BF}$

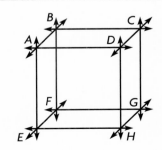

PROBLEM SOLVING SKILL
Estimate or Find Exact Answer

Analyze
Choose
Solve
Check

Learn how to decide when to estimate and when to find an exact answer.

QUICK REVIEW

Estimate the sum or difference to the nearest whole number.

1. $6.2 + 8.62$ **2.** $12.73 + 7.41$

3. $4.42 - 1.48$ **4.** $34.9 - 23.04$

5. $253.4 + 8.03$

Alex is a radio-station disk jockey. He is making a list of songs that should last about a half hour, but no longer. Below is his first list of songs and their playing times. Does he have enough music?

SONG	LENGTH	SONG	LENGTH
Color Me Blue	4.5 min	Smile on Me	5.7 min
Top Dog	3.6 min	Kelso Blues	4.3 min
Hittin' the Road	7.2 min	A Long Time Ago	6.4 min
Stand Up and Shout	2.6 min		

To find out if he has enough music, Alex can estimate the total amount of time for the songs in his list. To estimate, he rounds each amount of time down.

$$4 + 3 + 7 + 2 + 5 + 4 + 6 = 31$$

Since his estimate is 31 min, he has more music than he needs.

Alex also has to play 5.7 min of commercials. How much music time does he need to cut?

Now Alex needs to know the exact amount of time. He adds the lengths of the songs and the lengths of the commercials.

$$4.5 + 3.6 + 7.2 + 2.6 + 5.7 + 4.3 + 6.4 + 5.7 = 40$$

He has 40 min of music and commercials, so he needs to cut the music by 10 min.

Math **I**dea ▶ Sometimes an estimate is all you need to answer a problem and sometimes you need to find an exact answer.

Talk About It ▶ • Which songs could Alex remove from his list so he has 30 min of music and commercials? Is an estimate or exact answer needed?

PROBLEM SOLVING PRACTICE

Decide whether you need an estimate or an exact answer. Solve.

1. Eric is having a party. He is planning for each of his six guests to have two 0.25-lb meat patties. He buys four packages of meat weighing 6 oz, 9 oz, 4.5 oz, and 11.5 oz. Does he have enough meat?

2. Sally uses cereal, $\frac{1}{2}$ c of nuts, $\frac{1}{4}$ c of coconut, and 1 c of raisins to make trail mix. She wants to make a total of 1 qt of mix. How many cups of cereal does she need to add?

3. Sherry took $20.00 to spend at the mall. She paid $8.95 for a blouse and $5.25 for lunch at the food court. Will she be able to spend $10.00 at another store?

4. Ronny takes $50.00 to the music store to buy three books of music. He spends $13.95, $18.99, and $15.75 on the music. How much money does Ronny have left?

MIXED APPLICATIONS

Karen has a checking account at her bank. The bank charges $4 per month plus $0.25 for each check she writes.

5. Which of the following expressions can be used to determine the amount Karen pays each month? Let $c =$ the number of checks.

   A $4 \times 0.25c$ **C** $4 + 0.25c$

   B $4c + 0.25$ **D** $4 - 0.25c$

6. Karen is charged $6.00 by the bank during the month of September. How many checks did she write in September?

   F 2   **H** 8

   G 6   **J** 24

Use Data   **For 7–9, use the table at the right.**

Precipitation In Inches

Nov.	Dec.	Jan.	Feb.	Mar.	Apr.
$5\frac{2}{5}$	$6\frac{3}{4}$	$8\frac{1}{2}$	$10\frac{1}{4}$	$5\frac{5}{8}$	$1\frac{1}{10}$

7. How much more rain fell during the month with the most rainfall than the month with the least rainfall?

8. Jon kept records of the rainfall at his home for six months. Estimate the total amount of precipitation from November through April.

9. The record rainfall for the months November through April is 40 inches. How much above or below the record is this year's rainfall?

10. How many of the numbers from 1 to 30 are prime numbers? How many of those are even numbers?

11. The sum of Maris's and Ramona's ages is 40 yr. Maris is 6 yr older than Ramona. How old is Maris?

12. Thirty-six students try out for baseball and basketball. If 20 students try out only for baseball and 8 try out for both sports, how many try out only for basketball?

13. ✎ **Write a problem** about measurement for which an estimate would be appropriate as an answer. Then write a related problem for which an exact answer is needed.

435

Set A (pp. 420–422)

Convert to the given unit.

1. 15 ft = ▩ yd

2. 12 c = ▩ pt

3. 8 gal = ▩ qt

4. 120 oz = ▩ lb

5. 6 days = ▩ hr

6. 12 in. = ▩ yd

Set B (pp. 423–425)

Convert to the given unit.

1. 0.22 m = ▩ km

2. 450 mm = ▩ cm

3. 0.0030 kL = ▩ L

4. 1,800 g = ▩ kg

5. 10,000 cm = ▩ m

6. 0.35 L = ▩ mL

7. Paul buys 2 L of orange juice. He drinks 250 mL with breakfast. How many milliliters are left?

8. Tiffany runs 5,000 m. Ashley runs 3.5 km. Who runs farther and by how many meters?

Set C (pp. 426–427)

Estimate the conversion.

1. 9 in. ≈ ▩ cm

2. 156 in. ≈ ▩ m

3. 20 mi ≈ ▩ km

4. 5 L ≈ ▩ qt

5. 45 cm ≈ ▩ ft

6. 3.5 kg ≈ ▩ lb

7. Eve weighs 51 kg. Beth weighs 116 lb. About how many more pounds does Beth weigh than Eve?

8. Zack has a board that is 6 ft long. He wants to cut a length that is 200 cm long. Is the board long enough? Explain.

Set D (pp. 428–431)

Measure the line segment to the given length.

1. nearest half inch; nearest inch

2. nearest centimeter; nearest millimeter

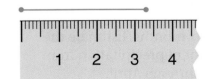

Tell which measurement is more precise.

3. 7 fl oz or 1 cup

4. 2 qt or 9 c

5. 1,245 m or 1 km

Name an appropriate customary or metric unit of measure for each item.

6. weight or mass of a bag of sugar

7. length of a shoelace

8. water in a fishbowl

Convert to the given unit. (pp. 420–422)

1. 5 ft = ■ in.

2. 4 yd = ■ in.

3. 8 qt = ■ gal

4. 40 oz = ■ lb

5. 6 c = ■ pt

6. 2.3 T = ■ lb

Convert to the given unit. (pp. 423–425)

7. 50 mm = ■ cm

8. 3,000 mg = ■ g

9. 100 g = ■ kg

10. 3.7 L = ■ mL

11. 1.25 km = ■ m

12. 4,700 mm = ■ m

Estimate the conversion. (pp. 426–427)

13. 2 ft ≈ ■ cm

14. 4 oz ≈ ■ g

15. 6 L ≈ ■ qt

16. 12.5 cm ≈ ■ in.

17. 7 in. ≈ ■ cm

18. 3.5 fl oz ≈ ■ mL

Measure the line segment to the given length. (pp. 428–431)

19. nearest centimeter; nearest millimeter

20. nearest half inch; nearest quarter inch

21. nearest centimeter; nearest millimeter

22. nearest quarter inch; nearest eighth inch

Tell which measurement is more precise. (pp. 428–431)

23. 2 cm or 21 mm

24. 4 ft or 49 in.

25. 27 lb or 427 oz

26. 4,210 g or 4 kg

27. 4,827 mL or 5 L

28. 785 mg or 1 g

29. Use a ruler to measure the lengths of the two line segments below to the nearest millimeter. Use < or > to compare the measurements. (p. 432)

30. Mike is having a party. He wants each of his guests to have at least 3 cups of punch. If there are 40 guests, how many gallons of punch are needed? (pp. 420–422)

31. The newspaper reported that the new courthouse was 97 ft tall. A television reporter said the courthouse was 32 yd tall. Which measurement is more precise? (pp. 428–431)

Tell whether you need an estimate or an exact answer.
Solve. (pp. 434–435)

32. Marla has 5 fl oz of lime juice, 16 fl oz of orange juice, 12 fl oz of white grape juice, and 6 c of pineapple juice for a punch. Does she have enough for twenty 5-fl oz servings?

33. Amy and 3 friends are working on a craft project. Each person needs 39 cm of ribbon. They have 1.25 m of ribbon. How much more do they need?

★ NUMBER SENSE, CONCEPTS, AND OPERATIONS

1. Just over $\frac{2}{5}$ of the states in the 50 United States border on the Atlantic Ocean, the Pacific Ocean, or the Gulf of Mexico. The exact fraction is given below. Which fraction is it?

A $\frac{3}{10}$ **C** $\frac{12}{25}$

B $\frac{7}{20}$ **D** $\frac{11}{30}$

2. Julie removed $\frac{1}{3}$ of the eggs from a carton containing one dozen eggs. Which of the following shows the carton after the eggs were removed?

F

G

H

J

3. Earth is one of nine planets in the solar system. Of the other eight planets, $\frac{3}{4}$ are farther from the Sun than Earth is. Which of the following pairs is equivalent to $\frac{3}{4}$?

A $33\frac{1}{3}\%$ and 0.33

B 0.075 and 7.5%

C 1.33 and 133%

D 75% and 0.75

4. Explain It There are 30 rows of seats in the Metropolitan Auditorium. Each row has 20 seats. Explain how you can use mental math to find the total number of seats in the auditorium.

★ MEASUREMENT

5. What is the length of this insect to the nearest $\frac{1}{4}$ inch?

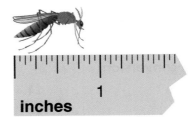

F $\frac{1}{4}$ inch **H** $\frac{5}{8}$ inch

G $\frac{1}{2}$ inch **J** $\frac{3}{4}$ inch

6. The Verrazano-Narrows Bridge is the longest suspension bridge in the United States. The length of the main span is 4,260 feet. Which is the length of the main span in yards?

A   355 yards

B   1,420 yards

C   12,780 yards

D   51,120 yards

7. In the Olympic shot-put event, contestants throw a metal ball having a mass of approximately 7,260 grams. Which is the mass of the ball in kilograms?

F   7.26 kilograms

G   726 kilograms

H   726,000 kilograms

J   7,260,000 kilograms

8. Explain It Justin works 1,440 minutes per week at his part-time job. How many hours does he work? Explain how you found the answer.

9. According to the stem-and-leaf plot below, how many members of the Investor Club are older than 30?

Ages of Investor Club Members

Stems	Leaves
1	8 9 9
2	2 4 4
3	0 1 6 6
4	2 3 4
5	0 2

A 6   **C** 8

B 7   **D** 9

10. The 50 cards in a game are numbered from 1 to 50. Seth must pick a number greater than 24 to win the game. What are Seth's chances of winning the game?

F $\frac{1}{24}$

G $\frac{1}{2}$

H $\frac{24}{50}$

J $\frac{26}{50}$

11. There are 6 sixth-grade classes at Jan's school.

NUMBER OF 6ᵀᴴ GRADERS PER CLASS						
Class	1	2	3	4	5	6
Number	28	32	33	29	31	29

Which is the median number of students in these classes?

A 31   **B** 30   **C** 29   **D** 28

12. Explain It For a survey, 1,500 randomly selected doctors from the United States were asked their opinions on medical insurance. Identify the sample and the population. Explain the difference.

13. The road sign shown below means "two-way traffic ahead." Which type of transformation can be used to transform the first arrow into the second?

F translation

G rotation

H reflection

J tessellation

14. Doug made this rectangular design. Inside the rectangle is a yellow quadrilateral with four congruent sides. Which is the **best** name for the quadrilateral?

A rectangle

B trapezoid

C rhombus

D isosceles triangle

TIP **Eliminate Choices.** See item 14. Look for answers that cannot be correct. Which choice does not have four sides? Which choices do not have congruent sides?

15. Explain It The figure at the right is from a made-to-scale jigsaw puzzle map of the United States. Is the puzzle piece congruent to the shape of the state of Idaho? Is it similar? Explain your answer.

IDAHO

20 Length and Perimeter

≡FAST FACT • SOCIAL STUDIES The first Ferris wheel was made for the Chicago World's Fair of 1893 by bridge builder George W. Ferris. It had 36 wooden cars that each held 60 people. Rides cost $0.50 each.

PROBLEM SOLVING The diameter of the Ferris wheel was 250 ft and the circumference was 785 ft. About how many times as great as the diameter was the circumference?

DIAMETERS AND CIRCUMFERENCES OF BIG WHEELS		
Wheel	**Diameter (in feet)**	**Circumference (in feet)**
1893 Chicago Ferris Wheel	250	785
Largest carousel	27.5	86
Portable merry-go-round	20	63
2000 London Millennium Wheel	443	1,391

Check What You Know

Use this page to help you review and remember important skills needed for Chapter 20.

✓ Perimeter

Find the perimeter of the figure.

1.
8 ft
8 ft

2.
12.5 m
6 m

3.
6 cm   5 cm
9 cm

4.
1.3 m
0.5 m
1.2 m

5.
26 in.
26 in.

6.
$3\frac{1}{3}$ yd
$6\frac{1}{2}$ yd

7. 212 yd   98 yd

8.
$8\frac{1}{2}$ ft $8\frac{1}{2}$ ft
5 ft

9.
15.9 m
15.9 m

✓ Multiply with Fractions and Decimals

10. $3\frac{1}{7} \times 28$

11. $2\frac{2}{3} \times 112$

12. $12\frac{1}{2} \times 210$

13. 3.7×9

14. 21.06×25

15. 3.14×8

16. $3\frac{3}{4} \times 16$

17. 5.25×14

18. 0.8×92

19. $15 \times 9\frac{4}{5}$

20. $\frac{22}{7} \times 42$

21. 3.14×12.5

VOCABULARY POWER

REVIEW

perimeter [pə•rim′ə•tər] *noun*

The word *perimeter* comes from the Greek root words *peri*, meaning "around," and *metron*, meaning "measure." Explain how these root words can help you understand how to find the perimeter of a figure.

PREVIEW

circumference

pi

 www.harcourtschool.com/mathglossary

Estimate Perimeter

MATH LAB

Explore how to estimate perimeter.

You need metric ruler, string, perimeter worksheet.

Mrs. Johnson is working with the Jackson Middle School student council to clean up the shores of Pine Lake. She gives all the members drawings of the lake and asks them to estimate the perimeter. Mrs. Johnson can then assign teams of students to clean portions of the lake's shore.

You can estimate the perimeter, or distance around a figure, by using string and a ruler.

Activity

- Lay a piece of string around the perimeter of the drawing of the lake. Mark the string where it meets itself.

- Decide on a metric unit of measure. Use the ruler to measure the string from its beginning to the mark you made on the string.

- Compare your measurement with those of the other students.

Pine Lake

Think and Discuss

- **Explain** why there are different estimates for the perimeter of the drawing of the lake.

- **REASONING**   Suppose the scale of the drawing is 1 cm = 100 m. How many meters would your estimate represent? How many kilometers?

Practice

Use string and a ruler to estimate the perimeter of each.

1. the outline of your hand

2. the outline of your shoe sole

LESSON 20.2

Perimeter

Learn how to find the perimeter of a polygon.

QUICK REVIEW

1. $2(19) + 2(12)$
2. $2(16) + 2(5)$
3. $(2 \times 18) + 3.4 + 6.02$
4. $2.5 + 3.7 + 4.9 + 5.8 + 4.6$
5. $7.04 + 3.5 + 5 + 2.40$

MATH LAB

Activity

You need: metric ruler

- Use the rectangle below. Measure the length of each side to the nearest centimeter.

Think and Discuss

- What is the perimeter to the nearest centimeter?

- How could you get a more precise measurement for the perimeter? What would the perimeter be then?

- Write a formula you could use to find the perimeter of a rectangle.

Math Idea ▶ The perimeter, P, of a polygon is the distance around it. To find the perimeter of any polygon, you can use a formula stating that the perimeter is equal to the sum of the lengths of the sides.

EXAMPLE 1

Tony is building a brick patio with a wooden frame. The lengths of the sides are $8\frac{1}{3}$ ft, $7\frac{1}{2}$ ft, $5\frac{3}{4}$ ft, $4\frac{2}{3}$ ft, and $6\frac{1}{4}$ ft. Tony needs to find the perimeter so he will know how much wood he needs for the frame. What is the perimeter?

$P = a + b + c + d + e$ *Write a formula.*

$P = 8\frac{1}{3} + 7\frac{1}{2} + 5\frac{3}{4} + 4\frac{2}{3} + 6\frac{1}{4}$ *Replace the variables with the lengths.*

$P = \left(8\frac{1}{3} + 4\frac{2}{3}\right) + \left(5\frac{3}{4} + 6\frac{1}{4}\right) + 7\frac{1}{2}$ *Use the Commutative and Associative Properties.*

$P = 13 + 12 + 7\frac{1}{2}$ *Use mental math to add.*

$P = 32\frac{1}{2}$

So, the perimeter is $32\frac{1}{2}$ ft.

443

Since the opposite sides of a rectangle are equal in length, you can find the perimeter by finding 2 times the sum of the length and the width. You can write a formula to find the perimeter of a rectangle. The formula is $P = 2(l + w)$, or by the Distributive Property, $P = 2l + 2w$.

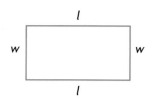

EXAMPLE 2

Find the perimeter of Sara's rectangular yard.

$P = 2l + 2w$	*Write the formula.*
$P = (2 \times 28) + (2 \times 15)$	*Replace l with 28 and w with 15.*
$P = 56 + 30$	*Add the products.*
$P = 86$	

So, the perimeter is 86 yd.

15 yd

28 yd

Sometimes you know the perimeter of a figure, but the length of one side is unknown.

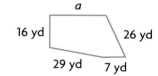

EXAMPLE 3

The polygon at the right has a perimeter of 105 yd. Find the unknown length.

$P = a + b + c + d + e$	*Write the formula.*
$105 = a + 16 + 29 + 7 + 26$	*Use the values you know.*
$105 = a + 78$	*Add the known lengths.*
$105 - 78 = a + 78 - 78$	*Solve for a.*
$27 = a$	

So, the unknown length is 27 yd.

a

16 yd   26 yd

29 yd   7 yd

EXAMPLE 4

The length of a rectangle is 1 cm more than 3 times the width. What is the perimeter of the rectangle if the width is 32 cm?

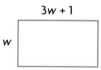

First find the length.

$l = 3w + 1$	*Length is 1 more than 3 times the width.*
$l = (3 \cdot 32) + 1$	*Replace w with 32.*
$l = 96 + 1$	*Multiply.*
$l = 97$	*Add.*

Find the perimeter.

$P = 2l + 2w$	*Write the formula.*
$P = 2(97) + 2(32)$	*Replace w with 32 and l with 97.*
$P = 194 + 64$	
$P = 258$	

So, the perimeter is 258 cm when the width is 32 cm.

Think and Discuss ▶ Look back at the lesson to answer each question.

1. **Explain** how to find the unknown length of one side of a triangle when you know the perimeter and the lengths of the other two sides.

2. **Tell** what formula you could write to find the perimeter of a regular pentagon.

Guided Practice ▶ Find the perimeter.

3.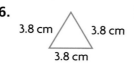
   5.56 m
   3.8 m
   4.21 m

4.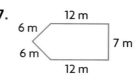
   $4\frac{3}{4}$ in. $4\frac{3}{4}$ in.
   $4\frac{3}{4}$ in. $4\frac{3}{4}$ in.
   $4\frac{3}{4}$ in.

5.
   3 ft
   18 in.

Independent Practice ▶ Find the perimeter.

6.
   3.8 cm   3.8 cm
   3.8 cm

7.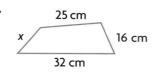
   12 m
   6 m
   7 m
   6 m
   12 m

8.
   $4w + 3$
   w
   width = 28 in.

The perimeter is given. Find the unknown length.

9.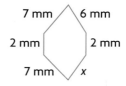
   25 cm
   x 16 cm
   32 cm
   perimeter = 86.5 cm

10.
   7 mm   6 mm
   2 mm   2 mm
   7 mm x
   perimeter = 30 mm

Problem Solving Applications ▶

11. **ALGEBRA** Write a formula to find the perimeter of the square at the right. If $x = 31$, what is the perimeter?
    x ft

12. **Write a problem** that can be solved by finding perimeter.

13. Solve. 15 cm ≈ ■ in. (p. 426)

14. Name the figure. ▱ (p. 362)

15. Solve. $316 = \frac{a}{4}$ (p. 291)

16. Write an expression for 43.8 times a number, p. (p. 258)

⭐ 17. **TEST PREP** The graph of which inequality is shown below? (p. 300)

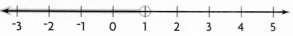

A $x < 1$ **B** $x > 1$ **C** $x \leq 1$ **D** $x \geq 1$

EXTRA PRACTICE page 452, Set A

PROBLEM SOLVING STRATEGY
Draw a Diagram

Learn how to use the strategy *draw a diagram* to solve problems.

QUICK REVIEW

1. $(2 \times 12) + (2 \times 7)$ **2.** $4\frac{3}{4} + 2\frac{1}{4} + 7\frac{1}{4}$

3. 4×9.8 **4.** $23 + 47 + 42$

5. $62.03 + 12.7 + 5.19 + 35.28$

Roy has a rectangular piece of land that he wants to put a barbed wire fence around. He will place a post every 9 ft along the perimeter. Each post is 5 ft tall. The land is 63 ft long and 45 ft wide. How many posts is Roy going to need ?

Analyze

What are you asked to find?

What information are you given?

Is there information you will not use? If so, what?

Choose

What strategy will you use?

Use the strategy draw a diagram to find the number of posts needed to go around the perimeter of Roy's land.

Solve

How will you solve the problem?

Draw a rectangle that is similar to the shape of Roy's land. Place marks along the perimeter of the rectangle to represent the posts.

Count the number of marks you placed around the rectangle. Each corner should have only one mark. So, Roy will need 24 posts.

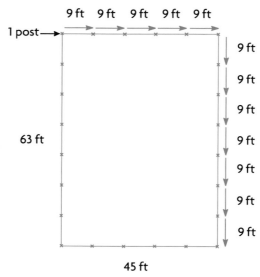

Check

How can you check your answer?

What if Roy wanted to place a post every 8 ft along a straight 64 ft-long boundary between his property and his neighbor's property? How many posts would he need?

PROBLEM SOLVING PRACTICE

Solve the problem by drawing a diagram.

1. Each hexagon on a quilt is made up of six congruent equilateral triangles with 11-in. sides. Each triangle shares two sides with other triangles in the hexagon. What is the perimeter of one hexagon?

2. Darin's pool is 4 yd wide and 10 yd long. He wants to put a cement deck around the pool. It will be $5\frac{1}{2}$ ft wide on all sides. What will be the perimeter of the deck?

For 3–4, use this information.
A window is in the shape of a square with an isosceles triangle attached at the top. The side of the triangle that is attached to the square is the same length as one side of the square.

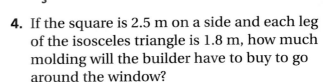

3. Use s for the length of a side of the square and l for the length of a leg of the isosceles triangle. Which expression can you use to find the window's perimeter?

   A $2s + 2l$ **C** $4s + 2l$
   B $3s + 2l$ **D** $4s + 3l$

4. If the square is 2.5 m on a side and each leg of the isosceles triangle is 1.8 m, how much molding will the builder have to buy to go around the window?

   F 6.8 m   **H** 11.1 m
   G 8.6 m   **J** 13.6 m

PROBLEM SOLVING STRATEGIES

▶ **Draw a Diagram or Picture**
   Make a Model
   Predict and Test
   Work Backward
   Make an Organized List
   Find a Pattern
   Make a Table or Graph
   Solve a Simpler Problem
   Write an Equation
   Use Logical Reasoning

MIXED STRATEGY PRACTICE

Use Data   **For 5–7, use the circle graph.**

5. Which three categories make up about 50% of the expenses? Explain.

6. Sharon spent a total of $98 this year and a total of $81 last year for her fall party. She spent the same percent for pumpkins this year as last year. How much more did she spend on pumpkins this year?

7. What percent of the expenses was spent on decorations, entertainment, and costumes?

EXPENSES FOR FALL PARTY

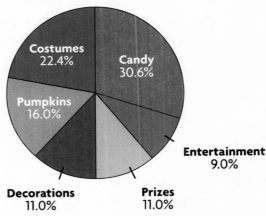

8. There are 90 ft between bases on major league baseball diamonds and 60 ft between bases on Little League diamonds. How much farther does a major league player have to run if he hits a home run?

9. Kathy wants to work on her car. She needs a 25-mm wrench but her wrenches are all in customary units. Estimate the size of a customary wrench she should use.

10. Ali and Walt are taking a 50-question test. Ali answers every sixth question incorrectly and Walt answers every eighth question incorrectly. Which questions do both Ali and Walt answer incorrectly?

11. ❓ **What's the Question?** May, Kevin, and Sean chopped wood. May chopped $\frac{2}{5}$ of the wood, Kevin chopped $\frac{1}{10}$ of it, and Sean chopped the rest. The answer is $\frac{1}{2}$.

Circumference

Vocabulary

circumference

pi

QUICK REVIEW

1. 3.14×8 **2.** 5.5×2 **3.** $14 \div 2$ **4.** $2 \times 3 \times 3.14$ **5.** $2 \times 5 \times 3.14$

Find the **circumference** , or distance around a circle, by using a compass, string, and a ruler.

Activity 1

You need: compass, string, ruler, calculator

Estimate the circumference of a circle with a radius of 4 in.

- Open the compass to a width of 4 in. Use the compass to construct a circle with a radius of 4 in.

- Lay the string around the circle. Mark the string where it meets itself.

- Use the ruler to measure the string from its beginning to the mark you made.

- What is the diameter of the circle? What is the circumference of the circle? Divide the circumference by the diameter. About how many times as long as the diameter is the circumference?

- Share your results with those of other students. What do you notice about the relationship between the diameter and the circumference of circles with different diameters?

- Write a formula to approximate the circumference of a circle.

4 in.

mark

When the circumference is divided by the diameter, $C \div d$, the quotient is the same for any circle. This number is called **pi**, or π. The value of π is usually approximated as 3.14 or $\frac{22}{7}$.

EXAMPLE 1

The Space Needle is about 605 ft high.

The revolving circular restaurant at the top of the Space Needle in Seattle has a diameter of 94.5 ft. To the nearest foot, how far will a person seated at the edge of the restaurant travel in one revolution?

You need to find the circumference of the restaurant. When you know the diameter of a circle, you can use the formula $C = \pi d$.

$C = \pi d$ *Write the formula.*

$C \approx 3.14 \times 94.5$ *Replace π with 3.14 and d with 94.5.*

$C \approx 296.73$

$C \approx 297$ *Round to the nearest foot.*

So, a person would travel about 297 ft.

Since $d = 2r$, you can write $C = \pi d$ as $C = \pi(2r)$, or $C = 2\pi r$.
Use $C = 2\pi r$ when you know the radius of the circle.

EXAMPLE 2

The Vienna Giant Ferris wheel was completed in 1897. It has a radius of 30.48 m. What is the circumference of the Ferris wheel? Round to the nearest whole number.

$C = 2\pi r$ *Write the formula.*

$C \approx 2 \times 3.14 \times 30.48$ *Replace π with 3.14*

$C \approx 191.4144$ *and r with 30.48.*

$C \approx 191$ *Round to the nearest whole number.*

So, the circumference is about 191 m.

Sometimes it makes sense to use the approximation $\frac{22}{7}$ for π.

EXAMPLE 3

Sean has a circular outdoor wooden planter with a radius of $3\frac{1}{2}$ in. He wants to put trim around the top. What is the length of the trim he will need?

$C = 2\pi r$ *Write the formula.*

$C \approx 2 \times \frac{22}{7} \times 3\frac{1}{2}$ *Replace π with $\frac{22}{7}$ and r with $3\frac{1}{2}$.*

$C \approx \frac{2}{1} \times \frac{\overset{11}{\cancel{22}}}{\underset{1}{\cancel{7}}} \times \frac{\overset{1}{\cancel{7}}}{\underset{1}{\cancel{2}}}$ *Write 2 and $3\frac{1}{2}$ as fractions. Simplify.*

$C \approx \frac{2}{1} \times \frac{11}{1} \times \frac{1}{1}$ *Multiply.*

$C \approx 22$

So, Sean will need about 22 in. of trim.

You can also use the π key on a calculator. If you use a calculator, you may have to round your answer.

EXAMPLE 4

Use a calculator with a π key. Find the circumference of a circle with diameter 12.7 m. Round to the nearest tenth.

Use this key sequence.

   12.7   39.8982267

$C \approx 39.8982267$

$C \approx 39.9$ *Round to the nearest tenth.*

So, the circumference is about 39.9 m.

Think and ▸
Discuss

Look back at the lesson to answer each question.

1. **Compare and contrast** the two formulas you can use to find the circumference of a circle.

2. **Express** $\frac{22}{7}$ as a decimal rounded to the nearest hundredth. How does it compare to 3.14?

Guided ▸
Practice

Find the circumference of the circle. Use 3.14 or $\frac{22}{7}$ for π. Round to the nearest whole number.

3.

5 m

4.

$4\frac{3}{8}$ ft

5.

1.9 cm

6. $r = 12.9$ mm

7. $d = 90$ yd

8. $r = 14$ mi

9. $d = 8.6$ in.

10. $r = 9.9$ m

11. $d = 10.6$ cm

Independent ▸
Practice

Find the circumference of the circle. Use 3.14 or $\frac{22}{7}$ for π. Round to the nearest whole number.

12.

14 m

13.

$6\frac{1}{2}$ in.

14.

7.6 cm

15.

$1\frac{2}{5}$ yd

16.

$2\frac{1}{3}$ in.

17.

35 cm

18. $r = 29.62$ km

19. $d = 100.5$ in.

20. $r = 6\frac{2}{3}$ yd

21. $d = 7$ ft

22. $r = 3.5$ m

23. $d = 5.1$ cm

24. Look at the figure of a circle inside a square. The length of each side of the square is 3.5 ft. What is the circumference of the circle to the nearest whole number?

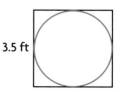
3.5 ft

Find the radius for each circumference.

25. $C \approx 28.26$ ft

26. $C \approx 47.1$ m

27. $C \approx 58.404$ cm

Problem Solving ▶
Applications

28. **Vocabulary Power** *Diameter* is from the Greek words *dia* and *metron*, meaning "across, through" and "measure." How does this help you understand the meaning of *diameter* of a circle?

29. **REASONING** How do the circumferences of two circles compare if the diameter of one circle is twice the diameter of the other? Give an example to explain your reasoning.

30. **? What's the Error?** Rhonda and Caren each used 3.14 to find the circumference of a circle with a radius of 34 mm. Rhonda's answer is 213.52 mm and Caren's is 106.76. Which girl made an error? What is the error?

31. George Ferris created the first Ferris wheel in 1893. The wheel had a maximum height of 264 ft. How many yards is this?

32. A garden shaped like the figure at the right will be fenced in. If there will be a 4-ft gate along the straight part, how much fencing is needed?

14 ft

MIXED REVIEW AND TEST PREP

33. Find the perimeter of a rectangle that is 46.3 m long and 28.2 m wide. (p. 443)

34. Is 131 prime or composite? (p. 166)

⭐ 35. **TEST PREP** $12\frac{2}{3} \div 5\frac{3}{5}$ (p. 236)

    A $2\frac{11}{42}$ **B** $2\frac{1}{2}$ **C** $3\frac{11}{42}$ **D** $7\frac{1}{2}$

⭐ 36. **TEST PREP** A quadrilateral has a perimeter of 19.5 yd. Three of the sides have lengths of 5 yd, 7 yd, and 2.25 yd. Find the length of the fourth side. (p. 443)

    F 14.25 yd   **H** 5 yd

    G 5.25 yd   **J** 4.25 yd

PROBLEM SOLVING   LiNKUP to Social Studies

Making Money The United States uses the dollar as the basic unit of money. France uses the euro and Mexico uses the peso. Artists play a big part in producing money. A new coin begins with an artist's design. The artist makes a clay model of the coin, and a mold is made from that model. A plaster cast is made from the mold. The artist then carves the details of the coin into the plaster.

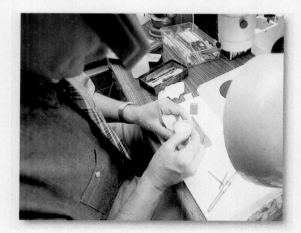

1. Use a metric ruler to measure the diameter of a penny, nickel, dime, and quarter to the nearest millimeter. Find the circumference of each coin to the nearest millimeter.

2. Research different countries to find the sizes of the coins they use. Compare the sizes of their coins with the ones used in the United States.

EXTRA PRACTICE page 452, Set B

Set A (pp. 443–445)

Find the perimeter.

1.
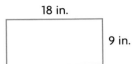
18 in.

9 in.

2.
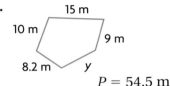
3.3 cm
3.3 cm   3.3 cm
3.3 cm   3.3 cm
3.3 cm

3.
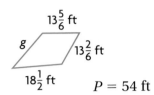
490 cm
6.5 m
9.8 m

The perimeter is given. Find the unknown length.

4.
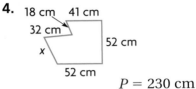
18 cm   41 cm
32 cm
52 cm
x
52 cm
P = 230 cm

5.
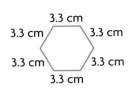
15 m
10 m
9 m
8.2 m   *y*
P = 54.5 m

6.
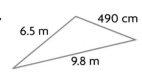
$13\frac{5}{6}$ ft
g $13\frac{2}{6}$ ft
$18\frac{1}{2}$ ft
P = 54 ft

7. Tanya wants to put a string of lights around a rectangular window that is 40 in. wide and 48 in. high. How long will the string of lights need to be to go around the window one time?

8. Linda is building a raised flowerbed $10\frac{1}{2}$ ft long and 4 ft wide. How many feet of lumber will she need to go around the flowerbed?

Set B (pp. 448–451)

Find the circumference of the circle. Use 3.14 or $\frac{22}{7}$ for π. Round to the nearest whole number.

1.

7 in.

2.

12 ft

3.

49 cm

4.

$4\frac{1}{2}$ in.

5.

2.7 cm

6.

15.4 ft

7. *r* = 1.6 ft

8. *d* = 23.5 cm

9. *d* = 28 ft

10. *r* = 25.9 m

11. *d* = 82.1 mm

12. *d* = 3.21 m

13. A blue circular rug in Dominique's room has a diameter of $6\frac{1}{2}$ ft. To the nearest foot what is the circumference of the rug?

14. A child's hat has a radius of 8 cm. To the nearest centimeter, what is the circumference of the hat?

1. **VOCABULARY** The distance around a polygon is the ___?___ .
(p. 443)

2. **VOCABULARY** The distance around a circle is called the ___?___ .
(p. 448)

3. **VOCABULARY** The ratio of the circumference of a circle to its diameter is called ___?___ . (p. 448)

Find the perimeter. (pp. 443–445)

4.
35 yd
19 yd

5.
$9\frac{1}{4}$ ft
5 ft
$12\frac{1}{2}$ ft

6.
8.2 cm   8.2 cm
14.7 cm   14.7 cm
10.5 cm

7.
19 in.
6 in.   14 in.
24 in.

8.
5.8 m
5.8 m   5.8 m
5.8 m   5.8 m
5.8 m

9. $4\frac{1}{10}$ ft $5\frac{1}{5}$ ft
$6\frac{7}{10}$ ft $8\frac{1}{2}$ ft

The perimeter is given. Find the unknown length. (pp. 443–445)

10.
13.4 m   11.9 m
11.06 m   11.06 m
x
$P = 65.7$ m

11.
13.8 cm   13.8 cm
22.2 cm   22.2 cm
x
$P = 84$ cm

12.
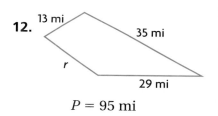
13 mi
35 mi
r
29 mi
$P = 95$ mi

Find the circumference of the circle. Use 3.14 or $\frac{22}{7}$ for π. Round to the nearest whole number. (pp. 448–451)

13.
14 in.

14.
35 ft

15.
4.3 m

16.
12.5 in.

17.
15.6 m

18.
60.8 km

Solve.

19. An official tournament-size dartboard has a radius of 9 in. Find its circumference to the nearest whole number. (pp. 448–451)

20. Julie has a rectangular piece of fabric 32 in. long and 25 in. wide. What is its perimeter? (pp. 443–445)

⭐ MEASUREMENT

1. The map gives approximate dimensions of North Dakota and South Dakota. Which is the **most** reasonable estimate of the perimeter around the Dakotas?

| 300 mi |
| North Dakota |
| 210 mi | 210 mi |
| 350 mi |
| 200 mi | 210 mi |
| South Dakota |
| 370 mi |

- **A** 350 miles
- **C** 1,800 miles
- **B** 1,500 miles
- **D** 1,850 miles

2. Using a yardstick, Marie found that the diameter of her bicycle wheel was 26 inches. Which of the following methods will give her the **best** approximation of the wheel's circumference?

- **F** Multiply the diameter by 2.
- **G** Multiply the diameter by 3.
- **H** Divide the diameter by 3.
- **J** Divide the diameter by 2, then multiply the quotient by 3.

3. A rectangular advertising billboard in Barcelona, Spain, was once the world's biggest sign. It had a length of 476 feet and a perimeter of 1,050 feet. What was the sign's width?

- **A** 49 feet
- **C** 287 feet
- **B** 98 feet
- **D** 574 feet

4. **Explain It** Franco's soccer game began at 11:15 A.M. and ended at 1:05 P.M. Explain how you can use mental math to find how long the game lasted.

⭐ ALGEBRAIC THINKING

5. Population counts show increasing numbers of elk in a wildlife refuge.

NUMBER OF ELK					
Year	1999	2000	2001	2002	2003
Number	24	26	30	36	44

If the trend continues, how many elk will make their home in the refuge in 2004?

- **F** 52
- **H** 54
- **G** 53
- **J** 55

6. The graph shows the relationship between the number of ounces of water, x, given to a flowering plant daily, and the number of blossoms produced, y.

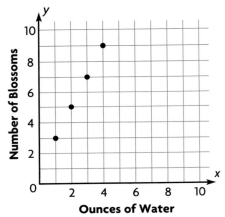

Which table shows the relationship between x and y?

A

x	1	2	3	4
y	2	3	4	5

C

x	1	2	3	4
y	3	4	5	6

B

x	1	2	3	4
y	1	2	3	4

D

x	1	2	3	4
y	3	5	7	9

7. **Explain It** Pete started with $10. In Week 1 he saved $2. In Week 2 he saved $4. In Week 3 he saved $6. If the pattern continues, in which week will he have a total of $52? Explain your reasoning.

DATA ANALYSIS AND PROBABILITY

8. Jay had a choice of rye or wheat bread and salami, ham, or turkey. How many different kinds of sandwiches could he make if he used one bread and one sandwich meat?

> **TIP** **Decide on a plan.** See item 8. Use a tree diagram or make a list.

F 5   **G** 6   **H** 7   **J** 8

9. The graph shows the number of meteors that Denise counted during four nights.

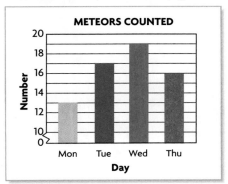

On Friday, Denise counted 9 fewer meteors than she did on Tuesday. How many meteors did she count on Friday?

A 4   **B** 7   **C** 8   **D** 10

10. Explain It Nick read the graph below and said it showed that there are more students in Grade 6 than in any other grade. Was he right? Explain.

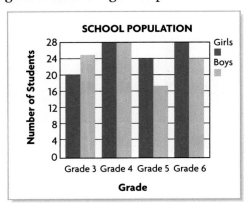

GEOMETRY AND SPATIAL SENSE

11. Highways connecting the towns of Grogan, Milton, and Plover form a triangle. Two of the angles of the triangle measure 32° and 49°. Which is the **best** way to classify the triangle?

F acute   **H** obtuse

G right   **J** straight

12. Jeri drew a design that included a circle.

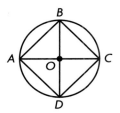

Which word describes $\overline{CD}$?

A diameter   **C** chord

B radius   **D** ray

13. A beach towel has the design shown below. Which line segment is a line of symmetry for the design?

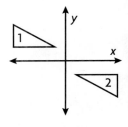

F $\overline{AF}$ **H** $\overline{CG}$

G $\overline{AD}$ **J** $\overline{JE}$

14. Explain It A triangle was rotated from position 1 to position 2. Explain how the change in position could have been made using reflections.

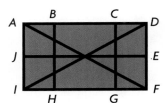

455

CHAPTER 21

Areas of Plane Figures

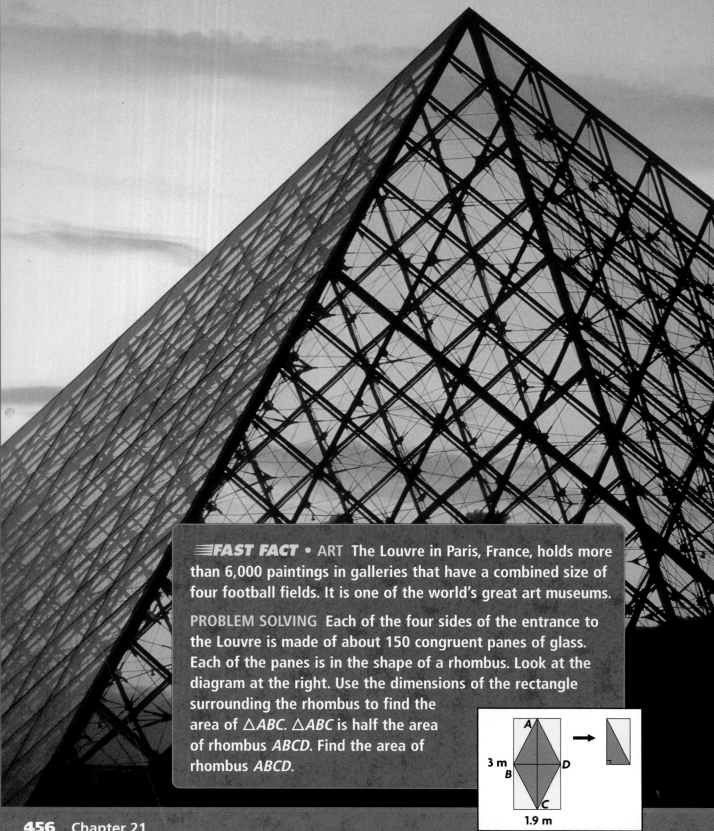

≡FAST FACT • ART The Louvre in Paris, France, holds more than 6,000 paintings in galleries that have a combined size of four football fields. It is one of the world's great art museums.

PROBLEM SOLVING Each of the four sides of the entrance to the Louvre is made of about 150 congruent panes of glass. Each of the panes is in the shape of a rhombus. Look at the diagram at the right. Use the dimensions of the rectangle surrounding the rhombus to find the area of △ABC. △ABC is half the area of rhombus ABCD. Find the area of rhombus ABCD.

Check What You Know

Use this page to help you review and remember important skills needed for Chapter 21.

✔ Evaluate Expressions

Evaluate the expression for the given value of the variable.

1. $a + b$ for $a = 12$ and $b = 4$

2. $h - g$ for $h = 27$ and $g = 9$

3. $5n$ for $n = 4$

4. $\frac{1}{2}k$ for $k = 30$

5. $13p$ for $p = 6$

6. $144 \div v$ for $v = 36$

7. $(6 + 9)c$ for $c = 11$

8. r^2 for $r = 8$

9. lw for $l = 6$ and $w = 9$

10. $\frac{1}{2}bh$ for $b = 5$ and $h = 10$

11. $2ab$ for $a = 4$ and $b = 12$

12. $3c^2$ for $c = 8$

13. $3(w + 5)$ for $w = 7$

14. $6(x + y)$ for $x = 12$ and $y = 3$

15. $\frac{1}{2}s^2 + 2s$ for $s = 4$

16. $\frac{1}{2}h(8 + m)$ for $h = 10$ and $m = 4$

✔ Multiply Fractions and Whole Numbers

Find the product.

17. $\frac{1}{2} \times 40$

18. $\frac{1}{4} \times 32$

19. $\frac{1}{3} \times 42$

20. $\frac{1}{7} \times 63$

21. $32 \times \frac{1}{8}$

22. $80 \times \frac{1}{5}$

23. $\frac{1}{2} \times 24$

24. $\frac{1}{3} \times 54$

25. $\frac{7}{2} \times 20$

26. $\frac{22}{7} \times 14$

27. $\frac{22}{7} \times 49$

28. $28 \times \frac{22}{7}$

29. $\frac{1}{2} \times 84$

30. $\frac{1}{2} \times 176$

31. $\frac{1}{2} \times 168$

32. $\frac{1}{2} \times 500$

VOCABULARY POWER

REVIEW

circle [sûr′kəl] *noun*

The Latin root of the word *circle* is *circus*. Roman chariot races were held in structures that were referred to as a *circus*. In what shape do you think the chariot races were run?

PREVIEW

area

 www.harcourtschool.com/mathglossary

Estimate and Find Area

Learn how to estimate area and find the area of rectangles and triangles.

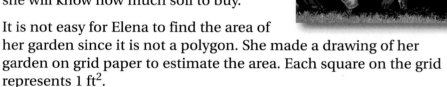

Vocabulary

area

Elena wants to put a layer of new soil on her garden to help the garden grow. She needs to know the area of her garden so she will know how much soil to buy.

It is not easy for Elena to find the area of her garden since it is not a polygon. She made a drawing of her garden on grid paper to estimate the area. Each square on the grid represents 1 ft^2.

The **area** of a figure is the number of square units needed to cover it. Use this drawing of Elena's garden to estimate the area.

Remember that area is measured in square units such as square feet (ft^2) and square meters (m^2).

There are 12 full red squares.

There are 6 almost-full blue squares.

There are 4 about half-full orange squares. Combine the half-full squares to make 2 more full squares. Do not count the squares

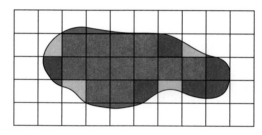

with green in them. They are less than half full and they combine with the almost-full blue squares to come close to 6 full squares.

Add the number of squares counted as full.

$12 + 6 + 2 = 20$

So, the area of Elena's garden is about 20 ft^2.

Activity

You need: ruler, scissors, square tiles or 1-inch graph paper

• Use a ruler to draw a rectangle with a length between 4 in. and 5 in. and a width between 2 in. and 3 in.

• Use square tiles or cut out enough 1-in. squares from 1-in. graph paper to cover the rectangle.

• Use the 1-in. squares to estimate the area of the rectangle.

• Count the squares along the length and along the width. Find the product. How does the product compare to your estimate of the area?

You can use the formula $A = lw$ to find the area of a rectangle and the formula $A = s^2$ to find the area of a square.

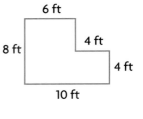
13 in. (width)

16 in. (length)

EXAMPLE 1

Find the area of the rectangle shown at the right.

$A = lw$ *Write the formula.*

$A = 16 \times 13$ *Replace l with 16 and w with 13.*

$A = 208$ *Multiply.*

So, the area of the rectangle is 208 in.^{2}

EXAMPLE 2

Cinzia is going to wallpaper a wall shown in the figure at the right. How many square feet of wallpaper will she need?

Think of the wall as a rectangle that is 8 ft × 6 ft and a square that is 4 ft × 4 ft.

Find the area of each figure and then find the sum.

Rectangle	Square
$A = lw$	$A = s^2$
$A = 8 \times 6$	$A = 4^2 = 4 \times 4$
$A = 48$	$A = 16$

Total area: $48 + 16 = 64$

So, Cinzia will need 64 ft^2 of wallpaper.

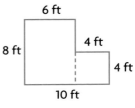
6 ft
8 ft
4 ft
4 ft
10 ft

6 ft
8 ft
4 ft
4 ft
10 ft

The figure at the right shows how two congruent right triangles can be used to model a rectangle. The area of each triangle is half that of the rectangle. The area of each right triangle is

$\frac{1}{2}lw$, or $\frac{1}{2} \times 14 \times 8 = 56$.

In a right triangle, the dimensions of the two legs are the base, b, and the height, h. So, the formula for the area of a right triangle is written as $A = \frac{1}{2}bh$.

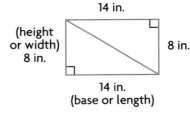
14 in.
(height or width) 8 in.
8 in.
14 in. (base or length)

height (h)
base (b)

EXAMPLE 3

Use the formula $A = \frac{1}{2}bh$ to find the area of the triangle at the right.

$A = \frac{1}{2}bh$ *Write the formula.*

$A = \frac{1}{2} \times 8 \times 5$ *Replace b with 8 and h with 5.*

$A = \frac{1}{2} \times 40$ *Multiply.*

$A = 20$ So, the area is 20 cm^2.

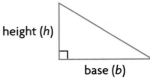
5 cm
8 cm

Use what you know about right triangles to find the area of other triangles. Look at triangle *ABC* below.

Area of right triangle *ABD*: $A = \frac{1}{2}bh = \frac{1}{2} \times 4 \times 6$.

Area of right triangle *CBD*: $A = \frac{1}{2}bh = \frac{1}{2} \times 7 \times 6$.

To find the area of triangle *ABC*, find the sum of those areas.

$A = \left(\frac{1}{2} \times 4 \times 6\right) + \left(\frac{1}{2} \times 7 \times 6\right)$

$A = 12 + 21$ *Add.*

$A = 33$ So, the area of triangle *ABC* is 33 in.²

The formula $A = \frac{1}{2}bh$ works for all triangles.

- Find the area of triangle *ABC* by using 4 in. + 7 in., or 11 in., as the base and 6 in. as the height. Compare your answer to 33 in.²

Sometimes the height is shown outside the triangle. The height of this triangle is 1.8 m.

$$A = \frac{1}{2} \times 2.8 \times 1.8 = 2.52$$

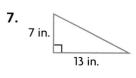

CHECK FOR UNDERSTANDING

Think and ▶
Discuss

Look back at the lesson to answer the question.

1. **Tell** how the areas of a rectangle and a triangle with the same base and height are related.

Guided ▶
Practice

Estimate the area of the figure. Each square represents 1 m².

2.   3.   4.

Find the area.

5. 13 in. / 9 in.   6.   7. 7 in. / 13 in.

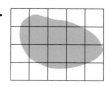

PRACTICE AND PROBLEM SOLVING

Independent ▶
Practice

Estimate the area of the figure. Each square represents 1 m².

8.   9.   10.

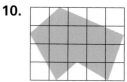

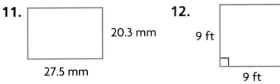
Find the area.

11.

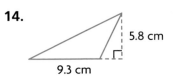
20.3 mm
27.5 mm

12.

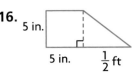
9 ft
9 ft

13.

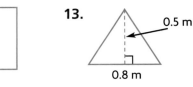
0.5 m
0.8 m

14.

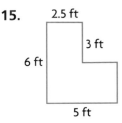
5.8 cm
9.3 cm

15.
2.5 ft
3 ft
6 ft
5 ft

16.
5 in.
5 in.
$\frac{1}{2}$ ft

Problem Solving ▶
Applications

17. The diagram shows a backyard. It will be covered with grass. How many square yards of grass are needed?

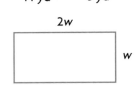
20 yd
15 yd
9 yd
3 yd
14 yd
3 yd

18. **?** **What's the Error?** The length of this rectangle is twice the width. Jeri says the area of the rectangle is 6*w* units. What error did Jeri make? What is the area?

2*w*
w

19. *REASONING* Rectangle *A* has a length of 8 cm. Rectangle *B* has a length of 6 cm. Both rectangles have areas of 24 cm². Find the perimeter of each rectangle. Are the perimeters the same?

MIXED REVIEW AND TEST PREP

20. Evaluate $\frac{1}{2} \times c$ for $c = 24$. (p. 260)

21. Evaluate $2d - 6$ for $d = 7$. (p. 260)

22. Write $\frac{3}{5}$ as a percent. (p. 191)

★23. TEST PREP If Rod is twice as tall as Cathy, and Rod's height is *x*, what expression represents Cathy's height? (p. 36)

A $2x$ **C** $\frac{1}{2}x$

B x **D** $x - 2$

★24. TEST PREP Which shows the circumference of a circle with a radius of 13 cm? Use 3.14 for π. (p. 448)

F about 23.55 cm   **H** about 81.64 cm

G about 40.82 cm   **J** about 93.01 cm

PROBLEM SOLVING 💡 Thinker's Corner

A Box of Triangles Here is another way to explore the relationship between triangles and rectangles.

Materials: ruler

• Draw and label rectangle *ABCD* as shown at the right. Draw points *M* and *N* anywhere on $\overline{AB}$.

• Draw △*DAC*, △*DMC*, △*DNC*, and △*DBC*.

• Find the area of the rectangle and each of the triangles. What do you notice about your results?

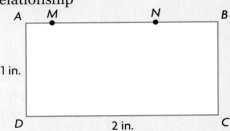
A M   N B
1 in.
D   2 in.   C

ALGEBRA
Areas of Parallelograms and Trapezoids

Learn how to find the areas of parallelograms and trapezoids.

A contractor has to put glass tiles on the side of an escalator. The side has the shape of a parallelogram. How many square feet of tiles will the contractor need?

Activity 1

You need: scissors, graph paper

• The parallelogram at the right is a drawing of the side of the escalator. Draw the parallelogram on a piece of graph paper and cut it out.

height (h)   3 ft
base (b)   22 ft

• Cut along the dotted line. Move the triangle to the right side to form a rectangle.

width (w) 3 ft
length (l)   22 ft

• What is the area of the rectangle? What is the area of the parallelogram?

• How are the dimensions and area of the parallelogram related to those of the rectangle?

• What formula can you write for the area of a parallelogram?

You can use the formula for the area of a rectangle to write a formula for the area of a parallelogram.

$A = lw$ *The length of the rectangle is the base of the parallelogram.*
    ↓ *The width of the rectangle is the height of the parallelogram.*
$A = bh$

Use $A = bh$ to find the area of the side of the escalator.

$A = bh$
$A = 22 \times 3$ *Replace b with 22 and h with 3.*
$A = 66$

So, the area of the side of the escalator is 66 ft².

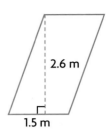

EXAMPLE 1

Find the area of the parallelogram at the right.

$A = bh$ *Write the formula.*

$A = 1.5 \times 2.6$ *Replace b with 1.5 and h with 2.6.*

$A = 3.9$ *Multiply.*

So, the area is 3.9 m².

You can also find the area of a trapezoid.

MATH LAB

Activity 2

You need: paper, scissors

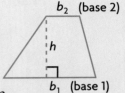

• Trace the trapezoid shown at the right twice. Label both trapezoids using h, b_1, and b_2 as shown. Cut them out.

• Arrange the trapezoids to form a parallelogram. The length of the parallelogram is $b_1 + b_2$. The height is h, the height of the trapezoid.

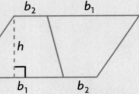

• The formula for the area of a parallelogram is $A = bh$. Use the expression $b_1 + b_2$ for the base and h for the height to write a formula for the area of this parallelogram.

• How does the area of one trapezoid relate to the area of the parallelogram?

Since each trapezoid is half of the parallelogram, you can use $\frac{1}{2} \times (b_1 + b_2) \times h$, or $\frac{1}{2}h(b_1 + b_2)$ to find the area.

EXAMPLE 2

Find the area of the trapezoid.

$A = \frac{1}{2}h(b_1 + b_2)$ *Write the formula.*

$A = \frac{1}{2} \times 12 \times (18 + 7)$ *Replace h with 12, b_1 with 18, and b_2 with 7.*

$A = \frac{1}{2} \times 12 \times 25$ *Multiply.*

$A = \frac{1}{2} \times 300$

$A = 150$ So, the area is 150 in.²

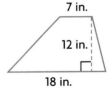

CHECK FOR UNDERSTANDING

Think and ▸ Discuss

Look back at the lesson to answer each question.

1. **Explain** which formula you would use to find the area of a rhombus.

2. **Tell** how to find the area of the trapezoid at the right.

463

Guided ▸ Practice Find the area of each figure.

3.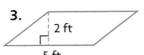
2 ft
5 ft

4.
3 in.
10 in.
12 in.

5.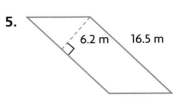
6.2 m   16.5 m

PRACTICE AND PROBLEM SOLVING

Independent ▸ Practice Find the area of each figure.

6.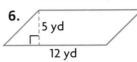
5 yd
12 yd

7.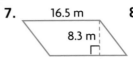
16.5 m
8.3 m

8.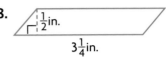
$\frac{1}{2}$ in.
$3\frac{1}{4}$ in.

9.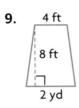
4 ft
8 ft
2 yd

10.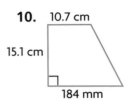
10.7 cm
15.1 cm
184 mm

11.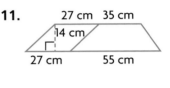
27 cm   35 cm
14 cm
27 cm   55 cm

Problem Solving ▸ Applications

12. When triangular flaps are raised on opposite sides of the square table at the right, it has the shape of a parallelogram. The base of each triangle is 2 ft. What is the area of the table top?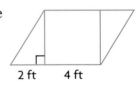
2 ft   4 ft

13. **REASONING** Copy the parallelogram in Exercise 6 and the trapezoid in Exercise 9. Show how you can divide each figure into 2 triangles to find the area. Then find the areas and compare your answers to the answers you originally got for Exercises 6 and 9.

14. Four months ago James had $1,480 in his savings account. Three months ago the balance was $1,590 and two months ago it was $1,700. Describe the pattern. Then find the account balance one month ago if the pattern continued.

MIXED REVIEW AND TEST PREP

15. Find the area of a triangle where $b = 4$ m and $h = 12$ m. (p. 458)

16. $7\frac{1}{6} \times \frac{3}{4}$ (p. 232)   17. 3 g = ▇ kg (p. 423)

18. Is the number 87 prime or composite? (p. 166)

⭐ 19. **TEST PREP** A bakery has a 40-lb bag of flour. Six pounds of flour are used to make cakes. Half of what is left is used to make cookies. How much flour remains in the bag after the cookies are made? (p. 24)

A 14 lb   B 17 lb   C 18 lb   D 19 lb

EXTRA PRACTICE page 472, Set B

Area of a Circle

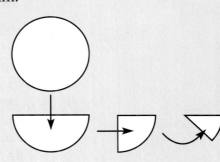

Explore how to find the area of a circle.

You need compass, scissors.

Activity

To see how the area of a circle and its radius are related, you can rearrange the cut-up parts of the circle to approximate a parallelogram.

- Use the compass to construct a circle on a piece of paper.

- Cut out the circle. Fold it three times as shown.

- Unfold it, and trace the folds. Shade one half of the circle as shown.

- Cut along the folds. Fit the pieces together to make a figure that approximates a parallelogram.

Think and Discuss

Think of the figure as a parallelogram. The base and the height of the parallelogram relate to the parts of the circle.

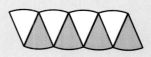

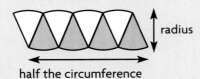
half the circumference / radius

base $(b) = \frac{1}{2}$ the circumference of the circle, or $\frac{1}{2} \times 2\pi r$, or πr

height $(h) =$ the radius of the circle, or r

Remember that the formula for the circumference of a circle is $C = \pi d$ or $C = 2\pi r$.
π is approximately 3.14, or $\frac{22}{7}$.

- What is the formula for the area of a parallelogram?

- Use the formula for the area of a parallelogram to write a formula for the area of a circle. Since the pieces of the parallelogram are the pieces of the circle, substitute πr for the base and r for the height.

- Use your formula to find the area, to the nearest whole number, of a circle with a radius of 7 yd.

Practice

Find the area of each circle with the given radius. Use your formula for the area of a circle, and round to the nearest square meter. Use 3.14 or $\frac{22}{7}$ for π.

1. $r = 1$ m   **2.** $r = 3$ m   **3.** $r = 8$ m   **4.** $r = 4$ m

ALGEBRA
Areas of Circles

Learn how to use a formula to find the area of a circle.

Jackie is on the girls' wrestling team at her high school. The photo at the right shows wrestling mats used for practice and competition. Square mats used for high school students have sides measuring 38 ft long. The large circle inside the square is the wrestling circle.

EXAMPLE 1

Find the area of the wrestling circle with a radius of 14 ft. Use the formula for the area of a circle, $A = \pi r^2$. Use $\frac{22}{7}$ for π.

$A = \pi r^2$	*Write the formula.*
$A \approx \frac{22}{7} \times (14)^2$	*Replace π with $\frac{22}{7}$ and r with 14.*
$A \approx \frac{22}{7} \times 196$	
$A \approx \frac{22}{7} \times \frac{\overset{28}{196}}{\underset{1}{1}}$	*Simplify.*
$A \approx \frac{22}{1} \times \frac{28}{1}$	*Multiply.*
$A \approx \frac{616}{1}$, or 616	

So, the area of the wrestling circle is about 616 ft^2.

• **What if** you use 3.14 for π? What do you get as the area of the wrestling circle, to the nearest whole number?

Sometimes you are given the diameter of a circle.

EXAMPLE 2

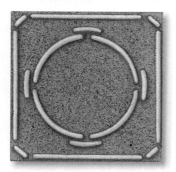

The wrestling circle for sumo, a Japanese form of wrestling, has a diameter of 4.6 m. What is the area of the circle, to the nearest whole number? Use 3.14 for π.

$4.6 \div 2 = 2.3$	*Find the radius.*
$A = \pi r^2$	*Write the formula.*
$A \approx 3.14 \times (2.3)^2$	*Replace π with 3.14 and r with 2.3.*
$A \approx 3.14 \times 5.29$	
$A \approx 16.6106$	

So, the area of the circle is about 17 m^2.

**Think and ▶
Discuss**

Look back at the lesson to answer the question.

1. **Explain** how to find the area of a circular dartboard with a diameter of $1\frac{1}{2}$ ft. Then find the area.

**Guided ▶
Practice**

Find the area of each circle to the nearest whole number. Use 3.14 or $\frac{22}{7}$ for π.

2.
3 cm

3.
20 m

4.
24 ft

5.
4.5 m

**Independent ▶
Practice**

Find the area of each circle to the nearest whole number. Use 3.14 or $\frac{22}{7}$ for π.

6.
8 yd

7.
56 in.

8.
1.5 m

9.
10.6 cm

10. $r = 4$ mm   **11.** $r = 0.9$ m   **12.** $d = 66$ in.   **13.** $d = 100$ ft

Find the area of the partial circle to the nearest whole number.

14.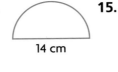
14 cm
$\frac{1}{2}$ circle

15.
8 cm
$\frac{1}{4}$ circle

16.
3 in.
$\frac{1}{3}$ circle

17.
12 in.
$\frac{2}{3}$ circle

**Problem Solving ▶
Applications**

18. College wrestling rules require that the mat have a wrestling circle with a minimum diameter of 32 ft. What is the minimum area of the wrestling circle to the nearest whole number?

19. **Vocabulary Power** *Radius* is from the Latin word *radius* meaning "spoke of a wheel." Compare the spoke of a wheel to the radius of a circle.

20. Find the area of a parallelogram with a base of 12.5 ft and height of 8 ft. (p. 462)

21. Solve. $17 = \frac{x}{12}$ (p. 291)

22. Complete. $\frac{16}{24} = \frac{2}{\blacksquare}$ (p. 182)

23. Find the LCM of 5, 8, and 20 (p. 170)

24. **TEST PREP** Rectangle *A* is 12 ft by 18 ft. Rectangle *B* is 9 ft by 13 ft. How much greater is the perimeter of *A* than the perimeter of *B*? (p. 443)

A 16 ft   **B** 44 ft   **C** 60 ft   **D** 99 ft

EXTRA PRACTICE page 472, Set C

ALGEBRA
Changing Dimensions

Learn how the perimeters and areas of figures change as the dimensions change.

QUICK REVIEW

Evaluate the expression for $l = 6$ and $w = 2$.

1. lw **2.** $2l + 2w$ **3.** $\frac{1}{2}lw$ **4.** l^2 **5.** $\frac{1}{2}(16)(l + w)$

Kerry plans to reduce his rectangular garden into a rectangular garden of half its present area. One way would be to halve the length. Another way would be to halve the width. Would these changes divide the perimeter in half as well?

Activity 1

You need: rectangular sheet of paper, ruler

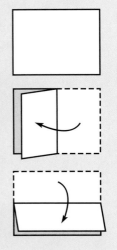

- Measure the length and width of the paper. Then find its perimeter and area.

- Fold the paper in half along its length to form a new rectangle with half the area of the original. Find the new perimeter. Is it half the perimeter of the original rectangle, more than half, or less than half?

- Unfold and repeat the above step, this time folding along the width.

- Compare the two results. In what ways are the results of folding in half along the length different from folding in half along the width?

- Will the perimeter of Kerry's garden be half the perimeter of the original garden? Explain.

EXAMPLE 1

A 4-in. by 6-in. index card has a perimeter of 20 in. and an area of 24 in.² The card is cut in half along its shorter side. Find the perimeter and area of the new rectangles formed.

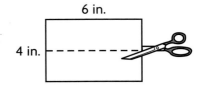

6 in.

4 in.

Both halves are rectangles that measure 6 in. × 2 in.

Perimeter		**Area**	
$P = 2l + 2w$	*Write the formula.*	$A = lw$	*Write the formula.*
$P = 2(6) + 2(2)$	$l = 6, w = 2$	$A = 6 \times 2$	$l = 6, w = 2$
$P = 16$	*Multiply and add.*	$A = 12$	*Multiply.*

So, the perimeter is 16 in. and the area is 12 in.²

- How do the new perimeter and area compare with the original perimeter and area?

Computer graphics tools allow artists to make new figures by changing the dimensions of existing figures. As the dimensions of the figures change, so do the perimeters and areas.

EXAMPLE 2

Suzy uses computer graphics tools to draw this design. Then she increases the length to 150%, or 1.5 times the original length. She also increases the width to 125%, or 1.25 times the original width.

Find the area of the new shaded triangle.

First, find the dimensions of the new rectangle.

150% of 8 $1.5 \times 8 = 12$, or 12 cm
125% of 4 $1.25 \times 4 = 5$, or 5 cm

Then find the area of the new shaded triangle.

$A = \frac{1}{2}bh$ *Write the formula.*

$A = \frac{1}{2} \times 12 \times 5$ *b = 12, h = 5*

$A = 30$ *Multiply.*

So, the area of the new shaded triangle is 30 cm².

- Will the area be the same if the length of the triangle is increased to 125% of the original, and the width to 150%?

Activity 2

You need: large paper isosceles triangle, ruler, scissors

Follow these instructions to make two trapezoids.

- Find the vertex formed by the congruent sides of the triangle. Fold it to the midpoint of the opposite side. Unfold and cut along the crease. Label the trapezoid *A*.

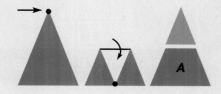

- The piece you cut off to form the trapezoid is another isosceles triangle. Repeat the process for this triangle. Label the new trapezoid *B*.

- Find and compare the perimeters of trapezoids *A* and *B*.

- Find and compare the areas of trapezoids *A* and *B*.

469

EXAMPLE 3

A trapezoid has bases measuring 4 in. and 5 in. and a height of 3 in. If the bases and the height are doubled, how does the new area compare with the original area?

The new bases measure 2 × 4 in. = 8 in. and 2 × 5 in. = 10 in. The new height measures 2 × 3 in. = 6 in.

Original Area		New Area
$A = \frac{1}{2}h(b_1 + b_2)$	*Write the formula.*	$A = \frac{1}{2}h(b_1 + b_2)$
$A = \frac{1}{2} \times 3 \times (4 + 5)$	*Replace h, b_1, and b_2.*	$A = \frac{1}{2} \times 6 \times (8 + 10)$
$A = \frac{1}{2} \times 3 \times 9$	*Simplify.*	$A = \frac{1}{2} \times 6 \times 18$
$A = 13\frac{1}{2}$		$A = 54$

Divide to compare. $\qquad 54 \div 13\frac{1}{2} = 4$

So, the new trapezoid has 4 times the area of the original trapezoid.

CHECK FOR UNDERSTANDING

Think and Discuss ▶ **Look back at the lesson to answer these questions.**

1. **Explain** how the area of a parallelogram changes when the height is reduced to half of the original height.

2. **Explain** how the perimeter of a rectangle changes if the length and width are both doubled.

Guided Practice ▶ **Find the area and the new area when the dimensions are doubled.**

3.
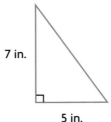
7 in.
5 in.

4.
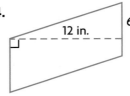
12 in.
6 in.

5.
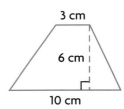
3 cm
6 cm
10 cm

PRACTICE AND PROBLEM SOLVING

Independent Practice ▶ **Find the area and the new area when the dimensions are doubled.**

6.

9ft
6 ft

7.
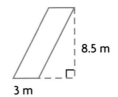
8.5 m
3 m

8.
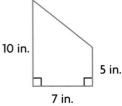
10 in.
5 in.
7 in.

Problem Solving Applications ▶ 9. The dimensions of a 12-in. square are tripled. How do the perimeter and area of the new square compare with the perimeter and area of the original square?

480 in.

228 in.

Puppy by Jeff Koons

10. A trapezoid has a height of 10 cm and bases measuring 11 cm and 3 cm. If the height is doubled and the length of each base is increased by 2 cm, what is the area of the new trapezoid?

11. The radius of a circle is 8 in. If the radius is halved, how does the area of the new circle compare with the area of the original?

12. **REASONING**   The height of a trapezoid is 4 cm, 5 cm, or 6 cm. The bases are the other two measurements. In order for the trapezoid to have the maximum possible area, which measurement must be the height?

13. **FAST FACT** • ART Artist Jeff Koons's *Puppy*, the largest flower sculpture in the world, contains over 70,000 plants and 25 T of soil. The approximate height and width of the sculpture are shown. Find the area of the rectangle around the sculpture in square feet.

MIXED REVIEW AND TEST PREP

14. Write 15% as a decimal. (p. 68)

15. Evaluate $3ab$ for $a = 3.6$ and $b = 4.2$ (p. 94)

16. What is the sum of the measures of the three angles of a triangle? (p. 356)

17. **TEST PREP**   Which dimensions give an area of 16 in.^{2} for a triangle? (p. 458)

A $b = 4, h = 4$ C $b = 2, h = 16$

B $b = 8, h = 2$ D $b = 16, h = 1$

18. **TEST PREP**   Write the product $\frac{7}{8} \times \frac{2}{3}$ in simplest form. (p. 228)

F $\frac{14}{24}$ H $\frac{7}{12}$

G $\frac{9}{11}$ J $\frac{14}{11}$

PROBLEM SOLVING

Thinker's Corner

Area Measurement After you find the area of a figure, you may need to convert it to another unit. Some conversions for units of area are shown in the table at the right. You can convert between units of area the same way you convert between linear measurements.

UNITS OF AREA	
1 m^2 = 10,000 cm^2	1 yd^2 = 9 ft^2
1 km^2 = 1,000,000 m^2	1 acre = 4,840 yd^2
1 ft^2 = 144 in.^{2}	1 mi^2 = 3,097,600 yd^2

A. 8 yd^2 = ■ ft^2

THINK: Since 1 yd^2 = 9 ft^2 and a square yard is a larger unit than a square foot, multiply by 9.

$8 \times 9 = 72$

So, there are 72 ft^2 in 8 yd^2.

B. 200,000 cm^2 = ■ m^2

THINK: Since 1 m^2 = 10,000 cm^2 and a square centimeter is a smaller unit than a square meter, divide by 10,000.

$200,000 \div 10,000 = 20$

So, there are 20 m^2 in 200,000 cm^2.

Convert to the given unit.

1. 5 mi^2 = ■ yd^2 2. 15 km^2 = ■ m^2 3. 1,728 in.^{2} = ■ ft^2 4. 24,200 yd^2 = ■ acres

EXTRA PRACTICE page 472, Set D

Set A (pp. 458–461)

Estimate the area. Each square on the grid represents 1 cm².

1.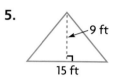

2.

3.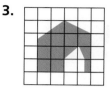

Find the area.

4.
24 cm
32 cm

5.
9 ft
15 ft

6.
5 in.
8 in.

7.
9.5 m
5.2 m

Set B (pp. 462–464)

Find the area of each figure.

1.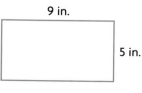
12 yd
7 yd

2.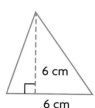
6 ft
4 ft
10 ft

3.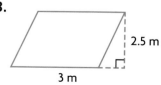
5.3 m
8.6 m

4.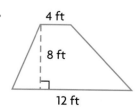
18 cm
12 cm
23 cm

5. A wall plaque is shaped like a trapezoid with a height of 6 in. and bases that measure 3.5 in. and 9.5 in. Find the area.

Set C (pp. 466–467)

Find the area of each circle to the nearest whole number. Use 3.14 or $\frac{22}{7}$ for π.

1. 9 yd

2. 12 mm

3. 7 ft

4. 4.2 in.

5. $d = 24$ cm

6. $r = 9.2$ mm

7. $d = 8$ yd

8. $d = 7\frac{1}{2}$ ft

Set D (pp. 468–471)

Find the area and the new area when the dimensions are doubled.

1. 9 in.
5 in.

2. 6 cm
6 cm

3. 2.5 m
3 m

4. 4 ft
8 ft
12 ft

Find the area. (pp. 458–464)

1.
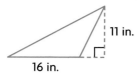
11 in.
16 in.

2.
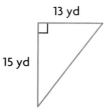
13 yd
15 yd

3.
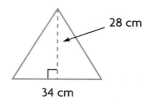
28 cm
34 cm

4.
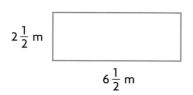
$2\frac{1}{2}$ m
$6\frac{1}{2}$ m

5.

9.1 cm
6.5 cm

6.

2 ft
20 in.

7.
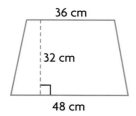
36 cm
32 cm
48 cm

8.
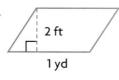
2 ft
1 yd

9.
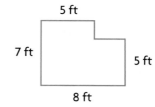
5 ft
7 ft
5 ft
8 ft

Find the area of each circle to the nearest whole number. Use 3.14 or $\frac{22}{7}$ for π. (pp. 466–467)

10. $r = 6$ m

11. $r = 12$ ft

12. $d = 18$ cm

13. $d = 10.5$ m

14. $r = 1\frac{1}{2}$ yd

15. $d = 15$ in.

16. $r = 2.9$ cm

17. $d = 8.4$ m

Find the area and the new area when the dimensions are doubled. (pp. 468–471)

18.
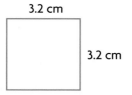
3.2 cm
3.2 cm

19.
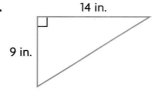
14 in.
9 in.

20.
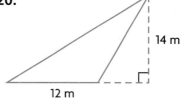
14 m
12 m

21.
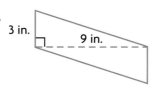
3 in.
9 in.

22.
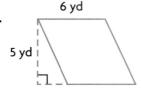
6 yd
5 yd

23.
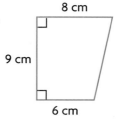
8 cm
9 cm
6 cm

24. Deanna wants to plant grass in three circular plots in her garden. The three plots have diameters of 9 ft, 8 ft, and 3 ft. To the nearest square foot, how much grass must she buy? Use 3.14 for π. (pp. 466–467)

25. The dimensions of a 5-in. by 8-in. rectangle are doubled. How does the area of the new rectangle compare with the area of the original rectangle? (pp. 468–471)

MEASUREMENT

1. A rectangular piece of stage scenery measures 12 feet by 10 feet. Triangular supports are also built. Their bases are half the length of the rectangle. How does the area of the rectangle compare to the area of one triangle?

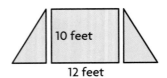

10 feet

12 feet

A one-fourth the area of one triangle

B one-half the area of one triangle

C two times the area of one triangle

D four times the area of one triangle

2. Serena is tiling a circular border around a planter. The radius of the large circle is 18 inches. The radius of the small circle is 12 inches. What is the area of the region Serena must tile? Use 3.14 for π.

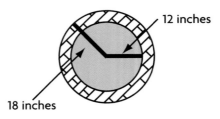

12 inches

18 inches

F 37.68 square inches

G 452.16 square inches

H 565.2 square inches

J 1,017.36 square inches

3. **Explain It** There are seven days in a week. The ancient Romans used an eight-day week. Is the number of eight-day weeks in a 365-day year more or less than the number of seven-day weeks? Explain your reasoning.

DATA ANALYSIS AND PROBABILITY

4. The table below gives the number of students in each of four classes at the Rembrandt School of Art.

ART CLASSES	
Class	**Number of Students**
Crafts	11
Quilts	9
Painting	14
Drawing	16

Which circle graph correctly displays the data in the table?

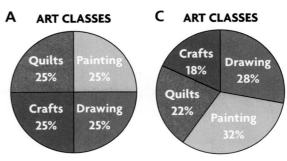

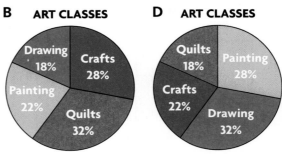

5. David can schedule a weekly tuba lesson for any day, Monday through Friday, at either 3, 4, 5, or 6 P.M. How many choices does he have for when he can schedule his lesson?

F 9   **H** 20

G 16   **J** 24

6. **Explain It** Brenda scored 18, 20, 17, 21, 2, 20, 22, and 20 points in 8 basketball games this season. Is the mean or the median the most useful to describe the data? Explain your reasoning.

GEOMETRY AND SPATIAL SENSE

7. On the Grid City map below, numbers on the *x*-axis represent avenues. Numbers on the *y*-axis represent streets. If you go to the point (3,5), what will you find?

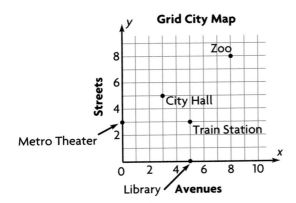

Grid City Map

A Library

C Train Station

B City Hall

D Zoo

8. On the Grid City map above, what are the coordinates of the point where the Metro Theater is located?

F (3,0)

H (3,1)

G (0,3)

J (1,3)

9. Jessica wants to make four paintings, one for each of four friends. She wants to use tessellations of the first letters of the names of her friends. Which block capital letter can she NOT use?

A I

C N

B T

D H

10. Explain It Choose a block letter from Problem 9. Draw a sketch to show a tessellation using that letter. Explain how you tessellated the letter.

ALGEBRAIC THINKING

11. The motto at the 88-Cent Store is "We never charge more than 88 cents." Which graph represents the prices at the store?

F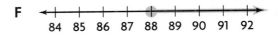
84 85 86 87 88 89 90 91 92

G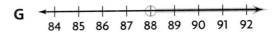
84 85 86 87 88 89 90 91 92

H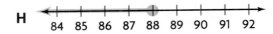
84 85 86 87 88 89 90 91 92

J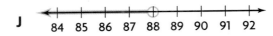
84 85 86 87 88 89 90 91 92

12. A gill is a rarely used unit of measure.

$$1 \text{ pint} = 4 \text{ gills}$$

A container has a volume of 36 gills. Solve the equation $4x = 36$ to find x, the volume of the container in pints.

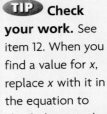

TIP Check **your work.** See item 12. When you find a value for *x*, replace *x* with it in the equation to check that it is the solution.

A $x = 9$

C $x = 40$

B $x = 32$

D $x = 144$

13. Look at the table below. What is the value of *y* when *x* = 10?

x	6	7	8	9	10
y	19	22	25	28	■

F $y = 10$

H $y = 31$

G $y = 30$

J $y = 34$

14. Explain It Kyle says that the expression 12*f* can be used to find the number of inches in *f* feet. Is he right? Explain why or why not.

IT'S IN THE BAG!

Perimeter Patterns

PROJECT Make squares to practice finding the least and greatest perimeter and make a box to hold the squares.

Materials

- Small box
- Two sheets of colored card stock
- Markers
- Glue
- Scissors
- Ruler

Directions

1. Make a label for the small box. Write *Perimeter Patterns* on the label. Decorate it and glue the label on one side of the box. *(Picture A)*

2. Make a label for the other side of the box. Write *What is the greatest perimeter you can make?* and *What is the least perimeter you can make?* on the label. Decorate the label and glue it on the other side of the box.

3. Cut out the card stock to form eight 1-in. by 1-in. squares. *(Picture B)*

4. Arrange the eight squares to make a figure with the greatest possible perimeter and then the least possible perimeter. A side of each square must be touching a side of at least one other square. What is the perimeter of each figure? What is the area of each figure? *(Picture C)*

5. Store the squares in the box.

The Pythagorean Theorem

An important and famous relationship in mathematics involves the three sides of a right triangle.

Look at the right triangle below, formed by using graph paper.

- Find the sum of the areas of the red squares. Then find the area of the blue square.

- What is the relationship between the areas of the red squares and the area of the blue square?

- What are the lengths of the sides of the triangle?

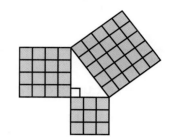

The sides of a right triangle have special names. The sides that form the right angle are the **legs**. The other side is the **hypotenuse**.

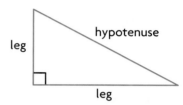

The relationship you discovered is called the **Pythagorean Theorem**. It states that if a and b are the lengths of the legs of a right triangle and c is the length of the hypotenuse, then $a^2 + b^2 = c^2$.

When you know the lengths of any two sides of a right triangle, use the Pythagorean Theorem to find the length of the third side.

EXAMPLE

The lengths of the legs of a right triangle are 6 ft and 8 ft. Find the length of the hypotenuse.

$$a^2 + b^2 = c^2$$
$$6^2 + 8^2 = c^2 \qquad \textit{Replace the variables.}$$
$$36 + 64 = c^2 \qquad \textit{Solve for c.}$$
$$100 = c^2$$
$$\sqrt{100} = c$$
$$10 = c \qquad \textit{The hypotenuse has length 10.}$$

So, the hypotenuse is 10 ft long.

TRY IT

Find the length of the hypotenuse of the right triangle.

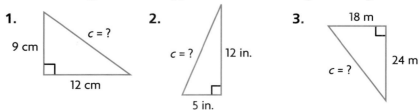

1. 9 cm, c = ?, 12 cm

2. c = ?, 12 in., 5 in.

3. 18 m, 24 m, c = ?

UNIT 6 Study Guide and Review

VOCABULARY

1. The distance around a circle is called the __?__. (p. 448)

2. The __?__ of a figure is the number of square units needed to cover it. (p. 458)

EXAMPLES

Chapter 19

- **Convert units of measurement.** (pp. 420–425)

Convert 20 ounces to pounds.

20 oz = ■ lb

20 ÷ 16 = 1.25

Since an ounce is a smaller unit than a pound, and 1 lb = 16 oz, divide by 16.

So, 20 oz = 1.25 lb, or $1\frac{1}{4}$ lb.

EXERCISES

Convert to the given unit.

3. 32 qt = ■ gal

4. 15,000 lb = ■ T

5. 15 ft = ■ in.

6. 42 m = ■ cm

7. 56 oz = ■ lb

8. 50 m = ■ km

9. 0.9 kg = ■ g

10. 60 km = ■ m

- **Relate customary and metric measurements.** (pp. 426–427)

Estimate the conversion.

6 in. ≈ ■ cm

6 × 2.5 = 15

Since 1 in. ≈ 2.5 cm, multiply by 2.5.

So, 6 in. ≈ 15 cm.

Estimate the conversion. Use the table.

1 in. ≈ 2.5 cm
1 ft ≈ 30 cm
1 mi ≈ 1.6 km
1 kg ≈ 2.2 lb
1 L ≈ 1 qt

11. 4 qt ≈ ■ L

12. 20 kg ≈ ■ lb

13. 5 ft ≈ ■ cm

14. 8 mi ≈ ■ km

15. 15 cm ≈ ■ in.

Chapter 20

- **Find the perimeter of polygons.** (pp. 443–445)

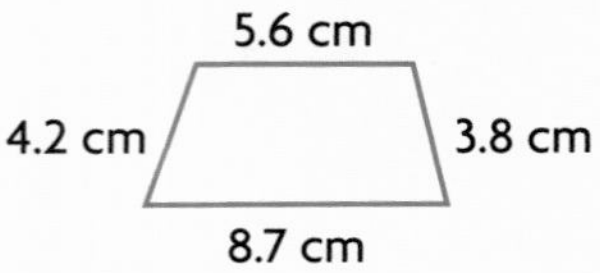
5.6 cm
4.2 cm
3.8 cm
8.7 cm

Add the lengths.

5.6 + 3.8 + 8.7 + 4.2 = 22.3 cm

Find the perimeter.

16.

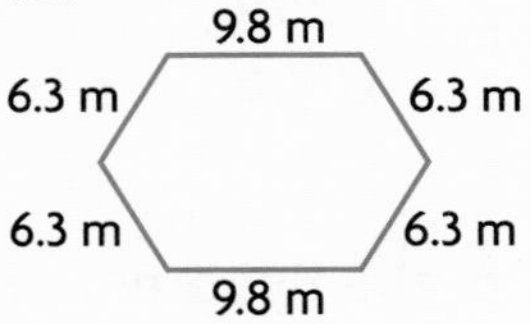
9.8 m
6.3 m
6.3 m
6.3 m
6.3 m
9.8 m

17. a regular pentagon with sides of $12\frac{1}{4}$ in.

The perimeter is given. Find the unknown length.

18.

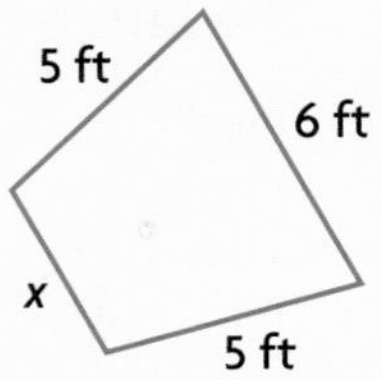
5 ft
6 ft
x
5 ft

perimeter = 20 ft

19.

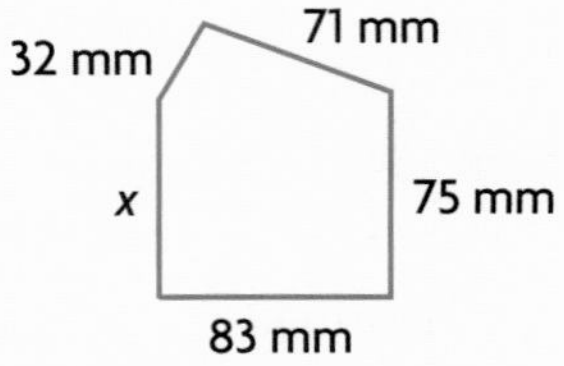
32 mm
71 mm
x
75 mm
83 mm

perimeter = 324 mm

- **Find the circumference of circles.** (pp. 448–451)

4.6 cm

Use the formula $C = 2\pi r$.
$C \approx 2 \times 3.14 \times 4.6$
$C \approx 28.888$ *Round to the nearest*
$C \approx 29$ cm   *whole number.*

Find the circumference to the nearest whole number. Use $\pi = 3.14$ or $\pi = \frac{22}{7}$.

20.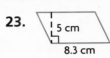
11.6 cm

21. $r = 42$ ft

22. $d = 125$ m

Chapter 21

15 cm

- **Find the area of polygons.**
  (pp. 458–464)

13 cm

$A = l \times w$ *Write the formula.*

$A = 15 \times 13$ *Replace l with 15 and w with 13.*

$A = 195$ *Multiply.*

So, the area is 195 cm².

Find the area.

23.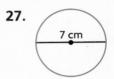
5 cm
8.3 cm

24.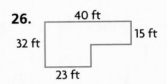
$6\frac{1}{2}$ in.
8 in.

25.
18.3 m
12 m
24.7 m

26.
40 ft
32 ft   15 ft
23 ft

- **Find the area of circles.**
  (pp. 466–467)

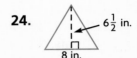
2.5 cm

Use the formula $A = \pi r^2$.

$A \approx 3.14 \times 2.5 \times 2.5$
$A \approx 19.625$ *Round to the nearest*
$A \approx 20$ *whole number.*

So, the area is about 20 cm².

Find the area to the nearest whole number. Use $\pi = 3.14$ or $\pi = \frac{22}{7}$.

27.
7 cm

28.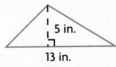
28 m

29. $r = 26$ in.

30. $d = 42$ m

- **Find the area of a figure when the dimensions are changed.** (pp. 468–471)

Double the dimensions of the triangle and compare the areas.

10 cm
6 cm

Original Area	New Area

$A = \frac{1}{2}bh$ $A = \frac{1}{2}bh$

$A = \frac{1}{2} \times 6 \times 10$ $A = \frac{1}{2} \times 12 \times 20$

$A = 30$ $A = 120$

So, the new triangle has 4 times the area of the original.

Find the new area when the given dimensions are changed as indicated. Compare the new area to the original area.

31. doubled
65 m
86 m

32. tripled
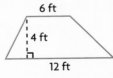
5 in.
13 in.

33. halved
6 ft
4 ft
12 ft

34. increased by 2 cm
7 cm
16 cm

PROBLEM SOLVING APPLICATIONS (pp. 446–447)

35. Kwan framed a rectangular picture that measured 15 in. × 12 in. The framing strips were $2\frac{1}{2}$ in. wide. What was the perimeter of the frame?

36. Li has two sheets of $8\frac{1}{2}$-in. × 11-in. paper. She cuts a 3-in. square from the center top edge of one of the sheets. Which sheet has the greater perimeter?

Performance Assessment

TASK A • Adding the Trim

Materials: calculator

Kate has decorated a box in which to store photos. She wants to trim the top edge of the box with ribbon. To do this, Kate needs to find the perimeter of a rectangle with length 8 in. and width 5 in.

- Write the formula for the perimeter of a rectangle.

- Show the steps needed to find the perimeter on a calculator by using the formula.

- Use the Distributive Property to write the perimeter formula in another form.

- Show the calculator steps needed to find the perimeter by using this formula.

- Write a sentence comparing the way you use the two formulas on your calculator.

TASK B • Measuring Up

Materials: inch ruler, metric ruler, plain paper

Draw a composite figure using squares, rectangles, triangles, other polygons, or circles. Draw the figure large enough so you can measure all the dimensions.

- Describe how you formed your figure.

- Measure the dimensions of your figure to the nearest inch. Determine the perimeter of your figure.

- Convert the perimeter measurement to centimeters.

- Measure the dimensions of your figure to the nearest half inch, to the nearest centimeter, and to the nearest millimeter. Copy and complete the table.

Unit	in.	cm (converted)	$\frac{1}{2}$ in.	cm (measured)	mm
Perimeter					

Technology Linkup

Use a Spreadsheet to Find
the Perimeter and Area of Rectangles

Vernetta is making a stained-glass window. She uses a spreadsheet to compute the perimeter and area of each rectangular piece of glass.

LENGTH AND WIDTH OF GLASS				
Rectangle	Length (l)	Width (w)	Perimeter (P)	Area (A)
A	12.25 cm	6.5 cm		
B	19.6 cm	12.75 cm		
C	12.4 cm	18.5 cm		
D	16.7 cm	11.25 cm		
E	6.21 cm	4.11 cm		

- Enter the column headings. Then enter the rectangle letters and their lengths and widths.

- To find the perimeter, type = 2*B2 + 2*C2 in cell D2.

	A	B	C	D	E
1	Rectangle	Length (l)	Width (w)	Perimeter (P)	Area (A)
2	A	12.25	6.5		
3	B	19.6	12.75		
4	C	12.4	18.5		
5	D	16.7	11.25		
6	E	6.21	4.11		

- Use the *Fill Down* command to enter the formula in cells D3 through D6.

- To find the area, type = B2*C2 in cell E2.

	A	B	C	D	E
1	Rectangle	Length (l)	Width (w)	Perimeter (P)	Area (A)
2	A	12.25	6.5	37.5	79.625
3	B	19.6	12.75	64.7	249.9
4	C	12.4	18.5	61.8	229.4
5	D	16.7	11.25	55.9	187.875
6	E	6.21	4.11	20.64	25.5231

- Use the *Fill Down* command to enter the formula in cells E3 through E6.

Practice and Problem Solving

Make a spreadsheet to find the perimeter and area of each rectangle.

1. length: 4.35 in.
width: 9 in.

2. length: 22.7 in.
width: 35.6 in.

3. length: 7.49 in.
width: 3.5 in.

4. length: 55.3 cm
width: 3.8 cm

5. length: 5.51 in.
width: 5.62 in.

6. length: 43.8 cm
width: 37.5 cm

7. length: 4.1 in.
width: 1.9 in.

8. length: 83.3 cm
width: 15.2 cm

9. **STRETCH YOUR THINKING** Explain how you could use a spreadsheet to compute the area of a circle.

GO ON-LINE **Multimedia Math Glossary** www.harcourtschool.com/mathglossary
Vocabulary Power Look up *circumference*, *diameter*, and *pi* in the Multimedia Math Glossary. Using the definition and illustration for each of them, describe the relationship among the circumference and diameter of a circle and the number pi.

Cincinnati Zoo and Botanical Garden

The Cincinnati Zoo and Botanical Garden opened in 1875, more than 125 years ago. The Zoo and Botanical Garden has over 700 animal species and over 3,000 types of plants. Polar bears and harbor seals are two kinds of animals you can see at the zoo.

Use Data   For 1–8, use the data in the table below. The data show typical weights and lengths for polar bears and harbor seals.

1. Find the weights shown for female polar bears in ounces.

2. Find the weights shown for female harbor seals in ounces.

3. Find the weights shown for male harbor seals in ounces.

4. Find the lengths shown for female polar bears in yards.

5. Find the lengths shown for male polar bears in inches.

6. Estimate the weights shown for male polar bears in kilograms. (1 kg ≈ 2.2 lb)

7. Estimate the weights shown for male harbor seals in kilograms. (1 kg ≈ 2.2 lb)

Adult harbor seals eat from 10 to 18 pounds of food each day.

POLAR BEARS AND HARBOR SEALS				
Measures	**Polar Bears**		**Harbor Seals**	
	Male	Female	Male	Female
Typical Weight (lb)	775–1,500	330–650	154–375	110–331
Typical Length (ft)	8–11	6	4.6–6.6	3.9–5.6

8. Estimate the lengths shown for male polar bears in centimeters. (1 ft ≈ 30 cm)

9. A harbor seal can dive about 90 m deep, and a polar bear can dive about 6 m deep. About how many feet deeper can a harbor seal dive than a polar bear? (1 ft ≈ 30 cm)

Lords of the Arctic Exhibit

One of the most popular attractions at the Zoo and Botanical Garden is the Lords of the Arctic exhibit. Visitors can see polar bears underwater through large windows.

Polar bears can remain underwater for as long as two minutes.

Use Data **For 1–6, use the drawing, which shows a typical exhibit viewing window.**

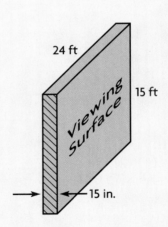

24 ft

15 ft

Viewing Surface

15 in.

1. What is the perimeter of the viewing surface?

2. What is the area of the viewing surface?

3. Suppose the dimensions were halved. How would the new perimeter and area compare with the original perimeter and area?

4. The top part of the viewing surface is 24 ft long and 15 in. wide. What is its area in square feet?

5. The side part of the viewing surface is 15 ft long and 15 in. wide. What is its area in square inches?

6. ✒ **Write About It** Explain how you could find the area of the viewing surface in square inches. Then find it.

7. The polar bear pool holds 70,000 gal of water. How many quarts of water does the pool hold?

8. The Lords of the Arctic exhibit covers 21,000 ft². If the exhibit is rectangular in shape and one side of the rectangle measures 150 ft, what is the length of the other side?

9. Suppose the exhibit is 200 ft long and 105 ft wide. What would be the area of the exhibit if the dimensions were doubled. How would the new area compare to the original area?

22 Solid Figures

FAST FACT •

SOCIAL STUDIES The Aon Center, at more than 1,100 ft, is the second-tallest building in Chicago.

PROBLEM SOLVING The tallest building in the center of the photo is the Aon Center. What solid figure does the building resemble?

TYPES OF SOLID FIGURES

Rectangular prism	Cylinder	Cone

Check What You Know

Use this page to help you review and remember important skills needed for Chapter 22.

✔ Identify Solid Figures

Name each solid figure.

1.

2.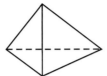

3.

4.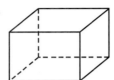

5.

6.

7.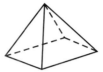

8.

✔ Faces, Vertices, and Edges

Write the number of faces, vertices, and edges for each solid figure.

9.

Faces: ▪

Vertices: ▪

Edges: ▪

10.

Faces: ▪

Vertices: ▪

Edges: ▪

11.

Faces: ▪

Vertices: ▪

Edges: ▪

12.

Faces: ▪

Vertices: ▪

Edges: ▪

VOCABULARY POWER

REVIEW

pyramid [pir′ə•mid] *noun*

The Great Pyramid in Giza, Egypt, is one of the Seven Wonders of the Ancient World. Why is it called a pyramid? What else can you think of that is shaped like a pyramid?

PREVIEW

polyhedron
lateral faces
bases
vertex
net

 www.harcourtschool.com/mathglossary

Types of Solid Figures

Learn how to name solid figures.

Vocabulary

polyhedron
lateral faces
bases
vertex

QUICK REVIEW

Draw each polygon.

1. rectangle   **2.** triangle
3. pentagon   **4.** hexagon
5. octagon

You see many solid figures every day.

All solid figures are three-dimensional. In the following activity, you'll explore ways that solid figures can be alike and ways they can be different.

Activity

You need: isometric dot paper, colored pencils

- Copy the rectangular prism on isometric dot paper. Use three different colors: one for length, one for width, and one for height.

- Draw a rectangular prism with different dimensions.

- Copy the pyramid. Then draw a rectangular pyramid with different dimensions.

- How are your rectangular prisms alike? How are they different?

- How are your pyramids alike? How are they different?

Math Idea ▶ Many common geometric shapes have special names.

A **polyhedron** is a solid figure with flat faces that are polygons.

A prism is a polyhedron with two congruent, parallel bases. Its **lateral faces**, or faces that are not bases, are rectangles. A prism is named for the shape of its **bases**.

Prisms can have any polygon as a base.

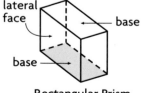

Rectangular Prism

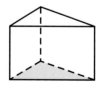

Triangular Prism

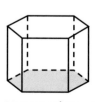

Hexagonal Prism

EXAMPLE 1

Name the figure.

All the faces are flat and are polygons, so the figure is a polyhedron.

The lateral faces are rectangles, so the figure is a prism.

The bases are congruent pentagons.

So, the figure is a pentagonal prism.

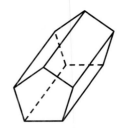

A cylinder is not a polyhedron. It has two flat, parallel, congruent circular bases and a curved lateral surface. Many cans are examples of cylinders.

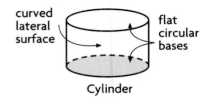

Cylinder

Remember that a *pyramid* is a solid figure whose one base is a polygon and whose faces are triangles that have a common vertex.

If you use line segments to connect the single center point on the top base of a cylinder to all the points around the bottom base, you form a cone.

A cone is not a polyhedron. It has one flat circular base, a curved lateral surface, and a **vertex**. The vertex is opposite the circular base.

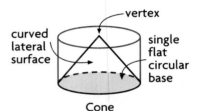

Cone

A pyramid is related to a prism as a cone is related to a cylinder.

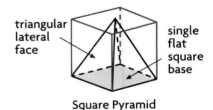

Square Pyramid

EXAMPLE 2

Name the figure.

All the faces are flat and are polygons, so the figure is a polyhedron.

The lateral faces are triangles with a common vertex, so it is a pyramid.

The base is a rectangle.
So, the figure is a rectangular pyramid.

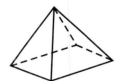

CHECK FOR UNDERSTANDING

Think and ▶ Discuss

Look back at the lesson to answer each question.

1. **Tell** the name of each solid figure: a prism with octagonal bases; a pyramid with a pentagon as a base; a solid figure with flat faces that are polygons.

2. **Explain** how a cylinder and a prism are alike. How are they different? Explain how a cone and a cylinder are alike. How are they different?

Guided ▶ Practice

Name the figure. Is it a polyhedron?

3.

4.

5.

6.

PRACTICE AND PROBLEM SOLVING

Independent ▶ Practice

Name the figure. Is it a polyhedron?

7. 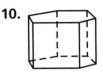   8.   9.   10.

Write *true* or *false* for each statement. Rewrite each false statement as a true statement.

11. A cone has no flat surfaces.

12. A cylinder is a polyhedron.

13. A cube is a rectangular prism.

14. The bases of a cylinder are congruent.

15. All pyramids have triangular bases.

16. A hexagonal prism has six faces.

Draw each figure.

17. rectangular pyramid

18. cylinder

19. hexagonal prism

20. cone

TECHNOLOGY LINK

More Practice:
**Harcourt Mega Math
Ice Station Exploration,**
Frozen Solids, Level L

Problem Solving ▶ Applications

21. **Vocabulary Power** In math, a cone is a solid figure with a circular base and a vertex. Explain how this meaning can be used to describe an ice cream cone or a traffic cone.

22. Gina made two square pyramids and glued the congruent bases together to make an ornament. How many faces does her ornament have? Is it a prism? Is it a pyramid? Is it a polyhedron?

23. **REASONING** The lateral faces of a pyramid are equilateral triangles. Is the base a regular polygon? Draw a diagram to explain.

MIXED REVIEW AND TEST PREP

24. Name the part of a circle that is a line segment with its endpoints on the circle. (p. 368)

25. Let *a* represent Alan's age. Write an equation stating that Alan's age 5 years ago was 13. (p. 274)

26. Write $\frac{27}{7}$ as a mixed number. (p. 186)

27. 600 m = ■ km (p. 423)

28. **TEST PREP** Maury worked 9.25 hours and earned $7.45 per hour. Which is the total amount he earned, to the nearest cent? (p. 80)

    A $16.70   **B** $68.91   **C** $74.50   **D** $689.13

EXTRA PRACTICE page 496, Set A

Views of Solid Figures

Learn how to draw and identify different views of a solid.

QUICK REVIEW

Name the base of each solid figure.

1. rectangular prism
2. cone
3. cylinder
4. triangular prism
5. square pyramid

Car designers use computer-aided design (CAD) to view their designs from different angles. These differing views help designers to create cars that are safe, efficient, and attractive.

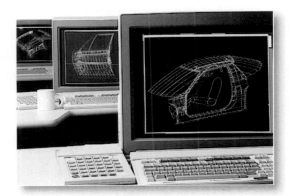

You can draw different views of a solid.

Activity 1

You need: cylinder

• Look at the top of the cylinder. Draw the top view.

• Look at the front of the cylinder. Draw the front view.

• Look at a side of the cylinder. Draw the side view.

Math Idea ▶ You can use different views of a solid figure to identify the figure.

EXAMPLE 1

Name the solid figure that has the given views.

top view

The top view shows that the base is square and that the faces come together at a point.

front view   side view

The front and side views show that the solid has triangular sides.

So, this solid is a square pyramid.

489

Activity 2

How would this solid look if you viewed it from the top, the front, and the side? You can build a model to find out.

You need: centimeter cubes, centimeter graph paper

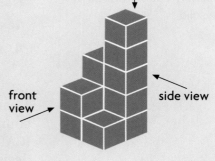

top view

front view

side view

• Use centimeter cubes to build the solid at the right.

• The top view of the solid is shown below:

Draw the front view and the side view on graph paper.

• How many cubes do you see in the top view? the front view? the side view?

• Which views show how tall the solid is?

EXAMPLE 2

Draw the front view of the above stack of cubes without building a model.

Think of the front view of each numbered cube. In your drawing, show only the numbered faces, placing them in correct relationship to one another.

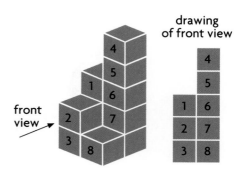

front view

drawing of front view

CHECK FOR UNDERSTANDING

Think and Discuss ► **Look back at the lesson to answer each question.**

1. **Explain** how the views of a cone and a cylinder are alike.

2. **Draw** a top view of the triangular prism.

Guided Practice ► **Name the solid figure that has the given views.**

3.
top

front   side

4.
top

front   side

5.
top

front   side

PRACTICE AND PROBLEM SOLVING

Independent ▶
Practice

Name the solid figure that has the given views.

6.
top

front   side

7.
top

front   side

8.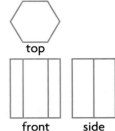
top

front   side

TECHNOLOGY LINK

More Practice:
Harcourt Mega Math
Ice Station Exploration,
Frozen Solids, Level M

Draw the front, top, and side views of each solid.

9.

10.

11.

12.

Each solid is made with 10 cubes. On graph paper, draw a top view, a front view, and a side view for each solid.

13.

14.

15.

16.

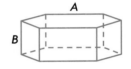

17. Draw the back and side views of the hexagonal prism as seen from *A* and *B*.

Problem Solving ▶
Applications

18. Pick an object in your classroom. Draw the top, front, and side views.

19. Every side view of a cylinder shows what shape?

20. ✏ **Write About It** Name objects in the classroom or at home that have a top view of a rectangle.

MIXED REVIEW AND TEST PREP

21. Name the figure. (p. 486)

22. Name a parallelogram that has four congruent sides. (p. 362)

23. Evaluate $x^2 + 3x$ for $x = 7$. (p. 260)

24. $\dfrac{3}{8} + \dfrac{3}{4}$ (p. 206)

⭐ **25. TEST PREP** Find the difference in the sums $22.7 + 27.9 + 24.3 + 25.1$ and $140.1 + 36 + 45.6$. (p. 76)

A 25   **B** 50.3   **C** 121.7   **D** 200.78

Models of Solid Figures

Explore how to build models of prisms and pyramids.

You need 4 in. × 6 in. index card, inch ruler, tape, scissors, protractor, patterns for cylinder and cone, graph paper.

Vocabulary

net

QUICK REVIEW

Tell the number of faces each solid figure has.

1. cube   **2.** triangular prism

3. square pyramid   **4.** pentagonal prism

5. triangular pyramid

You can build a solid figure by cutting its faces from paper, taping them together, and then folding them to form the solid.

3 in.

2 in.   1 in.

Activity 1

• Follow these steps to make a pattern for the prism.

Step 1: Draw the faces on the index card.

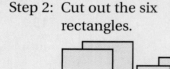

Step 2: Cut out the six rectangles.

Step 3: Tape the pieces together to form the prism.

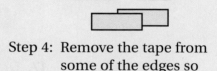

Step 4: Remove the tape from some of the edges so that the pattern lies flat.

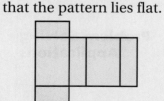

A pattern of polygons that can be folded to form a polyhedron is called a **net** for the polyhedron.

Think and Discuss

• Can you make a different net for the same rectangular prism? Draw a sketch to explain.

• Are the nets for a cube and a rectangular prism different?

Practice

On graph paper, draw four nets that can be folded to form a cube. Then draw four nets that cannot form a cube. One of each type is shown at the right.

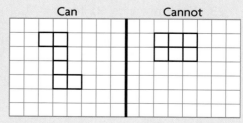

Can   Cannot

- How many triangles make up the pyramid at the right?

- Draw an equilateral triangle on a sheet of paper. Cut out the triangle.

- Use the triangle as a pattern to trace seven more triangles. Cut out these triangles.

- Using tape, make two different nets that form triangular pyramids.

- Fold and tape each of them to form triangular pyramids.

60°

60°   60°

Equilateral
triangle

Think and Discuss

- What shapes will always appear in the net of a pyramid? of a prism?

- What solid figure could you make from the net shown at the right? How do you know?

- Explain why the nets shown below cannot be folded to make solid figures.

a. 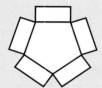   b.   c.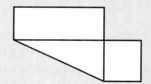

Practice

1. Draw a net for a pentagonal pyramid.

2. Draw a net for a pentagonal prism.

3. Use the cylinder pattern to build a cylinder.

4. Use the cone pattern to build a cone.

MIXED REVIEW AND TEST PREP

5. Draw a top view of a square pyramid. (p. 489)

6. A triangle contains two 48° angles. Find the measure of the third angle. (p. 356)

7. Find the mean, median, and mode of the data: 349, 350, 360, 350, 346. (p. 118)

8. $2\frac{2}{3} \times 1\frac{7}{8}$ (p. 232)

★9. **TEST PREP**   Let *t* represent today's temperature. If tomorrow's temperature is 8 degrees less than today's temperature, which expression represents tomorrow's temperature? (p. 258)

   A $t - 8$ **B** $t \times 8$ **C** $8 - t$ **D** $t + 8$

PROBLEM SOLVING STRATEGY
Solve a Simpler Problem

Learn how to use the strategy *solve a simpler problem* to solve problems.

Andrew is building models of prisms. He is using balls of clay for the vertices and straws for the edges. How many of each will he need to make a prism with 15-sided bases?

Analyze   What are you asked to find?

What information is given?

Is there information you will not use? If so, what?

Choose   What strategy will you use?

You can use the strategy *solve a simpler problem*. Find the number of vertices and edges for some prisms whose bases have fewer sides. Then use what you learn to solve the harder problem.

Solve   How will you solve the problem?

Find the number of vertices and edges there are on prisms whose bases have 3, 4, and 5 sides. Record your findings in a table.

Sides on base	3	4	5	
Vertices	3 + 3, or 6	4 + 4, or 8	5 + 5, or 10	*top + bottom*
Edges	3 + 3 + 3, or 9	4 + 4 + 4, or 12	5 + 5 + 5, or 15	*top + bottom + sides*

The table shows that the number of vertices is twice the number of sides on the base, and the number of edges is three times the number of sides on the base. Use this information for a prism whose bases each have 15 sides.

Vertices: $2 \times 15 = 30$ Edges: $3 \times 15 = 45$

So, Andrew will need 30 balls of clay for the vertices and 45 straws for the edges.

Check   What other strategy could you use to solve the problem?

What if the prism had bases with 25 sides each? How many vertices and how many edges would it have?

PROBLEM SOLVING PRACTICE

Solve the problem by first *solving a simpler problem*.

1. Margo wants to make a model of a prism whose bases have 10 sides each. She will use balls of clay for the vertices and straws for the edges. How many balls of clay will she need?

2. Amy wants to make a model of a pyramid whose base has 10 sides. She will use balls of clay for the vertices and toothpicks for the edges. How many balls of clay will she need? How many toothpicks will she need? How many faces will her pyramid have?

PROBLEM SOLVING STRATEGIES

Draw a Diagram or Picture

Make a Model

Predict and Test

Work Backward

Make an Organized List

Find a Pattern

Make a Table or Graph

▶ **Solve a Simpler Problem**

Write an Equation

Use Logical Reasoning

3. By drawing 1 vertical line and 1 horizontal line, you can divide a sheet of paper into 4 sections. Into how many sections can you divide a sheet of paper using 8 vertical and 8 horizontal lines?

1	2
3	4

A 10   **B** 16   **C** 64   **D** 81

4. Boxes are stacked with 1 box in the first row, 3 in the second, 5 in the third, adding 2 each time. How many boxes are needed altogether to make a 10-row stack?

F 12   **G** 19   **H** 81   **J** 100

MIXED STRATEGY PRACTICE

Use Data   **For 5–7, use the graph.**

5. On which day was the difference between the high and low temperatures the greatest? What was the difference?

6. Between which two days was the temperature change the greatest? Did the high or low temperature change more?

7. ✏️ **Write a problem** that can be solved by using the graph.

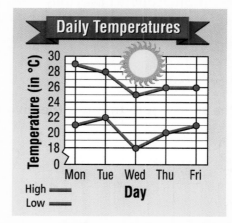

Daily Temperatures

High ━━
Low ━━

8. Corbin centered a table against a wall that was 13 ft wide. The table was $3\frac{1}{2}$ ft wide. How far was the left end of the table from the left end of the wall?

9. **FAST FACT** • SOCIAL STUDIES
There are 110 stories in Chicago's Sears Tower. The Aon Center has 25 more than half as many stories as the Sears Tower. How many stories are in the Aon Center?

10. Keith, Fran, and Lanni divided a basket of tennis balls among themselves. Keith took half of the balls. Fran took half of those that remained. Lanni took the remaining 5 balls. How many balls were in the basket to begin with?

Set A (pp. 486–488)

Name the figure. Is it a polyhedron?

1.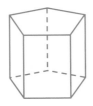

2.

3.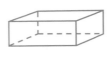

4.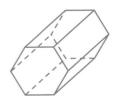

5.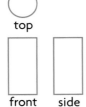

6.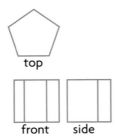

7.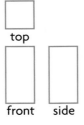

8.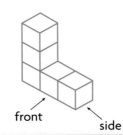

Write *true* or *false* for each statement. Rewrite each false statement as a true statement.

9. In a pentagonal prism, the bases are congruent.

10. A cylinder may have a polygon as its base.

11. All pyramids have rectangular bases.

12. The lateral surface of a cylinder is curved.

13. A prism with square bases may be a cube.

14. A prism with congruent square bases must be a cube.

Set B (pp. 489–491)

Name the solid figure that has the given views.

1.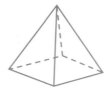
   top, front, side

2.
   top, front, side

3.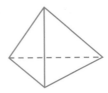
   top, front, side

Draw the top, front, and side views of each solid.

4.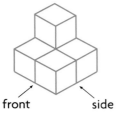
   front, side

5.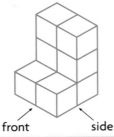
   front, side

6.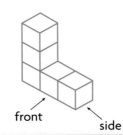
   front, side

1. **VOCABULARY**   A solid figure with flat faces that are polygons is called a(n) __?__ . (p. 486)

2. **VOCABULARY**   A pattern of polygons that can be folded to form a polyhedron is called a(n) __?__ . (p. 492)

3. **VOCABULARY**   A solid figure with two flat, parallel, congruent circular bases and a curved lateral surface is a(n) __?__ . (p. 487)

Name the figure. Is it a polyhedron? (pp. 486–488)

4.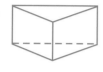
5.
6.
7.

Name the solid figure that has the given views. (pp. 489–491)

8.
top
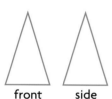
front   side

9.
top

front   side

10.
top

front   side

Draw the front, top, and side views of each solid. (pp. 489–491)

11.
12.
13.
14.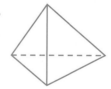

Will the net fold to form a cube? Write *yes* or *no*. (pp. 492–493)

15.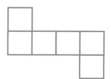
16.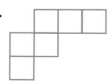
17.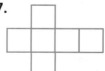
18.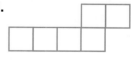

Solve. (pp. 494–495)

19. April made a model of a prism whose bases have 9 sides each. How many vertices and how many edges did her model have?

20. Mark made a model of a pyramid with 16 edges. How many sides did the base of his pyramid have?

DATA ANALYSIS AND PROBABILITY

1. The cumulative frequency table below shows the number of bicycles that Joseph sold at his store each week in July.

NUMBER OF BICYCLES SOLD		
Week	Frequency	Cumulative Frequency
1	13	13
2	6	19
3	11	30
4	8	38

How many bicycles did Joseph sell by the end of Week 3?

A 11 **C** 30

B 19 **D** 38

2. The following data represent the number of states that Jill and each of her six friends have visited: 8, 20, 6, 9, 11, 13, 10. What is the median number of states visited by Jill and her friends?

F 12 **H** 10

G 11 **J** 9

3. **Explain It** The graph below shows car sales of two different models for one year. Explain why the graph is misleading.

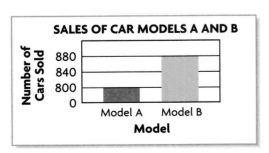

★ **ALGEBRAIC THINKING**

4. Carmen bought bags of ice that cost $0.98 each. Let b represent the number of bags she bought. Which expression represents the total cost of the bags of ice?

A $0.98 + b$

B $0.98 - b$

C $0.98 \times b$

D $0.98 \div b$

5. A display in the window of a bookstore has 1 book in the top row, 5 books in the second row, 9 books in the third row, and 13 books in the fourth row. If the pattern continues, how many books will there be in the seventh row?

F 4

G 17

H 21

J 25

6. Victoria has 2 more brothers than sisters. She has 3 brothers. Which shows the correct equation to find the number of sisters she has and the correct solution?

A $s - 2 = 3; s = 5$

B $s + 2 = 3; s = 1$

C $2s = 3; s = 1.5$

D $s \div 2 = 3; s = 6$

7. **Explain It** If $x + 8 = 35$, what is the value of $x + 6$ and $x - 6$? Explain how you found your answers.

8. Which is the measure of angle *B*?

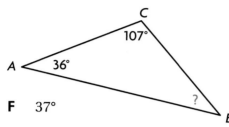

F 37°

G 54°

H 73°

J 217°

9. The distance between two cities on a map is 3 inches. The actual distance is 120 miles. What is the scale on the map?

>  **Check your work.** See item 9. After you choose your answer, test it in the original problem. Using your scale, will 3 map inches represent 120 actual miles?

A 1 in. = 360 mi

B 1 mi = 40 in.

C 1 in. = 40 mi

D 120 mi = 40 in.

10. Which is the **best** estimate of the width of your calculator?

F 3 meters

G 3 feet

H 3 inches

J 3 yards

11. Explain It The width of Lily's rectangular garden is 5 feet and the perimeter is 21 feet. Explain how you can find the area of Lily's garden.

12. The populations of four neighboring towns are shown in the table. What is the **best** estimate for the total population of the four towns?

TOWN POPULATIONS	
Town	**Population**
Pine Ridge	3,204
Deer Hills	3,593
Palm Lake	7,428
Maplewood	5,991

A 17,000

B 20,000

C 23,000

D 24,000

13. A new jogging track at Jake's high school is 580 feet longer than the old jogging track. The new track is 1,320 feet long. How long was the old track?

F 740 feet   **H** 1,740 feet

G 860 feet   **J** 1,900 feet

14. Miles has 1,288 beads to put in boxes. Each box holds 46 beads. How many boxes does Miles need to hold all of the beads?

A 30   **C** 26

B 28   **D** 24

15. Explain It The Statue of Freedom, which sits on top of the dome of the U.S. Capitol Building in Washington, D.C., is 234 inches tall. ESTIMATE the height of the statue in feet. Explain how you made your estimate.

23 Measure Solid Figures

≡FAST FACT • SCIENCE

Pure gold melts at a temperature of 1,064.43°C. Gold bars called bullion are made by melting gold and then pouring it into a mold.

PROBLEM SOLVING The dimensions of a 400-oz gold bar are shown below. How tall would a stack of 3 bars be?

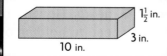

$1\frac{1}{2}$ in.

3 in.

10 in.

Check What You Know

Use this page to help you review and remember important skills needed for Chapter 23.

✔ Areas of Squares, Rectangles, and Triangles

Find the area of each figure.

1.

9 cm
6 cm

2.
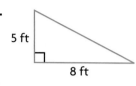
5 ft
8 ft

3.
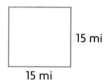
15 mi
15 mi

4.
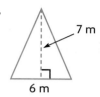
7 m
6 m

5.
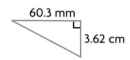
60.3 mm
3.62 cm

6.
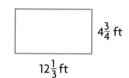
$4\frac{3}{4}$ ft
$12\frac{1}{3}$ ft

7.
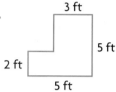
3 ft
5 ft
2 ft
5 ft

8.
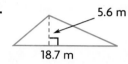
5.6 m
18.7 m

✔ Areas of Circles

Find the area to the nearest whole number. Use 3.14 for π.

9.

4 cm

10.

6.7 cm

11.

13 cm

12.

21 cm

13.

3 ft

14.

6 ft

15.

20 m

16.

200 m

VOCABULARY POWER

REVIEW

cylinder [sil′in•dər] *noun*

Look up the word *cylinder* in a dictionary, and write down the definition. Then list three things you could find in your home or at school that have the shape of a cylinder.

PREVIEW

surface area
volume

 www.harcourtschool.com/mathglossary

ALGEBRA
Surface Area

Learn how to find the surface areas of prisms, pyramids, and cylinders.

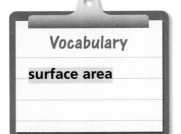

Vocabulary

surface area

21 in.
11 in.   5 in.

Sam wants to paint the box shown above. He wants to find the total area of the outside of the box. How many square inches will Sam have to paint?

You can use the formula for the area of a rectangle to find the surface area of a rectangular prism. The **surface area** is the sum of the areas of the surfaces of a solid figure.

EXAMPLE 1

Use a net to find the surface area.
Use the formula $A = lw$.

face A: $A = 11 \times 5 = 55$

face B: $A = 21 \times 11 = 231$

face C: $A = 21 \times 5 = 105$

face D: $A = 21 \times 11 = 231$

face E: $A = 21 \times 5 = 105$

face F: $A = 11 \times 5 = 55$

$55 + 231 + 105 + 231 + 105 + 55 = 782$ *Find the sum.*

So, Sam will paint 782 in.²

	A	5 in.
11 in.	5 in.	11 in.	5 in.
B	C	D	E
		F	5 in.

21 in.

Use the formula for the area of a rectangle to find the area of each face.

• **What if** the height of the box were 10 in.? How many more square inches would Sam have to paint?

Another way to find the surface area, S, of a prism is to remember that opposite faces have the same area.

EXAMPLE 2

Find the surface area of the prism at the right.
Use the formula $A = lw$.

front and back: $(6 \times 8) \times 2 = 96$ *Multiply by 2 to include opposite faces.*

top and bottom: $(6 \times 4) \times 2 = 48$

left and right sides: $(4 \times 8) \times 2 = 64$

$S = 96 + 48 + 64 = 208$ *Find the sum.*

So, the surface area is 208 cm².

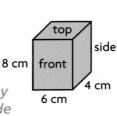

top
side
8 cm front
4 cm
6 cm

Remember that a pyramid is named by the shape of its base.

To find the surface area of a pyramid, think about its net.

The surface area of a pyramid equals the sum of the areas of the triangular faces and the area of the base. This pyramid has 4 triangular faces and a square base.

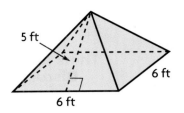

5 ft
6 ft
6 ft

EXAMPLE 3

Find the surface area of the pyramid.

$S = \text{area of square} + 4 \times (\text{area of triangle})$

$S = s^2 + 4 \times \left(\frac{1}{2} bh\right)$ *Replace s with 6, b with 6, and h with 5.*

$S = 6^2 + 4 \times \left(\frac{1}{2} \times 6 \times 5\right)$

$S = 36 + 4 \times 15$

$S = 36 + 60$

$S = 96$

So, the surface area is 96 ft².

5 ft
6 ft
6 ft

To find the surface area of a cylinder, think about the pattern you would use to make a cylinder. The surface area equals the sum of the areas of its lateral surface and two circular bases. When laid flat, the lateral surface is a rectangle. The length of the rectangle is equal to the circumference of the circular base.

base *r*

←circumference→
(2πr)

lateral surface   *h*

base

EXAMPLE 4

Find the surface area of the cylinder. Use 3.14 for π.

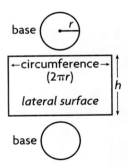

3 cm
5 cm

$S = \text{area of lateral surface} + 2 \times (\text{area of circle})$

$S = (l \times h) + 2 \times (\pi r^2)$

$S = (2\pi r \times 5) + 2 \times (\pi r^2)$ *Replace l with 2πr and h with 5.*

$S \approx (2 \times 3.14 \times 3 \times 5) + 2 \times (3.14 \times 3^2)$ *Replace π with 3.14 and r with 3.*

$S \approx 94.2 + 2 \times (28.26)$

$S \approx 94.2 + 56.52$

$S \approx 150.72$

So, the surface area of the cylinder is about 151 cm².

Think and ▶ Discuss

Look back at the lesson to answer each question.

1. **Explain** how you would find the surface area of a pentagonal prism.

2. **Explain** how to find the surface area of a square pyramid.

Guided ▶ Practice

Find the surface area. Use 3.14 for π.

3.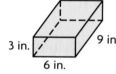
6 ft
2 ft
10 ft

4.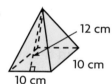
6 cm
16 cm

5.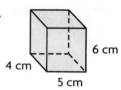
8 cm
12 cm
12 cm

Independent ▶ Practice

Find the surface area. Use 3.14 for π.

6.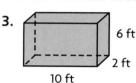
3 in.
9 in.
6 in.

7.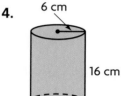
12 cm
10 cm
10 cm

8.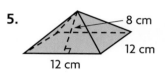
6 cm
4 cm
5 cm

9.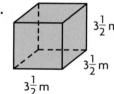
$3\frac{1}{2}$ m
$3\frac{1}{2}$ m
$3\frac{1}{2}$ m

10.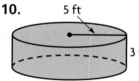
5 ft
3 ft

11.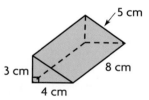
5 cm
3 cm
8 cm
4 cm

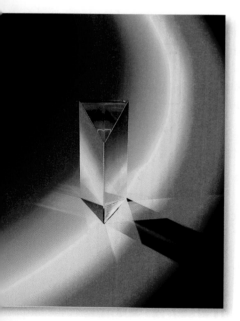

Find the surface area of the cube with the given side length, s.

12. $s = 1\frac{1}{2}$ m

13. $s = 3.4$ cm

14. $s = 28$ ft

15. Find the dimensions of each rectangular prism. Then find the surface area of each.

   a. The length is twice the width. The height is twice the length. The width is 3 meters.

   b. The width is half the length. The height is twice the width. The length is 6 feet.

   c. The height is three times the length. The length is half the width. The width is 10 inches.

   d. The length is four times the height. The width is one fourth the height. The height is 8 centimeters.

Problem Solving ▶ Applications

For 16–17, use the figure at the right.

16. Tamara is painting a 12 ft × 10 ft × 10 ft room. She will not paint the ceiling or the floor. What is the total area she is painting?

17. One can of paint covers 350 ft². How many cans of paint will Tamara need to paint the 4 walls?

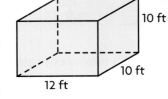

10 ft
10 ft
12 ft

Use Data **For 18–19, use the graph at the right.**

18. About how many more square inches of cardboard are used for Box C than Box A?

19. If Box A is a cube, what is the length of each side?

20. **What's the Question?** The surface area of a cube is 96 m². The answer is 4 m.

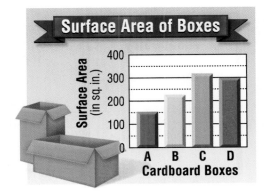

Surface Area of Boxes

MIXED REVIEW AND TEST PREP

21. Find the area of the circle at the right. (p. 466)

22. Evaluate $3\frac{1}{3} \times 4\frac{1}{2}$. (p. 232)

23. Which is greater, $\frac{1}{5}$ or 0.25? (p. 191)

12 ft

24. **TEST PREP** Lydia wants to sew a ribbon along the edge of a circular tablecloth with a radius of $1\frac{1}{2}$ yards. The ribbon costs $0.45 per yard. What is the cost of the ribbon to the nearest cent? (p. 448)

   A $3.20   **B** $4.24   **C** $4.71   **D** $12.20

25. **TEST PREP** Which shows the perimeter of a regular hexagon with sides $9\frac{1}{2}$ ft long? (p. 443)

   F 38 ft   **G** $47\frac{1}{2}$ ft   **H** 57 ft   **J** $66\frac{1}{2}$ ft

---

PROBLEM SOLVING THINKER'S CORNER

REASONING Look at the large cube at the right. It is made up of 27 unit cubes. Each unit cube is 1 in. long, 1 in. wide, and 1 in. high.

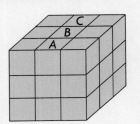

1. What is the surface area of the large cube?

2. What would happen to the surface area if you removed one cube from each of the eight corners? Explain.

3. What would happen to the surface area if you removed the cubes labeled *A*, *B*, and *C*? Explain.

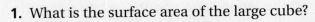

Estimate and Find Volume

Learn how to estimate and find the volumes of rectangular prisms and triangular prisms.

Vocabulary

volume

Jean wants to estimate how much sand will fill a sandbox. To estimate, Jean needs to think of the volume of the sandbox.

The **volume** is the number of cubic units needed to occupy a given space.

Jean will use a net to make an open box to estimate the volume.

Activity

You need: box net, scissors, tape, 30 centimeter cubes

• Cut out the net. Fold along the dashed lines, and tape the sides to make an open box.

• Estimate how many cubes will fit in the box. Put as many cubes as you can in the box.

• Is your estimate greater than or less than the actual number of cubes you put in the box?

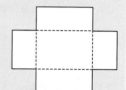

You can visualize how many cubes will fill a prism.

EXAMPLE 1

Use the centimeter cube to estimate the volume.

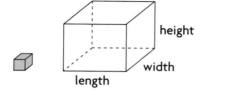
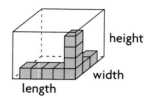

About 5 cubes fit along the length and about 3 cubes along the width. The bottom layer has about 15 cubes. There are about 4 layers of about 15 cubes each.

4 layers × 15 cubes = 60 cubes

So, the volume is about 60 cubic cm, or 60 cm³.

A layer of centimeter cubes has been placed on the base of the rectangular prism below. It takes 10, or 5 × 2, centimeter cubes to make the bottom layer.

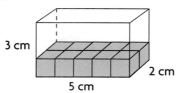

The picture below shows the prism filled with centimeter cubes.

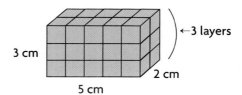

There are 3 layers of 10 cubes each. It takes 30, or 3 × 5 × 2, cubes to fill the prism.

- Look at the table below. What relationship do you see among the length, width, height, and volume? What formula can you write for the volume of a rectangular prism?

LENGTH	WIDTH	HEIGHT	VOLUME
5	2	3	30
3	3	6	54
7	4	3	84

The relationship between the dimensions and the volume of each prism can be written as Volume = length × width × height, or $V = lwh$.

The formula $V = Bh$ can also be used to find the volume of a rectangular prism. In this formula, B is equal to $l \times w$, which is the area of the base of the prism, and h is the height of the prism.

EXAMPLE 2

Find the volume of the prism at the right.

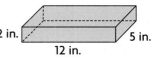

$V = Bh$, where $B = l \times w$ *Write the formula.*

$V = (12 \times 5) \times 2$ *Replace B with 12 × 5 and h with 2. Multiply.*

$V = 120$

So, the volume of the rectangular prism is 120 in.^{3}

- **What if** you cut the rectangular prism into two congruent triangular prisms? What would be the volume of one triangular prism?

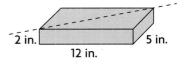

Remember that a triangular prism has bases that are congruent triangles.

The volume of a triangular prism is one half the volume of a rectangular prism with the same length, width, and height. To find the volume of a right triangular prism, you can use the formula $V = \frac{1}{2}lwh$. To find the volume of any triangular prism, you can use the formula $V = Bh$, where B is the area of the triangular base.

EXAMPLE 3

Find the volume of the prism at the right.

One Way

$V = \frac{1}{2}lwh$

$V = \frac{1}{2} \times 2.8 \times 4.2 \times 5$

$V = 29.4$

Another Way

$V = Bh$

$V = \left(\frac{1}{2} \times 2.8 \times 4.2\right) \times 5$

$V = 5.88 \times 5$

$V = 29.4$

So, the volume is 29.4 m³.

- **What if** the dimensions of the prism were tripled? What would the volume be?

TECHNOLOGY LINK
More Practice:
Harcourt Mega Math Ice Station Exploration, *Arctic Algebra,* Level DD

CHECK FOR UNDERSTANDING

Think and Discuss ▶ Look back at the lesson to answer each question.

1. **Tell** how to find the volume of a cereal box that measures 26 cubes by 3 cubes by 18 cubes.

2. **Explain** how to find the height of a rectangular prism if you know the length, width, and volume of the prism.

Guided Practice ▶ Find the volume.

3. 4 in. 3 in. 2 in.

4. 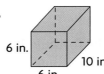 6 in. 6 in. 10 in.

5. 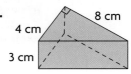 8 cm 4 cm 3 cm

PRACTICE AND PROBLEM SOLVING

Independent Practice ▶ Find the volume.

6. 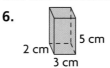 5 cm 2 cm 3 cm

7. 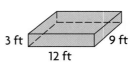 3 ft 9 ft 12 ft

8. 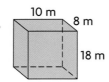 10 m 8 m 18 m

9. 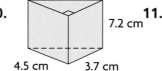 3 ft 7 ft 14 ft

10. 7.2 cm 4.5 cm 3.7 cm

11. 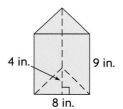 4 in. 9 in. 8 in.

Find the unknown length.

12.

9 cm

5 cm

x

V = 900 cm³

13.

x

8.2 m   9 m

V = 369 m³

14. 6 cm   6 cm

x

V = 162 cm³

Problem Solving ▶
Applications

15. Bobby is ordering sand to fill the long-jump pit. The pit is 14 ft long, 9 ft wide, and $1\frac{1}{2}$ ft deep. How much sand does Bobby need to order?

16. ✎ **Write a problem** in which you have to find the surface area and the volume of a rectangular prism. Then explain the difference between surface area and volume.

17. A model of a rectangular prism is made using the scale 1 in. = 3 ft. The model measures 4 in. by 3 in. by 2 in. What is the volume of the actual prism?

18. Vocabulary Power *Prism* comes from the Greek word *prisma* meaning "something sawed off." Look up *prism* in the Glossary. Could parts of a cylinder be "sawed off" to form a prism? Explain.

MIXED REVIEW AND TEST PREP

19. Find the surface area of a rectangular prism 8.2 ft long, 6.4 ft wide, and 4.5 ft high. (p. 502)

20. Evaluate $3y^2$ for $y = 3.9$. (p. 266)

21. Solve $8.1t = 49.41$. (p. 291)

22. TEST PREP Which type of angle is formed by two perpendicular lines?
(p. 344)

   A straight   **C** right
   B obtuse   **D** acute

23. TEST PREP Find the area of a circle with a diameter of 12 m. Use 3.14 for π. (p. 466)

   F 452.16 m²   **H** 75.36 m²
   G 113.04 m²   **J** 37.68 m²

PROBLEM SOLVING   LiNKUP to Reading

Analyze Information When you analyze details in a problem, look for information that is needed to solve the problem.

Calvin is mailing a model car to a friend. To make sure the model box does not move around in the mailing box, he must fill the empty space with packing material. How many cubic inches of packing material will he need?

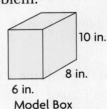

10 in.

8 in.

6 in.

Model Box

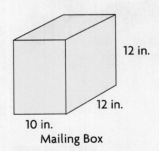

12 in.

12 in.

10 in.

Mailing Box

1. What information do you need to solve the problem?

2. Solve the problem. Explain how you solved it.

3. **What if** Calvin uses a mailing box that is 1 ft by $\frac{3}{4}$ ft by $\frac{3}{4}$ ft? Will he have more or less space to fill? How much more or less?

PROBLEM SOLVING STRATEGY
Make a Model

Learn how to use the strategy *make a model* to solve problems.

A rice company uses different-sized boxes. A small box of rice is 2 in. wide, 4 in. long, and 6 in. high. How does the volume of the small box change when the length, width, and height are halved to make a sample box?

Analyze What are you asked to find?

What information are you given?

Is there information you will not use? If so, what?

Choose What strategy will you use?

You can use the strategy *make a model*.

Solve How will you solve the problem?

Make a model of each box. Compare the volumes.

Use cubes to make a model of each box. Count the cubes to find the volume of each box.

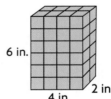

6 in.   4 in.   2 in.

3 in.   2 in.   1 in.

The volume of the small box is 48 in.^{3}
The volume of the sample box is 6 in.^{3}

Now compare the volumes.

$$\frac{sample\ box \rightarrow}{small\ box \rightarrow} \frac{6}{48} = \frac{1}{8}$$

So, the volume of the sample box is 6 in.^{3}, or $\frac{1}{8}$ the volume of the small box.

Check How can you check your answer?

What if the dimensions of the small box are doubled to make a larger box? How will the volume of the box change?

PROBLEM SOLVING PRACTICE

Solve the problem by making a model.

1. The volume of the box at the right is 240 in.³ Double the height of the box. How does the volume of the box change?

10 in. 3 in. 8 in.

2. The dimensions of the large box at the right are halved to make a smaller box. How does the volume change?

12 in. 6 in. 8 in.

PROBLEM SOLVING STRATEGIES

Draw a Diagram or Picture

▶ **Make a Model**

Predict and Test

Work Backward

Make an Organized List

Find a Pattern

Make a Table or Graph

Solve a Simpler Problem

Write an Equation

Use Logical Reasoning

For 3–4, a rectangular box is 6 cm wide, 8 cm long, and 13 cm high.

3. The length and width of the rectangular box are halved. The height remains the same. How does the volume of the smaller box compare to the volume of the larger box?

 A $\frac{1}{8}$ of the volume   **C** $\frac{1}{3}$ of the volume

 B $\frac{1}{4}$ of the volume   **D** $\frac{1}{2}$ of the volume

4. The length, width, and height of the rectangular box are doubled. How does the volume of the larger box compare to the volume of the smaller box?

 F equal to the volume

 G 2 times the volume

 H 4 times the volume

 J 8 times the volume

MIXED STRATEGY PRACTICE

Use Data   For 5–6, use the line graph at the right.

5. About how much did Howie make in sales during the six months shown on the graph?

6. At what point were sales and costs the same?

7. Grander's Clothes Shop sells shirts for $12 and shorts for $15. Terance will spend $120. How many different combinations of shirts and shorts can Terance buy with no money left over?

8. Ana makes a circular pattern of stars on a piece of paper. Adjacent stars are the same distance apart. The sixth star is directly opposite the eighteenth star. How many stars form the circle?

9. Jasmine, Hugh, Sharon, and Mike are standing in line. A girl is not first or last in line. Mike is before Hugh. Jasmine is directly in front of Hugh. Who is first, second, third, and fourth in line?

10. A side of square A is 6 times the length of a side of square B. How many times as great as the area of square B is the area of square A?

11. ❓ **What's the Question?** The volume of a cube is 216 cm³. The length of each side is halved. The answer is 27 cm³.

ALGEBRA
Volumes of Pyramids

Learn how to use a formula to find the volumes of pyramids.

When it was built, the Great Pyramid of Khufu was 145.75 m (481 ft) high. Each side measured 229 m (751 ft) in length.

Juan wants to use what he knows about the volume of a prism to find the volume of his model of the Great Pyramid of Khufu.

Activity

You need: prism and pyramid nets, tape, rice

- Cut out the nets for the prism and the pyramid. Fold along the dashed lines and use tape to make an open prism and an open pyramid.
- Compare the height of the prism with the height of the pyramid.
- Compare the base of the prism with the base of the pyramid.
- Fill the pyramid with rice. Pour the rice into the prism. Repeat until the prism is full.
- What is the relationship between the heights and bases of the prism and pyramid?
- What is the relationship between the volume of the pyramid and the volume of the prism?

To find the volume of a pyramid, use the formula $V = \frac{1}{3}Bh$.

EXAMPLE

Find the volume of Juan's pyramid model at the right to the nearest tenth.

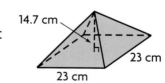

$V = \frac{1}{3}Bh$, where $B = l \times w$ *Write the formula.*

$V = \frac{1}{3}(23 \times 23) \times 14.7$ *Replace B with 23 × 23 and h with 14.7. Multiply.*

$V = \frac{1}{3} \times 529 \times 14.7$

$V = \frac{1}{3} \times 7,776.3$

$V = 2,592.1$ So, the volume is 2,592.1 cm³.

Think and ▸
Discuss

Look back at the lesson to answer the question.

1. **Compare** the formulas for the volume of a prism and the volume of a pyramid.

Guided ▸
Practice

Find the volume.

2.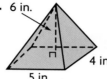
6 in.
4 in.
5 in.

3.
5 m
5 m
3 m

4.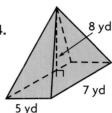
8 yd
7 yd
5 yd

Independent ▸
Practice

Find the volume.

5.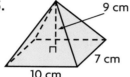
9 cm
7 cm
10 cm

6.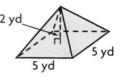
2 yd
5 yd
5 yd

7.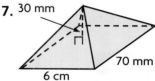
30 mm
70 mm
6 cm

8. square pyramid:
$l = 12$ cm, $w = 12$ cm,
$h = 25$ cm

9. rectangular pyramid:
$l = 18$ ft, $w = 25$ ft,
$h = 30$ ft

10. rectangular pyramid:
$l = 10$ dm, $w = 4$ dm,
$h = 7.5$ dm

11. rectangular pyramid: $l = 9$ ft,
$w = 5$ yd, $h = 4\frac{4}{5}$ yd

Problem Solving ▸
Applications

12. **≡FAST FACT • SCIENCE** The weight of a cubic foot of steel is 490 lb. What is the weight of a solid steel rectangular pyramid that is 2 ft by 3 ft by 18 in.?

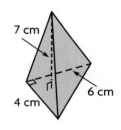
7 cm
6 cm
4 cm

13. **Write About It** Tell how you would find the volume of the triangular pyramid at the right.

14. Ken has $8.40 in nickels, dimes, and quarters. He has the same number of each coin. How many of each coin does he have?

15. $13\frac{1}{5} \times 8\frac{1}{3}$ (p. 232)

16. $4\frac{1}{2} + 3\frac{4}{5}$ (p. 210)

17. Write 79% as a decimal. (p. 68)

18. Volume = ■ (p. 506)

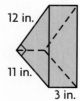
12 in.
11 in.
3 in.

★ 19. **TEST PREP** Which list shows $\frac{3}{4}$, $\frac{2}{3}$, and $\frac{5}{8}$ in order from least to greatest? (p. 188)

A $\frac{2}{3}, \frac{5}{8}, \frac{3}{4}$

B $\frac{5}{8}, \frac{3}{4}, \frac{2}{3}$

C $\frac{5}{8}, \frac{2}{3}, \frac{3}{4}$

D $\frac{2}{3}, \frac{3}{4}, \frac{5}{8}$

Volume of a Cylinder

MATH LAB

In geometry, a cylinder is a solid figure that has two congruent, parallel circles as its bases. In the activity below, you will estimate the volume of a cylinder.

Explore how to use manipulatives to estimate the volume of a cylinder.

You need 2 pieces of centimeter graph paper, scissors, tape.

Activity

• Use one piece of graph paper to cut out a rectangle 20 cm long and 8 cm wide. Without overlapping, roll the rectangle the short way and tape it to form a cylinder.

20 cm

8 cm

• Stand the cylinder on the second piece of graph paper. Trace around the base of the cylinder. Count the whole centimeter squares and the parts of centimeter squares inside the tracing.

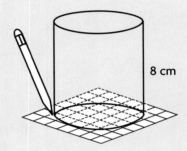

8 cm

Think and Discuss

• About how many cubes would fit on the bottom layer of the cylinder?

• How many layers of cubes can fit inside the cylinder?

• What is the approximate volume of the cylinder?

Practice

Draw the following rectangles on centimeter graph paper. Cut out each one, roll it, and tape it to make a cylinder. Estimate the volume of each cylinder.

1.

6 cm

12 cm

2.

4 cm

18 cm

ALGEBRA
Volumes of Cylinders

Learn how to find the volume of a cylinder.

You can find the volume of a rectangular prism by multiplying the area of the base by the height. You can use the same method to find the volume of a cylinder.

Math Idea ▶ Volume of a cylinder = area of base × height

$$V = Bh$$

$$V = \pi r^2 h \qquad \pi r^2 \text{ is the area of the base, which is a circle.}$$

EXAMPLE 1

Larisa has a flower vase like the cylinder shown at the right. To the nearest cubic inch, what is the volume of water the vase will hold?

$V = \pi r^2 h$	*Write the formula.*
$V \approx 3.14 \times 4^2 \times 15$	*Replace π with 3.14 or $\frac{22}{7}$, r with 4, and h with 15.*
$V \approx 3.14 \times 16 \times 15$	
$V \approx 753.6$	*Multiply.*

So, the volume of water the vase will hold is about 754 in.³

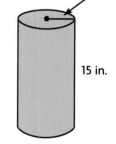

4 in.

15 in.

The volume of a cylinder can also be found if you know the diameter and the height of the cylinder.

EXAMPLE 2

Find the volume to the nearest cubic centimeter.

$5 \div 2 = 2.5$	*Find the radius.*
$V = \pi r^2 h$	*Write the formula.*
$V \approx 3.14 \times (2.5)^2 \times 30$	*Replace π with 3.14 or $\frac{22}{7}$, r with 2.5, and h with 30.*
$V \approx 3.14 \times 6.25 \times 30$	
$V \approx 588.75$	*Multiply.*

So, the volume is about 589 cm³.

5 cm

30 cm

• **What if** you have a cylinder with a diameter of 6.5 cm and a height of 12.5 cm? What is the volume of the cylinder?

Sometimes you may have to find the volume of part of a cylinder.

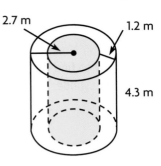

2.7 m 1.2 m

4.3 m

EXAMPLE 3

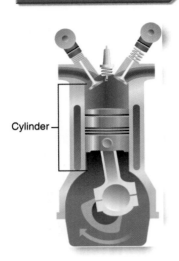

Cylinder

Look at the water tank at the right. The wall is 1.2 m thick. To the nearest cubic meter, how much water can the inside cylinder hold?

Find the radius of the inside cylinder.

$2.7 - 1.2 = 1.5$ ← radius

Use the radius to find the volume of the inside cylinder.

$V \approx 3.14 \times (1.5)^2 \times 4.3$

$V \approx 3.14 \times 2.25 \times 4.3$

$V \approx 30.3795$

Replace π with 3.14, r with 1.5, and h with 4.3. Multiply.

So, the water tank can hold about 30 m³ of water.

CHECK FOR UNDERSTANDING

Think and Discuss ▸ Look back at the lesson to answer each question.

1. **What if** the dimensions of Larisa's vase are doubled? What is the volume of the vase to the nearest cubic inch?

2. **Explain** how the formula for the volume of a cylinder is similar to the formula for the volume of a rectangular prism.

3. **Explain** in your own words which parts of a cylinder are represented by πr^2 and h in the formula $V = \pi r^2 h$.

Guided Practice ▸ **Find the volume. Round to the nearest whole number. Use 3.14 for π.**

4.
4 cm
7 cm

5.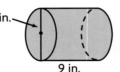
7 in.
9 in.

6.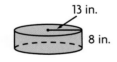
13 in.
8 in.

PRACTICE AND PROBLEM SOLVING

Independent Practice ▸ **Find the volume. Round to the nearest whole number. Use 3.14 for π.**

7.
10 in.
12 in.

8.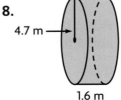
4.7 m
1.6 m

9.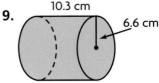
10.3 cm
6.6 cm

Find the volume. Round to the nearest whole number. Use 3.14 for π.

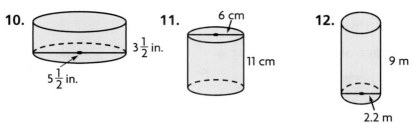

10. $5\frac{1}{2}$ in. $3\frac{1}{2}$ in.

11.   6 cm   11 cm

12.   9 m   2.2 m

Find the volume of the inside cylinder to the nearest whole number. Use 3.14 for π.

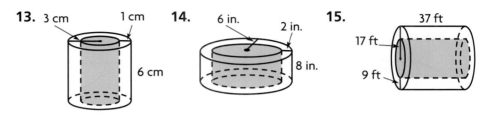

13.   3 cm   1 cm   6 cm

14.   6 in.   2 in.   8 in.

15.   37 ft   17 ft   9 ft

Problem Solving ▶ Applications

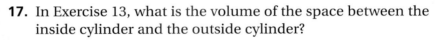
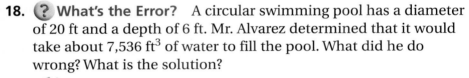
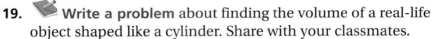
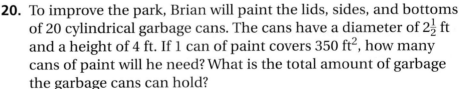

16. Nicole bought a decorative outdoor planter with a diameter of 21 in. and a height of 28 in. She wants to fill it with potting soil. How much potting soil will Nicole need, to the nearest cubic inch?

17. In Exercise 13, what is the volume of the space between the inside cylinder and the outside cylinder?

18. **? What's the Error?** A circular swimming pool has a diameter of 20 ft and a depth of 6 ft. Mr. Alvarez determined that it would take about 7,536 ft³ of water to fill the pool. What did he do wrong? What is the solution?

19. **Write a problem** about finding the volume of a real-life object shaped like a cylinder. Share with your classmates.

20. To improve the park, Brian will paint the lids, sides, and bottoms of 20 cylindrical garbage cans. The cans have a diameter of $2\frac{1}{2}$ ft and a height of 4 ft. If 1 can of paint covers 350 ft², how many cans of paint will he need? What is the total amount of garbage the garbage cans can hold?

MIXED REVIEW AND TEST PREP

21. Find the volume, to the nearest cubic foot, of a rectangular pyramid 1.2 ft long, 2.8 ft wide, and 3.6 ft high. (p. 512)

22. Find the surface area of a cylinder that has a top and bottom, a height of 12 in., and a radius of 7 in. (p. 502)

23. Which has the greater value, $\frac{1}{10} \div \frac{1}{2}$ or $\frac{1}{2} \div \frac{1}{10}$? (p. 236)

24. Write the algebraic expression for 6.9 more than 5 times d. (p. 258)

25. **TEST PREP** The volume of a rectangular prism is 360 cm³. The length is 12 cm and the width is 10 cm. Which is the height? (p. 506)

   A 3 cm   **B** 10 cm   **C** 30 cm   **D** 36 cm

EXTRA PRACTICE page 518, Set D

Set A (pp. 502–505)

Find the surface area. Use 3.14 for π.

1.
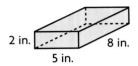
2 in.   8 in.   5 in.

2.

4 m   2 m   2 m

3.
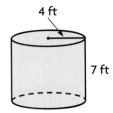
4 ft   7 ft

4.
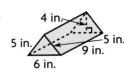
4 in.   5 in.   5 in.   9 in.   6 in.

Set B (pp. 506–509)

Find the volume.

1.
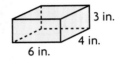
3 in.   4 in.   6 in.

2.
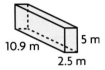
5 m   10.9 m   2.5 m

3.

5 m   10.2 m   12 m

4.
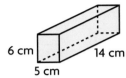
6 cm   14 cm   5 cm

Set C (pp. 512–513)

Find the volume.

1.

18 ft   8 ft   8 ft

2.

9.5 m   6 m   7 m

3.

79 in.   41 in.   42 in.

4.
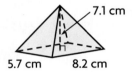
7.1 cm   5.7 cm   8.2 cm

5. Find the volume of a rectangular pyramid with a length of 18 cm, a width of 16 cm, and a height of 12 cm.

6. Find the volume of a rectangular pyramid with a base of 300 ft² and a height of 50 ft.

Set D (pp. 515–517)

Find the volume. Round to the nearest whole number. Use 3.14 for π.

1.

17 ft   5 ft

2.
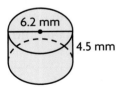
6.2 mm   4.5 mm

3.
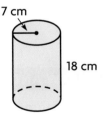
7 cm   18 cm

Find the volume of the inside cylinder to the nearest whole number. Use 3.14 for π.

4.
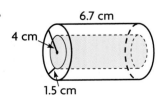
6.7 cm   4 cm   1.5 cm

5.
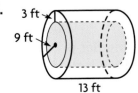
3 ft   9 ft   13 ft

6.

5 mm   2 mm   9 mm

Find the surface area. Use 3.14 for π. (pp. 502–505)

1.
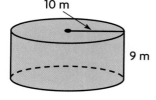
10 m
9 m

2.
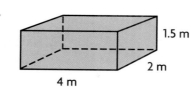
1.5 m
2 m
4 m

3.
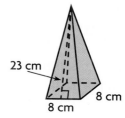
23 cm
8 cm
8 cm

Find the volume. (pp. 506–509)

4.
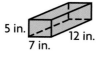
5 in.
12 in.
7 in.

5.
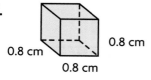
15 cm
13 cm
7 cm

6.
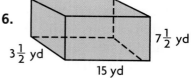
7½ yd
3½ yd
15 yd

7.

0.8 cm
0.8 cm
0.8 cm
0.8 cm

8.
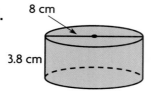
4 ft
12 ft
8 ft

9.
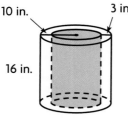
5.6 m
9.3 m
7.8 m

Find the volume of the pyramid. (pp. 512–513)

10.
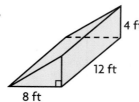
8 in.
6 in.
6 in.

11.
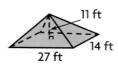
11 ft
14 ft
27 ft

12.
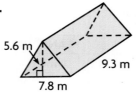
22.8 m
17 m
11.4 m

Find the volume. Round to the nearest whole number. Use 3.14 for π. (pp. 515–517)

13.
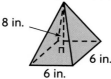
4 m
9.6 m

14.
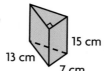
8 cm
3.8 cm

15.
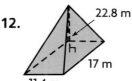
5 in.
7 in.

Find the volume of the inside cylinder to the nearest whole number.
Use 3.14 for π. (pp. 515–517)

16.
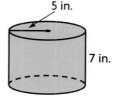
10 in.
3 in.
16 in.

17. 9 ft
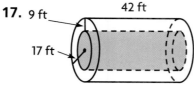
42 ft
17 ft

18.
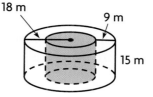
18 m
9 m
15 m

Solve. (pp. 510–511)

19. A box is 8 in. high, 2 in. wide, and 4 in. long. The length and the width of the box are doubled to make a larger box. How does the volume of the larger box compare to the volume of the smaller box?

20. A box is 12 cm long, 8 cm wide, and 9 cm tall. Each dimension is halved to make a smaller box. How does the volume of the smaller box compare to the volume of the larger box?

★ NUMBER SENSE, CONCEPTS, AND OPERATIONS

1. The diameter of Earth is about 12,756 kilometers. The table below compares the diameters of four other planets with the diameter of Earth. Which planet in the table has a diameter of about 2,296 kilometers?

> **TIP Eliminate choices.** See item 1. Since 2,296 is less than 12,756, eliminate the planets with diameters greater than Earth's diameter.

PLANET DIAMETERS	
Planet	**Diameter Compared to Earth**
Mercury	0.382 times as long
Saturn	9.4 times as long
Neptune	3.9 times as long
Pluto	0.18 times as long

A Mercury   **C** Neptune

B Saturn   **D** Pluto

2. The Hope Diamond can be seen at the Smithsonian Institution in Washington, D.C. It weighs 45.52 carats. One carat equals 0.2 grams. What is the mass of the Hope Diamond in grams?

F 9.104 grams   **H** 45.52 grams

G 22.76 grams   **J** 91.04 grams

3. During a 24-hour period, the average person will speak about 4,800 words. How many words per hour is that?

A 200   **C** 20,000

B 2,000   **D** 115,200

4. Explain It Carla sold three pairs of sneakers for $19.99 each, and two pairs for $39.99 each. Explain how you can ESTIMATE the average price of all the sneakers she sold.

★ GEOMETRY AND SPATIAL SENSE

5. Barbara used a computer program to draw a design for a Web page.

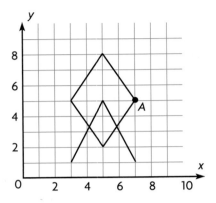

Which ordered pair represents point *A*?

F (5,5)   **H** (7,5)

G (5,7)   **J** (7,7)

6. The figures below show the outlines of four sites in the Washington, D.C. area. Which figure is NOT a quadrilateral?

A

Franklin Park

C

Union Station Plaza

B
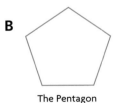
The Pentagon

D

Phitzner Stadium baseball diamond

7. Explain It Locations in XY-town are written as ordered pairs, with avenues written first and streets written last. The ordered pair (3,7) means the corner of 3rd Avenue and 7th Street. Is (2,5) the same location as (5,2)? Explain your reasoning.

⭐ ALGEBRAIC THINKING

8. A cubical carton is packed tightly with individually boxed baseballs. The figure at the right shows that the carton holds $4 \times 4 \times 4$ baseballs. Each baseball costs \$4, so the value of all the balls in the carton is $4 \times 4 \times 4 \times 4$ dollars. What is another way to write $4 \times 4 \times 4 \times 4$?

F $4 + 4 + 4 + 4$ **H** 44^2

G 4^4 **J** $4,444$

9. Jerry had a box that contained 25 bottles of juice. He removed ten of the bottles from the box. Use b to represent the number of bottles that are still in the box. Which equation could be used to find the number of bottles that are still in the box?

A $b = 10 + 25$

B $b - 10 = 25$

C $b + 10 = 25$

D $b \times 10 = 25$

10. **Explain It** The bar graph shows the number of runs scored by players on a softball team. For which players does the inequality $n \geq 9$ represent the runs they scored? Explain your reasoning.

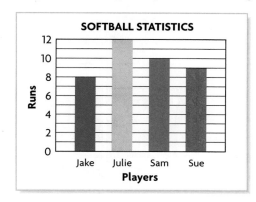

⭐ DATA ANALYSIS AND PROBABILITY

11. Kyle scored 121, 132, and 113 while bowling. What was his mean score?

F 113 **H** 122

G 121 **J** 366

12. The histogram shows the results of a survey about the number of hours students in a sixth-grade class spend exercising each month.

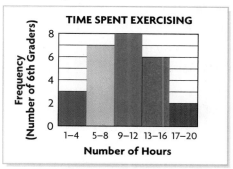

How many more students exercise from 9 to 16 hours than exercise from 5 to 8 hours each month?

A 7 **B** 8 **C** 15 **D** 22

13. Mary has 2 red, 3 orange, 1 green, and 2 yellow pencils in a bag. If she randomly draws one pencil, which colors is she equally likely to choose?

F red and orange

G green and yellow

H orange and green

J red and yellow

14. **Explain It** Kent, Luis, Don, Jan, Lori, and Tony are tied for first place in a fund raising drive. To determine the winner, a student's name will be randomly drawn from a hat. What is the probability that either Lori or Tony will win? Explain how you found the answer.

IT'S IN THE BAG!

Cereal Box Suitcase

PROJECT Make a cereal box suitcase to practice finding the volume and surface area of solid figures.

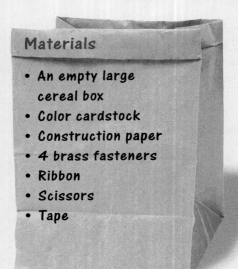

Materials

- An empty large cereal box
- Color cardstock
- Construction paper
- 4 brass fasteners
- Ribbon
- Scissors
- Tape

Directions

1. Tape the box closed around the edges. Make a lid on one side of the box by cutting a slit $\frac{3}{4}$ in. from three of the edges.

2. Attach a brass fastener to the lid and to the opposite side of the cereal box. Attach a ribbon to the brass fastener on the lid. *(Picture A)*

3. Fold a piece of construction paper to form a handle $8\frac{1}{2}$ in. long. Insert brass fasteners into each end of the handle and attach to the side of the box. *(Picture B)*

4. Measure the length, width, and height of the suitcase. Use construction paper to label these measurements on the suitcase. Find the volume and surface area of the suitcase. *(Picture C)*

5. Halve the measurement of the length, width, and height of the suitcase. Use cardstock and tape to make a box with these new measurements. Find the volume and surface area of the new box. Compare the volume and surface area of the new box to that of the suitcase.

Learn how to identify and perform transformations of solid figures.

Remember that a transformation can be a rotation, a reflection, or a translation.

You perform a transformation of a solid figure when you move your math book from your backpack to your desk.

Activity

- Place your textbook in the upper left corner of your desk, and imagine vertical and horizontal lines that divide the desk into fourths.

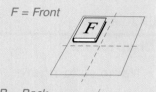

- Perform a 180° rotation of the textbook around the desk's vertical center line.

- Perform a 180° rotation around the desk's horizontal center line.

- Translate the textbook from the lower right to the lower left of the desk.

- Perform a 180° rotation around an axis that runs through the middle of the book, perpendicular to the desktop.

TALK ABOUT IT

- How many different ways can you place your textbook on a piece of paper of the same size so that the paper is completely covered?

- Explain whether a solid figure and its transformation are congruent.

TRY IT

Tell how many ways you can place the solid figure on the outline.

1.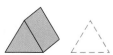

2.

3.

4.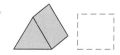

VOCABULARY

1. A solid figure with flat faces that are polygons is a(n) __?__ . (p. 486)

2. The sum of the areas of the faces of a solid figure is the __?__ . (p. 502)

3. The number of cubic units needed to occupy a given space is the __?__ . (p. 506)

EXAMPLE	EXERCISES

Chapter 22

• Name solid figures. (pp. 486–488)

Name the figure.
Is it a polyhedron?

square pyramid
It is a polyhedron.

cone
It is not a polyhedron.

Name the figure. Is it a polyhedron?

4.

5.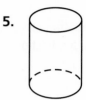

6.

7.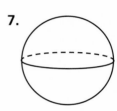

• Identify different views of a solid.
(pp. 489–491)

Name the
solid figure.

triangular
pyramid

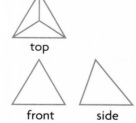

Name the solid figure that has the given views.

8.

9.

• Identify nets for solid figures.
(pp. 492–493)

Name the figure that
can be formed from
the net.

triangular pyramid

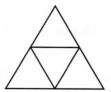

Will the arrangement of squares fold to form a cube? Write *yes* or *no*.

10.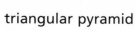

11.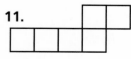

12.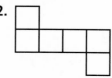

13.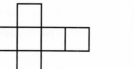

Chapter 23

- **Find the surface area of prisms, pyramids, and cylinders.** (pp. 502–505)

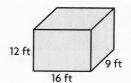

$2 \times 12 \times 9 = 216$ *area of sides*
$2 \times 12 \times 16 = 384$ *area of front and back*
$2 \times 9 \times 16 = 288$ *area of top and bottom*

$216 + 384 + 288 = 888$
So, the surface area is 888 ft².

Find the surface area. Use 3.14 for π.

14.

15.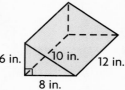

16.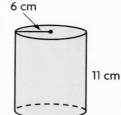

17.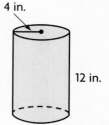

- **Find the volume of prisms, pyramids, and cylinders.**
  (pp. 506–517)

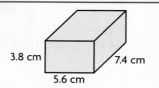

$V = B \times h$ *Base is a rectangle.*
$V = l \times w \times h$ *Area of a rectangle is l × w.*
$V = 5.6 \times 7.4 \times 3.8$
$V = 157.472$
So, the volume is about 157 cm³.

Find the volume. Use 3.14 for π.

18.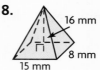

19.

20.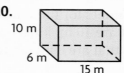

21.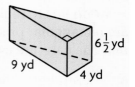

PROBLEM SOLVING APPLICATIONS

22. Susan made a model of a prism. Its base has 5 sides. What kind of prism is her model? (pp. 486–488)

23. Juan made a model of an octagonal prism. How many vertices and how many edges did his model have? (pp. 494–495)

24. A circular swimming pool has a radius of 10 ft and a depth of 6 ft. How many cubic feet of water does it take to fill the pool? (pp. 514–517)

25. A box is 8 m × 6 m × 9 m. If each dimension is doubled, how does the volume change? (pp. 510–511)

Performance Assessment

TASK A • Building Blocks

Constance is teaching her younger brother, Eric, about different solid figures.

Figure A   Figure B   Figure C

a. Constance picks up blocks shaped like Figure A and Figure B. Name each solid figure. Explain your answer.

b. Draw a net of Figure A and a net of Figure B.

c. How are Figures A and B alike? How are they different?

d. Eric uses cubes to build the solid shown in Figure C. On graph paper, draw a top view, a front view, and a side view for the solid.

TASK B • Arts and Crafts Time

Several students are using boxes with flip-tops and cans with snap-on lids to make containers for their art supplies. The boxes are rectangular prisms that are 10 in. long, 6 in. wide, and 4 in. tall. The cans are cylinders that are 8 in. tall with a diameter of 6 in.

a. The students are painting the tops and sides of their boxes. Then they will decorate the boxes with beads. Draw a net of the box. Shade the parts that will be painted. What is the surface area of the part being painted?

b. Some students will keep art supplies inside the boxes. How much space is inside each box to store art supplies? Explain.

c. The students are painting only the lateral surfaces of the cans. Draw a pattern for the can. Shade the parts that will be painted. What is the surface area of the part being painted? Explain. (Use π = 3.14.)

d. Some students will use the cans to store paintbrushes. How much space is inside each can to store paintbrushes? Explain. (Use π = 3.14.)

Draw Nets of Solid Figures

Many nets and patterns for solid figures are made up of squares, rectangles, and circles. You can use the drawing toolbar of word processing software to draw nets and patterns.

In the drawing toolbar, you can use the rectangle icon to draw rectangles and squares. You can use the oval icon to draw ovals and circles. Or you can click *AutoShapes* to choose from a variety of figures, including triangles, rectangles, and squares.

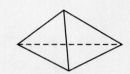

Draw a net for the triangular pyramid above.

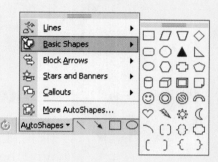

- All the faces of a triangular pyramid are triangles. Click *AutoShapes* on the drawing toolbar. Select *Basic Shapes*. Then click the isosceles triangle.

- Move the cursor to the place where you want the triangle. Press the mouse button while dragging the cursor to size the triangle.

- You need four equilateral triangles for the net. Copy and paste three more triangles.

- One of the triangles must be rotated. To rotate the triangle, find the shaded square located at the top vertex. Move the cursor until you see the curved arrow. Drag to rotate the triangle into position.

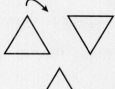

- Drag the triangles into the correct positions to form the net.

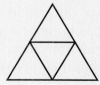

Practice and Problem Solving

Use drawing tools to draw the net or pattern for each solid figure.

1. 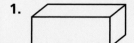 2.   3.

4. Explain how you can use a net or pattern you drew to make the solid figure it represents.

Multimedia Math Glossary www.harcourtschool.com/mathglossary
Vocabulary Power Look up *surface area* in the Multimedia Math Glossary. Using the picture of the rectangular prism as a model, draw a picture of a square pyramid and its net. Label the dimensions of the square pyramid and find the surface area.

Lake Okeechobee was formed about 6,000 years ago.
Okeechobee is a Seminole Indian word that means "big water."

PROBLEM SOLVING ON LOCATION
In Florida

Lake Okeechobee

Nowhere in the United States is water more a part of the scenery than it is in Florida. Florida has 1,350 miles of coastline on the Atlantic Ocean and the Gulf of Mexico. This places Florida second only to Alaska in the length of its coastline. There are more than 30,000 lakes in Florida. One of them, Lake Okeechobee, is the largest lake in the southeastern United States.

1. About $\frac{2}{5}$ of Florida's coastline is on the Atlantic Ocean. Estimate the length of Florida's Atlantic coastline.

Use Data For 2–3, use the circle graphs.

2. If 100,000 gallons of water flowed into Lake Okeechobee, how much would you expect to come from sources *other than* rainfall or the Kissimmee River?

3. How many times as great is the amount of water that flows out of Lake Okeechobee by way of the Caloosahatchee River as the amount that flows from the St. Lucie River? Explain.

The figure at the right shows the area and average depth of Lake Okeechobee. To find the volume of the lake, think of it as a cylinder with a base of 730 mi² and a height of 3 yd.

4. To the nearest thousandth, the average depth of Lake Okeechobee is 0.002 mi. Find the volume of Lake Okeechobee in cubic miles.

LAKE OKEECHOBEE WATER

INFLOW

Rainfall 39%

30%

31%

Other rivers and creeks

Kissimmee River

OUTFLOW

Evaporation 66%

18%

12%

Drains into Everglades

4% St. Lucie River

Caloosahatchee River

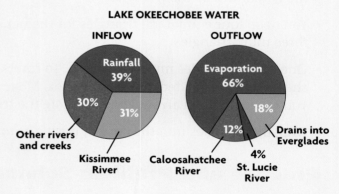

area = 730 mi²

average depth, 3 yd

Lake Okeechobee

5. REASONING Since 1992, the average depth of Lake Okeechobee has been 9 ft. Due to evaporation, the lake can lose up to 1 in. of water a day. What fraction of its volume can the lake lose in one day? Explain your reasoning.

The Everglades

Water from Lake Okeechobee flows south to the marshes and grasslands of Everglades National Park. The Everglades is the largest remaining subtropical area in the United States. Many rare and unusual wildlife species, including alligators, manatees, and Florida panthers, make their homes in the park.

Alligators may live to be 50 years old. The largest known specimen was 19 ft 2 in. long.

The photo shows the visitor center that is located at the main entrance to Everglades National Park. Visitors can stop at the pyramid-roofed gazebos to get information and view maps of the park.

Use Data For 1–2, use the figure at the right.

1. The dimensions are shown for one of the triangles that form the roof of one of the gazebos. What is the surface area of the entire roof? Explain.

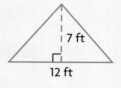

7 ft

12 ft

2. The gazebo roofs are examples of open pyramids. Draw a net for one roof.

Ernest F. Coe Visitor Center

Use Data For 3–4, use the figure at the right. Use 3.14 for π.

3. The approximate dimensions are shown for one of the support poles of a gazebo. To the nearest cubic inch, what is the volume of concrete needed to make one pole?

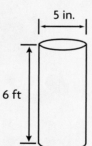

5 in.

6 ft

4. **Stretch Your Thinking** Draw a pattern for one of the poles. Label it with the correct dimensions.

Visitors to the Everglades can hike, bike, drive, or take a boat to see the park's attractions. The map shows a section of the southern area of the park.

5. Hikers on the Snake Bight Trail can see many examples of tropical trees. Estimate the length of the trail.

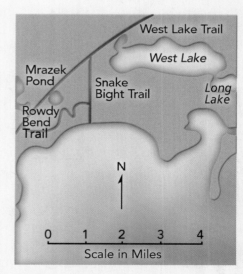

6. Suppose you row a boat around West Lake at a rate of 2 mph. About how long would the trip take?

24 Ratio and Proportion

≡FAST FACT • ART It took over 19,000 hours to make some of the scale models at Mini-Europe, an attraction in Belgium. The models in the display are made using the scale 1:25. The tall building is a replica of the Brussels Town Hall in Brussels, Belgium, and is about 3.8 m tall. The actual building is about 96 m tall.

PROBLEM SOLVING Another model in Mini-Europe is the Eiffel Tower. The actual Eiffel Tower is 320.75 m tall. Using the scale 1:25, about how tall is the model?

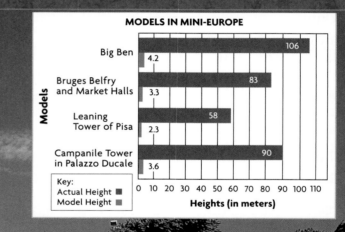

MODELS IN MINI-EUROPE

Models

Big Ben — 106 / 4.2

Bruges Belfry and Market Halls — 83 / 3.3

Leaning Tower of Pisa — 58 / 2.3

Campanile Tower in Palazzo Ducale — 90 / 3.6

Key:
Actual Height ■
Model Height ■

Heights (in meters)
0 10 20 30 40 50 60 70 80 90 100 110

Check What You Know

Use this page to help you review and remember important skills needed for Chapter 24.

 ## Write Equivalent Fractions

Complete each number sentence.

1. $\frac{4}{5} = \frac{\blacksquare}{20}$ 2. $\frac{5}{9} = \frac{15}{\blacksquare}$ 3. $\frac{\blacksquare}{3} = \frac{28}{21}$ 4. $\frac{5}{6} = \frac{\blacksquare}{24}$

5. $\frac{\blacksquare}{9} = \frac{2}{3}$ 6. $\frac{5}{\blacksquare} = \frac{25}{30}$ 7. $\frac{3}{4} = \frac{12}{\blacksquare}$ 8. $\frac{\blacksquare}{6} = \frac{45}{54}$

9. $\frac{1}{2} = \frac{15}{\blacksquare}$ 10. $\frac{3}{\blacksquare} = \frac{21}{49}$ 11. $\frac{\blacksquare}{25} = \frac{3}{5}$ 12. $\frac{24}{64} = \frac{\blacksquare}{16}$

 ## Solve Multiplication Equations

Solve.

13. $5x = 20$ 14. $2p = 14$ 15. $48 = 3k$ 16. $45 = 9m$

17. $96 = 8b$ 18. $65 = 2.5d$ 19. $0.4n = 6$ 20. $187 = 11y$

21. $\frac{1}{2}h = 21$ 22. $7.2 = 0.03m$ 23. $12 = \frac{2}{3}a$ 24. $23h = 23$

Similar and Congruent Figures

Write *similar* or *congruent* to compare the figures. If the figures appear not to be similar or congruent, write *neither*.

25.   26.   27.    28.

29.   30.    31.   32.

Ratios and Rates

Learn how to write ratios and rates and how to find unit rates.

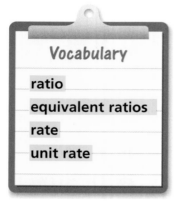

Vocabulary

ratio

equivalent ratios

rate

unit rate

A model of the Liberty Bell on a scale of 1:45 is small enough to hold in your hand. A scale of 1:45 means that each measurement on the model is $\frac{1}{45}$ as long as the corresponding measurement on the real bell. Both 1:45 and $\frac{1}{45}$ are ratios.

A **ratio** is a comparison of two numbers, a and b, and can be written as a fraction $\frac{a}{b}$. You can write a ratio in three ways.

Write: 1 to 45 or 1:45 or $\frac{1}{45}$ ← $\dfrac{\text{first term}}{\text{second term}}$ **Read:** one to forty-five

You can write a ratio to compare two amounts—a part to a part, a part to the whole, or the whole to a part.

EXAMPLE 1

The world's largest bells are made from "bell metal." In every 4 pounds of bell metal, there are 3 pounds of copper and 1 pound of tin. Write the following ratios.

a. pounds of copper to pounds of tin   → $\frac{3}{1}$ *part to part*

b. pounds of copper to total pounds   → $\frac{3}{4}$ *part to whole*

c. total pounds to pounds of tin   → $\frac{4}{1}$ *whole to part*

Equivalent ratios are ratios that name the same comparison.

EXAMPLE 2

Write three equivalent ratios to compare the number of stars with the number of stripes.

$\dfrac{\text{number of stars}}{\text{number of stripes}}$ → $\frac{6}{9}$

$\frac{6}{9}$ → $\frac{6 \div 3}{9 \div 3} = \frac{2}{3}$ *Divide both terms by a common factor.*

$\frac{6}{9}$ → $\frac{6 \times 2}{9 \times 2} = \frac{12}{18}$ *Multiply both terms by the same number.*

So, $\frac{6}{9}$, $\frac{2}{3}$, and $\frac{12}{18}$ are equivalent ratios comparing stars to stripes.

Math Idea ▶ A **rate** is a ratio that compares two quantities having different units of measure.

Suppose 24 ounces of cereal costs $4.32.

rate: $\dfrac{\text{price}}{\text{weight}} \rightarrow \dfrac{\$4.32}{24\text{ oz}}$ $4.32 for 24 oz

A **unit rate** is a rate that has 1 unit as its second term.

unit rate: $\dfrac{\$4.32}{24} = \dfrac{\$4.32 \div 24}{24 \div 24} = \dfrac{\$0.18}{1}$ $0.18 for 1 oz

The unit rate for the cereal is $0.18 per ounce.

Average speed is average distance traveled in 1 unit of time, such as 1 hour or 1 second. So, average speed is a unit rate.

EXAMPLE 3

The Howards are driving their car from Richmond, VA, to Philadelphia, PA, a distance of 250 mi. They have traveled 200 mi in 4 hr. At this rate, how long will it take them to make the complete trip?

$\dfrac{\text{miles}}{\text{hours}} \rightarrow \dfrac{200}{4}$ *Write a ratio to compare miles to hours.*

$\dfrac{200}{4} = \dfrac{200 \div 4}{4 \div 4} = \dfrac{50}{1}$ ← miles ← hours   *Find the unit rate, or average speed.*

$\dfrac{50}{1} = \dfrac{50 \times 5}{1 \times 5} = \dfrac{250}{5}$ ← miles ← hours   THINK: *50 × 5 = 250. Multiply each term by 5 to find the number of hours for 250 mi.*

So, it will take the Howards 5 hr to travel 250 mi.

CHECK FOR UNDERSTANDING

Think and ▶
Discuss

Look back at the lesson to answer each question.

1. **Explain** how to find equivalent ratios.

2. **Tell** which is the better buy, 14 oz of cereal at $2.52 or 20 oz of cereal at $3.20. Explain.

Guided ▶
Practice

Write two equivalent ratios.

3. $\dfrac{4}{8}$ 4. $\dfrac{6}{10}$ 5. $\dfrac{9}{12}$ 6. $\dfrac{10}{15}$

Write a ratio in fraction form. Then find the unit rate.

7. 150 points in 10 games   8. $64 in 16 hr

9. 90 words in 2 min   10. $2.56 for 4 pencils

11. $15 for 6 lb   12. 120 mi in 3 hr

Independent ▶
Practice

Write two equivalent ratios.

13. $\frac{2}{4}$ **14.** $\frac{4}{5}$ **15.** $\frac{3}{9}$ **16.** $\frac{15}{21}$

17. $\frac{6}{16}$ **18.** $\frac{21}{30}$ **19.** $\frac{5}{9}$ **20.** $\frac{14}{24}$

Write each ratio in fraction form. Then find the unit rate.

21. $15 for 5 tapes   **22.** 8 pages in 2.5 hr

23. 60 mi on 3 gal   **24.** $1.89 for 3 pens

25. $2.10 for 6 fish   **26.** 900 students for 30 teachers

For 27–28, use the figure at the right.

27. Find the ratio of red sections to blue sections. Then write three equivalent ratios.

28. Find the ratio of blue sections to all the sections. Then write three equivalent ratios.

Find the missing term, *m*, that makes the ratios equivalent.

29. 5 to 4; *m* to 12   **30.** 20:*m*; 10:8   **31.** $\frac{9}{12}$; $\frac{45}{m}$

32. Write the following ratio: number of tricycles to number of tricycle wheels.

33. Write the following ratio: number of tires to number of cars.

Problem Solving ▶
Applications

34. Of the 10 members on a team, 4 are girls. What is the ratio of girls to all the members? of boys to girls?

Use Data   **For 35–38, use the table.**

35. ***REASONING*** How can you decide if Brand B or Brand C is the better buy without dividing?

36. Which brand is the best buy?

37. Find the cost of 6 boxes of Brand D.

38. **?** **What's the Question?** The answer is $0.42 per box.

Brand	Cost	Number of Boxes
A	$1.17	3
B	$1.23	3
C	$2.52	6
D	$3.15	9

HOW JUICES COMPARE

MIXED REVIEW AND TEST PREP

39. Describe the pattern. Then find the next term. 1, 4, 9, 16, ■ (p. 360)

40. If $k = 4p - 3t$, what is the value of k when $p = 3$ and $t = 2$? (p. 260)

41. Give the prime factorization of 54. (p. 168)

42. Write 45.6% as a decimal. (p. 68)

43. TEST PREP Solve. $n + 3 = 11$ (p. 277)

     A $n = 1$ **B** $n = 2$ **C** $n = 6$ **D** $n = 8$

EXTRA PRACTICE page 550, Set A

ALGEBRA
Explore Proportions

Explore how to find equivalent ratios to form a proportion.

You need two-color counters.

The ratio of oxygen atoms to hydrogen atoms in 1 molecule of water is $\frac{1}{2}$. The ratio of oxygen atoms to hydrogen atoms in 2 molecules of water is $\frac{2}{4}$, which is equivalent to $\frac{1}{2}$.

These ratios can be used to write a proportion. A **proportion** is an equation that shows two equivalent ratios.

$$\frac{1}{2} = \frac{2}{4} \leftarrow \text{ proportion}$$

You can use counters to model proportions.

Vocabulary

proportion

Activity

- Make the model shown here. Write the ratio of red counters to yellow counters.

- Separate the red counters into three equal groups. Do the same with the yellow counters. Write the ratio of red to yellow in each group.

- Separate the counters into six equal groups. Write the ratio of red to yellow in each group.

Think and Discuss

- Is $\frac{4}{8} = \frac{3}{4}$ a proportion? Use your counters to explain your reasoning.

You can also determine whether two ratios form a proportion by finding common denominators or by finding the cross products. Equivalent ratios have equal cross products.

$$\frac{2}{3} \overset{?}{=} \frac{9}{16}$$

$$\frac{2 \times 16}{3 \times 16} \overset{?}{=} \frac{9 \times 3}{16 \times 3}$$

$$\frac{32}{48} \neq \frac{27}{48} \leftarrow \text{common denominators}$$

The ratios do not form a proportion.

$$\frac{2}{3} \overset{?}{\underset{}{\longleftrightarrow}} \frac{8}{12}$$

$$2 \times 12 \overset{?}{=} 8 \times 3 \leftarrow \text{cross products}$$

$$24 = 24$$

The ratios form a proportion.

Practice

Determine whether the ratios form a proportion.

1. $\frac{1}{3}$ and $\frac{4}{12}$ **2.** $\frac{3}{4}$ and $\frac{6}{9}$ **3.** $\frac{2}{4}$ and $\frac{3}{6}$ **4.** $\frac{2}{5}$ and $\frac{6}{8}$

ALGEBRA
Solve Proportions

Learn how to write and solve proportions.

Your weight depends on where you are. Because the moon is smaller than Earth and has less mass, you would weigh less there than on Earth. An object that weighs 60 lb on Earth would weigh only 10 lb on the moon. This ratio of weights remains the same for all objects.

Remember that a proportion is an equation that shows two equivalent ratios.

Morgan weighs 90 lb. How much would she weigh on the moon?

Step 1 Write a proportion. Let m represent Morgan's weight on the moon.

$$\frac{\text{weight on Earth}}{\text{weight on moon}} \rightarrow \frac{60}{10} = \frac{90}{m} \leftarrow \frac{\text{Morgan's weight on Earth}}{\text{Morgan's weight on moon}}$$

Step 2 Use cross products to solve the proportion.

$$\frac{60}{10} = \frac{90}{m} \qquad \textit{Find the cross products.}$$

$$60 \times m = 10 \times 90 \qquad \textit{Multiply.}$$

$$60m = 900$$

$$\frac{60m}{60} = \frac{900}{60} \qquad \textit{Divide to solve the equation.}$$

$$m = 15$$

So, Morgan would weigh 15 lb on the moon.

EXAMPLE

Solve the proportion.

$$\frac{5}{2} = \frac{50}{a}$$

$$\frac{5}{2} = \frac{50}{a} \qquad \textit{Find the cross products.}$$

$$5 \times a = 2 \times 50 \qquad \textit{Multiply.}$$

$$5a = 100$$

$$\frac{5a}{5} = \frac{100}{5} \qquad \textit{Divide to solve the equation.}$$

$$a = 20$$

$$\frac{5}{2} = \frac{50}{a} \qquad \textit{Check your solution}$$

$$\frac{5}{2} \overset{?}{=} \frac{50}{20} \qquad \textit{Replace a with 20. Find the cross products.}$$

$$5 \times 20 \overset{?}{=} 2 \times 50 \qquad \textit{Multiply.}$$

$$100 = 100 \checkmark \qquad \textit{The solution checks.}$$

Think and Discuss ▶ Look back at the lesson to answer the question.

1. **Tell** what the cross products are in the proportion $\frac{2}{3} = \frac{y}{12}$.

Guided Practice ▶ Solve the proportion.

2. $\frac{3}{5} = \frac{x}{20}$

3. $\frac{5}{6} = \frac{15}{y}$

4. $\frac{z}{8} = \frac{9}{24}$

PRACTICE AND PROBLEM SOLVING

Independent Practice ▶ Solve the proportion.

5. $\frac{3}{4} = \frac{12}{x}$

6. $\frac{2}{3} = \frac{k}{18}$

7. $\frac{x}{12} = \frac{7}{4}$

8. $\frac{8}{20} = \frac{y}{5}$

9. $\frac{10}{6} = \frac{60}{p}$

10. $\frac{1}{w} = \frac{8}{24}$

11. $\frac{a}{50} = \frac{3}{2}$

12. $\frac{20}{b} = \frac{15}{30}$

13. $\frac{3}{400} = \frac{9}{c}$

Problem Solving Applications ▶

14. Maggie drinks 2 qt of milk every 6 days. How many days will it take her to drink 5 qt of milk?

15. Jerome earns 3 credits for every 500 points he scores on the pinball machine. How many points will he need to score in order to earn 15 credits?

16. **FAST FACT • SCIENCE** The weight of an object on Mars is less than its weight on Earth, but greater than its weight on the moon. A person who weighs 150 lb on Earth would weigh 57 lb on Mars. Look back at the lesson. How much more would Morgan weigh on Mars than on the moon?

17. Abdul won 8 of his first 12 games. At that rate, how many of the next 30 games will he win?

18. **What's the Question?** Astronaut Neil Armstrong, the first person to walk on the moon, weighed $27\frac{1}{2}$ lb on the moon. The answer is 165 lb.

MIXED REVIEW AND TEST PREP

19. Find the area. (p. 458)

3.9 cm

8.1 cm

20. Find the measure of $\angle A$. (p. 356)

21. Evaluate $3n - 7$ for $n = 17$. (p. 260)

22. Solve. $x - 29.3 = 23.9$ (p. 280)

⭐ 23. **TEST PREP** Which ratio is equivalent to $\frac{4}{7}$? (p. 532)

A $\frac{7}{4}$ B $\frac{6}{9}$ C $\frac{12}{21}$ D $\frac{3}{8}$

ALGEBRA
Ratios and Similar Figures

Learn how to use ratios to identify similar figures.

QUICK REVIEW
Simplify.

1. $\frac{6}{8}$ 2. $\frac{6}{12}$ 3. $\frac{8}{12}$ 4. $\frac{15}{18}$ 5. $\frac{9}{15}$

Vocabulary

corresponding sides

corresponding angles

The larger soccer ball and the soccer ball on the key ring have similar black pentagons on them. What other similar polygons can you find on the soccer balls?

Similar figures have **corresponding sides** and **corresponding angles**. The corresponding sides and angles for similar rectangles *ABCD* and *EFGH* are shown below.

$\overline{AB}$ corresponds to $\overline{EF}$.
$\overline{BC}$ corresponds to $\overline{FG}$.
$\overline{CD}$ corresponds to $\overline{GH}$.
$\overline{DA}$ corresponds to $\overline{HE}$.

Remember that similar figures have the same shape.

∠*A* corresponds to ∠*E*.
∠*B* corresponds to ∠*F*.
∠*C* corresponds to ∠*G*.
∠*D* corresponds to ∠*H*.

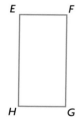

It is usually easier to find the corresponding sides and corresponding angles of similar figures if they are oriented the same way on the page.

Activity

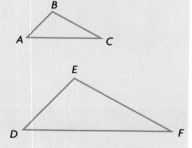

You need: metric ruler

- Do these triangles appear to be similar? Explain.

- Measure and record the lengths of the sides of both triangles in centimeters.

- Write the ratios *AB* to *DE*, *BC* to *EF*, and *AC* to *DF*.

- Write each of the ratios in simplest form. What do you notice about the ratios?

- Measure and record the angles in both triangles.

- What do you notice about the angle measures?

Math **I**dea ▶ If polygons are similar, their corresponding angles are congruent, and the lengths of their corresponding sides have the same ratio.

EXAMPLE 1

△MNP and △HJK are similar. Find the measures of ∠M, ∠N, and ∠P and the ratio of the lengths of the corresponding sides.

∠M corresponds to ∠H, so ∠M measures 35°.

∠N corresponds to ∠J, so ∠N measures 23°.

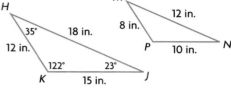

∠P corresponds to ∠K, so ∠P measures 122°.

$\overline{MN}$ corresponds to $\overline{HJ}$, $\overline{NP}$ corresponds to $\overline{JK}$, and $\overline{PM}$ corresponds to $\overline{KH}$.

$$\frac{MN}{HJ} \to \frac{12}{18} = \frac{2}{3} \qquad \frac{NP}{JK} \to \frac{10}{15} = \frac{2}{3} \qquad \frac{PM}{KH} \to \frac{8}{12} = \frac{2}{3}$$

So, the ratio of the lengths of the corresponding sides is $\frac{2}{3}$.

Two triangles are similar if their corresponding angles are congruent *or* if the ratios of their corresponding sides are equal. Other polygons are similar only if their corresponding angles are congruent *and* the ratios of their corresponding sides are equal.

EXAMPLE 2

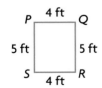

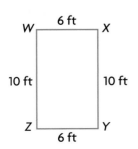

A. Tell if △ABC is similar to △DEF.

Since these are triangles, check either the measures of the corresponding angles *or* the ratios of the corresponding sides.

∠A and ∠D are congruent.
∠B and ∠E are congruent.
∠C and ∠F are congruent.

Check whether corresponding angles are congruent.

So, △ABC is similar to △DEF.

B. Tell if rectangle PQRS is similar to rectangle WXYZ.

Since these are rectangles, check the measures of the corresponding angles *and* the ratios of the corresponding sides.

All angles in rectangles measure 90°, so the corresponding angles are congruent.

$$\frac{PQ}{WX} \to \frac{4}{6} = \frac{2}{3} \qquad \frac{QR}{XY} \to \frac{5}{10} = \frac{1}{2}$$

Write the ratios of the corresponding sides in simplest form.

$$\frac{RS}{YZ} \to \frac{4}{6} = \frac{2}{3} \qquad \frac{SP}{ZW} \to \frac{5}{10} = \frac{1}{2}$$

$$\frac{2}{3} \neq \frac{1}{2}$$

Compare the ratios.

The corresponding angles are congruent but the ratios of the corresponding sides are not equal. So, PQRS is not similar to WXYZ.

Think and ▶ Discuss

Look back at the lesson to answer each question.

1. **Explain** whether the ratio of corresponding sides in Example 2A is $\frac{2}{3}$.

2. **Choose** the one correct statement:
   A All similar figures are also congruent.
   B All congruent figures are also similar.

Guided ▶ Practice

3. Name the corresponding sides and angles. Write the ratio of the corresponding sides in simplest form.

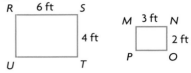

Independent ▶ Practice

Name the corresponding sides and angles. Write the ratio of the corresponding sides in simplest form.

4.
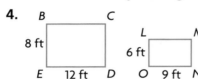

5.
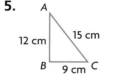

Tell whether the figures in each pair are similar. Write *yes* or *no*. If you write *no*, explain.

6.
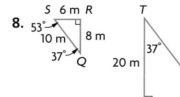

7.
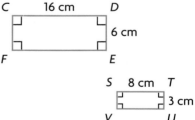

8.
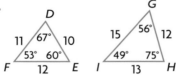

9.
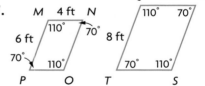

The figures in each pair are similar. Find the unknown measures.

10.
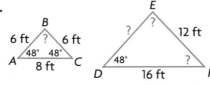

11.
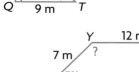

Write _yes_ or _no_. Explain your answer.

12. Are all squares similar?   **13.** Are all rectangles similar?

14. Are all rhombi similar?   **15.** Are all right triangles similar?

Problem Solving ▶
Applications

Use the following information for 16–17: The rectangular front of the North End Mall is 60 ft tall and 80 ft wide. The front of the Eastside Mall has sides that are $\frac{3}{4}$ the lengths of the sides of the North End Mall.

16. Are the fronts similar?

17. Find the dimensions of the front of the Eastside Mall.

18. Most basketball courts are 94 ft long and 50 ft wide. A half court is 47 ft by 50 ft. Is a half court similar to a full court? Explain.

19. **Write About It** Explain how you know that _ABCD_ is similar to _AEFG_.

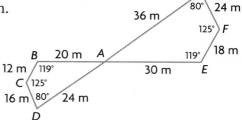

MIXED REVIEW AND TEST PREP

20. What is the unit rate if 5 cans cost $3? (p. 532)   **21.** If $5y = 15$, what does y equal? (p. 291)

22. How many faces does a rectangular pyramid have? (p. 486)

★**23. TEST PREP** Evaluate $4x + x + 9$ for $x = 3$. (p. 260)

  A 19   **B** 21   **C** 24   **D** 25

★**24. TEST PREP** Evaluate. $7^2 - \sqrt{49}$ (p. 266)

  F 7   **G** 14   **H** 42   **J** 56

PROBLEM SOLVING ⚡ ThiNker's CorNer

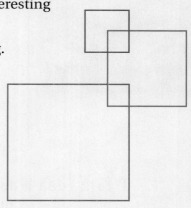

Hip to be square! All squares are similar. You can find an interesting relationship between the perimeter and area of similar squares.

1. Find the perimeter and area of a square with sides 5 units long. Double the lengths of the sides of the square and find the new perimeter and area. Write a ratio comparing the new perimeter and area to the old perimeter and area. Describe the relationship.

2. Triple the lengths of the sides of the original square and find the new perimeter and area. Write a ratio to compare this perimeter and area to the original perimeter and area. Draw a picture to illustrate the relationship.

3. What happens to the perimeter and area of a square when the sides are increased k times?

EXTRA PRACTICE page 550, Set C

ALGEBRA
Proportions and Similar Figures

Learn how to use proportions and similar figures to find unknown measures.

Vocabulary

indirect measurement

Arizona's Grand Canyon is more than 1 mile deep and 217 miles long. It has been called one of the Seven Natural Wonders of the World. Each year, tourists snap millions of photos of the canyon. A photo is similar to the scene it depicts.

If two figures are similar and you know the lengths of two corresponding sides, you can use proportions to find the lengths of other sides.

EXAMPLE 1

Remember that a proportion is an equation which states that two ratios are equivalent.

Armando made an enlargement that is similar to a 4-in. × 6-in. photo he took of the Grand Canyon. The enlargement is 12 in. wide. How long is it?

Write the ratios of the corresponding sides. Let x = the length of $\overline{EF}$.

$$\frac{AB}{EF} \rightarrow \frac{6}{x} \qquad \frac{AD}{EH} \rightarrow \frac{4}{12}$$

$\dfrac{6}{x} = \dfrac{4}{12}$ *Use the ratios to write a proportion.*

$4 \cdot x = 6 \cdot 12$ *Find the cross products.*

$4x = 72$ *Solve the equation.*

$\dfrac{4x}{4} = \dfrac{72}{4}$

$x = 18$

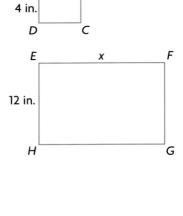

So, the enlargement is 18 in. long.

Math **I**dea ▶ In Example 1, similar figures and a proportion were used to find an unknown length. This method of finding a measurement is called **indirect measurement**. It can be used to find lengths and distances that are too great to be measured with a ruler.

EXAMPLE 2

On a sunny day, one saguaro cactus casts a shadow that is 56 ft long. At the same time, a yardstick casts a shadow that is 4 ft long. Use the similar right triangles shown below to find the height of the cactus.

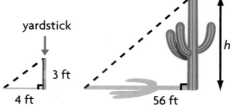

yardstick

3 ft

4 ft

h

56 ft

$$\frac{3}{h} = \frac{4}{56} \begin{array}{l}\leftarrow \text{ small triangle}\\ \leftarrow \text{ large triangle}\end{array}$$ *Write a proportion.*

$$4 \times h = 3 \times 56$$ *Find the cross products.*
Solve the equation.

$$4h = 168$$

$$\frac{4h}{4} = \frac{168}{4}$$

$$h = 42$$

So, the cactus is 42 ft tall.

The saguaro cactus, the world's tallest cactus, is native to Arizona.

CHECK FOR UNDERSTANDING

Think and Discuss ▶ **Look back at the lesson to answer each question.**

1. **Explain** why you can use similar figures to measure objects indirectly.

2. **Name** three objects that would be difficult to measure directly.

3. **Determine** how long the picture in Example 1 would be if it were 8 in. wide.

Guided Practice ▶ **The figures are similar. Write a proportion. Then find the unknown length.**

4.

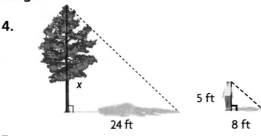

x

24 ft

5 ft

8 ft

5.

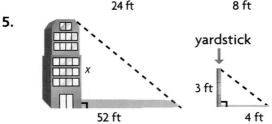

x

52 ft

yardstick

3 ft

4 ft

PRACTICE AND PROBLEM SOLVING

Independent ▶ Practice

The figures are similar. Write a proportion. Then find the unknown length.

6.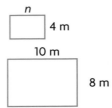
   n
   4 m
   10 m
   8 m

7.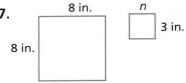
   8 in.
   n
   3 in.
   8 in.

8.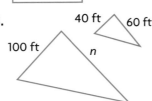
   40 ft
   60 ft
   100 ft
   n

9.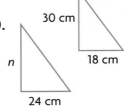
   30 cm
   18 cm
   n
   24 cm

10. 7 m
    n
    1.8 m
    4.5 m

11.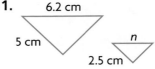
    6.2 cm
    5 cm
    n
    2.5 cm

Problem Solving ▶ Applications

12. **REASONING**   Two common envelope sizes are $3\frac{1}{2}$ in. × $6\frac{1}{2}$ in. and 4 in. × $9\frac{1}{2}$ in. Are these envelopes similar? Explain.

13. **Art**   The famous painting known as "Red Interior, Still-life on a Blue Table" was painted by Henri Matisse in 1947. The copy at the left measures 1 in. tall by $\frac{3}{4}$ in. wide. The height of the real painting is 32 in. Find the width of the real painting.

14. **Vocabulary Power**   On page 530, the people in the model are *in proportion* to the buildings because they are the correct size in relation to the building. Name other examples of things that are *in proportion*.

15. **(?) What's the Error?**   The shadow of a 6-ft man measures 5 ft at the same time his son's shadow is 2 ft. Taylor used a proportion to find the son's height as $1\frac{2}{3}$ ft. Explain Taylor's mistake.

MIXED REVIEW AND TEST PREP

16. Triangle 1 is acute. Triangle 2 is obtuse. Can the triangles be similar? Explain.
    (p. 538)

17. The base of a prism has 20 sides. How many vertices does the prism have? (p. 494)

For 18–19, use the box-and-whisker graph.

18. What is the median? (p. 143)

19. What is the range? (p. 143)

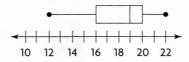
10 12 14 16 18 20 22

⭐ 20. **TEST PREP**   Solve. $0.4p = 20$ (p. 291)

   A 5   **B** 19.6   **C** 20.4   **D** 50

EXTRA PRACTICE page 550, Set D

ALGEBRA
Scale Drawings

Learn how to use scale to find the dimensions for a drawing or the actual dimensions of an object.

QUICK REVIEW

1. 490 ÷ 7   **2.** 800 ÷ 10 **3.** 540 ÷ 6   **4.** 3 × 120   **5.** 70 × 11

Vocabulary

scale drawing
scale

Floor plans, road maps, and diagrams are examples of scale drawings. A **scale drawing** is a drawing of a real object that is smaller than (a reduction of) or larger than (an enlargement of) the real object. Measurements on a scale drawing are proportional to measurements of the real object.

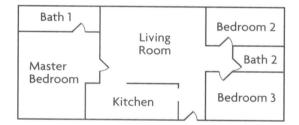

The above floor plan and other types of architectural drawings are called blueprints. A blueprint can be a reduction or an enlargement of an object.

Activity

You need: centimeter graph paper, metric ruler

- Measure the length and width of the scale drawing above in centimeters.

- On graph paper, make a drawing with measurements that are twice those in the scale drawing.

- Write the ratio of length to width for the original drawing.

- Write the ratio of length to width in your drawing. Are the two ratios equal? Are the drawings similar? Explain.

- Make a drawing with measurements that are half those in the original scale drawing.

- Write the ratio of length to width for your new drawing. Is the ratio equal to the ratio for the original scale drawing? Are the drawings similar? Explain.

- Suppose you made a drawing of the floor plan that was 21 cm long. If your drawing was similar to the original floor plan, how wide would it be? Explain.

A **scale** is a ratio of two sets of measurements. The scale 1 in. = 3 ft on this drawing of a bicycle means that 1 in. on the drawing represents 3 ft on the actual bike.

scale: 1 in. = 3 ft

EXAMPLE 1

Measure the length of the bike in the scale drawing. Then use the scale to find the actual length of the bike.

scale drawing length: 2 in.

$$\underset{\text{actual (ft)}}{\overset{\text{scale}}{\text{drawing (in.)}}} \rightarrow \frac{1}{3} = \frac{2}{n}$$ *Write a proportion. Let n represent the actual length of the bike.*

$$1 \times n = 3 \times 2$$ *Find the cross products and solve.*

$$n = 6$$

So, the actual length of the bike is 6 ft.

If an object is very small, a scale drawing might be larger than the object.

scale: 8 cm = 1 mm

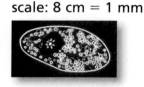

EXAMPLE 2

A paramecium is a tiny organism whose entire body consists of a single cell. Use the scale and the scale drawing to find the length of the paramecium.

scale drawing length: 2.4 cm

$$\underset{\text{actual (mm)}}{\overset{\text{scale}}{\text{drawing (cm)}}} \rightarrow \frac{8}{1} = \frac{2.4}{n}$$ *Write a proportion. Let n represent the actual length of the paramecium.*

$$8 \times n = 1 \times 2.4$$ *Find the cross products and solve.*

$$n = \frac{2.4}{8}$$

$$n = 0.3$$

So, the paramecium is about 0.3 mm long.

CHECK FOR UNDERSTANDING

Think and ▶ Discuss

Look back at the lesson to answer each question.

1. **Compare** the actual length of the bike in Example 1 with the length of the bike in the scale drawing.

2. **Make** a scale drawing of a square microchip that has a side of 2 mm. Use a scale of 4 cm:1 mm. How long will the side on your drawing be?

3. **Explain** how the scale drawing of a microchip is different from the scale drawing of the bicycle.

Find the unknown dimension.

4. scale: 1 in. = 8 ft
drawing length: 3 in.
actual length: ■ ft

5. scale: 2 in. = 7 yd
drawing length: 8 in.
actual length: ■ yd

PRACTICE AND PROBLEM SOLVING

Independent ▶
Practice

Find the unknown dimension.

6. scale: 1 in. = 4 ft
drawing length: ■ in.
actual length: 28 ft

7. scale: 1 in. = 6 ft
drawing length: 5 in.
actual length: ■ ft

8. scale: 3 in. = 4 ft
drawing length: ■ in.
actual length: 14 ft

9. scale: 4 cm = 3 mm
drawing length: ■ cm
actual length: 15 mm

10. scale: 2 in. = 5 ft
drawing length: $\frac{1}{2}$ in.
actual length: ■ ft

11. scale: 6 cm = 3 mm
drawing length: ■ cm
actual length: 2 mm

Problem Solving ▶
Applications

12. A hallway is 15 ft long. How long is it on a floor plan drawn to the scale 2 in. = 3 yd?

13. A model of a storage shed is shown at the right. The model measures 8 in. × 3 in. × 4 in. How many cubical boxes measuring 2 ft on a side can be stacked in the actual shed?

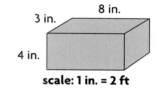

scale: 1 in. = 2 ft

14. **FAST FACT** • SCIENCE The diameter of the sun is about 900,000 miles. Gail wanted to make a scale drawing of the solar system. She drew the sun in the center with a diameter of 1 in. What problem did Gail run into in drawing the planet Pluto at its average distance of 3.6 billion miles from the sun?

15. **Write About It** Explain what the scale 1 cm = 2 m on a scale drawing means.

MIXED REVIEW AND TEST PREP

16. Two rectangles measure 9 cm by 12 cm and 12 cm by 16 cm. Are the rectangles similar? (p. 538)

17. True or false? A cone is a polyhedron. (p. 486)

For 18–19, use the stem-and-leaf plot at the right.

18. What is the greatest data value shown? (p. 140)

19. What is the mean of the data? (p. 140)

Stem	Leaves
3	0 0 3 9
4	2 3 8
5	3 6 7

⭐**20.** **TEST PREP**   Ted recorded these scores on 10-point history quizzes: 8, 7, 10, 9, 7, 7. What was his median score? (p. 118)

A 3 **B** 7 **C** 7.5 **D** 8

ALGEBRA
Maps

Learn how to read and use map scales.

Mapmakers are called cartographers. Cartographers use ratios, proportions, and scales to convert actual distances on Earth to map distances. You can use the same method to convert map distances into real distances.

EXAMPLE

Use the Maryland map to determine the actual straight-line distance from Washington, DC, to Columbia, MD. The map scale is 1 in. = 20 mi.

Use a ruler to measure the distance from Washington to Columbia.

map distance → $1\frac{1}{4}$, or 1.25 in.

Let n represent the actual distance in miles. Write a proportion.

$$\frac{\text{in.}}{\text{mi}} \rightarrow \frac{1}{20} = \frac{1.25}{n}$$

Find the cross products.
$1 \times n = 1.25 \times 20$

Multiply.
$n = 25$

So, it is 25 mi from Washington to Columbia.

- Philadelphia, PA, is about 130 mi from Washington. If you were a cartographer making a map with the same scale, how far from Washington would you place Philadelphia?

CHECK FOR UNDERSTANDING

Think and ▸ Discuss

Look back at the lesson to answer each question.

1. Find the actual straight-line distance from Washington, DC, to Baltimore, MD.

Guided ▸ Practice

2. Tell the map distance that represents 90 mi on the Maryland map.

The map distance is given. Find the actual distance. Use a map scale of 1 in. = 100 mi.

3. $\frac{1}{2}$ in.   **4.** 5 in.   **5.** $4\frac{1}{4}$ in.

Independent ▶ Practice

The map distance is given. Find the actual distance. The scale is 1 in. = 80 mi.

6. $1\frac{1}{2}$ in. **7.** 3 in. **8.** $2\frac{1}{2}$ in. **9.** $5\frac{1}{4}$ in.

10. $\frac{1}{2}$ in. **11.** 18 in. **12.** $2\frac{3}{4}$ in. **13.** $4\frac{5}{8}$ in.

The actual distance is given. Find the map distance. The scale is 1 in. = 25 mi.

14. 100 mi **15.** 150 mi **16.** $12\frac{1}{2}$ mi **17.** $62\frac{1}{2}$ mi

Problem Solving ▶ Applications

For 18–20, use the map of Colorado. The scale is $\frac{1}{2}$ in. = 46 mi.

18. Find the straight-line distance in miles from Pueblo to Denver and then from Denver to Steamboat Springs.

19. Stefano drove from Denver to Vail. If he drove 55 mi per hour, about how long did the trip take him?

20. Fran drove for 2.3 hours at 50 mi per hour. If you drew her route as a line on the Colorado map, how long would it be?

21. **REASONING** The auto club map of Alabama has a scale of 1 in. = 20 mi. The tourist map has a scale of 1 in. = 40 mi. On which map does the state of Alabama appear larger?

22. ✏️ **Write About It** Explain how you can find the actual distance between two cities if you know the map distance and the scale.

MIXED REVIEW AND TEST PREP

23. Scale: 1 in. = 5 ft; actual length: 20 ft; drawing length: ___?___. (p. 545)

24. How many bases does a cone have? (p. 486)

For 25–26, use the line plot at the right. (p. 118)

25. What is the mode of the data?

26. What is the median of the data?

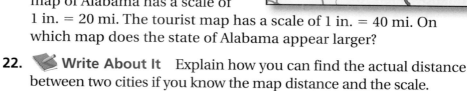

27. TEST PREP Which fraction is greatest? (p. 188)

A $\frac{3}{8}$ **B** $\frac{7}{24}$ **C** $\frac{5}{12}$ **D** $\frac{1}{3}$

Set A (pp. 532–534)

Write each ratio in fraction form. Then find the unit rate.

1. $2.50 for 10

2. $2.76 for 12

3. 360 people in 3 sq mi

4. 240 miles in 6 hr

5. $2.75 for 25

6. 500 miles on 20 gallons

Set B

Solve the proportion. (pp. 536–537)

1. $\frac{1}{2} = \frac{x}{14}$

2. $\frac{2}{3} = \frac{y}{33}$

3. $\frac{5}{6} = \frac{25}{z}$

4. $\frac{8}{9} = \frac{32}{a}$

5. $\frac{b}{10} = \frac{2}{5}$

6. $\frac{c}{24} = \frac{1}{6}$

7. $\frac{3}{p} = \frac{9}{27}$

8. $\frac{32}{q} = \frac{4}{9}$

Set C (pp. 538–541)

The figures in each pair are similar. Write the ratio of the corresponding sides in simplest form.

1.
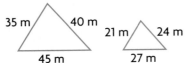

2.

3.
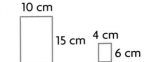

Set D (pp. 542–544)

The figures are similar. Write a proportion. Then find the unknown length.

1.
24 ft
16 ft
12 ft
n

2.
9 m
6 m
12 m
n

3.

Set E (pp. 545–547)

Find the unknown dimension.

1. scale: 1 in. = 5 ft
drawing length: 7 in.
actual length: ■ ft

2. scale: 1 in. = 5 ft
drawing length: 4 in.
actual length: ■ ft

3. scale: 1 in. = 5 ft
drawing length: ■ in.
actual length: 15 ft

Set F (pp. 548–549)

The map distance is given. Find the actual distance. The scale is 1 in. = 25 mi.

1. $1\frac{1}{2}$ in.

2. 3 in.

3. $5\frac{1}{2}$ in.

4. 7 in.

1. **VOCABULARY**   A comparison of two numbers is a(n) __?__ . (p. 532)

2. **VOCABULARY**   An equation that shows two equivalent ratios is a(n) __?__ . (p. 535)

3. **VOCABULARY**   A __?__ is a ratio of two sets of measurements. (p. 546)

Write each ratio in fraction form. (pp. 532–534)

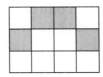

4. white sections to all sections

5. yellow sections to white sections

6. all sections to yellow sections

Solve the proportion. (pp. 536–537)

7. $\frac{3}{5} = \frac{x}{35}$

8. $\frac{2}{7} = \frac{16}{y}$

9. $\frac{z}{42} = \frac{9}{14}$

10. $\frac{35}{a} = \frac{7}{8}$

Tell whether the figures in each pair are similar. Write *yes* or *no*. If you write *no*, explain. (pp. 538–541)

11.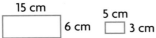

15 cm, 5 cm, 6 cm, 3 cm

12.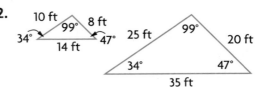

10 ft, 8 ft, 99°, 34°, 47°, 14 ft, 25 ft, 99°, 20 ft, 34°, 47°, 35 ft

The figures are similar. Write a proportion. Then find the unknown length. (pp. 542–544)

13.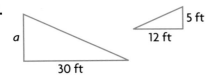

a, 30 ft, 5 ft, 12 ft

14.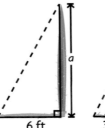

a, 6 ft, 3 ft, 5 ft

Find the unknown dimension. (pp. 545–547)

15. scale: 2 in. = 5 ft
    drawing length: 8 in.
    actual length: ▇ ft

16. scale: 2 in. = 5 ft
    drawing length: ▇ in.
    actual length: 40 ft

17. scale: 2 in. = 5 ft
    drawing length: 13 in.
    actual length: ▇ ft

The map distance is given. Find the actual distance. The scale is 1 in. = 150 mi. (pp. 548–549)

18. 5 in.

19. 12 in.

20. $3\frac{1}{2}$ in.

21. $6\frac{3}{4}$ in.

22. $\frac{1}{2}$ in.

23. 0.4 in.

Solve. (pp. 536–537)

24. Beach towels are on sale at 2 for $17.98. Rich buys 5 of them. How much does he pay?

25. Oranges are selling for $3.00 a dozen. Find the cost of 2 oranges.

★ ALGEBRAIC THINKING

1. In the 2000 Summer Olympics, the country of Great Britain won a total of 28 gold, silver, and bronze medals. The total included 11 gold and 10 silver medals. Let b represent the number of bronze medals. Which shows the correct equation to find the number of bronze medals won by Great Britain and also shows the correct solution?

   A $b + 21 = 28; b = 7$

   B $b + 11 = 28; b = 17$

   C $b + 10 = 28; b = 18$

   D $b + 22 = 28; b = 6$

2. A recipe calls for 2 tablespoons of sugar for every 3 cups of flour. How many tablespoons of sugar are needed when 18 cups of flour are used?

   F 18 tablespoons

   G 12 tablespoons

   H 6 tablespoons

   J 2 tablespoons

3. Each car in the parking lot at Central Elementary School has 4 tires plus a spare tire in the trunk. If c represents the number of cars in the parking lot, which expression represents the total number of tires in the parking lot?

   A $4 + c$ **C** $4c + 1$

   B $5c$ **D** $4c$

4. **Explain It** Two-fifths of people in the United States have blood type A. The proportion given below can be used to find how many out of 40 people in the United States have blood type A. Explain how to solve the proportion.

$$\frac{2}{5} = \frac{n}{40}$$

★ MEASUREMENT

5. Based on the scale provided, which is the **best** estimate of the **shortest** distance between Tara's home and her school?

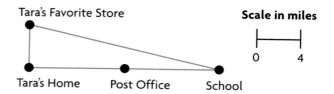

   F 4 miles

   G 8 miles

   H 12 miles

   J 16 miles

6. How much space is needed to store 60 boxes, if each box measures 30 inches × 20 inches × 13 inches?

   A 3,780 cubic inches

   B 7,800 cubic inches

   C 36,000 cubic inches

   D 468,000 cubic inches

7. The game board in backgammon has 24 "points." Each point is a triangle with dimensions 5 inches × 5 inches × 1 inch. What type of triangle is a "point"?

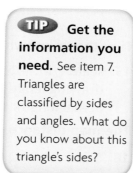

TIP **Get the information you need.** See item 7. Triangles are classified by sides and angles. What do you know about this triangle's sides?

   F right   **H** isosceles

   G scalene   **J** equilateral

8. **Explain It** Jed knows the perimeter and the length of a rectangular doorway. Explain how he can find the width.

9. The graph below displays the number of participants for each of the fall activities at the Recreation Center. The chess club wants to have the most participants. How many more participants does the chess club need in order to achieve this goal?

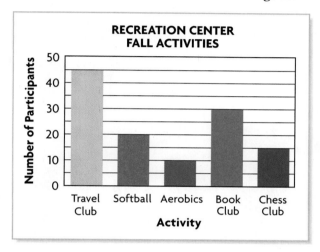

A 6

B 15

C 30

D 31

10. Look at the graph above. How does the number of participants in aerobics compare to the number of participants in the book club?

F $\frac{1}{2}$ as many participate in aerobics.

G $\frac{1}{3}$ as many participate in aerobics.

H Twice as many participate in aerobics.

J Three times as many participate in aerobics.

11. Explain It Joyce wants to make a graph to show changes in movie-ticket prices over the past 4 years. Which type of graph would be best? Explain your choice.

12. The dimensions of a photograph are shown at the right. Which of the photographs below is similar to the photograph above?

2.5 inches

1.5 inches

A 7.5 inches

4.5 inches

B 1.5 inches

0.5 inches

C 5.5 inches

3 inches

D 10 inches

3 inches

13. Which type of angle is ∠1?

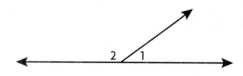

F acute

G obtuse

H right

J straight

14. Explain It Explain how you could find the coordinates of point *D* to form rectangle *ABCD*. Name the coordinates.

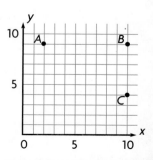

FAST FACT • SOCIAL STUDIES

In 2002, Alaska, Delaware, Montana, New Hampshire, and Oregon had no state sales tax. All other states had sales taxes varying from 2.9% to 7%.

PROBLEM SOLVING Suppose you have $65.00 and you want to buy a dictionary for $18.75, a map for $6.00, a magazine for $4.50, and a book on tape for $34.00. Based on the graph, if you are in Michigan, would you have enough money after adding sales tax? Why or why not?

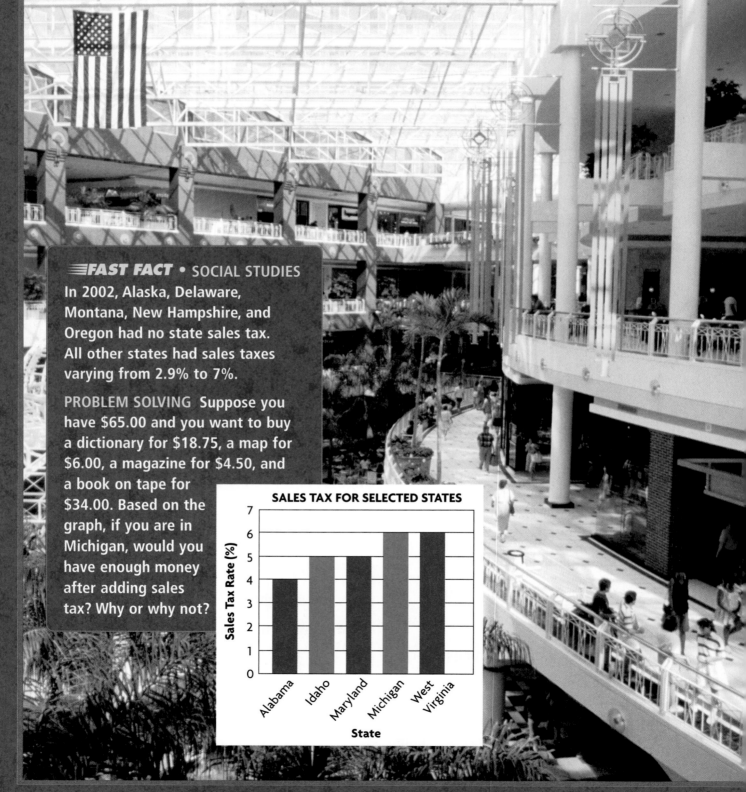

SALES TAX FOR SELECTED STATES

Sales Tax Rate (%)

State: Alabama, Idaho, Maryland, Michigan, West Virginia

Check What You Know

Use this page to help you review and remember important skills needed for Chapter 25.

 ## Write Fractions as Decimals

Write each fraction as a decimal.

1. $\frac{1}{4}$ 2. $\frac{3}{5}$ 3. $\frac{1}{10}$ 4. $\frac{7}{20}$ 5. $\frac{4}{5}$

6. $\frac{9}{10}$ 7. $\frac{1}{5}$ 8. $\frac{13}{25}$ 9. $\frac{81}{100}$ 10. $\frac{31}{50}$

 ## Multiply with Decimals and Fractions

Find the product.

11. $\begin{array}{r} 3.6 \\ \times 4.8 \\ \hline \end{array}$ 12. $\begin{array}{r} 9.2 \\ \times 4.9 \\ \hline \end{array}$ 13. $\begin{array}{r} 6.5 \\ \times 4.1 \\ \hline \end{array}$ 14. $\begin{array}{r} 2.7 \\ \times 4.3 \\ \hline \end{array}$

15. $\begin{array}{r} 72 \\ \times 0.4 \\ \hline \end{array}$ 16. $\begin{array}{r} 22.4 \\ \times 0.16 \\ \hline \end{array}$ 17. $\begin{array}{r} 19 \\ \times 1.8 \\ \hline \end{array}$ 18. $\begin{array}{r} 0.043 \\ \times\ 240 \\ \hline \end{array}$

Find the product. Write the answer in simplest form.

19. $\frac{1}{2} \times \frac{1}{3}$ 20. $\frac{3}{8} \times \frac{3}{5}$ 21. $\frac{2}{3} \times \frac{1}{7}$ 22. $\frac{4}{5} \times \frac{1}{6}$

23. $\frac{3}{4} \times \frac{4}{5}$ 24. $\frac{4}{9} \times \frac{3}{8}$ 25. $\frac{6}{7} \times \frac{8}{9}$ 26. $\frac{5}{12} \times \frac{3}{10}$

 ## Percents and Decimals

Write the corresponding decimal or percent.

27. 45% 28. 0.8 29. 0.14 30. 73%

31. 40% 32. 0.39 33. 53% 34. 3%

VOCABULARY POWER

REVIEW

percent [pər•sent′] *noun*

Percent often refers to a part of a larger amount. What other mathematical words refer to part of a larger amount?

 www.harcourtschool.com/mathglossary

PREVIEW

discount

sales tax

principal

simple interest

Percent

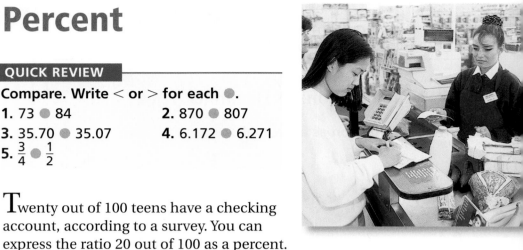

Learn how to write, compare, and order percents.

Twenty out of 100 teens have a checking account, according to a survey. You can express the ratio 20 out of 100 as a percent.

Math Idea ▶ A percent is the ratio of a number to 100. Percent, %, means "per hundred."

So, 20% of teens have a checking account.

EXAMPLE 1

What percent of the squares are shaded?

$\frac{\text{shaded} \to}{\text{total} \to} \frac{46}{100}$ *Write the ratio of shaded squares to total squares.*

$\frac{46}{100} = 46\%$ *Write the ratio as a percent.*

So, 46% of the squares are shaded.

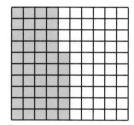

You can compare percents just as you compare other numbers.

EXAMPLE 2

The average weekly allowance for 9–11-year-olds in a recent survey was $5. Gina gets 85% of the average. Ricky gets 60% of the average. Compare the percents.

85 > 60, so 85% > 60%.

Allowance Amounts, 9–11-year-olds

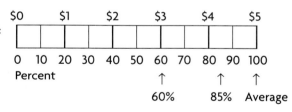

You can order percents just as you do other numbers.

EXAMPLE 3

Ben scored 75%, 83%, 82% and 86% on four tests. Order Ben's percentages from least to greatest. Compare every possible pair of percentages.

75% < 83%   75% < 82%   75% < 86%
83% > 82%   83% < 86%   82% < 86%

So, Ben's percentages in order from least to greatest are 75%, 82%, 83%, 86%.

CHECK FOR UNDERSTANDING

Think and Discuss ▶ **Look back at the lesson to answer the question.**

1. **Draw** a model to show 63 out of 100. Then write the ratio as a percent.

Guided Practice ▶ **Write the percent that is shaded.**

2. 

3. 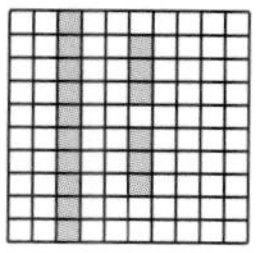

4. 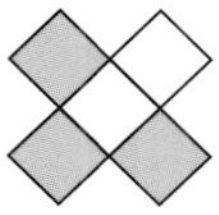

Compare. Write <, >, or = for each ●.

5. 30% ● 25% **6.** 99% ● 100% **7.** 54% ● 54.0%

Order from least to greatest.

8. 37%, 33%, 35%, 27% **9.** 46%, 24%, 44%, 40%

PRACTICE AND PROBLEM SOLVING

Independent Practice ▶ **Write the percent that is shaded.**

10. 

11. 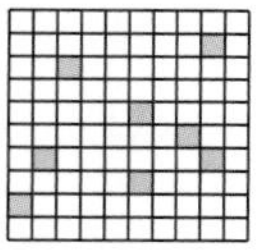

12. 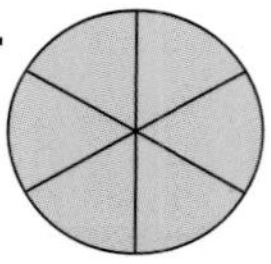

Compare. Write <, >, or = for each ●.

13. 6% ● 12% **14.** 50.0% ● 50% **15.** 0.4% ● 0.04%

Order from greatest to least.

16. 23%, 28%, 38%, 32% **17.** 65%, 96%, 56%, 69%

Problem Solving Applications ▶

18. Out of 100 students in the cafeteria, 38 wanted chicken and 29 wanted roast beef. What percent did not want either one?

19. The Geckos won 4 out of their 8 games in April, 7 out of 9 in May, and 5 out of 8 in June. What percent of all their games did they win?

20. **Write a problem** that involves money and can be solved using percents.

MIXED REVIEW AND TEST PREP

21. If a map scale is 1 in. = 60 mi, what map distance represents 150 mi? (p. 548)

22. Write an expression for the phrase "21 decreased by y." (p. 258)

23. $1.5 + 0.51 + 11 + 0.005$ (p. 76)

24. $\frac{9}{16} - \frac{3}{8}$ (p. 206)

25. TEST PREP What is the solution of the equation $8 = 2 + n$? (p. 277)

A $n = \frac{1}{4}$ **B** $n = 4$ **C** $n = 6$ **D** $n = 16$

EXTRA PRACTICE page 574, Set A

Percents, Decimals, and Fractions

Learn how to convert among percents, decimals, and fractions.

Every day, data appear in newspapers, on television, and on the Internet. Some data are given in decimal form, some in fraction form, and some in percent form. To fully understand the data you see in your everyday life, you should be able to change from one number form to the others.

Below are two ways to write a decimal as a percent.

One Way   Use place value.

EXAMPLE 1

About 0.8 of young people between the ages of 12 and 17 use the Internet to e-mail friends. Write 0.8 as a percent.

$0.8 = \frac{8}{10}$ *Use place value to express the decimal as a ratio in fraction form.*

$= \frac{8 \times 10}{10 \times 10} = \frac{80}{100}$ *Write an equivalent fraction with a denominator of 100.*

$= 80\%$ *Since percent is the ratio of a number to 100, write the ratio as a percent.*

• Write 0.6 as a percent.

Another Way   Multiply by 100.

EXAMPLE 2

Write the decimal as a percent.

A. 0.2
   $0.2 = 0.20 = 20\%$ *Multiply by 100 by moving the decimal point two places to the right.*

B. 0.87
   $0.87 = 0.87 = 87\%$ *Multiply by 100 by moving the decimal point two places to the right.*

• Write 0.3 and 0.94 as percents.

Remember that when multiplying decimal numbers by powers of 10, you move the decimal point one place to the right for each factor of 10.

Write Fractions as Percents

Below are two ways to write a fraction as a percent.

One Way Write an equivalent fraction with a denominator of 100.

EXAMPLE 3

In 2001, about $\frac{2}{5}$ of the people surveyed said they use the Internet to download games. What percent of the people surveyed use the Internet to download games?

$$\frac{2}{5} = \frac{2 \times 20}{5 \times 20} = \frac{40}{100}$$ *Write an equivalent fraction with a denominator of 100.*

$$= 40\%$$ *Since percent is the ratio of a number to 100, write the ratio as a percent.*

So, about 40% of the people surveyed download games.

Another Way Use division to write the fraction as a decimal.

$$\frac{2}{5} \rightarrow 5\overline{)2.00} \quad 0.40$$ *Divide the numerator by the denominator.*

$$0.40 = 40\%$$ *Multiply by 100 by moving the decimal point two places to the right.*

You can also write a percent as a fraction.

EXAMPLE 4

> **R**emember that *percent* means "per hundred."

In 2000, about 42% of all homes in the United States had Internet access. Write 42% as a fraction.

$$42\% = \frac{42}{100}$$ *Write the percent as a fraction with a denominator of 100.*

$$\frac{42}{100} = \frac{42 \div 2}{100 \div 2} = \frac{21}{50}$$ *Write the fraction in simplest form.*

So, 42% written as a fraction is $\frac{21}{50}$.

You can write a percent as an equivalent decimal.

EXAMPLE 5

Over a period of two years, the number of websites on the Internet increased 218%. Write 218% as a decimal.

$$218\% = \frac{218}{100}$$ *Write the percent as a fraction with a denominator of 100.*

$$= 2.18$$ *Write the fraction as a decimal.*

So, 218% written as a decimal is 2.18.

The key sequence below shows how to change a percent to a decimal or a fraction by using a calculator.

70 ÷ 100 = = 0.7 F↔D $\frac{7}{10}$

Sometimes it takes several steps to rewrite in a different form a percent that is less than 1.

EXAMPLE 6

In 2000, about 0.8% of the people in China were Internet users. Write 0.8% as a fraction and as a decimal.

To write 0.8% as a fraction, recall that *percent* means "per hundred."

$$0.8\% = \frac{0.8}{100}$$ *Write the percent as a fraction with a denominator of 100.*

$$\frac{0.8}{100} \times \frac{10}{10} = \frac{8}{1,000}$$ *Multiply numerator and denominator by 10 to remove the decimal from the fraction.*

$$= \frac{8 \div 8}{1,000 \div 8}$$ *Simplify.*

$$= \frac{1}{125}$$

So, about $\frac{1}{125}$ of the people in China used the Internet.

To write 0.8% as a decimal, divide by 100.

$$0.8\% = 00.8\%$$ *Divide by 100 by moving the decimal point two places to the left.*

$$= 0.008$$

So, about 0.008 of the people in China used the Internet.

CHECK FOR UNDERSTANDING

Think and Discuss ▶

Look back at the lesson to answer the question.

1. **Explain** how to write a percent as a decimal and a decimal as a percent.

Guided Practice ▶

Write as a percent.

2. 0.8   **3.** 0.25   **4.** 1.2   **5.** $\frac{3}{5}$ **6.** $1\frac{1}{2}$

Write each percent as a fraction or mixed number in simplest form.

7. 50%   **8.** 40%   **9.** 75%   **10.** 15%   **11.** 180%

Write each percent as a decimal.

12. 33%   **13.** 8%   **14.** 19%   **15.** 0.2%   **16.** 240%

PRACTICE AND PROBLEM SOLVING

Independent Practice ▶

Write as a percent.

17. 0.15   **18.** 0.9   **19.** 0.09   **20.** 0.483   **21.** 0.007

22. 1   **23.** 2.5   **24.** $\frac{1}{5}$ **25.** $\frac{1}{8}$ **26.** $\frac{1}{400}$

Write each percent as a fraction or mixed number in simplest form.

27. 88% **28.** 73% **29.** 4% **30.** 700% **31.** $33\frac{1}{3}$%

Write each percent as a decimal.

32. 58% **33.** 7% **34.** 2.5% **35.** 220% **36.** 0.03%

Compare. Write <, >, or = for each ●.

37. 3 ● 3% **38.** $\frac{1}{2}$ ● 50% **39.** 7% ● 0.7 **40.** 12% ● 1.2

Problem Solving ▶ Applications

41. John says that 20% and 20 are equal. Jim says they are not equal. Who is correct and why?

42. Carlo has $10 more than Erin, and Erin has $5 more than Minh. Altogether they have $50. What percent of the money does Erin have?

43. **What's the Question?** If the answer is "32% of the instruments," what is the question? Use the table.

Central Avenue School Band	
Instruments	**Number**
Brass	28
Woodwinds	16
Percussion	6

MIXED REVIEW AND TEST PREP

44. If 4 of 25 students are absent, what percent are absent? (p. 556)

45. Joe read 78 pages in 3 hours. What was his unit rate? (p. 532)

46. Estimate the quotient: 47.96 ÷ 6.03. (p. 66)

47. TEST PREP Which is the prime factorization of 45? (p. 168)

　A $3 \times 3 \times 5$　　**B** 9×5　　**C** 45×1　　**D** 3×5

48. TEST PREP Kendra counted cars passing her school each hour. She made this stem-and-leaf plot. What is the median number? (p. 140)

　F 55　　　**G** 45　　　**H** 44　　　**J** 18

Number of Cars

Stem	Leaves
3	3 8
4	0 1 7
5	1 5 5

PROBLEM SOLVING　　💡 Thinker's Corner

Math Match Play this game with a partner. Write each percent shown at the right on an index card, and put the cards down as shown. Then write each fraction and decimal shown below on an index card.

$\frac{1}{20}$	$\frac{1}{2}$	$\frac{3}{5}$	$\frac{4}{100}$	$\frac{25}{100}$	$\frac{8}{50}$	$\frac{10}{200}$	$\frac{5}{10}$	$\frac{6}{10}$	0.040

0.05	0.50	0.60	0.04	0.25	0.16	0.050	0.5	0.6	0.250

$\frac{1}{25}$	$\frac{1}{4}$	$\frac{4}{25}$	$\frac{5}{100}$	$\frac{5}{10}$	$\frac{60}{100}$	$\frac{2}{50}$	$\frac{4}{16}$	$\frac{12}{75}$	0.160

50%	
60%	
5%	
4%	
25%	
16%	

Shuffle the fraction and decimal cards. Place them in two equal stacks. Each player draws a card. The first player to place his or her card on the correct equivalent percent card earns 1 point. Continue until all cards have been used. The player with more points is the winner.

EXTRA PRACTICE page 574, Set B

Estimate and Find Percent of a Number

Learn how to estimate and find a percent of a number.

Remember that to change a percent to a ratio in fraction form, write the percent over 100. Then simplify.

$$36\% = \frac{36}{100}$$
$$= \frac{9}{25}$$

QUICK REVIEW

Write each percent as a fraction.

1. 50%   2. 25%   3. 10%
4. $33\frac{1}{3}\%$ 5. 20%

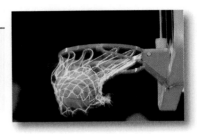

In 2002, basketball star Tracy McGrady made about 75% of his free throws. At that rate, how many of 20 free throws would he make?

To find the answer, you need to find 75% of 20.

Activity

You need: two-color counters or colored paper squares

- To find 75% of 20, use 20 yellow counters.

- 75% equals $\frac{3}{4}$, so separate the counters into four groups. Change the color of three groups to red.

- Count the number of red counters. How many free throws would Tracy McGrady make?

- Use two-color counters to find 50% of 16.

One way to find a percent of a number is to change the percent to a fraction and multiply.

EXAMPLE 1

Due to an injury, Josh played in only 60% of his team's 25 hockey games. In how many games did he play?

Find 60% of 25.

$60\% = \frac{60}{100}$ *Write the percent as a ratio in fraction form.*

$= \frac{3}{5}$ *Write the ratio in simplest form.*

$\frac{3}{5} \times \frac{25}{1} = \frac{75}{5} = 15$ *Multiply the ratio by the number.*

So, Josh played in 15 games.

Sometimes it is easier to change a percent to a decimal.

EXAMPLE 2

In one year, Randall Cunningham threw 425 passes, and 8% of them resulted in touchdowns. How many touchdown passes did he throw?

Find 8% of 425.

8% = 0.08   *Change the percent to a decimal.*

0.08 × 425 = 34   *Multiply the number by the decimal.*

So, Randall Cunningham threw 34 touchdown passes.

It is customary to leave a tip when you eat in a restaurant.

EXAMPLE 3

Katie's lunch bill came to $13.79. She wants to leave a 15% tip. How much should she leave?

You can estimate the amount of the tip.

Estimate. $13.79 is about $14.
THINK: 15% = 10% + 5%

      10% of $14 is $1.40.
      5% of $14 is half of $1.40, or $0.70.

So, 15% of $13.79 is about $1.40 + $0.70, or $2.10.

To find the amount of the tip to the nearest cent, use a proportion.

Let t = amount of tip.   **THINK:** $15\% = \frac{15}{100}$

So, the tip (t) is to the total bill ($13.79) as 15 is to 100.

$$\frac{t}{13.79} = \frac{15}{100}$$
$$100 \times t = 15 \times 13.79$$
$$100t = 206.85$$
$$t = 206.85 \div 100 = 2.0685$$

To the nearest cent, a 15% tip would be $2.07.

You can use a calculator to find a percent of a number.

EXAMPLE 4

Use a calculator to find 15% of 13.79.

Use the key sequence below.

13.79 ✕ 15 **SHIFT** **%**   `2.0685`

So, 2.0685 is 15% of 13.79.

You can use mental math to estimate the percent of a number.

EXAMPLE 5

Estimate 15% of 81.

THINK: 81 is about 80.

15% = 10% + 5%

10% of 80 = 8.
5% of 80 is half of 10% of 80, or half of 8, or 4.

So, 15% of 81 is about 8 + 4, or 12.

- In Example 2, 8% of 425 is given as 34. Use estimation to determine if 34 is reasonable.

CHECK FOR UNDERSTANDING

Think and ▶ Discuss

Look back at the lesson to answer each question.

1. **Explain** how you can easily find 50% of a number if you know 25% of the number.

2. **Explain** how you can tell whether a percent of a number should be less than or greater than the number.

Guided ▶ Practice

Use a fraction in simplest form to find the percent of the number.

3. 20% of 30   4. 50% of 80   5. 75% of 48   6. 15% of 20

Use a decimal to find the percent of the number.

7. 52% of 15   8. 40% of 90   9. 28% of 75   10. 76% of 25

PRACTICE AND PROBLEM SOLVING

Independent ▶ Practice

Use a fraction in simplest form to find the percent of the number.

11. 25% of 80   12. 45% of 10   13. 80% of 55   14. 90% of 120

Use a decimal to find the percent of the number.

15. 12% of 9   16. 28% of 20   17. 71% of 84   18. 95% of 18

Use the method of your choice to find the percent of the number.

19. 21% of 88   20. 35% of 92   21. 40% of 106   22. 2% of 12

23. 51% of 30   24. 99% of 99   25. 82% of 150   26. 63% of 85

27. 5.5% of 70   28. 200% of 100   29. 150% of 38   30. 0.5% of 400

Estimate a 15% tip for each amount.

31. $8.00   32. $12.25   33. $15.75   34. $18.09   35. $32.18

Find a 20% tip to the nearest cent.

36. $12.00   **37.** $25.00   **38.** $18.14   **39.** $3.95   **40.** $46.12

 **ALGEBRA**   Each proportion shows *n* as a percent of a number. What is the percent? What is *n*?

41. $\frac{25}{100} = \frac{n}{60}$ **42.** $\frac{40}{100} = \frac{n}{280}$ **43.** $\frac{n}{6} = \frac{10}{100}$ **44.** $\frac{n}{240} = \frac{75}{100}$

Problem Solving ▶
Applications

Mille Lacs Lake

45. **FAST FACT** • GEOGRAPHY   The surface area of Earth is about 200,000,000 mi². If 70% of the surface is water, about how many square miles of Earth's surface are water?

46. The largest lakes in Minnesota are Red Lake and Mille Lacs Lake. Red Lake is about 218% as large as Mille Lacs Lake. If Mille Lacs Lake covers 207 square miles, how much area do the two lakes cover together?

47. Arnold wants to leave a 15% tip on a bill of $32. He has $35. Does he have enough money for the tip? Explain.

48. *REASONING*   Find 28% of 75 and 75% of 28. Explain why the answers are the same. Make up another problem where it is easier to find the changed problem than the given one.

MIXED REVIEW AND TEST PREP

49. Write 0.001 as a percent. (p. 558)

50. $3\frac{2}{5} - 1\frac{7}{10}$ (p. 210)

51. Do the figures appear to be *similar*, *congruent*, or *neither*? (p. 384)

52. **TEST PREP**   An obtuse triangle contains an angle __?__ 90°. (p. 356)

A greater than   **B** less than   **C** equal to   **D** less than or equal to

53. **TEST PREP**   Two perpendicular lines form an angle which is __?__. (p. 344)

F straight   **G** right   **H** obtuse   **J** acute

PROBLEM SOLVING 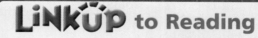 to Reading

Strategy • Sequence   Sometimes the events in a problem are given in an order which is different from the order in which they occurred. To solve the problem, you must first *sequence* the events in the correct order.

The Brainiac computer was introduced in 1981. Today, a Brainiac sells for 40% of its original price. The price increased an average of $200 per year during the first 6 years. The price topped out at $3,600 in 1987 and has dropped steadily ever since. How much does a Brainiac sell for today?

• Use the words *increased* and *decreased* to sequence the changes in the price of a Brainiac from 1981 till today.

EXTRA PRACTICE page 574, Set C

565

Construct Circle Graphs

Explore how to construct circle graphs.

You need compass, protractor, straightedge.

Write each fraction as a percent.

1. $\frac{1}{2}$ 2. $\frac{1}{4}$ 3. $\frac{1}{10}$ 4. $\frac{1}{5}$ 5. $\frac{27}{100}$

A circle graph shows parts of a whole. If you think of a complete circle as 100%, you can express portions of a circle graph as percents.

- Ms. Shipley's class earned $400 at the school fair. What fraction of the $400 did the class earn at the bake sale?

- What percent of the $400 did the class earn at the bake sale?

MONEY RAISED AT SCHOOL FAIR

Activity

People in the United States spend over $1.1 billion per year on pasta. The table gives the approximate total weights of the three most popular shapes sold.

- Use a compass to draw a circle on a piece of paper. Mark the center.

- Find the combined weight of the three shapes of pasta.

- Find the percent of the total weight represented by each shape.

  spaghetti: $\frac{310}{\text{total weight}} = \blacksquare\%$

  elbows: $\frac{115}{\text{total weight}} = \blacksquare\%$

  noodles: $\frac{75}{\text{total weight}} = \blacksquare\%$

- Since there are 360° in a circle, multiply each of the percents by 360° to find the degrees in each sector of the circle graph. Round your answers to the nearest degree.

- Use a protractor to draw each angle of 180° or less. If there is an angle greater than 180°, it is what remains.

- Label the sectors and write a title.

ANNUAL PASTA SALES

Shape	Pounds Sold (millions)
Spaghetti	310
Elbows	115
Noodles	75

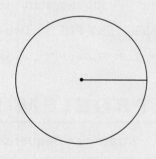

TOP-SELLING PASTA (in millions of lb)

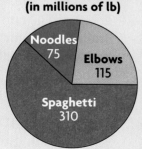

Think and Discuss

- In the circle graph you drew, what does the whole circle represent?

- Suppose the combined weight of the three shapes of pasta was 930 million pounds but the weight of the spaghetti remained the same. Find the number of degrees in the sector representing spaghetti.

Practice

Use Data **Make a circle graph of the data.**

1. The table shows how Shari budgets her earnings from her job.

MONTHLY BUDGET	
Item	**Percent**
Rent	30%
Food	25%
Clothes	12.5%
Other	32.5%

2. The table shows the number of videos rented in one week.

VIDEOS RENTED			
Drama	**Comedy**	**Kids**	**Classics**
250	250	300	200

3. The table records the results of a survey.

FAVORITE SPORTS SURVEY				
Tennis	**Soccer**	**Baseball**	**Golf**	**Other**
50	20	30	80	20

4. Collect data from your classmates about their favorite color. Use the data to make a circle graph with no more than five categories. Compare your graph with those of your classmates.

MIXED REVIEW AND TEST PREP

5. Find 20% of 30. (p. 562)

6. Evaluate $(6 - 2m)^2$ for $m = 2$. (p. 260)

7. A rectangle is 16 in. long and 12 in. wide. A similar rectangle is 4 in. long. Find the perimeter of the similar rectangle. (p. 542)

8. Is this survey question biased? "Do you agree that our excellent mayor should be re-elected?" Explain. (p. 112)

9. TEST PREP Which shows the value of y for the equation $3y = 15$? (p. 291)

A $y = 3$ **B** $y = 4$ **C** $y = 5$ **D** $y = 6$

Discount and Sales Tax

Learn how to solve problems involving discounts and sales tax.

Vocabulary

discount

sales tax

Anthony wants to buy a backpack for summer camp. He saw the newspaper ad shown below. How much will the pack cost with a 30% discount?

Backpack Sale!
Regular Price $129
NOW 30% OFF!!

Math **I**dea ▶ To find the sale price, you can first find the discount. A **discount** is an amount that is subtracted from the regular price of an item.

discount = regular price × discount rate
= $129 × 30%
= $129 × 0.30   *Write the percent as a decimal.*
= $38.70

So, the amount of the discount is $38.70.

To find the sale price of the backpack, subtract the discount from the regular price.

Regular Price
Discount
Sale Price

sale price = regular price − discount
= $129.00 − $38.70
= $90.30

So, the sale price of the backpack is $90.30.

• What would the sale price of the backpack be with an additional 10% off?

EXAMPLE 1

A volleyball set that regularly sells for $32 is on sale at a 25% discount. Find the amount of the discount and the sale price of the set.

You can use mental math to find the discount if you change 25% to the fraction $\frac{1}{4}$. **THINK:** $\frac{1}{4}$ of $32 is $8.

You can also find the discount by writing the percent as a decimal.

discount = $32 × 25%
= $32 × 0.25
= $8

sale price = regular price − discount
= $32 − $8
= $24

So, the discount is $8 and the sale price is $24.

In Example 1, you found the sale price when you knew the regular price and the discount rate. Sometimes you may want to find the regular price when you know the sale price and the discount rate.

EXAMPLE 2

Find the regular price of the in-line skates.

All In-line Skates On Sale!!
40% Off!
Now Only $72!!

The regular price has been discounted 40%. That means the sale price must be 60% of the regular price, since 100% − 40% = 60%.

Regular Price
|← 100% →|
60% | 40%
Sale Price | Discount

THINK: sale price = 60% × regular price

Let n = the regular price.

$72 = 60% × n   *Write an equation relating the sale price and the regular price.*

$72 = 0.6 × n   *Write the percent as a decimal.*

$\frac{\$72}{0.6} = \frac{0.6 \times n}{0.6}$ *Divide both sides of the equation by 0.6.*

$120 = n

So, the skates regularly sell for $120.

569

Most states charge a **sales tax** on purchases. A sales tax is calculated as a percent of the cost of an item. To find the amount of the sales tax, multiply the amount of the purchase by the sales tax rate.

EXAMPLE 3

Martina bought a table-tennis table for $119. The sales tax rate was 5%. How much did she pay in sales tax?

Estimate. **THINK:** 10% of $119 is about $12.00, so 5% of $119 is about $6.

$119 × 5% = $119 × 0.05   *Multiply the price by the percent.*
            = $5.95

So, she paid $5.95 in sales tax. This is close to the estimate of $6, so the answer is reasonable.

You can find the total cost of a purchase that includes sales tax.

EXAMPLE 4

The Carduso family purchased a pool table for $825. The sales tax rate was 7%. What was the total cost of the purchase?

One Way Add the sales tax to the price.

$825 × 7% = $825 × 0.07
           = $57.75

$825 + $57.75 = $882.75

Another Way Multiply the price by 107% since 7% is added to the cost.

$825 × 107% = $825 × 1.07
            = $882.75

So, the total cost of the purchase was $882.75.

CHECK FOR UNDERSTANDING

Think and Discuss

Look back at the lesson to answer each question.

1. **Explain** how you can estimate the 25% discount on a $96.50 coat.

2. **Explain** how to find the regular price of an item that has been discounted 50%, if you know the discount price.

Guided Practice

Find the sale price.

3. regular price: $80

4. regular price: $55

5. regular price: $96

6. regular price: $110

 Find the regular price.

7. sale price: $80
   discount rate: 20%

8. sale price: $150
   discount rate: 40%

Independent ▶
Practice

Find the sale price.

9. regular
price:
$47.90

DISCOUNT
30%

10. regular
price:
$120.00

SAVE
40%

11. regular
price:
$51.80

SALE
10% OFF

12. regular
price:
$88.50

20% OFF

 ALGEBRA **Find the regular price.**

13. sale price: $28.56
discount rate: 25%

14. sale price: $595.63
discount rate: 30%

Find the sales tax for the given price. Round to the nearest cent.

15. $512.00
tax: 6%

16. $24.95
tax: 7.5%

17. $84.50
tax: 5.5%

18. $260.00
tax: 6.75%

Find the total cost of the purchase. Round to the nearest cent.

19. price:
$44.00
tax: 5%

20. price:
$125.00
tax: 7%

21. price:
$56.95
tax: 8%

22. price:
$899.99
tax: 8.75%

Problem Solving ▶
Applications

Use Data   For 23–24, use the graph.

23. In February, apples cost 12% less per
pound than they cost in January.
Estimate the cost per pound in
February.

24. Maureen bought 15 lb of apples in
January and paid 4% sales tax.
What was the cost of her purchase?

25. *REASONING*   A refrigerator that
regularly sold for $800 was discounted
25%. After the sale, the sale price was raised 25%. Was the new
price less than, greater than, or equal to $800? Explain.

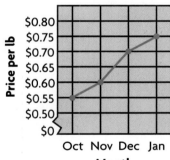

PRICE OF APPLES

MIXED REVIEW AND TEST PREP

26. Find 80% of 12.5. (p. 562)

27. Solve for b: $2 = b - 15$. (p. 280)

28. On a scale of 2 in.:3 ft, what is the actual length of a room that is
12 in. long in a scale drawing? (p. 545)

⭐**29. TEST PREP**   Which is $\frac{37}{8}$ written as a mixed number? (p. 186)

A $3\frac{5}{8}$ **B** $4\frac{3}{8}$ **C** $4\frac{5}{8}$ **D** $8\frac{29}{37}$

⭐**30. TEST PREP**   The part of a circle shown in red is a ___?___ . (p. 368)

F chord   **G** radius   **H** diameter   **J** circumference

Simple Interest

Learn how to find simple interest.

Vocabulary

principal

simple interest

When money is in a savings account, the bank regularly adds money to the account. The original amount you put in the account is called the **principal**. The amount the bank adds is called interest.

Simple interest is a fixed percent of the principal and is paid yearly. Use the formula $I = prt$ to calculate simple interest, where I = interest earned, p = principal, r = interest rate per year, and t = time in years.

> **EXAMPLE 1**

Katrina put $500 in a savings account at a simple interest rate of 6% per year for 2 years. How much interest will she earn?

$I = prt$	$p = \$500$, $r = 6\%$, $t = 2$ years
$I = \$500 \times 0.06 \times 2$	*Multiply.*
$I = \$60$	

So, she will earn $60 in interest.

Activity

You need: 12 index cards, as shown

Shuffle and stack the principal cards and turn them face down. Do the same with the interest-rate and time cards.

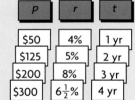

P	r	t
$50	4%	1 yr
$125	5%	2 yr
$200	8%	3 yr
$300	$6\frac{1}{2}\%$	4 yr

- Each player draws one card from each pile and computes the interest earned. The player with the most interest earns points equal to the total interest of all the players.

- Play for five rounds. What is the most interest a player could earn in one round? What is the least?

> **EXAMPLE 2**

Bill borrows $500. He will repay it in 2 years at a simple interest rate of 8%. How much will he have to repay at the end of 2 years?

$I = prt$	*Find the amount of interest.*
$I = \$500 \times 0.08 \times 2 = \$80$	
$\$80 + \$500 = \$580$	*Add the interest to the loan.*

So, Bill will have to repay $580.

Think and ▶
Discuss
Look back at the lesson to answer each question.

1. **Explain** what $I = prt$ means.

2. **Explain** how to find the simple interest earned on $500 for 6 months at an annual interest rate of 5%. Then find the simple interest.

Guided ▶
Practice
Find the simple interest.

3. principal: $100
   rate: 4%
   time: 1 year

4. principal: $750
   rate: 8%
   time: 4 years

5. principal: $2,400
   rate: 12%
   time: 6 years

PRACTICE AND PROBLEM SOLVING

Independent ▶
Practice
Find the simple interest.

6. principal: $12,000
   rate: 8%
   time: 2 years

7. principal: $640
   rate: 6.5%
   time: 5 years

8. principal: $21,000
   rate: 5.25%
   time: 18 years

Find the simple interest.

	Principal	Rate	1 Year	5 Years
9.	$70	2%	▪	▪
10.	$250	3.5%	▪	▪
11.	$1,200	6.9%	▪	▪

Problem Solving ▶
Applications

12. **Vocabulary Power** Find *rate* in the Glossary. Then name two other words in the Glossary that are related to rate. Explain how they are related to rate.

13. Amber put $2,000 in an account at a simple interest rate of 6%. Haines put $2,400 in an account at a simple interest rate of 4%. How many years would Amber and Haines have to invest their money until their principal is doubled?

14. **REASONING** Jake earned $54 in simple interest on a principal of $900 invested for 1 year. What was the interest rate?

15. **?** **What's the Error?** Jeff found simple interest of $360 for a principal of $200, interest rate of 6%, and a time of 3 years. Find his error and the correct amount of simple interest.

MIXED REVIEW AND TEST PREP

16. What is the sale price on a $150 item discounted 20%? (p. 568)

17. Two towns are 125 mi apart. How far apart do they appear on a map with a scale of 2 in. = 50 mi? (p. 548)

18. Solve $4x = 96$. (p. 291)

19. Evaluate $12 + 24 \div 12 - 4$. (p. 48)

20. **TEST PREP** Which is the best estimate of the quotient $618.6 \div 5.914$? (p. 88)

   A 1   **B** 10   **C** 100   **D** 1,000

Set A (pp. 556–557)

Write the percent that is shaded.

1.

2.

3.

4.

Set B (pp. 558–561)

Write as a percent.

1. 0.3   **2.** 0.09   **3.** 0.43   **4.** $\frac{7}{20}$ **5.** $\frac{3}{8}$

Set C (pp. 562–565)

Find the percent.

1. 20% of 8   **2.** 30% of 90   **3.** 45% of 75   **4.** 50% of 58

5. Of all the cookies Wendy baked, 40% were chocolate chip. If she baked 200 cookies, how many were chocolate chip?

Set D (pp. 568–571)

Find the sale price.

1. regular price: $31.00
25% off

2. regular price: $65.00
50% off

3. regular price: $42.00
75% off

Find the regular price.

4. sale price: $45.00
discount rate: 25%

5. sale price: $24.95
discount rate: 50%

6. sale price: $14.40
discount rate: 20%

Set E (pp. 572–573)

Find the simple interest.

	Principal	Rate	Interest for 1 Year	Interest for 5 Years
1.	$65,000.00	4%	■	■
2.	$735.00	7%	■	■
3.	$1,300.00	3.9%	■	■
4.	$2,250.00	2.3%	■	■

5. Nancy put $2,500 in a savings account for 3 years at a simple interest rate of 8%. How much interest did she earn?

1. **VOCABULARY**   An amount subtracted from the regular price of an item to give the sale price is called the __?__. (pp. 568)

2. **VOCABULARY**   A fixed percent of the principal, paid yearly, is the __?__. (p. 572)

Write the percent that is shaded. (pp. 556–557)

3.

4.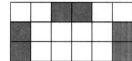

5.

Write as a percent. (pp. 558–561)

6. 0.38   7. $\frac{1}{4}$ 8. 0.09   9. $\frac{2}{5}$

Write each percent as a decimal and as a fraction in simplest form. (pp. 558–561)

10. 20%   11. 18%   12. 75%   13. 10%

Find the percent. (pp. 562–565)

14. 40% of 300   15. 25% of 24   16. 1% of 350   17. 100% of 80

18. 200% of 7   19. 15% of 24   20. 11% of 80   21. 90% of 300

22. Use these data to make a circle graph of the Vernon family's monthly budget of $2,000: clothing and entertainment, 25%; food, 10%; rent, 35%; other, 30%. (pp. 566–567)

23. Find the amount spent on food in the Vernon family's budget.

24. Find the amount spent on rent in the Vernon family's budget.

Find the sale price. (pp. 568–571)

25. regular price: $40

26. regular price: $79

Find the regular price. (pp. 568–571)

27. sale price: $36
    discount rate: 20%

28. sale price: $95
    discount rate: 50%

29. What is the sales tax on an item that costs $33.50 if the sales tax rate is 6%?

30. What is the total cost of an item that costs $98 if the sales tax rate is 8%?

Find the simple interest. (pp. 572–573)

31. principal: $200
    rate: 6%
    time: 1 year

32. principal: $8,000
    rate: 7.5%
    time: 4 years

33. Julia put $1,500 in a savings account. The yearly simple interest rate was 5%. How much did she have in her account after 3 years?

NUMBER SENSE, CONCEPTS, AND OPERATIONS

1. A survey showed that $\frac{1}{20}$ of those attending a concert did not enjoy it. What percent of those attending enjoyed the concert?

   > **TIP** **Understand the problem.** See item 1. You are told the *fraction* of those who did *not* enjoy the concert. You must use that information to find the *percent* of those who *did* enjoy it.

   A 5%

   B 20%

   C 80%

   D 95%

2. The table shows the original price and the discount for the same video game at each of four stores. Which store has the lowest sale price?

VIDEO GAME DISCOUNTS		
Store	**Original Price**	**Discount Percent**
Tom's	$50	15%
Big Sale	$60	20%
Top Buy	$55	25%
Manny's	$58	18%

   F Tom's

   G Big Sale

   H Top Buy

   J Manny's

3. **Explain It** On average, Sue makes 85% of her basketball free throws. Out of 12 free throws, how many would you expect her to make? Explain your reasoning.

 MEASUREMENT

4. What is the measure of angle *x* in the figure below?

   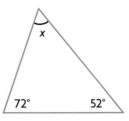

   A 36°   **C** 88°

   B 56°   **D** 124°

5. Four students measured the width of the same maple leaf in the science lab. The results are shown in the table below.

MAPLE LEAF MEASUREMENTS	
Student	**Measurement**
Jason	$2\frac{7}{8}$ inches
Ashley	$2\frac{13}{16}$ inches
Tan	3 inches
Roberto	$2\frac{3}{4}$ inches

   Which student made the **most** precise measurement?

   F Jason

   G Ashley

   H Tan

   J Roberto

6. **Explain It** On a map of his neighborhood, Dominic drew a triangle connecting his house, his school, and West Side Park. He told his mother that the figure he drew was a "right equilateral triangle." Does his description make sense? Explain your reasoning.

7. The stem-and-leaf plot shows the number of points Josh scored in each of his last 15 basketball games.

JOSH'S BASKETBALL SCORING

Stem	Leaves
1	0 2 3 6 6 7 9
2	0 0 0 1
3	1 1 1 2

Based on the data in the plot, which of the following statements about Josh's scoring in his last 15 games is true?

A Josh never scored fewer than 12 points.

B Josh scored more than 15 points in most of his games.

C Josh scored fewer than 16 points in most of his games.

D Josh never scored more than 30 points.

8. The table below shows the range of heights of players on Gina's baseball team.

BASEBALL PLAYERS' HEIGHTS		
Height (in inches)	Frequency	Cumulative Frequency
55–58	12	12
59–62	8	20
63–66	2	22

Gina is 63 inches tall. How many players are shorter than she is?

F 22 **G** 20 **H** 12 **J** 2

9. Explain It Brad had the following scores for five games of golf: 78, 80, 69, 75, 73. He thought the range of his scores was 5. Explain the mistake Brad made. Then explain the correct way to find the range.

10. Rangers in Blue Lake Park use a grid system to locate features in the park. Eagle nests have been found at (3,4) and (4,5). Which grid shows the locations of the nests?

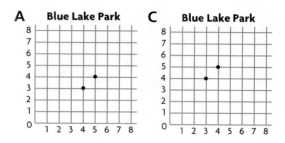

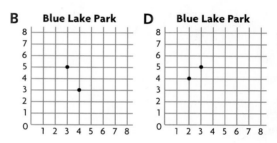

11. A lapel pin is in the shape of a quadrilateral. A line of symmetry is drawn on the pin. Which of the following figures could be the shape of the pin?

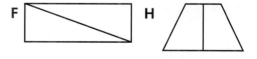

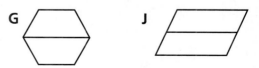

12. Explain It Oak Street is parallel to Birch Road. Creek Lane is perpendicular to Birch Road. How are Oak Street and Creek Lane related? Explain your reasoning.

26 Probability of Simple Events

PAULA'S JAZZ COLLECTI

Musician	Number
Benny Goodman	2
Billie Holiday	3
Ella Fitzgerald	5
Louis Armstrong	6
Miles Davis	4

FAST FACT • MUSIC New Orleans, Louisiana is considered the birthplace of jazz. Each spring, about 500,000 people attend the New Orleans Jazz & Heritage Festival, more commonly known as Jazz Fest. This outdoor festival lasts about 10 days and features the music and food of New Orleans.

PROBLEM SOLVING Paula has a collection of jazz CDs as shown in the table. If she selects one CD at random, what is the probability that it features Louis Armstrong? Miles Davis?

Check What You Know

Use this page to help you review and remember important skills needed for Chapter 26.

✔ Fractions, Decimals, and Percents

Write each fraction as a decimal and a percent.

1. $\frac{2}{5}$ 　　2. $\frac{1}{2}$ 　　3. $\frac{7}{10}$ 　　4. $\frac{3}{4}$ 　　5. $\frac{9}{20}$

6. $\frac{1}{10}$ 　　7. $\frac{1}{4}$ 　　8. $\frac{3}{5}$ 　　9. $\frac{1}{5}$ 　　10. $\frac{18}{25}$

11. $\frac{3}{8}$ 　　12. $\frac{3}{25}$ 　　13. $\frac{5}{8}$ 　　14. $\frac{19}{20}$ 　　15. $\frac{3}{50}$

✔ Simplest Form of Fractions

Write each fraction in simplest form.

16. $\frac{4}{12}$ 　　17. $\frac{9}{6}$ 　　18. $\frac{32}{64}$ 　　19. $\frac{40}{15}$ 　　20. $\frac{36}{54}$

21. $\frac{9}{75}$ 　　22. $\frac{22}{55}$ 　　23. $\frac{96}{60}$ 　　24. $\frac{49}{56}$ 　　25. $\frac{81}{120}$

26. $\frac{25}{75}$ 　　27. $\frac{72}{60}$ 　　28. $\frac{70}{120}$ 　　29. $\frac{155}{200}$ 　　30. $\frac{200}{800}$

✔ Certain, Impossible, Likely, Unlikely

Tell if the event is *certain*, *impossible*, *likely*, or *unlikely*.

31. The month of May having 34 days next year

32. Having homework this week

33. The sun rising today

34. Reading 3 novels in one day

Vocabulary Power

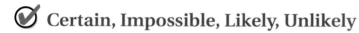

REVIEW

random [ran′dəm] *adjective*

When an item is selected at random from a group of items, each item in the group has an equal chance of being selected. You can use a computer to select items at random. Describe another way to select something at random.

PREVIEW

outcome

sample space

theoretical probability

odds in favor of an event

odds against an event

experimental probability

 www.harcourtschool.com/mathglossary

Theoretical Probability

Learn how to find the theoretical probability of an event.

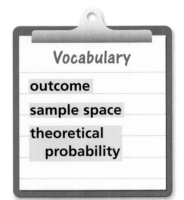

Vocabulary

outcome

sample space

theoretical probability

Each color on the spinner shown represents one equally likely **outcome**, or possible result, of spinning. The **sample space**, or set of all possible outcomes, is white, purple, red, yellow, and green.

Math Idea ▶ The **theoretical probability**, P, of an event is a comparison of the number of favorable outcomes to the number of possible, equally likely outcomes. It can be written as a ratio.

$$P(\text{event}) = \frac{\text{number of favorable outcomes}}{\text{number of possible, equally likely outcomes}}$$

EXAMPLE 1

Students created a game using the spinner above. If the pointer lands on red, you get an extra turn. What is the probability that you get an extra turn?

1 favorable outcome: red   *Count the favorable outcomes.*

5 possible outcomes   *Count the possible outcomes.*

$P(\text{red}) = \dfrac{1 \text{ favorable outcome}}{5 \text{ possible outcomes}} = \dfrac{1}{5}$ *Write the probability as a ratio.*

So, the probability that you get an extra turn in the game is $\frac{1}{5}$.

Probabilities can be expressed as fractions, decimals, and percents.

EXAMPLE 2

Lauren rolled a number cube labeled 1 to 6. Find each probability. Express your answers as fractions, decimals, and percents.

A. $P(2) = \frac{1}{6}$, $0.1\overline{6}$, or $16\frac{2}{3}\%$ *1 choice out of 6*

B. $P(2 \text{ or } 3) = \frac{2}{6}$ *2 choices out of 6*

$\qquad = \frac{1}{3}$, $0.\overline{3}$, or $33\frac{1}{3}\%$

C. $P(\text{greater than } 3) = \frac{3}{6}$ *3 choices out of 6*

$\qquad = \frac{1}{2}$, 0.50, or 50%

The number line below shows that the probability of an event ranges from 0, or impossible, to 1, or certain. The closer a probability is to 1, the more likely the event is to occur.

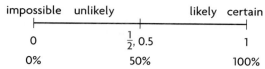

impossible   unlikely   likely   certain

0                    $\frac{1}{2}$, 0.5   1

0%   50%   100%

EXAMPLE 3

Each letter of the word *OUTCOMES* is written on a card and placed in a bag. One card is chosen at random. Which outcome is more likely to occur, an *M* or an *O*?

$P(M) = \frac{1}{8}$ *Find each probability.*

$P(O) = \frac{2}{8} = \frac{1}{4}$

$\frac{1}{4} > \frac{1}{8}$ *Compare the probabilities.*

So, the outcome *O* is more likely to occur than the outcome *M*.

EXAMPLE 4

Use the spinner at the right to find each probability.

A. $P(\text{blue}) = \frac{0}{4}$. None of the sections are blue.

B. $P(\text{green}) = \frac{1}{4}$

C. $P(\text{not green}) = \frac{3}{4}$

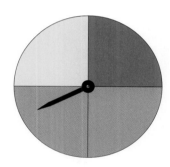

Look at P(green) and P(not green) in Example 4.
The sum of those probabilities is $\frac{1}{4} + \frac{3}{4}$, or 1. If *P* is the probability of an event occurring, $1 - P$ is the probability of an event not occurring.

EXAMPLE 5

Use the spinner above to find each probability. Write each answer as a fraction, a decimal, and a percent.

A. $P(\text{not yellow}) = 1 - P(\text{yellow})$

$$= 1 - \frac{1}{4}$$

$$= \frac{3}{4}$$

So, P(not yellow) is $\frac{3}{4}$, 0.75, or 75%.

B. $P(\text{not orange}) = 1 - P(\text{orange})$

$$= 1 - \frac{1}{2}$$

$$= \frac{1}{2}$$

So, P(not orange) is $\frac{1}{2}$, 0.50, or 50%.

581

Think and ▶ Discuss

Look back at the lesson to answer each question.

1. Write the sample space for the number cube in Example 2.

2. Explain why the probabilities computed in Example 4 are reasonable.

Guided ▶ Practice

Use the spinner at the right to find each probability. Write each answer as a fraction, a decimal, and a percent.

3. P(yellow)

4. P(purple)

5. P(red)

6. P(red or purple)

7. P(not yellow)

8. P(green)

PRACTICE AND PROBLEM SOLVING

Independent ▶ Practice

Use the spinner at the right to find each probability. Write each answer as a fraction, a decimal, and a percent.

9. P(L)

10. P(T)

11. P(B)

12. P(E or R)

13. P(L, F, or T)

14. P(vowel)

A number cube is labeled 1 to 6. Find each probability. Write each answer as a fraction.

15. P(2)

16. P(not 5)

17. P(4 or 6)

18. P(less than 4)

19. P(1, 2, or 3)

20. P(even)

21. P(multiple of 3)

22. P(divisible by 6)

23. P(integer)

Cards numbered 1, 1, 2, 3, 3, 4, 5, and 6 are placed in a box. You choose one card without looking. Compare the probabilities. Write <, >, or = for each ●.

24. P(1) ● P(2)

25. P(1) ● P(5 or 6)

26. P(6) ● P(2)

27. P(1 or 3) ● P(3 or 4)

28. P(even) ● P(odd)

29. P(multiple of 3) ● P(multiple of 2)

Use P(A), the probability of event A, to find P(not A).

30. P(A) = $\frac{1}{2}$

31. P(A) = 0.4

32. P(A) = 80%

33. P(A) = $\frac{7}{12}$

34. P(A) = 0.61

35. P(A) = 23%

Problem Solving ▶
Applications

36. A rental car agency has 55 blue cars, 32 red cars, and 70 white cars. If a customer selects at random, what is the probability that she will select a green car? Write your answer as a percent.

37. Suppose the probability of an event is $\frac{5}{12}$. Which is greater, the probability that the event will occur or the probability that it will not occur?

38. You are given a choice of three answers to a trivia question. If you don't know the answer, what is the probability of guessing the correct answer?

39. **What's the Question?** Stephen has a number cube labeled 1 to 6. The answer is 1.

40. *REASONING* Brenda has a bag with 8 cubes all the same size: 1 red, 4 yellow, and 3 blue. She chooses a blue cube without looking and does not put it back in the bag. What is the probability of choosing a yellow cube after the blue cube has been removed?

41. A box has 24 marbles. If $\frac{3}{8}$ of the marbles are blue, find the number of marbles that are not blue.

MIXED REVIEW AND TEST PREP

42. Li invested $420 at a simple interest rate of $3\frac{1}{2}$%. How much interest will she earn in 5 years? (p. 572)

43. Order $7\frac{3}{8}$, $7\frac{3}{4}$, $7\frac{1}{4}$, and $7\frac{1}{2}$ from least to greatest. (p. 188)

44. Divide. $135.892 \div 6.41$ (p. 88)

45. TEST PREP Evaluate $3p$ for $p = 7.8$.
(p. 94)

   A 2.6   **B** 4.8   **C** 10.8   **D** 23.4

46. TEST PREP How many sides does a decagon have? (p. 354)

   F 6   **G** 8   **H** 10   **J** 12

PROBLEM SOLVING Thinker's Corner

Geometric Probability
You can use the areas of geometric figures to find probabilities.

In a certain game, students throw a quarter onto a target that looks like the square at the right. To find the probability that the quarter lands on the green section, compare the areas. Assume that the center point of the quarter lands on the target at some random point and that all points are equally likely.

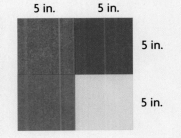

area of green section
$5 \text{ in.} \times 5 \text{ in.} = 25 \text{ in.}^2$

area of target
$10 \text{ in.} \times 10 \text{ in.} = 100 \text{ in.}^2$

$P(\text{green}) = \dfrac{\text{area of green section}}{\text{area of target}} = \dfrac{25}{100} = \dfrac{1}{4}$

• If the center point of a randomly thrown quarter lands on the target at the right, what is the probability of its being in the blue section?

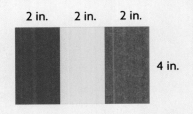

PROBLEM SOLVING SKILL
Too Much or
Too Little Information

Learn how to use the skill of determining whether there is *too much or too little information* to solve problems.

QUICK REVIEW

Write each fraction in simplest form.
1. $\frac{8}{12}$ 2. $\frac{6}{9}$ 3. $\frac{15}{20}$ 4. $\frac{12}{21}$ 5. $\frac{35}{100}$

Karyn is waiting in line with 14 other people to ride the bumper cars at a carnival. Each person in line is randomly assigned to one of 15 bumper cars. There are 3 blue, 5 red, 4 yellow, and 3 green bumper cars. What is the probability that Karyn is assigned to a red bumper car?

If a problem has too much information, you must decide what to use to solve the problem.

1. **Want to know:** P(red bumper car)

2. **Know:** number of red bumper cars, total number of bumper cars

3. **Don't need to know:** number of people waiting in line; number of blue, yellow, and green bumper cars

4. **Missing and need to know:** none

Decision: Too much information

Solve: 5 red bumper cars, 15 bumper cars total; P(red) $= \frac{5}{15} = \frac{1}{3}$

So, the probability that Karyn is assigned to a red bumper car is $\frac{1}{3}$.

Sometimes there is too little information to solve a problem.

What fraction of the people waiting in line to ride the bumper cars are females?

1. **Want to know:** fraction of people in line who are females

2. **Know:** 15 people waiting in line

3. **Don't need to know:** number of blue, yellow, green, and red bumper cars; number of bumper cars

4. **Missing and need to know:** number of females in line

Decision: Too little information

Solve: can't; need more information

Tell if each problem has *too much*, *too little*, or *the right amount* of information. Then solve the problem if possible, or describe the information needed to solve it.

1. A club has 32 female members and 24 male members. The members range in age from 22 years to 51 years. If a club member is randomly selected to be president, what is the probability that a female is chosen?

2. The Jenkins family is trying to decide on a name for their dog. They place the names Rusty, Sporto, and Buddy in a box and randomly select one name. What is the probability that they select the name Rusty or Buddy?

3. G. de Chasseloup-Laubat held the official land speed record in 1898. He drove a vehicle, the Jeantaud, at a speed of 39.24 mi per hr. How many times as fast was the land speed record in 1970?

4. Lina is saving to buy a bicycle and a helmet. The price of the bike is $199. So far, she has $155 saved. How much more does she need to save?

MIXED APPLICATIONS

Use Data For 5–6, use this table.

5. What is the difference between the average high temperature and the average low temperature for the 4 cities?

   A 88°F   **B** 85°F   **C** 63°F   **D** 22°F

6. **ALGEBRA** Choose the high temperature in Greenville in °C. Use the formula $C = \frac{5}{9} \times (F - 32)$.

   F 17°C   **G** 30°C   **H** 54°C   **J** 86°C

TEMPERATURES IN JUNE (°F)		
City	Low	High
Asheville, NC	58	80
Charlotte, NC	69	88
Greenville, NC	62	86
Winston-Salem, NC	63	86

7. Lydia studies twice as long as Jorge. Jorge and Olga study a total of 7 hr, but Olga studies 3 hr longer than Jorge. How long does Lydia study?

8. A bus travels 55 mi per hour. Misty starts out by bus at 11:45 A.M. to go to the carnival. How many miles does she travel if she arrives at the carnival at 1:15 P.M.?

9. There are 164 steps in the Astoria Column on Coxcomb Hill in Astoria, Oregon. Rick decided to climb to the top once a week for a year. How many steps must he climb up to do that?

10. The Stefan family spent a total of $42.75 at the carnival. They bought food for $12.50, souvenirs for $5.25, and show tickets for $5.00 each. How many tickets did they buy?

11. ✎ **Write a problem** about probability and include too much information. Then write a related problem, giving too little information.

Astoria Column

Odds

Learn how to find the odds in favor of an event and the odds against an event.

QUICK REVIEW

A number cube labeled 1 to 6 is rolled. Find each probability.

1. P(3) **2.** P(2) **3.** P(not 1) **4.** P(odd) **5.** P(2 or 4)

In Lesson 26.1, you used the spinner at the right to find the probability of an event. You can also use the spinner to find the odds in favor of an event and the odds against an event.

The **odds in favor of an event** compare the number of favorable outcomes to the number of unfavorable outcomes. These odds can be written as a ratio.

$$\text{odds in favor of an event} = \frac{\text{number of favorable outcomes}}{\text{number of unfavorable outcomes}}$$

The **odds against an event** compare the number of unfavorable outcomes to the number of favorable outcomes. These odds can also be written as a ratio.

$$\text{odds against an event} = \frac{\text{number of unfavorable outcomes}}{\text{number of favorable outcomes}}$$

EXAMPLE 1

In Lesson 26.1, you found P(red) for the spinner above. Use the spinner to find the odds in favor of and the odds against the pointer landing on red.

1 favorable outcome: red	*Count and list the*
4 unfavorable outcomes: yellow, green,	*favorable and*
white, purple	*unfavorable outcomes.*
Odds in favor of red $= \frac{1}{4}$	*Write the odds as ratios.*
Odds against red $= \frac{4}{1}$	

So, the odds in favor of the pointer landing on red are $\frac{1}{4}$, and the odds against the pointer landing on red are $\frac{4}{1}$.

Odds can be expressed as fractions, with the word *to,* or with a colon.

EXAMPLE 2

Each letter of the word *BOOKKEEPER* is written on a card and placed in a bag. One card is chosen at random. Find the odds.

A. odds in favor of choosing *O*   **B.** odds in favor of choosing *K* or *P*

    favorable: 2   unfavorable: 8   favorable: 3   unfavorable: 7

    $\frac{2}{8}$, 2 to 8, or 2:8 $\frac{3}{7}$, 3 to 7, or 3:7

CHECK FOR UNDERSTANDING

Think and Discuss ▶ Look back at the lesson to answer each question.

1. **Explain** how odds and theoretical probability are different.

Guided Practice ▶ Use the spinner at the right to find the odds in favor of and the odds against the pointer landing on the given color. Write the answer in three different ways.

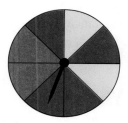

2. yellow   3. purple   4. red

5. red or purple   6. red or yellow

PRACTICE AND PROBLEM SOLVING

Independent Practice ▶ Use the spinner at the right to find the odds in favor of and the odds against the pointer landing on the given letter. Write the answer in three different ways.

7. *A*   8. *R*   9. *O*

10. *A* or *O*   11. *R* or *O*   12. vowel

A number cube is labeled 1, 2, 3, 4, 5, and 6. Find the odds in favor of rolling the given number.

13. 1, 2, or 4   14. a number less than 5

15. a number divisible by 3   16. not 3

Problem Solving Applications ▶

17. Natasha has a bag containing 35 red marbles, 20 green marbles, and 25 yellow marbles. If she selects one marble at random, what are the odds against selecting a red marble?

18. *REASONING* Tom has a spinner with two colors, blue and red. If the odds in favor of the pointer landing on red are 1:2, on which color is the pointer more likely to land, blue or red? Explain your thinking.

19. **(?) What's the Error?** Carlton says that the odds in favor of rolling an odd number on a number cube labeled 1 to 6 are $\frac{3}{6}$. What error did Carlton make? What is the correct answer?

MIXED REVIEW AND TEST PREP

20. A number cube is labeled 1 to 6. Find P(less than 3). (p. 580)

21. Find the area of a parallelogram with $b = 20$ ft and $h = 14$ ft. (p. 462)

22. Is 161 prime or composite? (p. 166)

23. Solve for *n*. 9 days = *n* hours (p. 420)

24. **TEST PREP** A computer that normally sells for $800 is on sale at 20% off. What is the total cost if the sales tax rate is 5%? (p. 568)

 A $780   **B** $672   **C** $640   **D** $168

EXTRA PRACTICE page 594, Set B

Simulations

Explore how to use a simulation to model an experiment.

You need a 5-section spinner and a calculator.

QUICK REVIEW

Find the mean.

1. 4, 5, 4, 6, 6 **2.** 2, 3, 1, 2, 3, 1

3. 10, 9, 17, 10 **4.** 15, 10, 14

5. 250, 200, 150

A cereal company is having a contest. To win a prize, you have to collect five cards that spell *PRIZE*. One of the five letters is put into each cereal box when the cereal is produced. The letters are divided equally among the cereal boxes.

You can conduct an experiment to simulate how many boxes of cereal you have to buy to get all five letters.

Activity 1

- Use a spinner to generate random numbers. Each of the numbers 1 to 5 will represent one of the letters.

- Spin the pointer on the spinner, and tally the numbers you get.

- Continue to spin the pointer until you get every number at least once.

- Repeat the experiment.

P	R	I	Z	E
1	2	3	4	5

NUMBER	TALLY
1	///
2	///
3	/
4	/
5	///

Think and Discuss

- How many spins did it take in the first experiment to get all five numbers? in the second experiment?

- What is the mean of the spins in your two experiments?

- How many boxes of cereal do you expect you will have to buy to get all five letters? If you bought this many boxes, would you be sure to win? Explain.

- Use the results of your experiments to estimate the probability that you will get the letter *Z*. Explain your solution.

Practice

- Repeat the experiment three more times.

- Combine your data with data from four classmates. Find the mean of the spins from all five sets of data.

- How many boxes of cereal do you expect you will have to buy to get all five letters? How does this differ from what you expected after the first two experiments?

You can use a calculator to produce random numbers.

Activity 2

- Predict how many students you need to survey to find two students who were born in the same month.

- Let the numbers 1 through 12 represent the 12 months. Use this key sequence on some calculators to produce random numbers from 1 to 12.

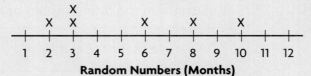

- Record the number you get each time.

- Continue to press until you get a duplicate number. For example: 8, 3, 10, 2, 6, 3.

- Make a line plot to show the results.

```
              X
        X     X           X        X        X
    +---+---+---+---+---+---+---+---+---+---+---+
    1   2   3   4   5   6   7   8   9  10  11  12
              Random Numbers (Months)
```

Think and Discuss
- How many times did you have to use the key sequence to get a duplicate month?

- How do your results compare with your prediction? How do your results compare with those of your classmates?

Practice
- Predict how many students you need to survey to find two students who were born on the same day of the week. Design and carry out a simulation using a calculator. Then compare your results with your prediction.

- Use a calculator to produce random numbers from 1 to 25. Record the number of times you get each number. Continue until you get all the numbers from 1 to 25.

MIXED REVIEW AND TEST PREP

1. A spinner has 8 equal sections numbered 1, 2, 1, 3, 2, 4, 1, 5. Find P(1 or 2). (p. 580)

2. The regular price of an item is $140. The discount rate is 25%. Find the amount of discount and the sale price. (p. 568)

3. Evaluate $y^2 + 8$, for $y = 9$. (p. 260)

4. Evaluate $b^2 \div (6 + 4)$, for $b = 8$. (p. 260)

5. **TEST PREP**   How much greater is the product 8.42×13.1 than the product 6.507×14? (p. 80)

   A 19.204   **B** 20.507   **C** 26.028   **D** 71.098

Experimental Probability

Learn how to find the experimental probability of an event.

Vocabulary

experimental probability

QUICK REVIEW

1. $\frac{1}{3} \times 27$ 2. $\frac{1}{5} \times 55$ 3. $\frac{3}{4} \times 24$ 4. $\frac{4}{5} \times 100$ 5. $\frac{2}{10} \times 3,000$

Pablo put some red, yellow, and green marbles in a box. He randomly selected a marble and recorded the color. He returned the marble to the box each time. Pablo did this a total of 25 times.

By performing an experiment, Pablo can find the experimental probability of selecting each marble color.

Math Idea ▶ The **experimental probability** of an event is the number of times a favorable outcome actually occurs compared with the total number of trials, or the total number of times you do the activity.

$$\text{experimental probability} = \frac{\text{number of favorable outcomes that occur}}{\text{total number of trials}}$$

EXAMPLE 1

Pablo recorded his results in a table. Use these results to find the experimental probability of selecting each color. Express your answers as fractions, decimals, and percents.

COLOR	Green	Red	Yellow
SELECTIONS	2	10	13

$P(\text{green}) = \frac{2}{25}$, 0.08, 8% $P(\text{red}) = \frac{10}{25} = \frac{2}{5}$, 0.40, 40%

$P(\text{yellow}) = \frac{13}{25}$, 0.52, 52%

You can compare experimental and theoretical probabilities.

Suppose Pablo has 10 green, 50 red, and 40 yellow marbles in his box. Make a table to compare the experimental and theoretical probabilities of selecting each color.

EXAMPLE 2

COLOR	EXPERIMENTAL PROBABILITY	THEORETICAL PROBABILITY	COMPARE
Green	0.08	$\frac{10}{100} = 0.10$	0.08 < 0.10
Red	0.40	$\frac{50}{100} = 0.50$	0.40 < 0.50
Yellow	0.52	$\frac{40}{100} = 0.40$	0.52 > 0.40

So, the experimental probabilities of selecting green and red are less than the theoretical probabilities. The experimental probability of selecting yellow is greater than the theoretical probability.

You can design an activity to find and compare experimental and theoretical probabilities.

Activity 1

You need: square tiles, box

- Put 20 square tiles in a box. Use at least two different colors.

- Find the theoretical probability of selecting each color.

- Decide how to randomly select a tile each time. Then select and replace a tile at least 25 times. Record the outcome of each selection.

- Use your results to find the experimental probability of selecting each color.

- Make a table to compare your experimental probabilities with the theoretical probabilities.

Think and Discuss

- Are your experimental probabilities close to the theoretical probabilities? Explain.

You can use experimental probabilities to predict future events.

EXAMPLE 3

Elaine has a box of buttons that are all the same size. She randomly selects one button and then replaces it. She does this a total of 40 times. Her results are shown in the table below.

COLOR	Blue	Brown	Red	Green	Black
TIMES SELECTED	5	12	5	8	10

Based on her experimental results, how many times can Elaine expect to select a green button in her next 10 selections?

$P(\text{green}) = \frac{8}{40} = \frac{1}{5}$, 0.20, 20% *Find the experimental probability of selecting green.*

$\frac{1}{5} \times 10 = 2$ *Multiply 10 selections by the experimental probability, $\frac{1}{5}$.*

So, Elaine can expect to select a green button 2 times.

CHECK FOR UNDERSTANDING

Think and ▶
Discuss

Look back at the lesson to answer the questions.

1. **Explain** the difference between theoretical probability and experimental probability.

2. **What if** Pablo selected a marble 50 more times? Do you think the experimental probabilities would be the same as in Example 1? Explain.

Celia rolled a number cube 30 times. For 3–8, use her results shown in the table below to find the experimental probability of each event. Write the answer as a fraction and a decimal.

NUMBER	1	2	3	4	5	6
TIMES ROLLED	2	6	7	3	8	4

3. P(1)   **4.** P(2)   **5.** P(3)

6. P(4)   **7.** P(5)   **8.** P(6)

9. What is the theoretical probability of rolling each number? How does the experimental probability of rolling each number compare with the theoretical probability?

PRACTICE AND PROBLEM SOLVING

Vincent spun the pointer of a 4-section spinner 40 times. For 10–15, use his results shown in the table below to find the experimental probability. Write the answer as a fraction and a decimal.

COLOR	Red	Yellow	Blue	Green
SPINS	10	6	16	8

10. P(red)   **11.** P(yellow)   **12.** P(blue)

13. P(green)   **14.** P(yellow or red)   **15.** P(not red)

16. Based on his experimental results, how many times can Vincent expect a result of yellow in the next 100 spins?

17. Suppose the spinner is divided into four equal sections. What is the theoretical probability of spinning each color? How does the experimental probability of spinning each color compare with the theoretical probability?

18. Conduct an experiment in which you toss a coin 50 times. Keep a tally of the number of times you toss heads. Combine your results with those of five other students to find the experimental probability of tossing heads. How does it compare with the theoretical probability?

19. The table below shows the results of 80 tosses of a dime and a nickel at the same time. Find the experimental probability of getting heads on both coins. How does it compare with the theoretical probability, which is 25%?

OUTCOME	TIMES TOSSED
heads on both coins	16
heads on dime, tails on nickel	21
tails on dime, heads on nickel	19
tails on both coins	24

20. **Vocabulary Power** You conduct *experiments* in your math and science classes. Give an example of a science experiment and a mathematical experiment. Explain how they are similar.

21. Tyrone has had 45 hits and 30 strikeouts in his last 150 times at bat. How many hits can Tyrone expect to get in his next 50 times at bat?

22.  **Write About It** Explain how to find the experimental probability of rolling a 4 using a number cube labeled 1 to 6.

23. **FAST FACT • SCIENCE** On a plant called the four o'clock, the flowers may be red, white, or pink. Pink flowers are twice as common as either red or white flowers. If a four o'clock has 140 flowers, how many can you expect to be red? white? pink?

MIXED REVIEW AND TEST PREP

Find the percent of the number. (p. 562)

24. 82% of 150

25. 7.5% of 130

26. 200% of 95

27. **TEST PREP** Which type of graph would you use to show the lengths of the five longest rivers? (p. 136)

   A circle   **B** bar   **C** histogram   **D** line

28. **TEST PREP** For a certain experiment, P(vowel) = $\frac{3}{7}$. Find P(consonant). (p. 580)

   F 0   **G** $\frac{3}{7}$ **H** $\frac{4}{7}$ **J** 1

PROBLEM SOLVING LiNKUP to Social Studies

Toss-Up In the days before computers, mathematicians performed experiments by hand. Around 1900, the English statistician Karl Pearson tossed a coin 24,000 times, recording 12,012 heads. In the 1940s, the English mathematician John Kerrich tossed a coin 10,000 times. The table at the right shows the results of Kerrich's experiment.

Number of Tosses	Number of Heads
10	4
50	25
100	44
500	255
1,000	502
5,000	2,533
10,000	5,067

For 1–4, use the table to find the experimental probability of tossing heads. Write your answer as a decimal.

1. after 10 tosses

2. after 100 tosses

3. after 1,000 tosses

4. after 10,000 tosses

5. Were John Kerrich's experimental results close to the theoretical probability of tossing heads? Explain.

EXTRA PRACTICE page 594, Set C

593

Set A (pp. 580–583)

For 1–5, use the spinner at the right. Find each probability. Write each answer as a fraction, a decimal, and a percent.

1. P(Dee)
2. P(Miles or Lili)
3. P(not Cara)
4. P(Marta)
5. P(Hugo, Miwa, or Chen)
6. P(name that begins with *M*)

Cards showing pictures of team mascots are placed in a hat. There are 3 lions, 5 bears, 4 cheetahs, and 8 tigers. You choose one card without looking. Find each probability.

7. P(bear)
8. P(tiger or lion)
9. P(member of cat family)
10. P(tiger)
11. P(cheetah or bear)
12. P(lion, bear, or tiger)

Set B (pp. 586–587)

A number cube is labeled 5, 10, 25, 50, 100, and 200. Find the odds in favor of and the odds against rolling the given number. Write the answer in three different ways.

1. 25
2. 5 or 25
3. 5, 10, or 100
4. not 50
5. an even number
6. a number ending in zero

Set C (pp. 590–593)

Anna has a box of color tiles. She randomly selects one tile and then replaces it. She does this a total of 100 times. Her results are shown in the table below. Find the experimental probability.

Color	red	yellow	blue	green
Times Selected	24	25	22	29

1. P(red)
2. P(yellow)
3. P(blue)
4. P(green)

5. Based on her experimental results, how many times can Anna expect to select a red tile in the next 50 spins? in the next 200 spins?

6. Suppose Anna has 25 tiles of each color in her box. What is the theoretical probability of selecting each color? How does the experimental probability of selecting each color compare with the theoretical probability?

1. **VOCABULARY**   A comparison of the number of favorable outcomes to the number of possible equally likely outcomes is called the ___?___ . (p. 580)

A bag has slips of paper numbered 2–10. Find the probability of randomly drawing the number from the bag. Write each answer as a fraction. (pp. 580–583)

2. P(5)

3. P(7 or 9)

4. P(1)

5. P(2, 5, or 9)

6. P(even number)

7. P(not 8)

8. P(5 or 6)

9. P(multiple of 5)

A bag has 10 new pencils: 3 red, 4 yellow, 1 blue, and 2 green. Find the odds in favor of and the odds against randomly choosing the given color from the bag. Write the answer in three different ways. (pp. 586–587)

10. green

11. red

12. blue

13. red or green

14. not yellow

15. red, blue, or yellow

Corey has a box of cards each labeled with a number from 1 to 6. He randomly selects one card and then replaces it. He does this a total of 100 times. His results are shown in the table below. For 16–21, find the experimental probability. (pp. 590–593)

NUMBER	1	2	3	4	5	6
TIMES SELECTED	8	12	24	13	17	26

16. P(1)

17. P(2)

18. P(3)

19. P(4)

20. P(5)

21. P(6)

22. Based on his experimental results, how many times can Corey expect to select a 1 or a 2 in his next 500 selections?

23. Suppose Corey has 48 cards with an equal number of cards for each number. What is the theoretical probability of selecting each number? How does the experimental probability of selecting each number compare with the theoretical probability?

Tell if each problem has *too much*, *too little*, or *the right amount* of information. Then solve the problem if possible, or describe the information needed to solve it. (pp. 584–585)

Forty-two people are eligible to win the grand prize in a random drawing. Sixteen of the people are male. Five of the people are from Alaska.

24. What is the probability that the grand prize winner will be a female?

25. What is the probability that the winner will be a male from Alaska?

MEASUREMENT

1. What is the measure of $\angle AOE$ in the figure below?

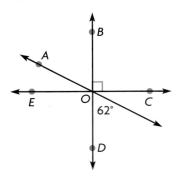

A 28°   **C** 62°

B 38°   **D** 118°

2. The free-throw lane used in international basketball is wider than the free-throw lane used in the United States, as shown below. How much greater is the area of the international lane than the area of the U.S. lane?

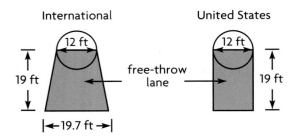

F 8.4 square feet   **H** 146.3 square feet

G 73.15 square feet   **J** 301.15 square feet

3. Explain It Gina has a tent shaped like the square pyramid at the right. What is the volume of the tent? Explain your answer.

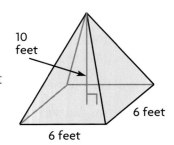

★ **ALGEBRAIC THINKING**

4. Jake is reading a book that is 128 pages long. The table below shows the number of pages he has read each day.

Day	Jan 5	Jan 6	Jan 7
Number of Pages	2	6	18

If the pattern continues, on which date will Jake finish reading the book?

A January 8   **C** January 10

B January 9   **D** January 11

5. The graph represents the number of hours of practice that the Barracudas have remaining this week. Which statement describes the inequality shown on the graph?

F The Barracudas have 5 hours of practice remaining.

G The Barracudas have less than 5 hours of practice remaining.

H The Barracudas have no more than 5 hours of practice remaining.

J The Barracudas have at least 5 hours of practice remaining.

6. Explain It Arizona has more national monuments than any other state. It also has 3 national parks, which is $\frac{1}{4}$ of the number of national monuments that it has. Kitt wrote $3n = \frac{1}{4}$, where $n =$ the number of national monuments, to relate the number of national parks in Arizona to the number of national monuments. Explain her error. Then write a correct equation and solve it to find the number of national monuments.

7. Of the first 42 men to serve as President of the United States, 12 were born in either Virginia or Massachusetts. Suppose the name of each President is written on a slip of paper and placed in a box. If you choose a name at random, what is the probability that the President you choose will NOT have been born in Virginia or Massachusetts?

> **TIP** **Decide on a plan.** See item 7. Find the number of Presidents who were not born in Virginia or Massachusetts. Then compare that number with the total number of Presidents.

A $\frac{2}{7}$

B $\frac{2}{3}$

C $\frac{5}{7}$

D $\frac{3}{4}$

8. For which spinner below are the odds in favor of the pointer landing on an even number equal to the odds in favor of the pointer landing on an odd number?

F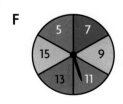

H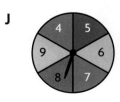

G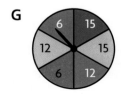

J

9. Explain It Fran randomly surveyed 100 girls in her school to find out what type of movie is most popular among students at her school. Is her sample biased or unbiased? Explain your answer.

10. In 1666, the English scientist Isaac Newton shone a beam of light through a glass prism. He discovered that the beam separated into a rainbow of colors called a spectrum. Which of the solid figures shown below could represent the solid figure that Newton used in his experiment?

A

C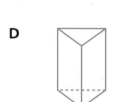

B

D

11. Which two triangles appear to be similar?

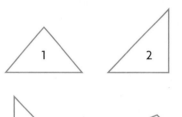

F triangle 1 and triangle 2

G triangle 2 and triangle 3

H triangle 1 and triangle 4

J triangle 3 and triangle 4

12. Explain It The figures below show the two types of frames that Carlos ordered from the craft store. Which figure has rotational symmetry? Explain your reasoning.

Figure A Figure B

27 Probability of Compound Events

≡FAST FACT • SOCIAL STUDIES

Great Smoky Mountains National Park, created in 1934, covers 800 square miles of mountainous land in Tennessee and North Carolina. With more than 9.1 million visitors in 2001, it is the most frequently visited national park in the United States.

PROBLEM SOLVING Suppose you were to ask two people who had visited the park in the past year to name the month they went there. What is the probability that both people were there during the period October 1–December 31?

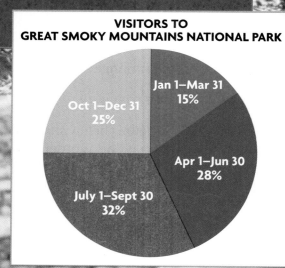

VISITORS TO GREAT SMOKY MOUNTAINS NATIONAL PARK

Oct 1–Dec 31
25%

Jan 1–Mar 31
15%

Apr 1–Jun 30
28%

July 1–Sept 30
32%

Check What You Know

Use this page to help you review and remember important skills needed for Chapter 27.

✓ Multiply Fractions

Multiply. Write your answer in simplest form.

1. $\frac{1}{3} \times \frac{1}{2}$

2. $\frac{1}{2} \times \frac{2}{3}$

3. $\frac{1}{4} \times \frac{1}{8}$

4. $\frac{3}{8} \times \frac{1}{2}$

5. $\frac{1}{3} \times \frac{3}{7}$

6. $\frac{1}{2} \times \frac{4}{5}$

7. $\frac{1}{9} \times \frac{2}{5}$

8. $\frac{3}{4} \times \frac{1}{6}$

9. $\frac{3}{5} \times \frac{1}{5}$

10. $\frac{1}{10} \times \frac{2}{5}$

11. $\frac{2}{3} \times \frac{1}{4}$

12. $\frac{1}{8} \times \frac{3}{5}$

13. $\frac{2}{3} \times \frac{2}{3}$

14. $\frac{3}{5} \times \frac{1}{10}$

15. $\frac{2}{7} \times \frac{1}{2}$

16. $\frac{3}{4} \times \frac{2}{3}$

✓ Solve Proportions

Solve for _n_.

17. $\frac{n}{6} = \frac{5}{6}$

18. $\frac{14}{7} = \frac{8}{n}$

19. $\frac{n}{3} = \frac{15}{5}$

20. $\frac{9}{36} = \frac{n}{48}$

21. $\frac{3}{n} = \frac{18}{48}$

22. $\frac{14}{16} = \frac{21}{n}$

23. $\frac{n}{2} = \frac{21}{6}$

24. $\frac{n}{2} = \frac{35}{14}$

25. $\frac{40}{n} = \frac{16}{6}$

26. $\frac{36}{n} = \frac{18}{8}$

27. $\frac{13}{6} = \frac{n}{6}$

28. $\frac{3}{n} = \frac{12}{16}$

29. $\frac{8}{12} = \frac{18}{n}$

30. $\frac{n}{24} = \frac{15}{30}$

31. $\frac{4}{n} = \frac{5}{25}$

32. $\frac{9}{8} = \frac{n}{56}$

VOCABULARY POWER

REVIEW

sample [sam′pəl] _noun_

A sample is a part of a population. Explain how a mathematical sample is similar to a sample of a product that you might receive at a store.

 www.harcourtschool.com/mathglossary

PREVIEW

compound event

tree diagram

Fundamental Counting Principle

permutation

combination

independent events

dependent events

PROBLEM SOLVING STRATEGY
Make an Organized List

Learn how to use the strategy *make an organized list* to solve problems.

The 5 members of the Montoya family are planning their next vacation. They will travel in June or July to New Orleans, LA; Nashville, TN; Miami, FL; or Charlotte, NC. How many different vacations involving one place and one month are possible?

Analyze　What are you asked to find?

What facts are given?

Is there any numerical information you will not use? If so, what?

Choose　What strategy will you use?

You can use the strategy *make an organized list* to show the sample space.

Solve　How will you solve the problem?

List the two months and pair each with the four places the Montoyas might visit.

June, New Orleans	**July, New Orleans**
June, Nashville	**July, Nashville**
June, Miami	**July, Miami**
June, Charlotte	**July, Charlotte**

So, there are 8 possible choices for the Montoyas' next vacation.

Check　How can you check your answer?

What if the Montoya family adds Indianapolis as a choice? How many different vacations are possible?

PROBLEM SOLVING STRATEGIES

Draw a Diagram or Picture

Make a Model

Predict and Test

Work Backward

▶ **Make an Organized List**

Find a Pattern

Make a Table or Graph

Solve a Simpler Problem

Write an Equation

Use Logical Reasoning

Solve by making an organized list.

1. Mrs. Chen is making a dental appointment. It can be on Monday, Tuesday, Wednesday, or Thursday, at 9:30 A.M., 11:00 A.M., or 2:00 P.M. How many choices does Mrs. Chen have?

2. Gilbert is packing for a ski trip. He has 2 jackets, 2 pairs of ski pants, and 2 hats. How many different outfits can Gilbert make if each outfit consists of a jacket, pants, and a hat?

MIXED STRATEGY PRACTICE

For 3–4, use this information. Chad spends $44.39 on two packages of computer disks and a cartridge for his printer.

3. If each package of disks costs $9.95, what equation could you use to find the cost of the cartridge for his printer?

   A $9.95 + c = 44.39$

   B $2(9.95) + c = 44.39$

   C $44.39 - 9.95 = c$

   D $9.95 + 2c = 44.39$

4. Chad's total includes $2.89 in sales tax. What would you do first to find the cost of the items he buys?

   F Add $2.89 to $44.39.

   G Subtract $2.89 from $44.39.

   H Multiply $44.39 by $2.89.

   J Divide $44.39 by $2.89.

5. **Use Data** Use the graph below. How many more visits did Great Smoky Mountains National Park have than Olympic National Park and Yosemite National Park combined? Estimate to determine if your answer is reasonable.

6. Yumi arranged five of her friends in line for a photograph. Alberto stood between Harley and Joshua. Eleni stood between Joshua and Merrill. Merrill was on the left. Starting from the left, write the order in which Yumi's friends were arranged for the photo.

7. A dance company performs in nonoverlapping groups of 8 and 10. There are 64 dancers in all. There are more groups of 10 than groups of 8. How many groups of each size are there?

8. **?** **What's the Error?** Jay's lunch cost $7.55. He left $0.15 for a 20% tip. Describe his error. How much should a 20% tip be?

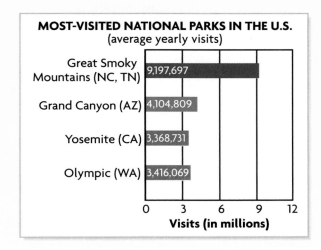

MOST-VISITED NATIONAL PARKS IN THE U.S.
(average yearly visits)

Great Smoky Mountains (NC, TN) 9,197,697

Grand Canyon (AZ) 4,104,809

Yosemite (CA) 3,368,731

Olympic (WA) 3,416,069

Visits (in millions)

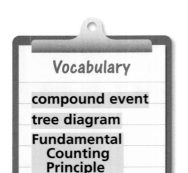

Compound Events

Learn how to find all possible outcomes for compound events.

LUNCH MENU
BEVERAGE
● Milk
  ● Juice
SANDWICH
● Chicken ● Tuna
  ● Vegetable
DESSERT
● Fruit Cup ● Pudding

Vocabulary

compound event
tree diagram
Fundamental Counting Principle

How many choices of a beverage, a sandwich, and a dessert does Carmella have for lunch?

Choosing three different items for lunch is an example of a **compound event**. A compound event includes two or more simple events.

One Way   Find the number of possible outcomes for a compound event by drawing a **tree diagram**.

Beverage	Sandwich	Dessert	Outcome
milk (M)	chicken (C)	fruit cup (F) →	M, C, F
		pudding (P) →	M, C, P
	tuna (T)	fruit cup (F) →	M, T, F
		pudding (P) →	M, T, P
	vegetable (V)	fruit cup (F) →	M, V, F
		pudding (P) →	M, V, P
juice (J)	chicken (C)	fruit cup (F) →	J, C, F
		pudding (P) →	J, C, P
	tuna (T)	fruit cup (F) →	J, T, F
		pudding (P) →	J, T, P
	vegetable (V)	fruit cup (F) →	J, V, F
		pudding (P) →	J, V, P

So, Carmella has 12 choices of a beverage, a sandwich, and a dessert.

Another Way   Find the number of possible outcomes for 2 or more events by using the **Fundamental Counting Principle**.

Fundamental Counting Principle	If one event has m possible outcomes and a second event has n possible outcomes, then there are $m \times n$ total possible outcomes for the two events together.

EXAMPLE 1

What if the school cafeteria adds 2 more desserts to the menu? Find the total number of beverage-sandwich-dessert selections.

	Beverages		Sandwiches		Desserts	
	2	×	3	×	4	= 24

So, there are 24 beverage-sandwich-dessert selections.

You can also show the sample space by using a grid to make a table.

EXAMPLE 2

Find the number of possible outcomes if Brianna selects one card at random and spins the pointer on the spinner.

Spinner

Card	1	2	3	4
A	(A,1)	(A,2)	(A,3)	(A,4)
B	(B,1)	(B,2)	(B,3)	(B,4)
C	(C,1)	(C,2)	(C,3)	(C,4)
D	(D,1)	(D,2)	(D,3)	(D,4)

List the card choices in rows and the spinner choices in columns.

So, there are 16 possible outcomes if Brianna selects one card at random and spins the pointer on the spinner.

CHECK FOR UNDERSTANDING

Think and Discuss ▶ **Look back at the lesson to answer each question.**

1. **What if** Brianna spins the pointer on the spinner in Example 2 and rolls a number cube labeled 1 to 6? Find the number of possible outcomes.

2. **Draw** a tree diagram to show all possible outcomes for tossing three coins.

Guided Practice ▶ **Draw a tree diagram or make a table to find the number of possible outcomes for each situation.**

3. a choice of vanilla, chocolate, or strawberry yogurt in a small, medium, or large cup

4. spinning the pointers on these two spinners

Use the Fundamental Counting Principle to find the number of possible outcomes for each situation.

5. rolling two number cubes labeled 1 to 6

6. a choice of 5 cards, 3 envelopes, and 2 stickers

PRACTICE AND PROBLEM SOLVING

Independent Practice ▶ **Draw a tree diagram or make a table to find the number of possible outcomes for each situation.**

7. a choice of a car or a van with a blue, black, white, or silver exterior, and a black or gray interior

8. tossing a coin and rolling a number cube labeled 1 to 6

Use the Fundamental Counting Principle to find the number of possible outcomes for each situation.

9. a choice of 3 pizza crusts and 6 toppings

10. a choice of 2 ties, 5 shirts, 3 trousers, 2 belts

11. rolling 3 number cubes

12. tossing a coin 4 times

Problem Solving ▶ Applications

13. A cafe offers 12 different sandwiches, 4 different salads, and 8 different soups. If the cafe is open every day of the year, is it possible to have a different combination of sandwich, salad, and soup for lunch every day of the year? Explain.

14. 📖 **Write About It**   Is it easier to draw a tree diagram, make a table, or use the Fundamental Counting Principle to find the number of possible outcomes for a compound event? Explain.

MIXED REVIEW AND TEST PREP

15. Out of 60 rolls of a number cube, Alicia rolls a six 12 times. What is the experimental probability of rolling a six? (p. 590)

Find the measure of the supplement of each angle. (p. 340)

16. 86°   17. 17°   18. 39°

⭐ 19. **TEST PREP**   Which is the least fraction greater than the sum of $\frac{3}{16}$ and $\frac{1}{4}$? (p. 206)

   A $\frac{1}{4}$ B $\frac{1}{3}$ C $\frac{5}{8}$ D $\frac{7}{8}$

PROBLEM SOLVING 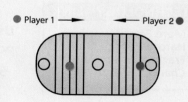 to Social Studies

Totolospi The Hopi Indians of Arizona invented a game called Totolospi. They used a board like the one shown at the right. A player tossed 3 playing pieces. Each playing piece had a round side and a flat side. With a toss of 3 "rounds," the player moved forward 2 lines. With 3 "flats," the player moved forward 1 line. Otherwise, the player lost his or her turn. The object was to reach the opposite end of the board first.

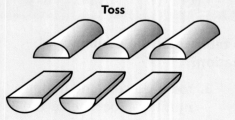

1. Draw a tree diagram to find the number of possible outcomes for tossing 3 playing pieces. Write *R* for *round* and *F* for *flat*.

2. What is the probability that a player will be able to advance 1 or 2 lines after tossing the playing pieces?

EXTRA PRACTICE page 614, Set A

Permutations and Combinations

Learn how to find the number of permutations and combinations of a set of items.

Vocabulary

permutation
combination

1. 7 × 6   **2.** 5 × 4 × 3   **3.** 4 × 5 × 6   **4.** 36 ÷ 2   **5.** 39 ÷ 3

Tanya wants different flavors in her 2-scoop ice cream cone. How many different ways can she make an ice cream cone if the order of the flavors is important?

ICE CREAM FLAVORS
Chocolate
Mint
Strawberry
Vanilla

A selection of different items in which the order of the items is important is called a **permutation**.

One Way Draw a tree diagram to find the number of permutations.

Since the order is important, "chocolate, vanilla" is different from "vanilla, chocolate."

Bottom	Top	Permutation
chocolate (C)	mint (M) →	C, M
	strawberry (S) →	C, S
	vanilla (V) →	C, V
mint (M)	chocolate (C) →	M, C
	strawberry (S) →	M, S
	vanilla (V) →	M, V
strawberry (S)	chocolate (C) →	S, C
	mint (M) →	S, M
	vanilla (V) →	S, V
vanilla (V)	chocolate (C) →	V, C
	mint (M) →	V, M
	strawberry (S) →	V, S

Remember that you can use the Fundamental Counting Principle to find the total number of possible outcomes for two or more events by multiplying the number of outcomes for each event.

So, there are 12 different ways for Tanya to make an ice cream cone.

Another Way Use the Fundamental Counting Principle to find the number of permutations.

There are 4 possible choices for the bottom flavor. Once the bottom flavor has been chosen, there are 3 choices remaining for the top flavor. Multiply, using the Fundamental Counting Principle:

Bottom   Top
4   ×   3   =   12 permutations

EXAMPLE 1

Del wants 3 different ice cream flavors in his 3-scoop cone. How many different ways can he make his cone if the order of the flavors is important?

Bottom   Middle   Top
4   ×   3   ×   2   =   24

So, there are 24 different ways that Del can make his cone.

Combinations

A **combination** is a selection of items in which the order of the items is *not* important.

EXAMPLE 2

Tanya decides to get her ice cream in a cup. The order of the flavors is not important to her. If she chooses from the ice cream flavors listed at the top of page 605, how many combinations of 2 ice cream flavors are possible?

Choose an ice cream flavor. Pair it with each of the other flavors. Do not use any combinations that reverse the pairs already listed.

chocolate and mint	*(C, M)*	*mint and strawberry*	*(M, S)*
chocolate and strawberry	*(C, S)*	*mint and vanilla*	*(M, V)*
chocolate and vanilla	*(C, V)*	*strawberry and vanilla*	*(S, V)*

So, there are 6 possible combinations of 2 flavors.

You can also use the number of permutations to find the number of combinations in Example 2. Look at the tree diagram on page 605. Each pair of ice cream flavors is listed twice on the tree diagram. If the order is not important, then (C, S) and (S, C) are the same. So, divide 12 by 2 to eliminate duplicates. $12 \div 2 = 6$ flavors.

Math Idea ▶ To decide whether a selection is a permutation or a combination, decide whether or not order is important. If it is, choose a permutation. If it is not, choose a combination.

CHECK FOR UNDERSTANDING

Think and ▶ Discuss

Look back at the lesson to answer each question.

1. **Explain** how combinations and permutations are alike and how they are different.

2. **Describe** two methods you can use to find the number of ways that 3 students can sit in a row of 3 seats.

Guided ▶ Practice

For 3–4, tell whether the selection is a permutation or a combination.

3. selection of toppings for a pizza

4. selection of players for the lineup of a baseball game

5. How many different 2-scoop ice cream cones can you make using 5 flavors if the order of the flavors is important?

6. How many different 2-scoop ice cream cones can you make using 5 flavors if the order of the flavors is *not* important?

7. Jo has 5 photos of her dog. She hangs 3 of them in a row on her wall. How many arrangements of 3 photos are possible?

8. Frank's favorite pizza toppings are pepperoni, mushrooms, olives, and sausage. Make a list to find how many different ways Frank can order pizza with 3 of these toppings.

Independent ▶ Practice

For 9–12, tell whether the selection is a permutation or a combination.

9. selection of 5 friends to come to a party

10. selection of license plate numbers

11. selection of 8 numbers for a password

12. selection of ingredients for a soup you plan to make

13. How many different 2-scoop ice cream cones can you make using 6 flavors if the order of the flavors is important? if the order of the flavors is *not* important?

14. How many different ways can Matt, Nan, Dale, Bill, and Pat form teams of three people? Make a list to solve.

15. Sharon has 7 books about cats. How many ways can she arrange them on a bookshelf?

Problem Solving ▶ Applications

16. **Vocabulary Power** A tree diagram shows all possible outcomes of a compound event. A factor tree shows the prime factors of a number. Why is the word *tree* appropriate for both of these mathematical terms?

17. *REASONING* How many different 3-scoop ice cream cones can you make using 4 flavors if the order of the flavors is important and each flavor can be chosen more than once? Explain your reasoning.

18. At the movie theater, there are 3 seats together in one row. In how many different ways can Martha, Danielle, and Anthony sit in the seats? Make a tree diagram to show the different arrangements.

19. ▬▬**FAST FACT** • SOCIAL STUDIES Nine-digit ZIP codes were first introduced in 1983. Using the digits 1–9, how many different ZIP codes can you make without repeating the digits within a ZIP code?

MIXED REVIEW AND TEST PREP

20. Find the number of possible outcomes for selecting from 5 entrees, 3 salads, and 3 beverages. (p. 602)

21. The table at the right shows the number of movies that each of Mrs. Becker's students has seen since the start of the year. Use the data to make a line plot. (p. 114)

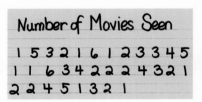

Number of Movies Seen

1 5 3 2 1 6 1 2 3 3 4 5
1 1 6 3 4 2 2 2 4 3 2 1
2 2 4 5 1 3 2 1

22. Solve. $6.36 = 6b$ (p. 291)

23. Find 70% of 30. (p. 562)

24. **TEST PREP** A store received a box of eggs. The box had 20 cartons of eggs, and each carton had a dozen eggs. A store clerk found 8 broken eggs. How many eggs were not broken? (p. 52)

A 160   **B** 200   **C** 232   **D** 240

EXTRA PRACTICE page 614, Set B

LESSON 27.4

Independent and Dependent Events

Learn how to identify and find probabilities of dependent and independent events.

QUICK REVIEW

1. $\frac{1}{4} \times \frac{1}{2}$ **2.** $\frac{2}{3} \times \frac{1}{6}$ **3.** $\frac{1}{5} \times \frac{1}{4}$ **4.** $\frac{1}{2} \times \frac{1}{2}$ **5.** $\frac{3}{5} \times \frac{1}{6}$

To calculate the probability that two events will occur, you must first decide whether the outcome of the second event depends on the outcome of the first event.

Activity 1

You need: 6 index cards, box

- Write the numbers 1 to 6 on the index cards, one number to a card. Place the cards in the box.
- Without looking, draw a card, replace it, and draw another card.
- Was the number of possible outcomes the same or different on the two times you drew a card? What was the probability of choosing a 4 on your first draw? on your second draw?
- Did your second choice depend on the first card you drew? Explain.

Vocabulary

independent events

dependent events

The table below shows the contents of a bag of marbles. Juan randomly selects a marble from the bag, replaces it, and selects again.

RED	BLUE	GREEN	YELLOW
3	8	5	4

Because Juan replaces the marble after the first selection, the outcome of the second event does not depend on the outcome of the first event. These are **independent events**.

To find the probability of two independent events, multiply their probabilities.

Marbles have been around for at least 4,000 years.

> If A and B are independent events, then
> P(A, B) = P(A) × P(B).

EXAMPLE 1

Remember that the theoretical probability of an event is a comparison of the number of favorable outcomes to the number of possible, equally likely outcomes.

What is the probability that Juan selects a blue marble, replaces it, and then selects a yellow marble?

Find P(blue, yellow).   *First blue, then yellow.*

first selection: P(blue) = $\frac{8}{20}$, or $\frac{2}{5}$ *Find the probability of blue.*

second selection: P(yellow) = $\frac{4}{20}$, or $\frac{1}{5}$ *Find the probability of yellow.*

P(blue, yellow) = $\frac{2}{5} \times \frac{1}{5} = \frac{2}{25}$ *Multiply the probabilities.*

So, the probability is $\frac{2}{25}$, 0.08, or 8%.

EXAMPLE 2

Lisa spins the pointer on the spinner two times.
Find the probability of each event.

A. $P(1, 2) = P(1) \times P(2) = \frac{1}{5} \times \frac{1}{5} = \frac{1}{25}$

B. $P(\text{not } 3, \text{not } 4) = P(\text{not } 3) \times P(\text{not } 4) = \frac{4}{5} \times \frac{4}{5} = \frac{16}{25}$

C. $P(1 \text{ or } 2, 2) = P(1 \text{ or } 2) \times P(2) = \frac{2}{5} \times \frac{1}{5} = \frac{2}{25}$

D. $P(1 \text{ or } 2, 4 \text{ or } 5) = P(1 \text{ or } 2) \times P(4 \text{ or } 5) = \frac{2}{5} \times \frac{2}{5} = \frac{4}{25}$

Dependent Events

Activity 2

You need: 6 index cards, box

• Write the numbers 1 to 6 on the index cards, one number to
a card. Place the cards in the box.

• Without looking, draw a card, do not replace it, and draw
another card.

• Was the number of possible outcomes the same or different on the
two times you drew a card?

• What was the probability of choosing a 4 on your first draw? What
was the probability of choosing a 4 on your second draw if you did
not choose it the first time? What was the probability of choosing
a 4 on your second draw if you did choose it the first time?

• Did your second choice depend on the first card you drew? Explain.

Without looking, Isabella selects a magnet
from a box, does not replace it, and then
passes the box to Jason, who also selects a
magnet. Since Isabella does not replace
the magnet, Jason's selection depends on
the result of Isabella's selection.

If the outcome of the second event
depends on the outcome of the first event,
the events are called **dependent events**.
To find the probability of two dependent
events, use the formula below.

> If A and B are dependent events, then
> $P(A, B) = P(A) \times P(B \text{ after } A)$.

$P(B \text{ after } A)$ is the probability that event B will occur after event A has
occurred. When Jason makes his selection (event B), the number of
magnets in the box is 1 less than the number of magnets when
Isabella made her selection (event A). So, the number of possible
outcomes for Jason is 1 less than the number of possible outcomes
for Isabella.

EXAMPLE 3

The contents of Isabella's magnet collection are shown in the table. Assuming that Isabella and Jason select without replacement, find the probability that they both select animal magnets.

FLOWERS	ANIMALS	CITIES
4	5	16

Find P(animal, animal).

Isabella's selection:

$P(animal) = \frac{5}{25} = \frac{1}{5}$ *There are 5 animal magnets and 25 equally likely outcomes.*

Jason's selection:

$P(animal\ after\ animal) = \frac{4}{24} = \frac{1}{6}$ *There are now 4 animal magnets and 24 equally likely outcomes.*

$P(animal, animal) = \frac{1}{5} \times \frac{1}{6} = \frac{1}{30}$ *Multiply the probabilities.*

So, the probability of Isabella and Jason both selecting animal magnets is $\frac{1}{30}$, $0.0\overline{3}$, or $3\frac{1}{3}\%$.

TECHNOLOGY LINK

More Practice:
**Harcourt Mega Math
Fraction Action,**
Last Chance Canyon,
Levels N and O

Math Idea ▶ Compound events consist of either independent events or dependent events. To find the probability of a compound event, multiply the probabilities of the simple events. For independent events, P(A, B) = P(A) × P(B). For dependent events, P(A, B) = P(A) × P(B after A).

CHECK FOR UNDERSTANDING

**Think and ▶
Discuss**

Look back at the lesson to answer each question.

1. **Find** the probability of spinning two even numbers in Example 2. Find the probability of spinning two odd numbers. Express your answers as percents. Are your computed probabilities reasonable? Explain.

2. **Give** an example of two events that are dependent.

**Guided ▶
Practice**

Write *independent* or *dependent* to describe the events.

3. Draw one card from a box, do not replace it, and draw another card.

4. Choose a table in a restaurant and an entree from the menu.

John rolls two number cubes labeled 1 to 6. Find the probability of each event.

5. P(1, 3) 6. P(not 2, 4) 7. P(7, 3) 8. P(1 or 2, 4)

A bag contains five lettered tiles labeled *P, I, Z, Z, A*. Without looking, Lin selects a tile, does not replace it, and selects another tile. Find the probability of each event.

9. P(*P, A*) 10. P(*Z,* not *I*) 11. P(*A* or *P, Z*) 12. P(vowel, *U*)

**Independent ▶
Practice**

Write *independent* or *dependent* to describe the events.

13. Draw a card from a deck of cards, do not replace it, and draw a second card.

14. Toss a coin three times.

Without looking, you take a card out of the jar and replace it before selecting again. Find the probability of each event. Then find the probability, assuming the card is not replaced after each selection.

15. P(1, 3) **16.** P(2, 4) **17.** P(4, 1 or 2)

18. P(4, not 2) **19.** P(1, 2 or 4) **20.** P(3, odd)

21. P(2, 2, 2) **22.** P(2, 1, 2) **23.** P(4, 1, 1)

Jared has a quarter and a spinner with 8 equal sections numbered 1 to 8. Find the probability of each event.

24. P(heads, 5) **25.** P(tails, not 6) **26.** P(heads, odd)

27. Leah flipped a penny 6 times and it landed heads up every time. If she flips the penny one more time, what is the probability that the penny will land heads up?

**Problem Solving ▶
Applications**

28. *REASONING* Michael has two numbered spinners. The probability of spinning a 5 on both spinners is 0.075. If the probability of spinning a 5 on the first spinner alone is 0.375, what is the probability of spinning a 5 on the second spinner alone?

29. (?) **What's the Question?** Owen rolls two number cubes labeled 1 to 6. The answer is $\frac{1}{9}$.

30. Donte and his two sisters collect stamps. Donte has twice as many as his older sister, who has 21 stamps, and three times as many as his younger sister. How many stamps do they have in all?

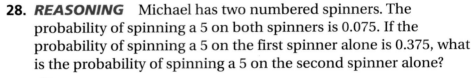

MIXED REVIEW AND TEST PREP

Find the number of possible outcomes for each situation. (p. 602)

31. 5 shirts, 3 pairs of slacks **32.** 4 cards, 6 envelopes **33.** 3 beverages, 6 entrees

34. A bag contains 3 blue, 4 yellow, 5 purple, and 3 red marbles. One marble is chosen at random. Find P(not yellow). (p. 580)

⭐**35. TEST PREP** Which figure can always be described as a rectangle? (p. 362)

A rhombus **B** square **C** parallelogram **D** trapezoid

Make Predictions

Learn how to use sample data to make predictions about a population.

Kevin and Shaundra conducted a survey of a random sample of sixth graders at Washington Middle School. The table below shows the results of the survey.

Remember that a population is a group being studied. A sample is a representative part of that group.

FAVORITE PETS	
Pet	**Number of Students**
Cat	30
Dog	25
Hamster	9
Rabbit	5
Bird	3
Other	3

Math Idea ▶ You can use the results from a sample to make predictions about preferences or actions of the population.

EXAMPLE 1

What is the probability that a randomly selected sixth grader at Washington Middle School chooses a cat as his or her favorite pet?

$$P(cat) = \frac{\text{number of students who prefer cats}}{\text{number of students surveyed}} = \frac{30}{75}, \text{ or } \frac{2}{5}$$

So, the probability that a sixth grader chooses a cat as his or her favorite pet is about $\frac{2}{5}$, 0.40, or 40%.

EXAMPLE 2

There are 210 sixth graders at Washington Middle School. Predict about how many of them would choose cats as their favorite pets.

$\frac{2}{5} = \frac{n}{210}$ *Write and solve a proportion.*

$2 \times 210 = 5 \times n$ *Find the cross products.*

$420 = 5n$ *Solve the equation.*

$\frac{420}{5} = \frac{5n}{5}$

$84 = n$

So, about 84 sixth graders would choose cats as their favorite pets.

Think and ▶
Discuss

Look back at the lesson to answer each question.

1. **Explain** how to predict how many sixth graders from Washington Middle School would choose rabbits as their favorite pets.

2. **What if** there were 300 sixth graders at Washington Middle School? About how many of them would you predict would choose cats as their favorite pets?

Guided ▶
Practice

The results of a survey of 500 randomly selected teenagers in Iowa indicate that 175 of them use the Internet regularly.

3. What is the probability that a randomly selected teenager in Iowa uses the Internet on a regular basis?

4. Predict about how many Iowa teenagers out of 4,500 use the Internet on a regular basis.

PRACTICE AND PROBLEM SOLVING

Independent ▶
Practice

Use Data   For 5–6, use the graph.
The graph shows the favorite colors of 100 randomly selected sixth graders from Glenville Middle School.

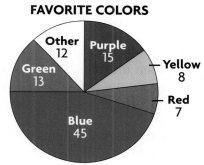

FAVORITE COLORS

Other 12 · Purple 15 · Yellow 8 · Green 13 · Red 7 · Blue 45

5. If there are 340 sixth graders at Glenville Middle School, about how many more would prefer the color blue than would prefer the color purple?

6. If there are 400 sixth graders at Glenville Middle School, about how many would prefer a color that is not green?

Problem Solving ▶
Applications

7. In a random sample of 400 remote control cars, the quality control department found that 24 were defective. If the company manufactures 10,000 remote control cars, about how many of them would you predict would be defective?

8. 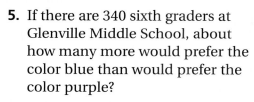 **Write a problem** that involves making a prediction about a population of 150 sixth graders based on a sample.

MIXED REVIEW AND TEST PREP

There are 6 cards that spell out *DIVIDE*. Suppose you choose one card at random. Find the probability of each event. (p. 580)

9. P(*D*)

10. P(*I* or *D*)

11. P(vowel)

12. Two number cubes labeled 1 to 6 are rolled. Find P(3, not 4). (p. 608)

⭐ 13. **TEST PREP**   Find $4^3 \div 2^2 + 4$. (p. 266)

A 6   **B** 8   **C** 20   **D** 64

Set A (pp. 602–604)

Draw a tree diagram or use the Fundamental Counting Principle to find the number of possible outcomes for each situation.

1. a choice of pancakes, French toast, or waffles, and juice, milk, or tea

2. a choice of 6 salads and 10 dressings

3. rolling 2 number cubes labeled *A* to *F*

Set B (pp. 605–607)

Tell whether the situation involves permutations or combinations. Then solve.

1. Sean can choose 2 toppings from 6 toppings to make a taco. How many ways can he make a taco?

2. There are 6 finalists in a tennis competition. How many ways can the first, second, and third prizes be awarded?

Set C (pp. 608–611)

Write *independent* or *dependent* to describe the events.

1. You have a bag of 6 red marbles and 4 green marbles. You draw one marble, record the color, place the marble back in the bag, and draw again.

2. Ana draws one name from a box to select the winner of a movie pass and then draws another name from the same box for the winner of a CD.

A box contains five cards labeled *C, L, A, S, S*. Without looking in the box, you select a card, replace it, and then select again. For 3–8, find the probability of each event. Then find the probability assuming the first card is not replaced.

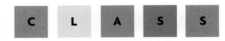

3. P(C, L)

4. P(L, C)

5. P(A, S)

6. P(S, L)

7. P(C, L or S)

8. P(C or L, S)

Set D (pp. 612–613)

Seventy-five students from Park Middle School were randomly surveyed about favorite pizza toppings. The results are shown in the table.

1. Suppose there are 225 students who attend Park Middle School. Predict the number of students who prefer black olives as a pizza topping.

2. Suppose there are 314 students at Park Middle School. Predict the number of students who prefer sausage as a pizza topping.

FAVORITE PIZZA TOPPINGS	
Topping	**Number of Students**
Pepperoni	30
Black Olives	15
Sausage	12
Mushrooms	10
Other	8

1. **VOCABULARY** If the outcome of the second event depends on the outcome of the first event, the events are called __?__ events. (p. 609)

2. **VOCABULARY** If the outcome of the second event does not depend on the outcome of the first event, the events are called __?__ events. (p. 608)

Draw a tree diagram or use the Fundamental Counting Principle to find the number of possible outcomes for each situation. (pp. 602–604)

3. Miguel tosses a coin and selects 1 marble at random from a jar containing 1 red, 1 blue, 1 yellow, and 1 green marble.

4. To get to work, Lea can walk or ride the subway to Central Station. From there, she takes either a bus, a cab, or a train.

For 5–6, tell whether the situation involves permutations or combinations. Then solve. (pp. 605–607)

5. In how many ways can Eliza line up her 5 bowling trophies on a shelf?

6. There are 6 boys in a gym class. In how many ways could teams of 2 boys be formed?

For 7–10, suppose you spin the pointer and select a card at random. (pp. 608–611)

7. Find P(green, 1).
8. Find P(red, 2).
9. Find P(red, odd).
10. Find P(blue, 4).

A bag contains 1 green, 2 purple, and 2 white blocks. Without looking in the bag, you choose a block, do not replace it, and then choose another block. **For 11–14, find the probability. Write your answer as a fraction, a decimal, and a percent.** (pp. 608–611)

11. P(green, white)
12. P(purple, black)
13. P(white or green, purple)
14. P(purple, not white)

Sixty students from Center Middle School were randomly surveyed about their favorite types of movies. The results are shown in the table. **For 15–18, find the probability that a student picked at random from Center Middle School prefers each type of movie.** (pp. 612–613)

15. drama
16. comedy
17. action
18. horror

19. Suppose there are 300 students at Center Middle School. Predict the number of students who prefer horror movies.

Favorite Types of Movies

Movies	Number of Students
Action	18
Comedy	12
Drama	15
Horror	7
Other	8

Make an organized list to solve. (pp. 600–601)

20. Armand is making a haircut appointment. It can be on Tuesday, Wednesday, or Friday, at 11:00 A.M., 1:00 P.M., 2:30 P.M., or 4:00 P.M. How many possible appointments are there?

★ GEOMETRY AND SPATIAL SENSE

1. How many lines of symmetry does the figure below have?

A 3   C 5

B 4   D 6

2. While playing a game of chess, Danny moved his playing piece by sliding it diagonally as shown in the figure. Which type of transformation does his move **most** resemble?

F tessellation   H rotation

G translation   J reflection

3. In the kite shown at the right, what type of angle is ∠y?

A acute

B right

C obtuse

D straight

4. Explain It Each team at the Math Fair is given a set of rules. The first rule reads: "Write all of your answers on a sheet of paper shaped like a trapezoid." Which of the figures shown below should the teams use? Explain your reasoning.

Figure 1   Figure 2   Figure 3   Figure 4

★ ALGEBRAIC THINKING

5. Marcus arranged counters in the pattern below.

Figure 1   Figure 2   Figure 3

How many counters will Marcus need for the eighth figure in his pattern?

F 20   H 36

G 28   J 64

6. A sign at the beginning of the line for a roller coaster ride reads: "You must be at least 50 inches tall to go on this ride." Which inequality shows this rule?

A $y \geq 50$

B $y > 50$

C $y \leq 50$

D $y < 50$

7. The fare, in dollars, for a ride in a Metro Blue taxi is given by $2.00 + 0.50m$, where m is the number of miles traveled. Maddie traveled 10 miles in a Metro Blue taxi. What was her total fare?

F $2.00   H $5.00

G $2.50   J $7.00

8. Explain It Bonnie wrote the following sequence in her notebook:

12, 36, 108, 324, . . .

Explain a possible rule used to make the sequence. Then find the next three terms.

9. A 2000 survey showed that Internet users spend an average of 8 hours online each week. About how many days do Internet users spend online in 7 weeks?

A $\frac{3}{7}$ day

B $1\frac{1}{3}$ days

C $2\frac{1}{3}$ days

D $7\frac{1}{3}$ days

10. Sue has 30 pens and 48 magnets. She will put them in bags with the same number of each item. What is the greatest number of bags she can make?

> **TIP** **Decide on a plan.** See item 10. List the factors of 30 and the factors of 48. Find the common factors. Then find the GCF, or greatest common factor.

F 3

G 6

H 8

J 12

11. Jim wants to buy 2 pairs of shoes that cost $24.95 each and 4 shirts that cost $14.95 each. Which is the **best** estimate of the amount of money that Jim needs?

A $200.00

B $110.00

C $50.00

D $30.00

12. **Explain It** Tina bought a television on sale at 20% off. The regular price was $250.00. What was the sale price? Explain how you found your answer.

13. The scale on Mr. Anderson's map is 1 inch = 2.5 miles. He is driving between two cities that are 5 inches apart on the map. How far will he drive?

F 2 miles

G 10 miles

H 12.5 miles

J 25 miles

14. What is the area of the triangular sail on the sailboat?

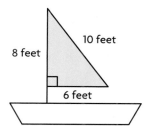

8 feet
10 feet
6 feet

A 16 square feet

B 24 square feet

C 40 square feet

D 48 square feet

15. The Great Pyramid of Khufu in Gaza, Egypt, is one of the Seven Wonders of the Ancient World. It is 150 yards tall. What is the pyramid's height in feet?

F 450 feet

G 300 feet

H 75 feet

J 50 feet

16. **Explain It** Ostrich eggs, the biggest eggs laid by any bird, can have a mass as great as 2.3 kilograms. Explain how to convert 2.3 kilograms to grams.

IT'S IN THE BAG!

Dot-to-Dot Ratios

PROJECT Make ratios to compare quantities.

Materials

- Six colors of dot stickers
- Ratio worksheet
- Construction paper
- Markers
- Glue

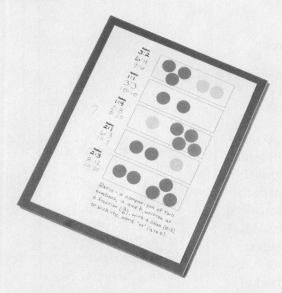

Directions

1. Use the dots to show the ratios written on the worksheet. Use different colors for the two parts of each ratio. For example, if the ratio is 5:1, you can use 5 blue dots for the first number and 1 red dot for the second number. *(Picture A)*

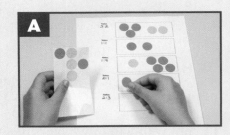

2. Glue the worksheet to the construction paper. Write the definition of the word *ratio* at the bottom of the worksheet. *(Picture B)*

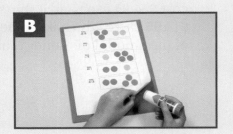

3. Write equivalent ratios for the ratios shown on the worksheet. Write your answers below the appropriate ratios on the worksheet. *(Picture C)*

Challenge Percent of Increase and Decrease

Learn how to find the percent of increase or decrease when given the amount of increase or decrease and the original amount.

The city of Sandville is increasing bus fares. The cost of a monthly bus pass for students will increase from $25 to $26.

Use this formula to find the percent of increase.

$$\% \text{ increase} = \frac{\text{amount of increase}}{\text{original amount}}$$

You divide by the original amount since you are comparing the increase to the original amount.

EXAMPLE 1

Find the percent of increase in a student's bus pass.

$\% \text{ increase} = \frac{\text{amount of increase}}{\text{original amount}}$ *Write the formula.*

$\% \text{ increase} = \frac{26 - 25}{25} = \frac{1}{25}$ *Amount of increase: 26 − 25 = 1*
Original amount: 25

$\% \text{ increase} = 0.04, \text{ or } 4\%$ *Write the fraction as a percent.*

So, the percent of increase is 4%.

Use this formula to find the percent of decrease.

$$\% \text{ decrease} = \frac{\text{amount of decrease}}{\text{original amount}}$$

You divide by the original amount since you are comparing the decrease to the original amount.

EXAMPLE 2

Beth observed that 64 elephants drank from a water hole this week. Last week, 80 elephants drank from the water hole. What is the percent of decrease?

$\% \text{ decrease} = \frac{\text{amount of decrease}}{\text{original amount}}$ *Write the formula.*

$\% \text{ decrease} = \frac{80 - 64}{80} = \frac{16}{80}$ *Amount of decrease:*
80 − 64 = 16
Original amount: 80

$\% \text{ decrease} = 0.20, \text{ or } 20\%$ *Write the fraction as a percent.*

So, the percent of decrease is 20%.

TRY IT

Find the percent of increase or decrease.

1. 30 is increased to 39.

2. 88 is decreased to 66.

3. $72 is increased to $99.

4. 50 is increased to 169.

VOCABULARY

1. A ratio that compares two quantities having different units of measure is a __?__. (p. 532)

2. A fixed percent of the principal, paid yearly, is called __?__. (p. 572)

3. The set of all possible outcomes is called the __?__. (p. 580)

EXAMPLES	EXERCISES

Chapter 24

- **Find the unit rate.** (pp. 532–534)
  Apples cost $2.97 for 3 lb. What is the cost per pound?

  $\frac{\text{cost}}{\text{pounds}} = \frac{\$2.97}{3}$ *Write a ratio to compare cost to pounds.*

  $\frac{2.97 \div 3}{3 \div 3} = \frac{0.99}{1}$ *Find the cost per pound.*

  So, the cost is $0.99 per pound.

Find the unit rate.

4. 480 mi in 6 hr

5. $51.96 for 4 CDs

6. 15 books in 5 months

7. 540 mi on 30 gal

8. $1.80 for a dozen rolls

9. 468 tickets for 3 games

- **Use proportions to solve problems using scale drawings.** (pp. 545–547)

  Find the actual length if the drawing length is 6 cm and the scale is 1 cm:5 m.

  $\frac{\text{drawing (cm)}}{\text{actual (m)}} \rightarrow \frac{6}{n} = \frac{1}{5}$ *Write a proportion. Let n represent the actual length.*

  $6 \times 5 = n \times 1$ *Find the cross products.*
  $n = 30$

  The actual length is 30 m.

Find the unknown dimension.

10. scale: 3 cm:5 mm
    drawing length: 12 cm
    actual length: ■ mm

11. scale: 1 in.:4 ft
    drawing length: 6 in.
    actual length: ■ ft

12. scale: 2 in.:10 ft
    drawing length: ■ in.
    actual length: 5 ft

13. scale: 4 cm:1 mm
    drawing length: ■ cm
    actual length: 12 mm

Chapter 25

- **Convert among percents, decimals, and fractions.** (pp. 558–561)

  Write 0.4 as a percent.

  0.4 = 40%

  Move the decimal point two places to the right.

  Write $\frac{3}{4}$ as a percent.

  $\frac{3}{4} = \frac{75}{100} = 75\%$

  Write an equivalent fraction with a denominator of 100.

Write as a percent.

14. 0.9   15. 0.34   16. 2.5

17. $\frac{4}{5}$ 18. $\frac{1}{200}$ 19. $\frac{5}{8}$

Write as a decimal.

20. 45%   21. $\frac{1}{4}$ 22. 135%

Chapter 26

- **Find the theoretical probability of a simple event.** (pp. 580–583)

  A cube is numbered 1 to 6. What is the probability that you will roll a number greater than 4?

  $$P(event) = \frac{\text{number of favorable outcomes}}{\text{number of possible outcomes}}$$

  $$P(\text{number greater than 4}) = \frac{2}{6} = \frac{1}{3}$$

A bag has 10 red marbles, 5 blue marbles, 6 yellow marbles, and 4 green marbles. Find each probability. Write each answer as a fraction, a decimal, and a percent.

23. P(green)

24. P(blue, yellow, or red)

25. P(white)

- **Make predictions based on experimental probabilities.** (pp. 590–593)

COIN	Heads	Tails
TOSS	15	35

  Based upon the experimental results, how many times would you expect to get heads if you tossed the coin 80 times?

  $$P(heads) = \frac{15}{50} = \frac{3}{10} \qquad \frac{3}{10} \times 80 = 24$$

  You would expect to get heads 24 times.

For 26–27, use the table to find the experimental probability.

26. If you tossed the coin 120 times, how many times would you expect to get tails?

27. If you tossed the coin 30 times, how many heads would you expect to get?

28. A baseball player hit the ball 42 times out of the last 150 times at bat. How many hits can he expect to get during his next 100 times at bat?

Chapter 27

- **Find the number of possible outcomes of a compound event.** (pp. 602–604)

  Find the number of possible outcomes for tossing a coin and selecting card A, B, C, or D.

  Coin: heads or tails—2 choices
  Card: A, B, C, D—4 choices

  $2 \times 4 = 8$; 8 possible outcomes

Find the number of possible outcomes for each situation.

29. picking chocolate or vanilla ice cream and sprinkles, hot fudge, nuts, or whipped cream toppings

30. picking a white, blue, striped, or plaid shirt and black, khaki, or navy pants

---

- **Find the probability of a dependent event.** (pp. 608–611)

  Find the probability of picking an X and then a Y from a bag of 5 cards labeled X, Y, Z, W, Q if you do not replace the card drawn.

  $$P(X) = \frac{1}{5} \qquad P(Y \text{ after } X) = \frac{1}{4}$$

  $$P(X, Y) = \frac{1}{5} \times \frac{1}{4} = \frac{1}{20}$$

Six cards labeled R, E, V, I, E, and W are in a jar. Suppose you pick a card, do not replace it, and then pick a second card. Find the probability of each event.

31. P(R, V)   32. P(W, E)

33. P(V, E)   34. P(E, E)

PROBLEM SOLVING APPLICATION

35. A drawing of a birdhouse has a scale of 1 in. = 4 in. If the height of the birdhouse on the drawing is 8 in., how high is the actual birdhouse? (pp. 545–547)

Performance Assessment

TASK A • Taxing Decision

James and his friends are shopping at the mall. They are browsing at the sporting goods store and are wondering if they could buy any of these items. Then they remember that there is sales tax on each item. Help James and his friends find the total cost of the items plus tax.

The sales tax on the bicycle is $15.

a. Find the rate of sales tax.

b. At the same rate, find the sales tax on the two other items.

c. If all bikes go on sale at 10% off and shoes are 5% off, how much will two bikes and two pairs of shoes cost, sales tax included?

d. Describe how to use your calculator to find the total cost of the bikes and the shoes.

TASK B • A Hairy Exercise

Collect data from the students in your class. Don't forget to include yourself. Copy and complete the table to show the number of students with each hair color.

Hair Color	Number of Students
Black	
Brown	
Red	
Blond	
Other	

a. Calculate the percent of students with each hair color.

b. Make a circle graph to show the results of your survey.

c. Find out how many students there are in your school. How many students would you expect to have each hair color?

Draw Similar Figures

You can use the drawing toolbar of a word processor to draw similar figures.

Draw three similar trapezoids.

- Open the drawing toolbar. Click the *AutoShapes* icon. Highlight *Basic Shapes* and click the trapezoid icon.

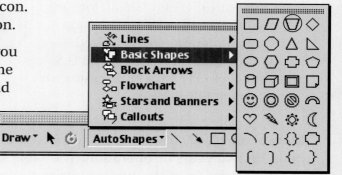

- Move the cursor to the place on the page where you want to draw the first trapezoid. Press and hold the mouse button. Move the cursor until the trapezoid is the size and shape you want.

- To draw similar trapezoids, copy the first trapezoid and paste two more trapezoids beside the original.

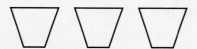

- Select the second trapezoid. On the standard toolbar, click *Format*, then click *AutoShapes*. Click the *Size* tab. Under *Scale*, change the height and width to 150%. Click *OK*.

- Repeat the process for the third trapezoid, but change the height and width to 200%.

Practice and Problem Solving

Use a drawing program to draw each figure. Then draw a similar figure.

1. rectangle
2. acute triangle
3. right triangle
4. obtuse triangle
5. isosceles triangle
6. square
7. rhombus
8. trapezoid
9. scalene triangle
10. pentagon
11. hexagon
12. circle
13. **REASONING** Give an example of a pair of real-life similar figures.

GO ON-LINE **Multimedia Math Glossary** www.harcourtschool.com/mathglossary
Vocabulary Power Look up *surface area* in the Multimedia Math Glossary. Sketch a rectangular prism. Label its dimensions, and explain how to find the surface area.

PROBLEM SOLVING ON LOCATION
In New York City

Ellis Island

From 1892 to 1954, Ellis Island, located in New York harbor, was the first stop for many immigrants to the United States. More than 40 percent of all U.S. citizens alive today have an ancestor who came through Ellis Island.

Where immigrants once entered, New Yorkers and tourists now visit the Ellis Island Museum.

More than 10,700,000 immigrants passed through Ellis Island in its first 40 years of operation. The table shows the number of immigrants from the two countries that sent the greatest number of people through Ellis Island. For 1–4, use the table.

1. About what percent of the immigrants came from Italy?

2. About what percent of the immigrants came from Russia?

3. During this period, about 500,000 immigrants came to Ellis Island from Ireland. Suppose you randomly choose the name of an immigrant from this period. Estimate the probability that the immigrant came from Ireland.

SOME ELLIS ISLAND IMMIGRANTS (1892–1932)	
Country	**Number of Immigrants**
Italy	2,500,000
Russia	1,900,000

4. Find the probability that an immigrant in this 40-year period came from a country other than Italy or Russia.

AVERAGE HIGH/LOW TEMPERATURE (IN °F) FOR NEW YORK CITY												
	Jan	**Feb**	**Mar**	**Apr**	**May**	**Jun**	**Jul**	**Aug**	**Sep**	**Oct**	**Nov**	**Dec**
High	38	42	51	65	74	82	84	84	79	70	48	46
Low	26	26	38	40	49	59	67	66	56	46	37	30

Use Data   For 5–8, use the table above.

5. What percent of the months have an average high temperature greater than 80°F?

6. What percent of the months have an average low temperature less than 70°F?

7. Write the ratio of the number of months with an average high temperature of 65°F or greater to the number of months with an average high temperature less than 65°.

8. Write the ratio of the number of months with an average low temperature of 50°F or less to the total number of months.

The tablet which the Statue holds in her left hand reads (in Roman numerals) "July 4th, 1776."

Statue of Liberty

As immigrants sailed toward New York harbor with dreams of a new life, their first sight in the distance was the Statue of Liberty. A gift from France in 1886, the Statue of Liberty stands directly across from Ellis Island in New York harbor.

1. When you visit the Statue of Liberty, you can climb 22 stories to the crown. In all, you will walk up 354 steps. Find the number of steps per story. Round your answer to the nearest whole number.

2. To get to the Statue of Liberty, you take a 2-mile ferry ride from Battery Park in New York City. If the ferry ride takes 15 minutes, what is your average speed in miles per hour?

3. The Statue of Liberty weighs 450,000 lb. Sixty percent of its weight is steel. How much of the Statue of Liberty's weight is steel?

Use Data   A popular New York City souvenir is a model of the Statue of Liberty. Suppose you made a scale drawing of the statue, using the scale 1 in. = 8 ft, for a school project. For 4–7, use the table.

Statue of Liberty	
Height of base	154 ft
Height of statue	151 ft
Length of hand	$16\frac{1}{2}$ ft
Length of index finger	8 ft

4. Explain what the scale 1 in. = 8 ft means.

5. What would be the length of the index finger in your drawing?

6. What would be the length of the hand in your drawing?

7. How tall would the drawing be from the bottom of the base to the tip of the torch?

28 Algebra: Number Relationships

≡FAST FACT • SCIENCE The elevation of Mount McKinley is 20,320 feet. It is the highest mountain in North America and has one of Earth's steepest vertical rises. With the high altitude, unpredictable weather, and steep, icy slopes, this mountain is a challenge to climb.

PROBLEM SOLVING Climbers are flown into base camp, where they start their climb at 7,200 ft. If a climb takes 20 days, what is the average altitude gained per day?

CLIMBING MOUNT McKINLEY		
Camp	**Altitude**	**Possible Time**
Base Camp	7,200 ft	0 day
Camp 2	9,500 ft	1st day
Camp 3	11,000 ft	3rd day
Camp 4	14,200 ft	10th day
Camp 5	16,200 ft	12th day
High Camp	17,200 ft	15th day
Summit	20,320 ft	20th day

Check What You Know

Use this page to help you review and remember important skills needed for Chapter 28.

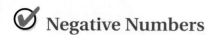 Negative Numbers

Copy the number line. Graph the numbers on the number line.

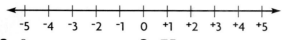

1. 4   **2.** 0   **3.** ⁻5   **4.** ⁻1   **5.** ⁻4

Use the number line to name the number each letter represents.

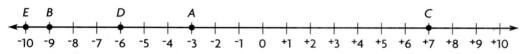

6. *A*   **7.** *B*   **8.** *C*   **9.** *D*   **10.** *E*

 Compare and Order Fractions

Compare. Write <, >, or = for each ●.

11. $9\frac{1}{2}$ ● $9\frac{3}{4}$ **12.** $\frac{2}{3}$ ● $\frac{3}{2}$ **13.** $\frac{3}{4}$ ● $\frac{3}{5}$ **14.** $\frac{16}{2}$ ● $\frac{24}{3}$ **15.** $2\frac{3}{5}$ ● $2\frac{1}{4}$

Order from least to greatest.

16. $\frac{5}{8}, \frac{1}{2}, \frac{1}{3}$ **17.** $1\frac{3}{4}, 2\frac{1}{8}, 1\frac{5}{6}$ **18.** $5\frac{4}{9}, 5\frac{5}{6}, 5\frac{2}{3}$ **19.** $\frac{5}{12}, \frac{1}{4}, \frac{5}{6}$ **20.** $\frac{1}{4}, \frac{7}{8}, \frac{11}{16}$

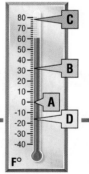

✓ Temperature

Tell the temperature shown by each letter on the thermometer.

21. A   **22.** B   **23.** C   **24.** D

VOCABULARY POWER

REVIEW

negative [neg′ə•tiv] *adjective*

Negative can mean "expressing opposition." In photography, *negative* can mean "having the light and dark parts in opposite order to those of the original photograph." How does this help you understand the relationship between negative and positive numbers?

 www.harcourtschool.com/mathglossary

PREVIEW

integers

opposites

positive integers

negative integers

absolute value

rational number

Venn diagram

Understand Integers

Learn how to identify integers and find absolute value.

New Orleans, Louisiana, is located along the Mississippi River.

Vocabulary

integers
opposites
positive integers
negative integers
absolute value

The mountain Clingmans Dome in Tennessee is 6,643 ft above sea level. New Orleans is 8 ft below sea level. Sea level equals 0 ft. You can use the integers $^{+}6,643$ and $^{-}8$ to represent these elevations.

Integers include all whole numbers and their **opposites**. Each integer has an opposite that is the same distance from 0 but on the opposite side of 0. The opposite of positive 8 ($^{+}8$) is negative 8 ($^{-}8$). The opposite of 0 is 0.

Integers greater than 0 are **positive integers**. Integers less than 0 are **negative integers**. The integer 0 is neither positive nor negative.

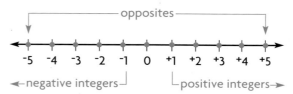

Negative integers are written with a negative sign, $^{-}$.

Positive integers can be written with or without a positive sign, $^{+}$.

EXAMPLE 1

Name an integer to represent the situation.
A. a gain of 12 yd   **B.** 30° below zero   **C.** a deposit of $100
   $^{+}12$ $^{-}30$ $^{+}100$

The **absolute value** of an integer is its distance from 0. Look at $^{+}3$ and $^{-}3$. They are both 3 units from 0.

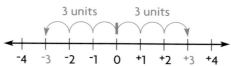

Write: $|^{-}3| = 3$ **Read:** The absolute value of negative three is three.
Write: $|^{+}3| = 3$ **Read:** The absolute value of positive three is three.

EXAMPLE 2

Use the number line to find each absolute value.
A. $|^{-}4|$ **B.** $|^{+}2|$ **C.** $|^{-}1|$ **D.** $|^{+}3|$
   4   2   1   3

CHECK FOR UNDERSTANDING

Think and ▶
Discuss

Look back at the lesson to answer each question.

1. Give an example of a scale in real life in which zero is used together with other integers.

2. Tell what the absolute value of an integer is.

Guided ▶
Practice

Write an integer to represent each situation.

3. 350 ft below sea level

4. an increase of 78 points

5. 14 degrees below zero

Write the opposite integer.

6. ⁻289   **7.** ⁻25   **8.** ⁺315   **9.** ⁺742   **10.** ⁺993

PRACTICE AND PROBLEM SOLVING

Independent ▶
Practice

Write an integer to represent each situation.

11. a $5.00 decline in value   **12.** an increased attendance of 477

13. a gain of 12,000 ft in altitude   **14.** a decrease of 50 points

Write the opposite integer.

15. ⁻2   **16.** ⁻14   **17.** ⁻31   **18.** ⁺88   **19.** ⁺207

Find the absolute value.

20. |⁺390| **21.** |⁻28| **22.** |⁻727| **23.** |⁺660| **24.** |⁺795|

Problem Solving ▶
Applications

25. ▤**FAST FACT** • SCIENCE The elevation of the Dead Sea is about 1,310 ft below sea level. Write the elevation using an integer.

26. *REASONING* What values can n have if $|n| = 5$?

27. Chris has a stack of coins containing 5 quarters, 5 dimes, and 15 nickels. What fraction of the number of coins are quarters? What fraction of the total value of the coins is in quarters?

28. **Vocabulary Power** A definition of *opposite* is "being the other of a pair that are corresponding in position." Describe an object that is in the opposite position of another object.

The Dead Sea

MIXED REVIEW AND TEST PREP

29. Multiply. $\frac{4}{5} \times \frac{3}{4}$ (p. 228)

30. Lisa works for $6.50 an hour, 3 hours a day, 4 days a week. How many weeks will it take her to earn more than $300? (p. 86)

31. Find the value of the expression.
$9 \times (12 - 4) \div 2^3 + 4$ (p. 48)

32. Write the prime factorization of 72. (p.168)

33. **TEST PREP** Jeff has $1,000 to landscape his yard. He plans to spend 35% of it on new trees. Each tree costs $55. How many trees can he buy? (p. 562)

A 6   **B** 7   **C** 8   **D** 9

EXTRA PRACTICE page 638, Set A

Rational Numbers

Learn how to classify rational numbers and find another rational number between two rational numbers.

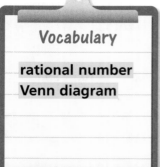

Vocabulary

rational number
Venn diagram

Write as a decimal and as a fraction.

1. eight tenths   2. fifty-four hundredths   3. three tenths
4. nineteen hundredths   5. forty thousandths

A ratio is a comparison of two numbers, a and b, written as a fraction $\frac{a}{b}$. A **rational number** is any number that can be written as a ratio $\frac{a}{b}$, where a and b are integers and $b \neq 0$. The numbers below are all rational numbers since each can be expressed as a ratio $\frac{a}{b}$.

$$3\frac{2}{5} \qquad 0.6 \qquad 42 \qquad {}^-2.5$$

Write each rational number as a ratio $\frac{a}{b}$.

EXAMPLE 1

A. $3\frac{2}{5}$ **B.** 0.6 **C.** 42 **D.** $^-2.5$

$3\frac{2}{5} = \frac{17}{5}$ $0.6 = \frac{6}{10}$ $42 = \frac{42}{1}$ $^-2.5 = \frac{^-5}{2}$

The **Venn diagram** shows how the sets of rational numbers, integers, and whole numbers are related.

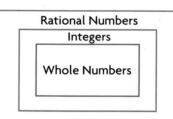

EXAMPLE 2

Use the Venn diagram to determine in which set or sets each number belongs.

A. 80   The number 80 belongs in the sets of whole numbers, integers, and rational numbers.

B. $^-2$ The number $^-2$ belongs in the sets of integers and rational numbers but not in the set of whole numbers.

C. $6\frac{1}{2}$ The number $6\frac{1}{2}$ belongs in the set of rational numbers but not in the set of integers or the set of whole numbers.

D. 7.09   The number 7.09 belongs in the set of rational numbers but not in the set of integers or the set of whole numbers.

• Name two integers that are not also whole numbers.

Christopher is training to run in a 5-km road race. Yesterday he ran $4\frac{1}{4}$ km, and he plans to run $4\frac{1}{2}$ km tomorrow. What distance could he run today if he wants to run between $4\frac{1}{4}$ km and $4\frac{1}{2}$ km?

Think of the distances of Christopher's training runs as rational numbers.

One Way You can use a number line to find numbers between two rational numbers.

EXAMPLE 3

Find a distance between $4\frac{1}{4}$ km and $4\frac{1}{2}$ km, using the number line.

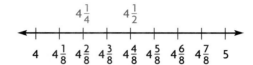

Notice that when the number line is marked in eighths, there is a mark between $4\frac{1}{4}$ and $4\frac{1}{2}$. That could be a distance Christopher could run.

So, Christopher could run $4\frac{3}{8}$ km today.

Another Way You can use a common denominator to find a number between two rational numbers.

EXAMPLE 4

Find a rational number between $4\frac{1}{4}$ and $4\frac{1}{2}$.

$4\frac{1}{4} = 4\frac{2}{8}$ $4\frac{1}{2} = 4\frac{4}{8}$ *Use a common denominator to write equivalent fractions.*

$4\frac{3}{8}$ is between $4\frac{2}{8}$ and $4\frac{4}{8}$.   *Find a rational number between the two numbers.*

So, $4\frac{3}{8}$ is between $4\frac{1}{4}$ and $4\frac{1}{2}$.

You can also find a number between two rational numbers in decimal form.

EXAMPLE 5

Find a rational number between $^-8.4$ and $^-8.5$.

$^-8.4 = {}^-8.40$ *Add a zero to each decimal.*

$^-8.5 = {}^-8.50$

Use a number line marked in hundredths to find a number between the two decimals.

So, $^-8.43$, $^-8.45$, and $^-8.48$ are some of the numbers between $^-8.4$ and $^-8.5$.

Remember that you can add a zero to the right of the digits to the right of the decimal point without changing the value of the decimal.

631

Think and ▶
Discuss

Look back at the lesson to answer each question.

1. **Explain** why every integer is a rational number. Give an example to support your answer.

2. **Tell** what numbers would be between $4\frac{1}{4}$ and $4\frac{1}{2}$ if you divided a number line into sixteenths.

Guided ▶
Practice

Write each rational number in the form $\frac{a}{b}$.

3. $^-0.37$ 4. $2\frac{4}{5}$ 5. 0.889 6. 7.31 7. $^-7\frac{1}{3}$

Use the number line to find a rational number between the two given numbers.

8. 1 and $1\frac{1}{2}$ 9. $^-\frac{3}{4}$ and $^-\frac{1}{4}$ 10. $\frac{1}{2}$ and 1 11. $^-\frac{1}{2}$ and $\frac{1}{2}$

TECHNOLOGY LINK

More Practice:
Harcourt Mega Math
Fraction Action,
Number Line Mine,
Levels U and V

Independent ▶
Practice

Write each rational number in the form $\frac{a}{b}$.

12. $9\frac{2}{3}$ 13. $^-0.71$ 14. 80.4 15. $^-2\frac{5}{8}$ 16. 3.18

Use the number line to find a rational number between the two given numbers.

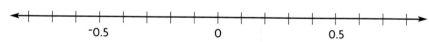

17. $^-0.2$ and $^-0.4$ 18. 0 and 0.2 19. $^-0.6$ and $^-0.8$

Find a rational number between the two given numbers.

20. $\frac{3}{4}$ and $\frac{1}{2}$ 21. $^-7$ and $^-\frac{15}{2}$ 22. 104.1 and $103\frac{7}{8}$

23. 16.1 and 16.01 24. $3\frac{5}{8}$ and $\frac{27}{8}$ 25. $^-\frac{3}{4}$ and $^-\frac{3}{8}$

Tell if the first rational number is between the second and third rational numbers. Write *yes* or *no*.

26. $\frac{1}{3}$; $\frac{1}{2}$ and $\frac{3}{4}$ 27. 0.97; 0.85 and 0.99 28. 3.29; 3.20 and 3.25

29. 3.07; 3.1 and 3.01 30. $^-8$; $^-\frac{29}{4}$ and $^-\frac{33}{4}$ 31. $^-\frac{1}{8}$; $^-\frac{1}{16}$ and $^-\frac{1}{4}$

Problem Solving ▶
Applications

32. Marie had already completed $\frac{1}{2}$ of the running race but had not yet reached the point $\frac{3}{4}$ of the way through the race. Could she have completed $\frac{5}{8}$ of the race? Explain.

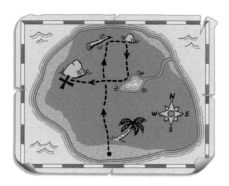

33. Susan follows the directions of a treasure map and walks 45 steps north, then $8\frac{1}{2}$ steps east, 22 steps south, and $14\frac{1}{2}$ steps west. How many steps does Susan walk?

34. Is it easier to find a rational number between $\frac{1}{2}$ and $\frac{3}{4}$ or between 0.50 and 0.75? Explain your reasoning.

35. **(?) What's the Error?** Jeff says that every whole number is an integer and that every integer is a whole number. Explain his error.

MIXED REVIEW AND TEST PREP

36. Find the absolute value. $|^-88|$ (p. 628)

37. Write the decimal and fraction equivalents of 34%. (p. 191)

38. $\frac{2}{5} + \frac{4}{10} + \frac{4}{5}$ (p. 206)

39. **TEST PREP** What is the difference between the means of the data sets 30, 8, 13, 20, and 24, and 17, 22, 29, and 20? (p. 118)

    A 0   **B** 1   **C** 2   **D** 3

40. **TEST PREP** Which triangle has one right angle and no congruent sides? (p. 356)

    F an obtuse scalene triangle   **H** a right isosceles triangle

    G a right scalene triangle   **J** an acute scalene triangle

PROBLEM SOLVING LINKUP to Reading

Strategy • Use Graphic Aids Graphic aids such as Venn diagrams, charts, and tables provide specific or important information in a visual form rather than in text. Sometimes, the information needed to solve a problem may be provided only in a graphic aid.

Look at the Venn diagram to the right. It shows the relationships among whole, prime, and composite numbers.

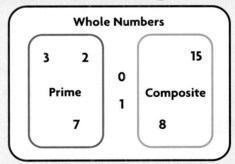

• Is a composite number always, sometimes, or never a whole number?

• Is a whole number always, sometimes, or never a prime number?

Use the Venn diagram to solve the following problems.

1. How would you describe the numbers 7 and 15? Are they whole numbers? Are they prime or composite?

2. Is 1 a whole number? Is it prime or composite? Explain.

EXTRA PRACTICE page 638, Set B

Learn how to compare and order rational numbers.

Compare and Order Rational Numbers

Temperature commonly is measured on a scale in units of degrees. The scale contains both negative and positive numbers, like a number line. For example, the temperature in Death Valley has reached a high of 132°F, and the record low in Alaska is $^-$80°F.

You can use a number line to compare integers. On a number line, each number is greater than any number to its left and less than any number to its right. The number line below shows that $^-$80° < 132° and 132° > $^-$80°.

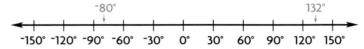

EXAMPLE 1

Compare the integers. Use < and >. Think about their positions on a number line.

A. 2 and $^-$3
   $^-$3 is to the left of 2 on the number line.
   So, $^-$3 < 2, or 2 > $^-$3.

B. $^-$2 and $^-$4
   $^-$2 is to the right of $^-$4 on the number line.
   So, $^-$2 > $^-$4, or $^-$4 < $^-$2.

It is easier to compare and order rational numbers when they are all expressed as decimals or as fractions with a common denominator.

EXAMPLE 2

Order $8\frac{1}{4}$, $^-8\frac{1}{2}$, and 8.3 from least to greatest.

Since $^-8\frac{1}{2}$ is the only negative number, it is the least number.

Compare $8\frac{1}{4}$ and 8.3.

$8\frac{1}{4} = 8.25$ and $8.3 = 8.30$ *Write the numbers as decimals with the same number of decimal places.*

$8.25 < 8.30$, or $8\frac{1}{4} < 8.3$ *Compare by looking at the place values.*

$^-8\frac{1}{2} < 8\frac{1}{4} < 8.3$ *Order the three numbers.*

So, from least to greatest the numbers are $^-8\frac{1}{2}$, $8\frac{1}{4}$, and 8.3.

CHECK FOR UNDERSTANDING

Think and ▶ Discuss

Look back at the lesson to answer each question.

1. **Explain** how you would compare 2.62 and $2\frac{3}{5}$.

2. **Give** an example of a rational number that is greater than ⁻2.5 and one that is less than ⁻2.5.

Guided ▶ Practice

Compare. Write <, >, or = for each ●.

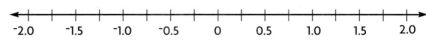

3. ⁻2 ● ⁻1   4. 0.5 ● ⁻1.0   5. $1\frac{1}{4}$ ● 1.5   6. ⁻2 ● ⁻$1\frac{1}{2}$

PRACTICE AND PROBLEM SOLVING

Independent ▶ Practice

Compare. Write <, >, or = for each ●.

7. $\frac{1}{2}$ ● $\frac{3}{4}$ 8. ⁻3 ● ⁻5   9. 0.5 ● $\frac{3}{8}$ 10. ⁻$\frac{1}{4}$ ● 0.25

11. 1.25 ● 1.75   12. ⁻$\frac{1}{4}$ ● ⁻$\frac{1}{3}$ 13. ⁻21 ● ⁻17   14. $\frac{4}{5}$ ● 0.9

15. $3.2 + 4.4$ ● $4\frac{3}{4} + 2\frac{3}{4}$ 16. $2\frac{3}{4} \times 4$ ● $3\frac{1}{4} + 8.5$

Order the rational numbers from least to greatest.

17. 4, ⁻8, ⁻9, ⁻3   18. ⁻$\frac{1}{8}$, ⁻$\frac{1}{2}$, ⁻$\frac{3}{8}$, ⁻$\frac{3}{4}$ 19. ⁻0.2, $\frac{1}{4}$, 0, ⁻$\frac{1}{4}$

Problem Solving ▶ Applications

20. Lynda's times for running a mile are $5\frac{1}{2}$ min, 5.48 min, 5.51 min, and $5\frac{2}{5}$ min. What is the longest she has taken to run a mile?

21. The mean temperatures for three days were ⁻3°, ⁻5°, and 1°. Order the temperatures from highest to lowest.

22. ✎ **Write About It** Explain how you would order three numbers that include a positive fraction, a decimal, and a negative integer.

MIXED REVIEW AND TEST PREP

23. Write an integer to represent 450 ft below sea level. (p. 628)

24. Round 2.0955 to the nearest thousandth. (p. 66)

25. Write $3\frac{3}{7}$ as a fraction. (p. 186)

26. $\frac{7}{8} - \frac{1}{2}$ (p. 206)

⭐ 27. **TEST PREP** The swim team practiced for 8 hours the first week, $1\frac{1}{4}$ times as long the second week, 12 hours the third week, and 6 hours the fourth week. What was the mean weekly practice time? (p. 118)

    A 8   **B** 9   **C** $9\frac{1}{2}$ **D** 10

EXTRA PRACTICE page 638, Set C

PROBLEM SOLVING STRATEGY
Use Logical Reasoning

Learn how to solve problems by using logical reasoning.

Stephen, Leticia, Shelley, and Ed emptied their banks. They found $7.50, $4.35, $5.00, and $10.00, but not necessarily in that order. Leticia has twice as much money as Shelley. Stephen has an amount between Shelley's and Leticia's. Who has $4.35?

Analyze

What are you asked to find?

What information are you given?

Choose

What strategy will you use?

You can *use logical reasoning*.

Solve

How will you solve the problem?

Take the clues one at a time. Use a table to help.

Only one box in each row and column can have a "yes."

	$4.35	$5.00	$7.50	$10.00
Stephen	no	no	yes	no
Leticia	no	no	no	yes
Shelley	no	yes	no	no
Ed	yes	no	no	no

Leticia has twice as much money as Shelley. So, Leticia must have $10.00 and Shelley $5.00. Fill in "yes" in those boxes, and fill in "no" in the rest of the boxes in those rows and columns.

Stephen has an amount between Shelley's and Leticia's. $7.50 is between $5.00 and $10.00, so Stephen must have $7.50. Fill in the rest of the boxes with "yes" and "no."

So, Ed has $4.35.

Check

How can you check your answer?

What if the amounts were $7.50, $4.35, $5.00, and $12.50? How could you change the clues in the problem?

PROBLEM SOLVING PRACTICE

Solve the problems by using logical reasoning.

1. Arthur, Victoria, and Jeffrey are in sixth, seventh, and eighth grades, although not necessarily in that order. Victoria is not in eighth grade. The sixth grader is in chorus with Arthur and in band with Victoria. Which student is in each grade?

2. Use the following information to tell which numbers in the box at the right are *A, B, C, D,* and *E.*

$^-3.5$	$2\frac{1}{2}$
	0.43
4.3	$^-0.43$

   • *A* is greater than *D* and less than *C.*
   • *A* and *D* are opposites.
   • *E* is the greatest number.

For 3–4, use this information.

Amir, Katherine, Patrick, and Lee are comparing their stamp collections. Lee has twice as many stamps as Amir. Patrick has 5 fewer stamps than Katherine. Their collections consist of 15, 20, 25, and 30 stamps.

3. How many stamps does Patrick have?

   A 30   **C** 20
   B 25   **D** 15

4. How many stamps does Katherine have?

   F 30   **H** 20
   G 25   **J** 15

Draw a Diagram or Picture
Make a Model
Predict and Test
Work Backward
Make an Organized List
Find a Pattern
Make a Table or Graph
Solve a Simpler Problem
Write an Equation
▶ **Use Logical Reasoning**

MIXED STRATEGY PRACTICE

5. To earn extra money, Mel makes and sells beanbag toys. He sold 25 beanbag toys at a fair. He sold some for $8 and some for $5 and made a total of $170. How many toys did he sell for $8?

6. The length of a side of square *C* is 8 times the length of a side of square *A.* How many times as great as the area of square *A* is the area of square *C*?

7. A guidebook costs $9.75 in Canadian dollars in a Vancouver, B.C., bookstore. It also has a price of $6.25 in United States dollars. If the exchange rate is $1.60 Canadian dollars for each U.S. dollar, would you rather pay in Canadian or U.S. dollars?

8. Shelters are located at regular intervals along a wilderness trail. The distance from the first shelter to the fourth shelter is 6 mi. What is the distance from the fourth shelter to the ninth shelter?

9. Marco has a garden that is 5 ft wide and 8 ft long. He decides to double the width. What is the difference in area of the gardens?

10. **? What's the Question?** The concession stand made a profit of $250, $327, $423, $196, and $334 for five games during football season. The answer is $306.

Set A (pp. 628–629)

Write an integer to represent each situation.

1. a temperature increase of 5°

2. the wind speed decreases by 12 mph

3. depositing $510 into a savings account

4. a temperature of 7° below zero

Write the opposite integer.

5. $^-3$

6. $^-12$

7. $^+360$

8. $^-1$

9. $^+160$

10. $^-3,047$

11. $^-1,119$

12. $^-942$

Set B (pp. 630–633)

Write each rational number in the form $\frac{a}{b}$.

1. $3\frac{1}{6}$

2. 0.5

3. 0.27

4. 13.4

5. $^-2\frac{2}{5}$

6. 3.18

7. $^-10.02$

8. 300

9. 0.36

10. $5\frac{1}{3}$

11. 312

12. $^-4\frac{1}{4}$

Find a rational number between the two given numbers.

13. $\frac{3}{4}$ and $\frac{5}{6}$

14. $\frac{1}{8}$ and $\frac{1}{4}$

15. $\frac{5}{9}$ and $\frac{11}{15}$

16. 1.8 and 1.9

17. $^-1.5$ and $^-1.3$

18. 4.23 and 4.235

19. 3.8 and 3.82

20. $^-5$ and $^-4.9$

21. $^-12\frac{1}{4}$ and $^-12\frac{1}{3}$

Set C (pp. 634–635)

Compare. Write $<$, $>$, or $=$ for each ●.

1. 0.4 ● 0.38

2. $\frac{2}{7}$ ● 0.25

3. $^-0.6$ ● $\frac{-2}{5}$

4. $^-13$ ● $^-10$

5. 0.28 ● $\frac{2}{7}$

6. $\frac{3}{13}$ ● 0.13

7. $\frac{-4}{9}$ ● $^-3.1$

8. $^-3$ ● 0.31

9. $2\frac{1}{5}$ ● $2\frac{4}{13}$

10. $^-125$ ● $^-130$

11. $\frac{-5}{8}$ ● $\frac{5}{8}$

12. $2\frac{1}{16}$ ● $2\frac{1}{10}$

Order the rational numbers from least to greatest.

13. $\frac{1}{3}, \frac{2}{5}, 0.38, \frac{1}{2}$

14. $\frac{2}{7}, \frac{1}{3}, \frac{1}{4}, 0.26$

15. $0.92, \frac{9}{8}, \frac{8}{9}, 0.924$

16. $0.23, \frac{2}{9}, \frac{1}{4}, \frac{1}{5}$

17. $\frac{-2}{5}, \frac{-1}{3}, \frac{-1}{2}, \frac{-3}{8}$

18. $\frac{1}{10}, ^-3, ^-0.3$

19. $^-7, 6, 1, ^-5$

20. $^-0.1, 0.01, 10, ^-10$

21. $^-12, ^-14, ^-8, 0$

1. **VOCABULARY**   Positive whole numbers, their opposites, and 0 make up the set of ___?___. (p. 628)

2. **VOCABULARY**   The distance an integer is from zero is its ___?___. (p. 628)

3. **VOCABULARY**   A number that can be written as a ratio $\frac{a}{b}$, where a and b are integers and $b \neq 0$, is a(n) ___?___. (p. 630)

Write an integer to represent each situation. (pp. 628–629)

4. an increase of 15 points

5. 6 degrees below zero

6. a loss of 20 pounds

7. a gain of 250 ft in altitude

Write the opposite integer. (pp. 628–629)

8. ⁻32

9. 12

10. ⁻289

11. 0

Find the absolute value. (pp. 628–629)

12. $|^-12|$

13. $|^-4|$

14. $|^+17|$

15. $|^+8|$

Write each rational number in the form $\frac{a}{b}$. (pp. 630–633)

16. 2

17. ⁻0.89

18. $3\frac{2}{3}$

19. 5.4

Find a rational number between the two given numbers. (pp. 630–633)

20. $\frac{1}{4}$ and $\frac{2}{3}$

21. 1.3 and 1.32

22. $3\frac{5}{8}$ and $3\frac{9}{10}$

23. ⁻4.3 and ⁻4.4

Compare. Write <, >, or = for each ●. (pp. 634–635)

24. $7\frac{5}{8}$ ● $7\frac{10}{16}$

25. ⁻3.4 ● ⁻4.3

26. $\frac{-25}{3}$ ● $\frac{-17}{2}$

27. $4\frac{3}{4}$ ● 4.77

Order the rational numbers from greatest to least. (pp. 634–635)

28. 3.7, 3.2, $3\frac{5}{8}$

29. ⁻8, ⁻3, $\frac{-77}{11}$

30. ⁻1.2, 1.2, 0.12

31. $\frac{5}{7}, \frac{9}{14}, \frac{11}{8}$

Solve.

32. Elizabeth, Doria, Emily, and Claudia each earned money doing odd jobs. They earned $4.50, $6.50, $8.00, and $9.00. Doria earned twice as much as Elizabeth. Emily earned $1.50 more than Claudia. How much did each person earn? (pp. 636–637)

33. Louisa, Chris, and Vicki have a dog, a cat, and an iguana, although not necessarily in that order. Each child has one pet. Louisa does not have a cat and Chris does not have a dog. Louisa's pet is a reptile. What pet does each girl have? (pp. 636–637)

★ NUMBER SENSE, CONCEPTS, AND OPERATIONS

1. The lowest point in Louisiana is found in New Orleans. The elevation is 8 feet below sea level. Which point on the number line marks Louisiana's lowest elevation?

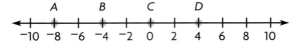

A point A

B point B

C point C

D point D

2. Rebecca saw an advertisement for 33% off the price of a pair of jeans. To help find her savings, she writes 33% as a decimal. Which is 33% written as a decimal?

F 33

H 0.33

G 3.3

J 0.033

3. The table shows the prices of four pieces of furniture in a local furniture store.

FURNITURE PRICES	
Piece	**Price**
Dresser	$350
Nightstand	$175
Chair	$190
Table	$425

Mr. Hitt bought a nightstand and a dresser. He paid 6% sales tax on the furniture. How much was his total bill?

A $493.50

C $540.25

B $525.00

D $556.50

4. Explain It A box contains 8 basketballs. Each ball weighs $1\frac{1}{4}$ pounds. Explain how you can use mental math to find the combined weight of all the basketballs.

★ ALGEBRAIC THINKING

5. Mr. Pearson drives 30 miles to work each day, and 30 miles home. He drives an average of 40 miles per hour. He takes the same time to drive to work as he does to drive home. How long does it take Mr. Pearson to drive to and from work each day?

F 45 minutes

G 1 hour

H 1 hour 15 minutes

J 1 hour 30 minutes

6. After the service club finished collecting newspapers, Jillian said that the club collected more than 500 pounds of newspapers. Which graph represents all the possible amounts of newspapers the service club collected?

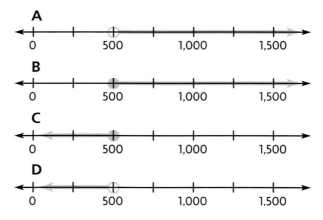

7. Explain It The table shows the population of Bay City for each of the past 4 years.

BAY CITY POPULATION	
Number of Years Ago	**Population**
4	23,812
3	24,201
2	24,605
1	25,008

ESTIMATE Bay City's population this year. Explain your reasoning.

DATA ANALYSIS AND PROBABILITY

8. Tim must spin a number less than 4 using the spinner below in order to win a game. What are the odds that he will succeed?

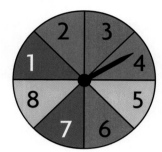

F 3 to 8 **H** 4 to 8

G 3 to 5 **J** 4 to 5

9. Mandy asked friends to suggest names for her new dog. She received these suggestions: Rex, Rover, Fido, Max, Blackie, King, Jet. Mandy wrote the names on a sheet of paper and chose one at random. What is the probability that the name she chose has fewer than 4 letters?

> **TIP** **Look for important words.** See item 9. You are looking for the probability that the name has *fewer than* 4 letters. That means it can have only 1, 2, or 3 letters.

A $\frac{3}{4}$

B $\frac{1}{3}$

C $\frac{5}{7}$

D $\frac{3}{7}$

10. Explain It On his last five math tests, Corey scored 95, 97, 96, 96, and 71. Explain why the mean is not a good measure to represent his last five scores.

GEOMETRY AND SPATIAL SENSE

11. The logo for the Bike Club includes a quadrilateral with four equal sides with the words "Bike Club" inside of it. Which is the **best** description of the quadrilateral in the Bike Club logo?

F parallelogram **H** rectangle

G rhombus **J** trapezoid

12. A wrapping paper design includes the four triangles below.

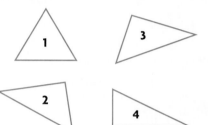

Which triangles appear to be congruent?

A triangle 1 and triangle 2

B triangle 2 and triangle 3

C triangle 3 and triangle 4

D triangle 1 and triangle 4

13. The angles below are complementary. Which is the unknown angle measure?

F 29°

G 61°

H 90°

J 151°

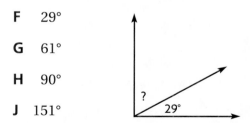

14. Explain It Ellen is planning to build a patio. She is deciding between a patio in the shape of a circle and one in the shape of a polygon. Explain how the shapes are alike and how they are different.

29 Algebra: Operations with Integers

≡FAST FACT • SCIENCE In Antarctica, the sun shines for only six months each year.

PROBLEM SOLVING The graph shows the average high and low temperatures at the South Pole, Antarctica. Which four months have the greatest difference between the average high and average low temperatures? What is the difference?

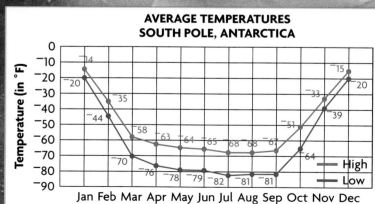

AVERAGE TEMPERATURES SOUTH POLE, ANTARCTICA

Check What You Know

Use this page to help you review and remember important skills needed for Chapter 29.

Understand Integers

Write a positive or negative integer to represent each situation.

1. 14° below zero

2. 62 degrees above zero

3. 10 ft above sea level

4. 13 m below sea level

5. bottom of a well, 50 ft below the surface

6. a gain of 12 yards

7. a bank deposit of $280

8. 3 ft below ground level

Opposites and Absolute Value

Write the opposite integer.

9. $^{+}15$

10. $^{-}8$

11. $^{-}42$

12. $^{+}229$

13. $^{+}99$

14. $^{-}112$

Find the absolute value.

15. $|^{+}12|$

16. $|^{-}19|$

17. $|^{-}43|$

18. $|^{+}728|$

19. $|^{+}88|$

20. $|^{-}65|$

Multiplication and Division Facts

Find the product or the quotient.

21. 4×6

22. 9×7

23. $81 \div 9$

24. $24 \div 3$

25. $120 \div 12$

26. 8×7

27. 12×6

28. $108 \div 9$

29. 3×11

30. $45 \div 9$

31. 7×12

32. $144 \div 12$

Find the value of the variable.

33. $2 \times x = 14$

34. $y \times 5 = 15$

35. $z \div 6 = 9$

36. $88 \div n = 11$

37. $42 = a \times 6$

38. $11 = b \div 12$

39. $9 = 108 \div n$

40. $56 = c \times 7$

VOCABULARY POWER

REVIEW

integer [inˈtə•jər] *noun*

The word *integer* comes from the Latin word *integer* which means "whole." How does this help you understand the meaning of integer?

PREVIEW

additive inverse

 www.harcourtschool.com/mathglossary

Model Addition of Integers

Explore how to use two-color counters to add integers.

You need two-color counters.

Vocabulary

additive inverse

Lin and Nina are playing a board game. To keep track of points, they are using yellow counters to represent positive points, or points gained, and red counters to represent negative points, or points lost.

Activity 1

• Lin earned 6 points during the first round. She earned 3 points during the second round. Use yellow counters to model Lin's total score.

First-round points   Second-round points

$6 + 3 = 9 \leftarrow$ total score

• Nina lost 2 points in the first round. Then she lost 5 points in the second round. Use red counters to model Nina's total score.

First-round points   Second-round points

$^-2 + {}^-5 = {}^-7 \leftarrow$ total score

Think and Discuss

• How is adding the scores like adding whole numbers? How is it different?

• Would changing the order when adding Lin's or Nina's points change their scores? Why or why not?

• How would you model $2 + 7$? $^-2 + {}^-7$?

Practice

Use counters to find the sum.

1. $4 + 9$
2. $^-3 + {}^-7$
3. $^-6 + {}^-4$
4. $5 + 8$

The **additive inverse** of an integer is its opposite. 1 and ⁻1 are the additive inverses of each other. When you add an integer and its additive inverse, the sum is always 0. You can model this using counters.

- Model the sum of 1 and its additive inverse, ⁻1.

 = 0

- Model the sum of 5 and its additive inverse, ⁻5.

 = 0

- During a game, Carmen gained 8 points and then lost 5 points. To find her total score, Carmen paired points gained with points lost. Use yellow and red counters to model Carmen's total score. Remember that pairs of red and yellow counters equal 0.

 $8 + {}^-5 = 3$

- Robert gained 3 points and then lost 7 points. Use yellow and red counters to model Robert's total score.

$3 + {}^-7 = {}^-4$

Think and Discuss

- Why is Carmen's score positive?

- Why is Robert's score negative?

Practice

Use counters to find each sum.

1. $5 + 2$ **2.** $3 + 1$ **3.** ${}^-4 + {}^-5$ **4.** ${}^-3 + {}^-8$

5. $4 + {}^-6$ **6.** ${}^-2 + 6$ **7.** $7 + {}^-7$ **8.** ${}^-3 + 8$

MIXED REVIEW AND TEST PREP

Order the rational numbers from least to greatest. (p. 634)

9. ${}^-6.4, {}^-6.2, {}^-6.8$ **10.** $\frac{1}{3}, \frac{2}{5}, \frac{1}{4}, \frac{3}{5}$ **11.** ${}^-3\frac{4}{7}, {}^-3.6, {}^-3\frac{1}{2}$

12. Evaluate the expression $c + \frac{1}{2}$ for $c = \frac{1}{3}$. (p. 206)

⭐**13. TEST PREP** Which shows the difference $6\frac{5}{6} - 5\frac{3}{4}$? (p. 210)

A $\frac{1}{9}$ **B** $1\frac{1}{12}$ **C** $1\frac{1}{2}$ **D** $1\frac{3}{4}$

Add Integers

Learn how to add integers.

Jeb and Raul made up a game using a number line. Play starts at 0. A spinner is used to show positive moves and negative moves.

Jeb's first spin was ⁻3, and his second spin was ⁻2. What is Jeb's position on the number line?

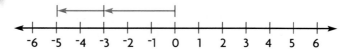

⁻3 + ⁻2 = ⁻5 ← Jeb is at ⁻5.

Remember that you can write a positive number without the ⁺ sign.

⁺7 = 7

Raul's first spin was 4, and his second spin was ⁻9. Where is Raul on the number line?

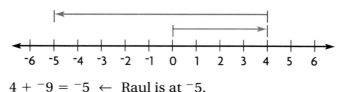

4 + ⁻9 = ⁻5 ← Raul is at ⁻5.

You can use a number line to find the sum of two integers.

EXAMPLE 1

Use a number line to find the sum 4 + ⁻6.

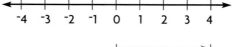

Draw a number line.

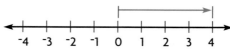

Start at 0. Move 4 units to the right to show 4.

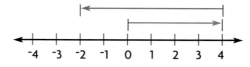

From 4, move 6 units to the left to show ⁻6. This takes you to ⁻2.

So, 4 + ⁻6 = ⁻2.

• When integers are added on a number line, when do the arrows point in the same direction and when do the arrows point in different directions?

Remember that the absolute value of an integer is its distance from 0 on the number line.

When adding integers, you can use their absolute values to find the sum.

> **Adding with the Same Sign**
> When adding integers with like signs, add the absolute values of the integers. Use the sign of the addends for the result.

EXAMPLE 2

Find the sum $^-7 + {}^-2$.

$^-7 + {}^-2$

$|{}^-7| + |{}^-2| = 7 + 2$ *Add the absolute values of the integers.*

$\qquad\qquad = 9$

So, $^-7 + {}^-2 = {}^-9.$ *Use the sign of the original addends.*

> **Adding with Different Signs**
> When adding integers with unlike signs, subtract the lesser absolute value from the greater absolute value. Use the sign of the addend with the greater absolute value for the result.

EXAMPLE 3

A. Find the sum $^-8 + 3$.

$^-8 + 3$

Subtract the lesser absolute value from the greater absolute value.

$|{}^-8| - |3| = 8 - 3$

$\qquad\qquad = 5$

Use the sign of the addend with the greater absolute value.

$|{}^-8| > |3|$ *The sum is negative.*

So, $^-8 + 3 = {}^-5.$

• Find the sum $9 + {}^-12$.

B. Find the sum $^-5 + 9$.

$^-5 + 9$

Subtract the lesser absolute value from the greater absolute value.

$|9| - |{}^-5| = 9 - 5$

$\qquad\qquad = 4$

Use the sign of the addend with the greater absolute value.

$|9| > |{}^-5|$ *The sum is positive.*

So, $^-5 + 9 = 4.$

EXAMPLE 4

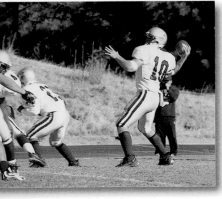

On the first play of a football game, the Cobras gained 21 yards. On the second play, they lost 9 yards. Find the total number of yards gained or lost by the Cobras on the first two plays.

$21 + {}^-9$ *Use 21 for yards gained and $^-9$ for yards lost.*

$|21| - |{}^-9| = 21 - 9 = 12$ *Subtract the lesser absolute value from the greater absolute value.*

$|21| > |{}^-9| \rightarrow 21 + {}^-9 = 12$ *Use the sign of the addend with the greater absolute value.*

So, the Cobras gained a total of 12 yards on the first two plays.

Think and ▶
Discuss

Look back at the lesson to answer each question.

1. **Explain** how you determine the sign of the sum of two integers with the same sign.

2. **Explain** how you determine if the sum of two integers with different signs is positive or negative.

Guided ▶
Practice

Write the addition problem modeled on the number line.

3.

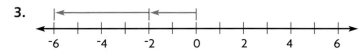

4.

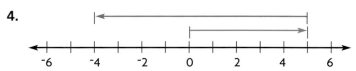

Find the sum.

5. $^-9 + 6$ 6. $^-3 + ^-4$ 7. $^-8 + 2$ 8. $5 + ^-7$

9. $^-3 + 7$ 10. $^-8 + ^-2$ 11. $11 + ^-5$ 12. $6 + ^-6$

Independent ▶
Practice

Write the addition problem modeled on the number line.

13.

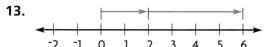

14.

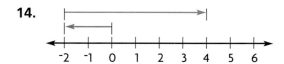

Find the sum.

15. $^-5 + 8$ 16. $2 + ^-3$ 17. $7 + 2$ 18. $^-1 + 4$

19. $8 + 7$ 20. $^-12 + ^-8$ 21. $^-15 + ^-10$ 22. $^-17 + 25$

23. $^-2 + 5$ 24. $^-12 + ^-16$ 25. $^-17 + 5$ 26. $25 + ^-37$

27. $24 + 12$ 28. $30 + ^-41$ 29. $|16| + |^-9|$ 30. $|^-64| + |36|$

Use the Commutative or Associative Property to help find the sum.

31. $17 + 19 + ^-7$ 32. $26 + ^-19 + ^-1$

33. $^-58 + ^-49 + 19$ 34. $^-34 + 9 + ^-16$

ALGEBRA Solve and check.

35. $^-5 + x = ^-7$ 36. $x + ^-6 = ^-13$

37. $x + ^-10 = ^-4$ 38. $^-8 + x = ^-3$

Problem Solving ▶
Applications

39. In the morning the temperature was ⁻6°F. By noon it had risen 11°F. What was the temperature at noon?

40. In the evening the temperature was ⁻9°F. By midnight it had dropped 3°F. What was the temperature at midnight?

41. Tina played a game in which she owned stock worth $33. During the game, the stock increased $11 in value and then decreased $15 in value. Write an addition sentence to find the new value of the stock.

42. On the first three plays of a football game, the Wildcats gained 15 yards, lost 9 yards, and lost 8 yards. Find the total number of yards gained or lost by the Wildcats on the first three plays.

43. **?** **What's the Error?** Ken says that ⁻6 + 2 = 8. What is his error? What is the correct sum?

44. **Geometry** A rectangle with an area of 180 cm² has a length of 15 cm. Find the width.

MIXED REVIEW AND TEST PREP

45. Is ⁻1.5 less than, greater than, or equal to ⁻1$\frac{3}{6}$? (p. 634)

46. Is 8$\frac{3}{5}$ less than, greater than, or equal to 8.5? (p. 634)

47. Is ⁻3.4 less than, greater than, or equal to ⁻3$\frac{1}{5}$? (p. 634)

48. **TEST PREP** Find the quotient 4$\frac{2}{3}$ ÷ 3$\frac{1}{2}$. (p. 236)

A $\frac{3}{4}$ **B** 1$\frac{1}{4}$ **C** 1$\frac{1}{3}$ **D** 1$\frac{1}{2}$

49. **TEST PREP** Find the sum 5$\frac{3}{4}$ + 6$\frac{1}{3}$. (p. 210)

F 11$\frac{1}{12}$ **G** 11$\frac{4}{7}$ **H** 12$\frac{1}{12}$ **J** 12$\frac{11}{12}$

PROBLEM SOLVING   Thinker's Corner

Math Fun • Opposites Distract Remember that every number has an opposite that is the same distance from zero but is on the opposite side on the number line. Use a number line to solve these riddles.

1. I am the opposite of a number between 3$\frac{2}{3}$ and 3$\frac{5}{6}$.

2. I am the first integer that is less than the opposite of a number between 2$\frac{1}{2}$ and 2$\frac{3}{4}$.

3. I am the opposite of a number between ⁻4.3 and ⁻4$\frac{3}{8}$.

4. We are between ⁻2.4 and ⁻2.6. If you add our opposites, you get 5.

5. I am the opposite of the integer between the sum ⁻5 + 2 and the sum ⁻15 + 10.

6. I am the second integer that is less than the sum ⁻22 + ⁻17.

7. I am the opposite of the even integer between the sum 35 + ⁻14 and the sum 12 + 6.

8. I am the integer that is 4 times the sum 42 + ⁻35.

EXTRA PRACTICE page 662, Set A

LESSON 29.3

Model Subtraction of Integers

Explore how to use two-color counters to subtract integers.

You need two-color counters.

You can use red and yellow counters to subtract integers. Subtracting integers is similar to subtracting whole numbers.

Activity 1

• Find $^-9 - ^-4$. First, make a row of 9 red counters.

• Then, take away 4 of them.

 $\rightarrow$ $^-9 - ^-4$

• How many counters are left? What is $^-9 - ^-4$?

Using red and yellow counters, model $^-7 - 5$.

• First, make a row of 7 red counters.

• Recall that a red counter paired with a yellow counter equals 0. Adding a red counter paired with a yellow counter does not change the value of $^-7$. Show another way to model $^-7$ that includes 5 yellow counters.

• Use your model to find $^-7 - 5$. Take away 5 yellow counters.

• What does your model show now? What is $^-7 - 5$?

Now model $7 - ^-2$.

• Model 7. Put down pairs of yellow and red counters until you can take away $^-2$. What is $7 - ^-2$?

Activity 2

Addition and subtraction of integers are related.

- Copy the model for ⁻7 below.

- Use the model to find ⁻7 − ⁻3. What is ⁻7 − ⁻3?

- Model ⁻7 again. Then add three yellow counters to find ⁻7 + 3. What is ⁻7 + 3?

Think and Discuss

- The models above show that ⁻7 − ⁻3 = ⁻7 + 3. How are ⁻3 and 3 related? How are subtraction and addition related?

- How are the two models different?

You can write a subtraction problem as an addition problem by adding the opposite of the number you are subtracting.

$$6 - {}^-2 = 6 + 2 \leftarrow \text{Add the opposite of } {}^-2.$$

- How can you write ⁻6 − 2 as an addition problem?

Practice

Use counters to find the difference.

1. ⁻7 − 4   **2.** ⁻8 − ⁻5   **3.** ⁻13 − 9   **4.** ⁻9 − 4

Complete the addition problem.

5. ⁻6 − ⁻2 = ⁻6 + ▮   **6.** ⁻9 − ⁻3 = ⁻9 + ▮   **7.** ⁻7 − 5 = ⁻7 + ▮   **8.** ⁻19 − 12 = ⁻19 + ▮

MIXED REVIEW AND TEST PREP

Find the sum. (p. 646)

9. ⁻3 + 9   **10.** 2 + ⁻7   **11.** ⁻1 + ⁻7

12. Write an integer to represent 217 m below sea level. (p. 628)

13. TEST PREP   Three friends shared a pizza that had 8 slices. There are $1\frac{1}{2}$ slices left. Alana had $2\frac{1}{2}$ slices, and Jill had $1\frac{1}{2}$ slices. How many slices did George have? (p. 210)

A $5\frac{1}{2}$ **B** 5   **C** 4   **D** $2\frac{1}{2}$

651

Subtract Integers

Learn how to subtract integers.

1. 29 − 24   **2.** 14 + 8
3. 217 − 12   **4.** 97 + 17
5. 365 − 295

During the summer of 1997, NASA landed the Mars Pathfinder on the planet Mars. On July 9, Pathfinder reported a temperature of ⁻1°F. On July 10, Pathfinder reported a temperature of 8°F. Find the range of temperatures reported by Pathfinder from July 9 to July 10.

Pathfinder endured temperatures as low as ⁻89°F.

To find the range of temperatures, you need to find the difference of 8 and ⁻1, or 8 − ⁻1. You can find the difference of two integers by adding the opposite of the integer you are subtracting. You can then use the rules for addition of integers.

The opposite of ⁻1 is 1. So, 8 − ⁻1 becomes 8 + 1.

8 − ⁻1 = 8 + 1 = 9

So, the range of temperatures was 9°F.

EXAMPLE

During an experiment, a scientist recorded a high temperature of ⁻9°C and a low temperature of ⁻22°C. What was the range of temperatures during the experiment?

⁻9 − ⁻22 = ⁻9 + 22   *Write the subtraction problem as an addition problem. Use the rules*
⁻9 + 22   *for addition of integers.*

|22| − |⁻9| = 22 − 9   *Subtract the lesser absolute value from the greater absolute value.*
         = 13

|22| > |⁻9| → ⁻9 − ⁻22 = 13   *Use the sign of the addend with the greater absolute value.*

So, the range of temperatures during the experiment was 13°C.

• During the afternoon, the temperature fell from 7°F to ⁻5°F. What was the range of temperatures?

Think and ▶
Discuss

Look back at the lesson to answer the question.

1. **Tell** how you would write the subtraction problem as an addition problem if the low temperature reached during the experiment in the example was ⁻40°C.

Guided ▶
Practice

Rewrite the subtraction problem as an addition problem.

2. $7 - 10$ 　　　 3. $3 - {}^-6$ 　　　 4. ${}^-1 - {}^-8$ 　　　 5. ${}^-4 - 6$

Find the difference.

6. $4 - 8$ 　　　 7. ${}^-7 - {}^-2$ 　　　 8. $4 - {}^-5$ 　　　 9. $1 - 8$

PRACTICE AND PROBLEM SOLVING

Independent ▶
Practice

Rewrite the subtraction problem as an addition problem.

10. $12 - 15$ 　　 11. $8 - {}^-11$ 　　 12. ${}^-6 - {}^-13$ 　　 13. ${}^-9 - 11$

Find the difference.

14. $6 - 11$ 　　 15. ${}^-9 - {}^-5$ 　　 16. $2 - {}^-1$ 　　 17. ${}^-5 - {}^-5$

18. $8 - {}^-3$ 　　 19. $31 - 37$ 　　 20. $|{}^-43| - |12|$ 　 21. $|{}^-27| - |{}^-32|$

Evaluate.

22. ${}^-3 - {}^-5 + {}^-8$ 　　 23. $6 - {}^-4 + {}^-5$ 　　 24. $8 - {}^-6 - 10$

ALGEBRA Solve and check.

25. $x + 12 = 7$ 　　 26. $y + 9 = {}^-42$ 　　 27. $z + 19 = {}^-57$

Problem Solving ▶
Applications

28. On Friday morning, the temperature was ⁻12°F. By that evening, the temperature had fallen 7°F. The temperature on Saturday morning was 5°F higher than the temperature on Friday evening. What was the temperature on Saturday morning?

29. The water level of a river was 3 ft above normal. After an unusually dry season, the water level is 6 ft below normal. Find the range of the water levels of the river.

30. **(?) What's the Question?** The temperature at noon was 15°F. By midnight the temperature was ⁻3°F. The answer is 18°F.

TECHNOLOGY LINK

More Practice:
Harcourt Mega Math
Fraction Action,
Number Line Mine,
Level W

MIXED REVIEW AND TEST PREP

31. Find the sum ⁻4 + 9. (p. 646)

32. Write the opposite integer for 213. (p. 628)

33. Find the quotient $5\frac{3}{4} \div 2\frac{1}{4}$. (p. 236)

34. Find the prime factorization of 84. (p. 168)

⭐ 35. **TEST PREP** Ty rolls a number cube labeled 1–6. Find P(2 or 4). (p. 580)

　　 A $\frac{2}{3}$ 　　 **B** $\frac{1}{2}$ 　　 **C** $\frac{1}{3}$ 　　 **D** $\frac{1}{6}$

Multiply and Divide Integers

Use red and yellow counters to model multiplication of integers. A red counter represents $^-1$ and a yellow counter represents $^+1$.

Activity 1

You need: two-color counters

- Use yellow counters to model the product 2×3.

      $\leftarrow$ 2 groups of $^+3$

  $2 \times 3 = 6$

- Use red counters to model the product $2 \times {^-3}$.

      $\leftarrow$ 2 groups of $^-3$

  $2 \times {^-3} = {^-6}$

- Use red counters to model the product $^-2 \times 3$. Using the Commutative Property, you can write $^-2 \times 3$ as $3 \times {^-2}$.

       $\leftarrow$ 3 groups of $^-2$

  $^-2 \times 3 = 3 \times {^-2} = {^-6}$

- How could you model the product 3×4?

- How could you model the product $3 \times {^-4}$?

- What do you notice about the product of two positive integers? of a positive integer and a negative integer?

The height of a submarine above the ocean floor is changing $^-30$ m every minute. If the submarine started at the surface of the ocean, how far below the surface is the submarine after 4 min?

Use a number line to find the product $4 \times {^-30}$.

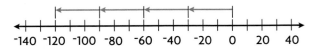

The number line shows that the height of the submarine changed $^-120$ m. So, the submarine is 120 m below the surface.

You can use patterns to find rules to multiply integers.

EXAMPLE 1

Complete the pattern.

$4 \times 3 = 12$
$4 \times 2 = 8$
$4 \times 1 = 4$
$4 \times 0 = 0$
$4 \times {}^-1 = \blacksquare$
$4 \times {}^-2 = \blacksquare$
$4 \times {}^-3 = \blacksquare$

Study the pattern. As the second factor decreases by 1, the product decreases by 4. Use this to complete the pattern.

$4 \times 3 = 12$
$4 \times 2 = 8$
$4 \times 1 = 4$
$4 \times 0 = 0$
$4 \times {}^-1 = {}^-4$
$4 \times {}^-2 = {}^-8$
$4 \times {}^-3 = {}^-12$

So, the missing products are ⁻4, ⁻8, and ⁻12.

• What is the sign of the product of a positive integer and a negative integer?

EXAMPLE 2

Complete the pattern.

${}^-4 \times 3 = {}^-12$
${}^-4 \times 2 = {}^-8$
${}^-4 \times 1 = {}^-4$
${}^-4 \times 0 = 0$
${}^-4 \times {}^-1 = \blacksquare$
${}^-4 \times {}^-2 = \blacksquare$
${}^-4 \times {}^-3 = \blacksquare$

Study the pattern. As the second factor decreases by 1, the product increases by 4. Use this to complete the pattern.

${}^-4 \times 3 = {}^-12$
${}^-4 \times 2 = {}^-8$
${}^-4 \times 1 = {}^-4$
${}^-4 \times 0 = 0$
${}^-4 \times {}^-1 = 4$
${}^-4 \times {}^-2 = 8$
${}^-4 \times {}^-3 = 12$

So, the missing products are 4, 8, and 12.

• What is the sign of the product of two positive integers? two negative integers?

Examples 1 and 2 lead to the rules below.

> The product of two integers with like signs is positive.
> The product of two integers with unlike signs is negative.

Multiplication and division are inverse operations. To solve a division problem, think about the related multiplication problem.

$$42 \div 7 = \blacksquare \quad \rightarrow \quad 7 \times 6 = 42, \text{ so } 42 \div 7 = 6.$$

Use related multiplication problems to determine the sign of the quotient when dividing integers.

$8 \times 3 = 24$, so $24 \div 8 = 3$. ${}^-8 \times {}^-3 = 24$, so $24 \div {}^-8 = {}^-3$.

${}^-8 \times 3 = {}^-24$, so ${}^-24 \div {}^-8 = 3$. $8 \times {}^-3 = {}^-24$, so ${}^-24 \div 8 = {}^-3$.

In the problems above, look at the sign of the quotient of two positive integers and the sign of the quotient of two negative integers. Then look at the sign of the quotient of a positive integer and a negative integer. The rules below apply when dividing integers.

> The quotient of two integers with like signs is positive.
> The quotient of two integers with unlike signs is negative.

EXAMPLE 3

Find the quotient.

A. ⁻84 ÷ ⁻7

⁻84 ÷ ⁻7 = 12

Divide as with whole numbers. The quotient is positive since the integers have like signs.

B. ⁻55 ÷ 11

⁻55 ÷ 11 = ⁻5

Divide as with whole numbers. The quotient is negative since the integers have unlike signs.

• Will the quotient ⁻72 ÷ 8 be positive or negative? Will the quotient ⁻72 ÷ ⁻8 be positive or negative?

EXAMPLE 4

The low temperatures for five days in Fairbanks, Alaska, were ⁻3°F, ⁻8°F, 2°F, 3°F, and ⁻4°F. Find the average low temperature for the five days.

Find the sum. Divide the sum by 5.

⁻3 + ⁻8 + 2 + 3 + ⁻4 = ⁻10

⁻10 ÷ 5 = ⁻2

So, the average low temperature was ⁻2°F.

CHECK FOR UNDERSTANDING

Think and Discuss ▶ Look back at the lesson to answer each question.

1. **Find** the product 5 × ⁻7. Find the product ⁻5 × ⁻7.

2. **Explain** how the rules for the sign of the product of two integers compare with the rules for the sign of the quotient of two integers.

Guided Practice ▶ Find the product or quotient.

3. ⁻9 × 6   **4.** ⁻3 × ⁻4   **5.** ⁻8 × 2   **6.** 8 × ⁻7

7. ⁻21 ÷ 7   **8.** ⁻16 ÷ ⁻2   **9.** 120 ÷ ⁻5   **10.** ⁻132 ÷ 6

PRACTICE AND PROBLEM SOLVING

Independent Practice ▶ Find the product or quotient.

11. ⁻5 × 8   **12.** 2 × ⁻3   **13.** 7 × 2   **14.** ⁻9 × 4

15. 84 ÷ 7   **16.** ⁻72 ÷ ⁻8   **17.** ⁻63 ÷ ⁻7   **18.** ⁻70 ÷ 7

19. 24 × 12   **20.** 30 × ⁻12   **21.** ⁻75 × 4   **22.** ⁻62 × ⁻20

23. 432 ÷ 12   **24.** 255 ÷ ⁻15   **25.** ⁻960 ÷ ⁻12   **26.** ⁻4,978 ÷ 19

TECHNOLOGY LINK

More Practice:
**Harcourt Mega Math
Fraction Action,**
Number Line Mine,
Level X

**Use the Commutative or Associative Property to help
find the product.**

27. $^-5 \times 13 \times ^-2$ **28.** $17 \times ^-50 \times 2$ **29.** $^-4 \times ^-7 \times ^-5$

ALGEBRA **Solve and check.**

30. $^-6x = ^-18$ **31.** $^-10y = 40$ **32.** $^-8z = 32$

33. $\frac{a}{6} = ^-3$ **34.** $\frac{b}{7} = 5$ **35.** $\frac{c}{12} = ^-9$

**Problem Solving ▶
Applications**

36. Drought conditions caused the water level in a lake to change by $^-3$ in. per month in May and June and by $^-4$ in. per month in July and August. Write the change in water level over these four months as a negative number.

37. The low temperatures for the four days of a winter festival were $^-8°F$, $^-6°F$, $^-9°F$, and $^-1°F$. Find the average low temperature for the four days.

38. During the first 6 months of business, a sporting goods store showed its losses as $^-\$3,054$. How would it show the average monthly loss?

39. The height of a submarine above the ocean floor changed $^-630$ ft over a period of 9 minutes. If the submarine descended at a constant rate, what was the change of height per minute?

40. The quotient $^-5 \div 2$ can be written as $^-2$ r$^-1$. Find the quotient $^-10 \div 7$.

41. **(?) What's the Question?** In a division problem, the divisor is $^-250$ and the dividend is 10. The quotient is negative.

42. **Number Sense** Joe picked a number, added 5, multiplied the sum by 3, subtracted 10, and doubled the result. His final result was 28. What number had Joe picked?

MIXED REVIEW AND TEST PREP

43. $16 - ^-6$ (p. 652) **44.** $^-32 + ^-42$ (p. 646) **45.** $5\frac{2}{3} \times 6\frac{3}{4}$ (p. 232)

46. TEST PREP Evaluate $2k$ for $k = 9.6$. (p. 94)

    A 19.2 **B** 11.6 **C** 7.6 **D** 4.8

47. TEST PREP Write the fraction $\frac{5}{8}$ as a percent. (p. 191)

    F 0.625% **G** 6.25% **H** 62.5% **J** 625%

EXTRA PRACTICE page 662, Set C

Explore Operations with Rational Numbers

Learn how to add, subtract, multiply, and divide with rational numbers.

QUICK REVIEW

1. $2 \times {}^-5$ 2. ${}^-7 \times {}^-3$

3. ${}^-4 \times 9$ 4. $18 \div {}^-6$

5. ${}^-24 \div {}^-8$

When you add, subtract, multiply, and divide rational numbers, use the same rules for determining signs as you use with integers.

LOW TIDES				
DATE	**A.M.**	**Feet**	**P.M.**	**Feet**
Dec. 7	6:41	2.6	7:35	⁻0.4
Dec. 8	7:19	3.1	8:09	⁻0.4
Dec. 9	7:56	3.3	8:43	⁻0.3
Dec. 10	8:32	3.4	9:15	⁻0.1
Dec. 11	9:10	3.5	9:47	0.1
Dec. 12	9:51	3.6	10:22	0.3
Dec. 13	10:37	3.6	11:01	0.6

EXAMPLE 1

Ocean tides are caused by the gravitational pull of the moon and the sun. On most days there are two high tides and two low tides. The table above shows the heights of the low tides, in feet, for one week in Astoria, Oregon. What is the range of the heights of the low tides?

The highest low tide measures 3.6 ft. The lowest measures ⁻0.4 ft.

$3.6 - {}^-0.4 = 3.6 + 0.4$ *Write the subtraction problem as an addition problem.*

$\qquad = |3.6| + |0.4|$ *Add the absolute values of the integers.*

$\qquad = 3.6 + 0.4$

$\qquad = 4.0$

So, the range of the heights of the low tides is 4.0 ft.

• The P.M. low tide on December 1 was 2.5 ft higher than the P.M. low tide on December 9. How high was the P.M. low tide on December 1?

EXAMPLE 2

Find the product. ${}^-3\frac{1}{2} \times {}^-4$

${}^-3\frac{1}{2} \times {}^-4 = \frac{{}^-7}{2} \times \frac{{}^-4}{1}$ *Write the mixed number as a fraction.*

$\qquad = \frac{28}{2}$ *Multiply. The fractions have like signs, so the product is positive.*

$\qquad = 14$ *Simplify.*

So, ${}^-3\frac{1}{2} \times {}^-4 = 14$.

EXAMPLE 3

As the tide went out, the water level dropped $15\frac{1}{2}$ in. in $2\frac{1}{2}$ hours. What was the average change in the water level per hour? Estimate to check that your answer is reasonable.

Find $^-15\frac{1}{2} \div 2\frac{1}{2}$.

Estimate. $^-16 \div 2 = ^-8$

$^-15\frac{1}{2} \div 2\frac{1}{2} = \frac{^-31}{2} \times \frac{2}{5}$ *Multiply by the reciprocal of the divisor. The numbers have unlike signs, so the product is negative.*

$\qquad = \frac{^-31}{5}$ *Simplify.*

$\qquad = ^-6\frac{1}{5}$ *Write the quotient as a mixed number.*

$^-6\frac{1}{5}$ is close to the estimate of $^-8$. The quotient is reasonable.

So, the average change in the water level was $^-6\frac{1}{5}$ in. per hour.

EXAMPLE 4

Remember the order of operations.

1. Operate inside parentheses.
2. Clear exponents.
3. Multiply and divide from left to right.
4. Add and subtract from left to right.

At 4 A.M. the air temperature was $^-5.2°F$. For the next 3 hours, the temperature fell 1.5° per hour. Then the sun came up and the temperature rose 4.6°. What was the final temperature?

Write an expression to find the change in temperature.

$^-5.2 + (3 \times ^-1.5) + 4.6$ *Operate inside parentheses.*

$^-5.2 + ^-4.5 + 4.6$ *Add from left to right.*

$^-9.7 + 4.6$

$^-5.1$

So, the final temperature was $^-5.1°F$.

CHECK FOR UNDERSTANDING

Think and Discuss ▶ **Look back at the lesson to answer each question.**

1. **Compare and contrast** multiplication of a positive decimal and a negative decimal with multiplication of a positive fraction and a negative fraction.

2. **Tell** if the order of operations process changes depending upon whether you are operating on positive or negative numbers. Give an example to illustrate your answer.

Find the sum or difference. Estimate to check.

3. $^-3\frac{4}{5} + 4\frac{1}{2}$ **4.** $7\frac{3}{4} - 8\frac{1}{2}$ **5.** $2.5 + ^-3.2$ **6.** $2.4 - ^-1.5$

7. $9\frac{2}{5} - ^-3\frac{4}{5}$ **8.** $\frac{1}{2} + ^-3\frac{1}{2}$ **9.** $^-3.9 - 4.1$ **10.** $^-10 + 8\frac{2}{3}$

Find the product or quotient. Estimate to check.

11. $^-4.5 \times 2.4$ **12.** $^-6 \div ^-1\frac{1}{2}$ **13.** $3.8 \div 0.2$ **14.** $\frac{4}{5} \times ^-2\frac{1}{2}$

15. $4.9 \div 1.4$ **16.** $^-\frac{1}{2} \times ^-6$ **17.** $1\frac{1}{4} \times ^-1\frac{3}{5}$ **18.** $^-4\frac{1}{2} \div \frac{1}{2}$

PRACTICE AND PROBLEM SOLVING

Find the sum or difference. Estimate to check.

19. $^-2.5 - ^-1.5$ **20.** $^-1.5 + 5.8$ **21.** $^-5\frac{1}{2} - 3\frac{3}{4}$

22. $6.5 + 0.9$ **23.** $3\frac{1}{2} + ^-7$ **24.** $10\frac{1}{2} - ^-12\frac{1}{2}$

25. $^-27.6 - ^-43.2$ **26.** $^-15\frac{1}{2} + ^-22$ **27.** $^-34.6 + ^-52.8$

Find the product or quotient. Estimate to check.

28. $\frac{3}{5} \times \frac{5}{6}$ **29.** $6.8 \div ^-0.4$ **30.** $^-1.4 \times ^-20$

31. $^-7\frac{1}{2} \div \frac{5}{8}$ **32.** $0.6 \times ^-2.5$ **33.** $^-\frac{2}{3} \div ^-3$

34. $8.8 \div 0.2$ **35.** $^-8 \div \frac{1}{6}$ **36.** $16\frac{2}{3} \times \frac{2}{5}$

Evaluate the expression.

37. $6.4 + 17.1 \div ^-3$ **38.** $\left(^-\frac{1}{2}\right)^2 - \left(^-3\frac{1}{2} + 2\right)$

39. $(3.6 - 5.4) \div (^-2.5 + 3.7)$ **40.** $^-7 - ^-5 - (^-3 \times ^-1)$

41. $8 \times ^-1.5 \div \left(^-\frac{2}{3} + \frac{1}{6}\right)$ **42.** $\frac{2}{3} + \frac{8}{9} \div ^-\frac{2}{3} + 1$

43. $4.4 \div (3.8 - 6) \div ^-0.5$ **44.** $\left(^-\frac{1}{2} + \frac{1}{3}\right)^2 \times ^-72$

ALGEBRA **Evaluate the expression for the given value of the variable.**

45. $x - 8.1$ for $x = ^-2.4$ **46.** $y + \frac{2}{3}$ for $y = ^-\frac{11}{12}$

47. $^-8z + 2\frac{1}{2}$ for $z = \frac{3}{4}$ **48.** $12 + (a - 1.2)$ for $a = ^-6.7$

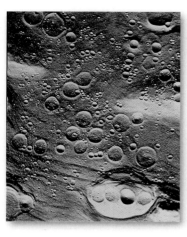

49. ≡**FAST FACT** • SCIENCE   The daytime temperature on the moon can reach 265.9°F. At night the temperature can fall to ⁻291.5°F. Find the difference between the daytime and nighttime temperatures.

50. In a football game, Sean gained $4\frac{1}{2}$ yd on one play, lost 8 yd on the next play, and gained $6\frac{1}{2}$ yd on the third play. What was his total gain?

51. Ellen had $5\frac{1}{2}$ lb of flour. She used $3\frac{1}{4}$ lb and gave half of what was left to Ruben. How much flour did she give to Ruben?

52. **Vocabulary Power**   The word *rational* begins with "ratio." Rational and ratio have the same origin. How does the meaning of ratio help you understand the meaning of rational number?

53. *REASONING*   For what values of *a* will $^-2 \times (a - 3)$ be positive? Explain.

MIXED REVIEW AND TEST PREP

54. Find the sum. $^-15 + 9$ (p. 646)

55. Write the percent for 0.085. (p. 68)

56. Evaluate the expression $3n - 8$ for $n = 25$. (p. 260)

57. **TEST PREP**   Mr. Tilson works 40 hours per week. One year he worked 50 weeks and earned $24,000. How much did he earn per hour? (p. 24)

   A $10.00   **B** $11.00   **C** $11.50   **D** $12.00

58. **TEST PREP**   Ari's test scores were 88, 79, 74, 79, and 90. What is the median of his scores? (p. 118)

   F 16   **G** 74   **H** 79   **J** 82

PROBLEM SOLVING   LiNKUP to Careers

Veterinarian   A veterinarian is a doctor who treats animals. Even though a veterinarian spends most of his or her time tending to patients, there is also some mathematics to be done. For example, after a dog undergoes surgery, it may need medication. The amount to give depends on the weight of the dog. Too much medicine could harm the dog. Figuring out the right amount of medicine requires mathematics.

• A certain medication is given at a rate of 0.2 mg per pound daily. Georgia's dog Barkum is undergoing surgery. Barkum weighs $30\frac{1}{2}$ lb. If needed, how much medicine should Barkum receive daily?

Set A (pp. 646–649)

Find the sum.

1. $^-3 + 9$ 2. $1 + {^-5}$ 3. $5 + 4$ 4. $^-2 + 8$

5. $^-9 + 17$ 6. $^-14 + {^-8}$ 7. $^-19 + 8$ 8. $22 + {^-36}$

9. $31 + 19$ 10. $32 + {^-45}$ 11. $63 + {^-47}$ 12. $^-71 + 32$

13. At 9:00 A.M., the temperature outside was $^-9°$C. By 3:00 P.M., the temperature had risen 5°C. What was the temperature at 3:00 P.M.?

Set B (pp. 652–653)

Find the difference.

1. $2 - 9$ 2. $^-8 - {^-3}$ 3. $4 - {^-2}$ 4. $4 - 9$

5. $8 - 19$ 6. $14 - {^-2}$ 7. $^-12 - {^-12}$ 8. $3 - 7$

9. $23 - 32$ 10. $14 - 29$ 11. $^-48 - 17$ 12. $^-24 - {^-39}$

13. The water level in the city water tower was 8 ft above normal. Three weeks later, the level was 4 ft below normal. Find the range of the water levels.

Set C (pp. 654–657)

Find the product or quotient.

1. $^-7 \times 6$ 2. $^-6 \times {^-8}$ 3. $^-20 \times 4$ 4. $50 \times {^-8}$

5. 32×10 6. $40 \times {^-9}$ 7. $^-27 \div 9$ 8. $^-64 \div {^-8}$

9. $^-140 \div 10$ 10. $225 \div {^-25}$ 11. $360 \div 15$ 12. $216 \div {^-12}$

13. The depth of a diver changed $^-5$ ft every 30 sec. How much of a depth change did the diver have after 2 min?

Set D (pp. 658–661)

Find the sum or difference.

1. $3.8 + 0.7$ 2. $8\frac{1}{2} - {^-17\frac{1}{2}}$ 3. $^-4.5 - {^-2.5}$ 4. $^-8.5 + 1.8$

5. $^-7\frac{1}{2} - 4\frac{3}{4}$ 6. $2\frac{1}{2} + {^-8}$ 7. $^-4.9 - 4.1$ 8. $^-17\frac{1}{2} + {^-34}$

Find the product or quotient.

9. $^-8 \div {^-2\frac{1}{2}}$ 10. $^-2.6 \times {^-20}$ 11. $7.7 \div 0.1$ 12. $\frac{4}{7} \times \frac{7}{8}$

13. $0.5 \times {^-2.6}$ 14. $85 \div {^-17}$ 15. $3\frac{1}{4} \times {^-1\frac{3}{5}}$ 16. $\frac{^-3}{4} \div {^-4}$

1. **VOCABULARY**   The opposite of an integer is its ___?___ . (p. 645)

Write the addition problem modeled on each number line. (pp. 646-649)

2.

3.

Find the sum. (pp. 646–649, 658–661)

4. $7 + {}^-6$

5. ${}^-5 + {}^-3$

6. ${}^-7 + 4$

7. ${}^-37 + 24$

8. ${}^-17 + {}^-41$

9. $6\frac{1}{2} + {}^-2\frac{1}{4}$

10. ${}^-2\frac{4}{5} + 1\frac{1}{5}$

11. ${}^-9.7 + {}^-1.3$

Find the difference. (pp. 652–653, 658–661)

12. $7 - 11$

13. $4 - {}^-4$

14. ${}^-1 - 4$

15. ${}^-6 - {}^-8$

16. ${}^-41 - 18$

17. ${}^-2\frac{1}{8} - 5\frac{1}{4}$

18. ${}^-16.2 - {}^-5.9$

19. ${}^-36.4 - {}^-25.1$

Find the product or quotient. (pp. 654–657, 658–661)

20. ${}^-9 \times {}^-5$

21. ${}^-12 \times 5$

22. ${}^-36 \div {}^-6$

23. $144 \div {}^-12$

24. $\frac{1}{3} \times {}^-\frac{1}{8}$

25. ${}^-4\frac{1}{2} \div \frac{1}{2}$

26. ${}^-9.6 \div 0.4$

27. ${}^-2.1 \times {}^-20$

Solve.

28. A submarine started one leg of its voyage at ${}^-300$ ft. At the end of that leg of the voyage, it was at ${}^-1{,}250$ ft. What was the difference between the two depths? (pp. 652–653)

29. Tasha needed to find the average temperature during three days in the winter. Her first step was to add the temperatures together. If the temperatures were ${}^-6°$, ${}^-8°$, and $11°$, what was the sum? (pp. 646–649)

30. At midnight the temperature was ${}^-15°$F. The temperature continued to fall until 7:00 A.M., when it was ${}^-22°$F. How many degrees had the temperature fallen during the seven hours? (pp. 652–653)

31. During the last glacial age, sea level in one body of water changed by an average of ${}^-3$ feet every 200 years. The glacial age lasted 10,000 years. What was the total change in sea level? (pp. 654–657)

32. During the first nine months of the year, a worldwide club showed its total loss of members as ${}^-2{,}718$. What integer shows the average loss of members per month? (pp. 654–657)

33. During a football game, the Mustangs lost 12 yd on the first play, lost another $7\frac{1}{2}$ yd on the next play, and gained $14\frac{1}{2}$ yd on the third play. What was the total number of yards lost or gained on the three plays? (pp. 658–661)

★ MEASUREMENT

1. A blue tablecloth and a red tablecloth are shaped like circles. The blue tablecloth has a diameter of 80 inches. The red tablecloth has a diameter 40 inches greater than that of the blue tablecloth. How much greater is the area of the red tablecloth than the area of the blue tablecloth?

> **TIP** **Get the information you need.** See item 1. Sketch the two tablecloths. Write what you know on the sketches. Find the diameters and radii of the tablecloths.

A 5,024 square inches

B 6,280 square inches

C 11,304 square inches

D 16,328 square inches

2. The table shows the capacities of some containers.

CAPACITY OF CONTAINERS	
Container	**Capacity**
Bowl	2.5 pints
Glass	20 ounces
Bottle	1 quart
Saucepan	3 cups

Which container holds the most liquid?

F bowl   **H** bottle

G glass   **J** saucepan

3. Explain It Kim drew a map of the three towns of Anderson, Baxter, and Central City and joined them with three line segments. She told her brother that the triangle that was formed contained one acute angle, one right angle, and one obtuse angle. Was she right? Explain why or why not.

★ ALGEBRAIC THINKING

4. The table below shows the relationship between the number of dictionaries, x, in a box, and the weight of the box, y, in pounds.

x	3	5	7	9
y	10	16	22	28

Which equation describes the relationship shown in the table?

A $y = x + 7$ **C** $y = 3x$

B $y = x + 11$ **D** $y = 3x + 1$

5. The diagram below shows different weights on a balance scale.

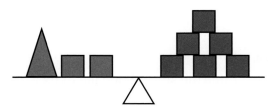

Each of the squares has the same weight. How many squares does it take to equal the weight of one triangle?

F 8

G 6

H 5

J 4

6. Explain It A scientist counts the number of bacteria in a Petri dish. She records her findings in a table.

POPULATION OF BACTERIA				
Time	4 P.M.	5 P.M.	6 P.M.	7 P.M.
Number	6	12	24	48

Predict the number of bacteria that will be in the dish at 8 P.M. Explain your answer.

DATA ANALYSIS AND PROBABILITY

7. The pictograph shows the results of the election for Student Council President.

ELECTION RESULTS	
Candidate	**Number of Votes**
P. Matthews	★★★★★★⸜
L. Martin	★★★★★⸜
W. Ruiz	★★★★★★★⸜
R. Washington	★★★★★★

Key: ★ = 6 votes

Last year the winning candidate received 51 votes. How many more votes did last year's winning candidate receive than this year's winning candidate?

A 6   **C** 15

B 12   **D** 38

8. Meg is playing a game that uses one of the spinners shown below. On the game spinner, the odds are 3:1 in favor of landing on a number between 10 and 20. Which is the game spinner?

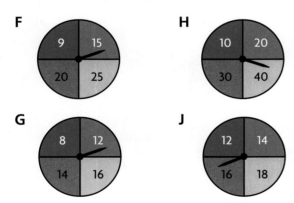

9. Explain It Paula is playing a game with a number cube numbered 1 to 6. She calculated that the probability she will win the game on her next roll is $\frac{1}{3}$. How many of the numbers on the cube will win the game for her? Explain your reasoning.

GEOMETRY AND SPATIAL SENSE

10. Which two nations have flags with exactly two lines of symmetry?

Japan   **Chile**

Jamaica   **Finland**

A Japan and Chile

B Jamaica and Japan

C Chile and Finland

D Finland and Jamaica

11. Jess used his woodworking tools to make a solid figure. The views of the figure are shown below.

    front   side   top

Which is the name of the figure?

F cone

G rectangular prism

H triangular pyramid

J square pyramid

12. Explain It Jason wants to use a tessellating shape to design a mural. Sketch a shape he can use. Explain what it means to say that a shape tessellates the plane.

CHAPTER 30

Algebra: Graph Relationships

≡FAST FACT • GEOGRAPHY Florida is the only state on the east coast of the United States that extends across two time zones. A plane could take off from one airport in Florida and land at another airport in Florida in a different time zone.

PROBLEM SOLVING East-west lines of latitude and north-south lines of longitude form a coordinate grid system on many maps. Suppose a plane to Pensacola departs from Miami, which has the approximate coordinates (26°N,80°W). What are the approximate coordinates of Pensacola?

Check What You Know

Use this page to help you review and remember important skills needed for Chapter 30.

☑ Ordered Pairs

Write the ordered pair for each point.

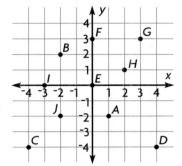

1. point A

2. point B

3. point D

4. point E

5. point G

6. point H

7. point C

8. point F

9. point I

10. point J

☑ Transformations

Identify the transformation as a reflection, rotation, or translation.

11.

12.

13.

14.

15.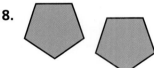

16.

17.

18.

19.

VOCABULARY POWER

REVIEW

equation [i•kwā′zhən] *noun*

An equation is a statement showing that two quantities are equal. The equation $9 + x = 54$ involves addition. Write an equation that involves multiplication.

 www.harcourtschool.com/mathglossary

PREVIEW

coordinate plane

x-axis

y-axis

axes

quadrant

origin

ordered pair

Graph on the Coordinate Plane

Learn how to use an ordered pair to describe a location on the coordinate plane.

Identify the number named by the point on the number line.

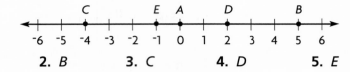

1. *A*   2. *B*   3. *C*   4. *D*   5. *E*

Vocabulary

coordinate plane

***x*-axis**

***y*-axis**

axes

quadrants

origin

ordered pair

Points on a map are often located using pairs of coordinates. On the map grid shown, the town of Dexter is located at point (3,*E*). The coordinates of the location are 3 and *E*.

Use the same method to locate points on a **coordinate plane** like the one below.

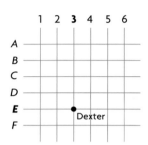

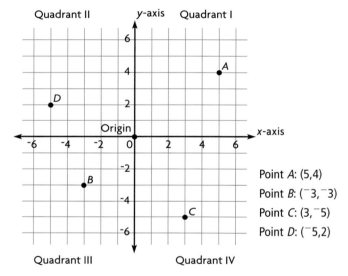

Point *A*: (5,4)

Point *B*: (⁻3,⁻3)

Point *C*: (3,⁻5)

Point *D*: (⁻5,2)

The coordinate plane is divided by a horizontal number line called the ***x*-axis** and a vertical number line called the ***y*-axis**. The two **axes** divide the plane into 4 pieces called **quadrants**. The point (0,0), where the axes intersect, is called the **origin**.

Math **I**dea ▶ Using an **ordered pair** of coordinates like (5,⁻2), you can locate any point on the coordinate plane. The first number of an ordered pair tells you how far to move right or left from the origin. The second number tells you how far to move up or down.

On the coordinate plane above, the coordinates of point *A* are (5,4), of point *B* are (⁻3,⁻3), of point *C* are (3,⁻5), and of point *D* are (⁻5,2). A point may be located at the origin, on the *x*-axis or *y*-axis, or in one of the four quadrants.

EXAMPLE 1

Describe how to locate the point represented by the ordered pair (6, ⁻5) on the coordinate plane.

From the origin, move 6 units to the right, since the 6 is positive. Then move 5 units down, since the 5 is negative.

- Is the point (3,4) the same as the point (4,3)? Explain.

EXAMPLE 2

Name the ordered pair and the quadrant where each point on the coordinate plane below is located.

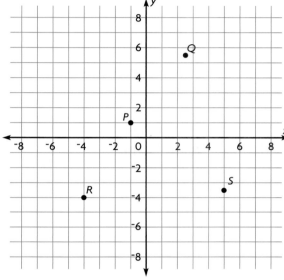

To find the ordered pair, first move right or left from the origin. Then move up or down.

Point P is located at (⁻1,1), in Quadrant II.

Point Q is located at about $(2\frac{1}{2}, 5\frac{1}{2})$, in Quadrant I.

Point R is located at (⁻4,⁻4), in Quadrant III.

Point S is located at about (5,⁻3.5), in Quadrant IV.

- Where would you find the point (0,6) on the coordinate plane? Where would you find (⁻5,0)?

You can use what you know about ordered pairs to plot points on a coordinate plane.

EXAMPLE 3

Sketch a coordinate plane, and plot the points A(4.5,2) and B(⁻3,3).

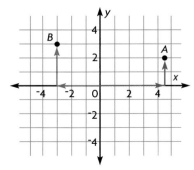

To locate point A, start at the origin and move 4.5 units to the right and 2 units up.

To locate point B, start at the origin and move 3 units to the left and 3 units up.

Think and ▶
Discuss

Look back at the lesson to answer each question.

1. **Explain** how the point (5,4) is different from the point (⁻5,⁻4).

2. **Decide** in which quadrant a point with two negative coordinates would appear. Explain your answer.

Guided ▶
Practice

Write the ordered pair for each point on the coordinate plane.

3. point *A*   4. point *B*

5. point *C*   6. point *D*

7. point *E*   8. point *F*

9. point *G*   10. point *H*

11. point *I*   12. point *J*

Use the coordinate plane at the right. Identify the points located in the given quadrant.

13. I   14. II

15. III   16. IV

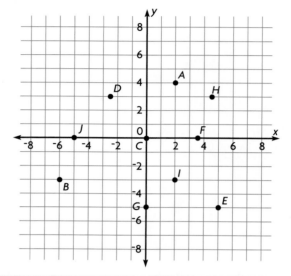

Independent ▶
Practice

Write the ordered pair for each point on the coordinate plane.

17. point *A*   18. point *B*

19. point *C*   20. point *D*

21. point *E*   22. point *F*

23. point *G*   24. point *H*

25. point *I*   26. point *J*

27. point *K*   28. point *L*

TECHNOLOGY LINK

More Practice:
Harcourt Mega Math
The Number Games,
ArachnaGraph, Level H

Use the coordinate plane at the right. Identify the points located in the given quadrant.

29. I   30. II

31. III   32. IV

Sketch and label a coordinate plane, and plot the points.

33. *F*(⁻7,3)   34. *L*(⁻4,6)   35. *Y*(⁻1,3)   36. *A*(⁻4,⁻4)

37. *K*(⁻2.5,⁻6)   38. *I*(0,⁻7)   39. *T*$\left(2\frac{1}{2}, -6\frac{1}{2}\right)$ 40. *E*(6,⁻3)

Problem Solving ▶
Applications

41. Geometry Locate and connect the points (5,5), (5,⁻3), and (⁻2,⁻3) on a coordinate plane. What kind of geometric figure do you have? What is the area of the figure?

42. Geometry Locate the points (2,3), (2,⁻3), and (⁻4,3) on a coordinate plane. What ordered pair tells the location of the fourth point that would make the figure a square? What is the area of the square? What is the perimeter?

43. Vocabulary Power We say a steep cliff is nearly vertical. Compare that use of vertical with the idea of a vertical axis in the coordinate plane.

44. ✎ **Write About It** What do all of the points in Quadrant II have in common? What do all of the points in Quadrant III have in common?

MIXED REVIEW AND TEST PREP

45. Solve. $5 + y \geq 18$ (p. 300)

46. A field is 249 ft long. Write the field's length in yards. (p. 420)

47. Find the circumference of a circle with radius 25 cm. Use 3.14 for π. (p. 448)

48. TEST PREP How much more is the sum of $6\frac{1}{2}$ and $3\frac{4}{5}$ than the sum of $2\frac{3}{4}$ and $3\frac{1}{5}$? (p. 210)

A $10\frac{3}{10}$ **B** $5\frac{19}{20}$ **C** $5\frac{13}{20}$ **D** $4\frac{7}{20}$

49. TEST PREP Which figure is a reflection of the figure at the right? (p. 394)

 F   **G**   **H**   **J**

PROBLEM SOLVING LiNKUP to Science

Astronomy Astronomers locate stars in the sky by using a coordinate grid system. Movements to the left and right are measured in hours (h). Movements up and down are measured in degrees (°).

Use the sky map of the Boötes constellation at the right.

1. Name the location of Arcturus, the brightest star in the constellation.

2. Give the letter of the star located at about $(14\frac{1}{2}$ h, 38°).

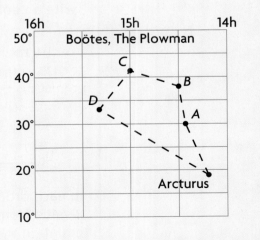

EXTRA PRACTICE page 684, Set A

671

Graph Functions

Learn how to represent functions with ordered pairs, graphs, and equations.

QUICK REVIEW

Find *y* for *x* = 2.

1. *y* = *x*   **2.** *y* = *x* + 4   **3.** *y* = *x* − 2

4. *y* = 8*x*   **5.** *y* = 3*x* − 1

When you see a flash of lightning, count the seconds until you hear thunder. A count of 5 seconds means you are 1 mile from the lightning.

ELAPSED TIME (sec)	5	10	15	20	25	30
DISTANCE TO LIGHTNING (mi)	1	2	3	4	5	6

The values in the table can also be given by using the ordered pairs (5,1), (10,2), (15,3), (20,4), (25,5), and (30,6).

The ordered pairs represent a function. You can use the ordered pairs to show the function on a graph.

HOW FAR AWAY IS THE LIGHTNING?

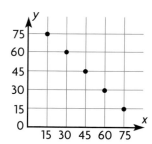

You can also use ordered pairs to graph data from a function table. Use the *x* and *y* values to form the ordered pairs.

EXAMPLE 1

The *x*- and *y*-values in the function table below represent the measures of the two acute angles in a right triangle. Graph the data on a coordinate plane. Then write an equation relating *y* to *x*.

x	15	30	45	60	75
y	75	60	45	30	15

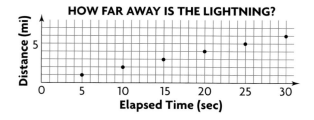

Write the data in the table as ordered pairs:

(15,75), (30,60), (45,45), (60,30), (75,15)

Then plot the points.

In each ordered pair, the *y*-value is found by subtracting the *x*-value from 90. This means that *x* and *y* are related by the equation *y* = 90 − *x*.

Several different methods can be used to show how two variables are related.

EXAMPLE 2

Kerry orders her music CDs through a website on the Internet. The CDs cost $10 each with a flat fee of $5 per order for shipping. Show how the number of CDs ordered, *n*, and the total cost in dollars, *C*, are related.

Method	Example
A. Words	Multiply *n* by 10 and add 5 to find the total cost, *C*.
B. Equation	$C = 10n + 5$

C. Function Table

n	1	2	3	4	5
C	15	25	35	45	55

D. Graph

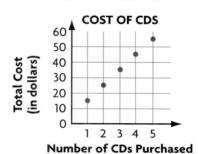

COST OF CDS

Total Cost (in dollars) / Number of CDs Purchased

• Can $n = 0$? Explain your thinking.

You can use a graph to estimate unknown values.

EXAMPLE 3

Duncan walks at a rate of 4 mi per hr, as shown by the table below. Estimate how long it will take Duncan to walk 24 mi at this rate.

Time (hr)	1	2	3	4	5
Distance (mi)	4	8	12	16	20

(1,4), (2,8), (3,12), (4,16), (5,20)

First, write the data in the table as ordered pairs.

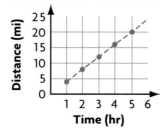

WALKING AT 4 MILES PER HR

Distance (mi) / Time (hr)

Then use the ordered pairs to show the function on a graph.

Look at the graph. If the points are connected and the line is extended, it looks as if it will take Duncan 6 hr to walk 24 mi.

• Write an equation and use it to find the distance Duncan will walk in 7 hr.

673

Think and Discuss ▶ Look back at the lesson to answer each question.

1. **Explain** why an order costing $30 is not possible in Example 2.

2. **Explain** whether it is possible for the *x*-value in Example 1 to be equal to $7\frac{2}{3}$.

Guided Practice ▶ For 3–4, copy and complete the function table. Then write the data in the table as ordered pairs.

3.
x	2	3	4	5	6
y	4	6	8	10	■

4.
x	2	4	6	8	10
y	7	9	11	■	15

For 5–6, use the function table to graph the data on a coordinate plane. Then write an equation relating *y* to *x*.

5.
x	5	6	7	8	9
y	3	4	5	6	7

6.
x	2	1	0	⁻1	⁻2
y	6	3	0	⁻3	⁻6

7. Use the given method to show how the variables in the equation $y = 16 - x$ are related. For **b** and **c**, use the integers from ⁻2 to 2 as values of *x*.

    a. words   **b.** function table   **c.** graph

Independent Practice ▶ For 8–9, copy and complete the function table. Then write the data in the table as ordered pairs.

8.
x	5	4	3	2	1
y	20	16	■	■	4

9.
x	⁻3	⁻2	⁻1	0	1
y	7	8	9	■	■

For 10–11, use the function table to graph the data on a coordinate plane. Then write an equation relating *y* to *x*.

10.
x	9	12	15	18	21
y	3	4	5	6	7

11.
x	⁻3	⁻2	⁻1	0	1
y	⁻7	⁻6	⁻5	⁻4	⁻3

12. Use the given method to show how the variables in the equation $y = 5x$ are related. For **b** and **c**, use the integers from ⁻2 to 2 as values of *x*.

    a. words   **b.** function table   **c.** graph

Problem Solving Applications ▶ 13. A website advertises videos for $15 each with a flat fee of $6 per order for shipping. Use a table, a graph, and an equation to show how the number of videos purchased, *v*, and the total cost in dollars, *C*, are related. Use 3, 4, 5, and 6 as the values of *v*.

For 14–15, use this information: Sue earns three coupons for each win in an arcade game.

14. Let w represent the number of wins. Use ordered pairs to show the number of coupons earned, c, for 7, 8, 9, and 10 wins. What equation relates c to w?

15. Let c represent the number of coupons earned. Use ordered pairs to show the number of wins, w, for 45, 48, 51, and 54 coupons. What equation relates w to c?

Alexander bikes at a rate of 8 mi per hr, as shown by the graph below. Use the graph for 16–17.

BIKING AT 8 MILES PER HR

16. Estimate how long it will take Alexander to bike 48 mi at this rate.

17. Estimate the distance Alexander travels in $2\frac{1}{2}$ hr.

18. **? What's the Error?** Jack is 8 and his brother Noah is 4. Jack let j represent his age and n represent Noah's age. Then he wrote the equation $j = 2n$ to relate their ages. Find his error and write the correct equation.

19. **FAST FACT • SCIENCE** Approximately 100 lightning strikes hit the Earth every second. About how many lightning strikes hit the Earth in 1 hour?

MIXED REVIEW AND TEST PREP

20. Name the quadrant containing the ordered pairs (4,3), (2,1), and (6,5). (p. 668)

21. A rectangle measures 8 cm by 5 cm. What is its area? (p. 458)

22. Describe the *greater than* symbol, $>$, as a transformation of the *less than* symbol, $<$, in two different ways. (p. 394)

23. **TEST PREP** Greg ran a 5-km race. How many meters did he run? (p. 423)

   A 50 m   **B** 500 m   **C** 5,000 m   **D** 50,000 m

24. **TEST PREP** What is the value of the expression $k^2 - 24 \div 3$ where k equals the perimeter of a square with sides of length 3? (p. 260)

   F 40   **G** 120   **H** 136   **J** 144

EXTRA PRACTICE page 684, Set B

675

PROBLEM SOLVING SKILL
Make Generalizations

Analyze
Choose
Solve
Check

Learn how to solve problems by making generalizations.

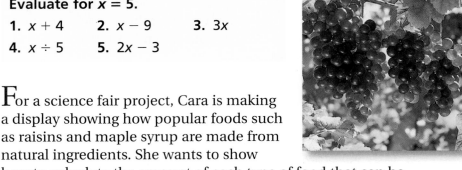

For a science fair project, Cara is making a display showing how popular foods such as raisins and maple syrup are made from natural ingredients. She wants to show how to calculate the amount of each type of food that can be produced from given amounts of ingredients.

It takes about 4 lb of grapes to make 1 lb of raisins. How many pounds of raisins can be made from 160 lb of grapes?

Pounds of Grapes, x	4	8	12	16	20
Pounds of Raisins, y	1	2	3	4	5

Notice that each y-value is $\frac{1}{4}$ of the corresponding x-value. So, the equation $y = \frac{1}{4}x$ describes this situation. Since the equation can be used to find the amount of raisins for any amount of grapes, it is called a generalization.

For 160 lb of grapes, $x = 160$. Then $y = \frac{1}{4} \times 160 = 40$.

So, about 40 lb of raisins can be made from 160 lb of grapes.

On average it takes about 40 gal of sap from maple trees to make 1 gal of maple syrup. How many gallons of sap does it take to make 25 gal of syrup?

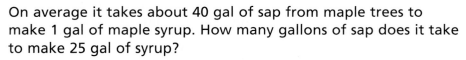

Gallons of Syrup, x	1	2	3	4	5
Gallons of Sap, y	40	80	120	160	200

Notice that each y-value is 40 times the corresponding x-value. So, the equation $y = 40x$ is a generalization.

For 25 gal of syrup, $x = 25$. Then $y = 40 \times 25 = 1,000$.

So, it takes about 1,000 gal of maple sap to make 25 gal of maple syrup.

Talk About It ▶ • **What if** Cara shows in her display that about 1 qt of apple juice can be made from 60 apples? What equation could she use to find the number of quarts that can be made from a given number of apples?

PROBLEM SOLVING PRACTICE

Solve by making a generalization.

Rod spent $6 on supplies to advertise his mowing business. The table shows his profit, *y*, for several income amounts, *x*.

x	$12	$13	$14	$15	$16
y	$6	$7	$8	$9	$10

1. Which equation can be used to show Rod's profit?

  A $y = 2x$ **C** $y = x - 6$

  B $y = \frac{1}{2}x$ **D** $y = x + 6$

2. How much profit did Rod make if he earned $80 mowing lawns?

  F $86   **H** $74

  G $83   **J** $40

Liz charges $9 for each lawn that she mows.

3. What equation can Liz use to show the amount that she earns, *y*, when she mows *x* lawns?

4. How much money will Liz earn if she mows 27 lawns?

MIXED APPLICATIONS

5. Eduardo is driving from New Orleans to Seattle, a distance of 2,639 mi. He drove 440 mi the first day, 380 mi the second day, and 425 mi the third day. How many miles does he have left to drive?

6. To celebrate school spirit week, Roosevelt School plans to paint every sixth locker blue and every tenth locker orange. If there are 300 lockers in the school, how many will be painted both blue and orange?

7. Mr. Wills needs to catch a flight that leaves at 1:00 P.M. It takes 45 min to get to the airport, and he wants to be there 1 hr 15 min early. At what time should Mr. Wills leave home?

8. Sandra used 60 ft of fencing to fence her garden. The garden is a rectangle that is twice as long as it is wide. What are the dimensions of the garden?

9. Use Data Use the graph at the right. The length of the main span of the Verrazano-Narrows Bridge is 4,260 ft. The lengths of several other suspension bridges are shown in the graph. About how much longer than the George Washington Bridge is the Verrazano-Narrows Bridge?

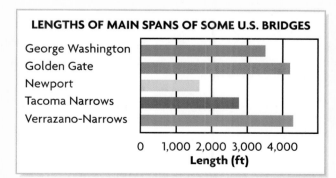

LENGTHS OF MAIN SPANS OF SOME U.S. BRIDGES

George Washington
Golden Gate
Newport
Tacoma Narrows
Verrazano-Narrows

0   1,000 2,000 3,000 4,000
Length (ft)

10. **(?) What's the Question?** Sally's Gifts sells an average of 9 beanbag animals each day. The answer is about 126 beanbag animals.

Explore Linear and Nonlinear Relationships

Explore linear and nonlinear relationships.

You need square tiles or paper squares, graph paper.

You can learn about linear relationships by looking at patterns.

Activity 1

The model at the right shows Stage 1 to Stage 3 of a pattern.

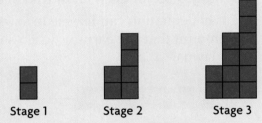

- Use square tiles or paper squares to build Stages 4, 5, and 6 of the pattern.

Stage 1   Stage 2   Stage 3

- Record each stage and the perimeter of each figure in a table.

- Graph the ordered pairs (x, y) from the table on a coordinate plane.

STAGE, x	PERIMETER, y
1	6
2	12
3	▪

Think and Discuss

- Describe the pattern of the points on the graph you drew.

- Write an equation to show the relationship between each stage and its perimeter.

Practice

- Make a table that shows the stage, x, and the perimeter, y, of each figure.

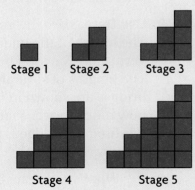

Stage 1   Stage 2   Stage 3

- Write an equation to find the perimeter. Graph the ordered pairs (x, y).

Stage 4   Stage 5

- What pattern do you see in the graph?

You can also use patterns to learn about nonlinear relationships, which have graphs that do not form straight lines.

You need: square tiles or paper squares, graph paper

The model at the right shows Stage 1 to Stage 3 of a pattern.

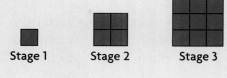

Stage 1   Stage 2   Stage 3

- Use square tiles or paper squares to build Stages 4, 5, and 6 of the pattern.

- Record each stage and the area of each figure in a table.

- Graph the ordered pairs (x, y) from the table on a coordinate plane.

STAGE, x	AREA, y
1	1
2	4
3	

Think and Discuss
- What pattern do you see in the y-values of the ordered pairs?

- Describe the pattern of the points on the graph you drew.

- The equation for this relationship is $y = x^2$. Use the equation to find the ordered pair for Stage 8.

Practice
Use the x-values 1, 2, 3, and 4 to find ordered pairs for each equation. Then graph the equation.

1. $y = 2x^2$

2. $y = {}^-2x^2$

3. $y = 3x^2$

4. $y = \dfrac{12}{x}$

MIXED REVIEW AND TEST PREP

5. Use the table to write an equation that relates x and y. (p. 672)

x	$^-2$	$^-1$	0	1	2
y	6	3	0	$^-3$	$^-6$

Evaluate the expression for $x = 1, 2,$ and 3. (p. 260)

6. $15 - 3x$

7. $0.25x + 6$

8. $\dfrac{18}{x} + 6$

⭐ **9. TEST PREP** A recipe for pumpkin cookies requires $1\frac{3}{4}$ c of pumpkin. Shana wants to triple the recipe. If Shana has 5 c of pumpkin, how much more does she need? (p. 232)

A $\frac{1}{4}$ c   **B** $\frac{1}{2}$ c   **C** $1\frac{1}{4}$ c   **D** $5\frac{1}{4}$ c

679

Graph Transformations

Learn how to use transformations to change positions of figures on a coordinate plane.

Remember that a rigid *transformation* is a movement that doesn't change the size or shape of a figure.

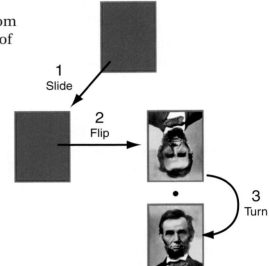

Marla has chosen a card from a pack of cards with pictures of Presidents to give to Matt.

First, she *slides* the card toward Matt, face down. This is a *translation*.

Next, she *flips* the card face up. This is a *reflection*.

Finally, she *turns* the card so that Matt can see it. This is a *rotation*.

1 Slide

2 Flip

3 Turn

Translations, reflections, and rotations are three types of transformations. You can use what you know about the coordinate plane to explore transformations on graph paper.

MATH LAB

Activity

You need: graph paper, scissors

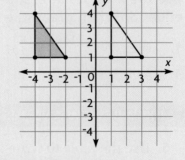

• Draw and number a coordinate plane as shown.

• Plot the points (1,4), (1,1), and (3,1) and connect them to form a triangle.

• Trace the triangle on a sheet of paper. Cut it out.

• Place your cutout triangle on the triangle in Quadrant I of the coordinate plane. Then translate it 5 units to the left, keeping the base parallel to the *x*-axis.

• Name the coordinates for the vertices of the new triangle.

• Again, place your cutout triangle on the original triangle in the coordinate plane. Translate the cutout 4 units down, keeping the left side parallel to the *y*-axis.

• Name the coordinates for the vertices of the new triangle.

You can translate a figure on a coordinate plane by sliding it horizontally, vertically, or both.

Translate square *ABCD* 6 units right and 5 units down. Find the coordinates of the new square, *A'B'C'D'*.

To find the coordinates of the new square, add 6 to each *x*-coordinate and subtract 5 from each *y*-coordinate of the original square.

ABCD			*A'B'C'D'*
$A(^-4,3)$	$\rightarrow$	$A'(^-4 + 6, 3 - 5)$	$\rightarrow A'(2, ^-2)$
$B(^-2,3)$	$\rightarrow$	$B'(^-2 + 6, 3 - 5)$	$\rightarrow B'(4, ^-2)$
$C(^-2,1)$	$\rightarrow$	$C'(^-2 + 6, 1 - 5)$	$\rightarrow C'(4, ^-4)$
$D(^-4,1)$	$\rightarrow$	$D'(^-4 + 6, 1 - 5)$	$\rightarrow D'(2, ^-4)$

original

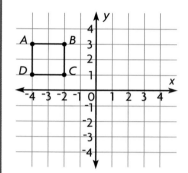

translation

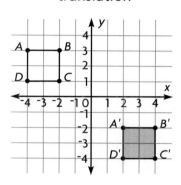

You can also draw the reflection of a figure on a coordinate plane. When you reflect a figure, you can flip it across the *x*-axis or the *y*-axis.

Reflect △*ABC* across the *x*-axis. Find the coordinates of the new figure, △*A'B'C'*.

original

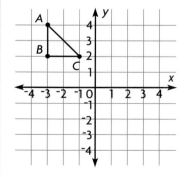

reflection

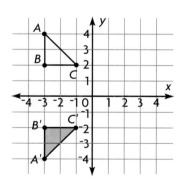

△*ABC*		△*A'B'C'*
$A(^-3,4)$	$\rightarrow$	$A'(^-3, ^-4)$
$B(^-3,2)$	$\rightarrow$	$B'(^-3, ^-2)$
$C(^-1,2)$	$\rightarrow$	$C'(^-1, ^-2)$

You can draw a rotation of a figure about the origin on a coordinate plane.

EXAMPLE 3

Rotate trapezoid *ABCD* clockwise 90° about the origin. Find the coordinates of the new figure, *A′B′C′D′*.

original

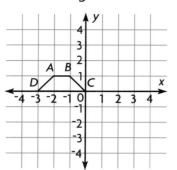

rotation

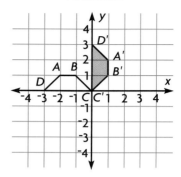

ABCD		*A′B′C′D′*
A(‾2,1)	→	*A′*(1,2)
B(‾1,1)	→	*B′*(1,1)
C(0,0)	→	*C′*(0,0)
D(‾3,0)	→	*D′*(0,3)

• **What if** you had rotated the trapezoid *counterclockwise* 90° about the origin? What would the coordinates of the new figure be?

CHECK FOR UNDERSTANDING

Think and Discuss ▶ **Look back at the lesson to answer each question.**

1. **Compare** the *x*- and *y*-coordinates of the original figure and the new figure in Example 2. How are they related?

2. **Explain** why the coordinates of vertex *C* in Example 3 above did not change from the original figure to the new figure.

Guided Practice ▶ **Copy the figure onto a coordinate grid. Transform the figure according to the directions given. Name the new coordinates.**

3. translate 2 units left

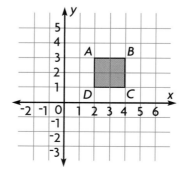

4. rotate 90° clockwise about (0,0)

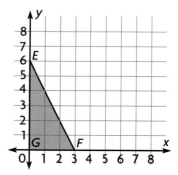

Independent ▶
Practice

Copy the figure onto a coordinate grid. Transform the figure according to the directions given. Name the new coordinates.

5.

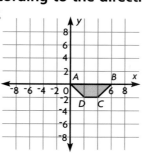

rotate 180°
counterclockwise
about (0,0)

6.

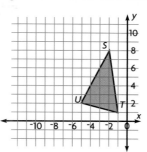

reflect across
the *y*-axis

7.

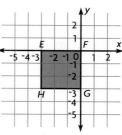

translate 3 units
right and 1 unit
down

TECHNOLOGY LINK

More Practice:
Harcourt Mega Math
Ice Station Exploration,
Polar Planes, Level T

Graph rectangle *EFGH* with coordinates (1,⁻2), (4,⁻2), (4,⁻4), and (1,⁻4).

8. Describe the transformation used to move rectangle *EFGH* to the coordinates (1,3), (4,3), (4,1), and (1,1).

9. Reflect the new rectangle in Exercise 8 across the *x*-axis. What are the new coordinates of the rectangle?

Problem Solving ▶
Applications

For 10–11, use the figure at the right.
Triangle *A* has been transformed into
triangle *B* by a 180° rotation about (0,0).

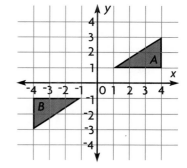

10. Could you complete the same transformation using only reflections? If so, how?

11. Could you complete the same transformation using only translations? Explain.

12. ❓ **What's the Question?** The coordinates of △*ABC* are *A*(1,⁻3), *B*(1,⁻1), and *C*(3,⁻1). The answer is that the new coordinates are *A'*(1,3), *B'*(1,1), and *C'*(3,1).

MIXED REVIEW AND TEST PREP

13. Use the table to write an equation that relates *x* and *y*. (p. 672)

x	0	1	2	3
y	0	7	14	21

14. Complete: 33, 24, 15, 6, ■ (p. 315)

15. $\frac{1}{2} \times \frac{2}{3} \times \frac{3}{4}$ (p. 228)

⭐**16. TEST PREP** What is the value of the expression $5v + 32 - 7v$ where *v* equals the volume of a rectangular prism with dimensions 2, 3, and 4? (p. 506)

A 152 **B** 24 **C** ⁻16 **D** ⁻24

⭐**17. TEST PREP** Find the greatest common factor of 35, 56, and 63. (p. 170)

F 6 **G** 7 **H** 8 **J** 9

EXTRA PRACTICE page 684, Set C

Set A (pp. 668–671)

Write the ordered pair for each point on the coordinate plane.

1. point *A*
2. point *B*
3. point *C*
4. point *D*
5. point *E*
6. point *F*
7. point *G*
8. point *H*
9. point *I*
10. point *J*

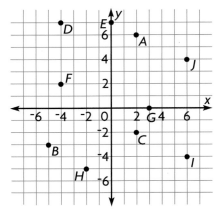

Set B (pp. 672–675)

Copy and complete the table. Then graph the data on a coordinate plane and write an equation relating *y* to *x*.

1.

x	1	2	3	4	5
y	3	4	5	▨	▨

2.

x	1	2	3	4	5
y	6	12	18	▨	▨

3.

x	8	9	10	11	12
y	1	2	3	▨	▨

4.

x	8	4	0	⁻4	⁻8
y	⁻2	⁻1	0	▨	▨

5. Jeff earns $6 per hour baby-sitting. Let *h* represent the number of hours worked. Use ordered pairs to show the amount of money earned, *m*, for 3, 4, 5, and 6 hours of work. What equation relates *m* to *h*?

Set C (pp. 680–683)

Copy the figure onto a coordinate grid. Transform the figure according to the directions given. Name the new coordinates.

1.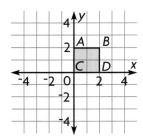

   translate 2 units right

2.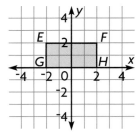

   rotate 90° clockwise about (⁻2,0)

3.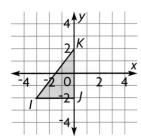

   reflect across the *y*-axis

4. Graph △*ABC* with vertices (⁻3,0), (0,0), and (0,4). Then describe the transformation used to move the triangle to the coordinates (⁻3,0), (0,0), and (0,⁻4).

1. **VOCABULARY**   The point where the *x*-axis and the *y*-axis intersect is called the __?__ . (p. 668)

2. **VOCABULARY**   The *x*-axis and the *y*-axis divide the coordinate plane into four __?__ . (p. 668)

Describe how to locate the point for the ordered pair on the coordinate plane. (pp. 668–671)

3. (2,4)

4. (3,⁻2)

5. (⁻1,⁻6)

6. (0,4)

Sketch and label a coordinate plane, and plot the points. (pp. 668–671)

7. $A(^-4,3)$

8. $B(5,5)$

9. $C(0,0)$

10. $D(6,0)$

11. $E(^-2,^-1)$

12. $F(0,^-4)$

13. Write the data in the table as ordered pairs. (pp. 672–675)

x	1	2	3	4
y	4	5	6	7

14. For the function table in Exercise 13, write an equation that relates *y* to *x*. (pp. 672–675)

15. Graph the data from the function table on a coordinate plane. Then write an equation that relates *b* to *a*. (pp. 672–675)

a	1	2	3	4
b	3	6	9	12

Solve. (pp. 680–683)

16. Trapezoid *DEFG* has coordinates *D*(3,3), *E*(4,3), *F*(5,1), and *G*(2,1). If it is reflected across the *x*-axis, what are the new coordinates?

17. Triangle *ABC* has coordinates *A*(0,0), *B*(3,2), and *C*(0,2). What are the new coordinates after it is rotated 90° clockwise about the origin?

18. Triangle *XYZ* has coordinates *X*(4,1), *Y*(7,1), and *Z*(6,2). It is translated 1 unit down and 3 units left. What are the new coordinates?

Solve. (pp. 676–677)

19. The table shows the total cost, *c*, for the number of tickets bought, *t*. Write an equation using *t* that gives the total cost, *c*.

t	1	2	3	4
c	$4	$8	$12	$16

20. Ella spends $3 on beads for each bracelet that she makes. The table shows her profit, *y*, when she sells a bracelet for price *x*. Write an equation using *x* that gives her profit, *y*.

x	$3	$4	$5	$6
y	$0	$1	$2	$3

NUMBER SENSE, CONCEPTS, AND OPERATIONS

1. With 80 million visitors each year, Hartsfield Airport in Atlanta, Georgia, is the world's busiest airport. The table below uses fractions to compare passenger totals at four foreign airports with Hartsfield's total.

AIRPORT PASSENGER TOTALS	
City	Fraction of Hartsfield's Passenger Total
Amsterdam	$\frac{1}{2}$
Paris	$\frac{3}{5}$
Seoul	$\frac{9}{20}$
Tokyo	$\frac{7}{10}$

Which list orders the fractions from **greatest** to **least**?

A $\frac{9}{20}, \frac{7}{10}, \frac{3}{5}, \frac{1}{2}$

B $\frac{7}{10}, \frac{3}{5}, \frac{1}{2}, \frac{9}{20}$

C $\frac{1}{2}, \frac{3}{5}, \frac{7}{10}, \frac{9}{20}$

D $\frac{7}{10}, \frac{1}{2}, \frac{9}{20}, \frac{3}{5}$

2. Theodore Roosevelt was the youngest man ever to serve as President of the United States. The expression $6^2 + 10 - (2^3 - 4)$ gives his age at his inauguration. Which of the following is equivalent to $6^2 + 10 - (2^3 - 4)$?

F 34 H 42

G 40 J 44

3. **Explain It** Movie tickets cost $7.50 for adults and $4.50 for children. How much will it cost for three adults and two children to go to the movies? Explain how you found your answer.

★ ALGEBRAIC THINKING

4. Sam drives at a rate of 50 miles per hour as shown by the graph below. Which is the **best** estimate of the distance Sam travels in $3\frac{1}{2}$ hours?

DRIVING AT 50 MILES PER HOUR

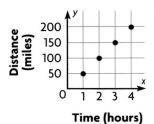

A 175 miles C 225 miles

B 200 miles D 250 miles

5. The number of pizzas that Carmen orders for the club luncheon depends on how many people will attend the luncheon.

Number of People	4	8	12	16
Number of Pizzas	1	2	3	4

If the pattern continues, how many pizzas will Carmen order for 28 people?

F 5

G 7

H 8

J 10

6. **Explain It** To find the distance from a bolt of lightning, count the number of seconds, n, from the moment you see the lightning until you hear thunder. Then divide by 5. The result is the approximate distance from the lightning in miles. Write an expression, using n, for the distance from a bolt of lightning. Explain how to use the expression to find the distance when $n = 20$.

GEOMETRY AND SPATIAL SENSE

7. An airplane lands at position *A* on the runway at Tri-City Airport. It then taxis to position *B* on the runway. Which describes the plane's movement from position *A* to position *B* in the drawing below?

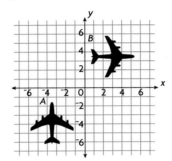

A rotation about the origin

B translation

C reflection across the *x*-axis, then reflection across the *y*-axis

D rotation 90° clockwise about the origin, then translation

8. Burt wants to lay patio bricks in a tessellation pattern. Which shape can he choose for the bricks?

F regular hexagon

G regular pentagon

H regular octagon

J circle

9. Explain It Darlene drew the shapes below.

Figure 1   **Figure 2**   **Figure 3**

Which of the shapes is a polygon? Explain your thinking.

MEASUREMENT

10. An ice hockey rink has a center circle and five red "face-off" circles. Each circle has a radius of 15 feet. What is the total area of the 5 circles? Use $\pi = 3.14$.

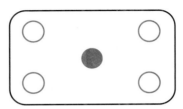

A 471 square feet

B 3,532.5 square feet

C 14,130 square feet

D 17,662.5 square feet

11. Standard copier paper is $8\frac{1}{2}$ inches wide by 11 inches long. "Oversize" paper is 11 inches wide by 17 inches long. What is the ratio of the area of standard paper to the area of oversize paper?

> **TIP** **Understand the problem.** See item 11. You are given the dimensions of each type of paper. You need to find the area of each type of paper and then use the areas to write a ratio.

F 1:2   **H** 1:4

G 1:3   **J** 1:8

12. What unit of measure would be the most appropriate to measure the weight of an adult cat?

A meters   **C** pounds

B milligrams   **D** tons

13. Explain It Jane measured the width of a bookshelf to the nearest half inch. Tessa measured it to the nearest quarter inch. Whose measurement is more precise? Explain your answer.

IT'S IN THE BAG!

Input/Output Bag

PROJECT Make a bag to practice completing input/output tables.

Materials

- Business size envelope
- Pipe Cleaner
- Markers
- Adding Machine paper
- Scissors
- Tape
- Hole Punch

Directions

1. Seal the envelope and cut it in half across the longer sides. Fold the sides back and forth and fold the bottom back and forth. *(Picture A)*

2. Put your hand in the bag and flatten the bottom. Fold back the two points on the bottom and tape them flat on the bottom.

3. Pinch the sides to make folded sides. Cut a 2-in. slit across the bottom of the bag. Write *Input Output Bag* on the front. *(Picture B)*

4. Cut the adding machine paper to form a point. Write *Pull out and solve* on the bottom. Above this, write a rule for a function. Then make an input/output table with at least four rows. Write question marks in some boxes. Write three more rules and tables. *(Picture C)*

5. Roll up the adding machine paper and insert it into the bag. Bring out the point through the slit. Punch four holes at the top of the bag and insert pipe cleaners to make handles. Ask another student to slowly pull the paper out of the bag and find the missing inputs and outputs.

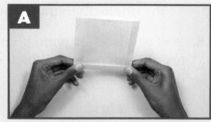

A

B

C

Negative Exponents

Learn how to work with negative exponents and how to write small numbers by using scientific notation.

Activity

Copy and complete the pattern. Use a calculator as needed.

$10^3 = 1,000$

$10^2 = 100$

$10^1 = 10$

$10^0 = \blacksquare$

$10^{-1} = \blacksquare$

$10^{-2} = \blacksquare$

$10^{-3} = \blacksquare$

Notice that as the value of the exponent decreases, each number is 0.1, or $\frac{1}{10}$, as great as the previous number.

- For powers of 10, how is the negative exponent related to the number of decimal places?

Negative exponents are used to write very small numbers in scientific notation.

$$0.004 = 4 \times 0.001 = 4 \times 10^{-3}$$

↑
Replace 0.001 with 10^{-3}.

Look at the relationship between 0.004 and 4×10^{-3}. To write 0.004 as 4, move the decimal point 3 places to the right, multiplying by 1,000. Use ⁻3 as the exponent of 10 to show the corresponding division by 1,000.

TECHNOLOGY LINK

You can use the key on a calculator to help you compute exponents. To find the value of 3^4, press

3 4 Enter .

The display will show 81.

EXAMPLE

Write 0.0000245 in scientific notation.

0.0000245
5 places

Count the number of places the decimal point must be moved to the right to form a number that is at least 1 but less than 10.

2.45×10^{-5}

Write the number. Since the decimal point moved 5 places to the right, the exponent of 10 is ⁻5.

TALK ABOUT IT

- When writing a very small number in scientific notation, how can you tell what the exponent should be?

TRY IT

Write in scientific notation.

1. 0.002   **2.** 0.00034   **3.** 0.06   **4.** 0.005365

5. 0.0084   **6.** 0.0000794   **7.** 0.0000008   **8.** 0.000202

VOCABULARY

1. All whole numbers and their opposites are the set of ___?___ . (p. 628)

2. A comparison of two numbers, a and b, written as a fraction $\frac{a}{b}$ is a ___?___ . (p. 630)

3. The horizontal number line in the coordinate plane is called the ___?___ . (p. 668)

EXAMPLES	EXERCISES

Chapter 28

- **Write the absolute value of an integer.** (pp. 628–629)

  $|^-5| = 5$ *Write the distance $^-5$ is from 0 on the number line.*

Write the absolute value.

4. $|^-8|$ 　5. $|^+6|$ 　6. $|^-28|$

7. $|^-73|$ 　8. $|^+49|$ 　9. $|0|$

- **Classify numbers as whole numbers, integers, or rational numbers.** (pp. 630–633)

  $^-5$ is an integer and a rational number.

  $\frac{3}{5}$ is a rational number.

Name the sets to which each number belongs.

10. $3\frac{5}{9}$ 　11. 0.35

12. $^-42$ 　13. $\frac{6}{3}$

- **Compare and order rational numbers.** (pp. 634–635)

  Compare. Write $<$, $>$, or $=$ for the ●.

  $^-5.8$ ● $^-5\frac{3}{4}$

  $^-5\frac{3}{4} = ^-5.75$ *Write the fraction as a decimal.*

  $^-5.80 < ^-5.75$ *Compare the decimals.*

  So, $^-5.8 < ^-5\frac{3}{4}$.

Compare. Write $<$, $>$, or $=$ for each ●.

14. $\frac{2}{5}$ ● 0.38 　15. $3\frac{3}{4}$ ● 3.89

16. $^-0.25$ ● $^-\frac{1}{4}$ 　17. $4\frac{3}{10}$ ● 4.03

Order from least to greatest.

18. 1.55, $\frac{2}{3}$, $^-3$, 4.2, $^-1.8$

19. $^-\frac{3}{4}$, 0, 6.5, $^-8$, $^-3.6$

Chapter 29

- **Add and subtract integers.** (pp. 644–653)

  Subtract. $6 - {}^-4$
  $6 - {}^-4 = 6 + 4$ *Write as an addition sentence.*
  $\quad = 10$

  Add. $15 + {}^-3$
  $|15| - |^-3| = 15 - 3$ *Subtract the absolute values.*
  $\quad = 12$ *The sum is positive.*

Find the sum or difference.

20. $^-3 + 9$ 　21. $^-8 + {}^-9$

22. $12 + {}^-5$ 　23. $^-4 - 10$

24. $^-9 - {}^-13$ 　25. $15 - {}^-6$

- **Multiply and divide integers.** (pp. 654–657)

  ⁻4 × 7 = ⁻28   *The product or quotient of a positive and a negative integer is negative.*

  ⁻72 ÷ ⁻9 = 8   *The product or quotient of two positive or two negative integers is positive.*

Find the product or quotient.

26. ⁻16 · 3   **27.** ⁻12 · ⁻12

28. 15 · ⁻6   **29.** ⁻14 · ⁻9

30. ⁻54 ÷ 9   **31.** 124 ÷ ⁻4

32. ⁻75 ÷ ⁻15   **33.** ⁻119 ÷ 7

Chapter 30

- **Use an ordered pair to describe a location on the coordinate plane.**

  (pp. 668–671)

  The first number of an ordered pair tells you how far right or left to move from the origin. The second number of an ordered pair tells you how far to move up or down.

  (⁻3,5)   *Move 3 units left and 5 units up.*

Write the ordered pair for each point on the coordinate plane.

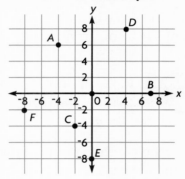

34. A   **35.** B

36. C   **37.** D

38. E   **39.** F

- **Use transformations to change positions of figures on the coordinate plane.**

  (pp. 680–683)

  Translate △ABC 5 units left and 2 units down.

  A(2,4) → (2 − 5,4 − 2)
  A′(⁻3,2)
  B(2,1) → (2 − 5,1 − 2)
  B′(⁻3,⁻1)
  C(4,1) → (4 − 5,1 − 2)
  C′(⁻1,⁻1)

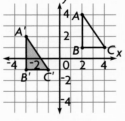

Copy the figure onto a coordinate grid. Transform the figure according to the directions given. Name the new coordinates.

40. rotate clockwise 90° about (⁻1,⁻4)

41. reflect across the y-axis

42. translate 6 units up and 5 units right

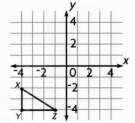

PROBLEM SOLVING APPLICATIONS

43. Four students spent money on books. The amounts they spent were $2.50, $3.25, $5.00, and $5.75. Ari spent $3.25 more than Nina. Nina spent half as much as Jamal. Kenny spent $1.75 less than Jamal. How much did each person spend? (pp. 636–637)

44. Frances claimed that the average of the low temperatures last week was greater than ⁻4°C. Patty says that the average was less than ⁻4°C. The low temperatures last week were ⁻6°C, ⁻8°C, ⁻3°C, ⁻4°C, 0°C, ⁻9°C, and ⁻5°C. Who is correct? Explain. (pp. 654–657)

Performance Assessment

TASK A • Waterfall Hike

Materials: graph paper

The Blake family is going on a three-day hiking and camping trip to see their favorite waterfall. The function $y = 2x$ shows the number of miles, y, that the Blakes hike in x hours.

a. Complete the function table below. Use the function table to sketch the graph of $y = 2x$ on graph paper.

hours, x	0	1	2	3	4
miles, y	0	2			

b. Explain how to use the graph to predict how long it will take the Blakes to hike 11 mi. About how long will it take?

c. The Blakes hiked for 3 hr the first day, 5 hr the second day, and 6 hr the third day. Sketch three different graphs on graph paper that show their progress each hour for the three days.

d. Do the graphs show linear relationships or nonlinear relationships? Explain.

TASK B • Transformations

Materials: graph paper

a. Graph the x- and y-axes on the graph paper. Then graph the points $(0,2)$, $(8,0)$, $(0,^-4)$, and $(^-4,0)$ and connect them in order so that the result is a quadrilateral.

b. Draw the quadrilateral with vertices $(^-4,0)$, $(^-8,2)$, $(^-16,0)$, and $(^-8,^-4)$. Is this quadrilateral a rotation, translation, or reflection of the first quadrilateral?

c. Draw a translation of the first quadrilateral. Give the new coordinates of the vertices.

d. Draw a transformation that is a combination of rotation and translation, rotation and reflection, or translation and reflection. Exchange drawings with a classmate and determine which two transformations he or she has used.

Technology Linkup

Calculator • Explore Graphing Equations

Chad works in a cafeteria. To make lemonade, he combines each scoop of lemonade mix with 8 ounces of water.

SCOOPS OF LEMONADE MIX	1	2	3	4	5	6
OUNCES OF WATER	8	16	24	32	40	48

If x equals the scoops of lemonade mix and y equals the ounces of water, then $y = 8x$.

You can use the ordered pairs to graph the equation on graph paper, or you can use a graphing calculator.

• Use the TI-73 graphing calculator to graph $y = 8x$.

Step 1
Press . Press , 8, , **ENTER** .

Step 2
Press **GRAPH** to show the graph on the coordinate plane.

Practice and Problem Solving
Use a graphing calculator to graph each equation. Then sketch the graph on a piece of paper.

1. $y = 6x$
2. $y = 32x$
3. $y = 57x$
4. $y = 0.14x$
5. $y = x - 6$

6. $y = 18x$
7. $y = 41x$
8. $y = 0.6x$
9. $y = x + 3$
10. $y = x + 8$

11. **Write a problem** involving a function. Write the equation and graph it. Draw the graph on your paper.

Multimedia Math Glossary www.harcourtschool.com/mathglossary

Vocabulary Power Look up *equation* in the Multimedia Math Glossary. Write some other algebraic sentences that have the same solution as the example shown in the glossary.

PROBLEM SOLVING ON LOCATION
In Michigan

Mt. Arvon

Although Michigan has 3,200 mi of shoreline, all of the state lies above sea level. Its highest point is Mt. Arvon, 1,979 ft above sea level. Its lowest point is along the shore of Lake Erie, 572 ft above sea level. In comparison, the lowest point in the United States is Death Valley, California, where the elevation is 282 ft below sea level (⁻282 ft). New Orleans, Louisiana, has an elevation of 8 ft below sea level (⁻8 ft).

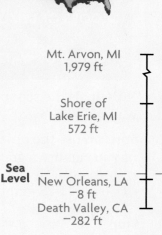

Mt. Arvon, MI
1,979 ft

Shore of
Lake Erie, MI
572 ft

Sea Level New Orleans, LA
⁻8 ft
Death Valley, CA
⁻282 ft

Use Data   For 1–6, use the diagram.

1. What is the difference in elevation between the lowest point in Michigan and the highest point in Michigan?

2. What is the difference in elevation between Death Valley and the top of Mt. Arvon?

3. What is the difference in elevation between Death Valley and the lowest point in Michigan?

4. About how many times the elevation of the lowest point in Michigan is the elevation of Mt. Arvon?

5. About how many times the elevation of New Orleans is the elevation of Death Valley?

6. **REASONING** Is the statement "The lowest point in Michigan is about twice as far above sea level as Death Valley is below sea level" reasonable? Explain.

Elevations in Michigan vary from the highest at Mt. Arvon (right) to the lowest along Lake Erie (below).

Outdoor Michigan

With 3.9 million acres of state forests, Michigan is a great place for people who enjoy the outdoors. Two of the most popular outdoor activities are skiing and bicycling. There are many places to ski in Michigan and with 96 state parks and recreation areas, there are plenty of trails for bicyclists of all ages.

The map at the right shows some of the cities in Michigan that have places to ski or have paved bike trails.

For 1–12, use the map above. Write the ordered pair for each city.

1. Hart
2. Monroe
3. Bessemer
4. Harbor Springs
5. Stockbridge
6. Otsego

Identify the city located at the given ordered pair.

7. $(4.2, ^-4.2)$
8. $(2.2, 1.8)$
9. $(3\frac{9}{10}, ^-1\frac{3}{4})$
10. $(1\frac{1}{2}, ^-\frac{1}{2})$
11. $(1, \frac{9}{10})$
12. $(^-2.2, 3.1)$

Use Data For 13–14, use the data in the tables. One day, Jon and Sara practiced cross-county skiing near Boyne Falls. The tables show the time, *t*, it took them to travel certain distances, *d*.

JON'S TIME AND DISTANCE					
t (sec)	3	6	9	12	15
d (ft)	21	42	63	■	■

SARA'S TIME AND DISTANCE					
t (sec)	7	14	21	28	35
d (ft)	■	■	168	224	280

13. Jon and Sara each traveled at a constant rate. Copy and complete the tables.

14. **Stretch Your Thinking** Use different colors to show Jon's and Sara's data on the same graph. Who traveled at a greater rate of speed? Explain.

Student Handbook

Troubleshooting H2

Prerequisite Skills Review Do you have the math skills needed to start a new chapter? Use this list of skills to review and remember your skills.

Troubleshooting

Multiplication and Division Facts

You can use an array to find a product or a quotient.

A. Find 5×9.

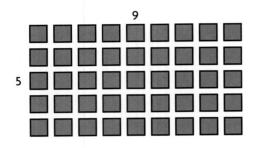

So, $5 \times 9 = 45$.

B. Find $18 \div 6$.

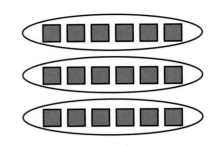

So, $18 \div 6 = 3$.

Practice

Find the product.

1. 3×6	**2.** 7×6	**3.** 4×9	**4.** 6×8
5. 9×8	**6.** 6×4	**7.** 8×5	**8.** 4×7

Find the quotient.

9. $21 \div 7$	**10.** $36 \div 6$	**11.** $18 \div 9$	**12.** $27 \div 9$
13. $54 \div 6$	**14.** $49 \div 7$	**15.** $48 \div 8$	**16.** $25 \div 5$

Represent Decimals

You can use decimal squares to represent decimals. A decimal square is divided into 100 parts. Each part represents 1 hundredth of the whole, or 0.01. Count the number of shaded parts. Write this number as hundredths.

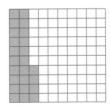

24 out of 100 small squares are shaded.
0.24 of the whole is shaded.

Practice

Write the decimal that is represented.

1.

2.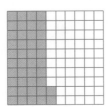

3.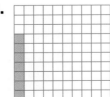

4.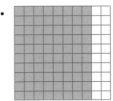

Evaluate Numerical Expressions

A **numerical expression** is a mathematical phrase that includes only numbers and operation symbols. To evaluate an expression, first perform any operations in parentheses ( ). Next, multiply and divide from left to right. Finally, add and subtract from left to right.

Examples

Evaluate each expression.

A. $14 + 3 \times 5$

1. There are no parentheses.

2. Multiply: $14 + 3 \times 5 = 14 + 15$

3. Add: $14 + 15 = 29$

So, $14 + 3 \times 5 = 29$.

B. $(19 + 6) - 12 \div 4$

1. Evaluate parentheses:
$(19 + 6) - 12 \div 4 = 25 - 12 \div 4$

2. Divide: $25 - 12 \div 4 = 25 - 3$

3. Subtract: $25 - 3 = 22$

So, $(19 + 6) - 12 \div 4 = 22$.

Practice

Evaluate each expression.

1. $24 - 8 \times 2$

2. $12 + 48 \div 8$

3. $(66 + 6) \div (4 + 5)$

4. $13 - (12 - 11)$

5. $(20 + 2) \div 2$

6. $15 - 2 + 18 \div 6$

Compare and Order Whole Numbers

You can compare and order numbers by comparing the digits in each place-value position.

Example

Write $<$, $>$, or $=$ to compare the numbers.   14,675 ● 14,228

Step 1

Compare the ten thousands.

14,675
↓   same number of
14,228   ten thousands

Step 2

Compare the thousands.

14,675
↓   same number of
14,228   thousands

Step 3

Compare the hundreds.

14,675
↓ $6 > 2$
14,228   So, $14,675 > 14,228$.

Practice

Write $<$, $>$, or $=$ to compare the numbers.

1. 3,919 ● 3,991

2. 188,937 ● 189,066

3. 70,001 ● 70,001

Order the numbers from greatest to least.

4. 9,774; 9,718; 9,762

5. 82,056; 82,856; 81,978

6. 23,091; 23,910; 23,109

Troubleshooting

Round Whole Numbers and Decimals

Follow these steps to round a number to a given place.

Example

Round 168,279 to the nearest ten thousand.

Step 1

Find the digit in the place being rounded, the ten thousands place.

1**6**8,279

Step 2

Look at the next digit to the right. If it is 5 or greater, round up. Otherwise, round down.

16**8**,279   8 > 5, so round up.

Step 3

Change to zero each digit to the right of the place being rounded.

168,279 → 170,000

Practice

Round to the nearest whole number.

1. 7.97   **2.** 15.58

Round to the nearest ten thousand.

5. 530,410   **6.** 12,677

Round to the nearest thousand.

3. 3,378   **4.** 7,607

Round to the nearest tenth.

7. 16.53   **8.** 2.96

Whole-Number Operations

When adding, subtracting, multiplying, and dividing whole numbers, align digits that have the same place value.

Examples

A. Find the sum. 247 + 1,496 + 89

```
  2 2    Think: 7 + 6 + 9 = 22
  247    Regroup 22 ones as
1,496    2 tens 2 ones.
+   89   Add the other columns
-------
1,832    in a similar way.
```

B. Find the difference. 31 − 12

```
  2 11  Regroup when necessary.
  3̸1̸
− 1 2
------
  1 9
```

C. Find the product. 27 × 86

```
     27  Multiply by the 6 ones.
   × 86  Multiply by the 8 tens.
   ----
    162  Add the products.
+ 2,160
  ------
  2,322
```

D. Find the quotient. 146 ÷ 9

```
       16 r2  Divide the 14 tens.
   9)146      Multiply and subtract.
    − 9       Bring down the 6 ones.
    ----      Divide the 56 ones.
     56       Multiply and subtract.
   − 54       Write the remainder.
   ----
      2
```

Practice

Add, subtract, multiply, or divide.

1. 700 − 388   **2.** 19 × 203   **3.** 155 + 9 + 4,823   **4.** 524 ÷ 31

H4 Prerequisite Skills Review

Number Patterns

To extend a number pattern, find the relationship between consecutive pairs of numbers. Then use the relationship to continue the pattern.

Examples

Find the next three numbers in the pattern.

A. 4, 12, 20, 28, ▒, ▒, ▒

Think: Each number is 8 greater than the previous number.

$4 + 8 = 12; 12 + 8 = 20; 20 + 8 = 28$

To find the next three numbers, add 8 to the previous number in the pattern.

$28 + 8 = 36; 36 + 8 = 44; 44 + 8 = 52$

So, the next three numbers are 36, 44, and 52.

B. 85, 75, 65, 55, ▒, ▒, ▒

Think: Each number is 10 less than the previous number.

$85 - 10 = 75; 75 - 10 = 65; 65 - 10 = 55$

To find the next three numbers, subtract 10 from the previous number in the pattern.

$55 - 10 = 45, 45 - 10 = 35, 35 - 10 = 25$

So, the next three numbers are 45, 35, and 25.

Practice

Find the next three numbers in the pattern.

1. 9, 13, 17, 21, ▒, ▒, ▒   **2.** 20, 25, 30, 35, ▒, ▒, ▒   **3.** 99, 90, 81, 72, ▒, ▒, ▒

4. 48, 42, 36, 30, ▒, ▒, ▒   **5.** 14, 17, 20, 23, ▒, ▒, ▒   **6.** 57, 50, 43, 36, ▒, ▒, ▒

Read a Table

Use the title of a table to understand what the data represent. Use the labels to understand what the items represent.

Example

How far did Angie jog on Tuesday?

DAILY JOGGING RECORD (IN MILES)							
Day	Sun	Mon	Tue	Wed	Thu	Fri	Sat
Milo	4	3	5	5	0	7	6
Angie	6	3	4	0	5	8	0

The number in the row marked "Angie" and the column marked "Tue" is 4. So, Angie jogged 4 miles on Tuesday.

Practice

Use the data in the table above to answer the questions.

1. How far did Milo jog on Friday?

2. On which day did Angie jog 6 miles?

3. Which person jogged 5 miles on Wednesday?

4. On which day did Milo and Angie jog the same distance?

5. How far did Angie jog on the two days that she jogged the same distance?

6. Who ran the greater total distance during the week?

Troubleshooting

Mean, Median, Mode, and Range

Example

Find the mean, median, mode, and range for this set of data.
6, 19, 6, 9, 11, 15

Mean Find the sum of the data items. Divide the sum by the number of items.	$6 + 19 + 6 + 9 + 11 + 15 = 66$ mean $= 66 \div 6 = 11$
Median Order the items from least to greatest. The median is the middle value. If there are two middle values, the median is the average of the two values.	6, 6, **9, 11**, 15, 19 9 and 11 are the middle numbers. median $= (9 + 11) \div 2 = 10$
Mode Order the items from least to greatest. The mode is the value or values that repeat most often. If no value repeats, there is no mode.	**6, 6**, 9, 11, 15, 19 mode $= 6$
Range Order the items from least to greatest. The range is the difference of the greatest and least values.	**6**, 6, 9, 11, 15, **19** range $= 19 - 6 = 13$

Practice

Find the mean, median, mode, and range for each set of data.

1. 2, 1, 3, 5, 9

2. 6, 52, 41, 21, 35

3. 11, 15, 6, 11, 22

4. 9, 5, 2, 5, 6, 1, 14

Read Bar Graphs

A **bar graph** uses bars of different lengths to show and compare data.

Example

How many books did Anita read last month?

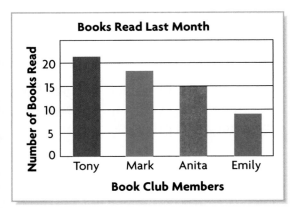

Find the bar representing Anita.

Look at the top of the bar. Read the scale at the left for the number the bar represents.

Anita read 15 books last month.

Practice

Use the bar graph to answer the questions.

1. How many books did Mark read?

2. Who read 22 books?

3. Who read the least number of books?

4. How many more books did Tony read than Anita?

Read Stem-and-Leaf Plots

In a **stem-and-leaf plot**, data are organized by "stems," or the tens digits, and "leaves," or the ones digits. The stems and leaves are listed in order.

Example

Each entry in the stem-and-leaf plot gives the number of cards that were stacked in a house of cards when it collapsed. How many times were there from 40 to 49 cards when the collapse occurred?

Stem	Leaves
1	2 5 7 8 8 9
2	0 0 1 3 5 8
3	1 2 4 7
4	2 8
5	1 6

The numbers from 40 to 49 have the stem of 4, because the tens digit is 4. There are two such numbers in the table:

Stem 4, leaf 2 shows **42**.
Stem 4, leaf 8 shows **48**.

So, twice there were from 40 to 49 cards. Once there were 42 cards, and once there were 48.

Practice

Use the stem-and-leaf plot to answer the questions.

1. How many times were there from 10 to 19 cards when the collapse occurred?

2. What was the greatest number of cards stacked? the least number?

3. How many houses of cards were built in this competition?

4. What are the mode, median, and range of the data in the table?

Repeated Multiplication

Some numbers can be written as products of repeated factors.

Example

Evaluate. $3 \times 3 \times 3 \times 3$

One Way

Find the products of pairs of factors.

$3 \times 3 \times 3 \times 3$
$\quad \downarrow \qquad \downarrow$
$\quad 9 \ \times \ 9 \ = 81$

Another Way

Step 1
Multiply the first two factors.

$3 \times 3 = 9$

Step 2
Multiply by the next factor.

$9 \times 3 = 27$

Step 3
Continue using all the factors.

$27 \times 3 = 81$

So, $3 \times 3 \times 3 \times 3 = 81$.

Practice

Evaluate.

1. $7 \times 7 \times 7$ **2.** $2 \times 2 \times 2 \times 2 \times 2 \times 2$ **3.** $4 \times 4 \times 4 \times 4 \times 4$ **4.** $8 \times 8 \times 8 \times 8$

Troubleshooting

Factors and Multiples

Multiples of a number are the products that result when the number is multiplied by 0, 1, 2, 3, 4, and so on.

27 is a multiple of 9 because $27 = 9 \times 3$.

Factors are numbers that divide a whole number evenly.

8 is a factor of 32 because 8 divides 32 evenly: $32 \div 8 = 4$.

Examples

A. List the next three multiples of 7: 7, 14, 21.

7,   14,   21,   **28,**   **35,**   **42**

↑   ↑   ↑   ↑   ↑   ↑

7×1 7×2 7×3 7×4 7×5 7×6

So, the next three multiples are 28, 35, and 42.

B. Find all the factors of 20.

Think: $1 \times 20 = 20$, so 1 and 20 are factors of 20. $2 \times 10 = 20$, so 2 and 10 are factors of 20. $4 \times 5 = 20$, so 4 and 5 are factors of 20.

So, the factors of 20 are 1, 2, 4, 5, 10, and 20.

Practice

List the next three multiples of the number.

1. 5: 5, 10, 15   **2.** 9: 9, 18, 27   **3.** 6: 12, 18, 24   **4.** 20: 40, 60, 80

Find all of the factors of the number.

5. 13   **6.** 12   **7.** 30   **8.** 24

9. 15   **10.** 22   **11.** 28   **12.** 36

Model Fractions

A **fraction** is a number that names a part of a whole or a part of a group.

Example

Write the fraction represented by the shaded part.

The group has 7 squares. The part that is shaded is 4 squares.

So, the fraction shaded is $\frac{4}{7}$.

Practice

Write the fraction represented by the shaded part.

1.   **2.**   **3.**   **4.**

Model Percents

Percent (%) means "per hundred." You can use a hundred square to model percents.

Example

Write the percent for the shaded part of the square.

There are 100 parts, and 75 of the parts are shaded. So, 75% of the parts are shaded.

Practice

Write the percent for the shaded part of the square.

1. 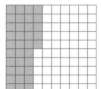 **2.** 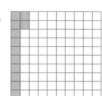 **3.** 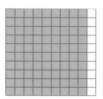 **4.**

Simplify Fractions

A fraction is in **simplest form** when the numerator and denominator have no common factors other than 1.

$\frac{10}{15}$ is not in simplest form, because 10 and 15 have the common factor 5.

$\frac{7}{12}$ is in simplest form, because 7 and 12 have no common factors other than 1.

You can write a fraction in simplest form by dividing the numerator and denominator by the greatest common factor (GCF).

Example

Write the fraction in simplest form. $\frac{16}{28}$

Step 1

Find the greatest common factor of 16 and 28.

factors of 16: 1, 2, 4, 8, 16
factors of 28: 1, 2, 4, 7, 14, 28

The *greatest* common factor is 4.

Step 2

Divide the numerator and the denominator by the GCF.

$\frac{16 \div 4}{28 \div 4} = \frac{4}{7}$ Since the GCF of 4 and 7 is 1, $\frac{4}{7}$ is in simplest form.

Practice

Write the fraction in simplest form.

1. $\frac{9}{15}$ **2.** $\frac{8}{12}$ **3.** $\frac{5}{20}$ **4.** $\frac{18}{6}$ **5.** $\frac{24}{32}$ **6.** $\frac{24}{30}$

Troubleshooting

Add and Subtract Like Fractions

Like fractions are fractions that have the same denominator.
To add or subtract like fractions, add or subtract the
numerators. Keep the same denominator.

Example

Find the sum. $\frac{4}{9} + \frac{2}{9}$

Step 1

Add the numerators. Write the sum over
the like denominator.

$\frac{4}{9} + \frac{2}{9} = \frac{4+2}{9} = \frac{6}{9}$

Step 2

If necessary, rewrite the fraction in
simplest form.

$\frac{6}{9} = \frac{6 \div 3}{9 \div 3} = \frac{2}{3}$

Practice

Find the sum or difference. Write the answer in simplest form.

1. $\frac{1}{7} + \frac{4}{7}$　　**2.** $\frac{4}{5} - \frac{2}{5}$　　**3.** $\frac{3}{8} + \frac{3}{8}$　　**4.** $\frac{3}{4} + \frac{1}{4}$　　**5.** $\frac{7}{10} - \frac{5}{10}$

6. $\frac{8}{12} - \frac{4}{12}$　　**7.** $\frac{15}{11} - \frac{9}{11}$　　**8.** $\frac{5}{9} + \frac{8}{9}$　　**9.** $\frac{2}{10} + \frac{6}{10}$　　**10.** $\frac{12}{8} - \frac{4}{8}$

11. $\frac{3}{6} + \frac{1}{6}$　　**12.** $\frac{5}{8} + \frac{1}{8}$　　**13.** $\frac{7}{16} + \frac{5}{16}$　　**14.** $\frac{17}{20} - \frac{9}{20}$　　**15.** $\frac{11}{25} + \frac{4}{25}$

Round Fractions

To round a fraction to 0, $\frac{1}{2}$, or 1, compare the numerator with
the denominator.

Examples

Round each fraction to 0, $\frac{1}{2}$, or 1.

A. $\frac{2}{11}$

2 is closer to 0 than to 11.

Round the fraction to 0.

B. $\frac{7}{15}$

7 is about half of 15.

Round the fraction to $\frac{1}{2}$.

C. $\frac{13}{16}$

13 is close to 16.

Round the fraction to 1.

Practice

Round each fraction to 0, $\frac{1}{2}$, or 1.

1. $\frac{3}{4}$　　**2.** $\frac{1}{5}$　　**3.** $\frac{2}{7}$　　**4.** $\frac{6}{13}$　　**5.** $\frac{5}{12}$

6. $\frac{14}{15}$　　**7.** $\frac{4}{18}$　　**8.** $\frac{3}{7}$　　**9.** $\frac{4}{5}$　　**10.** $\frac{12}{20}$

11. $\frac{11}{24}$　　**12.** $\frac{17}{20}$　　**13.** $\frac{11}{18}$　　**14.** $\frac{3}{25}$　　**15.** $\frac{15}{16}$

Mental Math and Equations

You can use mental math to solve equations. Try using a related equation to find the value of the variable.

Examples

Use mental math to solve the equation.

A. $k + 6 = 10$

Think: When 6 is added to k, the sum is 10. That means that $k = 10 - 6$.

So, $k = 4$. Check: **$4 + 6 = 10$** ✔

B. $m - 4 = 11$

Think: When 4 is subtracted from m, the difference is 11. That means that $m = 11 + 4$.

So, $m = 15$. Check: **$15 - 4 = 11$** ✔

C. $c \div 5 = 7$

Think: When c is divided by 5, the quotient is 7. That means that $c = 7 \times 5$.

So, $c = 35$. Check: **$35 \div 5 = 7$** ✔

D. $h \times 4 = 36$

Think: When h is multiplied by 4, the product is 36. That means that $h = 36 \div 4$.

So, $h = 9$. Check: **$9 \times 4 = 36$** ✔

Practice

Use mental math to solve the equation.

1. $g - 5 = 6$ **2.** $r \times 2 = 12$ **3.** $d \div 3 = 6$ **4.** $x + 9 = 17$

5. $v \div 6 = 5$ **6.** $y - 6 = 9$ **7.** $a + 3 = 15$ **8.** $n \times 3 = 21$

Fractions and Mixed Numbers

A **mixed number** is made up of a whole number and a fraction. You can write a mixed number as a fraction greater than 1, and a fraction greater than 1 as a mixed number.

Examples

A. Write $\frac{14}{3}$ as a mixed number.

$$\begin{array}{r} 4 \text{ r}2 \\ 3\overline{)14} \end{array}$$ Divide the numerator by the denominator.

$\frac{14}{3} = 4\frac{2}{3}$ Write the remainder as the numerator of a fraction.

B. Write $3\frac{4}{5}$ as a fraction.

$3 \times 5 = 15$ Multiply the denominator by the whole number.

$15 + 4 = 19$ Add the numerator.

$3\frac{4}{5} = \frac{19}{5}$ Write the sum over the denominator.

Practice

Write the fraction as a mixed number.

1. $\frac{13}{7}$ **2.** $\frac{18}{5}$ **3.** $\frac{10}{3}$ **4.** $\frac{22}{9}$ **5.** $\frac{17}{6}$

Write the mixed number as a fraction.

6. $2\frac{4}{5}$ **7.** $1\frac{3}{8}$ **8.** $3\frac{3}{4}$ **9.** $2\frac{22}{25}$ **10.** $2\frac{11}{16}$

Troubleshooting

Compare Fractions

To compare fractions with unlike denominators, rename the fractions so that they have like denominators. Then compare the numerators.

Examples

Compare. Use $<$, $>$, or $=$ for ●.

A. $\frac{5}{8}$ ● $\frac{7}{8}$

The denominators are like. Compare the numerators.

$5 < 7$, so $\frac{5}{8} < \frac{7}{8}$.

B. $\frac{7}{10}$ ● $\frac{3}{5}$

The denominators are unlike. Rename one or both fractions.

$\frac{3 \times 2}{5 \times 2} = \frac{6}{10}$

$7 > 6$, so $\frac{7}{10} > \frac{3}{5}$.

C. $2\frac{5}{12}$ ● $2\frac{1}{3}$

The whole numbers are equal. Rename one or both fractions.

$\frac{1 \times 4}{3 \times 4} = \frac{4}{12}$

$5 > 4$, so $2\frac{5}{12} > 2\frac{1}{3}$.

Practice

Compare. Use $<$, $>$, or $=$ for ●.

1. $\frac{4}{5}$ ● $\frac{3}{5}$

2. $\frac{11}{15}$ ● $\frac{13}{15}$

3. $1\frac{4}{6}$ ● $1\frac{2}{3}$

4. $2\frac{5}{8}$ ● $2\frac{1}{2}$

5. $\frac{2}{3}$ ● $\frac{5}{12}$

6. $\frac{7}{8}$ ● $\frac{3}{4}$

7. $\frac{5}{15}$ ● $\frac{2}{6}$

8. $\frac{8}{9}$ ● $\frac{2}{3}$

9. $\frac{13}{16}$ ● $\frac{7}{8}$

10. $\frac{5}{9}$ ● $\frac{14}{27}$

Understand Integers

The **integers** are the whole numbers and their opposites. Integers greater than 0 are **positive integers** and are found to the right of 0 on a number line. Integers less than 0 are **negative integers** and are found to the left of 0.

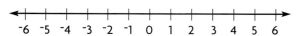

Example

Name the temperatures indicated by point A and point B.

The temperature at point A is $^-35°$. The temperature at point B is $^+68°$.

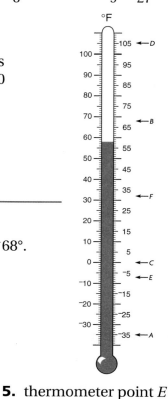

Practice

Give four examples from each set of numbers.

1. whole numbers

2. negative integers

Write a positive or negative integer for each situation.

3. thermometer point C

4. thermometer point D

5. thermometer point E

6. thermometer point F

7. 35 ft above sea level

8. a loss of $5

Explore Negative Numbers

Positive numbers are located to the right of 0 on the number line. **Negative numbers** are located to the left of 0 on the number line. Zero is neither positive nor negative.

Examples

Use the number line to name the number each letter represents.

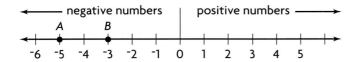

A. point *A*
Point *A* represents ⁻5.

B. point *B*
Point *B* represents ⁻3.

Practice

Use the number line to name the number each letter represents.

```
  Q  H  P  N      F      E  G      M
◄─●──●──●──●──┼──●──┼──●──●──┼──●──┼──►
 -9 -8 -7 -6 -5 -4 -3 -2 -1  0  1  2  3
```

1. point *M* **2.** point *N* **3.** point *P* **4.** point *Q*

5. point *E* **6.** point *F* **7.** point *G* **8.** point *H*

Multiply by 10, 100, 1,000

You can use a pattern to multiply a whole number by 10, 100, or 1,000. To multiply a decimal by a power of 10, move the decimal point one place to the right for each zero.

Examples

Find the product.

A. $24 \times 10 = 240$
$24 \times 100 = 2,400$
$24 \times 1,000 = 24,000$

B. $4.3 \times 10 = 43$
$4.3 \times 100 = 430$
$4.3 \times 1,000 = 4,300$

Practice

Find the product.

1. 56×10 **2.** 78×100 **3.** $11 \times 1,000$ **4.** 127×100 **5.** $238 \times 1,000$

6. 2.6×100 **7.** 4.8×10 **8.** $5.7 \times 1,000$ **9.** 7.13×100 **10.** 0.02×10

Troubleshooting

Classify Lines

Parallel lines are lines in a plane that are always the same distance apart. **Intersecting lines** cross at exactly one point. **Perpendicular lines** intersect to form 90° angles, or right angles.

Examples

Classify the lines.

A.

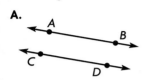

Line *AB* and line *CD* are in the same plane and are always the same distance apart. The lines are *parallel*.

$\overleftrightarrow{AB} \parallel \overleftrightarrow{CD}$ ($\parallel$ means "is parallel to.")

B.

Line *EH* and line *GF* cross at exactly one point, *J*. The lines are *intersecting*.

C.

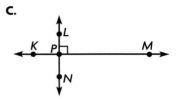

Lines *KM* and *LN* intersect at *P* to form right angles. The lines are *perpendicular* and *intersecting*.

$\overleftrightarrow{KM} \perp \overleftrightarrow{LN}$ ($\perp$ means "is perpendicular to.")

Practice

Classify the lines.

1.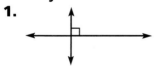

2.

3.

4.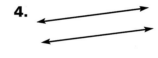

Patterns

Look for a rule for the pattern. Then use it to extend the pattern.

Example

Find the next three possible numbers in the pattern.   1, 2, 4, 8

Step 1 Find a rule.

Each number in the series is 2 times the number before it.
$1 \times 2 = 2; 2 \times 2 = 4; 4 \times 2 = 8$
The rule is "multiply by 2."

Step 2 Use the rule.

Multiply each number by 2 to find the next number:
$8 \times 2 = 16, 16 \times 2 = 32, 32 \times 2 = 64$
So, the next three numbers are 16, 32, and 64.

Practice

Find the next three possible numbers in the pattern. Write the rule.

1. 10, 14, 18, 22, 26

2. 729, 243, 81, 27

3. 1, 4, 16

4. 63, 55, 47, 39

5. 49, 37, 25, 13

6. $2\frac{1}{2}, 1\frac{3}{4}, 1, \frac{1}{4}$

Exponents

You can use exponents to express powers of numbers. An **exponent** tells how many times the **base** is used as a factor.

$$6 \times 6 \times 6 \times 6 = 6^4 \quad \leftarrow \text{exponent}$$
$$\uparrow \text{base}$$

The exponent 4 shows that the base 6 is used 4 times as a factor.

Examples

Find the value of 5^3.

A. $5^3 = 5 \times 5 \times 5 = 125$

Write 49 by using an exponent.

B. $49 = 7 \times 7 = 7^2$

Practice

Find the value.

1. 2^4 **2.** 4^3 **3.** 5^2 **4.** 10^3 **5.** 3^4

Write by using an exponent.

6. 9 **7.** 32 **8.** 36 **9.** 100 **10.** 27

Order of Operations

When more than one operation is used in an expression, follow these rules to evaluate the expression.

RULES FOR ORDER OF OPERATIONS	
1. First, do the operations **in parentheses**.	3. Next, **multiply and divide** from left to right.
2. Next, evaluate **exponents**.	4. Finally, **add and subtract** from left to right.

Examples

Evaluate each expression.

A. $3^2 + 5 \times 2$

1. There are no parentheses.

2. Evaluate exponents. $3^2 + 5 \times 2 = \mathbf{9} + 5 \times 2$

3. Multiply. $9 + \mathbf{5 \times 2} = 9 + \mathbf{10}$

4. Add. $\mathbf{9 + 10} = 19$

B. $(21 - 6) \div 3$

1. Evaluate parentheses. $\mathbf{(21 - 6)} \div 3 = \mathbf{15} \div 3$

2. There are no exponents.

3. Divide. $15 \div 3 = 5$

4. There is no addition or subtraction.

Practice

Evaluate each expression.

1. $4 + 6 \times 9$ **2.** $(5 + 4) \times 3$ **3.** $25 - 12 \times 3$ **4.** $2^2 + 3^2$

5. $(2 + 3)^2$ **6.** $\dfrac{10 - 4}{2} \times 4^2$ **7.** $5^2 \div (1^5 + 4)$ **8.** $2 + 3 \times 3 \times 3$

Troubleshooting

Multiply

An understanding of place value can help you find products.

Example

Multiply. 472 × 3

Step 1

Multiply the ones.

$$\begin{array}{r} 472 \\ \times\, 3 \\ \hline 6 \end{array}$$ 3 × 2 ones = 6 ones

Step 2

Multiply the tens. Regroup 21 tens as 2 hundreds 1 ten.

$$\begin{array}{r} \overset{2}{4}72 \\ \times\, 3 \\ \hline 16 \end{array}$$ 3 × 7 tens = 21 tens

Step 3

Multiply the hundreds. Add the regrouped hundreds. Regroup 14 hundreds as 1 thousand 4 hundreds.

$$\begin{array}{r} \overset{2}{4}72 \\ \times\, 3 \\ \hline 1{,}416 \end{array}$$ 3 × 4 hundreds = 12 hundreds

So, 472 × 3 = 1,416.

Practice

Multiply.

1. 218 × 4   **2.** 653 × 3   **3.** 8,394 × 7   **4.** 9,573 × 9   **5.** 4,721 × 5

Divide

An understanding of place value can help you find quotients.

Example

Divide. 683 ÷ 3

Step 1

Decide where to place the first digit in the quotient.

$$\begin{array}{r} 2 \\ 3\overline{)683} \\ -6 \\ \hline 0 \end{array}$$

6 > 3, so place the first digit in the hundreds place.

Divide. 6 ÷ 3
Multiply. 2 × 3
Subtract. 6 − 6
Compare. 0 < 3

Step 2

Bring down the 8 tens. Divide the 8 tens.

$$\begin{array}{r} 22 \\ 3\overline{)683} \\ -6\!\downarrow \\ \hline 8 \\ -6 \\ \hline 2 \end{array}$$

Divide. 8 ÷ 3
Multiply. 2 × 3
Subtract. 8 − 6
Compare. 2 < 3

Step 3

Bring down the 3 ones. Divide the 23 ones.

$$\begin{array}{r} 227\text{r}2 \\ 3\overline{)683} \\ -6\!\downarrow \\ \hline 8 \\ -6\!\downarrow \\ \hline 23 \\ -21 \\ \hline 2 \end{array}$$

Divide. 23 ÷ 3
Multiply. 7 × 3
Subtract. 23 − 21
Compare. 2 < 3

So, 683 ÷ 3 = 227 r2.

Practice

Divide.

1. 710 ÷ 8   **2.** 941 ÷ 3   **3.** 862 ÷ 9   **4.** 412 ÷ 7   **5.** 336 ÷ 8

Words for Operations

Many different words and phrases can be used to represent the operations of addition, subtraction, multiplication, and division.

Examples

Write the operation described by the phrase.

A. the sum of 6 and 7

To find a sum means to add. The operation is addition.

B. the product of k and 15

To find a product means to multiply. The operation is multiplication.

Practice

Write the operation described by the phrase.

1. k greater than 75

2. 42 less than m

3. the sum of h and 6

4. the quotient of 11 and b

5. c times w

6. the difference of a and 45

7. 9 increased by 7

8. the product of 12 and p

9. 2 reduced by m

Words and Equations

You can write equations to represent some sentences. Use a variable to represent what is unknown in the sentence. Use operation signs or other mathematical signs to represent words or phrases in the sentence.

Example

Write an equation for this sentence: A number increased by 7 is 12.

Represent "a number" with a variable such as x.
Represent "increased by" with a plus sign.
Represent "is" with an equal sign.

So, the equation is $x + 7 = 12$.

Practice

Write an equation for the sentence.

1. The product of a number and 7 is 49.

2. 8 less than a number is 50.

3. 12 and a number have a quotient of 2.

4. 13 times a number is 91.

5. 7 more than a number is 12.

6. 16 divided by a number is $\frac{4}{5}$.

7. A number reduced by 13 is 9.

8. 45 more than a number is 26.

Troubleshooting

Evaluate Algebraic Expressions

An expression that includes one or more variables is called an **algebraic expression**. To evaluate algebraic expressions, replace the variables with the given numbers. Then evaluate as you would with a numerical expression. Follow the rules for the order of operations.

Example

Evaluate $3 + m \times 2$ for $m = 6$.

$3 + m \times 2 = 3 + 6 \times 2$ Replace m with 6.

$ = 3 + 12$ Multiply before adding.

$ = 15$ Add.

Practice

Evaluate the expression for the given value of the variable.

1. $4m$ for $m = 9$ **2.** $\frac{3}{4}p$ for $p = 8$ **3.** $\frac{z}{24}$ for $z = 96$

4. $t - 5$ for $t = 19$ **5.** $6h$ for $h = 9$ **6.** $5 + c$ for $c = 13$

7. $72 \div k$ for $k = 6$ **8.** $p - 14$ for $p = 27$ **9.** $8f$ for $f = 7$

Classify Angles

You can classify angles by their measures.

An *acute* angle has a measure greater than 0° and less than 90°.

A

A *right* angle forms a square corner. It measures 90°.

B

An *obtuse* angle has a measure greater than 90° and less than 180°.

C

A *straight* angle has a measure of 180°.

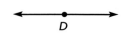
D

Practice

Classify each angle by stating whether it is *acute*, *obtuse*, *right*, or *straight*.

1.
K

2.
P

3.
Z

4.
N

5.
V

6.
M

7.
Q

8.
T

Name Angles

You can name an angle by using one letter, three letters, or a number.

Examples

Name the angle formed by the blue rays.

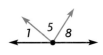

Use the vertex letter to name the angle. ∠G

There are two angles with vertices at *N*. So, use three letters. ∠*ANV* or ∠*VNA*

Use a number. ∠5

Practice

Name the angle formed by the blue rays.

1.

2.

3.

4.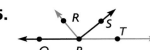

5.

6.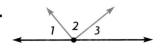

Identify Polygons

A **polygon** is a closed plane figure with straight sides that are connected line segments. A polygon is classified by its number of sides.

Examples

State whether the figure is a polygon or not. If it is, classify it.

A. The figure is not closed, so it is not a polygon.

B. The figure is a 5-sided polygon called a pentagon.

Practice

State whether the figure is a polygon or not. If it is, classify it.

1.

2.

3.

4.

Troubleshooting

Identify Solid Figures

A **polyhedron** is a solid figure with flat faces that are polygons. A **prism** is a polyhedron with two congruent, parallel **bases**. Its **lateral faces** are rectangles. A **pyramid** has a polygon for its base and triangles for its lateral faces.

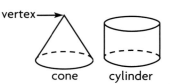

pentagonal prism   square pyramid

A **cone** has a circular base. A **cylinder** has two congruent parallel circular bases. Cones and cylinders have curved lateral surfaces.

cone   cylinder

Practice

Identify each solid figure.

1.

2.

3.

4.

5.

6.

7.

8.

Faces, Edges, and Vertices

Each polygon that forms a solid figure is a **face** of the figure. A line segment where two faces meet is an **edge**. A point where three or more edges meet is a **vertex**.

Face
Vertex
Edge

Example

Tell the number of faces, vertices, and edges of the cube above.

The cube has 6 faces, 8 vertices, and 12 edges.

Practice

Give the number of faces, edges, and vertices of each solid figure.

1.

2.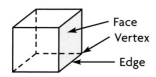

3.

4.

Write Equivalent Fractions

To write a fraction equivalent to a given fraction, multiply or divide the numerator and denominator by the same number.

Examples

Complete the number sentence to find an equivalent fraction.

A. $\frac{18}{24} = \frac{3}{\blacksquare}$

Think: To change 18 to 3, divide the numerator of $\frac{18}{24}$ by 6. Then divide the denominator by 6.

$$\frac{18}{24} = \frac{18 \div 6}{24 \div 6} = \frac{3}{4}$$

So, the equivalent fraction is $\frac{3}{4}$.

B. $\frac{3}{5} = \frac{\blacksquare}{20}$

Think: To change 5 to 20, multiply the denominator of $\frac{3}{5}$ by 4. Then multiply the numerator by 4.

$$\frac{3}{5} = \frac{3 \times 4}{5 \times 4} = \frac{12}{20}$$

So, the equivalent fraction is $\frac{12}{20}$.

Practice

Complete each number sentence to find an equivalent fraction.

1. $\frac{1}{2} = \frac{\blacksquare}{8}$

2. $\frac{12}{18} = \frac{2}{\blacksquare}$

3. $\frac{3}{4} = \frac{15}{\blacksquare}$

4. $\frac{\blacksquare}{6} = \frac{25}{30}$

5. $\frac{8}{24} = \frac{\blacksquare}{12}$

6. $\frac{\blacksquare}{15} = \frac{30}{45}$

7. $\frac{3}{5} = \frac{48}{\blacksquare}$

8. $\frac{\blacksquare}{40} = \frac{7}{8}$

9. $\frac{27}{36} = \frac{\blacksquare}{12}$

10. $\frac{\blacksquare}{16} = \frac{8}{32}$

11. $\frac{12}{\blacksquare} = \frac{6}{10}$

12. $\frac{\blacksquare}{100} = \frac{11}{20}$

Solve Multiplication Equations

To solve a multiplication equation, use an inverse operation. Divide both sides of the equation by the number that multiplies the variable.

Example

Solve and check. $8n = 40$

$$8n = 40$$
$$\frac{8n}{8} = \frac{40}{8} \quad \text{Divide both sides by 8.}$$
$$n = 5 \quad \text{Simplify.}$$

Check: $8n \stackrel{?}{=} 40$
$8 \times 5 \stackrel{?}{=} 40$
$40 = 40 \; ✔$

Practice

Solve and check.

1. $6k = 18$

2. $3h = 27$

3. $5e = 75$

4. $10d = 700$

5. $120 = 8m$

6. $24y = 108$

7. $40 = 160b$

8. $1p = 12$

9. $15n = 135$

10. $4k = 30$

11. $1.2\,t = 96$

12. $5b = 35$

13. $198 = 18s$

14. $9 = \frac{1}{2}p$

15. $7f = 98$

16. $84 = 14q$

Troubleshooting

Congruent and Similar Figures

Two figures are **similar** if they have the same shape. One may be an enlargement or a reduction of the other. Two figures are **congruent** if they have the same size and shape.

Examples

Tell if the figures in each pair appear to be similar or congruent. If they appear not to be similar or congruent, write *neither*.

A.

neither

B.

The figures are similar.

C.

The figures are congruent.

Practice

Tell if the figures in each pair appear to be similar or congruent. If they appear not to be similar or congruent, write *neither*.

1.

2.

3.

Write Fractions as Decimals

To write a fraction as a decimal, divide the numerator by the denominator. Or, write an equivalent fraction with a denominator of 10, 100, or 1,000. Then rewrite the fraction as a decimal.

Example

Write $\frac{3}{4}$ as a decimal.

One Way

$$\begin{array}{r} 0.75 \\ 4\overline{)3.00} \\ -28 \\ \hline 20 \\ -20 \\ \hline 0 \end{array}$$ Divide 3 by 4. So, $\frac{3}{4} = 0.75$.

Another Way

$\frac{3}{4} = \frac{3 \times 25}{4 \times 25} = \frac{75}{100}$ Write an equivalent fraction with a denominator of 100.

$\frac{75}{100} = 0.75$ Write the equivalent fraction as a decimal.

So, $\frac{3}{4} = 0.75$.

Practice

Write the fraction as a decimal.

1. $\frac{1}{2}$ **2.** $\frac{7}{10}$ **3.** $\frac{1}{4}$ **4.** $\frac{3}{8}$ **5.** $\frac{7}{20}$

6. $\frac{2}{5}$ **7.** $\frac{17}{25}$ **8.** $\frac{43}{50}$ **9.** $\frac{48}{250}$ **10.** $\frac{19}{50}$

Multiply with Fractions and Decimals

When you multiply decimals, the number of decimal places in the product is the total of the decimal places in the two factors. When multiplying fractions, write the product of the numerators over the product of the denominators.

Find the product.

A.
$$\begin{array}{r} 2.57 \\ \times\ \ 1.2 \\ \hline 514 \\ +\ 2570 \\ \hline 3.084 \end{array}$$
2.57 **2 decimal places**
× 1.2 **1 decimal place**

3.084 **2 + 1 = 3 decimal places**

B. $\frac{3}{4} \times \frac{8}{9} = \frac{3 \times 8}{4 \times 9} = \frac{24}{36}$ Multiply numerators. Multiply denominators.

$\frac{24 \div 12}{36 \div 12} = \frac{2}{3}$ Simplify.

Find the product. Write the answer in simplest form.

1. 7.2×0.9 **2.** 8.4×1.1 **3.** 112.3×0.15 **4.** 17.55×1.05 **5.** 15.82×25

6. $\frac{1}{3} \times \frac{2}{3}$ **7.** $\frac{5}{6} \times \frac{3}{4}$ **8.** $\frac{2}{3} \times \frac{5}{12}$ **9.** $\frac{5}{8} \times \frac{3}{5}$ **10.** $\frac{1}{2} \times \frac{1}{4}$

Fractions, Decimals, and Percents

You can write a percent as a decimal and a decimal as a percent. You can write a percent as a fraction and a fraction as a percent.

A. Write 42% as a decimal.

42% = 42 ÷ 100 Divide by 100.

So, 42% = 0.42.

B. Write 0.781 as a percent.

0.781 = 0.781 × 100% Multiply by 100.

So, 0.781 = 78.1%.

C. Write 24% as a fraction.

$24\% = \frac{24}{100} = \frac{6}{25}$ Write the percent over 100. Simplify.

So, $24\% = \frac{6}{25}$.

D. Write $\frac{11}{25}$ as a percent.

$\frac{11}{25} = 11 \div 25 = 0.44$ Divide numerator by denominator.

So, $\frac{11}{25} = 44\%$. Write the percent.

Write each decimal and each fraction as a percent.
Write each percent as a decimal and as a fraction.

1. $\frac{2}{5}$ **2.** 10% **3.** 0.34 **4.** 25% **5.** $\frac{1}{2}$

6. 0.81 **7.** $\frac{7}{25}$ **8.** 60% **9.** $\frac{18}{50}$ **10.** 0.02

Troubleshooting

Certain, Impossible, Likely, Unlikely

An event is **certain** if it is sure to happen. It is **impossible** if it can never happen. It is **likely** if there is a strong chance that it will happen. It is **unlikely** if there is a strong chance that it will not happen.

Examples

Tell if the event is *certain*, *impossible*, *likely*, or *unlikely*.

A. 2 + 2 will equal 5 next Tuesday.

    2 + 2 can never equal 5.

    So, the event is *impossible*.

B. You toss a penny 10 times and get at least 1 head.

    The probability of getting a head is $\frac{1}{2}$ each time you toss a coin.

    So, the event is *likely*.

Practice

Tell if the event is *certain*, *impossible*, *likely*, or *unlikely*.

1. Rain will fall at least once this year.

2. There will be no June next year.

3. You toss a quarter and get either a head or a tail.

4. A person who does not know you will guess your phone number.

Opposites and Absolute Value

Every number on a number line has an **opposite** that is the same distance from 0 but on the opposite side of 0.

The **absolute value** of a number is its distance from 0 on the number line. The symbol for absolute value is | |.

    |⁻2| means "the absolute value of ⁻2."

Examples

A. Find the opposite of ⁻4.
⁻4 and 4 are both 4 units from 0. So, the opposite of ⁻4 is 4.

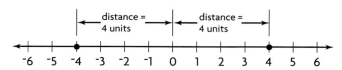

B. Find |⁻4|.
The distance between 0 and ⁻4 is 4 units. So, |⁻4| = 4.

Practice

Find the opposite of each number.

1. 6   **2.** ⁻2   **3.** 8   **4.** ⁻1   **5.** ⁻5

Find each absolute value.

6. |⁻3| **7.** |⁻9| **8.** |1| **9.** |⁻7| **10.** |0|

Customary Units

The table shows equivalents in the customary system of measurement. To change from a larger unit to a smaller one, multiply. To change from a smaller unit to a larger one, divide.

UNITS OF LENGTH
12 inches (in.) = 1 foot (ft)
3 feet = 1 yard (yd)
5,280 feet = 1 mile (mi)
1,760 yards = 1 mile

UNITS OF CAPACITY
2 cups (c) = 1 pint (pt)
2 pints = 1 quart (qt)
4 quarts = 1 gallon (gal)

UNITS OF WEIGHT
16 ounces (oz) = 1 pound (lb)
2,000 pounds = 1 ton (T)

Examples

Change to the given unit.

A. 24 in. = ▧ ft **Think:** An inch is smaller than a foot. To change from inches to feet, divide by 12.

$24 \div 12 = 2$, so 24 in. = 2 ft.

B. 4 gal = ▧ qt **Think:** A gallon is larger than a quart. To change from gallons to quarts, multiply by 4.

$4 \times 4 = 16$, so 4 gal = 16 qt.

Practice

Change to the given unit.

1. 2 yd = ▧ ft **2.** 4 c = ▧ pt **3.** 4 lb = ▧ oz **4.** 2.5 gal = ▧ qt

Multiply Fractions and Whole Numbers

To multiply a fraction and a whole number, first write the whole number as an equivalent fraction with 1 as the denominator. Then multiply as you would any two fractions.

Example

Find the product. $4 \times \frac{7}{8}$

Step 1

Write 4 as a fraction.

$4 = \frac{4}{1}$

Step 2

Multiply the numerators. Multiply the denominators.

$\frac{4}{1} \times \frac{7}{8} = \frac{28}{8}$

Step 3

Write the product in simplest form.

$\frac{28}{8} = \frac{28 \div 4}{8 \div 4} = \frac{7}{2}$, or $3\frac{1}{2}$

Practice

Find the product. Write it in simplest form.

1. $3 \times \frac{5}{6}$ **2.** $\frac{7}{10} \times 8$ **3.** $5 \times \frac{3}{5}$ **4.** $\frac{1}{8} \times 12$

5. $\frac{11}{12} \times 9$ **6.** $15 \times \frac{3}{10}$ **7.** $6 \times \frac{5}{7}$ **8.** $\frac{2}{5} \times 10$

Troubleshooting

Solve Proportions

A **proportion** is an equation which states that two ratios are equal. You can solve a proportion by using the fact that in a proportion, the **cross products** are equal.

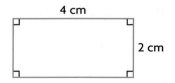

cross products

$2 \times 6 = 3 \times 4$

Example

Solve for n. $\frac{2}{3} = \frac{n}{12}$

$\frac{2}{3} \ \diagdown\!=\!\diagup \ \frac{n}{12}$ Find the cross products.

$2 \times 12 = 3 \times n$ Use the cross products to write an equation.

$24 = 3 \times n$ Simplify.

$\frac{24}{3} = \frac{3 \times n}{3}$ Divide both sides of the equation by 3.

$8 = n$ Write the solution.

Practice

Solve for n.

1. $\frac{n}{3} = \frac{6}{9}$

2. $\frac{4}{n} = \frac{5}{10}$

3. $\frac{8}{10} = \frac{n}{15}$

4. $\frac{20}{15} = \frac{12}{n}$

5. $\frac{n}{6} = \frac{25}{30}$

6. $\frac{n}{5} = \frac{9}{15}$

7. $\frac{8}{n} = \frac{32}{16}$

8. $\frac{48}{36} = \frac{n}{9}$

Perimeter

Perimeter is the distance around a figure. To find the perimeter of a polygon, find the sum of the lengths of the sides.

Example

The opposite sides of a rectangle are congruent, so the sides of the figure that are not labeled measure 4 cm and 2 cm.

$P = 4 \text{ cm} + 2 \text{ cm} + 4 \text{ cm} + 2 \text{ cm}$

So, the perimeter is 12 cm.

4 cm

2 cm

Practice

Find the perimeter of the figure.

1.
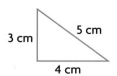
3 cm
5 cm
4 cm

2.

11 cm
11 cm

3.
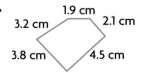
1.9 cm
3.2 cm
2.1 cm
3.8 cm
4.5 cm

4.
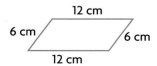
12 cm
6 cm
6 cm
12 cm

5.
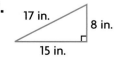
17 in.
8 in.
15 in.

6.
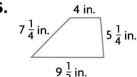
4 in.
$7\frac{1}{4}$ in.
$5\frac{1}{4}$ in.
$9\frac{1}{2}$ in.

Pictographs

A *pictograph* is a type of graph that uses pictures or symbols to show and compare information. A *key* is used to show the value of each picture or symbol in the graph.

This pictograph shows the number of hours four employees at the Ice Creamery worked last week.

NUMBER OF HOURS WORKED	
Cassie	🕐 🕐 🕐 🕐 🕐 🕐
Kristen	🕐 🕐 🕐 🕐 🕐
Leticia	🕐 🕐 🕐 🕐 🕐 🕐 🕐
Morgan	🕐 🕐 🕐 🕐 🕐 🕐

Key: Each 🕐 = 5 hours.

Example

How many more hours did Cassie work than Kristen?

Step 1

Find the number of hours that Cassie worked.

Each clock represents 5 hr worked. Cassie worked $6 \times 5 = 30$, or 30 hr.

Step 2

Find the number of hours that Kristen worked.

Each clock represents 5 hr worked. Kristen worked $4\frac{1}{2} \times 5 = 22\frac{1}{2}$, or $22\frac{1}{2}$ hr.

Step 3

Subtract.

$$30 - 22\frac{1}{2} = 7\frac{1}{2}$$

So, Cassie worked $7\frac{1}{2}$ more hours than Kristen.

Practice

For 1–2, use the pictograph above.

1. How many hours did the employee with the most hours work last week?

2. How many hours in all did the four employees work last week?

For 3–4, use the pictograph below.

NUMBER OF VIDEOS RENTED	
Week 1	▭ ▭ ▭ ▭ ▭ ▭ ▭
Week 2	▭ ▭ ▭ ▭
Week 3	▭ ▭ ▭ ▭ ▭ ▭ ▭
Week 4	▭ ▭ ▭ ▭ ▭ ▭

Key: Each ▭ = 100 videos.

3. How many more videos were rented during Week 4 than during Week 2?

4. What was the total number of videos rented during the four weeks?

Troubleshooting

Areas of Squares, Rectangles, and Triangles

The area of a rectangle or square is the product of the length and the width. The area of a triangle is *half* the product of the base and the height.

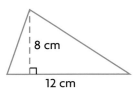

$A = l \times w$

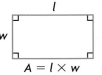

$A = \frac{1}{2} \times b \times h$

Examples

Find the area of the figure.

A.

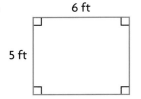

6 ft

5 ft

$A = 6 \times 5 = 30$, or 30 ft^2

B.

9 in.

9 in.

$A = 9 \times 9 = 9^2 = 81$, or 81 in.^{2}

C.

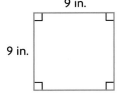

8 cm

12 cm

$A = \frac{1}{2} \times 12 \times 8 = 48$, or 48 cm^2

Practice

Find the area of the figure.

1.

13 yd

13 yd

2.

12 ft

7 ft

3.

15 cm

10.4 cm

4.

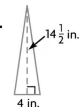

$14\frac{1}{2}$ in.

4 in.

Areas of Circles

The area of a circle is the product of π and the square of the radius. Use 3.14 for the value of π.

r

$A = \pi r^2$

Examples

Find the area of the circle.

A. radius = 3 cm

$A \approx 3.14 \times 3^2$

$\approx 3.14 \times 9$

≈ 28.26 cm^2

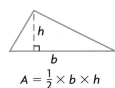

3 cm

B. The radius is half the diameter, or 8 in.

$A \approx 3.14 \times 8^2$

$\approx 3.14 \times 64$

≈ 200.96 in.^{2}

16 in.

Practice

Find the area of the circle. Use 3.14 for π.

1.

10 cm

2.

12 in.

3.

18 cm

4.

42 in.

Compare Numbers

| To compare integers, use a number line. The number to the right on the line is greater. | To compare decimals, align the decimal points. Then compare the digits from left to right. | To compare fractions, rename unlike fractions, then compare the numerators. |

Examples

Compare. Write $<$ or $>$ for each ⬤.

A. 2 ⬤ $^-3$

2 is to the right of $^-3$, so $2 > {}^-3$.

B. 6.25 ⬤ 6.179

6.25

6.179

$0.2 > 0.1$, so $6.25 > 6.179$.

C. $\frac{1}{2}$ ⬤ $\frac{2}{3}$

$\frac{1 \times 3}{2 \times 3} = \frac{3}{6}$ $\frac{2 \times 2}{3 \times 2} = \frac{4}{6}$

$3 < 4$, so $\frac{1}{2} < \frac{2}{3}$.

Practice

Compare. Write $<$ or $>$ for each ⬤.

1. 485 ⬤ 579 **2.** 3.03 ⬤ 3.3 **3.** $\frac{1}{2}$ ⬤ $\frac{1}{3}$ **4.** $^-11$ ⬤ $^-3$ **5.** 5 ⬤ $^-4$

6. 14.97 ⬤ 14.9 **7.** 523.6 ⬤ 532.8 **8.** 0.007 ⬤ 0.01 **9.** $^-0.5$ ⬤ $^-0.4$ **10.** $\frac{3}{4}$ ⬤ $\frac{5}{8}$

Function Tables

To find an output value for a function table, replace the variable with an input value. Then evaluate the algebraic expression.

Example

Complete the function table.

k	$k + 4$
7	⬜
9	⬜
11	⬜
16	⬜

Replace k in $k + 4$ with 7: $k + 4 = 7 + 4 = 11$.

Replace k in $k + 4$ with 9: $k + 4 = 9 + 4 = 13$.

Replace k in $k + 4$ with 11: $k + 4 = 11 + 4 = 15$.

Replace k in $k + 4$ with 16: $k + 4 = 16 + 4 = 20$.

Input Output
↓ ↓

k	$k + 4$
7	11
9	13
11	15
16	20

Practice

Copy and complete the function table.

1.

x	$x + 7$
9	16
13	⬜
18	⬜
24	⬜

2.

b	$b \times 16$
2	⬜
5	⬜
8	⬜
13	⬜

3.

m	$m \div 6$
192	⬜
150	⬜
90	⬜
51	⬜

4.

r	$r - 7.4$
25.8	⬜
19.2	⬜
13.05	⬜
9.1	⬜

Troubleshooting

Slides, Flips, and Turns

There are three ways that you can **transform** a figure. You can **slide,** or **translate,** the figure along a straight line. You can **flip,** or **reflect,** the figure over a line. Or you can **turn,** or **rotate,** the figure around a point.

Examples

Identify the transformation as a *slide, flip,* or *turn.*

A.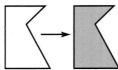

The figure has been translated along a straight line to the right. This is a *slide.*

B.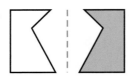

The figure has been reflected across a vertical line. This is a *flip.*

C.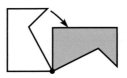

The figure has been rotated clockwise around a point. This is a *turn.*

Practice

Identify the transformation as a *slide, flip,* or *turn.*

1.

2.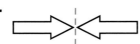

3.

4.

Line Symmetry

A figure has **line symmetry** if it can be folded along a line, or reflected, so that the two parts of the figure match, or are congruent. A figure can have more than one line of symmetry.

Examples

Is the dashed line a line of symmetry? Write *yes* or *no.*

A. 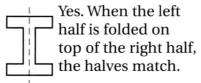 Yes. When the left half is folded on top of the right half, the halves match.

B. No. When the lower left is folded on top of the upper right, the halves do not match.

Practice

Is the dashed line a line of symmetry? Write *yes* or *no.*

1.

2.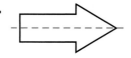

3.

4.

Measure Angles

To measure ∠ABC with a protractor, place the center of the protractor at B.

Align the 0° mark on the protractor with one ray of the angle.

Read the angle measure where the other ray passes through the scale on the protractor.

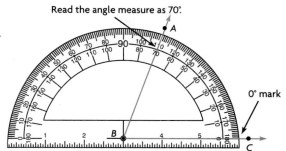
Read the angle measure as 70°.

0° mark

> ### Practice

Use a protractor to measure the angle.

1.

2.

3.

4.

Ordered Pairs

You can use two numbers called an **ordered pair** to locate a point on a grid. The first number tells you how far to move horizontally from (0,0). The second number tells you how far to move vertically from (0,0).

> ### Example

Write the ordered pair for point A.

To reach point A from (0,0), go
$^{+}3$ units right (horizontally) and
$^{-}2$ units down (vertically).

So, the ordered pair is $(3, ^{-}2)$.

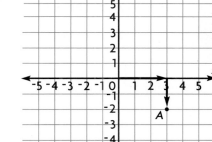

> ### Practice

Write the ordered pair for each point.

1. point A

2. point C

3. point D

4. point E

5. point F

6. point G

7. point I

8. point J

9. point B

10. point H

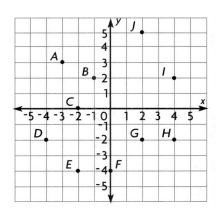

Sharpen Your Test-Taking Skills

TIPS FOR TAKING MATH TESTS

Being a good test-taker is like being a good problem solver. When you answer test questions, you are solving problems. Remember to **ANALYZE, *CHOOSE*, *SOLVE*, and CHECK.**

Analyze
Choose
Solve
Check

Analyze

Read the problem.

- Look for math terms and recall their meanings.
- Reread the problem and think about the question.
- Use the details in the problem and the question.

1. The difference between two numbers is 37. Their sum is 215. What are the numbers?

A 37 and 178   **C** 89 and 126

B 83 and 120   **D** 107 and 108

TIP **Understand the problem.**
The problem requires you to find two numbers for which the difference and sum are given. Reread the problem to compare the details to the answer choices. You can use estimation instead of calculating the sum and difference of each pair of numbers. The answer is **C**.

- Each word is important. Missing a word or reading it incorrectly could cause you to get the wrong answer.
- Pay attention to words that are in **bold** type, all CAPITAL letters, or *italics* and words like *round, best,* and *least to greatest*.

2. Florinda took $\frac{1}{2}$ hour to complete a race. Doris took $\frac{3}{8}$ hour and Violet took $\frac{2}{3}$ hour to complete the same race. Which lists the three runners from fastest to slowest?

F Florinda, Doris, Violet

G Doris, Violet, Florinda

H Violet, Florinda, Doris

J Doris, Florinda, Violet

TIP **Look for important words.**
The words *fastest to slowest* are important. The fastest runner takes the least amount of time. Think about where each fraction would be placed on a number line between 0 and 1. Then put the times in order from least to greatest. The answer is **J**.

Think about how you can solve the problem.

- See if you can solve the problem with the information given.
- Pictures, charts, tables, and graphs may have the information you need.
- You may need to recall information not given.
- Sometimes the answer choices have information to help solve the problem.

3. Jeremy wants to make a graph to see the trend of the profit in his lawn-mowing business over the past 10 months. What type of graph would best show this?

A circle graph   **C** line graph

B histogram   **D** stem-and-leaf plot

TIP Get the information you need.

The answer choices give four different types of graphs or plots. Think about each one and the kind of data that is appropriate for it. The problem states that Jeremy wants to see the trend in his profit over the past 10 months, and line graphs show trends. The answer is **C**.

- You may need to write a number sentence and solve it to answer the question.
- Some problems have two steps or more.
- In some problems you need to look at relationships instead of computing an answer.
- If the path to the solution isn't clear, choose a problem solving strategy and use it to solve the problem.

4. A square tile with 4-inch sides is rotated along the line below. If the tile stopped with the letter **P** again in an upright position, which of these distances could it have been rotated?

P

F 40 in.   **H** 48 in.

G 44 in.   **J** 52 in.

TIP Decide on a plan.

From the distances given, you must find the one that could allow for complete rotations of the square tile. Since each side of the square is 4 inches long, it moves 16 inches in one complete rotation. If you *use logical reasoning*, you see that only one of the choices is a multiple of 16. The answer is **H**.

Follow your plan, working logically and carefully.

- Estimate your answer. Compare it to the answer choices.
- Use reasoning to find the most likely choices.
- Make sure you solved all the steps needed to answer the problem.
- If your answer does not match any of the answer choices, check the numbers you used. Then check your computation.

5. Glen and Doug painted a fence. It took Glen three times as long to paint one side of the fence as it took Doug to paint the other side. If h represents the number of hours Doug painted, which expression shows the number of hours Glen painted?

A $3 \div h$ **C** $3 + h$

B $3 - h$ **D** $3 \times h$

> **TIP** **Eliminate choices.**
> It is important to understand that h represents the hours it took Doug to paint one side of the fence. Since Glen painted three times as long as Doug, you can eliminate choices **A** and **B** because it does not make sense to divide by or subtract the hours Doug painted. Choice **C** means three more than h, so it can be eliminated. The answer is **D**.

- If your answer still does not match one of the choices, look for another form of the number, such as a decimal instead of a fraction.
- If answer choices are given as pictures, look at each one by itself while you cover the other three.
- Read answer choices that are statements and relate them to the information in the problem one by one.

6. Tanya and her class helped plant 120 tulip and daffodil bulbs in front of the school. If 30 of the bulbs were tulips, what percent of the bulbs were daffodils?

F 90%   **H** 25%

G $66\frac{2}{3}\%$ **J** 75%

> **TIP** **Choose the answer.**
> Since 30 of the bulbs were tulips, 90 were daffodils. The question asks what percent are daffodils, so you need to find what percent of 120 is 90 ($90 \div 120 = 0.75$). Choose the answer that is equivalent to 0.75. The answer is **J**.

Take time to catch your mistakes.

- Be sure you answered the question asked.
- Check for important words you might have missed.
- Be sure you used all the information you needed.
- Check your computation by using a different method.

7. The temperature was 6°F today. A forecaster predicted that the temperature would drop by 5°F each day for the next four days. Which sequence shows the predicted temperatures?

A 6°F, 11°F, 16°F, 21°F, 26°F

B 6°F, 1°F, 6°F, 11°F, 16°F

C 6°F, 1°F, ⁻6°F, ⁻11°F, ⁻16°F

D 6°F, 1°F, ⁻4°F, ⁻9°F, ⁻14°F

TIP **Check your work.**
You need to find the sequence that shows a drop of 5°F each day in temperature for the next four days. Draw a thermometer or a number line to check your computation. The answer is **D**.

Don't Forget!

Before the test...

- Listen to the teacher's directions and read the instructions.
- Write down the ending time if the test is timed.
- Know where and how to mark your answers.
- Know whether you should write on the test page or use scratch paper.
- Ask any questions you have before the test begins.

During the test...

- Work quickly but carefully. If you are unsure how to answer a question, leave it blank and return to it later.
- If you cannot finish on time, look over the questions that are left. Answer the easiest ones first. Then go back to answer the others.
- Fill in each answer space carefully. Erase completely if you change an answer. Erase any stray marks.
- Check that the answer number matches the question number, especially if you skip a question.

Adding and Subtracting

1. 70
+8

2. 43
+5

3. 58
+7

4. 67
+18

5. 24
+36

6. 264
+58

7. 836
+54

8. 1,641
+385

9. 3,231
+578

10. 4,605
+2,493

11. 5,619
+2,537

12. 84,520
+3,864

13. 274,051
+40,318

14. 68
−5

15. 74
−43

16. 50
−38

17. 149
−58

18. 394
−145

19. 560
−217

20. 750
−192

21. 1,460
− 316

22. 4,960
− 681

23. 8,000
− 562

24. 35,120
−6,299

25. 36,009
−19,148

26. 0.4
+0.9

27. 2.6
+8.1

28. 0.31
+2.04

29. 5.92
+3.15

30. 0.218
+2.143

31. 2.14
+6.08

32. 7.04
+0.13

33. 0.126
+0.408

34. 8.360
+5.216

35. 5.816
+3.215

36. 17.31
+12.06

37. 8.26
+26.15

38. 31.18
+125.50

39. 11.4
−6.2

40. 12.8
−4.1

41. 17.3
−16.5

42. 21.8
−17.4

43. 13.2
−8.17

44. 35.51
−23.17

45. 8.026
−7.317

46. 19.408
−1.582

47. 5.848
−5.261

48. 13.601
−10.311

49. 5
−3.21

50. 630.71
−527.21

Multiplying

1. $\begin{array}{r} 20 \\ \times 4 \\ \hline \end{array}$

2. $\begin{array}{r} 30 \\ \times 2 \\ \hline \end{array}$

3. $\begin{array}{r} 30 \\ \times 3 \\ \hline \end{array}$

4. $\begin{array}{r} 24 \\ \times 2 \\ \hline \end{array}$

5. $\begin{array}{r} 31 \\ \times 3 \\ \hline \end{array}$

6. $\begin{array}{r} 46 \\ \times 2 \\ \hline \end{array}$

7. $\begin{array}{r} 37 \\ \times 4 \\ \hline \end{array}$

8. $\begin{array}{r} 74 \\ \times 6 \\ \hline \end{array}$

9. $\begin{array}{r} 63 \\ \times 8 \\ \hline \end{array}$

10. $\begin{array}{r} 58 \\ \times 9 \\ \hline \end{array}$

11. $\begin{array}{r} 61 \\ \times 20 \\ \hline \end{array}$

12. $\begin{array}{r} 84 \\ \times 40 \\ \hline \end{array}$

13. $\begin{array}{r} 76 \\ \times 30 \\ \hline \end{array}$

14. $\begin{array}{r} 68 \\ \times 50 \\ \hline \end{array}$

15. $\begin{array}{r} 92 \\ \times 60 \\ \hline \end{array}$

16. $\begin{array}{r} 26 \\ \times 14 \\ \hline \end{array}$

17. $\begin{array}{r} 93 \\ \times 15 \\ \hline \end{array}$

18. $\begin{array}{r} 50 \\ \times 38 \\ \hline \end{array}$

19. $\begin{array}{r} 81 \\ \times 54 \\ \hline \end{array}$

20. $\begin{array}{r} 79 \\ \times 43 \\ \hline \end{array}$

21. $\begin{array}{r} 680 \\ \times 35 \\ \hline \end{array}$

22. $\begin{array}{r} 710 \\ \times 52 \\ \hline \end{array}$

23. $\begin{array}{r} 825 \\ \times 173 \\ \hline \end{array}$

24. $\begin{array}{r} 522 \\ \times 286 \\ \hline \end{array}$

25. $\begin{array}{r} 463 \\ \times 836 \\ \hline \end{array}$

26. $\begin{array}{r} 0.5 \\ \times 0.9 \\ \hline \end{array}$

27. $\begin{array}{r} 3.6 \\ \times 7.1 \\ \hline \end{array}$

28. $\begin{array}{r} 1.3 \\ \times 2.5 \\ \hline \end{array}$

29. $\begin{array}{r} 5.9 \\ \times 3.1 \\ \hline \end{array}$

30. $\begin{array}{r} 4.2 \\ \times 8.7 \\ \hline \end{array}$

31. $\begin{array}{r} 3.14 \\ \times 6.8 \\ \hline \end{array}$

32. $\begin{array}{r} 7.24 \\ \times 0.8 \\ \hline \end{array}$

33. $\begin{array}{r} 9.65 \\ \times 0.4 \\ \hline \end{array}$

34. $\begin{array}{r} 7.25 \\ \times 1.8 \\ \hline \end{array}$

35. $\begin{array}{r} 9.97 \\ \times 0.9 \\ \hline \end{array}$

36. $\begin{array}{r} 17.31 \\ \times 2.06 \\ \hline \end{array}$

37. $\begin{array}{r} 8.26 \\ \times 0.87 \\ \hline \end{array}$

38. $\begin{array}{r} 31.82 \\ \times 15.5 \\ \hline \end{array}$

39. $\begin{array}{r} 15.4 \\ \times 6.27 \\ \hline \end{array}$

40. $\begin{array}{r} 12.8 \\ \times 4.16 \\ \hline \end{array}$

41. $\begin{array}{r} 17.3 \\ \times 16.5 \\ \hline \end{array}$

42. $\begin{array}{r} 165.4 \\ \times 7.4 \\ \hline \end{array}$

43. $\begin{array}{r} 139.2 \\ \times 8.17 \\ \hline \end{array}$

44. $\begin{array}{r} 935.5 \\ \times 3.25 \\ \hline \end{array}$

45. $\begin{array}{r} 987.2 \\ \times 7.8 \\ \hline \end{array}$

46. $\begin{array}{r} 246.28 \\ \times 25.5 \\ \hline \end{array}$

47. $\begin{array}{r} 950.8 \\ \times 52.4 \\ \hline \end{array}$

48. $\begin{array}{r} 825.2 \\ \times 9.63 \\ \hline \end{array}$

49. $\begin{array}{r} 440.7 \\ \times 425.2 \\ \hline \end{array}$

50. $\begin{array}{r} 2,145.2 \\ \times 527.5 \\ \hline \end{array}$

1. $8\overline{)72}$ 2. $27\overline{)108}$ 3. $6\overline{)138}$ 4. $4\overline{)816}$ 5. $5\overline{)525}$

6. $6\overline{)624}$ 7. $7\overline{)763}$ 8. $4\overline{)836}$ 9. $5\overline{)205}$ 10. $2\overline{)164}$

11. $7\overline{)642}$ 12. $9\overline{)700}$ 13. $2\overline{)785}$ 14. $5\overline{)277}$ 15. $3\overline{)343}$

16. $90 \div 30$ 17. $40 \div 20$ 18. $160 \div 40$ 19. $360 \div 40$ 20. $540 \div 90$

21. $630 \div 70$ 22. $3,000 \div 60$ 23. $100 \div 20$ 24. $560 \div 70$ 25. $3,500 \div 50$

26. $630 \div 58$ 27. $4,801 \div 37$ 28. $100 \div 21$ 29. $560 \div 82$ 30. $1,875 \div 19$

31. $900 \div 300$ 32. $480 \div 240$ 33. $840 \div 105$ 34. $1,500 \div 300$ 35. $9,800 \div 800$

36. $1.2 \div 4$ 37. $0.12 \div 4$ 38. $3.5 \div 5$ 39. $6.4 \div 8$ 40. $0.18 \div 9$

41. $3.69 \div 3$ 42. $83.7 \div 9$ 43. $44.8 \div 4$ 44. $56.8 \div 8$ 45. $19.75 \div 5$

46. $2.24 \div 4$ 47. $4.48 \div 2.8$ 48. $3.78 \div 3$ 49. $12.1 \div 1.1$ 50. $229.6 \div 8.2$

51. $0.38\overline{)13.3}$ 52. $0.55\overline{)2.42}$ 53. $2.48\overline{)1.3392}$ 54. $6.41\overline{)135.892}$ 55. $15\overline{)10.8}$

56. $9\overline{)43.65}$ 57. $18.2\overline{)378.56}$ 58. $49.3\overline{)201.144}$ 59. $186.24 \div 29.1$ 60. $378.56 \div 18.2$

Pronunciation Key

a	add, map	f	fit, half	n	nice, tin	p	pit, stop	yoo	fuse, few
ā	ace, rate	g	go, log	ng	ring, song	r	run, poor	v	vain, eve
â(r)	care, air	h	hope, hate	o	odd, hot	s	see, pass	w	win, away
ä	palm, father	i	it, give	ō	open, so	sh	sure, rush	y	yet, yearn
b	bat, rub	ī	ice, write	ô	order, jaw	t	talk, sit	z	zest, muse
ch	check, catch	j	joy, ledge	oi	oil, boy	th	thin, both	zh	vision,
d	dog, rod	k	cool, take	ou	pout, now	t̶h̶	this, bathe		pleasure
e	end, pet	l	look, rule	o͝o	took, full	u	up, done		
ē	equal, tree	m	move, seem	o͞o	pool, food	û(r)	burn, term		

ə the schwa, an unstressed vowel representing the sound spelled *a* in **above**, *e* in **sicken**, *i* in **possible**, *o* in **melon**, *u* in **circus**

Other symbols:
• separates words into syllables
′ indicates stress on a syllable

absolute value [ab′sə•lo͞ot val′yo͞o] The distance of an integer from zero (p. 628)

acute angle [ə•kyo͞ot′ ang′gəl] An angle whose measure is greater than 0° and less than 90° (p. 338)

acute triangle [ə•kyo͞ot′ trī′ang•gəl] A triangle with all angles less than 90° (p. 356)

Addition Property of Equality [ə•dish′ən prä′pər•tē əv i•kwol′ə•tē] The property that states that if you add the same number to both sides of an equation, the sides remain equal (p. 280)

additive inverse [ad′ə•tiv in′vûrs] The opposite of a given number (p. 645)

adjacent angles [ə•jā′sənt ang′gəlz] Angles that are side by side and have a common vertex and ray (p. 340)
Example:

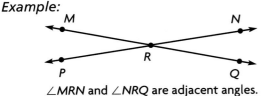

∠*MRN* and ∠*NRQ* are adjacent angles.

Word History

The root for *adjacent* is from the Latin word *jacere,* meaning "to throw." The prefix *ad-* means "near" or "toward." Adjacent angles were thought of as "thrown toward" or beside each other.

algebraic expression [al•jə•brā′ik ik•spre′shən] An expression that includes at least one variable (p. 36)
Examples: $x + 5$, $3a - 4$

algebraic operating system [al•jə•brā′ik ä′pə•rā•ting sis′təm] A way for calculators to follow the order of operations when evaluating expressions (p. 49)

alternate exterior angles [ôl′tər•nit ek•stir′ē•ər ang′gəlz] A pair of exterior angles on opposite sides of the transversal (p. 345)

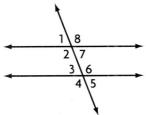

Angles 1 and 5 and angles 4 and 8 are pairs of alternate exterior angles.

alternate interior angles [ôl′tər•nit in•tir′ē•ər ang′gəlz] A pair of interior angles on opposite sides of the transversal (p. 345)

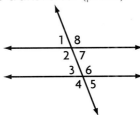

Angles 2 and 6 and angles 3 and 7 are pairs of alternate interior angles.

angle [an′gəl] A figure formed by two rays with a common endpoint (p. 338)
Example:

area [âr′ē•ə] The number of square units needed to cover a given surface (p. 458)

Associative Property [ə•sō′shē•ā•tiv prä′pər•tē] The property that states that whatever way addends are grouped or factors are grouped does not change the sum or the product (p. 40)
Examples: 12 + (5 + 9) = (12 + 5) + 9
(9 × 8) × 3 = 9 × (8 × 3)

axes [ak′sēz] The horizontal number line (*x*-axis) and the vertical number line (*y*-axis) on the coordinate plane (p. 668)

bar graph [bär′ graf] A graph that displays countable data with horizontal or vertical bars (p. 136)

base [bās] A number used as a repeated factor (p. 46)
Example: $8^3 = 8 \times 8 \times 8$; 8 is the base.

base [bās] A side of a polygon or a face of a solid figure by which the figure is measured or named (pp. 459, 486)
Examples:

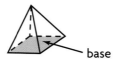

base
base

biased question [bī′əst kwes′chən] A question that suggests or leads to a specific response or excludes a certain group (p. 112)

biased sample [bī′əst sam′pəl] A sample is biased if certain groups from the population are not represented in the sample. (p. 112)

bisect [bī•sekt′] To divide into two congruent parts (p. 380)

box-and-whisker graph [bäks•and•hwis′kər graf] A graph that shows how far apart and how evenly data are distributed (p. 143)

Celsius [səl′sē•əs] A metric scale for measuring temperature (p. 295)

certain [sûr′tən] Sure to happen (p. 581)

chord [kôrd] A line segment with its endpoints on a circle (p. 368)
Example:

chord: $\overline{AB}$

circle [sûr′kəl] The set of all points a given distance from a point called the center (p. 368)
Example:

circle graph [sûr′kəl graf] A graph that lets you compare parts to the whole and to other parts (p. 138)
Example:

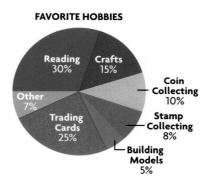

FAVORITE HOBBIES

circumference [sûr•kum′fər•əns] The distance around a circle (p. 448)

Word History

Circumference is the combination of the prefix *circum,* which means "around," and *ferre,* which means "to carry." Together, you get "to carry around."

clustering [klus′tər•ing] A method used to estimate a sum when all addends are about the same (p. 18)

combination [kom′bə•nā′shən] A selection of different items in which the order is not important (p. 606)

Commutative Property [kə•myoo′tə•tiv prä′pər•tē] The property that states that if the order of addends or factors is changed, the sum or product stays the same (p. 40)
Examples: 6 + 5 + 7 = 5 + 6 + 7
8 × 9 × 3 = 3 × 8 × 9

compensation [kom•pən•sā′shən] A mental math strategy in which you change one addend to a multiple of ten and then adjust the other addend to keep the balance (p. 43)

complementary angles [kom•plə•men′tər•ē ang′gəlz] Two angles whose measures have a sum of 90° (p. 341)
Example:

composite number [käm•pä′zət num′bər] A whole number greater than 1 that has more than two whole-number factors (p. 166)

compound event [käm′pound i•vent′] An event made of two or more simple events (p. 602)

congruent [kən•groo′ənt] Having the same size and shape (pp. 340, 376)

coordinate plane [kō•ôr′də•nit plān] A plane formed by a horizontal line (*x*-axis) that intersects a vertical line (*y*-axis) (p. 668)

corresponding angles [kôr•ə•spän′ding ang′gəlz] Angles that appear in the same positions in relation to a transversal and two lines crossed by the transversal (p. 345)

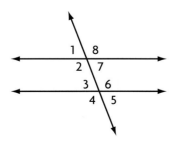

Pairs of Corresponding Angles
∠1 and ∠3   ∠2 and ∠4
∠5 and ∠7   ∠6 and ∠8

corresponding angles [kôr•ə•spän′ding ang′gəlz] Angles that are in the same position in different plane figures (p. 538)
Example:

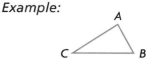

∠*A* and ∠*D* are corresponding angles.

corresponding sides [kôr•ə•spän′ding sīdz] Sides that are in the same position in different plane figures (p. 538)
Example:

$\overline{CA}$ and $\overline{FD}$ are corresponding sides.

cube [kyoob] A rectangular solid with six congruent faces (p. 486)
Example:

cumulative frequency [kyoo′myə•lə•tiv frē′kwən•sē] A running total of the number of subjects surveyed (p. 115)

D

decagon [dek′ə•gän] A polygon with 10 sides (p. 354)
Examples:

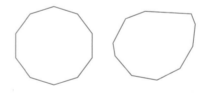

decimal [de′sə•məl] A number with one or more digits to the right of the decimal point (p. 60)

denominator [di•nä′mə•nā•tər] The part of a fraction that tells how many equal parts are in the whole (p. 182)
Example: $\frac{3}{4}$ ←denominator

dependent events [di•pen′dənt i•vənts′] Events for which the outcome of the second event depends on the outcome of the first event (p. 609)

diameter [dī•am′ə•tər] A line segment that passes through the center of a circle and has its endpoints on the circle (p. 368)
Example:

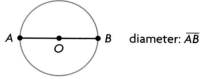

diameter: $\overline{AB}$

dimension [di•men′shən] The length, width, or height of a figure (p. 468)

discount [dis′kount] An amount that is subtracted from the regular price of an item (p. 568)

Distributive Property [di•strib′yə•tiv prä′pər•tē] The property that states that multiplying a sum by a number is the same as multiplying each addend by the number and then adding the products (p. 40)
Example: $14 \times 21 = 14 \times (20 + 1) = (14 \times 20) + (14 \times 1)$

dividend [di′və•dend] The number that is to be divided in a division problem (p. 86)
Example: In $56 \div 8$, 56 is the dividend.

Division Property of Equality [di•vi′zhən prä′pər•tē əv i•kwol′ə•tē] The property that states that if you divide both sides of an equation by the same nonzero number, the sides remain equal (p. 291)

divisor [di•vī′zər] The number that divides the dividend (p. 86)
Example: In $45 \div 9$, 9 is the divisor.

equally likely [ē′kwə•lē li′klē] Having the same chance of occurring (p. 580)

equation [i•kwā′zhən] A statement that shows that two quantities are equal (p. 38)

equilateral triangle [ē•kwə•la′tə•rəl tri′ang•gəl] A triangle with three congruent sides (p. 357)
Example:

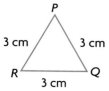

equivalent fractions [ē•kwiv′ə•lənt frak′shənz] Fractions that name the same amount or part (p. 182)

equivalent ratios [ē•kwiv′ə•lənt rā′shē•ōz] Ratios that name the same comparison (p. 532)

estimate [es′tə•mit] A number close to an exact amount (p. 18)

evaluate [i•val′yōō•āt] To find the value of a numerical or algebraic expression (p. 36)

event [i•vent′] A set of outcomes (p. 580)

experimental probability [ik•sper•ə•men′təl prä•bə•bil′ə•tē] The ratio of the number of favorable outcomes that occur to the total number of trials, or times the activity is performed (p. 590)

exponent [ik•spō′nənt] A number that tells how many times a base is used as a factor (p. 46)
Example: $2^3 = 2 \times 2 \times 2 = 8$; 3 is the exponent.

expression [ik•spre′shən] A mathematical phrase that combines operations, numerals, and/or variables to name a number (p. 36)

exterior angles [ik•stir′ē•ər ang′gəlz] Angles on the outside of two lines crossed by a transversal (p. 345)

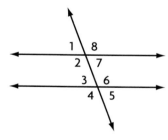

$\angle 1$, $\angle 4$, $\angle 5$, and $\angle 8$ are exterior angles.

face [fās] One of the polygons of a solid figure (p. 486)
Example:

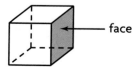

face

factor [fak′tər] A number that is multiplied by another number to find a product (p. 46)

Fahrenheit [fâr′ən•hit] A customary scale for measuring temperature (p. 295)

formula [fôr′myə•lə] A rule that is expressed with symbols (p. 294)
Example: $A = lw$

fractal [frak′təl] A figure with repeating patterns containing shapes that are like the whole but of different sizes throughout (p. 320)

frequency table [frē′kwən•sē tā′bəl] A table representing totals for individual categories or groups (p. 115)

function [funk′shən] A relationship between two quantities in which one quantity depends uniquely on the other (p. 315)

Word History

The word *function* comes from the Latin word *fungi* which means "perform." A mathematical function can be thought of as "performing" an operation or operations on a set of values.

Fundamental Counting Principle [fun•də•men′təl koun′ting prin′sə•pəl] If one event has *m* possible outcomes and a second event has *n* possible outcomes, then there are $m \times n$ total possible outcomes. (p. 602)

greatest common factor (GCF) [grā′təst kä′mən fak′tər] The greatest factor that two or more numbers have in common (p. 171)

height [hīt] A measure of a polygon or solid figure, taken as the length of a perpendicular from the base of the figure (p. 459)
Example:

height

hexagon [heks′ə•gän] A six-sided polygon (p. 354)

histogram [his′tə•gram] A bar graph that shows the number of times data occur in certain ranges or intervals (p. 141)

hypotenuse [hī•pot′ə•n(y) o͞os′] In a right triangle, the side opposite the right angle (p. 477)

Example:

hypotenuse

Identity Property of Addition [ī•den′tə•tē prä′pər•tē əv ə•dish′ən] The property that states that the sum of zero and any number is that number (p. 40)
Example: $25 + 0 = 25$

Identity Property of Multiplication [ī•den′tə•tē prä′pər•tē əv mul•tə•plə•kā′shən] The property that states that the product of any number and 1 is that number (p. 40)
Example: $12 \times 1 = 12$

impossible [im•pos′ə•bəl] Never able to happen (p. 581)

independent events [in•di•pen′dənt i•vents′] Events for which the outcome of the second event does not depend on the outcome of the first event (p. 608)

indirect measurement [in•di•rekt′ mezh′ər•mənt] The technique of using similar figures and a proportion to find a measure (p. 542)

inequality [in•i•kwäl′ə•tē] An algebraic or numerical sentence that contains the symbol $<, >, \leq, \geq$, or $\neq$ (p. 300)
Example: $x + 3 > 5$

integers [in′ti•jərz] The set of whole numbers and their opposites (p. 628)

interior angles [in•tir′ē•ər ang′gəlz] Angles between two lines crossed by a transversal (p. 345)

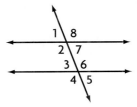

$\angle 2$, $\angle 3$, $\angle 6$, and $\angle 7$ are interior angles.

intersecting lines [in′tər•sekt′ing līnz] Lines that cross at exactly one point (p. 344)

isosceles triangle [ī•sä′sə•lēz trī′ang•gəl] A triangle with exactly two congruent sides (p. 357)
Example:

iteration [it•ə•rā′shən] A step in the process of repeating something over and over again (p. 320)

lateral faces [lat′ər•əl fās′əz] The faces in a prism or pyramid that are not bases (p. 486)

least common denominator (LCD) [lēst kä′mən di•nä′mə•nā•tər] The least common multiple of two or more denominators (p. 206)

least common multiple (LCM) [lēst kä′mən mul′tə•pəl] The smallest number, other than zero, that is a common multiple of two or more numbers (p. 170)

leg [leg] In a right triangle, either of the two sides that form the right angle (p. 477)
Example:

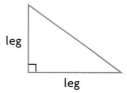

like terms [līk tûrmz] Expressions that have the same variable with the same exponent (p. 261)

line [līn] A straight path that extends without end in opposite directions (p. 336)
Example: ⟷

line graph [līn graf] A graph that uses a line to show how data change over time (p. 137)

line of symmetry [līn əv si′mə•trē] A line across which a figure is symmetric (p. 402)

line plot [līn plät] A graph that shows frequency of data along a number line (p. 114)
Example:

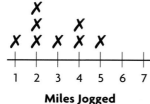

Miles Jogged

line segment [līn seg′mənt] A part of a line with two endpoints (p. 336)
Example: ●————————●

line symmetry [līn si′mə•trē] A figure has line symmetry if it can be folded or reflected so that the two parts of the figure match, or are congruent. (p. 402)

lower extreme [lō′ər ik•strēm′] The least number in a set of data (p. 143)

lower quartile [lō′ər kwôr′tīl] The median of the lower half of a set of data (p. 143)

mean [mēn] The sum of a group of numbers divided by the number of addends (p. 118)

median [mē′dē•ən] The middle value in a group of numbers arranged in order (p. 118)

Word History

Some people get the meanings of *mean* and *median* confused. Originally, they both meant the same thing. Both words come from the Indo-European root *medhyo*.

midpoint [mid′point] The point that divides a line segment into two congruent line segments (p. 380)

mixed number [mikst num′bər] A number represented by a whole number and a fraction (p. 186)

mode [mōd] The number or item that occurs most often in a set of data (p. 118)

multiple-bar graph [mul′tə•pəl bär′graf] A bar graph that represents two or more sets of data (p. 136)

multiple-line graph [mul′tə•pəl līn′graf] A line graph that represents two or more sets of data (p. 137)

multiple [mul′tə•pəl] The product of a given whole number and another whole number (p. 170)

Multiplication Property of Equality [mul•tə•plə•kā′shən prä′pər•tē əv i•kwol′ə•tē] The property that states that if you multiply both sides of an equation by the same number, the sides remain equal (p. 292)

negative integers [ne′gə•tiv in′ti•jərz] Integers to the left of zero on the number line (p. 628)

net [net] An arrangement of two-dimensional figures that folds to form a polyhedron (p. 492)
Example:

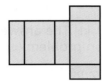

n-gon [en′gän] A polygon with *n* sides (p. 354)

numerator [noo′mə•rā•tər] The part of a fraction that tells how many parts are being used (p. 182)

Example: $\frac{3}{4}$ ←numerator

numerical expression [noo•mer′i•kəl ik•spre′shən] A mathematical phrase that uses only numbers and operation symbols (p. 36)

obtuse angle [äb•toos′ ang′gəl] An angle whose measure is greater than 90° and less than 180° (p. 338)

obtuse triangle [äb•toos′ trī′ang•gəl] A triangle with one angle greater than 90° (p. 356)
Example:

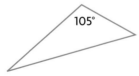
105°

odds [odz] A comparison of favorable outcomes and unfavorable outcomes (p. 586)

odds against an event [odz ə•genst′ ən i•vent′] A comparison of the number of unfavorable outcomes to the number of favorable outcomes (p. 586)

odds in favor of an event [odz in fā′vər uv ən i•vent′] A comparison of the number of favorable outcomes to the number of unfavorable outcomes (p. 586)

opposites [ä′pə•zəts] Two numbers that are an equal distance from zero on the number line (p. 628)

order of operations [ôr′dər əv ä•pə•rā′shənz] The process for evaluating expressions: first perform the operations in parentheses, clear the exponents, perform all multiplication and division, and then perform all addition and subtraction (p. 48)

ordered pair [ôr′dərd pâr] A pair of numbers that can be used to locate a point on the coordinate plane (p. 668)
Examples: (0,2), (3,4), (⁻4,5)

origin [ôr′ə•jən] The point where the *x*-axis and the *y*-axis in the coordinate plane intersect, (0,0) (p. 668)

outcome [out′kəm] A possible result of a probability experiment (p. 580)

overestimate [ō•vər•es′tə•mət] An estimate that is greater than the exact answer (p. 19)

parallel lines [pâr′ə•lel līnz] Lines in a plane that are always the same distance apart (p. 344)
Example:

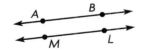

percent (%) [pər•sent′] The ratio of a number to 100; *percent* means "per hundred." (p. 68)

perimeter [pə•ri′mə•tər] The distance around a figure (p. 442)

permutation [pər•myü•tā′shən] A selection of different items in which the order is important (p. 605)

perpendicular bisector [pər•pen•dik′yə•lər bī•sek′tər] A line that intersects a line segment at its midpoint and forms a 90° angle (p. 380)

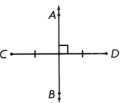

$\overleftrightarrow{AB}$ is the perpendicular bisector of $\overleftrightarrow{CD}$.

perpendicular lines [pər•pen•dik′yə•lər līnz] Two lines that intersect to form right, or 90°, angles (p. 344)
Example:

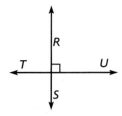

pi (π) [pī] The ratio of the circumference of a circle to its diameter; π ≈ 3.14 or $\frac{22}{7}$ (p. 448)

plane [plān] A flat surface that extends without end in all directions (p. 336)

point [point] An exact location in space, usually represented by a dot (p. 336)

point of rotation [point əv rō•tā′shən] The central point around which a figure is rotated (p. 403)

polygon [pä′lē•gän] A closed plane figure formed by three or more straight sides that are connected line segments (p. 354)

polyhedron [pä•lē•hē′drən] A solid figure with flat faces that are polygons (p. 486)
Example:

Hexagonal Prism

population [pä•pyə•lā′shən] The entire group of objects or individuals considered for a survey (p. 110)

positive integers [pä′zə•tiv in′ti•jərz] Integers to the right of zero on the number line (p. 628)

precision [pri•sizh′ən] A property of measurement that is related to the unit of measure used; the smaller the unit of measure used, the more precise the measurement (p. 428)

prime factorization [prim fak•tə•ri•zā′shən] A number written as the product of all of its prime factors (p. 168)
Example: 24 = 2^3 × 3

prime number [prim num′bər] A whole number greater than 1 whose only factors are 1 and itself (p. 166)

principal [prin′sə•pəl] The amount of money borrowed or saved (p. 572)

prism [priz′əm] A solid figure that has two congruent, polygon-shaped bases, and other faces that are all rectangles (p. 486)
Example:

probability [prä•bə•bil′ə•tē] See *theoretical probability* and *experimental probability*

product [prä′dəkt] The answer in a multiplication problem (p. 24)

proportion [prə•pôr′shən] An equation that shows that two ratios are equal (p. 535)
Example: $\frac{1}{3} = \frac{3}{9}$

Word History

Proportion comes from the Latin word *proportio*, a translation from the Greek word for *analogy*. Like a proportion in mathematics, an analogy refers to things that share a similar relation.

pyramid [pir′ə•mid] A solid figure with a polygon base and triangular sides that all meet at a common vertex (p. 487)
Example:

Pythagorean Theorem [pə•thag•ə•rē′ən thē′ə•rem] In any right triangle, if *a* and *b* are the lengths of the legs and *c* is the length of the hypotenuse, then $a^2 + b^2 = c^2$ (p. 477)

quadrants [kwäd′rənts] The four regions of the coordinate plane (p. 668)

quadrilateral [kwä•drə•lat′ə•rəl] A closed plane figure formed by four straight sides that are connected line segments (p. 362)

quotient [kwō′shənt] The number, not including the remainder, that results from dividing (p. 25)

R

radius [rā′dē•əs] A line segment with one endpoint at the center of a circle and the other endpoint on the circle (p. 368)
Example:

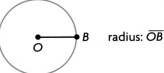

radius: $\overline{OB}$

random sample [ran′dəm sam′pəl] A sample in which each subject in the overall population has an equal chance of being selected (p. 110)

range [rānj] The difference between the greatest and least numbers in a group (p. 114)

rate [rāt] A ratio that compares two quantities having different units of measure (p. 533)

ratio [rā′shē•ō] A comparison of two numbers, *a* and *b*, that can be written as a fraction $\frac{a}{b}$ (p. 532)

rational number [ra′shə•nəl num′bər] Any number that can be written as a ratio $\frac{a}{b}$, where *a* and *b* are integers and $b \neq 0$ (p. 630)

ray [rā] A part of a line with a single endpoint (p. 336)
Example:

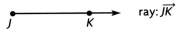

ray: $\overrightarrow{JK}$

reciprocal [ri•sip′rə•kəl] Two numbers are reciprocals of each other if their product equals 1. (p. 235)

reflection [ri•flek′shən] A movement of a figure by flipping it over a line (p. 394)

regular polygon [reg′yə•lər pä′lē•gän] A polygon in which all sides are congruent and all angles are congruent (p. 360)
Example:

relative frequency [rel′ə•tiv frē′kwən•sē] The frequency of a category divided by the sum of the frequencies (p. 116)

repeating decimal [ri•pēt′ing de′sə•məl] A decimal that doesn't end, because it shows a repeating pattern of digits after the decimal point (p. 191)

right angle [rīt ang′gəl] An angle that has a measure of 90° (p. 338)
Example:

right triangle [rīt trī′ang•gəl] A triangle with one right angle (p. 356)
Example:

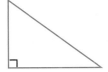

rotation [rō•tā′shən] A movement of a figure by turning it around a fixed point (p. 394)

rotational symmetry [rō•tā′shən•əl si′mə•trē] The property of a figure that can be rotated less than 360° around its center point and still look exactly the same as the original figure (p. 403)

S

sales tax [sālz taks] A percent of the cost of an item, added onto the item's cost (p. 570)

sample [sam′pəl] A part of a population (p. 110)

sample space [sam′pəl spās] The set of all possible outcomes (p. 580)

scale [skāl] A ratio between two sets of measurements (p. 546)

scale drawing [skāl drô′ing] A drawing that shows a real object smaller than (a reduction) or larger than (an enlargement) the real object (p. 545)

scalene triangle [skā′lēn trī′ang•gəl] A triangle with no congruent sides (p. 357)

scatterplot [skat′ər•plät] A graph with points plotted to show a relationship between two variables (p. 155)

sequence [sē′kwəns] An ordered set of numbers (p. 312)

similar figures [si′mə•lər fig′yərz] Figures with the same shape but not necessarily the same size (p. 384)

simple interest [sim′pəl in′trəst] A fixed percent of the principal, paid yearly (p. 572)

simplest form [sim′pləst fôrm] The form in which the numerator and denominator of a fraction have no common factors other than 1 (p. 183)

skew lines [skyo͞o linz] Lines that are not in the same plane, are not parallel, and do not intersect (p. 344)

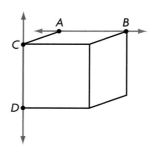

$\overleftrightarrow{AB}$ and $\overleftrightarrow{CD}$ are skew lines.

solution [sə•lo͞o′shən] A value that, when substituted for a variable in an equation, makes the equation true (p. 38)

square [skwâr] The product of a number and itself; a number with the exponent 2 (p. 264)

square [skwâr] A rectangle with four congruent sides (p. 362)

square root [skwâr ro͞ot] One of two equal factors of a number (p. 265)

stem-and-leaf plot [stem ənd lēf plät] A type of graph that shows groups of data arranged by place value (p. 140)

straight angle [strāt ang′gəl] An angle whose measure is 180° (p. 338)
Example:

Subtraction Property of Equality [sub•trak′shən prä′pər•tē əv i•kwol′ə•tē] The property that states that if you subtract the same number from both sides of an equation, the sides remain equal (p. 277)

sum [sum] The answer to an addition problem (p. 18)

supplementary angles [sup•lə•men′tə•rē ang′gəlz] Two angles whose measures have a sum of 180° (p. 341)
Example:

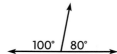

surface area [sûr′fəs âr′ē•ə] The sum of the areas of the faces of a solid figure (p. 502)

survey [sûr′vā] A method of gathering information about a group (p. 110)

term [tûrm] Each number in a sequence (p. 312)

terms [tûrmz] The parts of an expression that are separated by an addition or subtraction sign (p. 261)

terminating decimal [tûr′mə•nāt•ing de′sə•məl] A decimal that ends, having a finite number of digits after the decimal point (p. 191)

tessellation [tes•ə•lā′shən] A repeating arrangement of shapes that completely covers a portion of a plane, with no gaps and no overlaps (p. 397)

theoretical probability [thē•ə•re′ti•kəl prä•bə•bil′ə•tē] A comparison of the number of favorable outcomes to the number of possible equally likely outcomes (p. 580)

transformation [trans•fər•mā′shən] The moving of a figure by a translation, reflection, or rotation (p. 394)

translation [trans•lā′shən] A movement of a figure along a straight line (p. 394)

transversal [trans•vûr′səl] A line that crosses two or more lines (p. 345)

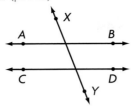

$\overleftrightarrow{XY}$ is a transversal.

tree diagram [trē dī′ə•gram] A diagram that shows all possible outcomes of an event (p. 602)

triangular number [trī•an′gyə•lər num′bər] A number that can be represented by a triangular array (p. 312)
Example:

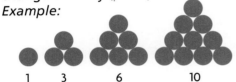

1   3   6   10

unbiased sample [un•bī′əst sam′pəl] A sample is unbiased if every individual in the population has an equal chance of being selected. (p. 112)

underestimate [un•dər•es′tə•mət] An estimate that is less than the exact answer (p. 19)

unit rate [yōō′nət rāt] A rate that has 1 unit as its second term (p. 533)
Example: $1.45 per pound

unlike fractions [un′līk frak′shənz] Fractions with different denominators (p. 204)

upper extreme [up′ər ik•strēm′] The greatest number in a set of data (p. 143)

upper quartile [up′ər kwôr′tīl] The median of the upper half of a set of data (p. 143)

variable [vâr′ē•ə•bəl] A letter or symbol that stands for one or more numbers (p. 36)

Venn diagram [ven dī′ə•gram] A diagram that shows relationships among sets of things (p. 630)

vertex [vûr′teks] The point where two or more rays meet; the point of intersection of two sides of a polygon; the point of intersection of three or more edges of a solid figure; the top point of a cone (pp. 338, 354, 487)
Examples:

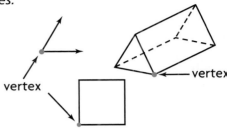

vertex   vertex

vertical angles [vûr′ti•kəl ang•gəlz] A pair of opposite congruent angles formed where two lines intersect (p. 340)
Example:

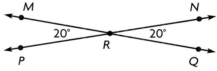

∠MRP and ∠NRQ are vertical angles.

volume [väl′yəm] The number of cubic units needed to occupy a given space (p. 506)

whole number [hōl num′bər] One of the numbers 0, 1, 2, 3, 4, ... The set of whole numbers goes on without end.

x-axis [eks•ak′səs] The horizontal number line on a coordinate plane (p. 668)

x-coordinate [eks•kō•ôr′də•nət] The first number in an ordered pair; it tells the distance to move right or left from (0,0).

y-axis [wī•ak′səs] The vertical number line on a coordinate plane (p. 668)

y-coordinate [wī•kō•ôr′də•nət] The second number in an ordered pair; it tells the distance to move up or down from (0,0).

Index

Associative Property
  of Addition, 40–45, 54, 261, 443, 648
  of Multiplication, 40–45
Average. *See* Mean, Median, *and* Mode
Average speed, 294–297, 533
Axes, 668

Bar graphs, 134–139, 146–149, 150, H6
Bases
  of plane figures, 459–460, 462–464
  of powers, 46–47, H15
  of solid figures, 486–488, 494–495, 496, H20
Biased sample, 112–113, 128
Binary number system, 318
Bisect
  angles, 381–382, 388
  line segments, 380–382, 388
Box-and-whisker graphs, 143–145, 150

Calculator, 25, 49–50, 88–90, 118, 185, 191–192, 242–243, 253, 264–265, 448, 449, 559, 563, 589, 689
  graphing, 693
Capacity
  customary, 420–422, 426–427, 436, H25
  estimating, 426–427, 432–433, 436
  measuring, 428–433, 436
  metric, 423–425, 436
Careers, 51, 239, 297, 661
Celsius temperature, 295–297, 304
Center, of circle, 368
Centimeters, 423–425, 436
Challenge
  Explore Scatterplots, 155
  Mixed Numbers and Time, 249
  Negative Exponents, 689
  Percent of Increase and Decrease, 619
  Pythagorean Theorem, 477
  Scientific Notation, 101
  Solving Two-Step Equations, 327
  Stretching Figures, 411
  Transformations of Solid Figures, 523
Changing dimensions, 385–387, 468–471, 510–511, 541
Chapter Review/Test, 31, 55, 71, 97, 129, 151, 177, 195, 221, 245, 269, 285, 305, 323, 349, 371, 389, 407, 437, 453, 473, 497, 519, 551, 575, 595, 615, 639, 663, 685
Check What You Know, 15, 35, 59, 75, 109, 133, 163, 181, 199, 225, 257, 273, 289, 309, 335, 353, 375, 393, 419, 441, 457, 485, 501, 531, 555, 579, 599, 627, 643, 667
Choose the Method, 242–243
Choose the Operation, 240–241
Chords, 368–369, 370
Circle graphs, 138–139, 566–567

Circles
  area of, 465–467, 472, H28
  as base of cylinder, 487–488
  center of, 368
  chord, 368–369, 370
  circumference of, 448–451, 452
  degrees in, 566–567
  diameter of, 368–369, 370
  drawing, parts of, 368–369
  fractions of, 182, 234
  radius of, 368–369, 370
  See also Geometry
Circumference, 448–451, 452
Clustering (in estimation), 18–19, 66–67
Combinations, 606–607, 614
Combined shapes, area of, 459–461
Common denominators, 204–209
Common factors, 171
Common multiples, 170, 188
Commutative Property
  of Addition, 40–45, 261, 443, 648
  of Multiplication, 40–45, 54, 654
Compare
  decimals, 61–63, H29
  decimals and fractions, 192–193, 194
  fractions, 188–189, 194, H12, H29
  graphs, 134–139, 146–149
  integers, 628–629, 638, H29
  measurements, 420–427, 432–433, 436, 468–471
  mixed numbers, 188–189, H12
  on a number line, 61, 188, 631–632, 634–635, H29
  percents, 556–557
  rational numbers, 634–635
  strategies, 12
  whole numbers, 16–17, H3
Compare Strategies, 12
Compass, 368, 376–379, 380, 383, 448, 465, 566–567
Compatible numbers, 19–21, 66–67, 86, 226
Compensation, 43–45
Complementary angles, 341–343, 348
Composite numbers, 166–168, 176
Compound events, 602–611, 614
Computer, 469, 489
  See also Cross-curricular connections *and* Technology
Computer software. *See* Harcourt Mega Math software *and* Technology
Cones, 484, 487–488, 496, H20
Congruent
  angles, 340, 377–379, 381, 388, 538–541
  figures, 384–387, 388, H22
  line segments, 376–379, 388
Constructing
  angles, 338–339, 566–567
  congruent angles, 377–379
  congruent figures, 385–387
  congruent line segments, 376–379
  parallel lines, 383
  similar figures, 385–387
Consumer, 60, 64–65, 66, 136–139, 258, 260, 288, 298–299, 554, 566–567, 568–571, 572–574
Coordinate grid. *See* Coordinate plane
Coordinate plane
  graphing on, 668–675, 678–679, 684
  quadrants of, 668–671
  transformations on, 680–683, 684
Corresponding
  angles, 345–347, 538–541
  sides, 538–544, 550
Counting principle. *See* Fundamental Counting Principle
Critical thinking. *See* Reasoning
Cross products, 535–537, 542–549, 550, H26
Cross-curricular connections
  architecture, 160, 255, 334, 417, 456, 484, 530, 625
  art, 51, 308, 334, 343, 347, 374, 456, 471, 530, 544

computer, 469, 489

consumer, 60, 64–65, 66, 136–139, 258, 260, 288, 298–299, 554, 566–567, 568–571, 572–574

geography, 147, 160, 200, 254, 274, 332, 379, 426, 548–549, 565, 626, 628, 666, 694, 695

history, 160, 174, 188, 333, 512, 624, 625

music, 578

reading, 27, 149, 213, 263, 365, 405, 509, 565, 633

science, 14, 16, 17, 22, 34, 42, 76, 79, 86, 90, 106, 107, 108, 114, 119, 132, 134, 136, 140, 161, 180, 183, 186, 187, 192, 211, 214, 215, 217, 226, 243, 256, 259, 275, 291, 297, 314, 352, 355, 356, 392, 396, 397, 402, 482, 500, 532, 535, 536, 537, 547, 593, 626, 629, 634, 642, 652, 661, 671, 672, 675

social studies, 38, 58, 69, 74, 121, 123, 139, 160, 162, 169, 198, 217, 224, 254, 255, 272, 288, 294, 332, 387, 416, 417, 418, 422, 440, 448, 451, 483, 484, 495, 528, 529, 542, 554, 560, 593, 598, 604, 624, 625, 658–659, 694, 695

sports, 18, 120, 272, 420–422, 423–425, 466, 562

Cubes, 486–488, H20

Cubic units, 506

Cumulative frequencies, 114–117

Cumulative Review. *See* Mixed Applications, Mixed Review and Test Prep, Mixed Strategy Practice, *and* Standardized Test Prep

Cups, 420–422, 436, H25

Customary system

capacity, 420–422, 426–427, 436, H25

changing units in, 420–422, 436, H25

equivalent measures in, 420–422, 436, H25

Fahrenheit temperature, 295–297, 304, 634, 642

length, 420–422, 436, H25

metric units compared to, 426–427, 436

relating units in, 420–422, 436, H25

weight, 420–422, 428–433, 436, H25

See also Table of Measures *on inside back cover*

Cylinders, 484, 487–488, 496, H20

bases of, 487–488, 496, H20

height of, 503–504, 515–517

model of, 514

surface area of, 503–504, 518

volume of, 514–517, 518

D

Data

analyzing, 114–127, 136–149, H5, H27

bar graphs, 134–139, 146–149, 150, H6

box-and-whisker graphs, 143–145, 150

circle graphs, 138–139, 566–567

collecting, 110–113, 126–127, 128

comparing measures of central tendency, 118–121, 123

conclusions based on, 122–127, 128

frequency tables, 114–117, 126–127, 128

histograms, 141–142, 150

interpreting, 136–149

line graphs, 137–139, 150

line plots, 114–117, 589

making tables, 64–65, 126–127

measures of central tendency

mean, 118–121, 128, H6

median, 118–121, 128, H6

mode, 118–121, 128, H6

misleading graphs, 146–149, 150

organized lists, 6, 174–175, 600–601

organizing, 64–65, 114–117, 126–127, 134–145

outcomes, 580–583, 586–587, 590–593, 602–604, 608–611, 614

range, 114–115, H6

representing, 134–145, 150

samples

biased, 112–113, 128

random, 110–111, 126–127, 128

unbiased, 112–113, 128

scatterplots, 155

stem-and-leaf plots, 140–142, 150, H7

surveys, 110–113, 126–127

tree diagrams, 602–607, 614

use data, 21, 23, 44, 47, 53, 63, 65, 67, 69, 83, 90, 106, 107, 124, 139, 160, 161, 185, 193, 203, 208, 212, 241, 254, 255, 281, 283, 297, 303, 318, 332, 361, 369, 401, 417, 431, 435, 447, 482, 483, 495, 505, 511, 528, 529, 571, 585, 601, 613, 624, 625, 677, 694, 695

Venn diagrams, 630, 633

Decagon, 354–355

Decimal points, placing, 60, 76–83, 86–91

Decimals

adding, 76–79, 96

annexing zeroes in, 61, 77, 631

calculators and, 88–90

comparing, 61–63, H29

dividing, 84–91, 96

equivalent, 61

estimating, 66–67, 70, 76–79

to fractions, 191–193, 194

fractions to, 190–193, 194, H22

metric measures and, 423–425

modeling, 80–85, H2

models of, 80–85, H2

money and, 76

multiplying, 80–83, 96, H23

ordering on a number line, 61, 631–632

patterns in, 88

to percents, 68–69, 192–193, 558–561, 574, H23

percents to, 68–69, 558–561, 563–565, H23

place value in, 60–63, H2

placing the decimal point, 60, 76–83, 86–91

and powers of ten, 101, 424–425, 558, 689, H13

probability and, 580–583, 590–593

repeating, 191–193, 194

rounding, 66, H4

subtracting, 76–79, 96

terminating, 191–193, 194

in words, 60–63

Decimeters, 423–425, 436

Degrees

in angles, 338–339, H18, H31

in a circle, 566–567

measuring with a protractor, 338–339, 378

in a quadrilateral, 360

on a thermometer, 295–297

in a triangle, 356–359, 370

Denominators

finding common, 204–209

least common, 206–213, 215

in like fractions, 204

in unlike fractions, 204

Dependent events, 609–611, 614

Diameters, 368–369, 370

Differences. *See* Subtraction

Digits, place value of, 16–17

Dimensions, changing, 385–387, 468–471, 510–511, 541

Discounts, 568–571

Distance formula, 294–297, 304

Distributive Property, 40–45, 54, 82, 232–233, 262, 444

Dividends. *See* Division

Divisibility rules, 164–165, 176

Division

with calculators, 88–90, 191–192, 242–243

changing units of measurement with, 420–427

connecting to multiplication, 236–239

of decimals, 84–91, 96

divisibility rules, 164–165, 176

equations, 292–293, 304

and equivalent fractions, 183

estimating quotients, 19–21, 66–67, 226–227

facts, H2

to find unit rates, 533–534, 550

of fractions, 234–239, 242–243, 244

of integers, 655–657, 662

interpreting remainders, 92–93

mental math and, 42–45, 54, 237–238, 242–243

of mixed numbers, 237–239, 242–243, 244

models of, 84–85, 234

facts, H2
of fractions, 228–231, 242–243, 244, H23
Identity Property of, 40–41, 54, 291–292
of integers, 654–657, 662
mental math and, 42–45, 54, 242–243
of mixed numbers, 232–233, 242–243, 244
models of, 80–83, 228, 264–265, 654
by multiples, 19–21, H8
on a number line, 654
patterns in, 655, H13
by powers of ten, 424–425, 558, 689, H13
properties of, 42–45, 291–293
Property of Equality, 292–293
of rational numbers, 658–661
of whole numbers, 24–27, 30, 42–45, H4
See also Measurement, changing units

Multistep problems, 13, 52–53
At least one multistep problem is provided in every exercise set. Some examples are 21, 39, 83, 111, 259, 297, 359, 488, 509, 649, 671.

Music, 578

Negative exponents, 689
Negative fractions, 630–635
Negative integers, 628–635, H12, H13, H24
as exponents, 689
Nets, 492–493, 502–503, 506, 512, 527
n-gon, 354–355
Nonlinear relationships, 678–679
Number lines
absolute value of numbers on, 628, H24
adding on, 646–648
comparing on, 61, 188, 631–632, 634–635, H29
decimals on, 61, 631–632
fractions on, 188–191, 200–202
inequalities on, 300–303, 304
integers on, 628–629, 646–648, 654, H12, H13, H24, H29
multiplying on, 654
ordering on, 61, 188, 191, 631–632, 634–635
percents on, 191
probability on, 581
rational numbers on, 631–632, 634–635
rounding on, 200
Number patterns, 88, 282–283, 312–318, 322, 655, H5, H14
Number sense.
The use of number sense to solve problems is a focal point at Grade 6 and is found throughout this book. Some examples are 217, 275, 657.

Number sentences. *See* Equations
Number theory
divisibility, 164–165, 176
least common multiple, 170–173
prime factorization, 168–169, 176
Numbers
absolute value, 628–629, H24
adding, 22–23, 76–79, 204–213, 644–649, H4
binary, 318
comparing, 16–17, 60–63, 188–189, 556–557, 628–629, 631–632, 638, H3, H12, H29
compatible, 19–21, 66–67, 86, 226
composite, 166–168, 176
decimal, 60–63, 66–69, 76–79, H2, H22
dividing, 24–27, 42–45, 84–91, 234–239, 242–243, 655–657, H4
expanded form of, 16–17, 60–63
factors of, H8
fractions, 182–193, 200–209, 226–231, 234–239, 242–243, H8, H10, H21, H22
integers, 628–629, H12
mixed, 186–189, 210–219, 226–227, 232–233, 237–239, 242–243, H11
multiples of, H8

multiplying, 24–27, 42–45, 80–83, 228–233, 242–243, 654–657, H4, H7, H21, H23, H25
negative, 628–635, H13
as exponents, 689
opposite, 628–629, H24
ordered pairs of, 668–675, 684
ordering, 16–17, 60–63, 188–189
percents of, 556–557, 562–565, 574, H9
pi, 91, 448, 465–467
place value in, 16–17, 60–63, 68
positive, 628–629
prime, 166–168, 176
random, 589
rational, 630–635
reading and writing, 16–17, 60–63, 628–629
reciprocal, 235
rounding, 18, 66, 200–202, H4, H10
square of, 264, 266–267, 268
square roots of, 265–267
standard form of, 16–17, 60–63
subtracting, 22–23, 43–45, 76–79, 205, 207–209, 211–217, 650–653, H4
triangular, 312
word form, 16–17, 60–63
Numerical expressions
evaluating, 36–37, 48–51, 54–55, H3
writing, 36–37
Numerical patterns. *See* Number patterns

Obtuse angles, 338–339, 356, H18
Obtuse triangles, 356–359, 370
Octagons, 354–355, 360
Odds
against an event, 586–587, 594
in favor of an event, 586–587, 594
Operations
choose the, 240–241
inverse, 225, 235, 277, 280, 291, 298, 655
order of, 48–51, 260–263, 659–661, H3, H15
words for, H17
Opposites, 628–629, H24
Order of operations, 48–51, 260–263, 659–661, H3, H15
Ordered pairs, 668–675
equations from, 672–675
graphing, 668–675, 678–679, 684
identifying on a graph, 668–675
writing, 668–675, H31
Ordering
combinations, 606–607, 614
decimals, 61–63, 631–632
fractions, 188–189, 194, 631–632, 638
integers, 628–629, 646–648, 654, H12, H13, H29
mixed numbers, 188–189
on a number line, 61, 188, 191, 631–632, 634–635
percents, 556–557
permutations, 605–607, 614
rational numbers, 634–635
whole numbers, 16–17, H3
Organized lists, 6, 174–175, 600–601
Origin, 668
Ounces, 420–422, H25
Outcomes, 580–583, 586–587, 590–593, 602–604, 608–611, 614
Overestimates, 19–21

Parallel lines, 344–347, 348, 383
Parallelograms
area of, 462–464, 472
properties of, 362

Photo Credits

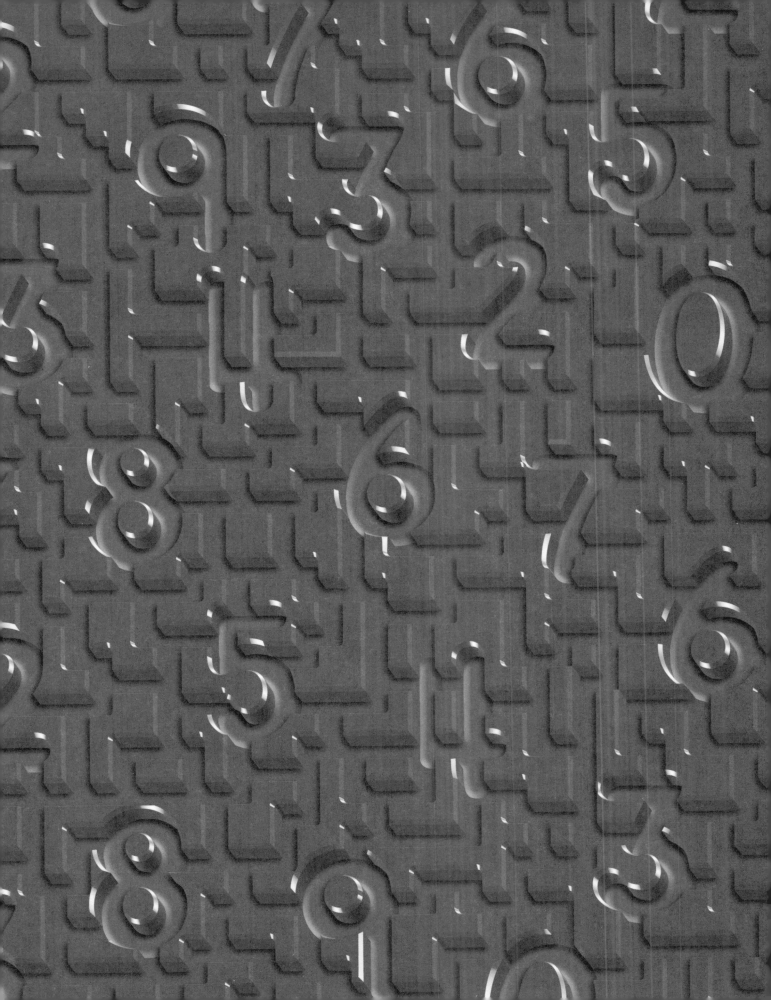

Table of Measures

METRIC	CUSTOMARY

Length

1 millimeter (mm) = 0.001 meter (m)	1 foot (ft) = 12 inches (in.)
1 centimeter (cm) = 0.01 meter	1 yard (yd) = 36 inches
1 decimeter (dm) = 0.1 meter	1 yard = 3 feet
1 kilometer (km) = 1,000 meters	1 mile (mi) = 5,280 feet
	1 mile = 1,760 yards
	1 nautical mile = 6,076.115 feet

Capacity

1 milliliter (mL) = 0.001 liter (L)	1 teaspoon (tsp) = $\frac{1}{6}$ fluid ounce (fl oz)
1 centiliter (cL) = 0.01 liter	1 tablespoon (tbsp) = $\frac{1}{2}$ fluid ounce
1 deciliter (dL) = 0.1 liter	1 cup (c) = 8 fluid ounces
1 kiloliter (kL) = 1,000 liters	1 pint (pt) = 2 cups
	1 quart (qt) = 2 pints
	1 quart (qt) = 4 cups
	1 gallon (gal) = 4 quarts

Mass/Weight

1 milligram (mg) = 0.001 gram (g)	1 pound (lb) = 16 ounces (oz)
1 centigram (cg) = 0.01 gram	1 ton (T) = 2,000 pounds
1 decigram (dg) = 0.1 gram	
1 hectogram (hg) = 100 grams	
1 kilogram (kg) = 1,000 grams	
1 metric ton (t) = 1,000 kilograms	

Volume/Capacity/Mass for Water

1 cubic centimeter (cm^3) → 1 milliliter → 1 gram

1,000 cubic centimeters → 1 liter → 1 kilogram

TIME

1 minute (min) = 60 seconds (sec)	1 year (yr) = 12 months (mo), or about 52 weeks
1 hour (hr) = 60 minutes	
1 day = 24 hours	1 year = 365 days
1 week (wk) = 7 days	1 leap year = 366 days